PURCHASING

Wiley Service Management Series

TOM POWERS, Series Editor

Introduction to the Hospitality Industry
Tom Powers

Introduction to Management in the Hospitality Industry
Tom Powers

Purchasing: Selection and Procurement for the Hospitality Industry
John M. Stefanelli

Marketing Hospitality
Tom Powers

Supervision in the Hospitality Industry
Jack E. Miller
Mary Porter
Karen Eich Drummond

The Management of Maintenance and Engineering Systems in the Hospitality Industry
Frank D. Borsenik
Alan R. Stutts

The Bar and Beverage Book: Basics of Profitable Management
Costas Katsigris
Mary Porter

PURCHASING

Selection and Procurement for the Hospitality Industry

FOURTH EDITION

JOHN M. STEFANELLI

University of Nevada, Las Vegas

JOHN WILEY & SONS, INC.

New York • Chichester • Weinheim • Brisbane • Singapore • Toronto

Library of Congress Cataloging-in-Publication Data
Stefanelli, John M.
    Purchasing : selection and procurement for the hospitality
  industry / John M. Stefanelli. — 4th ed.
        p.   cm.
    Includes bibliographical references and index.
    ISBN 0-471-13583-6 (cloth : alk. paper)
    1. Hospitality industry—Purchasing. I. Title.
  TX911.3.P8S73 1997
  647'.9'0687—dc21   96-46444

Printed in the United States of America

10 9 8 7 6 5 4 3 2

PREFACE

In 1976, I undertook a project that seemed, at the time, to defy conventional practice. Dr. Tom Powers, Consulting Editor for the Wiley Service Management Series, suggested that hospitality educators would appreciate a purchasing textbook that combined generally accepted purchasing principles and procedures with some description of the products and services normally purchased by the typical hospitality enterprise.

Since the first edition of this book, many hospitality educators have adopted this approach to purchasing instruction. Many of my colleagues, both in education and in industry, continue to find that it is valuable for their students, most of whom will not become purchasing agents but will be involved with some phase of purchasing throughout their careers. As one colleague put it, this book is a purchasing book for nonpurchasing agents. It provides a comprehensive and understandable view of the activity, as well as its relationship to the management of a successful operation.

This book has also proved useful to professional purchasing agents. In the *Journal of Purchasing and Materials Management,* Summer 1985, reviewer Richard L. Mooney, C.P.M., Materiel Manager at UCLA, stated, "This is a management book. But there is a tremendous amount of very valuable hands-on purchasing information here too. For those with hospitality-type responsibilities, or those who simply wish to expand their knowledge of the specialized aspects of food and beverage buying and management, this book will be an excellent investment."

One of the highlights of my life came recently when the late Patt Patterson, purchasing guru who penned a purchasing column for *Nation's Restaurant News* for many years, noted in April 1992 that the purchasing course offered by the Educational Foundation of the National Restaurant Association is "a complete, comprehensive and clearly written examination of the whole purchasing function plus the principles behind each phase." Mr. Patterson went on to say: "The course is built around an excellent book, the third edition of John M. Stefanelli's *Purchasing— Selection and Procurement for the Hospitality Industry.*" He further commented (and this is the best part) that "Stefanelli is with the University of Nevada in Las Vegas, and he knows his subject."

To say the least, you could have knocked me over with a purchase order. His compliment was equivalent to an actor reading that Orson Welles considered him the best actor he'd ever seen on the stage. It was the nicest compliment I have ever received. I shall never forget it.

The fourth edition of this book maintains the original objectives: It includes discussions of the purchasing activity and product information from a managerial perspective. Each chapter has been revised to include the most current concepts available. A few sections have been rearranged. And, since convenience foods have steadily become a way of life in our industry, the extensive discussion in the convenience foods chapter has been eliminated and the remaining pertinent information incorporated into other relevant areas.

A major change in this edition is the addition of a chapter on computer technology applications in the purchasing function. This new chapter comes at the tail end of the chapters on purchasing principles and offers students an excellent opportunity to explore purchasing techniques in an interactive computer environment.

Perhaps the most critical change in this edition, though, is the introduction of a new author, Andy Feinstein. Andy is a young academic who shares my enthusiasm for this subject. He begins his collaboration with me by writing the computer technology applications chapter and accompanying exercises. He also developed and produced the instructor aid package. The plan is for him to be firmly in the driver's seat when it comes time to create the fifth edition. By that time, I fully expect to be no more than a passenger trying to keep up with him.

Over the past three editions, I have received numerous comments from education and industry professionals regarding the usefulness of this text and its approach to the subject matter. I am gratified that so many people spent the time necessary to provide valuable input, particularly since most reactions have been favorable. I have used many of these comments in the revision of this fourth edition.

The appropriate methods of teaching purchasing to hospitality students continue to be subject to a great deal of opinion, discussion, and interpretation. This book remains a synthesis of generally accepted industry principles and practices, and our personal experiences and judgments. We hope it will continue to be seen as a worthy contribution to each reader's professional development.

JOHN STEFANELLI

William F. Harrah College of Hotel Administration
University of Nevada, Las Vegas

CONTENTS

Preface   v

PART 1 Gaining a Perspective on Selection and Procurement

Chapter 1 The Concept of Selection and Procurement   3
Chapter 2 Distribution Systems   10
Chapter 3 Forces Affecting the Distribution Systems   28
Chapter 4 An Overview of the Purchasing Function   56
Chapter 5 The Organization and Administration of Purchasing   74
Chapter 6 The Buyer's Relations with Other
            Company Personnel   86

PART 2 Principles of Selection and Procurement

Chapter 7 The Purchase Specification: An Overall View   108
Chapter 8 The Optimal Amount   136
Chapter 9 The Optimal Price   160
Chapter 10 The Optimal Payment Policy   194
Chapter 11 The Optimal Supplier   204
Chapter 12 Typical Ordering Procedures   236
Chapter 13 Typical Receiving Procedures   250
Chapter 14 Typical Storage Management Procedures   276
Chapter 15 Security in the Purchasing Function   306
Chapter 16 Computer Technology Applications in Purchasing   326

PART 3 Selection and Procurement of the Items

Chapter 17 Fresh Produce   340
Chapter 18 Processed Produce and Other Grocery Items   370
Chapter 19 Dairy Products   404
Chapter 20 Eggs   425

Chapter 21 Poultry   442
Chapter 22 Fish   462
Chapter 23 Meat   486
Chapter 24 Alcoholic and Nonalcoholic Beverages   530
Chapter 25 Nonfood Expense Items   564
Chapter 26 Services   588
Chapter 27 Furniture, Fixtures, and Equipment   616
Index   649

PART 1

GAINING A PERSPECTIVE ON SELECTION AND PROCUREMENT

CHAPTER 1

THE CONCEPT OF SELECTION AND PROCUREMENT

THE PURPOSE OF THIS CHAPTER

This chapter discusses:

- The major differences between purchasing, selection, and procurement
- The major differences between the types of hospitality operations

INTRODUCTION

To most hospitality students the term "purchasing" means paying for an item or service. This conveys a far too restrictive meaning; it fails to portray the complete scope of the buying function. Perhaps the terms "selection" and "procurement" are better.

"Selection" can be defined as choosing from among various alternatives on various levels. For example, a buyer can select from among several competing brands of applesauce; a buyer can select a specific quality of applesauce; a buyer can select from among several applesauce suppliers; and a buyer can select from among fresh and processed products.

One buyer may not perform all these activities—make all these choices—at one time. But he or she will be involved in most of them at some level.

"Procurement," as opposed to "selection," can be defined as an orderly, systematic exchange between a seller and a buyer. It is the process of obtaining goods and services, including all activities associated with determining the types of products needed, making purchases, receiving and storing shipments, and administering purchase contracts.

Most people see procurement as the "nuts and bolts" of the buyer's job. Once they know what they want, buyers set about locating the best suppliers that fit their needs. They then attempt to order the correct amounts of products or services at the appropriate times, see to it that shipments are timely, and ensure that the delivered items meet company requirements.

A host of related duties surround these activities—being on the lookout for new items and new ideas, learning the production needs of the other departments, appraising the reliability of suppliers, and so on.

Few operations have full-time buyers; most have managers and supervisors who do the buying in addition to their other duties. Buying, to these employees, means more than the term "procurement" by itself implies. These employees must also be aware of the relationship between purchasing and other related activities in the hospitality operation.

Because there are so few full-time purchasing agents in our field, a textbook that focuses solely on hospitality buying principles and procedures or product identification, although useful to some, would unnecessarily restrict operating managers and supervisors in hospitality. In other words, it is not enough to know how to procure applesauce. The typical operating manager must also consider what form of applesauce to purchase—and whether or not applesauce should be on the menu to begin with.

TYPES OF HOSPITALITY OPERATIONS

The hospitality industry includes three major segments. The first is the commercial segment—the profit-oriented companies. The second is the institutional segment—those facilities that are operated on a break-even basis. The third is the military segment, which includes troop feeding and housing as well as the various military clubs and military exchanges that are operated within military installations. The second and third segments are collectively referred to as *noncommercial* hospitality operations.

The following types of operations are generally considered part of the commercial segment:

1. Quick-service (limited-service) restaurants
2. Snack bars
3. Table-service restaurants
4. Hotels with food services
5. Casinos with food services
6. Motels with food services
7. Hotels, casinos, and motels without food services
8. Taverns and lounges
9. Cafeterias
10. Family restaurants
11. Steak houses
12. Social caterers

13. Mobile caterers
14. Vending machine companies
15. Buffets
16. Ice cream stands
17. In-transit food services (e.g., cruise ships and airlines)
18. Contract food-service companies, which typically operate in plants, office buildings, day-care facilities, senior care facilities, schools, recreation centers, hospitals, and sports centers
19. Convenience stores with food services
20. Supermarkets with food services
21. Department stores/discount stores with food services

The following types of operations are generally considered part of the noncommercial division of the hospitality industry:

1. Employee feeding operations
2. Public and parochial elementary and secondary school food services
3. College and university dormitories and food services
4. Transportation food services, such as the Meals on Wheels program
5. Hospitals
6. Extended-care facilities Nursing homes
7. Clubs
8. Self-operated community centers, such as senior centers and day-care centers
9. Military installations
10. Camps
11. Public institutions, such as the food services in some government facilities
12. Adult communities
13. Correctional facilities
14. Religious facilities

MAJOR PURCHASING DISTINCTIONS IN HOSPITALITY OPERATION TYPES

In Chapter 5, we offer a more detailed discussion of the distinctions in the purchasing function that the industry makes among the various types of hospitality operations. Here in this introductory chapter, however, we only attempt to provide you with sufficient understanding to carry you through to Chapter 5. When we discuss hospitality operations in their traditional mode, we think first of the independent operation. In addition, those in the trade usually arrange the independent operations according to size: the small, medium, and large independents. The other major type of hospitality operation includes the multiunits and the franchises, which we discuss second.

THE INDEPENDENT OPERATION

The small independent is typically run by an owner-manager who usually does all the buying for the business. He or she also oversees the other related purchasing activities, such as receiving deliveries and paying the bills.

The medium independent generally involves more than one person in the purchasing function. Usually, the general manager coordinates the various activities that are performed by other management personnel. For instance, he or she typically coordinates the purchases of department heads, such as the dining room manager who needs ashtrays, the bartender who requires liquor, and the chef who needs foodstuffs. The general manager also oversees other related purchasing activities.

The large independent, usually a hotel, follows the purchasing function in much the same way the medium independent does, except that it may employ a full-time buyer. This buyer purchases for the various production departments, such as housekeeping, maintenance, engineering, and food service. Or a designated employee from each of these departments may be doing the purchasing: for example, a hotel may employ an executive steward to order supplies and to supervise the sanitation crew. Most familiar is the large independent operation that has a full-time food buyer, beverage buyer, and equipment and nonfood supplies buyer. These three may or may not be supervised by a purchasing vice president or an equivalent official. They are, almost certainly, supervised by a management person.

An idea addressed more completely in Chapter 5 is co-op buying, a concept that enjoys popularity among some independent hospitality operations, particularly some food services. As the phrase implies, co-op buying is a system whereby hospitality operations come together to achieve savings by purchasing food and supplies in bulk. Either they rotate the purchasing duties among themselves, or they hire someone to coordinate all the purchasing for them. For instance, some lodging properties belong to referral groups that provide, among other things, some central purchasing activities.

THE MULTIUNITS AND FRANCHISES

The second major category of hospitality operations in the purchasing function includes the multiunit companies and franchises. These interlocking operations organize their purchasing somewhat differently from that found in independent organizations. One usually finds, when examining a chain of hospitals, for example, a centrally located vice president of purchasing. Moreover, the company may maintain one or more central commissaries or distribution warehouses. The managers of the company-owned outlets receive supplies from the central distribution points under the authority of the vice president of purchasing. But these managers may also do a minimal amount of purchasing from local or national suppliers approved by that officer; they may order from approved suppliers without consulting the vice president of purchasing, or they may order everything from a central commissary.

In company-owned unit outlets, the internal organization for buying, particularly for restaurants, stipulates that the unit manager order most products from the central commissary or approved suppliers. The unit managers may have authority to buy a few things on their own, like a cleaning service or some carpentry work. But when they do this sort of purchasing, they nevertheless need to follow company policies and procedures.

In the company-owned, large hotel properties, a system similar to that of the large independents generally exists. That is, the vice president of purchasing at corporate headquarters may draw up some national contracts, establish purchase specifications, and set general purchasing policy. He or she may also purchase the stock for the central distribution warehouses and/or the central commissaries that the company owns. But, by and large, vice presidents of purchasing handle overall policy, and the individual hotel units, although they do not have complete freedom, nevertheless exercise a great deal of purchasing discretion within established limitations.

The typical franchise receives a good many supplies from a central commissary, but many of these noncompany-owned units try to do some purchasing locally—to maintain good relations in the community if nothing else. However, they quickly discover that they save considerable time, money, and energy by using the central commissary and/or central distribution center as much as possible. If there are no central commissaries and distribution centers available, the franchises usually order their needed stock from suppliers who have been prescreened and approved by the vice president of purchasing. They are, however, usually free to buy from anyone as long as that supplier meets the company's requirements.

THE USE OF THIS BOOK

This book has been designed for those students who expect to have careers in the hospitality industry. Because we seek to address all those individuals, not merely the readers who expect to specialize in hospitality purchasing, we have added several areas of discussion not usually found in a book aimed specifically at the professional purchasing agent.

We emphasize the managerial principles of the purchasing function and intertwine the purchasing function with the other related management activities that are faced by the hospitality operator on a day-to-day basis. We also deemphasize product characteristics.

The typical way of instructing hospitality purchasing agents is to teach them all about the various products that will be purchased, that is, focusing on the development of product knowledge, since an item cannot be purchased effectively without the purchaser's knowing a lot about it. We have not eschewed the product knowledge approach in this volume, but we have presented it in such a way that the typical hospitality operator will learn just enough about the major product categories that he or she can easily take on the burden, if necessary, of preparing the appropriate product specification needed to select and procure an item adequately.

This book includes product information, but it also includes several related purchasing activities, such as bill-paying, that most purchasing agents do not perform. However, the typical hospitality manager does become involved with many of these related activities. Hence, it is with this person in mind that we begin our discussion of selection and procurement for the hospitality industry.

KEY WORDS AND CONCEPTS

A broad view of purchasing

Central distribution center

Commercial hospitality operations

Commissary

Co-op buying

Executive steward

Franchise

Noncommercial hospitality operations

Procurement

Purchasing

Referral groups

Selection

Varying purchasing organizations

QUESTIONS AND PROBLEMS

1. Define the term "selection."
2. Define "procurement."
3. Explain the advantages of studying the broad view of the purchasing function.
4. Briefly describe the major segments of the hospitality industry.
5. Briefly differentiate between the ways in which the small and the large independents generally do their purchasing.

6. Briefly describe "co-op buying."

7. Briefly describe two typical purchasing procedures found in the multiunits and franchises.

8. Briefly describe how a local hospital (part of a large hospital chain) probably does its purchasing.

9. Name one reason a franchise might do some local buying.

10. Describe three duties of a vice president of purchasing in a large hotel or restaurant chain.

11. Why might a small, independent hospitality operation be interested in co-op buying?

12. Under what conditions do you think a franchise operation might be interested in co-op buying?

13. Do you think that purchasing from the commissary will result in cost saving for the buyer? Why?

14. Do you think that purchasing from the commissary will result in no cost saving for the buyer? Why? If possible, ask a manager of a local franchise operation to review this answer and your answer to Question 13.

15. Define the term "purchasing."

16. What is a referral group?

CHAPTER 2

DISTRIBUTION SYSTEMS

THE PURPOSE OF THIS CHAPTER

This chapter discusses:

- The major sources of products and services
- The major middlemen encountered in the channel of distribution
- The economic values added to products and services as they journey through the channel of distribution
- The buyer's position in the channel of distribution
- The determination of optimal values and supplier services that accompany the products and services purchased by hospitality operators

INTRODUCTION

Food, beverages, nonfood supplies, furniture, fixtures, equipment, and services follow relatively specific distribution channels. In most instances, an item goes from its primary source through various intermediaries to the retailer, as Figure 2.1 illustrates. As shown, however, there is also the possibility of a retailer's bypassing the intermediaries and dealing directly with the primary source.

DISTRIBUTION SYSTEM FOR FOOD, NONALCOHOLIC BEVERAGES, AND NONFOOD SUPPLIES

This distribution system involves a tremendous number of primary sources, intermediaries, and hospitality retailers. In the United States, there are several thousand primary sources and intermediaries competing to serve approximately 750,000 food-service operations and about 50,000

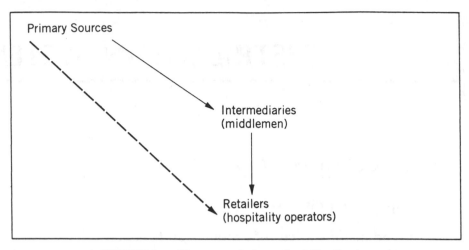

FIGURE 2.1. The general channel of distribution.

lodging facilities.[1] The typical nonchain hospitality property uses about 10 to 12 of these types of suppliers, but chain units generally use only about 6 to 8.[2]

SOURCES

Three major sources supply these products:

1. *Growers.* There are many farmers and ranchers who provide fresh food products to the hospitality industry.
2. *Manufacturers.* A manufacturer controls the production of an item from raw materials. For example, a paper products manufacturer can take wood materials and create paper napkins, bags, and place mats.
3. *Processors.* A processor (sometimes referred to as a "fabricator") takes one or more foods and assembles them into a new end product. For example, a processor could combine flour, water, yeast, tomato sauce, cheese, and seasonings to produce frozen pizzas. The new end product is usually referred to as a "convenience," "efficiency," or "value-added" food. Some processors are also manufacturers, but not all manufacturers are processors. The difference is that processors always work with food products.

INTERMEDIARIES

Several intermediaries, or middlemen, can be found in this distribution system:

1. *Distributors.* A distributor (sometimes referred to as a "merchant wholesaler") purchases products directly from growers, manufacturers, and/or processors for resale and delivery to customers. There are three major types of distributors:
   a. Specialty Distributor. A company that handles only one type or classification of products.
   b. Full-line Distributor. A company that provides foods and nonfood supplies.
   c. Broad-line Distributor. A company that provides foods, nonfood supplies, and equipment. It is more than likely that hospitality buyers purchase most of their product requirements from one or more distributors.

2. *Brokers.* An agent who represents one or more primary sources. Brokers neither buy nor resell. Their job is to promote products to potential buyers. They usually represent primary sources that do not employ their own sales forces.

   A broker most often works among hospitality operation buyers, generating enthusiasm for a particular product. If the broker is successful, he or she then convinces a distributor that there is a good "market" for the product and that the distributor can easily resell that product. In this example, the broker provides the sales effort, and the distributor provides the "end-user" services, that is, everything but the sales effort. The broker earns a sales commission, and the distributor earns a profit on the resale. The broker's objective is to provide the sales effort. In effect, he or she puts sellers in contact with buyers.[3]

3. *Manufacturer's Representatives.* These middlemen serve a function similar to that of brokers. One major difference is that they do more than simply get sellers and buyers together. They often provide such additional end-user services as actually carrying items in stock themselves, perhaps delivering items, and maybe also providing additional service to the buyers. Representatives seem to work more frequently with the equipment and furnishings trade, whereas brokers are usually found in the food and nonfood supplies trade.

4. *Manufacturer's Agents.* These intermediaries are similar to manufacturer's representatives. The major difference, though, is that they are employed by primary sources to represent them in a specific geographic area, and they work exclusively for one source. Usually, the agent is a manufacturer or processor who agrees to take on another primary source's products and try to sell them. This other primary source typically is a very small company that cannot afford to market and distribute its own products to a wide market area.

5. *Commissaries.* A commissary is usually owned and operated by a large food-service company. It processes food products according to exact requirements determined by the company. It is intended to sell and

ship products to company-owned restaurants or those owned by approved franchisees. Some commissaries, though, may also serve other types of restaurants that are not affiliated with the parent company.

6. *Wholesale Clubs.* A wholesale club is a type of "cash-and-carry" operation that is patronized primarily by small businesses who do not order enough product from distributors to qualify for deliveries. Distributors usually cannot make a profit on small-order deliveries. Some distributors have opened storefronts in their warehouses to provide cash-and-carry service, thereby accommodating the small businessperson as well as the large.[4]

7. *Buying Clubs.* A buying club (sometimes referred to as a "price club") is a group of independent purchasers who join together to purchase collectively in order to obtain more competitive prices that can save them money in the long run. The most typical kind of buying club is the purchasing co-op, which usually includes several small, independent food services and lodging properties. Some buying clubs, such as "contract houses," are operated by third parties that pass on some of the savings obtained through bulk purchasing to those buyers who are allowed to purchase from them. Buying clubs typically purchase directly from primary sources in order to obtain the lowest possible prices.

DISTRIBUTION SYSTEM FOR BEER, WINE, AND DISTILLED SPIRITS

SOURCES

Three major sources supply these products:

1. Brewers. They provide beer, ale, and other similar items.
2. Wine makers. They provide wine and other similar items.
3. Distillers. They provide bourbons, Scotches, and other similar high-alcohol-content items.

INTERMEDIARIES

Three major intermediaries, or middlemen, can be found in this distribution system:

1. Importers-Wholesalers. These intermediaries are responsible for importing alcoholic beverages into the United States as well as into each

state and local municipality. Most of them also act as liquor distributors, in that they buy the liquor from primary sources for resale to retail establishments such as restaurants, hotels, taverns, and supermarkets.

2. Distributors. Liquor distributors are specialized wholesalers who operate under a variety of legal sanctions. They purchase from sources and sell to retailers, and they are careful not to overstep their legal boundaries because their business is continually examined by regulatory authorities. In most states, these distributors are prohibited by so-called "tied-house laws" from becoming primary sources or retailers; tied-house laws mandate separate ownership for primary sources, intermediaries, and retailers.

   In many states, liquor distributors operate in exclusive territories; that is, they are the only suppliers to carry and offer particular brands to retail customers. As a result, there is little competition in the wholesale liquor trade.[5] In fact, the alcoholic beverage distribution system is defined so precisely that an individual purchaser has very little discretion in buying these items and almost no control over how the channel of distribution operates.

3. Alcohol Beverage Commissions (ABC). All states have one or more liquor control authorities, often referred to as the Alcohol Beverage Commission, or some similar title. The ABC controls rigidly the sale and purchase of alcoholic beverages. In some states, control is so tight that the state itself is the only purveyor of alcoholic beverages. When the state itself sells the alcoholic beverages, it is called a "control state" (as opposed to a "license state," where the ABC grants licenses to importers-wholesalers, distributors, and retailers who then handle the distribution of these products). When operating in a control state, the purchaser has no discretion. He or she must adhere exactly to the purchasing, receiving, and bill-paying procedures set forth by the governmental authority.[6]

DISTRIBUTION SYSTEM FOR FURNITURE, FIXTURES, AND EQUIPMENT (FFE)

SOURCE

There is one major source for FFE items—the manufacturer. The number of manufacturers of these items tends to be smaller than the number of sources in the other distribution systems.

INTERMEDIARIES

Six major intermediaries can be found in this distribution system:

1. Dealers. An equipment dealer typically functions much like a food distributor. Dealers usually buy equipment items from primary sources, earning their profit when they resell them to hospitality buyers. There are four major types of dealers:[7]

    a. Catalog House. This is typically a very small dealer that carries no inventory, or very little inventory, in stock. Items are selected by customers from one or more catalogs, and the dealer handles the ordering, delivery, setup, and so forth.

    b. Storefront Dealer. Storefront dealers (sometimes referred to as "discount operations") usually carry a minimum amount of inventory. They typically specialize in handling small, portable types of FFE.

    c. Heavy Equipment Dealer. Heavy equipment dealers specialize in handling large equipment installations. They carry inventory and are usually involved in the layout and design of new hospitality properties or major renovations.

    d. Full-service Dealer. Full-service dealers typically carry a full line of inventory and are able to provide all end-user services to their customers.

2. Brokers. FFE brokers are similar to brokers working in the distribution system for food, nonalcoholic beverages, and nonfood supplies. However, FFE brokers are not as numerous as their counterparts in other distribution systems.

3. Designers. These individuals typically work as consultants for hospitality operators. They are hired to design, say, an addition to an existing kitchen. During their work, they see to it that the appropriate FFE are ordered from the primary sources. They see to it that the required end-user services, such as delivery, are provided in a timely manner. Designers earn their income from the hospitality operator who employs them. They work for a fee.

4. Architects. They perform a function similar to that of designers.

5. Construction Contractors. They also perform a function similar to that of designers.

6. Distributors. Many distributors of food, nonalcoholic beverages, and nonfood supplies often supply several of the most commonly purchased FFE items. They typically sell replacement items and are not normally involved with the design and construction of new hospitality operations.

7. Leasing Companies. It is relatively common for retailers to lease furniture, fixtures, and equipment. For example, computers, ice machines, and video equipment are frequently leased or purchased on a rent-to-own plan.

DISTRIBUTION SYSTEM FOR SERVICES

Such services as advertising, consulting, and waste removal follow slightly different distribution patterns. There are few large national sources. Most sources are local and consist of many "mom and pop" operations or small partnerships. A few of these may be local offices of a national firm, or they may be franchisees of a national firm. For instance, the major accounting firms and printing companies have local offices or franchisees.

It is important to be sure that these small companies have actual expertise. Anyone can claim to be an accountant, for example, but normally a person qualified to provide a complete range of accounting and bookkeeping services is a certified public accountant (CPA).

RETAILERS

You, the hospitality operator, are generally classified as a retailer—someone who sells a product or service to its ultimate consumer.* You deal most often with one or more distributors. You probably make fewer contacts with brokers and manufacturer's representatives. As a rule, small operations rarely deal directly with a primary source. If they do, it is only when they purchase new equipment. Large corporations may, however, achieve economies of scale by purchasing large quantities of products directly from a primary source.

WHAT HAPPENS THROUGHOUT THE CHANNEL OF DISTRIBUTION?

We often hear that "the middleman makes all the money." For instance, it is suggested that the loaf of bread we buy contains only a few pennies' worth of food ingredients. What accounts for the rest of the price we pay for it?

As with most things purchased, the price paid is the sum total of several costs. Some cost is tacked on during the bread's journey through the distribution channel each time someone adds value to the original

---

* You could, of course, "sell" products in a not-for-profit organization, such as in most hospitals. Generally, though, both commercial and noncommercial operators adopt similar points of view concerning the management of any type of hospitality operation.

food ingredients. Four kinds of economic values may be added to a product as it passes from primary source to retailer: time, form, place, and information.

TIME VALUE

If you want to buy a product at the time you select, you must be willing to pay for this privilege. If, for instance, you wish to buy canned vegetables a little at a time instead of in bulk, your supplier will have to store these products and wait for you to order them. This is a major problem for the supplier, because he or she must assume the risk and cost of storing the items. The supplier also will have money sitting on the shelf.

Whoever pays money for a product, regardless of where in the distribution channel it may be, loses the use of that money for a while. For instance, a vegetable canner may have to pay cash for raw vegetables and may also have to store the finished products, the canned vegetables, for many weeks. During this time, money is tied up. And the longer the money is tied up, the more the vegetable canner has to charge for the canned vegetables. That is, the processor adds an interest cost for capital tied up in processing since he or she probably borrows money from a bank to carry inventory.

The time economic value can also include other types of financing. For example, the typical intermediary often provides credit financing to hospitality buyers. It is generally accepted procedure in the industry for a supplier to grant credit terms to his or her customers. These terms usually allow a buyer about 30 to 45 days after delivery before the bill must be paid. Obviously, this purveyor must earn an interest income for capital tied up in accounts receivable.

Some restaurant operators do the same thing when they price wines. They usually start with a certain price, and, for every year they must keep the wine in their wine cellar waiting for a buyer, they add a percentage markup to the price.

Thus, members of the distribution channel consider financing an investment. If they invest money in products, they cannot invest it elsewhere. Consequently, this investment must offer them a certain return at least equal to the amount of interest they would have to pay to borrow these same funds. And in a productive, profitable business, the expected rate would exceed the cost of borrowed capital.

FORM VALUE

Form is usually the most expensive value added to the products our industry purchases. Form is what turns a raw ingredient into something more user-friendly. For instance, a precut steak is much easier to purchase, store, and use than is a large cut of beef that must undergo quite a bit of processing in the restaurant kitchen. Unfortunately, the preprocessed item is much more expensive than the raw, unprocessed product.

The form value is also very expensive because highly processed items are normally packaged in costly containers. In fact, packaging becomes more expensive every day, especially for products that can be reconstituted in their own packages. In addition, buyers pay close attention to frozen food packaging, particularly if these products are to be stored on their premises for a while. The demand and the need for stronger and more effective packaging has increased the price that retailers must pay.

Another reason packaging and, hence, form value, adds so much to an item's final price is that there are numerous package sizes from which to choose. For example, catsup comes in several package types and sizes. You must be ready to pay more for individual servings of catsup than for catsup in large cans.

PLACE VALUE

If you want an item delivered to the place of your choice, you must pay for it. For instance, all other things being equal, it costs more to buy a car at the local dealership than if you traveled to Detroit to purchase it. Whoever moves a product from one place to another must recoup these costs in the selling price. This value is very expensive, especially when refrigerated and frozen products must be shipped.

INFORMATION VALUE

This is the least understood and, quite often, the most controversial economic value. An operator may be wiling to pay more for a product if some information, for example, directions for use, comes with it. This operator might not mind paying a little more for a dishwasher machine if the company sends an instructor for three or four days to instruct in how to use the machine. (On the other hand, most hospitality operators would not care to pay anything extra for the recipes on the backs of flour bags.)

SUPPLIER SERVICES VALUE

In addition to the four economic values just noted, there are the intangible supplier services that accompany the things you purchase. When you purchase something, you purchase not only whatever you desire, but also any additional services that come with it. For instance, a salesperson who puts a rush order in his or her car and runs it over to your operation in an emergency is a good friend; an accountant who prepares a special report "overnight" also is valuable to you. But how much more are you willing to pay for the added supplier services? This is not an easy question to answer. But one thing you can be sure of is that supplier services (sometimes referred to as "support functions") do work their way into an item's final price tag.

ULTIMATE VALUE

In the final analysis, a product's ultimate value consists of its quality and the values added to it. This final analysis does not always apply, especially when a perishable product must be price-discounted before it spoils. But, more often than not, the largest component of a product's final cost to the hospitality buyer can be attributed to the values added to that product as it journeys through the channel of distribution.

THE BUYER'S PLACE IN THE CHANNEL OF DISTRIBUTION

The buyers for most hospitality operations deal almost exclusively with middlemen, and the typical middleman is the distributor. Larger corporations normally break out of this strict pattern and purchase many of their items directly from the primary source, in effect bypassing some intermediaries.

The large firms feel that buying directly from the primary source offers considerable cost savings. Car prices in Detroit are generally cheaper than those in San Francisco, simply because the Detroit buyer takes advantage of the "place" value; in effect, he or she is compensated for receiving the car at its place of manufacture. Consider, too, the buyer who picks up food supplies in his or her own vehicle instead of waiting for the delivery. In this case, the price of the food should be lower because the buyer is providing the transportation value. (Notice, though, that the practice of picking up food oneself uses time and gasoline.) But assuming that the primary sources and middlemen would allow this choice, can you provide the economic values more cheaply yourself? Many large multi-unit corporations think so and have moved into what is called "direct buying with central distribution." They buy from the primary sources, take delivery of the products at central distribution centers, perhaps add some form value to the raw ingredients in their commissaries (e.g., clean, cut, and package raw vegetables), and then deliver them to their restaurants or hotel properties via their own transportation.

Some hospitality companies claim that buying directly in this manner saves a great deal of money.[8] In addition to cost reduction, these firms feel that they enjoy supply assurances, greater quality control, improved coordination, and an ability to overcome local suppliers' lack of technological capabilities.

Other firms, though, do not agree that eliminating the middlemen necessarily makes their operations easier and less costly.[9] For instance, many of them fear the considerable investment that may be necessary to launch such ventures. Some also feel that they may lack the necessary expertise and, thus, could become very inefficient and inflexible over time. Furthermore, these firms are not always eager to cut out local suppliers who may be able to provide unique supplier services, purchase discounts, and other competitive advantages.

Direct buying, central distribution, and the surrounding issues are controversial. The major problem seems to be that everyone has a different view of what it costs to provide the economic values. Historically, few companies have been able to usurp profitably the middleman's role. These activities can divert their attention away from the major part of their businesses, thereby causing them to lose sight of their customers.[10]

THE OPTIMAL ECONOMIC VALUES
AND SUPPLIER SERVICES

When the hospitality business is doing well, hospitality company officials are not usually eager to provide too many economic values and supplier services themselves. They would rather spend their time, for example, convincing retail customers to purchase hamburgers than concern themselves with the care and feeding of steers.

But when business takes a nosedive, hospitality company officials begin to examine, for example, the as-purchased (AP) price of preportioned steak per pound versus the AP price of a side of beef per pound. In other words, in recessionary periods, management may try to provide some of its own economic values and supplier services with the hope of restoring prerecessionary profits.

This type of thinking has cost many companies quite a bit of money. Middlemen are experts, and, in the long run, they can usually provide these values and services less expensively than the individual hospitality operation.

SELECTING ECONOMIC VALUES

Full-time buyers do not normally have complete control over which economic values their company provides for itself. As with the determination-of-quality issue, the owner-manager must make these decisions. Full-time buyers may, of course, make suggestions and help inform the decision-making process.

Part-time buyers, especially those who have other management responsibilities, often are expected merely to maintain the economic values decided upon by top management. Like full-time buyers, though, they may also make relevant suggestions and recommendations.

When managements do consider the feasibility of providing their own economic values, they tend to slant the analyses in the direction they desire. This skewing is easily done, since everyone has a particular idea of what it costs, for example, to cut his or her own steaks. Some managers include an extra labor expense; some assume no extra labor expense, thinking existing employees can absorb this extra task.

There is no doubt that it is very costly to provide your own economic values, particularly the form economic value. There are sound reasons that a precut, preportioned, New York sirloin steak sells for about $10.00 per pound, while the wholesale cut of beef (the short loin) that contains this type of steak, along with extra fat and trim, sells for about $6.00 per pound. To obtain the convenience of prefabrication, a buyer must compensate a primary source, and/or middleman, for the cost of payroll, payroll-related administrative expenses, the waste associated with meat processing, and the cost of energy needed to process and store the finished products.

But there are factors other than the "hard cost" figures that can enter the picture and haunt the manager later. Here are three of them:

1. Does the manager really want to get into the meat-packing business? Does he or she really want to buy a truck? Does the manager have the long-term desire, expertise, and time to engage in these activities?
2. Will there be antitrust problems? Large companies must consider this potentiality. For instance, some supermarket chains have expressed an interest in going way back in the channel of distribution for meat and becoming their own primary source. But no one is quite sure what the Justice Department would say about this plan. And it does not seem that too many want to find out.
3. What will other company employees, especially hourly employees and supervisors, say about taking on additional burdens? What will the labor unions say about it?

SELECTING SUPPLIER SERVICES

Buyers usually do have something to say about which supplier services their company should be willing to pay for. These supplier services are correlated with AP prices. Since buyers are not normally restricted to exact AP price limitations, they have a bit more discretion in deciding how much they are willing to pay for supplier services.

Generally, the arguments for and against supplier services are the same as those that center on the economic values issue. On one hand, there are owner-managers and buyers who are convinced that they can "do it all." On the other hand, there are those who see the supplier as a kind of "employee," and if the "employee" performs additional "service," he or she should be compensated for it. Thus, if the supplier performs additional service, they are willing to pay for it—and choose to do so if the supplier's cost for the service is less than the "in-house" cost.

Many analysts have searched futilely for a middle ground between these extremes. Perhaps there is no middle ground. But it is undoubtedly worthwhile to accept, and pay for, many supplier services. An executive in the hospitality industry once put it this way:

> Let's try to relate purchasing dollars to sales dollars to help us judge how much service is worth. Look at some hypothetical figures.

> ### Purchases per Month

> | | |
> |---|---|
> | Distributor's cost | $5,000.00 |
> | Average distributor markup 15% | +750.00 |
> | | $5,750.00 |
> | Monthly sales | $90,000.00 |
> | 12 hours per day, 30 days per month | 12 × 30 = 360 hours |
> | $90,000 ÷ 360 = $250.00 sales per hour | |

> Let's say we find a really great distributor who provides all those extras that we like, but who asks for a 17-percent markup on the same $5,000 monthly purchases. That's $850.00 or $100.00 more per month, or 28 cents per operating hour. Where should we devote our time and attention? To satisfying our customers and earning $250 worth of sales per operating hour? Or riding herd on our distributor to save 28 cents per operating hour? If you choose to cherry pick, have rigid receiving hours, and generally have a one-way relationship, you'll probably wind up paying more for less and spend more time at it.

> We believe that if we are to make a profit, we must give something of value to our customers. We know what we give our customers and [what we] must do to satisfy them. We hope that our distributors do also.[11]

In this example, it is assumed that the manager can increase sales by $250 if he or she spends more time with the restaurant's customers. Of course, many things contribute to sales volume; however, the point is well taken, and this example's approach is an honest attempt to quantify the difficult decision-making factors that surround the supplier services issue.

KEY WORDS AND CONCEPTS

ABC	Exclusive territories
AP price	Fabricators
Architects	FFE
Brewers	Full-line distributor
Broad-line distributor	Full-service dealer
Brokers	Growers
Buying clubs	Heavy equipment dealer
Cash-and-carry	Importers-wholesalers
Catalog house	Intermediaries
Central distribution	Leasing companies
Channel of distribution	License state
Commissary	Liquor distributors
Construction contractors	Manufacturer's agents and representatives
Control state	
Contract houses	Merchant wholesalers
Convenience foods	Middlemen
Co-op purchasing	Price club
Designers	Primary sources
Direct buying	Processors
Discount operations	Storefront dealer
Distillers	Supplier services
Distributors	Support functions
Economic values	Tied-house laws
Efficiency foods	Value-added foods
End-user services	Wholesale clubs
Equipment dealers	Wine makers

REFERENCES

1. National Restaurant Association (NRA) and American Hotel and Motel Association (AH&MA) estimates.
2. Patt Patterson, "Single Source of Supply: Does It Really Work?" *Nation's Restaurant News,* July 19, 1993, p. 109.
3. Michael Selz, "Independent Sales Reps Are Squeezed by the Recession," *The Wall Street Journal,* December 27, 1991, p. B2.

4. Jack Hayes, "Cash and Carry Wholesalers Pay Off for Small-Order Operators," *Nation's Restaurant News,* July 23, 1990, p. 27.

5. Mort Hochstein, "Questioning the Laws of Beverage Distribution," *Nation's Restaurant News,* May 9, 1994, p. 51.

6. Marj Charlier, "Existing Distributors Are Being Squeezed by Brewers, Retailers," *The Wall Street Journal,* November 22, 1993, p. 1A.

7. Patt Patterson, "Dealer Evolution Gives Rise to Many New Options," *Nation's Restaurant News,* September 21, 1992, p. 128.

8. See, for example, Carolyn Walkup, "New Chef-Owners Dodge Mistakes at Chicago Bistros," *Nation's Restaurant News,* December 16, 1991, p. 1. See also Ron Ruggless, "Furr's/Bishop's Tackles Food Manufacturing," *Nation's Restaurant News,* January 11, 1993, p. 7, and Jack Hayes, "CHPD Cuts Costs, Maintains Quality," *Nation's Restaurant News,* March 29, 1993, p. 74.

9. See, for example, Laurie P. Cohen, "The Man with the Midas Touch Meets His Match in the Nation's Steakhouses," *The Wall Street Journal,* January 3, 1994, p. B1. See also Richard Martin, "LaSalsa, Green Burrito Gear Up for Showdown," *Nation's Restaurant News,* February 8, 1993, p. 1.

10. Charles Bernstein, "Catch 22: Should Suppliers Operate Restaurants?" *Nation's Restaurant News,* May 28, 1990, p. 21.

11. George Topor, "What Price Service?" *Restaurant Business,* February 1977, p. 101.

QUESTIONS AND PROBLEMS

1. Define the major primary sources in the hospitality channels of distribution and explain how they differ from one another.

2. Describe the various intermediaries (the middlemen) with whom hospitality operators deal. How do these middlemen differ from one another?

3. How does the channel of distribution for services differ from the distribution channel for food?

4. Define the four economic values. Why might buyers be reluctant to pay for the information value?

5. Would it be profitable for a small restaurant owner to buy directly from a primary source? What specific items do you feel lend themselves particularly to this sort of buying?

6. Discuss how the need for financing adds to the ultimate cost of a product.

7. Assume that you are the buyer for a large corporation. Of the four specific values discussed in this chapter, which do you think you can provide more cheaply than the middleman? Why? Which do you think can be provided more cheaply by a middleman? Why?

8. What is the buyer's normal role in determining which economic values the company should provide for itself?

9. What is the buyer's normal role in determining which supplier services should be "purchased"?

10. What is the difference between a manufacturer's agent and a manufacturer's representative?

11. What is the difference between a price club and a wholesale club?

12. If possible, find one or two chain companies that provide many of their own economic values. Try to arrange a visit to their facilities. Also, try to get them talking about the costs and benefits of providing many of their own economic values. Before you go, see whether you can determine beforehand what they will say. (*Hint:* Even though many companies have lost money at this, they all seem to argue that their quality control has improved immensely. In addition, some firms are so insistent about certain types of services, usually those that suppliers are reluctant to provide, such as daily deliveries, that they embark on this difficult activity just to get exactly what they want; hang the cost!)

13. Assume that you are a small restaurateur. You have the opportunity to purchase your precut steaks less expensively from a competing restaurant chain's central commissary. Should you do this? Why?

14. What would be an advantage of purchasing a piece of equipment on the rent-to-own plan?

15. Assume that you have been purchasing your produce from one supplier for several years. You have been satisfied over the years. A new produce supplier seeks your business and offers you a $3\frac{1}{2}$ percent discount from what you currently are paying. What would you do?

16. Define the term "end-user services."

17. Give an example of each of the four economic values.

18. Give an example of a supplier service.

19. Briefly describe the typical distribution system for fresh meat.

20. What is the difference between a broker and a food distributor?

21. The food distributor normally earns a larger percentage of profit than the broker. What are some of the reasons you feel might account for this?

22. List three typical intermediaries you will find in the distribution system for FFE.

23. What is the primary function of a commissary?

24. What is the difference between a "control state" and a "license state"?

25. What is meant by the term "efficiency foods"?

CHAPTER 3

FORCES AFFECTING THE DISTRIBUTION SYSTEMS

THE PURPOSE OF THIS CHAPTER

This chapter discusses:

- The economic force and its effect on the channel of distribution
- The political force and its effect on the channel of distribution
- The ethical force and its effect on the channel of distribution
- The legal force and its effect on the channel of distribution
- The technological force and its effect on the channel of distribution

INTRODUCTION

In Chapter 2, we discussed the overall pattern of distribution in the hospitality business, as well as the values added throughout the distribution channel. That discussion did not take into consideration the forces that might interfere with the flow of products and services or with the final purchase price retailers must pay. In other words, several forces in the environment can have some effect on the price and availability of the products a hospitality operation needs. Figure 3.1 shows the major forces that affect the distribution channel, and the next sections discuss these forces.

ECONOMIC FORCE

Supply and demand considerations have a powerful effect on purchase prices, particularly the prices of perishable items. At the beginning of the channel of distribution, at the primary source level, supply and demand can be extremely important. Generally, at this level, the products are in their initial stages of production and are not readily distinguishable, re-

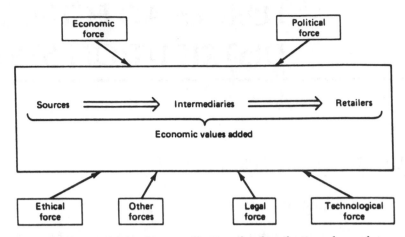

FIGURE 3.1. Major factors affecting the distribution channels.

gardless of the producer who has them. Little value has been added to these products; as a result, the prices at this stage are often set through a bidding procedure.

For example, many of the food products that eventually reach the retailer start out as such basic commodities as wheat, corn, cattle, poultry, and so on. Within the same product quality class, there may be little or no differences between Farmer Jones's wheat and Farmer Smith's. Consequently, if the amount of this wheat available exceeds the demand for it, the price drops until all the wheat is sold. Conversely, if the demand exceeds supply, prices rise until people quit bidding for the wheat. Supply and demand forces exert a major impact on commodity prices.

In many respects, the wheat farmers in this example occupy a precarious position unless they can do something to differentiate their products. This differentiation usually occurs when each primary source, or a middleman, attempts to apply his or her own version of the economic values. For instance, manipulating the form in which the product comes to market can earn a seller a stronger competitive position. Consequently, once a basic commodity gets into the channel of distribution, the rush is on to do something to make the product unique in the buyer's eyes.

If all products were sold strictly on a supply and demand basis, sellers would be forced to accept the price set by supply and demand conditions. Thus, they would worry constantly about producing an excessive supply. Wheat is wheat, period. Consequently, the wheat farmer must accept the established market price.

As products move along in the channel, they acquire various different values. In fact, by the time they reach middlemen, once-similar products may carry pronounced differences. This variety means that a seller begins to exercise a bit of control over the price; he or she need not always have to accept the price determined by supply and demand.[1]

But sellers cannot forget supply and demand conditions entirely. If a seller is overstocked, for example, he or she may have to lower the price to generate a demand—a situation often associated with perishable goods. Sellers try to avoid this problem, but they remain aware of the old axiom, "Sell it or smell it." And most of them would rather sell.

Buyers can expect to see varying prices for apparently similar products, even products that are in the same quality class. This situation is not so surprising once you realize that each seller can do something to differentiate the product.

Sellers normally strive to emphasize the product's overall value. Value is directly related to the quality of a product, but it also is directly related to the supplier services. Hence, a buyer supposedly would be willing to pay more for a product if the price included additional supplier services that the buyer felt provided increased value.

We use the term "value" intentionally, but to be even more accurate, we should use the term "perceived value," since value means different things to different people. Perceived value is equal to the "perceived quality" of a product or service plus the "perceived supplier services" divided by the "perceived edible portion (EP) cost." (See Figure 3.2 for a diagram of this equation.)

The perceived EP cost is the final cost to you of providing, for example, a finished steak dinner. Usually it is not equal to the AP price, since some products must normally occasion some waste: fat may have to be trimmed from the steak, resulting in an EP cost per pound higher than the AP price per pound; or, depending on the style in which you purchase steak, for example, precut and preportioned versus a whole beef carcass, you incur different labor costs as well as different energy costs utilized in the preparation of a steak dinner.

Traditionally, the EP cost of food included only the food ingredient cost, and the cost of nonfood supplies included only the cost of the usable product. Although difficult to assess, we think that it is more appropriate to expand the tradition and think of the EP cost in a different way. For instance, the labor cost associated with some food items may be higher than for other similar items. Also, the amount and cost of energy utilized in preparation can differ among similar food products. And the labor and energy required to clean can vary according to the type of cleaning solution used.

Throughout this book, we refer to the EP cost, not necessarily as the edible portion cost of food or beverage, but in the context of an as-served cost of food or beverage or an as-used cost per gallon of liquid cleaner. Our intent is not to provide mathematical formulas to compute these costs. But we want you to adopt a more panoramic view of the AP price—we wish to use the term "EP cost" to mean that the final cost of anything you

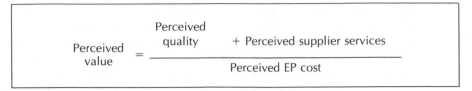

$$\text{Perceived value} = \frac{\text{Perceived quality} + \text{Perceived supplier services}}{\text{Perceived EP cost}}$$

FIGURE 3.2. Value as related to quality, supplier services, and EP cost.

buy includes several aspects, the least of which might be the initial AP price.

The relationship shown in Figure 3.2 is not a mathematical formula. We present it as an equation to emphasize the point that value is directly related to quality and supplier services but inversely related to the EP cost. For example, if quality and the supplier services remain the same while the EP cost drops, the value of the product increases. If quality decreases and the supplier services and EP cost remain constant, the value of the product decreases.

The possibilities for sellers' manipulation of the value equation and the ubiquitous supply and demand conditions create a market situation that economists refer to as "monopolistic competition." Monopolistic competition refers to the idea that each seller enjoys some sort of monopoly to the extent that he or she can manipulate products and services and make them seem to be unique. But the specter of supply and demand remains, and, ultimately, so does the need to be sensitive to price competition: suppliers cannot raise their prices that much higher than their competitors. Thus, most competitors have some sort of monopoly, but just enough to give them some control over prices and some flexibility in attracting customers.

Monopolistic competition is the most common type of marketing environment found throughout the hospitality industry. From the primary source to the retail level, all members of the distribution systems strive to highlight value over price. Suppliers do this in an attempt to convince retailers that there are no substitute suppliers capable of satisfying their needs. Restaurant managers likewise manipulate product quality, customer services, and menu prices in order to create repeat patronage. And hotel operators are quick to emphasize their unique sets of room quality, customer services, and room rates.

Buyers must realize that they might need to pay a bit more for a certain unique set of quality, supplier services, and EP cost. But this can easily be the most cost-effective alternative. There is no reason that buyers cannot enjoy considerable financial success by throwing in their lot with only those suppliers who provide the best perceived value. In the long run, a slightly higher AP price can very well generate the most profitable results.

POLITICAL FORCE

Large suppliers and hospitality enterprises exercise considerable political influence in state legislatures and even in the U.S. Congress. They frequently lobby for legislation that favors their business and against unfavorable legislation.

Generally, the primary sources in the channel of distribution have the most political influence. There are fewer sources than middlemen and hospitality operations; thus, the sources can make a well-organized, concentrated effort to assure that their interests are served.

The majority of members in the channels of distribution usually restrict their lobbying efforts to joining the local hospitality association and/or chamber of commerce. Since politics play a large part in how hospitality operators conduct their businesses, it should not be surprising to find many people trying to effect an easier business climate. One unfortunate aspect of this political reality is that as one channel member is accommodated, others may be hurt.

Political activity need not be restricted to local, state, and federal legislative bodies. Many political realities, or "unwritten laws," can affect a channel member's behavior. For instance, it may be politically unwise for a hospitality operator to provide some of his or her own specific values, thereby reducing some middleman's income, particularly if that operator may need the friendship of the middleman later. Or it may be unwise to delay paying your bills.

There is nothing inherently wrong with trying to influence legislation; this behavior is natural and often beneficial. Also, operators must constantly remember that politics are not restricted to government. Channel members must coexist, and the political force, as invisible as it may at times be, is there to influence product availability, prices, and channel member behavior.

ETHICAL FORCE

What is "the ethical force"? Better yet, what is "ethical"? Is it ethical for a large meat packer to restrict supply for a few days, hoping that the price for meat will rise? Is it ethical for buyers to browbeat suppliers, especially suppliers who may be in a slump and are, therefore, vulnerable? Is it ethical for a chef to return spoiled products if the products spoiled because the chef purchased too much and could not use them quickly enough? Is it ethical for a salesperson to keep quiet about a product's limitations if the buyer does not ask about them? No doubt most of us would agree that this is unethical behavior, but we must recognize that not everyone would view such practices as dishonest.

For instance, a recent study posed the following scenario: A beverage supplier offers a buyer a free case of wine for the buyer's personal use. What should the buyer do? Accept? Reject? Offer to buy it at a reduced price? Or take it and add it to the bar inventory instead of taking it home?

The results of the study indicated that approximately one-third of the respondents would accept the wine; just over one-half would say thanks, but decline the gift; about 1 percent would offer to purchase it at half-price; and approximately 8 percent would accept the wine, but add it to the bar inventory.[2]

Another study also indicated that there is no clear-cut definition of ethical behavior. Respondents were asked to indicate their perceptions of ethical issues in business practices. Interestingly enough, on the average, they felt that accepting gifts from suppliers was not considered very unethical.[3]

Some have suggested that questionable ethics are necessary speed bumps in the channel of distribution. The pressure on salespersons and buyers to consummate attractive deals practically compels members to behave unethically at times. The fact is that through the years a system of rebates and kickbacks has grown up among some traditional operators, and these may be thought of as an "unethical force" bearing on the channels. In large business firms, control systems quickly detect the inflation of cost, and the wise and ethical manager avoids these practices. An honest manager can advance more surely "playing by the rules" than can the dishonest person who must constantly devote energy to covering his or her tracks—and who constantly risks destroying his or her career.[4]

Several professional purchasing associations, among them the National Association of Purchasing Managers (NAPM) and the Foodservice Purchasing Manager's (FPM) Study Group of the National Restaurant Association (NRA), have developed codes of ethics to guide their members.[5] All buyers should be familiar with these codes. The buyers' supervisors should also examine these codes, since purchasing policies to guide a buyer's performance could inadvertently force the buyer toward unethical behavior.

Legislators continue to devote considerable attention to selling and buying practices, particularly the various rebate systems and other forms of economic favoritism. Adherence to sound ethics by channel members can ease this growing pressure, but, regardless of the future role of ethics in the hospitality channel of distribution, ethical and unethical forces continue to influence product availability and prices in the present.

LEGAL FORCE

Many buyers have discovered that a lawyer is a buyer's best friend. Channel members must accept a multitude of rules and regulations if they want to engage in buying and selling. And we have already seen how the political force works to influence legislation. The following paragraphs discuss the major pieces of legislation and their relevance to the hospitality channel of distribution.

THE SHERMAN ACT (1890)

The Sherman Act was America's first piece of antitrust legislation. Basically, it forbids any action that tends to eliminate or severely reduce competition. Interestingly, the language of this law is so general that just about anything relating to unfair competition could be covered under the Sherman Act.

MEAT SAFETY LEGISLATION

In 1906, Sinclair Lewis shocked the world with his book *The Jungle.* In it, he depicted the unspeakable sanitation conditions then prevalent in the meat-packing industry. His description of these horrendous conditions led immediately to a severe decline in meat consumption in the United States. It also forced the federal government to pass the Pure Food Act (1906) and the Meat Inspection Act (1907).

These acts allowed the U.S. Department of Agriculture (USDA), established by Congress in 1862, inspection powers throughout the channels of distribution. Although the USDA technically has the authority to inspect any channel member (except seafood production), it usually confines its activities to the inspection of red meat, poultry, and egg production.

The meat inspection legislation requires continuous antemortem and postmortem inspection of all meat intended for interstate and international commerce. State agriculture departments normally inspect meat plants that service customers located only within the particular states.

One of the major weaknesses in the original meat inspection laws was the lack of application to poultry products. Although voluntary poultry inspection was begun in 1926, required inspection of all poultry sold in interstate commerce did not take effect until the passage of the Poultry Products Inspection Act (1957) over 30 years later.

No further federal legislation affected red meat until 1967 when Ralph Nader and his "Nader's Raiders" focused attention on continuing abuses in the meat industry. Nader's efforts led to the passage of the Wholesome Meat Act (1967).

Current USDA food safety authority rests on a series of legislation based primarily on the Wholesome Meat Act (1967), the Poultry Products Inspection Act (1957), and the Wholesome Poultry Products Act (1968). The USDA enforces chemical residue standards and the standards dealing with wholesomeness, general sanitation, packaging, and labeling.

The current meat inspection system still relies on inspectors' observations of meat products. There is no testing of products for harmful bacteria that cannot be seen by the human eye, though the USDA has proposed adopting a procedure referred to as the Hazard Analysis and Critical Control Points (HACCP) system. This system (similar to one promulgated by local health districts for restaurant operators) requires food processors to identify places within their production cycle where the items can become contaminated (i.e., "critical points") and institute procedures to ensure food safety. It is thought that stronger regulations could reduce the number of food-borne illness outbreaks caused by meat and poultry products.[6]

There are approximately 7,000 federal meat and poultry plants and 2,900 state plants. There are approximately 7,400 federal inspectors employed to supervise the processing of approximately 6 million birds and 125 million beef, pork, and lamb animals per year.

Federal inspection is under the direction of a supervising veterinarian from the Food Safety Inspection Service (FSIS) division of the USDA. Approximately three-quarters of the FSIS's budget is allocated to meat and poultry inspections and operations.

THE FEDERAL FOOD, DRUG, AND COSMETIC ACT (1906)

Although meat inspection is primarily administered by the USDA, the Federal Food, Drug, and Cosmetic Act (FFDCA) provides the majority of food and drug regulation in the United States. The Food and Drug Administration (FDA) was created by Congress to administer this law.

The FDA is responsible for random inspections of approximately 50,000 food-processing plants in the United States. It employs about 350 inspectors. And, like the USDA, it has adopted the HACCP system to increase quality assurance.

The FDA has the power to inspect products, records, and premises of food and drug establishments to ensure compliance with the law. Among other powers, the FDA is granted the authority to establish maximum amounts permitted for various classes of contaminants whose presence in food cannot be avoided.

The FDA's power has been increased several times over the years. The major changes occurred in 1938, 1958, 1960, 1962, and 1967, perhaps the most significant one being the Cosmetics-Devices Act (1938). This law gave the FDA injunctive power and the authority to set food standards. Essentially, the FDA has the power to remove from the marketplace any product that does not meet its standards. Indeed, no other governmental agency can force a company to recall its products as quickly as the FDA can.

SEAFOOD SAFETY LEGISLATION

Seafood is not subject to the rigorous mandatory continuous inspection required for meat and poultry products. People have lobbied for a mandatory system,[7] but as of this writing, there is only a voluntary program.

A major continuous inspection program is housed in the United States Department of Commerce. For a fee, a fish processor can obtain continuous inspection of its processing plant. In return, the processor can label its packages as "Packed Under Federal Inspection" (PUFI). For an additional fee, the Commerce Department will provide a quality grading service.

Seafood is subject to the provisions of the FFDCA. This law allows the FDA to inspect periodically fish production to ensure that the foods are wholesome, sanitary, labeled correctly, and stored properly. Since there are approximately 5,000 fish-processing plants in the United States, a mandatory continuous inspection program is not feasible. However, the FDA requires seafood processors to use the Hazard Analysis Critical Control Point (HACCP) system when establishing and operating their production plants.

The FDA has the authority to examine seafood in interstate commerce and, if the product is defective, to seize it and prohibit its sale. In addition, the FDA is allowed to inspect imported seafood products before they are permitted entry into the United States.

There also is a cooperative program, involving federal and state agencies, that supervises the beds of water that are used to grow and harvest shellfish. This venture, referred to as the Interstate Shellfish Sanitation Commission, certifies areas that are suitable for the production of clams, oysters, and mussels and designates that they are in compliance with the Department of Commerce's voluntary inspection program.

Some seafood products are subject to legislation that, while not necessarily focused on seafood safety, nevertheless contributes to a safe, wholesome environment. For instance, the 1992 Marine Mammal Protection Act (a federal law) stipulates that only tuna harvested without endangering dolphins can be sold, distributed, or bought in the United States.

FEDERAL TRADE COMMISSION (FTC) (1914), AMENDED BY WHEELER-LEA ACT (1938)

This commission (FTC) deals with advertising, deceptive promotions, monopolies, and unprofessional conduct in the marketplace. It was established primarily to clarify the Sherman Act and to enhance its power.

THE CLAYTON ACT (1914)

The Clayton Act was yet another attempt by Congress to increase the federal government's control over antitrust violations. The Act essentially enumerates and amplifies the antitrust duties of the FTC.

Two illegal activities covered in this Act are of particular importance to channel members: (1) "Tying agreements," whereby sellers once forced retailers to purchase certain items (e.g., pickles) in order to gain the privilege of purchasing others (e.g., mustard), and (2) "exclusive dealing," whereby a salesperson forced a retailer to buy only his or her product (e.g., beer) and no other brands of that product. Exclusive dealing should not be confused with "exclusive selling," which is a perfectly legal type of franchise arrangement. For example, in most cases, a beer company can legally sell its beer to only a few select retailers, who then become the retailers that customers must contact if they want that particular brand of beer.

PERISHABLE AGRICULTURAL COMMODITIES ACT (1930)

The intent of this legislation is to control interstate commerce, specifically by prohibiting unfair and fraudulent practices in the sale of fresh and frozen produce. Wholesalers are required to be licensed by the government. If an individual hospitality operation does a bit of wholesale business on the side, it also may need such a license if the products sold in this manner cross state lines.

AGRICULTURAL ADJUSTMENT ACT (1933) AND AGRICULTURAL MARKETING AGREEMENT ACT (1937)

This legislation permits primary sources and intermediaries to work together in certain ways to solve their marketing problems and to ensure a steady flow of perishable products. The Acts exempt these sellers from some antitrust laws. For example, in certain cases, sellers of these products may join together to form seller co-ops, which market the products of each individual primary source.

THE ROBINSON-PATMAN ACT (1936)

This Act, known as the "small-business protection act," was designed to enhance further the power of the federal government to control antitrust violations. The primary thrust of the Act was the limitation placed on companies that used various types of price discounts when marketing their goods and services.

Among other things, this Act addressed three specific loopholes. (1) Up until 1936, sellers could give "promotional discounts" to buyers of their choice. After 1936, this became a form of illegal price discrimination if the discounts were not offered to all qualified buyers. (2) It is legal for sellers to offer a buyer a discount if the buyer purchases in large amounts. But it has been illegal since 1936 to set this amount so high that only one or two buyers can hope to reach it. In other words, the Robinson-Patman Act incorporated a "quantity limits provision" so that the quantity a buyer must purchase to qualify for a discount must be reasonable. (3) A supplier cannot practice "predatory pricing." That is to say, he or she cannot price goods or services so low that it would drive all other competitors out of the marketplace, thereby affording this lone supplier a monopoly and the opportunity to raise prices significantly in the future.

The Clayton Act and Robinson-Patman Act do not prohibit all types of price discrimination. Generally, two buyers can pay different prices for the same product if one buyer, for example, provides some value. For instance, purchasing large quantities of products is a way for buyers to provide their own financing as well as storage. As a reward for bulk purchasing, a supplier can legally charge a lower price. In general, sellers can manipulate the price if the goods are of unlike quality or quantity. Sellers also can reduce their prices at a moment's notice to meet a competitor's recently reduced price.

THE HART ACT (1966–1969)

The Hart Act altered the way products are packaged, particularly with regard to a package's pictorial aspects. The Act, enforced by the FDA, sought to eliminate misleading descriptions and illustrations. It also sought to force companies to adopt standard packaging sizes, which it failed to accomplish. The Hart Act has managed to frighten several channel members, especially primary sources, who quickly adopted many of the late Senator Hart's informal suggestions voluntarily.

PACKAGE LABEL REGULATIONS

The federal government requires the labels of packaged, processed foods to contain the following information:[8]

1. The common or legal name of the product.
2. The name and address of the food processor, or the distributor, of the items.
3. The net contents in the package, listed according to count, weight, or other appropriate measure.
4. A listing of ingredients, in descending order, from greatest proportion to least proportion. (This requirement may be unnecessary if a "standard of identity" has been established for the product. A standard of identity essentially establishes what a food product is—for example, what a food product must be to be labeled "strawberry preserves."

The federal government has developed standards of identity for approximately 235 products.)[9]

5. A notation of any artificial flavoring or chemical preservative added to the product.

6. Serving size (in typical measures, such as "cups") and number of servings per container. (The federal government has developed standard serving sizes for approximately 150 food categories.)

7. Number of calories per serving.

8. Number of calories derived from fat.

9. Amount of fat, saturated fat, cholesterol, sodium, sugars, dietary fiber, protein, total carbohydrates, and complex carbohydrates.

10. Amounts of important vitamins and minerals.

11. If the product is a beverage, the amount of juice (fruit or vegetable) it contains.

12. A notation that the product falls below the standard of fill, if relevant. (A "standard of fill" indicates to the processor how full a container must be to avoid deception. It prevents the selling of air or water in place of food; prescribed amounts of air and water, though, are permissible.)

13. Also, if relevant, a statement that the product falls below the standard of quality. (A "standard of quality" is the minimum standard a product must meet in order to earn the federal government's lowest possible quality grade. For instance, if canned green beans are excessively broken, the label could read "Below Standard of Quality: Excessively Broken.")

14. All label information must be noted in English unless an imported product with a foreign-language label will not deceive consumers, or if such a product will be distributed in an area where the foreign language is the predominant language.

15. If the food processor makes any nutritional or dietary claims, the package label must carry government-approved terminology. There are several terms that can be used as long as the processor meets their strict definitions. (See Figure 3.3.)

16. A standardized list of nutrition facts, as articulated by the Nutrition Labeling and Education Act (1990), must be included on the package label. (See Figure 3.4.) (Technically, the package labels of processed foods sold only to food services that will process them further and resell them to guests, do not have to include nutrition facts. However, it is unusual to see a package label today that does not include this standardized information.)

17. If the product is raw or partially cooked meat or poultry, it must contain safe-handling instructions on the package label, that is, in-

NUTRITION/HEALTH CLAIM	STANDARD DEFINITION
Calorie free	Fewer than 5 calories
Cholesterol free	Less than 2 milligrams cholesterol and 2 grams (or less) saturated fat
Fat free	Less than $1/2$ gram fat
Heart healthy	Contains 13 grams of oat bran or 20 grams of oatmeal and is low fat and low sodium
Light (lite)	One-third fewer calories (or 50 percent less fat)
Low calorie	40 calories (or less)
Low cholesterol	20 milligrams (or less) cholesterol and 2 grams (or less) saturated fat
Low fat	3 grams (or less) fat
Low sodium	140 milligrams (or less) sodium
Sodium free	Less than 5 milligrams sodium

FIGURE 3.3. Standard definitions of some nutrition/health claims.

structions that indicate how the product should be handled in order to avoid contamination.

In addition to federal government labeling requirements, many states and local municipalities issue their own label regulations. For instance, in California, a food processor must put a health warning on any food that contains an ingredient(s) suspected of causing cancer or birth defects.

FRANCHISE LAW

A franchisor can legally require franchisees to adhere to standards of quality set forth by the franchisor. For instance, franchisors normally prepare strict product specifications that franchisees must use when purchasing all food, beverage, and nonfood supplies. These specifications ensure quality and cost control as well as a consistent appearance.

Usually a franchisor will not force a franchisee to purchase from the franchisor's commissary and/or central distribution center; nor would a franchisee necessarily be required to buy from a supplier designated by the franchisor. However, it would appear that, under some circumstances, a franchisor can impose these types of restrictions on franchisees.[10] At one time, the courts held these restrictions illegal, citing them as violations of antitrust legislation. More recently, though, court rulings have eased these limitations on franchisors, as long as they do not derive an

Nutrition Facts

Serving Size 1 cup (228g)
Servings per Container 2

Amount per Serving

Calories 90	*Calories from Fat 30*

	% Daily Value*
Total Fat 3g	5%
Saturated Fat 0g	0%
Cholesterol 0mg	0%
Sodium 300mg	13%
Total Carbohydrate 13g	4%
Dietary Fiber 3g	12%
Sugars 3g	
Protein 3g	

Vitamin A 80%	•	Vitamin C 60%
Calcium 4%	•	Iron 4%

* Percent Daily Values are based on a 2,000 calorie diet. Your daily values may be higher or lower depending on your calorie needs:

	Calories:	2,000	2,500
Total Fat	Less than	65g	80g
Sat Fat	Less than	20g	25g
Cholesterol	Less than	300mg	300mg
Sodium	Less than	2,400mg	2,400mg
Total Carbohydrate		300g	375g
Dietary Fiber		25g	30g

Calories per gram:
Fat 9 • Carbohydrates 4 • Protein 4

FIGURE 3.4. Example of nutrition facts on a package label.

economic benefit from requiring franchisees to carry certain specified products.[11]

THE INTERNAL REVENUE SERVICE (IRS), THE BUREAU OF ALCOHOL, TOBACCO, AND FIREARMS (BATF)

These federal government agencies are responsible for the orderly and legal sale, distribution, and purchase of alcoholic beverages. They ensure that (1) no adulterated product enters the marketplace; (2) products are produced, sold, distributed, and purchased only by duly licensed entities; and (3) all appropriate taxes and fees are collected.

STATE AND LOCAL LEGISLATION

All the laws discussed so far are federal. Some states and municipalities have adopted somewhat stricter versions of them as well as additional legislation not found in the federal statutes. For instance, although the federal government does not mandate fish plant inspection, some states do. In addition, many channel members must contend with several state and county liquor codes.

CONTRACT LAW

A contract is "a voluntary and lawful agreement, by competent parties, for a good consideration, to do or not do a specified thing."[12] A completed purchase order, once accepted by a supplier, becomes a legally enforceable contract. If buyers renege on their promises, they may be sued by their suppliers and forced to perform according to the terms established in the contracts.

In some instances, a buyer purchases only a small amount of merchandise at one time and may not prepare a formal purchase order document. He or she may simply call in an order to a local supplier instead of mailing in or faxing a written order. In some cases, a verbal commitment of this type can carry the force of a written contract. Article 2-201 of the Uniform Commercial Code (UCC) states that a purchase order of $500 or more is not enforceable in a court of law unless the agreement is reduced to writing. Consequently, a small verbal order of, say, $100, could be considered legally binding on both parties.

After an order is made with the supplier, a buyer might request a written acknowledgement from the supplier. Technically, no contract exists if a supplier does not acknowledge his or her intent to enter into a legally binding agreement.

Presumably, once the goods are delivered, the buyer will deem them acceptable and will pay for the merchandise. However, legal problems might arise if the goods delivered do not meet the agreed-upon standards of quality, quantity, and price. A buyer is able to return these goods if he or she (1) inspects a representative sample of the goods; (2) indicates why the goods are not acceptable; and (3) informs the supplier that the goods are being rejected. If a buyer fails to inspect, reject, and indicate why this action is being taken, he or she will have accepted the merchandise and will be responsible for paying for them.[13]

A great deal of trust must exist between buyers and suppliers. In some situations, we cannot take time to create written documentation; we must rely on our suppliers to treat us honestly and with good faith. As long as all parties have each other's best interests at heart, all of them can coexist and achieve their long-term goals.

This brief discussion highlights the major issues that a purchasing agent needs to consider when preparing purchase orders. There are other laws, federal, state, and local, for a buyer to consider. In fact, an operator should immediately seek legal advice whenever a question arises. For instance, there may be unique deposit and refund laws in your area that must be considered before entering into a long-term purchase agreement.

AGENCY LAW

Salespersons need to know the precise authority operators delegate to their buyers. In general, buyers have the authority, as their company's agents, to bind legally their companies to purchase order contracts. Hospitality companies usually limit a buyer's authority by setting a dollar limit on the purchases he or she can contract for. If such a limitation exists, however, salespersons and their companies must be notified, or else they can rightfully assume that the buyer has unlimited authority.

TITLE TO GOODS

It is important for buyers to know the precise moment when the title to any product passes to their firm because, at the point of title transfer, the buyer's firm assumes responsibility for the item. Title can pass at any one of many points in the market channel. Usually, when purchasing from intermediaries, the hospitality operation takes title when the delivered merchandise is received, inspected, and signed for by a receiving agent. Under a direct-buying arrangement, the hospitality operation takes title when the merchandise leaves the primary source's premises; typically, the primary source places the merchandise on a common carrier "free on board" (FOB), which states that, once it is on board, the buyer now owns the property and takes responsibility for its safe transit.

If the buyer takes title before actually receiving the item, even though he or she may not have actually paid for the product, it, as well as the risk, belongs to his or her company. (Parenthetically, when taking a risk like this earlier than necessary, the buyer may earn a slightly lower AP price.)

CONSIGNMENT SALES

Although consignment sales are not common in the hospitality industry, and are not allowed for alcoholic beverages, they do appear now and then, especially in seasonal resort areas where buyers must stock up well before the doors are opened to cash-paying guests. Off-premises caterers also tend to rely on consignment sales from time to time, especially for big parties that are allowed to pay most of their catering bills after the functions are over.

A typical consignment sale stipulates that the buyer of a product need not pay until his or her company sells the product. This is a good way for a retailer to work with a supplier's money, but a desire to buy "on consignment" tends to imply that the buyer is in a precarious financial position.

WARRANTIES AND GUARANTEES

Warranties and guarantees may be either "expressed" or "implied." The express warranty or guarantee is written out in, ideally, straightforward language. The implied versions are, as the name suggests, either inferred by the buyer or implied by the seller. Courts of law have been known to allow salespersons to voice a degree of prideful exaggeration and to include a certain amount of subjectivity, or permissible puffery, in a sales pitch. Consequently, a buyer may face problems if he or she seeks retribution when the product is not, after all, "the best in the land."

PATENTS

Retailers must be careful to avoid adopting illegally someone else's patented procedures. For example, at one time, only a select few were authorized to use the pressure fryers. Nor can copyrights be violated. For instance, you cannot sell Pepsi for Coke.

REBATES

Rebates, gifts of cash or product, are legal as long as suppliers offer all buyers the same rebate possibility. An exception exists in the liquor trade, where all rebates are illegal on the wholesale level. Oddly enough, a buyer may unknowingly take a rebate, having assumed that all buyers have had the same opportunity. If he or she is, in fact, the only buyer receiving a rebate, he or she could be implicated in a legal action.

Rebates are also against the law when buyers and sellers conspire to inflate the price of a product and the buyer takes a personal rebate after the purchase. (See Chapter 15 for a more complete discussion of kickbacks, which is the term normally used to refer to illegal rebates.)

TECHNOLOGICAL FORCE

Many technological advances in the hospitality channel of distribution have taken place. The following paragraphs discuss some current developments.

GENETICALLY ENGINEERED FOODS

Food processing has advanced to the point whereby several foods can be altered genetically in order to improve their shelf life and increase their flavor and availability in the marketplace. For example, tomatoes that have been genetically engineered can remain much longer on the vine than those produced the traditional way.[14] While there is some question regarding the safety of these items, it would appear that, before too long, buyers will have several options from which to choose.

PRODUCT PRESERVATION

Foods reach us today in many forms, and one of the main reasons for this is the sophisticated level of preservation technology we have reached. Although some persons are wary of some preservation processes, no one can deny that we would not enjoy many of the foods we take for granted if these products deteriorated noticeably through the channel of distribution.[15]

Closely related to the genetic engineering of foods are techniques that can be used by food processors to increase productivity. For instance, government-approved irradiation techniques can reduce product spoilage.[16] And giving government-approved hormones to dairy cows can increase their output of milk significantly.[17] Once again, though, some persons are very leery of these practices and feel they result in foods that are unsafe for human consumption.

VALUE-ADDED FOODS

Product processing, from primary source to retailer level, has reached higher and higher levels of sophistication. There are a very large number of convenience foods on the market today. It is the rare hospitality operation that does not purchase some of these products.

Hospitality operators normally purchase these items in order to save money in the long run. While it is generally true that a value-added food is much more expensive than its raw counterpart, the potential savings in labor preparation time, energy usage, and storing and handling chores may reduce the EP cost to the point at which overall profit margins will be attractive.

In some cases, the AP price of a convenience food may actually be less than the AP price of the raw ingredients needed to fabricate the item. This is especially true with "first generation" convenience foods. For instance, frozen orange juice concentrate is a first-generation convenience food and, like many of the older convenience foods, is usually less expensive than its homemade equivalent. Since it usually takes about three oranges to produce one cup of orange juice, an eight-ounce serving of fresh-squeezed juice can easily cost twice as much as some processed products to prepare and serve.

Almost every food item purchased today has some degree of form value added to it. "Convenience," then, is all a matter of degree. The hospitality buyer can look forward to having an ever-increasing supply of convenience foods from which to choose.

TRANSPORTATION

In many respects, faster transportation constitutes a form of product preservation. But it is much more. Buyers today can expect faster, larger, and more predictable deliveries, which often reduces the number of purchase orders they must make. Also, the increased dependability of transportation allows the buyer companies, in turn, to fulfill more readily the promises they make to their customers.

COMPUTERIZATION

The computer is firmly entrenched in the hospitality industry. The selection and procurement function enjoys many of the labor-saving aspects of this form of technology.

For instance, suppliers now have the ability to use the computer to plot the most cost-effective delivery-truck routes. Salespersons can carry lap-top computers with them when making their sales calls in order to expedite the ordering process. And hospitality operators can use the computer to perform a whole host of purchasing-related duties, such as inventory valuation and control, menu planning and recipe costing, and purchase forecasting.[18]

Most large suppliers have computerized their total operations. The hospitality operator who has a touchtone phone and/or a personal computer can communicate directly with a supplier's warehouse computer, thereby hastening the ordering process as well as increasing order accuracy. Generally speaking, if a supplier has the desired products available in his or her warehouse, a call to the computer by 5:00 P.M. the day before a regularly scheduled delivery date will ensure delivery the next day.

The smaller, independently owned and operated hospitality operations typically deal with sales representatives, either in person or over the telephone. To some extent, all buyers enjoy some personal contact with their suppliers.

One of the more popular, cost-effective ordering procedures to come about is the use of the fax machine to enter orders with the approved suppliers. This technique ensures that the buyer will have a copy of the purchase order. It also eliminates any ambiguity or mistakes that can occur when orders are communicated personally to a sales representative.

The future of computerization of the selection and procurement function will probably resemble what is sometimes referred to as the "paperless office."[19] Large suppliers and hospitality operations will increasingly adopt an Electronic Data Interchange (EDI) system, a communications system that connects distributors and buyers via a computer network, allowing computers to communicate with a standardized format. Usually this type of system involves a third party providing the technological support, allowing sellers and buyers to concentrate on their main businesses and leave the record keeping to someone else. This type of system also enhances the inventory management procedure and tends to give all customers the best prices and most supplier services.[20] (See Chapter 16 for an extended discussion of computer technology applications in purchasing.)

PACKAGING

According to the USDA, packaging accounts for (on average) about 8 percent of the purchase price of food products. It also estimates that in about one-fourth of all food and beverages sold, packaging costs exceed the cost of the edible ingredients. In general, the more processed or complicated a food product is, the higher the packaging costs.

Packaging is extremely important to the hospitality operator because it directly impacts the quality, shelf life, and convenience of the food or beverage products. Unfortunately, the higher-quality packaging demanded by our convenience-oriented society has caused a consumer backlash in the United States. Our quest for more and more processed "instant" foods has led food fabricators to create packaging materials that may pose a long-term harmful effect on our environment.

Some packaging today not only can make a food product more convenient, but it can also contribute to better taste. For example, many products are packed in Controlled Atmosphere Packaging (CAP), which involves placing an item in waxboard, cardboard, aluminum, and/or plastic, removing all existing gases by pulling a vacuum, and then introducing a specially formulated mixture of gases that will extend the shelf life of the particular product in the package.

A common form of CAP is the aseptic packs that are used to package juices, wines, and unrefrigerated milk; shelf-stable, unrefrigerated convenience meals; and processed produce and other grocery products. These items are convenient to use. They do not require expensive refrigerated storage. They tend to taste better, because the aseptic sterilization process

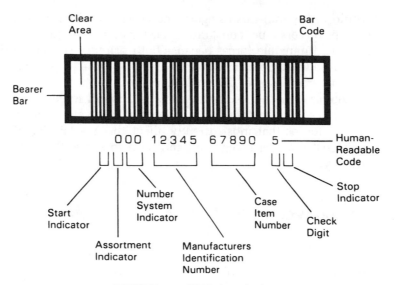

FIGURE 3.5. UPC description.

requires less heating time than the canning process. Another plus is that these types of containers usually can be stacked more readily and take up less storage space than regular cans or bottles.[21]

Some packaging can also increase the safety of the foods we purchase. For instance, some products have time- and temperature-sensitive food labels attached, which will change color if the products have been stored too long and/or have been subjected to unsafe storage temperatures.

Another welcome packaging advance is the application of the Universal Product Code (UPC) to the hospitality industry. (See Figure 3.5.) These familiar bar codes that are present on most grocery store product offerings are being introduced into the hospitality industry, thanks to the efforts of the International Foodservice Manufacturers Association (IFMA) and other like-minded business organizations. Eventually, the use of this technology will lead to more efficient order processing, improved receiving operations, more accurate inventory valuation and control, and increased opportunities to do business electronically, thereby saving a bit of labor cost.[22]

OTHER FORCES

It may be more appropriate to label other forces "intangible forces." For example, such factors as a supplier's advertising and promotion effectiveness, pricing policy, credit terms, and the conviviality of salespersons would fall within this category and certainly affect the channel of distribution. Buyers must constantly guard against reacting disproportionately to these intangible forces because both primary sources and middlemen use these intangibles to differentiate the products and services they sell. The buyer must be a "rational buyer."

Buyers and their superiors must accept all forces as part of the game they have elected to play. In the final analysis, though, the dynamic market forces that most directly affect the availability of products and their cost must be recognized and used to shape the overall purchasing strategy.

KEY WORDS AND CONCEPTS

Agency law

Agricultural Adjustment Act

Agricultural Marketing Agreement Act

Antitrust

AP price

Aseptic pack

As-served cost

As-used cost

Basic commodity

BATF

Business ethics

CAP

Clayton Act

Computerization

Consignment sale

Contract law

Convenience foods

Cosmetics-Devices Act

Economic force

EDI

EP cost

Ethical force

Exclusive dealing

Exclusive selling

FDA

FFDCA

First-generation convenience foods

FOB

Foodservice Purchasing Managers (FPM) Study Group of the NRA

Franchise law

FSIS

FTC

Genetically altered foods

Hart Act

HACCP system

IFMA

Intangible forces

Interstate Shellfish Sanitation Commission

Irradiation

IRS

Kickback

Legal force

Marine Mammal Protection Act

Meat Inspection Act

Monopolistic competition

National Association of Purchasing Managers (NAPM)

Nutrition Labeling and Education Act

Ordering procedures

Packaging

Paperless office

Patent	Standard of identity
Perceived value equation	Standard of quality
Perishable Agricultural Commodities Act	Supply and demand
	Technological force
Political force	Time- and temperature-sensitive food labels
Poultry Products Inspection Act	
Predatory pricing	Title to goods
Product preservation	Transportation
Product processing	Tying agreement
Promotional discount	UCC
PUFI	UPC
Pure Food Act	USDA
Quantity limits provision	US Department of Commerce
Rebate	Value-added foods
Robinson-Patman Act	Warranties and guarantees
Safe-handling instructions	Wheeler-Lea Act
Seller co-ops	Wholesome Meat Act
Sherman Act	Wholesome Poultry Products Act
Standard of fill	

REFERENCES

1. F. William Barnett, "Making Game Theory Work in Practice," *The Wall Street Journal,* February 13, 1995, p. A14.

2. Kim Johnson and Susan Pottorff, "Ethics and Hospitality: Perceptions of Hotel and Restaurant Management Students," *1992 Annual CHRIE Conference Proceedings* (Poster Session), Orlando, FL.

3. Craig C. Lundberg, "The Views of Future Hospitality Leaders of Business Ethics," *Hospitality & Tourism Educator,* Spring 1994, p. 11.

4. See, for example, Thomas L. Trace, John F. Lynch, Joseph W. Fisher, and Richard C. Hummrich, "Ethics and Vendor Relationships," in *Ethics in Hospitality Management: A Book of Readings* (edited by Stephen S. J. Hall), 1992, p. 155.

5. See, for example, Lendal H. Kotschevar and Richard Donnelly, *Quantity Food Purchasing,* 4th ed. (New York: Macmillan, 1994), pp. 113–114. See also, Patt Patterson, "Certification Adds Professionalism to Purchasing," *Nation's Restaurant News,* March 23, 1992, p. 36.

6. Marilyn Chase, "Food Poisoning Is No Picnic as Bugs Widen Their Reach," *The Wall Street Journal,* May 22, 1995, p. B1.

7. Robin Lee Allen, "New Senate Bill Backs Seafood Inspection Plan," *Nation's Restaurant News,* April 27, 1992, p. 3.

8. Rose Gutfeld, "Food-Label 'Babel' to Fall as Uniform System Is Cleared," *The Wall Street Journal,* December 3, 1992, p. B1.

9. Bruce Ingersoll, "Label Rules to Foster Healthful Foods," *The Wall Street Journal,* December 26, 1991, p. 9.

10. "A Big Franchiser of Hotels Wins Dismissal of Antitrust Charges," *The Wall Street Journal,* January 12, 1995, p. B2. See also, Jeffrey A. Tannenbaum, "Franchisees Balk at High Prices for Supplies from Franchisers," *The Wall Street Journal,* July 5, 1995, p. B1.

11. "District Court Rules McDonald's Can Require Licensees to Use Coke," *Nation's Restaurant News,* January 27, 1986, p. 84.

12. James O. Eiler, "Hotel Contracts and Words," *Hotel and Casino Law Letter,* September 1990, p. 87.

13. John R. Goodwin and Jolie R. Gaston, "Creating Sales Contracts in the Hospitality Industry," *Hospitality & Tourism Educator,* Spring 1994, p. 23.

14. Laurie McGinley, "U.S. Clears Calgene Tomato, the First Genetically Engineered Food to Be Sold," *The Wall Street Journal,* May 19, 1994, p. B8.

15. Richard Gibson, "'Shelf-Stable' Foods Seek to Freshen Sales," *The Wall Street Journal,* November 2, 1990, p. B1.

16. Bruce Ingersoll, "FDA Approves the Use of Irradiation for the Control of Bacteria on Poultry," *The Wall Street Journal,* May 2, 1990, p. B4.

17. Richard Koenig, "Wisconsin Bans Hormone to Raise Cows' Milk Output," *The Wall Street Journal,* April 30, 1990, p. B4.

18. Bill Eacho, "Quality Service Through Strategic Foodservice Partnerships: A New Trend," *Hosteur,* Spring 1993, p. 22.

19. Heidi Splete, "Paperless Processing," *F & B Business,* March/April 1995, p. 56.

20. Peter F. Drucker, "The Economy's Power Shift," *The Wall Street Journal,* September 24, 1992, p. A16.

21. "In Your Opinion, What Are the Three Most Important Advancements Made in Food Products and Packaging in the Past 10 Years?" *FoodService Director,* May 15, 1990, p. 16.

22. Carolyn Walkup, "Industry Buyers Learn About Inventory, Cost-Saving Advantages of UPC Systems," *Nation's Restaurant News,* June 4, 1990, p. 64.

QUESTIONS AND PROBLEMS

1. Define "monopolistic competition." How does this concept differ from a strict monopoly? From strict price competition?

2. Give an example of how the political force affects the hospitality channel of distribution.

3. Is it ethical for a buyer to cancel an order with one supplier because he or she just found out that the item can be purchased at a lower price from someone else? Why or why not?

4. Define the following:

(a) Sherman Act	(i) Consignment sale
(b) USDA	(j) Rebate
(c) FDA	(k) Value-added foods
(d) FTC	(l) Federal Meat Inspection Act
(e) Tying agreement	(m) Perishable Agricultural Commodities Act
(f) Exclusive dealing	(n) Poultry Products Inspection Act
(g) Quantity limits provision of the Robinson-Patman Act	(o) IRS
(h) Agency law	(p) BATF

5. Do rebates foster unethical behavior among channel members? Why or why not?

6. Explain how buyers and sellers might be influenced by advertising and promotion.

7. How are prices affected by supply and demand conditions? Is it ethical to hold products off the market in an attempt to increase their prices? Why or why not?

8. Assume you own a coffee shop that is open 24 hours a day. You have purchased a 2-month supply of chicken for a planned fried chicken promotion. Now you have changed your mind and would like to return the chicken. Your supplier refuses to take it back. What would you do?

9. If a customer ordered a Coke, but you were serving another type of cola, would you merely serve the customer the brand you carry without mentioning this to him or her? Why? If possible, obtain a copy of the National Restaurant Association's (NRA) booklet, *Accuracy in Menus*. Discuss what it has to say regarding the misrepresentation of a brand name.

10. What does the Robinson-Patman Act forbid?

11. Give an example of legal price discrimination practiced by a food distributor.

12. Give an example of illegal price discrimination practiced by a food distributor.

13. What is the major difference between the AP price and the EP cost?

14. Briefly describe the perceived value equation. How might a broker utilize this equation when selling foods?

15. How might a restaurant operator utilize the perceived value equation to increase patronage?

16. What is one difference between a basic commodity and a product that has additional form value added to it?

17. Why do you think the federal government exempts growers from some antitrust laws?

18. What are some advantages of using genetically engineered foods in a restaurant operation? What are some disadvantages?

19. What is the primary duty of the FSIS division of the USDA?

20. Which federal law grants injunctive power to the FDA?

21. If the label on a seafood package contained the notation "PUFI," what would this indicate to the buyer?

22. What is the difference between "exclusive dealing" and "exclusive selling"?

23. Which federal law is known as the "small-business protection act"?

24. What is "predatory pricing"? Why do you think it is outlawed by the federal government?

25. When would a verbal contract carry the same legal force as a written one?

CHAPTER 4

Preparation Date: _____		**MUST BE TYPED** **PURCHASE REQUEST (RX)**		DOC #: **2RXA** 0008858
▓▓▓ = *Optional entry*		(NOT FOR DATA ENTRY USE BY DEPARTMENT)		Page _____ of _____

DO NOT USE AN RX FOR UNDER $250. USE LIMITED PUR. ORDER	TRANS: **RX**	AREA:*	DEPT LOG: *	RESP AREA/ORGN:	PC #
	DOCUMENT ACTION: **E**	RESP PERSON:			PC #
REQUESTED BY: (DEPARTMENT)		PHONE # OF REQUESTOR:		BUILDING: ROOM #:	PC #
SUGGESTED VENDOR CODE.[a]		SUGGESTED VENDOR: _____			
DELIVERY DATE (MM/DD/YY):		VENDOR ADDRESS:*			
RX DATE (MM/DD/YY):		CITY/STATE/ZIP:*			
TYPE:[b] CWO? Y N FAX: Y N	TOLERANCE:[c] Y N	PHONE #:* ( ) - EXT:* FAX #:* ( ) - CONTACT:*			

Notes (left column):
a Required. Must be valid in either the VENA or VEN2 tables.
b Overstrike "N" if this is cash with the order or if the Purchase Order is to be faxed to the vendor. Insure fax # is entered.
c Overstrike "Y" to force a match between this unit cost and the subsequent Central Purchase Order unit cost. See 1 below.
d Account line total and commodity line total must agree to process this form.
e See reverse of this form for commodity codes.
f If the lowest or best bid exceeds this amount, the Buyer cannot place this order if a "N" is placed in the TOLERANCE field (c above).
g Place "Y" in this column if you added text (attach additional double-spaced typewritten text).

ACCOUNT DISTRIBUTION COMMODITY DATA

LINE	FUND	AREA	ORGN	SORG*	OBJT	SOBJ	JOB # *	TOTAL[d]
01								
02								
03								
04								
05								

LINE	QTY	U/I	COMMODITY CODE[e]	ITEM#*	UNIT COST[f]	TOT COST[d]	DESCRIPTION (Include catalog # if known)	TXT[g]	ACCT REF*
001									

Dean: _____ Date _____   Representative: _____ Date _____

Chairman: _____ Date _____   Commodity Approval Authority: _____ Date _____

PR/1033-11/6-92 (part 1)

Distribution: White-Purchasing/Yellow-Purchasing (returned to department)/ Pink-Department

Source: University of Nevada, Las Vegas

AN OVERVIEW OF THE PURCHASING FUNCTION

Ode to a Purchasing Agent

The Purchasing Agent stood at the Golden Gate,
His head was bending low.
He merely asked the man of fate,
Which way he ought to go.
"What have you done," St. Peter said,
"to seek admittance here?"

"I was a Purchasing Agent down on earth,
for many and many a year."
St. Peter opened wide the gate,
and gently pressed the bell.
"Come in," he said, "and choose your harp.
You've had your share of hell!!"

AUTHOR UNKNOWN

THE PURPOSE OF THIS CHAPTER

This chapter discusses:

- The major purchasing activities
- The major purchasing objectives
- The major problems that buyers encounter when performing these major activities in an attempt to attain these major objectives

INTRODUCTION

As we mentioned in our first chapter, each hospitality organization must come to grips with the purchasing function. Moreover, each operation, large or small, performs many purchasing activities common to all. Finally, all operations, regardless of size, strive for similar purchasing objectives. These are the unifying facts that this chapter addresses.

57

The hospitality industry is made up of a surprisingly large number of small operations. For instance, the majority of food-service operations are single-unit, independent businesses whose annual sales volumes are less than $500,000.[1] These small establishments do not have the resources to perform each operating activity in "textbook fashion." The small operator normally has to conduct some business procedures informally, and purchasing may be one of them. The large company may employ purchasing specialists, but the normal pattern is for an owner-manager to squeeze the purchasing activities into his or her schedule.

As we have said, every operation performs pretty much the same activities. The difference is in the degree of attention the activities receive and the thoroughness with which they are accomplished. Large companies tend toward completeness; smaller firms must trim somewhere. This chapter discusses these purchasing activities and purchasing objectives. Not every organization adheres to our outline, but all hospitality managers or owners must at least consider a definite procedure.

PURCHASING ACTIVITIES

Regardless of the size of a hospitality operation, a certain number of purchasing activities must be performed by someone. (See Figure 4.1.) The owner-manager does the best that he or she can under the circumstances. In some cases, though, we tend to abdicate our responsibilities by allowing a supplier and/or a salesperson to perform some activities for us. For instance, we should determine our own requirements and not allow a salesperson to do this for us. We are not implying that something unfortunate will occur if we enlist the help of a friendly salesperson, but, realistically, we must understand that the salesperson will be prone to enhancing his or her self-interest.

Buyers usually perform a number of activities common to all hospitality operations. One survey of hotel purchasing agents uncovered the following key purchasing responsibilities: "(1) determine when to order; (2) control inventory levels; (3) establish quality standards; (4) determine specifications; (5) obtain competitive bids; (6) investigate vendors; (7) arrange financial terms; (8) oversee delivery; (9) negotiate refunds; (10) handle adjustments; (11) arrange for storage."[2] A study of large food-service firms indicated that the purchasing activities center on "(1) recipe development; (2) menu development; (3) specification writing; (4) approval of buying source; (5) designation of approved brands; (6) supplier evaluation; (7) negotiation with suppliers; (8) change of suppliers; (9) change of brands; (10) substitution of approved items; (11) approve new products; (12) invoice approval; (13) invoice payment; (14) order placement with supplier."[3]

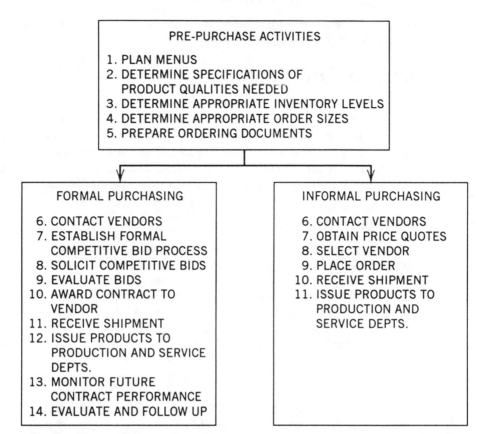

FIGURE 4.1. As this chart indicates, several activities must be accomplished to fulfill the purchasing function's responsibilities. Of course, the owner-manager can dictate the desired degree of formality. (Adapted from *Food Purchasing Pointers for School Foodservice.*)

To do an efficient buying job, hospitality organizations must usually perform, at a minimum, the activities discussed in the following paragraphs.

SELECTION AND PROCUREMENT PLAN

Typically, the person charged with purchasing responsibilities needs to determine relevant policies and procedures to guide the purchasing function. The plan should contain a description of how the organization intends to select and procure the products and services needed to conduct normal business activity. The plan should also explain the methods used, why they were selected, and its major goals and objectives. Ideally, it should also include discussion of supplier availability, purchasing trends that will have to be considered, and a procedure to follow to allow the plan to be revised when necessary.

DETERMINE REQUIREMENTS

In most cases, the buyer helps to determine the varieties and amounts of products, services, equipment, and furnishings the hospitality enterprise requires. It is unusual, though, for a buyer to make these decisions in a vacuum. Normally, they are made collectively—the buyers consult with other management officials and with those persons who will eventually use the purchased items to decide what the operation needs.

SUPPLIER SELECTION

Selecting dependable suppliers who will provide consistent values is a very difficult task. Generally speaking, the large hospitality firms wield considerable purchasing power and can therefore receive the attention and value commensurate with this power. Unfortunately, the smaller firm sometimes finds it difficult to enlist this type of consistency; while no supplier would intentionally ignore a customer, the fact is that the buyer who is not high on the priority list will eventually be disappointed.

SOURCING

For most products and services, there are a number of suppliers capable of meeting a buyer's needs. For some items, though, especially unique products that must be purchased in large quantities, it may be necessary for a buyer's company to help establish a supplier.[4]

When a supplier is established by a buyer, the process is usually referred to as "sourcing." It is typically a win-win situation, in that the buyer establishes a reliable source and the supplier enjoys a predictable amount of business.[5] It is also a good way for buyers to help establish and support minority-owned suppliers.[6]

MAINTAIN A CONVENIENT AND SUFFICIENT INVENTORY

An operation must practice optimal inventory management, which is nothing more or less than ensuring that an appropriate inventory of all items is always on hand. If we have too small an inventory, we could run out of some items, which often produces guest dissatisfaction. On the other hand, too large an inventory ties up extra dollars in these items and requires extra storage space.

An operation should strive to maintain an optimal, overall level of inventory items, although this is more easily said than done. As much as possible, though, a buyer must try to maintain this optimal level by determining the correct order size for each item and ordering this correct amount at the correct time.

CONDUCT NEGOTIATIONS

Someone has to negotiate specific AP prices, delivery schedules, and other supplier services. The general feeling in the industry is that "negotiating" should not be a euphemism for browbeating suppliers; firm but fair bargaining builds mutual respect. We should point out that your negotiating power is determined largely by the amount of money you expect to spend. Keep in mind, though, that all things, at least theoretically, are negotiable. In many cases, suppliers will provide something extra simply because a buyer asks about it. Although negotiating may require a certain degree of time and effort, the benefits can be considerable.

RESEARCH ACTIVITIES

Buyers often find it necessary to conduct research projects. Purchasing is a very dynamic activity, and, while the general principles and procedures remain the same, their applications may have to be altered to meet perceived trends. Similarly, product availability, prices, supplier services, and customer tastes may change quickly. The wise buyer will undertake research projects in order to improve future operations.

Value Analysis

One of the more common research activities, and one that is typically done very frequently, is value analysis. Value analysis involves examining a product in such a way as to identify unnecessary costs that can be eliminated without sacrificing overall quality or performance. For instance, a buyer who habitually purchases whole milk for cooking purposes may want to research the possibility of using less expensive low-fat milk instead. If the recipes can be prepared with the less expensive milk without a discernable loss of quality, he or she would recommend using the more economical low-fat product.

Value analysis usually centers on the perceived value equation noted in the previous chapter. Although the typical value analysis procedure may not be quite this formal, the ultimate purpose of this research activity is to increase value by manipulating quality, supplier services, and EP cost.

When he or she performs value analysis on a product or service, a buyer should make no changes without consulting the person who uses that product or service. There may be good reasons, for example, that the EP cost is a little higher than it could be—reasons known only to the user. Value analysis usually works best when it becomes a cooperative venture.

Forecasting

Forecasting can involve many things, but usually the buyer is most interested in predicting the kinds of products and services that will be available in the future and what their prices will be.

Buyers often center their forecasting efforts on "picking the brains" of friendly suppliers and salespersons. Informal chats with them can yield accurate and useful information quickly and easily.

These days, supply availability and future pricing can be tracked with one or more on-line computer services. For instance, the Restaurant Association Network (a division of the National Restaurant Association) includes a good deal of on-line, current commodities-pricing information that can be accessed by subscribers 24 hours a day.[7]

What-If Analysis

Many buyers use computer spreadsheet software to develop mathematical models that can test various "what-if" proposals. For instance, a simple model buyers can use predicts the overall effect that an increase in the purchase price of one food item will have on the overall food cost. For example, let us say that the price of prime rib will increase 10 percent and that prime rib represents 50 percent of the restaurant's overall food cost. We want to know what will happen to the overall food cost as a result of this increase. The model equation to use in this case is:

Increase in overall food cost = percentage price increase for the ingredient times the ingredient's percentage of overall food cost
= 10% × 50%
= 0.10 × 0.50
= 0.05 or 5%

Other more complicated formulas can be developed to show, for instance, the effect of a purchase price increase on overall profits.

Any model is an attempt to predict the future. Some models may be based on shaky estimates, but this has not curtailed their use. Most, if not all, operations rely on models. And some of these models become highly sophisticated mathematical devices.

Make-or-Buy Analysis

At times, management may consider making a product in-house instead of buying it already prepared, even though there are several types of value-added products on the market that can serve an operator's needs.

Make-or-buy analysis is one of the most critical types of research projects in which a buyer can become involved. There is a lot to lose if the wrong decision is made. There are usually several advantages and disadvantages peculiar to each situation.

For instance, value-added products usually offer the following advantages: (1) consistent quality; (2) consistent portion control; (3) an opportunity to serve diversified menu items regardless of the employee skill level, and thereby to attract patrons who enjoy diversity; (4) operating efficiencies such as less energy needed to reconstitute, rather than prepare from scratch, a menu item; (5) less food handler supervision, which gives the supervisor more time for merchandising, promoting, and otherwise increasing sales volume; (6) reduced employee skill requirements; (7) reduction in leftovers; (8) reduction of raw materials inventory, which implies less storage costs; (9) reduction in ordering costs, since you are not ordering and receiving several raw ingredients; (10) an increase in edible yields, since usually there is no waste with convenience items; and (11) with convenience foods usage, a possible reduction of the size of the storage and the kitchen facility, thereby allowing more room for dining patrons.

The major disadvantage of convenience foods is, of course, their high price.[8] Since most or all of the economic form value is included, the buyer expects to pay more for a value-added food than for the individual ingredients needed to produce the item in-house. However, there is no average rule of thumb to indicate whether the difference between these two prices favors the buyer or the food processor.

For instance, let us say that we cannot quite decide which alternative is better: cutting our own steaks from a side of beef or buying precut, portion-controlled steaks. The AP price of the uncut sides is cheaper. But considering the waste involved, additional labor costs, and investment in equipment, the precut steaks might represent the best EP cost.

There is no simple way to tell whether you should "make" or "buy." There are so many qualitative and quantitative factors to consider that the decision necessarily involves a great deal of research and analysis.

Plant Visits

Purchasing agents and buyers usually take the time to visit suppliers' facilities. Most industry members recommend this practice, particularly if there is some question about a supplier's ability to fulfill a need. In addition, a supplier who runs a sloppy store, experiences labor-management difficulties, or keeps erratic hours may be undependable and, therefore, undesirable.[9]

MAINTAIN SUPPLIER DIPLOMACY

A buyer works constantly with suppliers and salespersons; meanwhile, several other suppliers may wish for the buyer's business. Keeping every potential supplier content is impossible; a buyer should not even try it. Nevertheless, diplomatic, cordial relations help a buyer get along with suppliers and earn the best value from each.

Some operations concentrate heavily on maintaining amicable relations with all reputable suppliers, and many of these companies insist on instituting a trade relations function within the organization.[10] The objective of trade relations is to spread the purchase dollar among as many suppliers as possible. Although trade relations like this may diminish a buyer's alternatives, the goodwill generated throughout the channel of distribution might sometimes prove valuable in the long run—and in short-run emergencies. (Several operations purchase from only one or two purveyors for other reasons. In Chapter 11 we discuss the potential advantages of "one-stop" shopping.)

EDUCATE THE SUPPLIERS

Buyers must attempt to keep all potential suppliers informed about anything that can help improve their performance. Suppliers who stay abreast of your changing needs can provide the service to match those needs. Moreover, a buyer can continually test a supplier's flexibility and capability.

Another dimension of this issue is the advisability of buyers maintaining close contact with suppliers and salespersons to "pick their brains." This is a time-consuming activity, but it is thought by many people in our industry that it is absolutely necessary if a buyer hopes to maintain his or her knowledge of the rapidly changing hospitality market.

PURCHASE, RECEIVE, STORE, AND ISSUE PRODUCTS

Someone must be responsible for a product until it is ready to be used. No chef, for example, will take responsibility for expensive meat cuts before they actually come within his or her domain. In some cases, a buyer assumes the duties of selecting the supplier, purchasing and receiving the products, and, often, storing and eventually issuing them to the various departments.

Some firms do not like to link these activities together, especially the buying and receiving activities. These companies tend to relieve a buyer of the receiving activity and place this function under the direct supervision of the accounting department. This approach establishes a measure of control. The physical separation of these two activities substantially reduces the possibility of theft.

DISPOSAL OF EXCESS AND UNSALABLE ITEMS

At times, because of menu changes, overbuying, and obsolescence, a hospitality organization finds itself overstocked with certain products. Sometimes, too, when it purchases a new piece of equipment, it must dispose of the old piece. Buyers normally are expected to shoulder these responsibilities and trade the items, sell them, or give them away. Since buyers involve themselves directly in the marketplace, it is logical to expect them to fulfill these duties.

RECYCLING

In addition to disposing of excess and unsalable items, buyers may be responsible for ensuring that recyclable materials are gathered efficiently and delivered to an approved recycling center. If a buyer can sell these items, he or she may also have the additional responsibility of accounting for the receipts.

DEVELOP RECORD-KEEPING CONTROLS

The activities of purchasing, receiving, storing, and issuing normally require some sort of control. Although uncommon in smaller companies, large firms and, to a lesser extent, small ones strive to maintain a system of overlapping receipts connecting these activities. For example, as a product moves from one activity to the next, its movement may be traced by a variety of computerized and/or noncomputerized forms (bills, receipts, inventory records, issue slips, etc.). The objective of using these forms is to allow management to locate and monitor the product as it moves through the operation. (Chapters 12, 13, and 14 provide thorough discussions of these internal controls.)

A buyer may help design these forms. Alternatively, the accounting department takes charge of this duty as part of its overall responsibility for controlling all of the company assets. It is normal, though, for a buyer at least to contribute to the development of these forms.

ORGANIZE AND ADMINISTER
THE PURCHASING FUNCTION

Where applicable, the person in charge of purchasing must plan, organize, staff, direct, and control this function, especially in large companies that maintain a separate purchasing department. In addition, purchasing must be coordinated with other company activities such as accounting, marketing, production, and service. The purchasing agent, then, must not only see to it that products and services are efficiently and effectively purchased, received, stored, and, where appropriate, issued, he or she must also exert the managerial competence to organize and administer these activities expeditiously.

SELF-IMPROVEMENT

All buyers should continually strive to improve their buying performance. Association meetings, seminars, plant visits, trade show visits, and continuing education courses are among some of the more traditional self-improvement methods available. Full-time buyers should consider seriously obtaining the Certified Purchasing Manager (CPM) and the Certified Foodservice Purchasing Manager (CFPM) certifications offered by the Foodservice Purchasing Managers (FPM) Study Group of the National Restaurant Association (NRA) and the National Association of Purchasing Managers (NAPM). The Certified Foodservice Professional (CFP) certification, offered through the North American Association of Food Equipment Manufacturers (NAFEM), is available to qualified purchasing professionals specializing in the equipment side of the business.[11]

Many hospitality operations will reimburse their employees for this kind of self-improvement by paying tuition charges, the cost of books, seminar fees, and travel expenses. In addition, some operators provide in-house training. In the long run, employees who increase their competence usually return management's investment many times by improving their productivity and increasing their readiness to assume more responsible positions within the firm.

HELP COMPETITORS

Helping the competition does not always seem to be a logical part of a purchasing agent's duties. An operation is unlikely to go out of its way to aid competitors; nevertheless, competing buyers are in a position to help each other in mutually beneficial ways.

The type of help we refer to consists, for one thing, of lending products to competitors when a crucial need arises. If we run out of something we desperately need, we try to borrow the product from a neighbor. Moreover, in the role of a lender, we have little to gain by refusing such a service: it is unlikely that a competitor's customers will flock to our door simply because the competitor temporarily cannot serve them a particular item.

When we do lend, we set up a reciprocal arrangement by which we feel justified in borrowing. Of course, management needs to make the ultimate decision about these types of loan arrangements. Lending and borrowing are reasonable activities that often come under a buyer's purview.

A buyer might also help his or her less knowledgeable colleague gain the advantage of the more seasoned buyer's experience. Cordial, professional relations such as these will tend to make everyone's life a bit easier and will also increase significantly the ability of the industry to serve its customers more effectively and efficiently.

OTHER ACTIVITIES

As hospitality companies continue to downsize their managerial ranks, those managers remaining often need to shoulder nontraditional duties. In today's business environment, managers should be prepared to adapt to any situation. For instance, a purchasing manager working at company headquarters may have to take on responsibility for the mail room operation. Or a buyer working at a large hotel may have to oversee the gift shop.

PURCHASING OBJECTIVES

Industry experts suggest several goals for the purchasing function. Continuing research into this issue shows that there are five major objectives that must be achieved.

- *Maintain an Adequate Supply.* Few hospitality operators enjoy running out of products. Stockouts are intolerable. Since customer service is really the only thing sold, running out of a key item frustrates an operator's customer service goals. Thus, an adequate stock level, one that avoids running out of items between deliveries, is crucial to good management.

- *Minimize Investment.* This objective seems to conflict with the first. How can we maintain an uninterrupted supply while, at the same time, minimize the number of dollars we tie up in inventory? This question suggests that we must find some kind of trade-off between investment level and the risk of running out. Most operators expect a buyer to compromise by optimizing the investment level and, at the same time, ensure a continual flow of products.

- *Maintain Quality.* Maintaining quality is not quite the same thing as establishing the level of quality desired by the firm. Some buyers have comparatively little to say about the quality of products they must purchase. They do, however, have a major responsibility to make sure that, once set, the quality standards vary only within acceptable limits. For such products as liquor and soaps, brand names assure uniform quality. Unfortunately, the quality of fresh foods can change drastically from day to day and from one supplier to the next. This situation can make it particularly difficult to maintain quality standards. In addition, occasional overbuying or a sudden breakdown in storage facilities, particularly refrigeration facilities, can play havoc with quality standards. Regardless of the associated difficulties, however, operators insist on quality control by their buyers.

- *Obtain the Lowest Possible EP Cost.* As we mentioned earlier, the AP price is only the beginning. Unfortunately, some buyers are entranced by a low AP price and tend to overlook the fact that the EP cost is the relevant price consideration.

Many operators think in terms of steak price per pound or liquid detergent price per gallon. What should be paramount in their thinking is the steak cost per servable pound or the liquid detergent cost per square foot of dirty tile. In other words, the EP cost rules the price roost, and management understandably expects its buyers to recognize this fact on the way to achieving the lowest possible EP cost and, ultimately, the best possible value.

• *Maintain the Company's Competitive Position.* As far as we have been able to determine, management's main concern here is to get the same, or better, deal from a supplier as any other comparable hospitality enterprise gets. Unfortunately, this task is easier recited than accomplished. Although EP cost and quality may be more or less uniform, suppliers often apply their supplier services unevenly among buyers. You may recall that these supplier services add to the overall value of a product or service, provided that the quality and EP cost remain constant. If we receive fewer supplier services, theoretically we receive less value for our money. This value loss places us at a competitive disadvantage—a position not at all dear to management.

PROBLEMS OF THE BUYER

Buyers encounter several problems while working to attain their objectives. Some of the major problems are:

1. Backdoor selling, whereby a salesperson bypasses the appointed buyer and goes to some other employee, such as the dining room hostess, to make a sales pitch. The hostess then exerts pressure on the buyer to consummate a sale.

2. Excessive time spent with salespersons. Most operators set aside certain periods during the week to receive sales presentations. On the one hand, these may be time-wasting affairs, but you sometimes need to spend time with others to pick up a good bit of advice or information now and then.

3. The variety of ethical traps awaiting the buyer.

4. Buyers sometimes have full responsibility for purchasing, yet they may lack the commensurate authority needed to act accordingly.

5. Perhaps the buyer has full responsibility, but he or she does not have enough time to do the job right. This is particularly true for part-time buyers.

6. There sometimes is difficulty involved in working with other department heads and coordinating their needs.

7. Sometimes department heads, or other users of products and services, make unreasonable demands on the person in charge of buying.

8. Late deliveries and subsequent problems with receiving and storage can do a great deal in ruining the most efficient purchase.

9. Other company personnel do not always consider purchasing a profit-making activity. Actually, a penny saved in purchasing goes directly to the bottom line of the income statement, whereas the typical hospitality operation must sell about 50 cents worth of product or service to realize a 1-cent net profit, since, to generate this 50-cent sale, considerable expense must be incurred.

10. Suppliers do not always have what we order, sending a substitute that may or may not be acceptable.

11. Some suppliers may not be interested in your business if you are a "small stop" (i.e., do a small amount of business). No salesperson will intentionally avoid you, but, realistically, he or she must service the large customers first. This means that you may not be on the list of his or her top priorities.

12. Receiving and storage inadequacies make it difficult to protect the merchandise after it is purchased. Regardless of the effort expended to procure the best possible value, it could all go for naught if these inadequacies result in excessive spoilage, waste, and/or theft.

13. When a supplier does not have something that you have ordered, he or she may note on the delivery slip that the item is "back ordered." This means that you will usually receive the item when the next regularly scheduled delivery occurs and be charged for it at that time. Your major problem is the fact that you do not have the item ready for your customers.

14. Returns and allowances occur because some delivered merchandise will be unsuitable for one reason or another. The hospitality operator must then ensure that he or she receives fair credit for the rejected items and that this credit is ultimately reflected on the supplier's bills. This takes time and effort, two attributes that most of us have in short supply. Furthermore, as with back orders, there are the stockout problems that must be solved to avoid customer dissatisfaction.

EVALUATION OF THE PURCHASING FUNCTION

The purchasing function involves a great variety of activities and objectives. As noted earlier, all buyers, full-time or part-time, perform most of these activities, one way or another. They also attain, or fail to attain, what we have outlined as the major purchasing objectives.

How much should we be willing to spend to discharge the purchasing activities conscientiously enough to achieve these major objectives? This is an especially difficult question because, on the one hand, buyers' salaries and receiving costs are highly visible to management, but, on the other hand, the benefits associated with these costs are not so visible. A look at the income statement reveals immediately most of the costs of maintaining a top-flight purchasing function; unhappily, the benefits do not leap out at us quite so dramatically.

In our opinion, the benefits outweigh the costs for all but perhaps the smallest hospitality operations. The purpose of this book, however, is to present what we perceive to be the relevant aspects of selection and procurement. We leave it to you to decide gradually the value of the purchasing function and the relative justification for its cost.

KEY WORDS AND CONCEPTS

AP price

Backdoor selling

Back orders

CFP

CFPM

Company's competitive position

Convenience foods

CPM

Disposal of stock

EP cost

Forecasting

FPM

Make-or-buy analysis

Minimal inventory investment

NAFEM

NAPM

National Restaurant Association (NRA)

Negotiations

One-stop shopping

Optimal inventory level

Plant visits

Problems of the buyer

Product substitutions

Purchasing activities

Purchasing objectives

Quality standards

Record-keeping control documents

Recycling

Restaurant Association Network

Returns and allowances

Selection and procurement plan

Small stop

Sourcing

Stockout

Supplier diplomacy

Supplier selection

Trade relations

Trade show visits

Value-added foods

Value analysis

What-if analysis

REFERENCES

1. National Restaurant Association (NRA) estimate.

2. Gregory I. Bohan, "Purchasing for Hotels: A Changing Scene, Survey Reveals," *Lodging,* April 1986, p. 17.

3. R. Dan Reid and Carl D. Riegel, *Purchasing Practices of Large Foodservice Firms* (Tempe, AZ: Center for Advanced Purchasing Studies (CAPS), 1989), p. 19.

4. Patt Patterson, "Good Buyers Track Orders from Field to Kitchen," *Nation's Restaurant News,* October 5, 1992, p. 42.

5. "McDonald's Recruits Duo to Make Its McCroutons," *USA Today,* January 27, 1989, p. 7B.

6. Udayan Gupta, "Getting Together," *The Wall Street Journal,* February 19, 1993, p. R12. See also, Udayan Gupta, "Where the Money Is," *The Wall Street Journal,* May 22, 1995, p. R6.

7. "Urner Barry Commodity Pricing Now On Line," *Restaurants USA,* March 1995, p. 47.

8. Sarah Hart Winchester, "Cutting Costs Without Cutting Quality," *Restaurants USA,* March 1995, p. 12.

9. Tom Wood, "Total Quality Management," *Restaurants USA,* February 1993, p. 19. See also, Mary Clare Brady, "National Restaurant Association Executive Study Groups," *Restaurants USA,* January 1993, p. 15.

10. "Casinos Back Variation on Set-Aside Program," *The Wall Street Journal,* March 30, 1993, p. B1.

11. Patt Patterson, "Certification Adds Professionalism to Purchasing," *Nation's Restaurant News,* March 23, 1992, p. 36.

QUESTIONS AND PROBLEMS

1. Assume that two suppliers sell the same quality of meat for the same price. What type of supplier services would you seek from them? Why? Which supplier service would you value enough so that if one supplier provided it and the other did not, you would purchase your meat from the former? Why?

2. Assume that steak represents 30 percent of your overall food cost. If the purchase price of steak increases 10 percent, by how much will the overall food cost increase?

3. Name some potential benefits of trade relations. Name potential difficulties. Would you engage in trade relations? Why?

4. Do you think it is a good idea to allow your competitors to "borrow a cup of sugar" once in a while? Why?

5. Explain what is meant by the purchasing function's goal of "maintaining the company's competitive position."

6. Assume that you have decided to serve roast beef on your menu. The AP price of roast beef is $2.98 per pound. The edible yield per pound is approximately 9 ounces. You plan to serve a $4\frac{1}{2}$-ounce portion size.

   (a) Approximately how much raw roast beef must you purchase in order to serve 125 portions?

   (b) KWG Enterprises, a statewide food merchant wholesaler, offers a pre-cooked, presliced roast beef product for $6.00 per pound. The edible yield is 100 percent.

      (1) Under what conditions would you purchase this convenience item?

      (2) Under what conditions would it be advisable to purchase the raw roast beef product instead of this convenience item?

      (3) Approximately how much of this convenience roast beef must you purchase in order to serve 125 portions?

7. Name the five major objectives of the purchasing function.

8. Name three types of research activities that a buyer might perform.

9. Is it a good idea to allow a salesperson to assist us in carrying out the necessary purchasing activities? Why? If possible, ask a broker and a merchant wholesaler to comment on your answer. Also, if possible, ask a hotel or restaurant buyer to comment on your answer and the answers of the broker and the merchant wholesaler.

10. Define or explain:

(a) Value analysis	(e) CFPM
(b) Sourcing	(f) Stockouts
(c) CPM	(g) Backdoor selling
(d) Plant visits	(h) Back orders

11. What problems will a food-service operation incur if it experiences several back orders?

12. What is a major disadvantage associated with having excess inventory on hand?

13. When should the buyer visit a supplier's facilities?

14. List three advantages and three disadvantages of using convenience foods.

15. A purveyor has offered to sell you fudge cakes for $6.00 each. You try to determine whether you can make the cakes more cheaply. Assuming that you will need to pay an additional employee $9.25 per hour, plus about $1.50-per-hour fringe benefits, and further assuming that this employee can make 24 cakes per hour, what alternative should you select? Should you "make" or should you "buy"? Why?

The recipe for one cake is:

12 ounces shortening

2 pounds sugar

$\frac{1}{2}$ ounce vanilla

6 eggs

5 ounces cocoa

1 pound, 12 ounces cake flour

$\frac{1}{4}$ ounce salt

1 ounce baking soda

$1\frac{1}{2}$ pints buttermilk

The AP prices for these ingredients are:

Shortening	$0.32 per pound
Sugar	$18.22 per 50 pounds
Vanilla	$6.85 per pint
Eggs	$1.29 per dozen
Cocoa	$2.12 per pound
Cake flour	$11.09 per 50 pounds
Salt	$0.11 per pound
Baking soda	$0.24 per pound
Buttermilk	$2.45 per gallon

CHAPTER 5

THE ORGANIZATION AND ADMINISTRATION OF PURCHASING

THE PURPOSE OF THIS CHAPTER

This chapter discusses:

- Planning the purchasing function
- Organizing the purchasing function
- Staffing the purchasing function
- Training purchasing personnel
- Budgeting for the purchasing function
- Supervising the purchasing function
- Controlling the purchasing function

INTRODUCTION

Buyers, both full-time and part-time, must plan, organize, and administer their purchasing activities. This principle is crucial in large operations, especially chain organizations, where more than one person may be involved in purchasing. But small operations cannot afford to be casual about purchasing; even a part-time buyer needs a definite plan of action.

PLANNING

In the initial stages of developing a selection and procurement plan that will be consistent with the hospitality operation's overall thrust, buyers must understand the goals and objectives of the purchasing function. For instance, the five purchasing objectives we discussed in Chapter 4—maintain adequate supply, minimize investment, maintain quality, obtain lowest possible EP cost, and maintain competitive position—can serve as the initial goals to be achieved in the long run. But buyers devise several ways of working toward these goals. Thus, evaluating possible methods of achieving the goals and eventually selecting one becomes the major accomplishment in the planning stage.

Here's an example. A small operator may decide that the main objective of the purchasing function is to maintain adequate supplies at all times and that all other objectives are second to this one. The overall buying plan, then, must be tailored to ensure the attainment of this objective: The operator may decide to select only those suppliers with the most favorable delivery schedules and, if necessary, pay a little extra for this supplier service.

Decisions made at the initial planning stage set the tone for future activities. Planning for purchasing is not carried out in a vacuum. It is part of the overall plan of the hospitality organization and cannot exist apart from the overall goals and objectives of the operation. Furthermore, a buyer rarely determines the buying plan without receiving input from other company personnel.

ORGANIZING

Having formulated a general plan, a buyer must organize the human and material resources needed to follow that plan. At this second stage, however, the buyer's voice may still be only one of many. In some cases, he or she has little to say; superiors may decide how to do the operation's purchasing.

There are several ways to organize the buying activities of a hospitality firm. But, generally, we find only two major organizational patterns: one for the independent operator and one for the multiunit chain operations. Most other organizational patterns are variations of these two.

ORGANIZING FOR THE INDEPENDENT OPERATION

There are many very small hospitality operations. Often, these are referred to as "mom and pop" places. Most do not have a payroll; that is, they are operated completely by the owners with perhaps some assistance from family members. Usually the selection and procurement responsibilities fall directly on the owner-manager's shoulders. If there are hourly employees in these organizations, as shown in Figure 5.1, they normally are involved in these activities only sparingly. For instance, an hourly employee may have receiving and storing responsibility whenever the owner-manager is absent.

Medium-sized operations (Figure 5.2) rarely employ full-time buyers. Instead, they tend to designate one or more "user-buyers." Ordinarily, the head bartender, the chef, the dining room supervisor, and other supervisors all do some buying as part of their other responsibilities. The

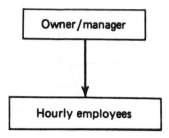

FIGURE 5.1. Typical purchasing organizational pattern for a very small independent hospitality operation.

owner-manager acts as a coordinator among these user-buyers to control their activity and, especially, to supervise the receipt of their orders. The owner-manager also oversees receiving and storing and bill payments.

In some independent properties, including the larger hotels, motels, and country clubs, an owner-manager may not coordinate the orders of each department head. Instead, a steward or assistant manager may be employed specifically to do this work. The owner-manager then controls and supervises this person's activities.

Another variation of this pattern occurs when a separate steward or food buyer works in the kitchen specifically to coordinate the chef's needs. A kitchen steward may also supervise the warewashing and cleaning employees. Large independents and, in some cases, large chain operations, may follow this pattern.

Organizational variations abound for independent operations; they are limited only by the imagination. But, as noted, a characteristic they share is the need for the owner-manager to be directly involved in purchasing. He or she cannot avoid this activity. And, in many cases, he or

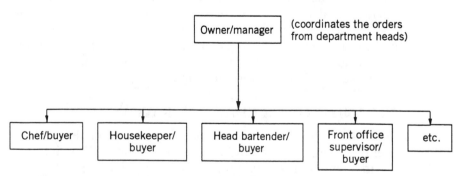

FIGURE 5.2. Typical purchasing organizational pattern for a medium-sized independent hospitality operation.

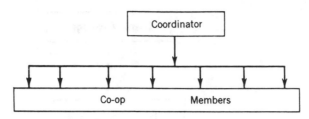

FIGURE 5.3. Typical purchasing organizational pattern for a co-op.

she is actually the owner-manager-chef, who not only buys for the kitchen but may also buy for, or at least coordinate the purchasing of, all the other departments.

Some small and medium-sized hospitality operations join a communal-buying network. As this term suggests, the independents join together and agree to pool their purchases. The idea is to place one larger order, thereby qualifying for a lower AP price. This scheme works not only with food and operating supplies but also with insurance, advertising, and other service purchasing. The concept works particularly well where independents agree to use the same brand of peas, bread, ice cream, detergent, accounting service, and so on.

The organizational pattern for communal buying, or "co-op purchasing" or "shared buying," as some call it, is relatively simple (Figure 5.3). Owners and managers from among the group of independents share the task of coordinating all the orders. Or the independents may hire someone to perform this coordination, to place large orders, and to arrange proper delivery schedules.

The concept of communal buying has its pros and cons.[1] We discuss the major advantages and disadvantages of co-op purchasing in Chapter 11.

The large independent is similar to the small one, the major difference being the physical presence of one or more persons assigned full-time to the purchasing, receiving, storing, and issuing of products and services. The most typical setup is to have a purchasing director, with specialists in food buying, beverage buying, and equipment and supplies buying working in the purchasing department. There also might be a receiving clerk working for the accounting department and a storeroom manager working for the purchasing director. (See Figure 5.4.)

ORGANIZING FOR CHAIN OPERATIONS

The major difference between independents and chains is the additional level of management found in the chain operation. The purchasing function in a hotel or restaurant that belongs to a chain operation often resembles the purchasing done by the independents. What is different is the presence of a vice president of purchasing (or a corporate purchasing

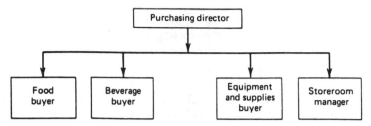

FIGURE 5.4. Typical purchasing organizational pattern for a large independent hospitality operation.

director) and a staff of buyers at headquarters overseeing the selection and procurement activities and, if applicable, monitoring the company-owned commissary and/or central distribution activities (Figure 5.5).

At the local unit level, in some cases, the unit manager performs all buying activities. In other cases, he or she may serve as coordinator for the users and buyers. In chain operations that have large units, there may be a purchasing system in each unit that is similar to the system of a large independent.

The unit manager in Figure 5.5 can be a franchisee or the manager of a company-owned store. If the former, he or she usually (1) buys from suppliers approved by the corporate vice president of purchasing; (2) buys from other suppliers, as long as they meet the company's quality standards; (3) buys from the franchisor's company-owned commissary and/or central distribution center; or (4) uses a combination of the three approaches. As mentioned previously, a franchisee typically buys from the commissary and/or central distribution center whenever possible, if only for convenience.

Managers of company-owned stores have the same options as franchisees, but, realistically, they have less flexibility. Once the buying procedure is decided by the company's top management, there is little chance for variation.

The vice president of purchasing serves as a central coordinator for purchases made by all the units. His or her major responsibilities usually include (1) setting purchasing guidelines for unit managers and (2) negotiating national, long-term contracts for items used by all the units. The vice president normally negotiates large-quantity buys with set prices—six-month supplies or longer. (Unit managers, by contrast, order and receive just what they need when they need it and then pay the AP price negotiated by the vice president.) The corporate vice president also (3) sets purchase specifications (to which we devote Chapter 7) for items that must be purchased at the unit level, (4) performs research activities, (5) serves as a resource person for all unit managers and unit buying

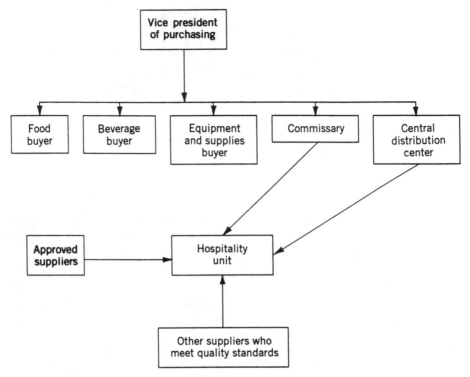

FIGURE 5.5. Typical purchasing organizational pattern for a multiunit hospitality operation.

personnel, and (6), if applicable, supervises the central distribution function and the commissary.

Some advantages and disadvantages accompany this kind of centralized purchasing. The major advantages are the reduction in the AP prices achieved by quantity buys, the presence of a strong negotiator, and cost and quality control. The main disadvantage seems to be the system's potential for alienating local suppliers, especially when the chain deals with one major supplier and bypasses all the locals.[2] But the corporate vice president of purchasing cannot purchase everything, nor can he or she negotiate contracts for all items. At least some buying must remain decentralized and in the hands of the local unit. This slight but inevitable degree of decentralization can soothe ruffled local suppliers as well as provide the unit personnel with some purchasing experience.

Another major difference between independents and chains is the propensity of the chains to develop a "central distribution and commissary network." This network really represents an effort by the chains to provide many of their own economic values and supplier services, that is, to bypass the middlemen. The chains feel it makes sense, dollars and "sense," to centralize their buying, to have products delivered to one location, to process these products (for example, to cut portion-controlled steaks), and to deliver these processed items to each unit.

As we noted in Chapter 2, there is little evidence to suggest that the commissary and central distribution network is a cost-effective system. There certainly are several quality control benefits, as well as the potential benefit of an uninterrupted supply. However, in light of the arguments for and against central distribution and commissary operation, managers who face this difficult decision must undertake a good deal of careful analysis.

STAFFING

Neither small nor medium-sized operations generally hire full-time purchasing employees. Large operations, especially chains, may hire several buyers, each an expert in one or two product areas. They are also more apt to employ full-time secretarial and clerical personnel in the purchasing department. And they may employ receiving clerks and storeroom managers. Again, the smaller operation would typically settle for a chef-buyer-storeroom manager and a well-trained, generously paid kitchen worker who doubles as a receiving clerk.

The job specification for these employees follows the typical pattern. It is divided into the three broad areas of technical, conceptual, and human skills. For some positions relating to the buying activity, technical skill and extensive experience are very important. For other positions, a desire to learn may be the only requirement. The complicating factor is that purchasing personnel often have other responsibilities besides purchasing, receiving, storing, and issuing; thus, these other responsibilities may take precedence when a manager undertakes to develop overall job specifications.

TRAINING

Entry-level purchasing personnel usually require training that consists of an orientation to the job and the company, formal instruction, and on-the-job experience. In addition, management training seminars and courses sometimes supplement in-house training. The National Restaurant Association (NRA), the National Association of Purchasing Managers (NAPM), the North American Association of Food Equipment Manufacturers (NAFEM), and the Foodservice Purchasing Managers (FPM) Study Group of the NRA normally sponsor several seminars and courses every year.

BUDGETING

In operations that employ a full-time buyer, it may be necessary to fund the buying function, which means that annual operating expenses, such as buyers' salaries and clerical costs, must be budgeted. The operations that employ user-buyers rarely construct a separate purchasing budget. (As you will learn in Chapter 6, though, part of a buyer's overall performance can be measured by comparing actual operating expenses with budgeted operating expenses.)

DIRECTING

In addition to their other responsibilities, full-time and part-time buyers must supervise the purchasing personnel assigned to them. Supervisory style is, of course, a personal matter; no two successful supervisors ever seem to follow identical supervisory styles. Generally speaking, though, top management, or an owner-manager, dictates some sort of supervisory policy.[3]

CONTROLLING

Buyers usually take responsibility for control over the products they buy until a user takes them from the storeroom and places them in the production flow. It is not always clear at exactly what point this responsibility shifts to the user. Nevertheless, everyone in a hospitality operation should be concerned with controlling waste, spoilage, and theft.

Small operations use a "direct control system" in which the owner-manager keeps a close eye on everything. Larger operations use an "indirect control system," often one in which a system of overlapping computerized and/or noncomputerized forms allows someone, usually the controller, to keep tabs on all the products. The manager can determine, from glancing at the controller's summary of issues and receipts, where these products are in the hospitality operation and how much of each is at its respective location. (Chapters 12, 13, and 14 contain thorough discussions of these controls.)

Control is complicated in the hospitality industry by the waste and spoilage factors. Furthermore, security takes on added difficulty because many of the products we buy are useful, convenient, and attractive to just about everyone. The buyer must do whatever possible to minimize losses—normally by adhering to the control system approved by company policy.

KEY WORDS AND CONCEPTS

Approved suppliers	Multiunit chain organization
Budgeting	NAFEM
Central distribution center	NAPM
Commissary	National contracts
Communal buying	NRA
Controlling	Organizing
Co-op coordinator	Planning
Co-op purchasing	Purchasing objectives
Corporate vice president of purchasing	Quality control
Cost control	Shared buying
Direct control system	Small independent organization
Directing	Staffing
FPM	Steward
Indirect control system	Supervisory style
Job specification	Training
Large independent organization	User-buyer
Medium-sized independent organization	

REFERENCES

1. Timothy L. O'Brien, "Franchises Spearhead Renewed Popularity of Co-Ops," *The Wall Street Journal,* November 29, 1993, p. B2. See also, "Co-Ops: Pool-Buying Grows for the Smaller Independent," *FoodService Director,* May 15, 1990, p. 42.

2. For an in-depth discussion of the advantages and disadvantages of centralized purchasing, see M. C. Warfel and Marion L. Cremer, *Purchasing for Food Service Managers,* 2d ed. (Berkeley, CA: McCutchan, 1990), pp. 44–46.

3. Three volumes that supervisors should consult are: Jack E. Miller, Mary Porter, and Karen Eich Drummond, *Supervision in the Hospitality Industry,* 2d ed. (New York: John Wiley & Sons, 1992); Susann Dowling, *Implementing the Supervisory Process: Theory and Practice* (Englewood Cliffs, NJ: Prentice-Hall, 1992); and Stan Kossen, *Supervision* (St. Paul, MN: West Publishers, 1991).

QUESTIONS AND PROBLEMS

1. Describe the typical organizational patterns for the independent operation and for the multiunit chain operation.

2. Explain how a co-op purchasing organization works.

3. Assume that you are the owner of a small restaurant and you have the opportunity to join a purchasing co-op. Should you do it? Why?

4. What are the major responsibilities of a vice president of purchasing?

5. Why do you think central distribution has been so unprofitable in the past? Are there any benefits, other than monetary, associated with central distribution? If so, what are they? If possible, ask an official of a multiunit chain operation to comment on your answer.

6. Develop a job specification for an assistant food buyer.

7. What is the main difference between a direct and an indirect control system? Assume that you are the owner of a small motel and that you use a direct control system. What advantages do you have with this system that you would not have with an indirect control system? What disadvantages?

8. List three critical issues that should be addressed in a company's selection and procurement plan.

9. A franchisee may purchase from a company commissary. If so, he or she will incur several advantages and disadvantages. (a) List some advantages. (b) List some disadvantages.

10. What do you feel is the major advantage to the purchasing co-op? Why?

11. What do you feel is the major disadvantage to the purchasing co-op? Why?

12. What would you think is the major advantage of centralizing the purchasing responsibilities in a hospitality operation? What would be the major disadvantage? If possible, ask an independent owner-operator of a full-service restaurant to comment on your answer. Also, if possible, ask the manager of a company-owned fast-food operation that is part of a chain to comment on your answer.

13. Develop a job specification for a full-time buyer.

14. Briefly describe a national contract. What is the primary advantage of such a contract?

15. When would it be advantageous for a franchisee to purchase from a local supplier instead of from the company-owned commissary?

CHAPTER 6

THE BUYER'S RELATIONS WITH OTHER COMPANY PERSONNEL

THE PURPOSE OF THIS CHAPTER

This chapter discusses:

- The buyer's relations with his or her supervisor
- The buyer's relations with his or her colleagues
- The buyer's relations with hourly employees

INTRODUCTION

In many cases, the buyer and the owner-manager are one and the same person. Only larger operations maintain part-time or full-time buyers. In large hotels, for example, it is common to find a full-time purchasing agent as well as several department heads who purchase specialized merchandise for their needs. And large multiunit chain restaurants usually employ a corporate purchasing agent with a buyer or a buyer-manager at each individual unit.

The full-time buyer is a member of management. He or she exercises line authority over those purchasing functions he or she is personally responsible for and, sometimes, exercises staff supervision over others, usually department heads who accomplish some or all of their own purchasing. In other cases, all buying is part-time in the sense that various department heads and other members of management include among their duties the purchasing function for their areas.

In this chapter, we explore both the relationship between the buyer and his or her supervisor and the buyer's relationship with the other supervisory, managerial, and staff persons and the hourly employees.

THE BUYER'S RELATIONS WITH THE SUPERVISOR

Regardless of the organizational pattern, a buyer or buyer-manager usually answers to a supervisor somewhere in the organization. In Chapter 5,

TECHNICAL SKILLS

Creating a recipe

Costing a recipe

Preparing a recipe

Preparing a work schedule

Developing a job description

INTERPERSONAL SKILLS

Conducting a performance appraisal

Interviewing a sales representative

Training an employee

Handling a customer complaint

Working with delivery agents

CONCEPTUAL SKILLS

Forecasting food trends

Marketing a restaurant

Organizing a banquet

Budgeting payroll expenses

Researching a new food item

FIGURE 6.1. Examples of technical, interpersonal, and conceptual skills.

we discussed the various ways of organizing and administering the purchasing function. These methods are a major concern for managers. Of equal concern are the issues that must be addressed before the buyer or buyer-manager can completely organize and administer the buying activity.

THE JOB SPECIFICATION

A job specification lists the qualities sought in a job candidate—in our case, a list of qualities to look for when evaluating the employment potential of an applicant for a buyer's position. A supervisor looks for at least four qualities before hiring a buyer. (See Figures 6.1 and 6.2.)

Technical Skill

Buyers must be extremely familiar with the items they will purchase. At the very least, they should have the aptitude to learn the intricate aspects

DIRECTOR OF PURCHASING

Our client, an acknowledged leader in the fast food industry, is seeking a dedicated professional to act as a corporate buying agent. Reporting directly to the President, you'll be responsible for negotiating long term manufacturing and distribution agreements and maintaining a network of contacts and sales personnel in the industry. The director will also supervise a purchasing and distribution specialist and secretary.

To qualify you should have at least 5-10 years' experience with emphasis in meat purchasing including product chemistry and processing as it relates to price, packaging, storage, distribution and preparation. Superior negotiation and communication skills are necessary. A degree in distribution or related field of study is a plus.

They are offering a competitive salary ($55-70,000), excellent benefits and an environment conducive to challenge and creativity.

If you're qualified and interested, send your resume in strictest confidence to:

Mr. Frank Coyle, Manager, Recruiting
Galardi Group
4440 Von Karman Ave.
Newport Beach, CA
92658-7460

EQUIP. PURCHASING AGENT

Seeking a career oriented individual with 3-5 yrs. of purchasing experience in Restaurant Equipment. Must be experienced in National Contract Negotiations and competitive bidding. College degree preferred. Salary $24-$34K. Full benefit package. Send resume to:

KFC National
Purchasing
Cooperative Inc.
P.O. Box 32033
Louisville, KY
40232
Attn.:
Tom Hutcherson
VP Purchasing

GILBERT/ROBINSON, INC.

DIRECTOR OF PURCHASING

Gilbert/Robinson, Inc., one of the nation's most progressive and diversified restaurant companies, is seeking a corporate staff member to direct all purchasing activities for its 116 restaurants nationwide. Among the Gilbert/Robinson concepts are Houlihans, Darryl's, Fedora and a variety of other full-service seafood and specialty restaurants in major markets throughout the country.

Responsibilities will include the establishing, monitoring and coordinating of field purchasing programs; interfacing with outside distributors in establishing distribution systems; working with our corporate support function on major commodity negotiations and purchases and resolving field purchasing problems; assisting food and beverage departments in establishing and insuring product specification; and on-going new product research and procurement for testing purposes.

Candidates must have 4+ years of comparable experience with a restaurant, hotel or food service corporation, a Bachelor's degree and/or culinary education, proven management ability and strong written communication skills. Salary and benefit package commensurate with qualifications.

Send resume in confidence to:

John P. Hawes
GILBERT/ROBINSON, INC.
P.O. Box 16000
Kansas City, MO 64112

Equal Opportunity Employer M/F

FIGURE 6.2. Examples of job specifications and job descriptions for purchasing positions. (Courtesy Gilbert/Robinson, Inc., KFC National Purchasing Cooperative, Inc., and Galardi Group.)

of all these products and services. In addition, a person cannot really aspire to a buyer's job unless he or she is familiar with the ways in which and the conditions under which the purchased items will be used by chefs, bartenders, housekeepers, and so on.

Interpersonal (or Human) Skill

The buyer must get along with other department heads and employees. After all, his or her performance affects colleagues' performance, since they must work with the items purchased. A buyer also must be firm but fair with all different types of sales representatives.

Conceptual Skill

A buyer should be able to conceptualize the entire hospitality operation and not see things exclusively from the point of view of purchasing. In other words, he or she must do the things that benefit the entire operation, not just his or her reputation. Sometimes it is difficult to see how, for example, a low AP price can turn into an exorbitant EP cost. But it is just this type of general perspective and systems mentality—the ability to view the whole operation and the multitude of relationships it contains— that supervisors tend to look for in a buyer.

Other Qualities

The three skills we just mentioned are fairly routine. Some other characteristics supervisors look for are not so easily discussed, but they are important. These include (1) the quality and types of an applicant's experience, (2) honesty and integrity, (3) desire to advance and grow with the operation, (4) ability to administer a purchasing department, if applicable, and (5) desire to work conscientiously for the operation.[1] In addition, a supervisor usually develops a set of questions he or she expects an applicant to answer satisfactorily. And a supervisor is almost certain to request some personal references.

LABOR POOL

The buyer's job can be a full-time position, or it can be part of another job. If a supervisor needs a full-time buyer, he or she may look among the current employees for someone with an aptitude for purchasing. Or a professional buyer may be sought through the newspaper and trade journal classified ads sections, by asking informally among trade association members, or by inquiring among friends and other professional colleagues. The supervisor must adhere to company policy and to federal, state, and local legislation throughout this recruiting process.

Part-time buyers spend relatively little time in purchasing. For example, chefs, kitchen stewards, and housekeepers often are required to do some purchasing. The labor pool for these jobs can be found in the same way employers look for full-time buyers. The main question, and major problem, when recruiting a part-time buyer is the degree of emphasis attached to individual aspects of the job. For instance, when recruiting a chef, how much emphasis should you place on the job candidate's purchasing skill, personnel skill, cooking expertise, and so on?

BUDGETING

As we pointed out in Chapter 5, the larger operations that employ full-time buyers may decide to fund their purchasing. This funding usually means that they decide to include annual salary expenses and other appropriate operating expenses (such as office supplies) as a part of the hospitality operation's overall budget. The operations that employ user-buyers tend to avoid this separate purchasing budget. Nevertheless, since a budget is always a measure of performance, a buyer's overall contribution can be measured by comparing actual operating expenses with budgeted operating expenses.

JOB DESCRIPTION

A job description constitutes a list of duties an employee must perform. It is usually prepared before, or in conjunction with, the job specification. In some cases, the supervisor develops the description personally. In others, some participation in this effort may arise between the supervisor and purchasing manager. Even here, however, the supervisor should set the tone of the job by stating its objectives and the broad guidelines a buyer must follow. The buyer, then, is left to iron out the specific details necessary to organize and administer the purchasing function.[2] (See Figure 6.3.)

Objectives of the Purchasing Function

We discussed the general objectives in Chapter 4, noting that buyers attain them by (1) purchasing the appropriate quality, (2) purchasing at the right price, (3) purchasing in the right amount, (4) purchasing at the right time, and (5) purchasing from the right supplier, who provides the needed supplier services. Additional objectives may be more specific. For example, someone in the operation may decide to set rigid quality standards for fresh produce and looser quality standards for the remaining food products. A specific goal, then, would be the maintenance of these various quality standards.

Establish selection and procurement policies
Forecast trends
Develop purchase specifications
Maintain supplier files, price lists, etc.
Negotiate contracts
Monitor deliveries
Select suppliers
Coordinate other departments' purchasing needs
Identify and research new products
Investigate suppliers' facilities
Establish inventory stock levels
Monitor storeroom inventories
Select and train purchasing staff
Monitor operating budget
Establish and monitor inventory and cost controls

FIGURE 6.3. Example of job description duties for a purchasing manager.

Selection and Procurement Policies

These are usually broad, flexible rules a supervisor expects a buyer to follow when selecting and procuring products and services. In general, policies guide a buyer in how to act and what to do in several types of situations. As becomes clear in the discussion that follows, precise policies are in the buyer's best interest. Some of these situations are presented next.

Accepting Gifts from a Supplier. (This also applies to accepting gifts, pooling them, and distributing them later to all company employees.) Strict rules against this practice are the norm. Drawing the line can, however, be difficult. For example, accepting bottles of liquor may be taboo, but what about a supplier who treats the buyer to a free lunch now and then? Or how about the supplier who always has complimentary tickets to major sports events? If the buyer picks up his or her share of the lunch tabs and tickets, everything is probably OK. But whatever the policy, a buyer must realize that accepting gifts, especially those that cannot be returned (such as complimentary meals and tickets) could create a psychological obligation to purchase goods or services from these generous suppliers.[3]

Favoring Suppliers. How many potential suppliers should you contact? Should you stick with one or two, or should you consider any reputable, capable purveyor? In some cases, other department heads may try to steer a buyer toward a certain supplier, usually a friend. This practice puts the buyer in a tough spot. But a strict policy can protect a buyer from undue pressure from, for example, the bartender who wants all the bar supplies to be purchased from his cousin's supply house. In most instances, the supervisor insists that an approved supplier list be developed, which then serves to restrict all personnel who have purchasing responsibilities.

Limiting Quantity. The typical buyer is restricted in the amount he or she can purchase at any one time. If a buyer wants to buy a larger-than-normal amount, generally permission must be obtained. This common policy is strictly enforced to help an operation avoid massive overstocks that tie up large sums of money and extra storage space.

Limiting Prices. A supervisor may suggest some flexible price limits for certain products, especially those products that represent the bulk of the purchasing dollar. And if, for instance, an item's price rises above that limit, it may be time to reevaluate its place on the menu.

Making Personal Purchases. Personal purchases (also referred to as "steward sales") occur whenever the hospitality company allows its employees to take advantage of the company's purchasing power to purchase goods for their personal, private use. Usually, a supervisor discourages a buyer from purchasing products for his or her own use. Buyers might be tempted to buy hams, or steaks, or roasts for a personal dinner party they are planning. And other employees might like to take advantage of the wholesale price. In some companies, employees may take advantage on such special occasions as holidays. And if employees must buy their own uniforms, they may be able to make these purchases through the buyer or purchasing agent. But if this practice is abused, it can lead to confusion and dishonesty.

Establishing Reciprocity. Basically, reciprocity means "you buy from me, I'll buy from you." It is also interpreted to mean "I'll buy from you if you do something special for me." This is a troublesome policy. Other department heads and employees may badger a buyer into entering into some sort of reciprocal arrangement. Not only may the arrangement be illegal, but the best a buyer can do, obviously, is to break even. In fact, the buyer usually winds up purchasing more items from a supplier than the supplier could ever reciprocate; keep in mind that suppliers can refer only so much room and food and beverage business, usually much less business than a buyer directs to them.

If there is a reciprocal arrangement, the superior normally establishes it, with the buyer then expected to purchase accordingly.

Free Samples. Some buyers collect all sorts of free samples; others accept them only when they have a sincere interest in buying the product;

Send for Free Samples and Special Introductory Offer.

Dear Scott Room Service:

Yes, I'd like to see how soft a soft amenity can be.

1. ☐ Please send me a FREE roll of Cottonelle and a FREE box of Scotties.

2. ☐ Please have a Scott representative contact me to discuss your special introductory offer: one free case of Scotties with every ten cases of Cottonelle bathroom tissue purchased on your initial order of Cottonelle.

FOR IMMEDIATE RESPONSE, CALL TOLL-FREE:
    1-800-FOR-INFO. (In PA: 1-215-337-1864) Ask for Ext. 10.

SCOTT
A HOUSEHOLD NAME, AT WORK.

Name _____ Title _____

Hotel/Motel Name _____

Address _____

City _____ State _____ Zip _____

Phone _____

Offer good in continental U.S. only.   ③① M37

FIGURE 6.4. Buyers have several opportunities to solicit free samples. Most suppliers use this sales technique very successfully. (Courtesy Scott Paper Company.)

still others purchase the samples they want to avoid obligating themselves to a particular supplier. Perhaps the best policy is to accept a free sample only when there is a serious interest in the product. (See Figure 6.4.)

Free equipment testing falls under the same guidelines: typically, you test it only if you have more than a casual interest.

The major difficulty with free samples and free equipment testing is the distinct possibility that suppliers will send their most expensive items and then pressure the user to pressure the buyer to purchase them. Consulting with a user of the equipment (the chef, for example) instead of the buyer is an example of "backdoor selling." This selling strategy can be effective, but it also helps to undermine efficiency and friendship. In any case, hospitality companies should adhere to a strict policy on free samples and test equipment.

Accepting Discounts. There are at least four separate types of discounts that a buyer could obtain from a supplier.

1. Quantity discount. This is granted by the supplier if a buyer agrees to purchase a large amount of one specific type of merchandise.

2. Volume discount. This is similar to the quantity discount. The buyer must agree to purchase a large volume of goods; however, he or she can buy more than one type of merchandise. This discount is sometimes referred to as a blanket-order discount, in that the purchase order contains a long list of several items, none of which is ordered in huge amounts; however, when all of these small amounts are totaled, there is a large dollar volume that a supplier might reward with a discount.

3. Cash discount. This is an award for prompt payment, for paying in advance of the delivery, or using a cash-on-delivery (COD) bill-paying procedure.

4. Promotional discount. A supplier might grant this type of discount if a buyer's company agrees to accept the discount and use it to promote the product in the operation. For example, this promotion might involve letting restaurant customers sample the product at a reduced menu price.

Quantity discounts and volume discounts are relatively common in the hospitality industry, but they often require purchasing amounts that cannot be stored easily. Buyers may or may not be permitted to bargain for cash discounts, since the accounting department or the financial officer usually sets up some sort of bill-paying schedule. (We discuss these schedules in Chapter 10.)

Some hospitality companies aggressively seek out suppliers who offer generous promotional discount opportunities.[4] For instance, some quick-service restaurants will allow a supplier to advertise brand name merchandise in the property if the supplier agrees to give them, free of charge, beverage dispensing equipment, menu sign boards, and/or countertop display shelving. Some table-service operations like promotional discounts because they can use them to reward servers who sell their quota of the particular item to guests. And caterers enjoy having suppliers construct attractive displays of their products in the caterers' sales offices that can be used to entice potential banquet customers into purchasing expensive parties.

Promotional discounts, though, represent a "loaded decision." Although a buyer may want to save the money, the company may not want the obligation to promote the product or even to be identified too closely with it.

Written Ethics Code. Most hospitality companies have established written ethical guidelines for their buyers. In many cases, these guidelines are adapted from those suggested by one or more professional purchasing associations. The typical code, though, is usually very explicit and pertains to all potential ethical dilemmas. It is normally a major part of a buyer's job description.

Controlling Products. When a product is purchased, the buyer is not relieved of the responsibility for that item. He or she may be responsible for its storage and use. In fact, in small operations, the buyer-user or part-time buyer generally takes responsibility for an item until it is used in production. Larger companies often split that responsibility. For example, the food buyer may be responsible for purchasing, storing, and then issuing the food to a user. In hotels, the receiving clerk is often part of the accounting department. He or she checks incoming merchandise and serves as a control on the buyer's purchases. Once users receive an item, they take responsibility for it.

The more times you split responsibility of this kind, the greater control you have, since more people check on each other's performance. This division is practically impossible in the smaller operations. But in the smaller places, the operator is usually on the premises to maintain strict supervision. A manager with a sharp eye suffers no loss of control whatsoever.

Supporting Local Suppliers. Some owner-managers like to support local suppliers and ensure that a certain amount of business stays in the community. Although this policy of trade relations can limit a buyer's alternatives, in the long run, some local purchasing may be a beneficial strategy.

Quality Standards. Usually, the owner-manager will set the quality standards, and the person who has ordering responsibilities will abide by them and see to it that, as much as possible, he or she purchases and receives such quality. It is unusual for most buyers to have the final say regarding the quality standards to be used in the hospitality operation, but quite often the person who has the major responsibility for ordering has some leeway and flexibility.

Shopping Procedures. The buyer's supervisor usually will want to note the exact type of buying procedures, especially the procedures to be used when selecting the appropriate supplier. The shopping procedures that most buyers must use require the buyer to consider the offerings of more than one approved supplier to make an intelligent decision regarding the available values and which approved supplier seems to be the best for the buyer's hospitality operation. In some instances, the buyer's supervisor will decide that, for one reason or another, some items should be purchased from one specific supplier, whereas other items should be purchased only from the supplier offering the best value. The supplier offering the best value is determined by shopping around.

COMPENSATION

Full-time and part-time buyers usually receive a straight salary, but in some situations they also receive a bonus. Corporate purchasing agents can expect to receive a good salary and to occupy a top management position within the company. Buyers, too, receive good salaries. Part-time buyers, though, tend to earn salaries based on several duties, not just their buying. For instance, a chef may receive a high salary primarily because of his or her staff supervision and culinary expertise.

Where purchasing has been concerned, the major aspect of the compensation issue has always been the bonus. A bonus can be tricky to assign because buyers may be tempted to work toward the bonus alone while sacrificing other important aspects of the job. For example, if a buyer receives a bonus based on the AP prices paid for food, he or she may be motivated to purchase foods with the lowest AP price, but with the highest EP cost.

TRAINING

A buyer should receive some type of training before being allowed to purchase products. If a new employee, he or she must be introduced to the philosophy and goals of the company, to all its operational aspects, and to the purchasing policies. These introductions actually represent an orientation rather than training.

Full-time buyers and buyer trainees undergo additional training, as needed, in the procedural elements of buying. On-the-job training (OJT) is probably most often used in the purchasing function.

PERFORMANCE EVALUATION

Buyers undergo two types of performance evaluations: (1) how well they operate the purchasing department, if there is one, and (2) how well they have carried out the procurement function.

"Operational performance" refers to how well the buyer has adhered to the budget allocated to the purchasing department, that is, how efficient the buyer has been in discharging the purchasing duties. This evaluation consists of comparing actual secretarial salaries, postage expenses, telephone costs, and so on, with their budgeted counterparts. Smaller operations tend to skip this type of evaluation, even though it can help a manager to isolate the operational costs of the buying function. Unfortunately, it is usually too difficult and costly to separate, for example, telephone calls to suppliers from the rest of the phone calls. It is not impossible, but in smaller places it may not be economical.

"Procurement performance" refers to how effectively a buyer has procured products and services. Procuring items is the heart of the buyer's job; thus, procurement performance is extremely important. Unfortunately, we can find little agreement about what to look at when evaluating procurement performance. We discuss several of these performance quality indicators next.

The Materials Budget

Some large companies forecast their sales and, concomitantly, the cost of goods sold. For example, the cost of food might be forecast at 35 percent of the food sales dollar. The food buyer might be expected to spend no more than, say, 30 percent of the sales dollar for food, the remaining 5 percent to be used to pay for the difference between the AP price and the EP cost—things such as trimming loss and other unavoidable waste.

A company could construct a materials budget for such items as advertising costs, detergent costs, and lobster costs. In fact, this procedure is relatively common, even in small operations. But it is uncommon to find a materials budget for all products and services. It would be convenient, however, to have these budgets; they make it easy to compare actual costs, thereby facilitating a fair procurement performance evaluation.

These budgets appear more commonly in hospitality organizations that serve "a captive audience": employee feeding, college feeding, hospital and prison food services, and so on. Indeed, whenever a food-service catering corporation bids on a food-service contract of this type, it usually must include the projected expenses as a part of its bid. Consequently, the buyer receives what amounts to a materials budget to work under for the duration of the contract. If, for example, the costs of some foods increase, he or she may be forced to try cheaper substitutes.

Inventory Turnover

"Inventory turnover" refers to the annual cost of goods sold divided by the average dollar value of inventory kept in stock during the course of that year. (The average inventory value is equal to the inventory value at the beginning of the year, plus the inventory value at the end of the year, divided by two.)

For example, if a restaurant's annual cost of goods sold equals $250,000, the beginning inventory is $12,000, and the ending inventory is $8,000, the inventory turnover calculation for that particular restaurant is:

$$\text{Average inventory} = \frac{\$12,000 + \$8,000}{2}$$

$$= \$10,000$$

$$\text{Inventory turnover} = \frac{\$250,000}{\$10,000}$$

$$= 25$$

The normal food turnover is between 20 and 25 times a year on the average; that is, it takes about two weeks for all foods to move from the receiving dock to a customer's stomach; for liquor it is from 7 to 10 times a year. But since there is no generally accepted, rule-of-thumb inventory turnover figure in the hospitality industry, an operation must decide what represents a good turnover figure for its business. And if 20 turns out to be ideal, 18 or 22 is unsatisfactory. Eighteen would be unsatisfactory because it indicates slow-moving stock. Twenty-two indicates a turnover so rapid that the operation risks the possibility of running out of stock. Most operations can fix an optimal number of turnovers that ensure an appropriate stock level, one that helps the business operate efficiently. (In Chapter 8 we provide further discussion of the optimal stock level.)

Percentage of Sales Volume

There are various rules of thumb regarding the appropriate amount of inventory that should be on hand at any one particular point in time to accommodate the hospitality operation's expected level of business. For instance, it is felt that the full-service restaurant should have an inventory of food, beverage, and nonfood supplies that is equal in dollar value to no more than 1 percent of the annual sales volume. An annual sales volume of $1,000,000, therefore, needs about $10,000 worth of inventory at all times to support it.

A related rule of thumb suggests that the food inventory should be no more than about one-third of the average monthly food costs. It is thought that the food inventory should not exceed this level unless there are other financial incentives to purchase unusually large quantities. As with all rules of thumb, though, generalizations can be dangerous. However, it is a quick method that can be used to evaluate the buyer's procurement performance.

Stockouts

A stockout occurs when you cannot serve a customer a particular item because you do not have it on hand. The number of stockouts an operation encounters indicates the amount of inventory held. Several stockouts suggest an unreasonably low stock level. Few or no stockouts indicate a high stock level. Again, an operation wants to reach an optimal stock level, which means it probably must accept some stockouts. How many to accept is, of course, a matter for managerial policy.

Number of Late Deliveries

A buyer may or may not be able to control a supplier's delivery schedule. But he or she certainly can complain when deliveries come late. If too many late deliveries occur, a supervisor may rightfully ask, "Why do you continue to buy from this purveyor?"

Number of Items That Must Be Returned to Suppliers

A buyer cannot always control defective deliveries, but he or she can complain about them. Also, a supervisor can pose the question: "Why continue to buy from a supplier who delivers defective goods?" Returned and late deliveries are to be avoided in the hospitality industry. If we run out of steak, we can hardly tell a customer to come back tomorrow for it.

Number of Back Orders

This issue is similar to the previous two. Usually, we do not like back orders, and we normally will not tolerate many of them.

Checking AP Prices

Some companies periodically check the AP prices of other suppliers against the AP prices they are paying their current suppliers. These prices may not always be equal because of differences in overall value between suppliers; but if wide disparities appear, the buyer is either negligent or dishonest. (Dishonesty in these situations usually takes the form of a buyer's overpaying with the operation's funds and then receiving a personal rebate directly from the supplier. This practice, a type of kickback, is discussed more thoroughly in Chapter 15.)

It is, of course, time-consuming and tedious for a supervisor to make these comparisons. It is not at all easy to compare values and EP costs. Also, if one does not deal in the marketplace every day, it is hard to keep track of current market prices. Nevertheless, supervisors exercise caution in this area because the practice of paying a little more and receiving a kickback is both tempting and easy to cover up.

Other Performance Indicators

There are many other performance indicators, but they are merely variations of the ones we have discussed. For instance, some large companies go to a lot of trouble to calculate such standard ratios as average inventory as a percentage of sales, average inventory as a percentage of total assets, or average inventory as a percentage of annual purchases. These standards, all variations on the materials budget, are subsequently compared with actual percentages.

When evaluating purchasing performance, the wise supervisor will establish clearly defined and easily measured goals. In view of the variety of performance evaluations used throughout the industry, the safest conclusion is that supervisors should continually evaluate a buyer's procurement performance by monitoring (1) the number of stockouts, (2) the inventory stock levels, (3) the percentage of returns, (4) losses due to overbuying, (5) losses due to the user's refusal of an item, and (6) inventory turnover.

Another major problem in performance evaluation is how to evaluate the part-time buyer. The measurements we have already discussed do apply, but the thorny question of how much emphasis to place on this part-time activity remains. For instance, a buyer-chef may be primarily involved in food production. Hence, his or her purchasing performance may be less important to the operation. If buying is a part-time activity, the chef may be unable to devote sufficient attention to it. Is this the chef's fault? Should he or she be reprimanded if the stock turnover is too low? Clearly, another dimension enters the picture whenever the part-time buyer's performance is measured.

OTHER RELATIONSHIPS BETWEEN BUYERS AND SUPERVISORS

Buyers and their supervisors rightfully have certain expectations of each other. Through this chapter so far, we have considered the straightforward aspects of the supervisor's role as it relates to the part-time or full-time buyer. But other more intangible expectations exist between these two employees.

Supervisors expect more than mere job competence. They also expect the buyer (1) to give pertinent advice when necessary, (2) to be loyal to the company, (3) to put the company's interests ahead of any personal interest, (4) to maintain effective and efficient working relationships with all purveyors and company personnel, (5) to bear in mind constantly that he or she represents the company in the marketplace, (6) to avoid the possibility of legal entanglements, and (7) to avoid the possibility of favoritism and discrimination when dealing with purveyors.

Buyers also have expectations. They expect their supervisor (1) to give them the necessary authority to perform their jobs adequately, (2) to give them adequate facilities and an adequate budget, (3) to give them a voice in such major decisions as menu planning, and (4) to have an appreciation for the profit potential of the buying activity.

THE BUYER'S RELATIONS WITH COLLEAGUES

All colleagues should strive to help each other. At the very least, a full-time buyer who purchases items for the kitchen, bar, housekeeping department, and so on can ensure a continual flow of supplies for all departments of the hotel or restaurant. We have stressed the fact that few operations employ a full-time buyer. Most depend on such buyer-users as the buyer-head bartender, the buyer-housekeeper, and the buyer-chef. But the buying aspect of their jobs can create an additional bond between these colleagues.

For instance, these user-buyers may want to combine some activities. They may agree that the buyer-chef will purchase writing supplies for everyone or that the buyer-housekeeper will purchase soaps and other cleaning supplies for all departments. Sometimes the owner-general manager makes these decisions. Or, all together, the part-time buyers iron out the details. However it is handled, a greater need for cooperation and coordination among colleagues enters the picture.

Buyers must also work closely with colleagues who have no buying authority. For instance, the buyer-chef may work with the accountant to develop various formats to be used for ordering, receiving, storing, and the like. The buyer-chef may work with the sales manager or the owner-manager whenever new menus are contemplated, since he or she can advise on food prices, the availability of various items, and the operation's capability of producing the new menu items given its kitchen facilities and employee skills.

POTENTIAL CONFLICTS WITH COLLEAGUES

Major conflict can, however, occur between buyers and production supervisors who use the products and services. For example, a full-time buyer may spend a lot of time tracking down good buys, only to see excessive waste and spoilage in food preparation. Although the control of purchased items eventually passes from the buyer to the user, the chef may blame the buyer for purchasing inferior merchandise if food costs are too high because of waste. Conversely, the buyer may blame the waste on the chef's lack of control over the kitchen employees. Either way, the owner-manager has a problem deciding whom or what to believe.

This kind of conflict has encouraged some operations to create several buyer-user positions, thereby keeping control and responsibility together. For example, some restaurants employ a buyer-chef, buyer-head bartender, buyer-wine steward, and buyer-maître d'. The drawback is the buyer-user who has no one checking up on his or her buying activities, no one to uncover buying mistakes. An alert owner-manager, though, can usually minimize this difficulty.

Other more minor conflicts can occur, but these usually involve the politics that arise whenever colleagues vie for favor with the boss. The major potential problem remains the control issue, which can lead to still larger problems and should never be taken lightly.

RELATIONS WITH HOURLY EMPLOYEES

The buyer's main responsibility to hourly employees is to provide the resources they need to carry out their duties properly. Buyers must ensure a continuity of supply. If employees do not have the raw materials, they cannot produce. And idle production workers lead to customer dissatisfaction somewhere down the line. When employees should be producing, but materials are late or not available, at some later point, when output is expected, guests will find that their guest rooms are not ready or their food is missing.

If the hospitality operation allows hourly employees to make personal purchases, the buyer generally incurs the responsibility for supervising and monitoring these purchases.

POTENTIAL CONFLICTS WITH HOURLY EMPLOYEES

The major potential conflict with hourly employees can occur when a buyer tries to exert control and authority over employees supervised by someone else. Generally, this conflict parallels the major conflict that occurs between a full-time buyer and his or her colleagues. Full-time buyers may unknowingly assume more authority than they are entitled to. For instance, if a buyer also manages the storeroom, he or she might alienate the chef's employees by forcing them to follow myriad rules and regulations to obtain the food and supplies they need in their work. These rules can indirectly affect the employees' work patterns; hence, they tend to give the buyer some control over these employees. In the long run, these conflicts must be ironed out between the buyer and his or her colleagues.

KEY WORDS AND CONCEPTS

AP price

Approved supplier list

Backdoor selling

Back orders

Beginning inventory

Bill-paying procedures

Blanket-order discount

Budgeting

Cash discount

COD

Compensation

Conceptual skill

Controlling products

Ending inventory

EP cost

Equipment testing

Ethics code

Evaluating the part-time buyer

Favoring suppliers

Food inventory value as a percentage of food costs

Free samples

Gifts from suppliers

Interpersonal skill

Inventory turnover

Inventory value as a percentage of sales volume

Job description

Job specification

Kickback

Labor pool

Late deliveries

Materials budget

OJT

Operational performance

Other expectations that exist between buyer and his or her supervisor

Performance evaluation

Personal purchases

Price limits

Procurement performance

Promotional discount

Purchasing objectives

Quality standards

Quantity discount

Quantity limits

Rebate

Reciprocity

Relations and conflicts between buyer and colleagues

Relations and conflicts between buyer and hourly employees

Relations between buyer and supervisor

Returns

Selection and procurement policies

Shopping procedures

Steward sales

Stockouts

Supporting local suppliers

Systems mentality

Technical skill

Trade relations

Training

Volume discount

REFERENCES

1. Patt Patterson, "What Qualities Make a Top-Notch Restaurant Food Buyer?" *Nation's Restaurant News,* January 19, 1987, p. 51.

2. For a detailed job description, see M. C. Warfel and Marion L. Cremer, *Purchasing for Food Service Managers,* 2d ed. (Berkeley, CA: McCutchan, 1990), pp. 50–52.

3. Pamela Sebastian, "Vendors' Gifts Pose Problems for Purchasers," *The Wall Street Journal,* June 26, 1989, p. B1. See also, Patt Patterson, " 'Tis the Season of Gift Giving, a Time to Show Appreciation," *Nation's Restaurant News,* November 23, 1992, p. 128.

4. Patt Patterson, "Distributor: Communication Key to Relationships," *Nation's Restaurant News,* February 25, 1991, p. 46.

QUESTIONS AND PROBLEMS

1. Define or briefly explain the following terms:

   (a) Job specification

   (b) Job description

   (c) Purchasing policies

(d) Quantity limits

(e) Price limits

(f) Reciprocal buying

(g) Performance evaluation

(h) Materials budget

(i) Inventory turnover

(j) Stockout

(k) Approved supplier list

2. Given the following data, compute the inventory turnover.

Beginning inventory: $15,000
Cost of goods sold: $325,000
Ending inventory: $12,000

3. Assume that you are a hotel manager and that you want to hire a food buyer. Prepare a newspaper ad advertising this position. If possible, ask a hotel manager to comment on your ad.

4. Assume that you are a hotel manager. Devise formal policies for the following:

(a) Accepting supplier gifts

(b) Establishing quantity limits

(c) Accepting free samples

Briefly discuss the reasoning that led to your policy statements.

5. Develop a two-week buyer's training program for a bartender who soon will be promoted to liquor buyer-bartender.

6. Assume you are a hotel manager. Develop a list of performance evaluation criteria you would use to evaluate the buyer-housekeeper's procurement activity. Briefly discuss the reasoning that led to your list.

7. Briefly describe the buyer's major working relationship with the accountant; with the sales manager.

8. What are some specific conflicts that can occur between the full-time buyer and the chef? the housekeeper?

9. Explain why a hospitality organization might create several buyer-user positions.

10. What is the buyer's typical responsibility regarding personal purchases by employees?

11. Should full-time buyers have control over a production supervisor's employees and their use of raw materials? Why?

12. Assume that you are a hotel manager. The food buyer and chef are blaming each other for the low quality of steak dinners. The chef claims that the

buyer is purchasing inferior meat. The buyer contends that the chef's employees are abusing the product. How would you solve this conflict? If possible, contact a local hotel manager and ask him or her to review your answer.

13. Assume that you have been instructed to purchase your fresh produce from one specific supplier, who happens to be a close friend of your employer. This supplier has back ordered you on several occasions. What would you do to improve this situation? If possible, ask a restaurant owner to comment on your answer.

14. Name three advantages of taking the time to shop around for the best value.

15. Name three disadvantages of taking the time to shop around for the best value.

16. What are some disadvantages of accepting promotional discounts from suppliers?

17. What would be the approximate food, beverage, and nonfood supplies inventory value of a full-service restaurant with an annual sales volume of $600,000?

18. If you had your preference, what method would you use to evaluate a buyer's procurement performance? What method would you ignore? If possible, ask a hotel manager to comment on your answer.

19. What are the major objectives of the purchasing function?

20. What are some advantages that a hospitality company gains if it insists that all company buyers use an approved supplier list?

P A R T **2**

PRINCIPLES OF
SELECTION AND
PROCUREMENT

CHAPTER 7

PURCHASE REQUISITION

MGM GRAND
WORLD'S LARGEST HOTEL, CASINO & THEME PARK
P.O. Box 77711
Las Vegas, Nevada 89177-7711

Telephone: (702) 891-1111
Fax: (702) 891-1112

REQUISITION NO.

☐ BYPASS DATE: _____
☐ EXPENSE
☐ CAPITAL EXPENDITURE - CER # _____
☐ FINANCIAL ANALYSIS ATTACHED
(REQUIRED FOR CAPITAL EXPENDITURE)

DEPARTMENT ORDERING: _____

ACCOUNT NUMBER CHARGE: _____
(REFER TO DEPARTMENT CHART OF ACCOUNTS)

THREE BIDS REQUIRED *

* If sole source give justification below.

QUANTITY	UNIT	COMPLETE ORDERING DESCRIPTION	SUPPLIER #1 PRICE	SUPPLIER #2 PRICE	SUPPLIER #3 PRICE	EXTENSION
		CAPITAL BUDGET AMOUNT: $			TOTAL	

REASON PURCHASE IS REQUIRED/EXPLANATION OF BYPASS OR SOLE SOURCE JUSTIFICATION

_____
DIRECTOR OF PURCHASING

_____
DEPT. HEAD

_____
VICE PRESIDENT

_____
SENIOR VICE PRESIDENT

PURCHASE ORDER NO. _____

SUPPLIER

_____
CFO

_____
CEO

PUR0060 (R 4/95)

DEPARTMENT

Source: MGM Grand Hotel, Casino & Theme Park

THE PURCHASE SPECIFICATION: AN OVERALL VIEW

THE PURPOSE OF THIS CHAPTER

This chapter discusses:

- The advantages of having purchase specifications
- Who decides what information to include on the purchase specification
- The information included on the purchase specification
- What influences the type of information included on the purchase specification
- Who writes the purchase specifications
- The potential problems with purchase specifications
- The optimal quality to include on the purchase specification
- The optimal supplier services to include on the purchase specification

INTRODUCTION

A "product specification" (sometimes referred to as "product identification") is a description of all the characteristics in a product required to fill certain production and/or service needs. It typically includes product information that can be verified on delivery and that can be communicated easily from buyers to suppliers.

Unlike the product specification (which includes only information about the product) the "purchase specification" implies a much broader concept. The purchase specification includes all product information, but, in addition, it includes information regarding the pertinent services buyers require from suppliers.

Large hospitality companies normally prepare purchase specifications. They usually seek long-term relationships with several primary sources and intermediaries and, before entering into these relationships, want to iron out every detail concerning product characteristics and desired supplier services. Smaller hospitality firms, on the other hand, tend to shop around for products on a day-to-day basis. They concentrate their efforts on preparing and using product specifications. If, for example, a particular supplier's supplier services are found lacking, these buyers will seek an alternative supplier who provides at least some of the desired supplier services.

Preparing detailed purchase specifications is not an easy task. It can be time-consuming, and a shortage of time is a major obstacle to getting this work done.

If you plan to invest the time, money, and effort needed to develop adequate purchase specifications, you must be prepared to study the product's characteristics. Among the best sources here are the references distributed by the U.S. Department of Agriculture. Many libraries contain these materials, or you can procure them from USDA offices or state Agriculture offices. (They are particularly attractive because you can reproduce them without violating a copyright.)

Other references are available. Purchasing guidelines are published by the U.S. government for use by school food services that participate in the subsidized school lunch program. The various product industries, like the apple growers, also publish literature depicting characteristics of their products. Industry associations, such as the Produce Marketing Association (PMA), similarly publish and distribute a significant amount of information that can be used to prepare specifications for fresh produce. And you can always find a supplier waiting to help you, especially if you buy from that supplier.

One thing you must usually do for yourself when preparing specifications is to choose the quality and supplier services you want. You cannot always expect to find a neat formula to guide you. This book offers several considerations that you should examine. But eventually you must make your own decisions concerning these other variables. You must also keep in mind that a purchase specification should contain more than just a brief description of a product.

WHY HAVE SPECS?

"Specs" (i.e., specifications) have several basic purposes and advantages, the primary ones being that (1) they serve as quality control standards and as cost control standards (in these respects, specifications are important aspects of a hospitality operation's overall control system); (2) they help to avoid misunderstanding between suppliers, buyers, users, and other company officials; (3) in a buyer's absence, they allow someone else to fill in temporarily; (4) they serve as useful training devices for assistant buyers and manager trainees; and (5) they are essential if a company wants to set down all relevant aspects of a product or service it wants to purchase, submit a list of these aspects to two or more suppliers, and ask these suppliers to indicate (bid) the price they will charge for the specific product or service.

In short, a specification is a sounding board for your ideas on which you detail every relevant consideration. By contrast, a purchase order is much less involved. After you know what you want and who you want it from, completing the purchase order is a formality. But it is a legal formality—a contract between you and a supplier that he or she will deliver goods at a specific time, for a specific price, to a specific place. The specification lays out the parameters of what you must have. The purchase order is a written or sometimes verbal—for example, over the phone—contract that arranges an actual transaction.

WHO DECIDES WHAT TO INCLUDE ON THE SPECS?

There are four potential decision-making entities here: (1) the owner-manager or another top management official, (2) the buyer, (3) the user, or (4) some combination of these three. It is unlikely that the buyer would write the specs alone, without the advice of the supervisor and of the users of the items to be purchased. All companies seem to take a different approach to this issue, but the buyers and users do most of the legwork, all the while staying within overall company guidelines. That is, a top company official normally sets the tone for the specs, and the buyers or users complete the details. The biggest problem with this participative approach is agreeing on what is a main guideline and what is a minute detail.

WHAT INFORMATION DOES A SPEC INCLUDE?

A spec can be very short; it might include only a product's brand name and nothing else. Or it might include several pages of detailed information, which is often the case with equipment specifications.

It should be noted that specifications are sometimes categorized as either "formal" or "informal." A formal specification is apt to be extremely lengthy—perhaps several pages of information. Government agencies typically prepare formal specifications. The average hospitality enterprise owner-manager may prepare informal specifications—perhaps just a bit of information regarding product yield, quality, and packaging. One should not assume that the person preparing an informal specification is not cognizant of all the other information normally found on a formal one. It is just that the typical operator does not spend so much time writing.

The buyer is apt to include at least some of the following pieces of information on a spec:

1. The performance requirement (i.e., the intended use) of the product or service. This is usually considered the most important piece of information. You must have a clear idea of what is supposed to happen.

2. The exact name of the product or service. You must note the exact name as well as the exact type of product you want. For example, you cannot note that you want olives; you must note that you want black olives, or green olives, or anchovy-stuffed olives, or whatever. In some instances, we must be extremely careful to indicate the correct name and/or type of merchandise desired, or we are apt to be disappointed at delivery time.

3. The packer's brand name, if appropriate. Packers' brands are an indication of quality. Some items, such as fresh produce, do not normally carry instantly recognizable brand-name identification. Many other items do, however, and a buyer may be interested primarily in only one or two brands and not any others. If you do indicate a brand name on the spec, you may want to add the words "or equivalent" next to it. This ensures that more than one supplier can compete for your business. By noting merely the brand name, you may reduce the opportunity to shop around since usually only one supplier in your area will carry that product.

   In lieu of the words "or equivalent," some buyers prefer to add the words "equal to or better" to their brand name preferences noted on the specs. This is a phrase used in conjunction with a brand name to indicate that the product quality characteristics desired must be similar or "superior" to the brand identified. The drawback with these words is the fact that there may be several superior brands and it may be very difficult for a buyer to make a sound purchase decision if he or she is unfamiliar with some of them.

   At times it is very important to insist on a certain brand name and avoid all other comparable brands. For instance, if a recipe has been developed that calls for a certain brand of margarine, the buyer should not purchase another brand unless it is compatible with that recipe. In this case, the finished product may be unacceptable if a different brand is used.

4. U.S. quality grade, if appropriate. U.S. grades have been developed by the federal government to allow the buyer the option of using an independent opinion of product quality when preparing specifications. Unfortunately, since grading generally is a voluntary procedure, many items in the channel of distribution may not be graded.

However, you can at least indicate a desired grade, along with the notation "or equivalent." This will allow suppliers who do not have graded merchandise to bid for your business. Also, these suppliers then have a quality standard to guide them. (Some states also have grading systems; for instance, Wisconsin has a grading procedure to use for some dairy items.)

5. Size information. In most instances you must indicate the size desired for a particular item. For some products, such as portion-cut steaks, the buyer can indicate an exact weight. For other items, though, such as large, wholesale cuts of beef or whole chicken, usually the buyer can only indicate the desired weight range. In some instances, the size of an item (such as lemons or lobster tails) is indicated by its "count," that is, the number of items per case, per pound, or per 10 pounds. (See Figure 7.1.)

6. Acceptable trim (i.e., acceptable waste). For some products, such as many fresh foods, you may need to indicate the maximum amount of waste you will tolerate. Another way of saying the same thing is to note the minimum edible yield of a product you will accept. For instance, fresh lettuce may have varying degrees of waste, depending on how it is processed by the food distributor. Some lettuce is a cleaned and chopped, ready-to-serve product, whereas the typical head of lettuce has an edible yield of much less than 100 percent. Of course, you expect to pay much more for the product that has little or no waste.

7. Package size. You will need to indicate, in most instances, the size of the container you desire. For instance, the can size must be noted when purchasing canned vegetables.

8. Type of package. In some cases, the type of packaging materials used is highly standardized. For example, dairy products packaging must meet minimum standards of quality. This is not the case for other items. Frozen products, for instance, should come in packaging sufficient to withstand the extreme cold without breaking. Some suppliers scrimp on this, and, while the quality of the product may meet your specification, the poor packaging will result in a rapid deterioration of this once-acceptable item.

Packaging can add considerable cost to the items we purchase. In some cases, the value of the packaging may exceed the value of the item. For instance, the cost of packaging of single-serve packets of salt can easily be higher than the cost of this food ingredient.

When specifying the desired type of packaging, some buyers may require suppliers to use recyclable packaging materials. Alternatively, buyers may request reusable packaging, such as the plastic tubs some suppliers use to deliver fresh fish.

CALIFORNIA CANNED RIPE OLIVES FOOD SERVICE PACK

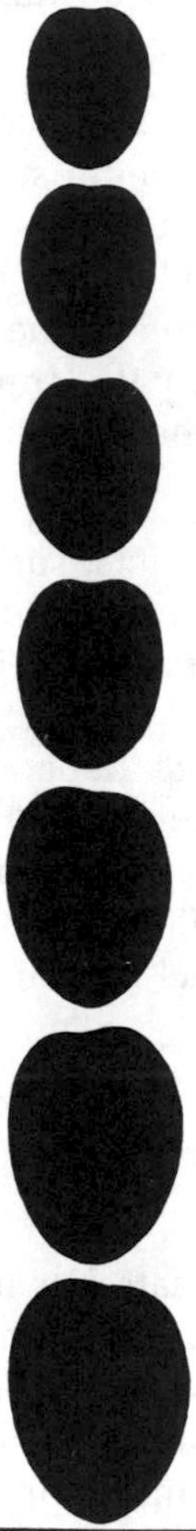

	Size Designation	PITTED			WHOLE-UNPITTED		
		Drained Net Weight No. 10 Can	Approx. Number Per Can	Average Number Per Lb.	Drained Net Weight No. 10 Can	Approx. Number Per Can	Average Number Per Lb.
	Small	51 oz.	578	177-193	66 oz.	557	128-140
	Medium	51 oz.	486	150-165	66 oz.	466	106-121
	Large	51 oz.	430	123-138	66 oz.	404	91-105
	Extra Large	51 oz.	350	105-120	66 oz.	288	65-88
	Jumbo	49 oz.	245	69-90	64 oz.	228	51-60
	Colossal	49 oz.	199	54-70	64 oz.	192	41-50
	Super Colossal	49 oz.	163	44-56	64 oz.	128	26-40

STYLE	DRAINED WEIGHT #10 CAN	CUPS PER CAN	WEIGHT PER CUP	CALORIES PER CUP
Sliced	55 oz.	13	135 gm	174
Wedged	55 oz.	11-¼	150 gm	193
Chopped	90 oz.	14-½	195 gm	251

California Olive Industry, P.O. Box 7796, Fresno, CA 93747

FIGURE 7.1. Trade associations provide information useful to buyers. (Courtesy California Olive Committee.)

9. Preservation and/or processing method. For some products, you will be able to identify two or more preservation methods. For instance, you could order refrigerated meats or frozen meats; canned green beans or frozen green beans; or refrigerated lettuce or nonrefrigerated lettuce.

   You also could specify unique types of preservation methods, such as smoked fish instead of salted fish; irradiated poultry instead of nonirradiated poultry; oil-cured olives instead of brine-cured olives; or genetically altered tomatoes instead of natural tomatoes.

   The type of preservation and/or processing method selected often influences the taste and other culinary characteristics of the finished food product. Consequently, it is important for the buyer to be familiar with recipe requirements before altering this part of the spec.

10. Point of origin. You may want to indicate the exact part of the country, or the world, that a specific item must come from. This is a rather important consideration for fresh fish. For instance, you may need to specify that your lobster must come from Maine and not from Australia.

    There are several reasons that buyers may want to note the point of origin on some specs. One is that the flavor, texture, and so forth of an item can differ dramatically among growing regions. Another reason is that the menu may state that an item comes from a particular producing region in the world; if so, it would be a violation of truth-in-menu regulations to serve an alternative product. Freshness can be another important consideration, in that buyers may specify nearby points of origin in order to ensure product quality. And, finally, a buyer may indicate where a product cannot come from, instead of where it must come from, in order to adhere to various company policies and/or legal restrictions. For instance, for political reasons, some companies may refuse to purchase products that come from certain parts of the world.

11. Packaging procedure. Some products are wrapped individually and conveniently layered in the case. Others are "slab" packed, that is, tossed into the container. The more care taken in the packaging procedure, the higher the AP price is apt to be. However, carefully packaged products will have a longer shelf life. And they will tend to maintain their appearance and culinary quality characteristics much longer than those products that are packaged indiscriminately.

    Another packaging consideration concerns the number of individual containers that normally come packaged in a case lot. For instance, it is traditional for no. 10 cans of foods to come packed six to a case. However, some buyers cannot afford to purchase six cans, or they cannot use six cans. Will the supplier sell fewer than six cans; that is, will he or she "bust" the case? Buyers who request busted cases run the risk of having few suppliers willing to compete for their business.

12. Degree of ripeness. This is important for fresh produce. The same concept applies to beef items; for example, you may desire a specific amount of "age" on the item. Wines also have a similar system that reflects, among other things, the year of production.

13. Form. This is an important consideration for many processed items. For instance, do you want your cheese in a brick, or would you rather have it sliced? Do you want your roast beef raw, or do you want it precooked?

14. Color. Some items are available in more than one color. For example, a buyer can order fresh red, green, or yellow peppers.

15. Trade association standards. Some trade associations establish minimum performance standards for items that carry their certification. For instance, the NSF International certification seal on a piece of food production equipment testifies to the equipment's sanitary acceptability.

16. Approved substitutes. Some buyers make it a habit to include on some specs a list of acceptable substitutes that the suppliers can deliver if they are out of the normal item. This can save a great deal of time and effort over the long haul, since suppliers would not have to call buyers every time a product shortage occurs. Buyers also may like this convenience. Unfortunately, before determining approved substitutes, buyers must ensure that they are compatible with production and service needs. So, while this notation on each spec saves time and trouble eventually, it can be more difficult in the short run to spend the time needed to test all potential substitute items.

17. Expiration date. Many buyers will not accept products if they are concerned about possible quality deterioration. To avoid this problem, they may indicate on some specs that suppliers must prove that the products delivered are not too old. For instance, some product labels list "sell-by" dates (sometimes referred to as "pull dates," "best-if-used-by dates," or "freshness dates"). For such items, buyers may want to add to their specs some reference to these dates.

18. Chemical standards. A buyer might decide to specify a particular level of acceptable chemical use for some of the items he or she purchases. For instance, it is possible to purchase organic produce that is grown in chemical-free soil. Meat and poultry products, raised without added chemicals in the animals' diets, are also available in the marketplace.

19. The test or inspection procedure you intend to use in checking the items delivered to you or the services performed for you. Generally, this is the logical outcome of specifying the intended use. After you

note the intended use, you should be prepared to indicate the tests or inspection procedures you will use to see whether your purchases will perform adequately.

20. The cost and quantity limitations. A buyer might indicate how much of the item or service is to be purchased at any one time. Also, he or she might require an item to be removed from production and a substitute item sought if the cost limits are approached.

21. General instructions. In addition to specific details, a buyer might include such general details as (a) delivery procedures, if possible, (b) credit terms, (c) the allowable number of returns and stockouts, (d) whether the product purchased must be available to all units in the hospitality company, regardless of a unit's location, and (e) other supplier services desired, like sales help in devising new uses for a product.

22. Specific instructions to bidders, if applicable. Suppliers who bid for your business may want to know (a) your bidding procedures, (b) your criteria for supplier selection, and (c) the qualifications and capabilities the buyer expects from the supplier.

WHAT INFLUENCES THE TYPES OF INFORMATION INCLUDED ON THE SPEC?

Several things must be assessed before determining what information to include on a specification. Eight of these are:

1. Company goals and policies. These are probably most important. Overall managerial guidelines must be consulted before writing specs.

2. The time and money available. The costs and benefits of written specifications are argued continually by industry members. Obviously, we consider the time and money preparing specifications well spent.

3. The production systems used by the hospitality operation. If a restaurant, for example, broils its hamburgers instead of grilling them, the fat content in its ground beef should be a bit higher to compensate for the additional loss of juices that can occur if meat is broiled to the well-done state.

4. Storage facilities. If, for example, freezer space is limited, a buyer may have to purchase larger amounts of fresh vegetables; a specification might carry this reminder.

5. Employee skill levels. Generally, the lower the skill level, the more buyers must rely on portion-controlled foods, one-step cleaners, and

other convenience items. The trade-off is between a higher AP price and a lower wage scale. The balance in these issues is not always clear-cut—this is a good example of the trade-off concept that usually arises in value analysis (which we discussed in Chapter 4).

6. Menu requirements. Live lobster on the menu forces a buyer to include the words "live lobster" on the specification.

7. Your sale prices or budgetary limitations. If, for example, a restaurant is located in a very competitive market, its menu prices may be fixed by its competition. This fact may force a buyer to include cost limits for some or all food specifications.

8. Service style. A cafeteria, for example, needs some food items that have a relatively long hot-holding life, since the food may remain on a steam table for a while. This type of information might be included on the specs, especially the specs for preprepared food entrées.

WHO WRITES THE SPECS?

Generally, four options are available to the hospitality operation, including:

1. Company personnel can write the specs. This option assumes that the necessary talent to write them exists in the company somewhere.

2. Many specifications can be found in industry publications, CD-ROMs, on-line services, and in government documents. Although they may not fit your needs exactly, they are at least a good starting point. (See Figures 7.2 and 7.3.)

3. You can hire an expert to help you write your specs. This is a reasonable alternative, as you can control the amount of money you care to spend for this service.

   The USDA operates an "Acceptance Service" that permits hospitality operators to hire USDA inspectors to help prepare specs. The inspectors check the products you buy at the supplier's plant to make sure they comply with your specifications. (See Figure 7.4.) They then stamp each item or sealed package to certify product compliance. This is often done for meat products. The acceptance service is provided for a fee, usually paid by the supplier. Although this expense may be

FIGURE 7.2. Some government and private agencies that provide product information useful to buyers.

American Bakers Association
American Beverage Institute
American Cutlery Manufacturers Association
American Egg Board
American Institute of Baking
American Meat Institute
American Poultry Association
American Restaurant China Council
American Seafood Distributors Association
Beer Institute
Canned Food Information Council
Canned Food Promotion Service
Florida Fruit and Vegetable Association
Food and Drug Administration
Foodservice Equipment Distributors Association
International Dairy Food Association
International Foodservice Manufacturers Association
Loading Dock Equipment Manufacturers Association
National Association of Food Equipment Manufacturers
National Association of Meat Purveyors
National Beverage Dispensing Equipment Association
National Beverage Packaging Association
National Cheese Institute
National Fisheries Institute
National Food Processors Association
National Frozen Food Association
National Live Stock and Meat Board
National Pasta Association
National Poultry and Food Distributors Association
National Seafood Educators
National Soft Drink Association
National Turkey Federation
North American Association of Food Equipment Manufacturers
NSF International
Produce Marketing Association
Quality Bakers of America Cooperative
Retail Bakers of America
Shellfish Institute of North America
United Egg Association
United Fresh Fruit and Vegetable Association
U.S. Department of Agriculture
    Agricultural Marketing Service
    Dairy Market News Branch
    Fruit and Vegetable Market News Branch
    Livestock Market News Branch
    Poultry Market News Branch
U.S. Department of Commerce
    National Marine Fisheries Service
Wine and Spirits Wholesalers of America
World Association of Alcohol Beverage Industries

ComSource Canned Goods Specifications Manual (Atlanta: ComSource Independent Foodservice Companies, Inc., 1994).

ComSource Frozen Food Specifications Manual (Atlanta: ComSource Independent Foodservice Companies, Inc., 1994).

Ian Dore, *The New Fresh Seafood Buyer's Guide*, 2d ed. (New York: VNR, 1991).

Lendal H. Kotschevar and Richard Donnelly, *Quantity Food Purchasing*, 4th ed. (New York: Macmillan, 1994).

National Association of Meat Purveyors, *Meat Buyers Guide* (McLean, VA: National Association of Meat Purveyors, 1988).

The Produce Marketing Association Fresh Produce Reference Manual for Food Service (Newark, DE: Produce Marketing Association, 1989).

Lewis Reed, *SPECS: The Comprehensive Foodservice Purchasing and Specification Manual*, 2d ed. (New York: VNR, 1993).

FIGURE 7.3. Some comprehensive reference materials buyers can use to prepare product specifications.

included in your AP price, the service could save you money by assuring you that you receive exactly what you want.

4. The buyer and supplier can work together to prepare the specifications. The problem with this arrangement is that the buyer usually neglects to send the specs out to other suppliers for their bids. Or the

FIGURE 7.4. An inspector employed by the USDA Acceptance Service will inspect the buyer's order on the supplier's premises. If the order meets the buyer's specifications, a stamp such as the one shown here will be applied to the package by the government inspector.

cooperating supplier may help slant the specs so that only he or she can provide the exact item wanted. Nevertheless, this is the option most independents find realistic, given their time resources and prospective order sizes.

The question of who writes the specs is important to hospitality operators because not many part-time buyers have enough time to learn this task thoroughly. If operators want to prepare their own specs, they often consult outside expertise.

The reasonable compromise seems to be to hire someone on a consulting basis to help write the specs, or if this is too expensive, to work with the specs you find in various trade and governmental sources. The usual approach, to huddle with a supplier, may actually be least advantageous, but it does allow operators to spend more time in other business activities.

POTENTIAL PROBLEMS WITH SPECS

As in most business activities, there are several costs in addition to benefits to consider in specification writing. There are, for example, a number of clearly identifiable costs, and there are some cleverly hidden problems. Some potential problems with specs are the following:

1. Delivery requirements, quality tolerance limits, cost limits, or quantity limits may appear in the specs. If these are unreasonable requirements, they usually add to the AP price, but it is questionable whether they add to the overall value.

2. There may be some inadvertent discrimination written into the specs. For example, the spec may read, "Suppliers must be within 15 miles to ensure dependable deliveries." Dealing with a supplier 16 miles away could cause legal trouble because of this.

    Worse, if a spec effectively cuts out all but one supplier, you have wasted your time, money, and effort if your intention was to use the spec to obtain bids from several sources. You do, of course, still have the value of having specified very precisely what you want. This does give you a receiving standard and a basis for returning unacceptable product.

3. The specifications may request a quality difficult for suppliers to obtain. This situation adds to cost, but not always to value. In some situations the quality you want cannot be tested or inspected adequately without destroying the item. In these cases, however, a sampling approach may ensure the requisite quality. Before embarking on such an expensive process, careful consideration is called for.

4. Some specs rely heavily on government grades. Unfortunately, some may not be specific enough for a food-service operator's needs. For example, USDA Choice beef covers a lot of possibilities: There are high, medium, and low-choice grades. Also, grades do not usually take into account packaging styles, delivery schedules, and so forth. Thus, U.S. grades alone are not adequate for most operations.

5. Food specifications are not static; they usually need periodic revision. For instance, a spec for oranges might include the term "Florida oranges," a perfectly reasonable requirement at certain times of the year. But during some seasons, Arizona oranges might be preferable. It costs time, money, and effort to revise specifications. Moreover, if you cannot determine exactly when to revise, not only might you receive what you do not want, but if you are forced to serve the food because you have no acceptable substitute, your customer also becomes dissatisfied.

6. The best specs in the world are of no use to us if the other personnel in the hospitality operation are not trained to understand and to use them appropriately. For instance, the buyer may be adept in the use of specs, but if the receiving agent does not have similar expertise, he or she may accept the delivery of merchandise that is not in accord with the properly prepared specifications.

7. The potential problems and costs multiply quickly if the spec is used in bid buying. Some of these additional problems include the following.

GETTING HIT WITH THE "LOWBALL"

The term "lowball" refers to a bid that is low for some artificial or possibly deliberately dishonest reason. For instance, bidders may meet your spec head on; that is, they may hit the minimum requirements and might even reduce their normal profit levels in order to win the bid. Once they are in, they usually try to trade up the users.

Lowballing is a fairly standard way of doing business for suppliers trying to woo buyers away from their regular suppliers. They are willing to sacrifice a bit of revenue in the short run for the opportunity to establish a long-term, potentially more profitable arrangement. Suppliers know that, once they get their foot in the door, buyers may get comfortable and stick with them through force of habit.

To avoid falling for lowball prices, buyers need to shop around frequently, which means they need to keep their specs current. This tends to keep suppliers competitive and more responsive.

INEQUALITY AMONG BIDDERS

If your specs are too loose, that is, if too many suppliers can meet the specs, you run the risk of finding several suppliers of differing reliability bidding for your business, and choosing one of the less reliable can result in serious operational problems.

This trouble is especially prevalent in the fresh produce trade, simply because the available qualities of fresh produce change continually and some buyers do not know exactly when to revise their specs. Several suppliers may bid for your lettuce contract, and several qualities may meet your specifications. One supplier may have a good product, and he bids 40 cents per pound. Another supplier may have lettuce that he could gain good profits on even if he sold it for 35 cents per pound. What he probably will do, though, is enter a bid for 39 cents per pound, because he has discovered that the other supplier will bid 40 cents. You gladly accept the 39-cent bid, and (who knows?) the quality may be satisfactory. To avoid this problem, do not use the costly bidding procedure unless you are willing to expend a great deal of effort to keep your specifications current.

A related problem occurs whenever an inexperienced buyer accidentally rigs the procedures by asking a supplier who has a high AP price and high quality to bid for the business. In our example, the 39-cent-per-pound bidder is very happy to include the 40-cent-per-pound bidder in the process. The wise buyer strives to include in the bidder pool only responsible, competent, and competitive suppliers who are able to follow through if they win his or her business.

Sometimes good suppliers may unintentionally differ significantly from others bidding for your business because of unanticipated changing business conditions. For instance, some suppliers who bid for your business may do so only when their regular business is slow. Consequently, you may be forced to change suppliers continually, which could cost you time, trouble, and money in the long run. In addition, although you may indeed receive an AP price break, when their regular business picks up, these suppliers may decide to stop bidding for yours.

SPECIFICATIONS THAT ARE TOO TIGHT

Tight specifications tend to eliminate variables and allow a buyer to concentrate on AP prices. Unfortunately, if only one supplier meets your specifications, you are in the position of spending a lot of time, money, and effort to engage in specification writing and bidding, only to find yourself with two choices: take it or leave it.

Large hospitality companies sometimes run into a similar problem when they demand things that only one or two suppliers are able to deliver. For instance, the typical large hospitality firm wants to purchase products that are available nationally; this ensures that all units in the company use the same products, and this, in turn, ensures an acceptable level of quality control and cost control. The number of suppliers who can accommodate national distribution, though, is limited.

ADVERTISING YOUR OWN MISTAKES

Bids may be entered on a three-month contract basis. If your specifications are in error, you can look forward to being reminded of your mistake whenever a delivery comes in.

REDUNDANT FAVORITISM

The buyer who writes several specs, sends them out for bid, and then rejects all bids except the one from the supplier he or she usually buys from anyway is a genuine annoyance. This practice is followed by some operations that must use bid buying. The buyer solicits a bid for, let us say, corn chips. Three companies bid. But the buyer decides to buy from supplier A because this supplier's product always is preferred. If this is the case, why seek bids?

SCHEDULING SEVERAL DELIVERIES

Another potential problem with bid buying is the possibility that you will have to adjust to several suppliers' ordering and delivering schedules. The large hospitality organization can handle this extra burden. But if he or she is accustomed to receiving produce at 10:00 A.M., it can be a difficult readjustment for a small operator to receive produce at 2:00 P.M. one week and at 9:00 A.M. the next. (We have seen this need to readjust operating procedures cause a great deal of trouble, especially when a delivery must sit on the loading dock for a while because no one is free to store it. When the receiving routine is broken, ordinary problems multiply.)

AND ALWAYS REMEMBER . . .

The object of bid buying is to obtain the lowest possible AP price, but if the lowest possible AP price does not, somehow, translate into an acceptable EP cost, you have gained little or nothing.

The costs and benefits of specification writing are never clear, and the subject becomes more confusing when you complicate it with a bid-buying strategy. We believe writing specs is generally necessary, as they help you to solidify your ideas on exactly what you want in an item. We are not so confident about the bid procedures, though. For some items, like equipment, bids may be economically beneficial to the hospitality operator. But on the whole, the buyer who uses this buying plan had better know as much or more about the items as the supplier. Only the large operations consistently approach this requirement.

THE OPTIMAL QUALITY TO INCLUDE ON THE SPEC

You frequently hear references to "quality" products. To most people, a "quality" product represents something very valuable. However, when business persons talk about quality, they are referring to some "standard" of excellence. This standard could be high quality, medium quality, or low quality. In other words, suppliers offer products and services that vary in quality. In most cases, they can sell you a "high quality," "highest quality," "substandard quality," or almost any quality you prefer.

It is important to keep in mind that quality is a standard: something to be decided on by company officials and then maintained throughout the operation.

We do not intend to second-guess the types of quality standards developed or decided upon by hospitality operators. Rather, our objective is to examine the typical process by which the optimal quality is determined.

WHO DETERMINES QUALITY?

Someone, or some group, must decide on a quality standard for every product or service the hospitality operation uses. If somebody decides to use a low choice grade of beef, this decision should reflect the type of customers the operation caters to, the restaurant type, and its location, among other factors.

Most analysts agree that a hospitality operator can hardly decide on quality standards without measuring the types of quality standards his or her customers expect. As the AP prices are translated into menu prices and room rates, customers are affected. The quality of the product purchased affects customers' perceptions of our operation, too. On the other hand, for the most part, supplier services are apparent principally to management. It is clear that value has many facets.

Most hospitality operations conduct some sort of market research to determine the types of value their customers, or potential customers, seek. The owner-manager's greatest responsibility is to interpret the results of the market research and translate them into quality standards. In other words, he or she must examine the overall value retail customers expect; "supplier" services, that is, the property's surroundings, service style, decor, and so on; and the typical menu or room price ranges attributable to his or her type of operation. Then the owner-manager must formulate a definition of quality standards. In the final analysis, then, the consumer really has the major say in determining the quality standards an operation establishes for most of its items.

Company officials may have a bit more latitude in determining the quality standards for those operating supplies and services retail customers do not directly encounter—things such as dish machine chemicals and pest control service. In these instances, it is interesting to note the number of people who may become involved in these determinations. A large group of company personnel may help work out these quality standards. The owner-manager, the department heads, and the buyer often influence the decision. Hourly employees may also be consulted, since they work with many of the products and services constantly and are, hence, most familiar with them.

Quality standards for supplies, services, and equipment normally come from the top of the company. Buyers exercise a lot of influence in these areas, though, because they get involved in such technical questions as "Is the quality standard available?" "What will it cost?" "Can it be tested easily?" The ultimate decision, though, usually rests with the owner-manager or, in the case of chain organizations, an executive officer.

MEASURES OF QUALITY

A buyer is expected to be familiar with the available measures of quality as well as their corresponding AP prices and ultimate values. Several objective measures of quality exist. Here are some of them.

FEDERAL GOVERNMENT GRADES

Under authority of the Agricultural Marketing Act of 1946 and related statutes, the Agricultural Marketing Service (AMS) of the U.S. Department of Agriculture (USDA) has issued quality grade standards for more than 300 food products. These grade standards for food, along with standards for other agricultural products, have been developed to identify the degrees of quality in the various products and thereby aid in establishing their usability or value.

Federal government grades are measurements that normally cannot be used as the sole indication of quality. This is true because federal governmental grading is not required by federal law, except for foods purchased by a government agency for an approved feeding program or commodities that are stored under the agricultural price support and loan programs; as a result, a buyer must use other measures of quality for ungraded items. Where possible, though, U.S. grades are the primary measures of quality most frequently used by buyers, at least at some point in the overall purchasing procedure.

The federal government, by legal statute, inspects most members of the channel of food distribution. Generally, the federal government's role is to check the sanitation of production facilities and the wholesomeness of the food products throughout the distribution channel. In some instances, states have set up additional inspector-powered agencies that either complement the federal agencies or supplant them.

Generally, to be graded, a product must be produced under continuous federal government inspection. Meat items and items that require egg breaking during their production process are always produced under continuous inspection, but other types of items may not be.

The federal government will provide grading services for food processors, usually those at the beginning of the channel of distribution, who elect to purchase this service. Some of these producers buy this service and some do not. Some opt for U.S. government grading because their customers include these grade stipulations in their specifications. Or, in some cases, the state requires federal grading. For example, several states require fresh eggs to carry a federal quality grade shield.

The grading procedure usually takes a scorecard approach with the products, beginning with a maximum of 100 points distributed among two or more grading factors. To receive the highest grade designation, a product must usually score 85 to 90 points or more. As the product loses points, it falls into a lower grade category. In addition, graders work under "limiting rules," which stipulate that if a product scores very low on one particular factor, it cannot be granted a high grade designation regardless of its total score. The grader usually takes a sample of product and bases his or her decision on that sample.

Grading can be a hurried process that can tax the resourcefulness of even the hardest grader. Although some food producers accuse graders of being capricious, unreasonable, and insensitive to production problems, the fact is that the grading system functions fairly well.

Several buyers in the hospitality industry have been conditioned to purchase many food products primarily on the basis of U.S. government grades. And the effect of government grading has ultimately been to create demand among retail consumers for specific quality levels; for example, homemakers are conditioned to buy USDA Choice beef or USDA Select beef in the supermarket.

A major problem with grading is the emphasis graders place on appearance. Although appearance is an overriding criterion used in U.S. government grading, this sole criterion is dangerous for food service because our customers are not making a purchase based solely on visual inspection but, rather, purchase and almost immediately evaluate the product on taste and other culinary factors.

There are a number of other problems associated with U.S. government grades. These additional difficulties include (1) the wide tolerance between grades—so much so that buyers quickly learn that when they indicate U.S. No. 1, they must also note whether they want a high 1 or a low 1 (this tolerance gap is especially wide for meat items); (2) grader discretion—graders operate under one or more "partial limiting rules," which allow them either to invoke a limiting rule or not; (3) the deceiving appearance of products—for example, some products can be dyed (like oranges), some can be waxed (like cucumbers), and some can be ripened artificially and inadequately (like tomatoes); (4) the possible irrelevance of grades to EP cost—for instance, a vine-ripened tomato may have a high grade and a good taste, but it may be difficult and wasteful to slice; (5) the fact that graders could slight such considerations as packaging and delivery schedules, which are important in preserving the grade—for example, a lemon may look good in the field, but if it is not packaged and transported correctly, it could be dry and shriveled when it arrives; (6) a raw food item is not a factory-manufactured product, and therefore its quality, as well as its U.S. quality grade, can fluctuate and may not be consistent throughout the year; (7) the lack of uniformity among terms used to indicate the varying grade levels—for instance, some items are labeled with a letter, some with a number, and some with other terminology; and (8) the lack of a specific regional designation. There is, for instance, a big difference between Florida and California oranges, particularly during certain times of the year.

AP PRICES

To some degree, graded quality and AP prices go hand in hand. The relationship, however, is not usually direct. One notch up in AP price does not always imply that quality has gone up one notch. AP prices, though, are considered good indicators of quality by many hospitality managers, especially novices.

PACKERS' BRANDS

Some food producers resort to their own brand names and try to convince buyers to purchase on the basis of these names.

The terms "brand names" and "packers' brand names," although often used interchangeably, do differ to some extent. For example, the word "Nifda" is a brand name, but the terms "Nifda Prime-Pak," "Nifda Chef-Pak," and "Nifda Econo-Pak" are the packer's brand names. In this case, the Nifda supplier offers several levels of quality, with Nifda Prime-Pak representing its highest quality and Nifda Econo-Pak its lowest. (See Figure 7.5.)

Both brand names and packers' brand names are indications of quality standards; however, packers' brand names are very specific quality indicators, whereas most brand names are much more general.

A packer's brand system is essentially a food processor's personal grading system; that is, the food processor uses his or her personal "grade" in lieu of a federal quality grade. Food processors identify their different

Brand Name	PACKERS' BRANDS			
	Premium Quality	First Quality	Second Quality	Third Quality
Nifda	Prime-Pak	Nifda	Chef-Pak	Econo-Pak
Frosty Acres	N/A	Frosty Acres	Garden Delight	N/A
Sysco	Imperial	Classic	Reliance	Value Line
Monarch	N/A	Blue*	Red*	Yacht Club
Nugget	N/A	Black*	Red*	Green*
S.E. Rykoff	N/A	S.E.R. Green	S.E.R. Blue	Glowing Star
		Golden Rey	Silver Rey	
White Swan	N/A	Red*	Blue*	Green*
CODE	N/A	Red*	Blue*	Green*
Golbon	N/A	Golbon Green	Golbon Red	Silbon Blue
S.S. Pierce	N/A	Red*	Blue*	Green*

* Color of package label

FIGURE 7.5. Example brand names and packers' brand names.

quality levels by using a particular nomenclature (such as that used by Nifda) or by using different colored package labels. (See Figure 7.5.)

Even though they are not widely known in many parts of the country, there are packers' brands for many products. And in some cases, the food processor uses the brand name in conjunction with the U.S. grade designation. For example, a fresh produce packer might stencil on a box the designation "No. 1." This would indicate that the product was not produced under continuous government inspection and that, in the opinion of the packer, not a government grader, the product meets all U.S. requirements for U.S. No. 1 graded products.

Packers' brands, too, present problems when they are designed to overlap U.S. grades so that, for example, a beef product that might be marked a high USDA Select instead of a low USDA Choice might be switched to the packer's brand, which permits it to carry a quality designation that might generally be thought among food buyers to be associated with USDA Choice. In addition, packers' branded merchandise, unless it is a meat or poultry item, may not be under continuous government inspection. However, even if a food processor does not purchase the U.S. government grading service, he or she must still undergo an inspection procedure. However, inspection is concerned only with safety and wholesomeness; it makes no quality statement. Only grading makes quality judgments.

Brand names may possibly be a little more reliable than government grades because the brand extends over several other considerations than just the food product's appearance. For example, the brand can also indicate a certain size of fruit and a certain packaging procedure. In addition, for products that do not come under the grading system, brand names may be the logical alternative.

Packers' brands are also thought by some to be a bit more consistent from day to day and month to month, though not everyone feels this is true. Some argue that the U.S. government graders are not always so consistent. A brand's supposed consistency should effect a more consistent and predictable EP cost. It is important to recall that the EP cost is most important, whereas the AP price represents only your starting point.

It should be noted that in this text, we use the term "packer's brand" a bit more frequently than the term "brand name" merely because it seems as if our industry uses such terminology more often.

SAMPLES

It may be necessary to rely on samples, and one or more relevant tests of these samples, when assessing the quality of new items in the marketplace. Samples and testing are commonly used to measure the quality of capital equipment.

ENDORSEMENTS

Several associations endorse items that we purchase. For instance, NSF International attests to the sanitary excellence of kitchen equipment. And the International Society of Food Service Consultants (ISFSC) is an association of food-service consultants whose members must achieve rigorous standards. We find, however, fewer associations endorsing foods and operating supplies.

TRADE ASSOCIATIONS

Organizations such as the National Live Stock and Meat Board, and other trade groups, help set quality standards that can be used by the buyer.

YOUR OWN SPECIFICATIONS

A buyer may use some combination of all the measures we have been discussing and work them into an extended measure of quality. This lengthy measuring exercise usually finds its way onto the specification. In many cases, particularly where a hospitality operation needs a special cut of meat, a unique type of paper napkin, or special cleaning agents, this extended measure is the only appropriate one.

As we imply throughout this discussion, few buyers consider only one of these quality measures. But, in our opinion, too many operators become overreliant on only one measure when it would be more appropriate to consider two or more.

IS THE QUALITY AVAILABLE?

Yet another aspect of quality a buyer must know is whether the quality desired is available at all, and this is quite a practical question. It is useless to determine quality standards if the quality you want is unavailable. Oddly enough, some types of quality are too often unavailable to the hospitality operation. A chef who wants low-quality apples to make homemade applesauce may find that suppliers do not carry such low quality. (The food canners usually purchase them all.)

A buyer must pay particular attention to the possibility that the quality desired is available from only one supplier. This may or may not be advantageous. In some cases, an owner-manager may take this opportunity to build a long-standing relationship with one supplier. But some company officials are not especially eager to lose flexibility in their supplier selection.

It is easier than you think to restrict yourself unknowingly to one supplier. If it does not happen because of the quality standards you set, it may happen because of the AP price you are willing to accept.

THE BUYER'S MAJOR ROLE

We have noted that the buyer usually provides his or her supervisors with the information they need to determine quality standards. Buyers normally do not set these standards by themselves, but they do generally participate in these decisions.

The buyer's major role here is to maintain the quality standards determined by someone else. Generally, the standards have some flexibility. But whatever the standards are, and whatever the degree of flexibility, a buyer must ensure that all the items purchased measure up to company expectations.

THE OPTIMAL SUPPLIER SERVICES TO INCLUDE ON THE SPEC

As we noted in Chapter 2, buyers normally have a major voice in determining supplier services, though they generally have less to say regarding economic values the company should bargain for.

If you want specific supplier services, chances are you will severely restrict the number of purveyors who can provide what you want. Consequently, if you like the bid-buying activity, you must be prepared to put up with a variety of supplier capabilities. In our experience, it is the supplier services that we become so attached to, since, for many items, there usually is not that much difference in quality.

KEY WORDS AND CONCEPTS

Advantages and purposes of specs
AMS
Approved substitutes
Best-if-used-by dates
Bid from a supplier
Busted case
Buyer's major role in setting quality standards
Chemical standards
Color of a product
Cost and quantity limitations
Count
Difference between "brand name" and "packer's brand name"
Endorsements
Equal to or better
Expiration dates
Form of a product
Formal versus informal spec
Freshness dates

General and specific instructions to bidders
Industry and government publications
Information included on a spec
Intended use
ISFSC
Limiting rule
Lowball bid
Measures of quality
NSF International
Optimal quality to include on a spec
Optimal supplier services to include on a spec
Package size and type
Packaging procedure
Packer's brand
Packer's "grade"
Partial limiting rule
Performance requirement of a product
PMA

Point of origin

Potential problems with specs

Preservation and/or processing method

Problems associated with the use of
  U.S. grades as a measure of quality

Product identification

Product specification

Product substitutions

Pull dates

Purchase specification

Returns

Ripeness

Samples

Sell-by dates

Slab packed

Size of a product

Standards of quality

Stockouts

Test procedures for delivered products

Trade association standards

Trim

Truth-in-menu regulations

USDA

USDA Acceptance Service

U.S. government quality grade

Waste

Weight range

What influences the information
  included on a spec?

Who determines quality?

Who should the spec writer be?

Yield

QUESTIONS AND PROBLEMS

1. What is a purchase specification? How does it differ from a product specification?

2. What are some of the reasons hospitality operations develop purchase specifications?

3. What information is included on the typical purchase specification?

4. Assume you are the owner of a small table service restaurant.

   (a) How much time, money, and effort would you spend to develop specifications? Why?

   (b) Assume that you do not want to write specifications; you want to rely strictly on packers' brands and government grades to guide your purchasing. What are the advantages and disadvantages of this strategy?

   (c) If possible, ask the owner of a small table service restaurant to comment on your answers.

5. Explain how the following factors influence the types of information included on the specification.

   (a) Company policies

   (b) Storage facilities

   (c) Menu requirements

   (d) Budgetary limitations

   (e) Employee skills

6. What are the costs and benefits of hiring an outside consultant to help you write specifications?

7. What are the costs and benefits of writing specifications and using them in a bid-buying strategy?

8. Which items do you think a buyer should receive bids on? Why?

9. Explain how company personnel normally determine quality standards for the food products they use.

10. How does a buyer normally get involved in determining quality standards? What is his or her major role once these quality standards are set?

11. Describe five measures of quality. Name some advantages and disadvantages of each.

12. What are some potential advantages of locking yourself to one supplier, the only one who can meet your quality standards? If possible, ask a hotel manager to comment on your answer.

13. Why do you think endorsements are used so much in measuring the quality of consulting services?

14. Are AP prices good measures of quality? Why?

15. It is thought that hospitality operators can set quality standards for some nonfood supplies without considering their customers' views. Do you think this is true? Why?

16. A product specification for fresh meat could include the following information:

   (a) _____

   (b) _____

   (c) _____

   (d) _____

   (e) _____

   (f) _____

17. Why are expiration dates important to include on fresh food specs?

18. Why would package quality be important to a food service buyer? Would you be willing to pay a bit more to ensure high-quality packaging? Why? If possible, ask a restaurant manager to comment on your answer.

19. A food processing plant normally must undergo continuous federal government inspection for wholesomeness if

   (a) _____

   (b) _____

   (c) _____

20. List some problems that the buyer will encounter if he or she is overreliant on U.S. grades.

21. What is the primary difference between a brand name and a packer's brand name?

22. Should a small hospitality operation prepare detailed purchase specifications, or should it prepare product specifications? Why?

23. What is the most important piece of information that can be included on a spec?

24. When should a buyer use packers' brands as an indication of desired quality in lieu of U.S. quality grades?

25. When should a buyer include on the specification "point of origin"?

CHAPTER 8

Source: K. Bendo

THE OPTIMAL AMOUNT

THE PURPOSE OF THIS CHAPTER

This chapter discusses:

* The optimal inventory level
* Procedures that can be used to determine the correct order size and the correct order time

INTRODUCTION

The correct order size and its counterpart, the correct time to order, are probably the most important keys to inventory management. Without a reasonable idea of the optimal order size and time, you cannot maintain an ideal inventory level of food, beverages, and nonfood supplies.

OPTIMAL INVENTORY LEVEL

Until recently, few hospitality operators concerned themselves with inventory management concepts. When the industry was smaller and less complex and competitive, and inventory costs were minor, the occasional overbuy or stockout was a forgivable offense. Such a casual attitude is rare these days. No longer is ordering haphazard. The emphasis is now on holding the optimal inventory; that is, management seeks to determine the amount of inventory that will adequately serve the operation without suffering the costs of excess inventory.

A principal objective of inventory management is to maintain only the necessary amount of food, beverages, and nonfood supplies to serve our guests without running out of anything, but not to have so much inventory that we suffer from occasional spoilage and other storage costs. We also need to develop a cost-effective ordering procedure; for example, a buyer does not want to spend an excessive amount of time, money, and effort to order merchandise, because this will increase the hospitality operation's cost of doing business.

These objectives are more easily recited than achieved. Quite commonly an individual manager may not know the exact value of inventory that should be on hand.

Over the years, hospitality operators have tried to devise ways of computing as accurately as possible the ideal amount of inventory that should be maintained to conduct business effectively and efficiently. A major portion of the inventory management skills utilized in our industry relies heavily on rules of thumb. For instance, as mentioned in Chapter 6, many practitioners rely on a percentage of sales to guide their inventory management decisions. Recall that this percentage-of-sales concept suggests, for instance, that a full-service restaurant operation requires an inventory of food, beverage, and nonfood supplies to be equal to about 1 percent of annual sales volume.

There are other rules of thumb that a buyer could use to determine the amount of inventory needed to service guests adequately. As mentioned in Chapter 6, the typical food-service operation could devise an inventory management strategy to ensure that the food inventory that is kept on hand at all times does not exceed about one-third of a normal month's total food costs. Also, in a fast-food restaurant, the general feeling is that the food inventory should turn over three times per week, or about 156 times per year. Consequently, the buyer's inventory management strategy should include an ordering procedure that maintains this approximate inventory turnover target.

Most industry practitioners view inventory as an investment. This investment must offer a return, like any other investment. Unfortunately, an inventory investment does not lend itself to a precise calculation of return, as does, say, a certificate of deposit, whereby an investor can depend on an exact percentage of return each year.

CORRECT ORDER SIZE AND ORDER TIME: A COMMON APPROACH

Most part-time and full-time buyers use a relatively simple approach to calculate the best order size and the best time to order. This approach is sometimes referred to as the "par stock approach." The buyer usually accepts the supplier's delivery schedule, for example, twice a week. The buyer then determines a par stock, that is, a level of inventory items that he or she feels must be on hand to maintain a continuing supply of each item from one delivery date to the next.

The buyer accepts the supplier's delivery schedule because he or she probably cannot change it without incurring an exorbitant delivery charge, or unless the buyer's company represents a very large order size, in which case the supplier might make concessions. In addition, the buyer normally accepts an ordering schedule dictated by the supplier; he or she places the order at a certain time prior to the actual delivery. For example, a call no later than Monday morning may be required to ensure a delivery on Tuesday morning.

As an example, assume that the buyer feels that he or she needs 6 cases of tomato paste on hand to last between orders. On Monday morning, just before placing the order, the buyer counts the number of cases of tomato paste on hand. Assume there are 1.5 cases left. If it is expected that a half case will be used that day, 1 case will be left on Tuesday morning. The par stock is 6. Subtracting what he or she feels will be on hand Tuesday morning from the par stock, 6 minus 1, the buyer orders 5 cases.

Another way of calculating the order size is for the buyer to subtract what is on hand, in this situation 1.5 cases, from the par stock of 6 cases and enter an order for 4.5 cases. Either way, the emphasis is on setting an acceptable par stock level and then ordering enough product to bring the stock up to that level. (This concept is a bedrock of our industry. For example, most bars set up a certain par stock level that must be on hand before opening for the afternoon or evening. The bartender on duty is responsible for counting what is on hand, subtracting this from what should be on hand, and then replenishing the overall inventory of beverages, foodstuffs, and nonfood supplies accordingly.)

Par stocks sometimes change. In a restaurant that does a lot of banquet business, the par stock for tomato paste might fluctuate monthly or even weekly. This fluctuation can complicate matters, but the problem can usually be dealt with by just adding to the par stock the extra amount of tomato paste needed specifically for any emergency or extra business volume, such as a banquet next week. For instance, we might order enough to reach our par stock level, plus additional product to be our "safety" stock or to use for the banquet.

The buyer, then, normally uses the following procedures when employing the par stock approach:

1. Accept the suppliers' stipulated ordering procedures and delivery schedules.
2. Decide when it would be desirable to order enough product to bring the stock level of any particular item up to par. This decision is normally influenced by the amount of storage facilities you have, how expensive the inventory item is, and the shelf life of the products you buy. For example, if a preferred supplier delivers meat twice a week, and if the meats are expensive, perishable items, a buyer would most likely set a par stock to last about three or four days. For some inexpensive, nonperishable operating supplies, paper towels, for example, the buyer might want to order once every three months. Consequently, he

or she sets the par stock large enough to last for three months under normal operating conditions.

3. Set par stocks for all food, beverages, and nonfood items—enough to last between regularly scheduled deliveries.

4. When ordering, subtract what is on hand from the par stock. Then add any additional amount necessary to cover extra banquets, increased room service, seasonal patronage, perhaps a "safety" stock, and so forth.

5. Shop around, if necessary, and enter this order size at the time designated by the supplier or at some agreed-upon time.

6. Periodically reevaluate the stock levels and adjust them as needed. For instance, if you change suppliers, and the new purveyor's delivery schedule is different, you must adjust accordingly.

There is no magic formula associated with the par stock concept. It is a trial-and-error process. If 6 cases are too many, the number can be adjusted downward. If it is too low, it can be increased. The trial-and-error procedure requires small amounts of management attention on a continuing basis, and, in time, these can add up to a significant amount. Nevertheless, the work involved is quite simple and lends itself to volume swings in overall sales as well as sales of individual products. The par stock concept works quite effectively in the hospitality industry.

There are several reasons that it does work so well. Most important, there is only a slight difference in annual storage and ordering costs between a theoretical order size and a more practical order size. (The appendix to this chapter provides an extended discussion of a theoretical calculation of optimal order size and order time.) A second reason is the relative predictability of deliveries. A third reason is the fact that most hospitality operations only occasionally undergo major modifications in their customer offerings. For the most part, menus, sleeping accommodations, and bar offerings remain unchanged, thereby allowing a buyer sufficient time to determine acceptable par stock levels for each inventory item. Finally, if you have already invested a considerable sum in a hospitality operation, an inventory level that is a few hundred dollars more than a theoretical optimal amount tends to generate little concern.

The major drawback to the par stock method is its emphasis on setting only the part stock level, to the possible detriment of the broader view of inventory management. Generally, the optimal amount of inventory on hand is related to annual storage costs, ordering costs, and the costs of running out of an item. If acceptable par stocks are achieved, these costs probably are minimized. But these concepts may not be examined directly, and, as a result, a buyer may be unaware of the total picture.

This innocence, or ignorance, can cause problems. For instance, buyers often have an opportunity to purchase large amounts of a product at reasonable savings. The problem arises when the buyer has little conception of the increase in storage costs that will accompany this huge order. (As with the par stock approach, though, some rule-of-thumb methods can be used to evaluate the economics of large orders, as you will see in Chapter 9.)

Regardless of its potential drawbacks, the par stock approach is common and works fairly well. It does not, however, represent the only approach to determining correct order size and order time.

CORRECT ORDER SIZE AND ORDER TIME: ANOTHER APPROACH

Another approach that is used in the hospitality industry is just a bit more complicated than the par stock approach. However, it would appear that its use (or a similar one) will become more common as our industry becomes fully computerized and computers can keep track of the data and perform the necessary calculations quickly.

We will call this approach the Levinson approach, since Charles Levinson was one of the very first persons to address these ideas formally in his book, *Food and Beverage Operation: Cost Control and Systems Management,* 2d ed. (Englewood Cliffs, NJ: Prentice-Hall, 1989). Much of the material in this section of our text is adapted from Levinson's volume.

Buyers using the Levinson approach will employ the following procedures:

1. Accept the suppliers' stipulated ordering procedures and delivery schedules.
2. On average, try to order most merchandise on a weekly basis. For instance, fresh dairy products may be ordered daily, fresh meats and produce may be ordered perhaps every third day, but other less perishable items may be ordered less frequently. Consequently, the buyers' work follows a reasonably predictable routine, in that they have enough work to keep busy each week, even though they are not ordering exactly the same items each day or each week.
3. Before ordering, forecast the amount of merchandise that will be needed during the period of time between regularly scheduled deliveries. The forecasting procedure includes the following steps:
   (a) Forecast the expected total number of customers, based usually on past history.
   (b) Forecast the expected number of customers who will order each specific menu offering, also based on past history—one way of doing this is to compute a "popularity index" for each menu item.

A menu item's popularity index is computed by taking the number sold of that particular menu item and dividing it by the total number of all menu items sold, thereby obtaining a percentage. This percentage is the menu item's popularity index.

For instance, if we project that we will serve 2,500 customers next week and we know that, based on past history, 25 percent of all customers eat T-bone steaks, then we can estimate that $0.25 \times 2,500$, or 625 customers, will eat a T-bone steak.

(c) Determine the number of raw pounds of each ingredient needed to satisfy our projected sales. To do this, first we must compute the "portion factor" (PF) and the "portion divider" (PD) for each ingredient that we need to satisfy our sales forecast. The PF is computed as follows:

$$PF = 16 \text{ oz} \div \text{ the amount of an ingredient} \\ \text{needed for one serving (in ounces)}$$

The PD is computed as follows:

$$PD = \text{the PF} \times \text{the ingredient's edible} \\ \text{(servable) yield percentage}$$

The edible yield percentage is computed in one of two ways: (1) We accept the supplier's estimate of edible yield. Or (2) we conduct our own yield tests for each and every ingredient; that is, we use the ingredients for a while and compute an average of unavoidable waste, thereby giving us a good idea of the edible yield percentage we can expect to derive from each ingredient.

(d) Compute the order sizes for all items. An order size is equal to the number of customers we feel will consume an ingredient divided by the PD for that ingredient—this will give us the order size in raw pounds. (Essentially, the PD is the expected number of servings per pound.)

4. Adjust this order size, if necessary, to account for stock on hand, extra banquets, increased room service, seasonal patronage, perhaps a "safety" stock, and so forth.

5. Shop around, if necessary, and enter the order size at the time designated by the supplier or at some agreed-upon time.

6. Periodically revise the order time, if necessary, and the PD of each ingredient if, for instance, it is decided to change suppliers and the new supplier's ingredients have a different yield percentage than those currently being purchased. (In Chapter 9, we will discuss the procedures used to determine whether another supplier's ingredient provides more value to you, even though it might appear that it has more waste. We will revisit the concept of the EP cost at that time.)

Example I

Given the following data, compute the number of raw pounds needed of each ingredient for a banquet of 500 persons.

Ingredient	Serving Size	Edible Yield (%)
Steak	12 oz	80
Beans	4 oz	90
Potatoes	4 oz	75

Solution

Compute each ingredient's PF:

$$PF_{(steak)} = \frac{16}{12} = 1.33$$

$$PF_{(beans)} = \frac{16}{4} = 4.00$$

$$PF_{(potatoes)} = \frac{16}{4} = 4.00$$

Compute each ingredient's PD:

$$PD_{(steak)} = 1.33 \times 0.80 = 1.06$$
$$PD_{(beans)} = 4.00 \times 0.90 = 3.60$$
$$PD_{(potatoes)} = 4.00 \times 0.75 = 3.00$$

Compute the order size, in raw pounds, for each ingredient:

$$Order\ size_{(steak)} = \frac{500}{1.06} = 472\ lb$$

$$Order\ size_{(beans)} = \frac{500}{3.60} = 139\ lb$$

$$Order\ size_{(potatoes)} = \frac{500}{3.00} = 167\ lb$$

Example II

Given the following data, compute the number of cases needed to serve 1,575 customers.

Ingredient: Iceberg lettuce
Serving size: 4 ounces

Edible yield: 75%
Minimum weight per case: 36 pounds

Solution

$$PF = \frac{16}{4} = 4.00$$

$$PD = 4.00 \times 0.75 = 3.00$$

$$\text{Number of raw pounds needed} = \frac{1,575}{3.00} = 525 \text{ pounds}$$

$$\text{Number of cases needed} = \frac{525 \text{ pounds}}{36 \text{ pounds per case}}$$

$$= 14.58 \text{ (say 15 cases)}$$

Example III

Given the following data, compute the number of gallons needed to serve 2,000 customers.

Ingredient: Prepared mustard
Serving size: ½ ounce
Edible yield: 95%

Solution

$$PF = \frac{16}{.5} = 32.00$$

$$PD = 32.00 \times 0.95 = 30.40$$

$$\text{Number of raw pounds needed} = \frac{2,000}{30.40} = 65.79 \text{ pounds}$$

$$\text{Number of raw ounces needed} = 65.79 \times 16 \text{ ounces per pound}$$
$$= 1,052.64$$

$$\text{Number of gallons needed} = \frac{1,052.64 \text{ ounces}}{128 \text{ ounces per gallon}}$$

$$= 8.22 \text{ (say 9 gallons)}$$

CORRECT ORDER SIZE AND ORDER TIME: VARIATIONS OF THE LEVINSON APPROACH

The procedures in the preceding Examples I, II, and III are appropriate for items purchased in pound units. However, the Levinson approach can be adapted for use with any purchase unit. The general formula for the portion factor (PF) needs to be altered to accommodate the specific purchase unit. The unit of purchase is divided by the portion size as depicted in that unit of purchase. For instance, if we purchase liter containers of liquor, the numerator for our PF calculation would be 1,000 milliliters (ml), and the denominator would be the portion size of liquor, in ml. The computation of the portion divider (PD) remains the same.

Example I

Given the following data, compute the number of liters needed to serve 250 customers.

    Ingredient: Gin
    Serving size: 55 ml
    Servable yield: 95%

Solution

$$PF = \frac{1,000}{55} = 18.18$$

$$PD = 18.18 \times 0.95 = 17.27$$

$$\text{Number of liters needed} = \frac{250}{17.27} = 14.48 \text{ (say 15 liters)}$$

Example II

Given the following data, compute the number of cases needed to serve 500 customers.

    Ingredient: Lobster tail
    Serving size: 2 tails
    Servable yield: 100%
    Number of tails per case: 50

Solution

$$PF = \frac{50}{2} = 25$$

$$PD = 25 \times 1.00 = 25$$

$$\text{Number of cases needed} = \frac{500}{25} = 20 \text{ cases}$$

Example III

Given the following data, compute the number of kilograms (kg)* needed to serve 125 customers.

 Ingredient: Fresh spinach
 Serving size: 90 grams
 Edible yield: 60%

Solution

$$PF = \frac{1,000}{90} = 11.11$$

$$PD = 11.11 \times 0.60 = 6.67$$

$$\text{Number of kilograms needed} = \frac{125}{6.67} = 18.74 \text{ (say 19 kg)}$$

CORRECT ORDER SIZE AND ORDER TIME: COMBINATION APPROACH

It is reasonable to expect the typical buyer to use a combination of the procedures just discussed to determine the proper order sizes and order times. For instance, a buyer could use the par stock approach to maintain sufficient stock for the normal, predictable business needs of the hospitality operation. However, when a buyer needs stock for special events, such as banquets and other similar functions, he or she could adopt the Levinson approach, or some variation thereof, when determining the correct order amount and order time.

APPENDIX

CORRECT ORDER SIZE: A THEORETICAL APPROACH

In centralized, multiunit purchasing operations, economies of scale make very large purchases realistic. When inventory value reaches the multi-million-dollar level, more formalized modes of analysis are useful in determining order size. This section suggests tools available for use in such cases.

---

* There are 1,000 grams in 1 kilogram.

The correct order size is influenced by two costs: the "storage cost" (sometimes referred to as the "carrying cost") and the "ordering cost." The storage cost is the sum of several little costs associated with holding inventory. The cost of maintaining storage facilities, inventory insurance, and risk of spoilage or obsolescence are three of the relatively minor aspects of the storage cost. The most important part of the storage cost— the largest element of the storage cost—is the need to tie up money in inventory, that is, the "capital cost." Economists refer to this as an "opportunity cost," which is a nice way of saying that if your money is tied up in canned goods on a shelf, you lose the opportunity to invest this money elsewhere, such as in a bank, in shares of stock, or in gold.

Attempts have been made to calculate the storage cost precisely. Unfortunately, no hard figures exist. Estimates run from 10 to 25 percent of the value of inventory, which is to say that for every dollar you tie up on the shelf, you can expect a storage cost of somewhere between 10 and 25 cents per year.

The ordering cost includes primarily the cost of paperwork, telephone, computer, fax, employee wages and salaries, receiving, and invoice processing.

There are differences of opinion concerning the dollar value of the ordering cost. One company estimates that it costs approximately $20 for each order it makes; another estimates the cost at $30 per order; and others set the cost as low as $3 to as high as somewhere between $100 and $130.[1] No matter. What is important is that we recognize the fact that placing orders is not a cost-free exercise and the potential savings of reducing the number of orders can and should be determined.

A large order size would ensure a large inventory amount and, hence, a huge annual storage cost. But, because we would not order a large amount so often as a small amount, the annual ordering cost would decrease. On the other hand, a small order size would result in a smaller inventory and a correspondingly smaller annual storage cost; but, unfortunately, our annual ordering cost would increase. This phenomenon is depicted in Figure 8.1.

The important point is that there is an *optimal* order size, one that leads to the lowest possible total cost per year (annual storage and ordering costs). We note that a small order size, any one to the left of the crosshatched area in Figure 8.1, carries a relatively high total cost per year, as does any order size to the right of the crosshatched area. There is an optimal range of order sizes, as represented by the crosshatched area. Theoretically, there is one optimal order size somewhere in that crosshatched area, at the point where the storage cost curve intersects the ordering cost curve.

In determining its one optimal order size, management must take into account the influence of these two costs. Basically, the intersection of the storage cost curve and the ordering cost curve represents the best balance

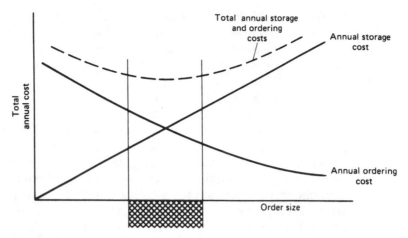

FIGURE 8.1. Annual storage and ordering costs related to order size.

between the cost of carrying inventory and the benefits derived from having the inventory available for sale to the customer. In calculating this intersection, management has two options. First, a manager could attempt to graph the operation's cost curves and then try to "eyeball" the optimal order size. Second, he or she might use a formula to determine the optimal order sizes.

The most common option is summarized in the Economic Order Quantity (EOQ) formula, which has been adopted by several industries. Relatively few hospitality operations use this formula directly. But they do find it useful as a reference insofar as the formula tends to identify the relevant costs and puts them in their proper perspective. Hence, a look at this formula will immediately drive home the concept of optimal order sizes.

There are two basic ways of calculating the EOQ, as noted in Figure 8.2. Assume that an operation currently uses 600 cases of tomato paste per year; the ordering cost per order is $3; the annual storage cost is 15 percent of the value of the tomato paste; and the cost of the tomato paste is $8 per case. The question: How many cases should the buyer purchase at one time, or what is the EOQ?

Applying the formulas noted in Figure 8.2, we determine that the EOQ is a little more than 54 cases, or approximately $438. The calculations follow:

$$\text{EOQ (in dollars)} \cong \sqrt{\frac{2 \times \$3 \times \$4,800^*}{0.15}}$$

$$\cong \$438^\dagger$$

* $4,800 = 600 \times \$8$
† $438/\$8$ per case $\cong 54$ cases

To calculate the EOQ, dollar value

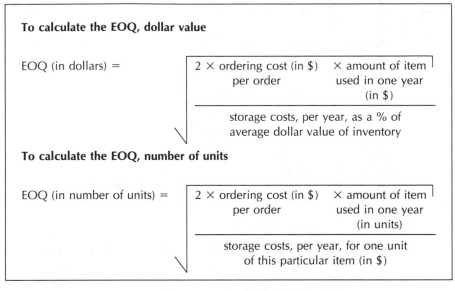

To calculate the EOQ, number of units

FIGURE 8.2. Ways of calculating the EOQ.

$$\text{EOQ (in units)} \cong \sqrt{\frac{2 \times \$3 \times 600 \text{ units}}{\$1.20^*}}$$

$$\cong 54 \text{ units (or cases)}$$

The total cost per year (annual storage and ordering costs) associated with this EOQ of 54 cases is calculated by using the formula depicted in Figure 8.3.

$$\text{Total cost per year} = \frac{\$3 \times 600 \text{ cases}}{54 \text{ cases}} + \frac{\$1.20 \times 54 \text{ cases}}{2}$$

$$= \$33.33 + \$32.40$$

$$= \$65.73$$

If we order fewer than 54 cases, say, 50 cases, the total cost per year is

$$\text{Total cost per year} = \frac{\$3 \times 600 \text{ cases}}{50 \text{ cases}} + \frac{\$1.20 \times 50 \text{ cases}}{2}$$

$$= \$36 + \$30$$

$$= \$66$$

* $1.20 = \$8 \times 15\% = \$8 \times 0.15$

$$\frac{\text{Total cost}}{\text{per year}} = \frac{\overset{*}{\text{Ordering cost}} \times \text{number of units used in one year}}{\text{Order size } \left(\begin{array}{c}\text{in}\\\text{units}\end{array}\right)} + \frac{\text{storage cost, per year, of one unit} \times \overset{\dagger}{\text{order size}} \left(\begin{array}{c}\text{in}\\\text{units}\end{array}\right)}{2}$$

* This is the total ordering cost per year.
† This is the total storage cost per year.

FIGURE 8.3. Calculation of annual total cost associated with a particular order size. (This formula is used in calculating the EOQ formula.)

If we order more than 54 cases, say, 60 cases, the total cost per year is

$$\text{Total cost per year} = \frac{\$3 \times 600 \text{ cases}}{60 \text{ cases}} + \frac{\$1.20 \times 60 \text{ cases}}{2}$$

$$= \$30 + \$36$$

$$= \$66$$

We have calculated the order size, 54 cases, that yields the least total cost per year. An order size of 50 cases gives us a lower annual storage cost, but our annual ordering cost increases, since we have to order more often during the year. Conversely, a larger order size yields a smaller annual ordering cost, but the increase in annual storage cost negates this slight saving.

As a practical matter, it may be inconvenient or impossible to order 54 cases at a time. In addition, some people are disturbed by the fact that too many aspects of the formulas are merely estimates, not hard-and-fast figures. The question is, then, of what value is this figure of 54 cases? Is it worthwhile to calculate the EOQ if it cannot be used?

Although it may be impractical to order 54 cases at a time, the fact that we know what the optimal order size is can help us make decisions about other more practical order sizes. For instance, if we can order only in blocks of 50 cases, we will have an idea of the annual ordering and storage costs associated with this order size and be able to plan our expenses accordingly.

We do not wish to leave the impression that this theoretical approach is simple or easy to use. It presents several potential problems, which we will point out later. But these difficulties notwithstanding, the concept of EOQ can be used in many productive ways to ensure an optimal overall level of inventory, which is the result of the optimal order size and the topic we turn to now, the optimal order time.

CORRECT ORDER TIME: A THEORETICAL APPROACH

Continuing with the tomato paste example, we should determine when to order our 54 cases, assuming 54 is a practical order size. If we could depend on instant delivery of our inventory items, we might be able to wait until we are completely out of tomato paste before we order the next batch of 54 cases. Unfortunately, a lag invariably exists between the time we place an order and the time it arrives. In some cases, this time lag is predictable; in other cases, it is not. As a result, we must reduce our supply of tomato paste to some level greater than zero if we want to ensure a continuing, uninterrupted supply.

This level is sometimes referred to as "the safety stock." It is also called "the reorder point" (ROP). We cannot wait until we are out of stock before ordering another batch; we must maintain a safety stock. But what this safety stock should be is open to hunches, theories, and educated guesses.

The trick to calculating the reorder point (ROP) is first to gain some idea of the usage pattern of the particular product in question. In our tomato paste example, we might experience the usage pattern outlined in Figure 8.4.

Normally, this type of pattern is not so predictable as Figure 8.4 implies. But if we keep track of our usage patterns for six months or so, we can determine how many cases we use, on the average, every day. For discussion purposes, assume that we have determined that, 40 percent of the time, we use 1 case of tomato paste or less per day; that 90 percent of

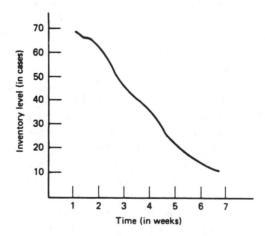

FIGURE 8.4. Hypothetical usage pattern for tomato paste.

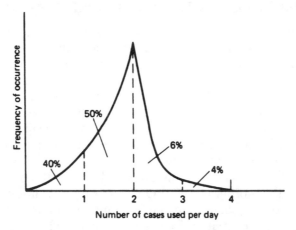

FIGURE 8.5. Percentage of times 1, 2, 3, or 4 cases are used per day.

the time, we use 2 cases or less; that 96 percent of the time, we use 3 cases or less; and that 100 percent of the time, we use 4 cases or less. These statistics are graphed in Figure 8.5.

Another way of looking at Figure 8.5 is to consider the possibility of using, on any given day, between 1 and 2 cases of tomato paste. We note that, in the past, we have used between 1 and 2 cases of tomato paste per day 50 percent of the time; hence, there is a 50 percent probability of selling more than 1 case but less than 2 cases per day. Similarly, we have sold less than 1 case per day 40 percent of the time; between 2 and 3 cases of tomato paste per day 6 percent of the time; and between 3 and 4 cases of tomato paste per day 4 percent of the time.

A conservative safety stock in this situation would be 4 cases for every day that lapses between the time we place our order of 54 cases and the time we receive this order. The interval of days is sometimes referred to as the "lead time." If we can safely assume that our lead time is three days, and we do not want to take a chance of running out of tomato paste, then we would place our order of 54 cases when our supply of tomato paste reaches 12 cases. This ordering decision appears graphically in Figure 8.6.

If we use all 12 cases during the three-day lead time, we will be out of stock when our order of 54 cases arrives. If we use only 10 cases, we will have 2 cases in inventory when our 54 cases are delivered. Our total inventory amount at this point then would be 56 cases.

After our order is delivered, we want to be as close as possible to a total inventory amount of 54 cases. Ideally, we will be right at 54 cases; that is, the moment we run out of inventory, the delivery van is pulling up at the unloading area with our 54-case order.

Hospitality operations that strive for this ideal arrangement practice what is generally referred to in the industry as "just-in-time inventory

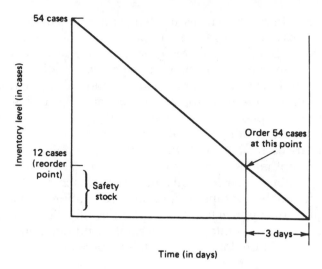

FIGURE 8.6. Graphical determination of the reorder point (ROP).

management." While they are trying to keep the total ordering and storage costs as low as possible, they are especially interested in minimizing the storage cost. For instance, if, using the figures in our example, they have 2 cases of inventory in stock when the delivery van arrives, they will have a then current inventory level of 56 cases. If they have 56 cases, they will incur an additional storage cost, which they are very eager to avoid. However, this additional storage cost must be weighed against the probability of running out of tomato paste and incurring various "stockout costs."

Stockout costs are those costs associated with being unable to serve a product because you do not have it. These costs are particularly irksome in our business: we cannot tell customers to come back for a steak tomorrow because we do not have any for them today. If we cannot provide a product, a customer usually selects another, the result being no apparent loss in profit. But we irritate a customer when we cannot supply the product wanted. In essence, we have diminished the customer's favorable opinion of our operation. The cost of goodwill is difficult to determine, and some operators harbor a greater disdain for stockouts than do others. For example, a more liberal manager, in our tomato paste example, might decide that he or she needs only 2 cases per day for the three-day period, thereby taking a slight chance on not needing more than 2 cases of tomato paste per day. The liberal manager would be willing to risk a stockout, since, according to Figure 8.5, there is a 10 percent chance that more than 2 cases of tomato paste per day will be needed during the lead time period.

Another problem associated with this safety stock concept is the exactness of the lead time. In most cases, deliveries are reasonably predictable. But the supplier may not have 54 cases of tomato paste. He or she may have only 30, or 40, or perhaps none at all.

The theoretical approach to the optimal order time rests on the assumptions you make about usage patterns, lead times, safety stocks, and supplier capabilities and dependability. By keeping historical records, you can determine the ROP you feel most comfortable with. If the numbers are correct, the ROP will be optimal. If not, at least you will be closer to the optimal ROP than you ever could be by relying on mere hunches.

Although the formality of the approach we have been discussing would not be appropriate for a single operation of modest size, clearly the logic of the approach has general application. This is a good way to think about reorder points, even if formulas and detailed records do not come into the picture for each hospitality operator.

CORRECT ORDER SIZE AND ORDER TIME: OTHER PROBLEMS WITH THEORETICAL APPROACHES

The basic overriding problem, alluded to earlier, is the need for certain assumptions and estimates. Any way you look at it, we deal here with some highly variable phenomena. Some additional variables that tend to detract from the usefulness of these approaches are given in the following list:

1. Usage rates vary from day to day and do not normally follow a steady pattern, unless the operation caters to a fairly predictable group of repeat customers. Although usage patterns can be approximated, they probably can never be calculated exactly.

2. Storage and ordering costs can vary; in addition, several opinions exist on the precise makeup of these costs.

3. Stockout costs are extremely difficult to assess. Management philosophy is the best guide in this case; consequently, the concept of correct order time can change according to management's tolerance of risk of stockouts.

4. Lead times are somewhat predictable, but you may qualify for only once-a-week delivery, which hurts any attempt to implement the EOQ and ROP concepts. In fact, the inability to control delivery times, either because of tradition or by law (e.g., some states have strict ordering and delivering schedules for alcoholic beverages), has done more to discourage the use of these concepts in the hospitality industry than any of the other difficulties. With the theoretical approach, the order size stays the same, but the order time varies. The opposite is true with the

par stock and Levinson approaches. As a result, since the typical buyer has no control over order times and delivery schedules, he or she cannot implement a theoretical approach.

5. What items should we consider for EOQ and ROP? All of them? This decision is not very easy when you consider that the average hospitality operation stocks a minimum of 600 to 800 items. Some people suggest considering only those few items that represent about 80 percent of the value of the total inventory. Others feel that it is possible to construct a few item categories and develop EOQs and ROPs for these categories. In any case, monitoring all items is impossible without the help of sophisticated computer technology. But as computer applications become increasingly feasible and economical, it is possible that we will be able to overcome this difficulty.

6. Keep in mind that your supplier normally buys from someone else. Your EOQ may not be consistent with your supplier's EOQ. As a result, you could encounter the problem of receiving an incomplete order. Or you might have to settle for certain substitutions, a situation that may or may not be compatible with your EOQ calculations.

7. At times, a supplier may be forced to discontinue an item—an item that you find especially profitable in your hospitality establishment. This problem is often associated with wines, particularly those of a certain vintage. As there is only so much of a certain type of wine produced in a certain year, the stock must run out sometime. Before reaching this point, you may decide to order as much as you can to maintain your supply as long as possible. Needless to say, this buying decision flies in the face of the EOQ and ROP concepts.

8. The EOQ assumes that you have adequate storage facilities. You may calculate an EOQ of 54 cases and then discover that you have space for only 30 cases.

9. Moreover, the EOQ assumes that the products you order will be used before they spoil or become obsolete. We have fewer problems with obsolescence in the hospitality industry than do other industries. But spoilage can be a giant problem. Although we can expect 54 cases of tomato paste to last two or three months, we cannot assume this storage life for all products.

CORRECT ORDER SIZE AND ORDER TIME: SOME BENEFITS OF THE THEORETICAL APPROACH

Theories can have shortcomings, of course, but they can also have numerous benefits. The EOQ and ROP concepts are cases in point. Some potential benefits associated with these approaches are presented in the following list:

1. A theoretical approach substitutes fact for fiction. Even if some of your estimates are off, at least you have been forced to consider these variables. This discipline in itself can easily lead to a more favorable profit performance.

2. There seems to be a range of order sizes in which the total cost per year (annual ordering and storage costs) does not vary dramatically. In our tomato paste example, the total cost per year for 50 cases was $66; for 54 cases, $65.73; and for 60 cases, $66. Notice that we could go down to 50 or up to 60 cases and incur an additional cost of only $0.27 per year. As a result, we gain insight by using the theory, and we do not have to be overconcerned if our estimates are a little off. And, as mentioned earlier in this chapter, this range is the major reason that the par stock approach to ordering is acceptable for many operations.

3. As computer services decline in cost, it becomes more feasible to monitor EOQs and ROPs, thereby extracting maximum benefit from these theoretical approaches while at the same time minimizing the time and paperwork involved with analyzing usage patterns, lead times, safety stock, and so on.

4. While the use of the EOQ and ROP concepts may not be feasible for a single-unit hospitality operation, the multiunit chain organizations, especially those with company-owned commissaries and/or central distribution centers, would be able to adopt these theories and use them to improve significantly their purchasing performance.

Theoretical approaches may or may not be completely useful in a specific hospitality operation. We believe, however, that all operations can derive more benefit than cost by considering these concepts. A thoughtful consideration of these concepts forces an operator to evaluate all the pertinent variables that influence an overall inventory level. By evaluating these variables, that operator comes as close as possible to an optimal overall inventory level, the ultimate objective of the EOQ and ROP concepts.

KEY WORDS AND CONCEPTS

A product's usage pattern

Capital cost

Carrying cost

Correct order size

Correct order time

Delivery schedules

Edible (servable) yield percentage

EOQ formula

EP cost

Food inventory amount as a percentage of monthly food costs

Forecasting

Inventory amount as a percentage of annual sales volume

Inventory turnover

Just-in-time inventory management

Lead time
Levinson approach to ordering

Opportunity costs

Optimal inventory level

Ordering costs

Ordering procedures

Par stock

Par stock approach to ordering

PD

PF

Popularity index

ROP

Safety stock

Stockout costs

Storage costs

Variations of the Levinson approach to ordering

REFERENCES

1. See, for example, Patt Patterson, "Effective Purchasing in Recessionary Times," *Nation's Restaurant News,* February 4, 1991, p. 48; Bill Eacho, "Quality Service Through Strategic Foodservice Partnerships: A New Trend," *Hosteur,* Spring 1993, p. 28; Steven Lipin, "Office Supplies Are Battlefield for Credit Cards," *The Wall Street Journal,* July 22, 1993, p. B8; Fred R. Bleakley, "When Corporate Purchasing Goes Plastic," *The Wall Street Journal,* June 14, 1995, p. B1.

QUESTIONS AND PROBLEMS

1. Briefly explain how the par stock approach to ordering works. Why does it work so well? What are some of the drawbacks of this method?

2. Fill in the blanks: Ordering the correct _____ at the correct _____ leads to _____.

3. Why would a general manager want to determine an optimal inventory amount?

4. Briefly describe EOQ and ROP. What benefits are there for managements that adopt these procedures? What drawbacks?

5. What are the elements of the ordering cost? Of the storage cost? How can either, or both, of these costs be decreased without harming the overall hospitality operation's profit performance?

6. You are currently using 750 cases of green beans per year. The cost of one purchase order is $75. Annual storage costs are approximately 25 percent of inventory value. The beans wholesale at $24 per case. Each case contains 6 No. 10 cans. How many cases should you purchase at one time?

7. Given the following data, determine the cost of one purchase order:

EOQ = 500 lbs (one-month supply)
Storage cost = 24% per year
Price of the product = $6 per pound

8. The typical owner-operator will accept suppliers' delivery and ordering procedures. The primary reason he or she would not try to change them is _____ .

9. What are some advantages and disadvantages of utilizing rules of thumb to direct your inventory management procedures? If possible, ask a restaurant manager to comment on your answer.

10. What is the most important part of the storage cost?

11. What is a safety stock? Why might an operator wish to maintain a safety stock?

12. Briefly describe the concept of an "opportunity cost."

13. One reason the EOQ concept is not particularly useful to the typical hospitality operation is _____ .

14. What is the objective of using the just-in-time inventory management procedure?

15. Given the following data, compute the number of raw pounds needed to serve 250 customers.

Ingredient: Pork chops
Serving size: 14 ounces
Edible yield: 75%

16. Given the following data, compute the number of liters needed to serve 500 customers.

Ingredient: Scotch
Serving size: 60 milliliters
Servable yield: 95%

17. Given the following data, compute the number of kilograms needed to serve 750 customers.

Ingredient: Belgian endive
Serving size: 75 grams
Edible yield: 65%

18. Given the following data, compute the number of cases needed to serve 1,000 customers.

Ingredient: Hash brown potatoes
Serving size: 4 ounces
Edible yield: 100%
Weight per case: 50 pounds

19. Given the following data, compute the number of cases needed to serve 1,250 customers.

Ingredient: Dinner rolls
Serving size: 2 rolls
Servable yield: 100%
Number of rolls per case: 250

20. Given the following data, compute the number of gallons needed to serve 1,500 customers.

Ingredient: Ice cream
Serving size: 4 ounces
Edible yield: 90%
Weight per gallon: 4.5 pounds

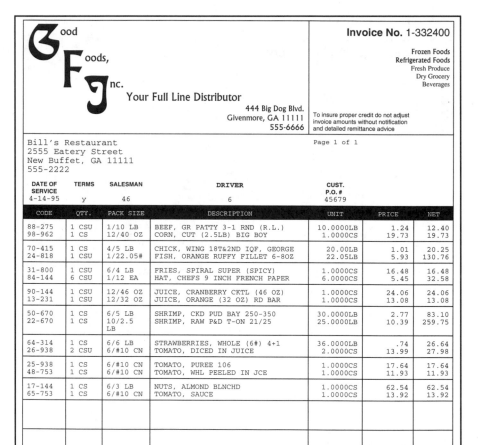

CHAPTER 9

Good Foods, Inc.
Your Full Line Distributor

444 Big Dog Blvd.
Givenmore, GA 11111
555-6666

Invoice No. 1-332400

Frozen Foods
Refrigerated Foods
Fresh Produce
Dry Grocery
Beverages

To insure proper credit do not adjust
invoice amounts without notification
and detailed remittance advice

Bill's Restaurant
2555 Eatery Street
New Buffet, GA 11111
555-2222

Page 1 of 1

DATE OF SERVICE	TERMS	SALESMAN	DRIVER	CUST. P.O. #
4-14-95	y	46	6	45679

CODE	QTY.	PACK SIZE	DESCRIPTION	UNIT	PRICE	NET
88-275	1 CSU	1/10 LB	BEEF, GR PATTY 3-1 RND (R.L.)	10.0000LB	1.24	12.40
98-962	1 CS	12/40 OZ	CORN, CUT (2.5LB) BIG BOY	1.0000CS	19.73	19.73
70-415	1 CS	4/5 LB	CHICK, WING 18T&2ND IQF, GEORGE	20.00LB	1.01	20.25
24-818	1 CSU	1/22.05#	FISH, ORANGE RUFFY FILLET 6-8OZ	22.05LB	5.93	130.76
31-800	1 CS	6/4 LB	FRIES, SPIRAL SUPER (SPICY)	1.0000CS	16.48	16.48
84-144	6 CSU	1/12 EA	HAT, CHEFS 9 INCH FRENCH PAPER	6.0000CS	5.45	32.58
90-144	1 CSU	12/46 OZ	JUICE, CRANBERRY CKTL (46 OZ)	1.0000CS	24.06	24.06
13-231	1 CSU	12/32 OZ	JUICE, ORANGE (32 OZ) RD BAR	1.0000CS	13.08	13.08
50-670	1 CS	6/5 LB	SHRIMP, CKD PUD BAY 250-350	30.0000LB	2.77	83.10
22-670	1 CS	10/2.5 LB	SHRIMP, RAW P&D T-ON 21/25	25.0000LB	10.39	259.75
64-314	1 CS	6/6 LB	STRAWBERRIES, WHOLE (6#) 4+1	36.0000LB	.74	26.64
26-938	2 CSU	6/#10 CN	TOMATO, DICED IN JUICE	2.0000CS	13.99	27.98
25-938	1 CS	6/#10 CN	TOMATO, PUREE 106	1.0000CS	17.64	17.64
48-753	1 CS	6/#10 CN	TOMATO, WHL PEELED IN JCE	1.0000CS	11.93	11.93
17-144	1 CS	6/3 LB	NUTS, ALMOND BLNCHD	1.0000CS	62.54	62.54
65-753	1 CS	6/#10 CN	TOMATO, SAUCE	1.0000CS	13.92	13.92

TERMS: ANY UNPAID BALANCE FROM PREVIOUS MONTH SUBJECT
TO INTEREST ON 15TH OF CURRENT MONTH AT THE RATE OF 1 ½%

THE OPTIMAL PRICE

Buying a cheap article
to save money is like stopping
the clock to save time.
JACOB M. BRAUDE'S COMPLETE SPEAKER'S
AND TOASTMASTER'S LIBRARY

Some people know the price of everything,
but the value of nothing.
ANONYMOUS

THE PURPOSE OF THIS CHAPTER

This chapter discusses:

- How purchase prices influence buyers
- How suppliers determine their purchase prices
- Methods that buyers might use to reduce purchase prices

INTRODUCTION

The optimal price is the price that, when combined with the optimal quality and supplier services, produces the optimal value. The optimal price represents the lowest possible EP cost consistent with the optimal value of a product, service, furnishing, or piece of equipment. As you recall, the best EP cost may or may not be related to the lowest AP price. When a buyer struggles to assess the optimal AP price, therefore, he or she must be able to translate a quoted AP price into the hospitality organization's relevant EP cost. The buyer could quickly make this conversion by using the following formula:

EP cost = AP price ÷ Edible (or servable, or usable) yield %

For example, if a roast beef has an AP price of \$2.45 per pound and an edible yield percentage of 75 percent, the EP cost per pound is \$3.27 (\$2.45/0.75 = \$3.27).

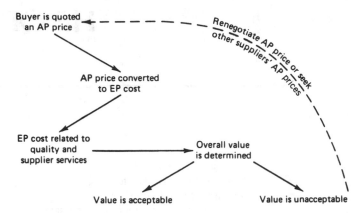

FIGURE 9.1. Conceptual process a buyer can use to relate AP price to value.

After computing the EP cost, the buyer must then relate it to product quality and supplier services, and conclude with the optimal value. (Figure 9.1 shows this progression.)

A buyer cannot evaluate AP price without concomitantly evaluating EP cost, product quality, and supplier services. All these components must be examined simultaneously, and buyers must seek the optimal value. Now let us see how the optimal price, or, more appropriately, the optimal EP cost, relates to this overall value.

HOW AP PRICES INFLUENCE BUYERS

The AP price can influence buyers in many ways. At one extreme are the buyers who shop entirely on the basis of AP price. This practice succeeds only if the buyers know exactly what they want in terms of quality and supplier services and can get two or more relatively similar suppliers to quote AP prices that permit adequate comparisons. At the other extreme are buyers concerned almost exclusively with quality and supplier services. These buyers do not hesitate to pay a premium AP price. The majority of buyers fall somewhere between these extremes, or, more realistically, some buyers may be close to one extreme for some products and close to the other extreme for other products.

The supplier, in turn, must obtain some measure of a buyer's reaction to AP prices. In Chapter 11, we will elaborate on "buyer profiles" (sometimes referred to as "buyer fact sheets"). These are diaries kept by suppliers and salespersons that include information on buyers' purchasing habits. Reactions to AP prices are invariably entered in the diaries.

Eventually, suppliers and salespersons can accurately gauge the influence of AP prices on various buyers. There are, however, certain predictable reactions to AP prices that suppliers and salespersons use to their advantage when selling the products and services to buyers for the first time. Some of the ways that buyers' and sellers' attitudes affect the purchasing process appear in the following paragraphs.

1. For the most part, novice buyers, and particularly novice managers, overrate AP prices. The AP price is, after all, a number—something that can be compared and measured. And the inexperienced shopper is more apt to grasp a number until he or she gains sufficient practice in relating AP prices to EP costs, quality, and supplier services. Top management is usually aware of the tendency to focus on numbers, which probably explains why buyers are expected to have previous experience in other areas of the hospitality firm. This previous experience generally helps a buyer relate AP prices to overall value.

2. Price normally follows quality; a higher quality is normally accompanied by a higher price. To a certain extent, most buyers accept this reasoning. Unfortunately, at a certain point the AP price keeps rising, and the quality fails to keep pace. Just when this difference between rising price and declining value occurs is not always clear, and inexperienced buyers and managers are liable to guess wrong. Even experienced purchasing personnel can be confused, especially if the products or services in question have just been introduced into the marketplace. Thus, suppliers and salespersons who are pushing a new item expect the AP price to receive more attention because no matter how much experience buyers have, they will have had little familiarity with new items.

    Price also may not necessarily correlate with quality if, for example, it is due primarily to the exemplary supplier services offered by a particular supplier. Nor will there be a significant relationship between price and quality if a supplier encounters considerable difficulty attaining an item and, therefore, must extract a higher price to compensate for this problem.

3. Generally, suppliers work under the assumption that the amount they sell to a hospitality firm is heavily influenced by a "derived demand." A buyer's demand for any particular item is derived from the ultimate customer's demand on the buyer's hospitality operation. As a result, an analysis by suppliers of their customers' customers can be enlightening. For example, price-conscious hospitality customers are a signal to the supplier that the buyer might become price conscious. Suppliers, then, would expect a budget motel buyer to be price conscious and would tailor their sales presentations and offerings accordingly.

4. Sometimes price is secondary. Suppliers sense this whenever an analysis of the buyer's customers shows that the ultimate consumers are not price conscious. Salespersons react by emphasizing other things. Prices may also be relatively unimportant to buyers when the suppliers

are the exclusive distributors for one or more items. Furthermore, if the supplier feels that a buyer is in dire need of something, he or she may expect a corresponding decrease in concern about the AP price.

5. A buyer who seeks an itemized bill is almost certainly price conscious. By "itemized" we mean a bill that notes separate charges for the item, for delivery, and for various other supplier services. In most cases, suppliers total all these charges and note only one AP price per item. But the buyer who asks for an itemized statement is thought to be one step from an attempt to provide many of his or her own economic values and supplier services.

6. If the products a buyer purchases represent a huge expense to the hospitality operation, chances are the buyer will be price conscious. Similarly, the AP prices of certain items are usually scrutinized more closely than others. Meat, for example, may receive disproportionate attention from a buyer.

7. Some buyers operate on a tight materials budget. If so, they are liable to become more price conscious than usual as the budget period approaches the end of its cycle. Also, some hospitality firms operate on a tight overall budget, and hard times cause them to examine AP prices more thoroughly. During difficult periods, in fact, some operators begin to assess the profit potential of providing their own economic values, such as purchasing raw food ingredients instead of a preprepared menu entrée, thereby providing their own form value in lieu of paying suppliers for it. Suppliers recognize this thought pattern, and many of them tailor their sales efforts to meet it.

HOW AP PRICES ARE DETERMINED

In Chapter 3 we considered economic forces and their probable effects on the channels of distribution. We suggested two main effects: availability of products and services and their relevant AP prices. Availability and AP prices usually go hand in hand as one factor, particularly for perishable food products and basic commodities. But additional price-setting procedures exist. Basically, suppliers use at least four general methods in determining AP prices.

AP PRICES AS A FUNCTION OF THE SUPPLIER'S COST

Suppliers add all their operating and nonoperating costs and attempt to allocate a certain portion of these costs to each product and service they sell. Then they add predetermined profit markups to these figures. The result is AP prices based on the suppliers' costs of doing business.

This approach is quite common, if only as a starting point in AP price determination. Hospitality operators, too, usually begin setting their retail prices in this way. For example, menu prices usually begin with the cost of food. To this cost, management may add labor and other variable costs. A markup to cover profit and overhead is the final touch to reach an initial retail price for the menu item.

In practice, of course, each item is not always approached as a separate case. Instead, the average cost of doing business is known in relationship to sales volume, and a standard profit markup percentage may be derived.

Some products in our channel of distribution include conventional profit markups, sometimes referred to as "rules." A rule is a numerical factor that suppliers use to set their AP prices. For example, in the fresh tomato market, one might find a "rule of 3," which tells the supplier to take his or her cost of tomatoes, multiply this cost by 3, and use the resulting figure for the AP price.

A cost-based AP price is a useful starting point. The supplier begins by applying a certain profit markup to the cost of his or her products. Then the supplier looks at his or her customers to see if they can pay, or will pay, this AP price. If they cannot, or will not, the supplier may lower the AP price, add additional supplier services to justify it, or, most typically, refuse to carry the item. The restaurant operator does much the same thing: he or she will be reluctant to offer a low-profit menu item unless, of course, it is traditional and is expected by customers.

It is important to keep in mind that while profit margins vary depending on the type of product, the average supplier in our industry earns an overall after-tax profit of only about 1 to 3 percent.[1] In many cases, a supplier earns only a few pennies per unit sold.[2]

AP PRICES AS A FUNCTION OF SUPPLY AND DEMAND

Supply and demand have a great effect on perishable food prices and on commodity prices. Generally, the supply and demand force has its greatest effect at the beginning of the channel of distribution. Bread prices, for example, do not vary so much as flour prices. Nor do flour prices vary so much as wheat prices.

To a certain extent, suppliers lower some AP prices to sell a slow-moving item. Hospitality operators do the same thing when they offer certain menu specials or special rates during the off-season.

Most of us would not prefer to participate in a market that sets prices strictly on the basis of supply and demand. After all, look at the yearly financial uncertainties farmers and cattle ranchers face. But supply and demand will be extremely influential as long as buyers perceive no differences among competing suppliers' offerings. Wheat is wheat and choice steak is choice steak.

Most sellers want to reduce the supply and demand effect; they consider it much too risky to carry several items other suppliers can duplicate exactly. The most common way of reducing the effect is somehow to differentiate the products. How can the same products be differentiated? Well, recall that quality is but one part of value. EP costs and supplier services are important too. Suppliers know this, and, as a result, most of them try to maintain profitable AP prices by manipulating supplier services. In other words, there are one or more attempts to differentiate the overall value, not just the AP price. And it is this differentiation that comes into play whenever suppliers use the following method of determining AP prices.

AP PRICE AS A FUNCTION OF COMPETITIVE PRESSURE

Suppliers operate in a reasonably competitive market, but there are ways to turn various sorts of competitive pressures to one's advantage. By differentiating a product's overall value, or by convincing buyers that a product's overall value is unique, suppliers can minimize competition.

In Chapter 3 we suggested that hospitality-related organizations operate in a market characterized by monopolistic competition. That is, price competition is a big factor, simply because many of the products we sell are so similar. But each of us has some type of monopoly. A steak served in a truck stop diner might be as good as or better than the same type of steak served in a gourmet restaurant. Yet the menu prices will be different because the supplier services—in this case, certainly, service style and physical surroundings—are different, so different that the overall value of each product might be quite acceptable to consumers. For the most part, many of us are willing to pay more for the same thing served in a gourmet restaurant because the different supplier services justify the higher price.

Suppliers seem more willing to operate under this third method of setting AP prices. It gives them an edge, since they can claim that there is no substitute for the value they provide. Moreover, it allows them numerous combinations of quality, supplier services, and AP prices sure to confuse even the most tight-fisted, objective buyer. The crucial factor, then, would seem to be supplier services. Delivery schedules, sales courtesy, general reliability—all these factors, and more, work their way into a product's overall value.

BUYER PRICING

Without a doubt, suppliers prefer this type of price determination. Unfortunately, the buyer who practices this procedure is almost certain to overpay.

Buyer pricing comes about in one of two ways. It will occur if a buyer does not have a detailed purchase or product specification; in this situation, the supplier "assists" the buyer in developing the spec which, of course, will tend to place him or her in a precarious financial position. Buyer pricing also will rear its ugly head if a buyer consistently engages in "panic buying," that is, he or she is constantly running out of products and relies on suppliers to make emergency deliveries. These emergencies will most assuredly result in significantly higher AP prices.

Price determination seems to be one of the last managerial "arts." It is something that is not entirely amenable to mathematical formulas. Hunches and experience come into play. Suppliers, though, normally want to maintain some perceived differences among one another's items. As long as they can, we will continue to see varying AP prices for the same type of product, unless their prices are controlled either directly or indirectly by state or product association bylaws or legislation. Theoretically, though, the resultant values should be acceptable to all concerned because of variations in supplier services.

WAYS TO REDUCE AP PRICE SO THAT OVERALL VALUE IS INCREASED

A quick way to increase a product's value is to pay less for that product yet keep the same quality and supplier services. This is not only a quick method, but it also leads to dramatic results: a lower AP price can be easily seen and appreciated by the buyer's superiors, whereas a bit more quality and supplier services do not make so deep an impression, at least not immediately.

Buyers in large organizations are quick to note that their superiors notice a lowered AP price. Chances are they will be asked to explain how they obtained the lower AP price, which gives them an opportunity to publicize their excellent performance. Consequently, buyers continually seek a lower AP price to increase an item's overall value.

Nevertheless, buyers should be cautious when seeking a lower AP price. The most important consideration is how well the purchased item fulfills its intended use. If a buyer pays a slightly higher AP price, all that is lost is money. But if an item performs poorly, a buyer has wasted money and time. In addition, he or she may have created some long-run employee or customer relations problems.

When seeking a lower AP price, the emphasis should be on increasing overall value. At no time should you accept a lower AP price if the overall value of a product or service is reduced disproportionately, unless this is done with management's approval. You should also fix a value on the time it takes to find or negotiate a lower AP price.

A buyer can use several methods in an attempt to decrease an AP price. A thorough value analysis of all products and services purchased will reveal the most feasible ones. Theoretically, a buyer can use some or all of the methods discussed in the following sections of this chapter.

MAKE-OR-BUY ANALYSIS

Buyers should periodically perform make-or-buy analyses, at least for the more expensive purchases. For example, it may be found that a hospitality operation might be able to save a great deal of money cutting its own steaks instead of purchasing them precut. When performing these analyses, though, a buyer must be absolutely certain to consider all relevant cost data, since it is very easy to overestimate these types of cost savings.

PROVIDE YOUR OWN SUPPLIER SERVICES AND/OR ECONOMIC VALUES

There are several possible cost-cutting opportunities. As is true with make-or-buy analysis, it behooves a buyer to consider the many alternatives available. For example, you can save money if you purchase products from a no-frills wholesale club, where you are expected to pay cash and provide your own delivery.

It also may be possible to select and pay for only those supplier services or economic values buyers desire. For example, some suppliers may offer high-priority, regular, and low-priority delivery options, with payment according to the speed of delivery. Some may offer price concessions for telephone orders as opposed to personal sales visits. And some may allow buyers to earn what is sometimes referred to as a "forklift discount" if they unload their deliveries instead of requiring the drivers to do the unloading.[3]

While these and other similar options may prove tempting, unfortunately many hospitality operations have not fared well when pursuing such cost-reduction strategies. Earlier we discussed the potential costs and benefits of providing many of your own supplier services and economic values. The conclusion seems to be that many firms attempting to do this have achieved mixed results and, in many cases, do not save nearly as much as they anticipated or have actually lost money.

SHOP AROUND MORE FREQUENTLY

Buyers who shop around frequently usually practice a technique sometimes referred to as "line-item purchasing." This purchasing strategy is a method used to obtain competitive bids for several products from two or more suppliers. The buyer will then select each individual product from the supplier who has given the lowest bid for it. For example, each supplier may bid on a total list of 10 products. However, the only products an individual supplier will be able to sell will be the ones priced lower than those offered by the competing bidders.

Suppliers do not like buyers to "cherry pick" their bids in this manner. They prefer buyers who use a purchasing technique sometimes referred to as "bottom-line, firm-price" purchasing. Using this buying procedure, buyers agree to purchase a group of products from the supplier who bids the lowest total price for the group. In this case, the successful bidder comes away with the complete order while the unsuccessful ones leave empty-handed.

Although it takes considerable time, money, and effort to shop around, the potential rewards may make this strategy very profitable. If a buyer has the time to develop specs and seek bids and does not mind dealing with several potential suppliers, generally he or she will acquire lower AP prices. As always, though, it is not quite clear whether the lower AP prices translate into increased values.

LOWER THE QUALITY STANDARD

Although it is possible to lower the quality one notch while lowering the AP price two notches, it is unlikely that this tactic will be successful. We have intimated elsewhere that buyers seldom have the authority to reduce unilaterally the quality standard. Management input is normally required. Also, some suppliers are unwilling to stock a product line of more than one or two qualities. Therefore, even if you decide to accept a lower quality, you may be unable to purchase it, though it is possible some suppliers might carry those qualities you desire.

Lowering the quality standard for all items purchased is unusual. But it is not uncommon to do this for a few items. Whenever you do this, though, you risk confusing or alienating your steady customers. A hospitality operation's image and reputation are very fragile and could easily be tarnished irreparably if quality standards are altered.

BLANKET ORDERS

A blanket order is a form of volume discount. It usually includes quite a few miscellaneous items, no one of which is particularly expensive. Taken together, however, the sum of the large number of low-cost items included in the blanket order makes it worth the supplier's time and effort, and some AP price concessions may be granted.

The basic questions with blanket orders seem to be whether you should try to order on an optimal size basis or order these items only a few times a year. In most cases it would probably pay you to place a large order once in a while because any optimal order size you might calculate would almost certainly be impractical. In fact, most buyers opt for a reasonably large par stock for these miscellaneous items and order up to par only once every three or four months.

When you place a blanket order for miscellaneous items, their AP prices may or may not decrease. Even without a decrease in AP prices, you can expect some savings if you use blanket orders, since you reduce significantly your annual ordering costs while experiencing only a slight increase in annual storage costs.

IMPROVED NEGOTIATIONS

It is possible to lower the AP price by adopting a stricter negotiating posture. For many products, AP prices are pretty well set and are not normally subject to negotiation. But supplier services and economic values can be manipulated, which might result in higher overall value. Also, it is possible to negotiate more favorable credit terms or payment schedules. Although this does not lower AP price, it does increase overall value, since you can delay paying your bills and can use that money elsewhere, if only for a little while.

AP prices are generally a little more flexible for long-term contracts and certain types of services. The AP price of a product purchased on a six-month contract basis is usually lower than the AP price for the same item purchased on a day-to-day basis. Also, such services as contract cleaning and consulting are not always accompanied by strict AP prices.

SUBSTITUTIONS

Whenever AP prices become too onerous, or appear to be heading that way, management can do at least one of four things: (1) pay the price and pass it on to the consumer; (2) lower the quality and/or reduce the supplier services and economic values provided to the hospitality operation's customers; (3) drop the item; or (4) stop offering the item but carry a substitute.

The fourth alternative is often used in the restaurant business and to some extent in the lodging industry. It does not necessarily lower the AP price of any item, but it could lower the total cost of operating the business. Buyers and suppliers should be encouraged to offer substitute possibilities to management, since they are the first to notice price trends, availability trends, and increased costs of preparation or service. They also are the first to evaluate new items on the market. And in some situations, these substitute items save money.

The big disadvantage with substitutes is that not all firms can use them. For instance, a family restaurant can manipulate menu offerings quite easily, but a steak house finds this substitution road a little rougher. Nevertheless, substituting products is a useful alternative often employed effectively by hospitality organizations.

CASH DISCOUNTS

A supplier may be willing to accept a lower AP price, provided he or she receives cash in advance, at the time of delivery, or shortly thereafter. This is particularly true if the supplier is cash starved. This practice is referred to as a "cash discount." The cash discount is a viable alternative only if the buyer has the authority to promise a quick payment and only if enough cash is available. In large firms, the accounting department or financial officer decides the payment schedule—in small operations, it is the owner-manager's decision—unless, of course, suppliers have strict payment demands or buyers have the authority to negotiate payment schedules that do not require a quick cash outlay. The accounting department usually does this as a part of its own cash management program and also because it may be more efficient to pay bills on a periodic basis. In addition, companies rarely have large amounts of cash available on a moment's notice. Nevertheless, paying cash "up front" can be extremely economical. The immediate cash payment, sometimes coupled with the proviso that you are buying an item "as is," can be such an attractive money-saving opportunity that sometimes it might even pay to borrow the funds to complete such a transaction.

A concept related to the cash discount is the cash rebate, sometimes referred to as a "coupon refund." Essentially, the supplier will charge you the full AP price, but later on, after you send him or her some proof of purchase, you will receive a bit of money back—a cash rebate. It does not appear to us that this activity saves as much money as it might seem to initially. Generally, there is postage to pay, costs of reproducing bills or other proof-of-purchase records, and the long wait for your money. Most large hospitality organizations do not like this procedure because of the extra work involved; they prefer bargaining for lower AP prices up front. Nevertheless, these types of rebates are quite common for most items, and, if economical, they should be pursued as much as possible.

HEDGING

The idea behind hedging is to maintain a specific AP price, not reduce it. (See Figure 9.2.) For example, assume that you wish to maintain the AP price of chicken for the next month. To do this, you would determine how much product you need for one month and enter into an agreement, usually a "futures contract," to purchase this amount one month from now at a specific price. During the month, you would purchase product as needed on the open market at the current AP price. If the AP price is higher than it was at the beginning of the month, you would be paying more for the product. However, your agreement, or futures contract, theoretically would be worth more. That is, the value of your agreement, which can be sold on the futures market, would increase. The increase

Food for Thought

Have you considered the hedging or speculative opportunities in "THE HAMBURGER?"

IMPORTED BEEF FUTURES
(The Hamburger)

It's the key commodity in America's food processing and fast-food industries. And subject to dramatic price movements in response to changes in supply and demand, political developments and trade policies.

If your business is exposed to risk due to fluctuations in the price of beef, Imported Lean Beef Futures, trading on the New York Mercantile Exchange, may be an important tool for hedging that risk.

And if you are interested in emerging speculative opportunities, the NYME contract may suit your trading strategy.

For more information contact your commodities broker or mail coupon, below.

nyme NEW YORK MERCANTILE EXCHANGE
Four World Trade Center
New York, N.Y. 10048
(212) 938-2222

NEW YORK MERCANTILE EXCHANGE
Department of Research and Education
Four World Trade Center, New York, N.Y. 10048

Please send me your informative booklet Imported Lean Beef Futures

Name _____
Address _____
City _____
State _____ Zip _____

FIGURE 9.2. Hedging offers an opportunity to smooth out AP price fluctuations. (Courtesy New York Mercantile Exchange.)

would offset the higher open-market AP price for the commodities. Consequently, you offset your high purchase price by selling your futures contract at a profit that would then be used to subsidize your "loss" on the open market. The tendency, where hedging is successful, is to maintain a stable AP price for the month.

But buyers should consider several problems associated with hedging: (1) a lot of cash may be necessary to buy futures contracts because the minimum amount of product involved in each agreement is relatively large; (2) hedging can be done for only a few items, though these items may account for the bulk of your purchasing dollar; (3) there are transactions costs—you must pay people to trade the contracts for you—you cannot do it yourself unless you own a seat on a commodity exchange; (4)

few of the smaller hospitality operations can muster the time necessary to engage in this activity; (5) the transactions costs might easily overpower the benefits you could derive from this type of protection against AP price fluctuations; and (6) it is possible, though unlikely, that no one would want to purchase your contract when you need to sell it to break even.

At one time it appeared that the hospitality industry was well on its way toward making the hedging procedure a common component of the overall procurement strategy. However, the industry has recently had second thoughts about this procedure. While some large hospitality organizations maintain at least a modicum of hedging as part of their overall purchasing arsenal, few companies currently seem to follow this pattern.[4]

ECONOMICAL PACKAGING

Every now and then, interest reemerges in changing some of the packaging methods manufacturers use. Some of the containers in use force an operator to waste storage space. For example, cylindrical cans and slope-necked bottles require more shelf space than do cube-shaped boxes. In addition, a lot of packaging contains such cosmetic touches as pictures and suggested recipes, which tend to increase its overall cost.

Since we buy products for production and not, like supermarkets, for immediate resale, we gain no benefit from attractive but inefficient packaging. Theoretically, more standardized packaging would reduce the AP price. Furthermore, efficient packaging reduces our storage capacity needs, thereby providing another saving. Nevertheless, manufacturers do not like to abandon this type of advertising and promotional appeal.

The buyer should consider purchasing products that are packed in adequate, not luxurious, packaging materials if at all possible. In addition, larger volume packs are normally cheaper per unit of weight than their smaller counterparts. For instance, a 1-gallon container of sliced peaches probably costs less than four 1-quart containers.

One other advantage to the larger containers is that they tend to decrease the possibilities for petty pilferage.

ODD-HOURS DELIVERIES

If a supplier delivers at night or very early in the morning, he or she should be able to handle more delivery stops because of the decrease in road traffic and other distractions. To some extent, these types of deliveries are done in large downtown urban areas that have particularly troublesome traffic jams during the day. It is not clear just what type of AP price reduction we could expect with these deliveries. Theoretically, we should gain some monetary benefit by increasing delivery efficiency.

Night deliveries might produce other cost savings, notably reductions in receiving costs. However, these savings would be available only if all receiving was done at night, as night deliveries by just one supplier probably would increase costs, since the receiving area and storage area would need to be open for an extended period of time.

A concept related to night deliveries is the possibility of receiving some monetary considerations from a supplier if you agree to receive deliveries during the "sacred hours." The sacred hours are those surrounding the lunch period, typically from 11:30 A.M. to 1:30 P.M. In some cases, the food-service buyer who agrees to receive deliveries during this time period may earn some price concessions.

CO-OP PURCHASING

Recall that a purchasing co-op is a group of buyers, each representing a different hospitality operation, who pool their individual small orders. The one large order more than likely qualifies the group for a lower AP price.

There are several advantages and disadvantages to co-op purchasing, and some of these are addressed in Chapter 11. It does seem clear that AP prices decrease whenever you purchase a large amount of a product or service. However, what is not clear is the effect on EP costs.

COST-PLUS PURCHASING

Under the cost-plus purchasing procedure, the AP price is equal to the supplier's cost of the product (sometimes referred to as the "landed cost") plus an agreed-upon profit markup. The markup can be a set dollar amount, or it can be a percentage of the supplier's cost. Either way, if the supplier's cost decreases, the buyer enjoys a price reduction. However, if the supplier's cost increases, so does the AP price.

Buyers must be willing to incur a bit of risk if they participate in this type of buying process. A sudden price increase is the most obvious risk. However, buyers must also be careful to monitor suppliers so that they do not subcontract products to their friends several times, thereby creating an artificial "daisy chain" type of distribution channel whereby the suppliers' costs are illegally inflated. In addition, if the profit markup is a percentage, suppliers have no incentive to control their costs. (It should be noted that government buyers usually are not allowed to enter into a cost-plus purchase agreement if the profit markup is a percentage of cost; however, they can usually agree to a set dollar amount.) The wise buyer normally has, and exercises, the right to audit the supplier's records to determine whether the correct AP price has, in fact, been charged.

Large hospitality operations generally prefer a long-term arrangement whereby the availability of a product, as well as its AP price, are predictable. While suppliers usually do not mind agreeing to provide a certain amount of product to a hospitality company, they do not wish to enter into a long-term, fixed-price contract. Hence, the use of a cost-plus arrangement seems to be the logical compromise. Negotiations center on the agreed-upon profit markup, and not on the actual AP price itself. It would appear that this is the strategy that must be followed if a hospitality corporation wishes to develop long-term contractual arrangements with its suppliers.

PROMOTIONAL DISCOUNT

A promotional discount is a rebate from the supplier that must be used by the buyer's company to promote the retail sale of the product. For example, a cheesecake manufacturer might grant a 2 percent rebate if you agree to promote his or her product in your food-service operation.

The traditional promotional discount is not so common these days. More commonly, suppliers provide free promotional materials now and then. (See Figure 9.3.) Many of them also like to do joint promotions with hospitality operations.[5] For example, a liquor distributor may split the cost of a special event with a local nightclub operator. In this case, while the nightclub operator does not receive a lower AP price, he or she does enjoy an increased promotional budget.

If the option does arise to gain a promotional discount, management should not jump too quickly. Certainly the extra money is tempting, but you need to do some serious thinking about how your operation's reputation will be affected by such a promotion. This decision can have several ramifications, and some of them may prove troublesome in the long run.

EXCHANGE BARTERING

Exchange bartering is simply the practice of trading your products or services for something you need, a relatively common practice in our industry.[6] (See Figure 9.4.) For instance, it is not unusual for a hotel company to exchange room nights, restaurant meals, and beverages for radio and billboard advertising. It is thought that as long as bartering represents no more than approximately 10 to 15 percent of a hospitality operation's total sales volume, it can be a very profitable arrangement.

Bartering, though, does have its costs. For instance, you may have to join a barter group. There are more than 400 such barter groups in the United States. A few charge a fee to join, but most typically charge a 10 to 12 percent commission for each transaction.[7] You may be able to avoid these costs if you engage in what is sometimes referred to as "direct bartering," whereby you personally make a deal with another business to swap goods and/or services.[8]

Bartering presents other potential difficulties. For example, there may be image problems with which to contend. At times, there may be price gouging and poor selections available. Furthermore, the Internal Revenue

A Tangy Taste Of The Tropics!

The traditional Italian pizza has come a long way in recent years. It's been redefined and reinvented in every possible way, from gourmet to breakfast pizzas! And, in keeping with the trend toward ethnic foods, more pizza chefs are adding tropical accents to traditional Italian pizzas.

They're adding Dole Pineapple!

Pizza chefs are creating new taste sensations by combining rich Italian flavors with the tropical taste and quality of Dole Pineapple. A quality that's evident in every bite!

COLOR: For sheer visual impact, no other topping compares to Dole Pineapple. It has a bright, rich color and smooth, consistent texture.

FLAVOR: Dole's sweet, tangy taste complements a wide variety of pizza toppings, including spicy meats, seafood, vegetables, and cheeses.

VARIETY OF CUTS: Our bite-sized tidbits and cubes are ready to serve, right from the can!

A Really Hot Item!

Just how hot is pineapple?

Pineapple pizza is fast becoming a mainstream menu item. In fact, a recent survey in *Pizza Today* magazine showed that 40% of all pizzerias carry at least one fruit topping, and it's usually pineapple.

Dole Pineapple is almost always paired with ham or Canadian bacon for a tasty combination that's called Hawaiian Pizza. And now, operations in the West are using Dole Pineapple to add zest to other specialty pizzas: Chinese, Japanese, seafood and even dessert pizzas.

This latest trend is sure to spread.

A Really Cool Offer!

Now's the time for you to introduce pizza with Dole Pineapple. And if you purchase Dole Pineapple between February 1 and July 30, 1990, you'll receive these colorful mitts and aprons.

They're free with purchases of Dole Pineapple!

OVEN MITT: Heavy-duty oven mitt, quilted for extra protection.

PIZZA APRON: Your customers will want to try Dole Pineapple pizza when they see your chef wearing this apron! One size fits all.

☐ YES! I've purchased Dole,

Pineapple and I'd like to order the **FREE** Pineapple Pizza Promotional Materials

2 cases purchased	=	**1 FREE Pineapple Pizza Oven Mitt**
5 cases purchased	=	**1 FREE Pineapple Pizza Oven Mitt *and* Pizza Apron**

LIMIT 20 aprons/mitts per foodservice operator

___ I've enclosed distributor invoices for ___ case purchases of 6/10 Dole Brand Pineapple between February 1 and July 30, 1990.

NAME _____

TITLE _____

ESTABLISHMENT _____

MAILING ADDRESS (No P.O. Boxes Please) _____

CITY _____ STATE _____ ZIP _____

PHONE (____) _____ DATE _____

NOTE: Your invoice(s) showing purchases between February 1 and July 30, 1990 must accompany this coupon. Requests must be postmarked no later than August 15, 1990. This offer is not valid in conjunction with any other offer or on cases offered for resale. It is available to Foodservice operators only. Chains or Affiliated Groups must participate on an individual outlet basis. Please allow 4 to 6 weeks for delivery of your mitt/apron. Mechanically reproduced coupons will not be honored. Offer good while supply lasts. LIMIT 20 aprons/mitts per foodservice operator

Mail this coupon with your distributor invoices to: Dole Packaged Foods Company Foodservice & Ingredients Division, P.O. Box 7319, San Francisco, CA 94120-7319

Dole
Life's a little fresher with Dole.

SP-PP-Fi

FIGURE 9.3. A promotional discount. There is no direct reduction in the AP price, but the buyer can receive free promotional materials. (Courtesy Dole Packaged Foods Company, San Francisco, CA.)

FIGURE 9.4. Announcement by an organization that matches individual businesses that want to trade. (Courtesy ITEX.)

Service (IRS) may be more apt to audit your income and expense records if you engage in a significant amount of bartering, because the agency suspects bartering might become the prelude to unreported income. In 1982, the IRS recognized barter as a legitimate purchase strategy so long as "trade" dollars are reported correctly for tax purposes.

The savings associated with bartering can be significant. For instance, when you pay a bill worth $100 with $100 worth of menu items, you have been able to discharge the obligation for much less out-of-pocket cost to you. Furthermore, if you restrict your trading partners' ability to exchange their meal credits, say, allowing them to eat only during the slow periods, you may gain even more financial benefit.

INTRODUCTORY OFFERS

New products constantly come on the market. Some suppliers move these items by selling them for an inexpensive AP price, at least for the first one or two orders. Or you might buy one, get one free. The obvious problem, of course, is that these offers are temporary. You can hardly make a career of moving from one introductory offer to the other. It is inconvenient, and suppliers do not like it. However, you could take advantage of an offer and stock up on the merchandise with the anticipation that you can use it later, for example, for special parties.

REEVALUATE EP COSTS

You should get into the habit of revising the portion divider (PD) and portion factor (PF), if necessary, of currently used ingredients and ingredients that you expect to use at some later time. This should be done for all ingredients that are being procured from current suppliers and for all ingredients that you might consider buying from other suppliers from whom you are not currently purchasing. Furthermore, you should occasionally consider purchasing an ingredient in some other form, say, in a form that provides less edible yield, because it just might turn out that the ingredient purchased in that form offers the lowest EP cost.

We can never ignore an ingredient's overall value, of which the EP cost is only one factor. But, assuming that the quality and the supplier services are the same across the board, and also assuming that our other expenses will not increase if we purchase different types of ingredients, we owe it to ourselves to examine the potential of purchasing another product that can be cheaper for us in the long run.[9]

It is necessary to have a storehouse of data to perform this type of analysis. Each ingredient that you currently purchase as well as each ingredient that you could conceivably purchase must be listed, along with its PF and PD. Hence, as we discussed in Chapter 8, this type of analysis is done primarily by food services that have sophisticated computer technology.

If you have these data, you can proceed to evaluate the EP costs of each ingredient. You need merely take the AP price per pound for any ingredient and divide it by its PD, and, instantly, you have the EP cost for one serving of that ingredient.

Example I

Given the following data, determine the EP cost for one serving of each ingredient.

Ingredient	Edible Yield (%)	Serving Size	AP Price per Pound
(a) Raw corned beef brisket	50	4 oz	$1.38
(b) Raw corned beef round	75	4 oz	$1.45
(c) Cooked corned beef brisket	90	4 oz	$2.98
(d) Cooked corned beef round	95	4 oz	$2.45

Solution

Compute each ingredient's PF:

$$\text{(a) PF} = \frac{16}{4} = 4 \qquad \text{(c) PF} = \frac{16}{4} = 4$$

$$\text{(b) PF} = \frac{16}{4} = 4 \qquad \text{(d) PF} = \frac{16}{4} = 4$$

Compute each ingredient's PD:

$$\text{(a) PD} = 4 \times 0.50 = 2.00 \qquad \text{(c) PD} = 4 \times 0.90 = 3.60$$

$$\text{(b) PD} = 4 \times 0.75 = 3.00 \qquad \text{(d) PD} = 4 \times 0.95 = 3.80$$

Compute each ingredient's EP cost:

$$\text{(a) EP cost} = \frac{\$1.38}{2.00} = \$0.69 \qquad \text{(c) EP cost} = \frac{\$2.98}{3.60} = \$0.83$$

$$\text{(b) EP cost} = \frac{\$1.45}{3.00} = \$0.48 \qquad \text{(d) EP cost} = \frac{\$2.45}{3.80} = \$0.64$$

Example II

Given the following data, determine the EP cost for one serving of each ingredient.

Ingredient	Edible Yield (%)	Serving Size	AP Price per Kilogram
(a) Fresh raw spinach	60	90 grams	$1.75
(b) Frozen leaf spinach	100	90 grams	$2.95
(c) Frozen chopped spinach	100	90 grams	$3.25

Solution

Compute each ingredient's PF:

$$\text{(a) PF} = \frac{1,000}{90} = 11.11$$

$$\text{(b) PF} = \frac{1,000}{90} = 11.11$$

$$\text{(c) PF} = \frac{1,000}{90} = 11.11$$

Compute each ingredient's PD:

$$\text{(a) PD} = 11.11 \times 0.60 = 6.67$$

$$\text{(b) PD} = 11.11 \times 1.00 = 11.11$$

$$\text{(c) PD} = 11.11 \times 1.00 = 11.11$$

Compute each ingredient's EP cost:

$$\text{(a) EP cost} = \frac{\$1.75}{6.67} = \$0.26$$

$$\text{(b) EP cost} = \frac{\$2.95}{11.11} = \$0.27$$

$$\text{(c) EP cost} = \frac{\$3.25}{11.11} = \$0.29$$

Example III

Given the following data, compute the servable portion cost for one serving of each ingredient.

Ingredient	Servable Yield (%)	Serving Size	AP Price per Liter
(a) Scotch (750 ml bottle)	95	50 ml	$8.25
(b) Scotch (1 liter bottle)	95	50 ml	$7.95
(c) Scotch (1.75 liter bottle)	100	50 ml	$7.25

Solution

Compute each ingredient's PF:

$$\text{(a) PF} = \frac{1{,}000}{50} = 20$$

$$\text{(b) PF} = \frac{1{,}000}{50} = 20$$

$$\text{(c) PF} = \frac{1{,}000}{50} = 20$$

Compute each ingredient's PD:

$$\text{(a) PD} = 20 \times 0.95 = 19$$

$$\text{(b) PD} = 20 \times 0.95 = 19$$

$$\text{(c) PD} = 20 \times 1.00 = 20$$

Compute each ingredient's servable portion cost:

$$\text{(a) Servable portion cost} = \frac{\$8.25}{19} = \$0.43$$

$$\text{(b) Servable portion cost} = \frac{\$7.95}{19} = \$0.42$$

$$\text{(c) Servable portion cost} = \frac{\$7.25}{20} = \$0.36$$

As mentioned earlier, unless you have access to specific computer technology, it is very difficult to maintain current EP costs per servings for all food and beverage ingredients. However, a buyer could develop some useful cost data in a relatively short amount of time if he or she knew each ingredient's (1) AP price per unit and (2) its edible (or servable, or usable) yield percentage. For instance, if you know that raw corned beef brisket carries an AP price of $1.38 per pound, and that its edible yield percentage is 50 percent, you could determine very quickly the EP cost per pound for this item by using the formula noted at the beginning of this chapter and repeated here.

EP cost = AP price/edible (or servable, or usable) yield %

$$\text{EP cost per pound of raw corned beef brisket} = \frac{\$1.38}{0.50} = \$2.76$$

This type of cost information is very useful to the buyer because it provides a solid base upon which sound purchasing decisions can be made. But buyers are not the only hospitality operation's managers and supervisors who rely on product cost data to perform their jobs. Production managers, for instance, also use these data when performing their menu planning duties. Specifically, product cost data are needed whenever a supervisor or manager needs to "precost" the menu and calculate suggested menu prices.

Precosting a menu involves costing out each menu offering. This is done by first calculating the EP cost of each ingredient included in a menu offering and then obtaining a total EP cost per serving. The result of this work is the calculation of each menu item's "standard cost," that is, the expected (or theoretical) cost of the menu item.

To see how a standard cost is calculated, consider the following example:

Example

Menu Item: Steak Dinner

Ingredient	Serving Size	Edible Yield (%)	AP Price per Pound
Steak	12 oz	80	$4.75
Beans	4 oz	90	$0.65
Potatoes	4 oz	75	$0.90

Solution

Compute each ingredient's PF:

$$PF_{(steak)} = \frac{16}{12} = 1.33$$

$$PF_{(beans)} = \frac{16}{4} = 4.00$$

$$PF_{(potatoes)} = \frac{16}{4} = 4.00$$

Compute each ingredient's PD:

$$PD_{(steak)} = 1.33 \times 0.80 = 1.06$$
$$PD_{(beans)} = 4.00 \times 0.90 = 3.60$$
$$PD_{(potatoes)} = 4.00 \times 0.75 = 3.00$$

Compute each ingredient's EP cost:

$$EP\ cost_{(steak)} = \$4.75 \div 1.06 = \$4.48$$
$$EP\ cost_{(beans)} = \$0.65 \div 3.60 = \$0.18$$
$$EP\ cost_{(potatoes)} = \$0.90 \div 3.00 = \$0.30$$

Compute the standard cost:

$$
\begin{array}{r}
\$4.48 \\
0.18 \\
+0.30 \\
\hline
\$4.96 \\
\hline
\end{array}
$$

Once a standard cost is computed, a manager can calculate a suggested menu price by dividing the standard cost by the target (i.e., desired) product cost percentage. For instance, if you wanted the food cost of the steak dinner menu item to be 30 percent of its menu price, the suggested menu price would be $16.53 ($4.96 ÷ .30 = $16.53).

Note that if $4.96 = .30 × menu price, then

$$
\text{Menu price} = \frac{\$4.96}{.30} = \$16.53
$$

The $16.53 figure is only a suggested menu price. The wise hospitality operator will usually begin with this price, but he or she typically will adjust it somewhat so that it is consistent with local market conditions. Furthermore, the manager would not normally adopt a menu price of $16.53; more than likely, he or she would use a price of $16.50 or $16.95, figures that are more recognizable to the typical customer.

The standard cost can also be used in a hospitality operation's overall cost control system. For instance, if we note that at the end of the month we sold 500 steak dinners, the total standard food cost for the ingredients needed to prepare and serve these meals would be $2,480 (500 × $4.96 = $2,480). This total standard cost can then be compared with the total actual cost,* which may be calculated in the following way:

> Inventory value (in $) at beginning of month
> + Purchases for the month (in $)
> ─────────────────────────────
> = Inventory available for the month (in $)
> − Inventory value (in $) at end of month
> ─────────────────────────────
> = Actual cost (in $)

The actual cost should be close to the total standard cost. If there is a significant "variance" between them, the hospitality operator will need to diagnose the situation, uncover the problem(s), and take corrective action.

OPPORTUNITY BUYS

One general category of purchases that can reduce AP prices dramatically deserves separate discussion. Some single event may occur that causes a

---

* See Chapter 14 for another example of actual cost calculation.

supplier to offer a bargain. A number of examples of the kind of opportunity we refer to appear in the discussion that follows.

Suppliers offer opportunity buys for several reason: (1) Sometimes they give a normal quantity discount. When you buy larger and larger amounts at one time of a particular item, the per unit AP price decreases. For example, when you buy 50 cases at one time, the AP price per case might be $8.00. But if you increase your order size to 100 cases, the AP price per case might be $7.95. (The figures 50 and 100 cases are sometimes referred to as "break points.") (2) Many suppliers offer volume discounts. In our experience, quantity discounts and volume discounts are the most common types of opportunity buys. (3) A supplier may have a "blowout sale," "buyout sale," or "closeout sale." These "sales" generally refer to merchandise that may be unsalable for one reason or another, or merchandise that must be sold at a loss. In most instances, the buyer of these "sales" is in a position to take advantage of someone's misfortune. (4) Some suppliers have move lists, or "muzz-go" lists, which include items that are on the verge of spoiling or, for one reason or another, are of poorer quality. These items, though, are wholesome and can be used by some hospitality operations. (5) A supplier might have received an excellent buy and wants to pass some of the savings on to his or her good customers. (6) A supplier may be cash starved and willing to offer cash discounts on large purchases. (7) A new supplier may be trying to break into the market and will sell items at a loss in order to introduce his or her company. Or your old supplier may be introducing a new product line and, while so doing, may reduce its AP price. (This is an introductory offer if the amount you can purchase is relatively small.)

To take advantage of an opportunity buy, a buyer must usually agree to buy in very large amounts. The buyer may have to purchase the item when he or she already has a complete stock. In addition, the buyer usually has to produce the cash in advance or on delivery.

Buyers must, of course, evaluate both the quantitative and qualitative factors when exploring the attractiveness of an opportunity buy. On the quantitative side, buyers first must consider the numbers. That is to say, they must determine the potential savings. If the savings are insufficient, there is no need to evaluate any qualitative factors.

For illustrative purposes, assume that we normally purchase 600 cases of canned peaches once a month. The AP price is $5 per case, a total of $3,000. We have an opportunity to purchase a two-month supply, 1,200 cases, for $4.95 per case, a total of $5,940. Our ordering cost for each order is $25. Storage costs are 24 percent per year, or 2 percent per month. What should we do?

Figure 9.5 depicts a quantitative analysis of this opportunity buy. In the normal situation, we would spend $6,050. In the proposed situation, we would spend only $6,023.80. We would save $25 with one less order. But, because we must buy next month's supply right now and store these 600 cases for one month, we would incur a 2 percent storage charge on

Normal situation
1 month supply $3,000 + $25 (order cost)

1 month supply $3,000 + $25 (order cost)

Total = $6,050

Proposed situation

2 months supply $5,940 + $25 (order cost)
58.80 (extra storage cost for 1 month, 2% of
$2,940*)

Total $6,023.80

Savings = $6,050 − $6,023.80 = $26.20

* $2,940 = $5,940 − $3,000

FIGURE 9.5. Quantitative analysis of an opportunity buy.

$2,940. We would not have to do this if we continued our monthly ordering schedule; that is, our normal storage costs would prevail. By deciding to take the option of buying 1,200 cases we make two savings but incur an additional cost. We save $0.05 a case on the price concession, and we eliminate the cost of one purchase order of $25.00. On the other hand, we incur an extra storage charge for one month of $58.80. The upshot of this quantitative analysis, assuming that our ordering and storage cost estimates are reasonably correct, is a savings of $26.20. It would appear that, based on the numbers, management could take this opportunity or leave it.

There is a simpler way of evaluating the quantitative aspects of this opportunity. In the first place, most buyers do not consider the ordering cost, mostly because there is confusion about the makeup and magnitude of this cost. Basically, these buyers look at the opportunity buy as an investment. In our peach example, we must buy an additional 600 cases for $2,940. And we have to store these cases for one month. In short, we have been asked to invest $2,940 in inventory for one month. If we do, we save $60. The return on this investment, then, is 2.04 percent ($60/$2,940) per month, or 24.48 percent per year. This percentage is normally compared with some cutoff percentage rate, usually a rate that represents the storage cost.

Regardless of which quantitative method the buyer uses, the emphasis should not be on a formula but on the estimates used in the calculations. Management must spend its time determining the relevant storage cost. (Recall that there are varying opinions surrounding the makeup of this cost.) And management must also determine what percentage rate of return it requires to take advantage of an opportunity buy. (In our experience, a buyer will usually be willing to purchase an additional one-month's supply of a product if the supplier discounts the AP price by 2 to 3 percent.)

Normally, management takes a conservative approach when setting this percentage rate and sets a relatively high rate. That way, if the savings of an opportunity buy exceed this high rate, the buy is indeed an excellent opportunity. But if it sets an unreasonably high rate, management may needlessly reject opportunity buys that, in reality, it should accept.

In our opinion, the percentage rate should differ according to the storage requirements of the product. Dry storage products could have a lower annual rate, perhaps 12 percent, whereas refrigerated and frozen products require a higher rate, perhaps 18 percent or more, to offset the higher costs of refrigerated storage.

These quantitative analyses can be more complex than the discussion so far has indicated. For instance, you may have to consider the probabilities of large AP price increases or decreases during the next month, as well as the possibility that you may suddenly start using less of the product. If management sets a reasonable cutoff percentage rate, however, there is usually no need to examine these additional possibilities. As noted, the conservative approach seems popular and is, in itself, normally sufficient to cover most of these extra potential costs.

Once a buyer is satisfied with the numbers, he or she can evaluate several qualitative aspects of the opportunity buy before making a purchasing decision, including:

1. Is the quality the same? Does it compare favorably with the normal purchase?
2. What is the probability of a large decrease in the item's AP price after the opportunity buy?
3. Are cash reserves available? How will the purchase affect the overall cash position of the company?
4. Are storage facilities available? Will there be an excessive burden on these storage facilities?
5. What is the storage life of the product?
6. Will insurance premiums, security risks, and the like increase dramatically, or will the current annual storage cost (in our peach example, 2 percent per month) remain pretty much the same?
7. Will personal property taxes increase now that the overall inventory level is higher?
8. Will the usage rate of the item remain the same over the next few weeks or months? Is there a possibility that management will discon-

tinue the item? Technically, you do not save money when you buy the product; you save money only when you use it.

9. Are the savings ridiculously high? Does the opportunity buy require a change of suppliers? If so, the current supplier may become disgruntled. And what happens if the new supplier cannot maintain the overall value?

10. Are the supplier services the same? How do they differ? Are these differences taken into consideration when evaluating the numbers?

11. Is the opportunity a legitimate one? Are you buying legitimate merchandise from licensed suppliers? You should never purchase anything if you doubt the legal status of that item.

12. Furthermore, a buyer should not engage in any illegal activity when trying to save money. For instance, you may save sales taxes on a piece of equipment if you buy it in another state and arrange to have it delivered to you. Or you may accomplish the same objective by purchasing equipment through an out-of-state mail-order supplier. However, even though you do not pay sales taxes to the supplier's state, you are required to pay them in your state (usually in the form of "use taxes").

13. Another problem is purchasing from unlicensed independent food distributors. You never know where they get their merchandise. Nor do you know whether they are under government inspection. Local producers often are not required to undergo federal inspection. Most states have laws preventing the purchase of home-canned and other home-prepared products. But local egg farmers and fishermen, who sell only in their local area market, usually require no inspection. Nor are they likely to obtain the necessary business license. Hence, you incur a risk by purchasing these products.

14. Sometimes a hospitality operation that is going out of business attempts to sell its inventories and equipment. Perhaps the operation is selling something that actually belongs to its creditors.

15. Another example is the salvage opportunity. For instance, a refrigerated railroad car overturns. Someone tries to sell the frozen food merchandise for 20 cents on the dollar. Should you take such a deal? Probably not, since buying food salvage or food from unlicensed purveyors is a violation of local health codes. The violation is purchasing food from an unapproved source.

It is permissible to purchase nonfood and nonbeverage salvage items. For example, you could purchase a freight-damaged table if the damage would not interfere with the hospitality operation's production and service, and if the damage would not tarnish the company's image. A buyer must realize, though, that he or she could be purchasing an item that suffers more than cosmetic bruises. Indeed, a freight-damaged item might be unusable and might not be a bargain at any price. And since products of this type generally are sold with no guarantee, the buyer must be willing to gamble that such a purchase will enhance the company's profits.

16. You may be able to save a great deal of money if you purchase used merchandise. Unfortunately, these items normally are sold or auctioned off in an "as is, where is" condition (i.e., there is no guarantee, and you would need to provide your own transportation). The high probability of a much shorter useful life for these types of items makes their purchase a risky endeavor. However, you may come out ahead if you are the lucky one who can spot a good opportunity. This is especially true if you can purchase a little-used demonstration model or a new one displayed only at a trade show exhibit.

Opportunity buys are clearly challenging. The quantitative aspects are relatively simple if the ordering and storage costs used are reasonably accurate. But the qualitative aspects are much more difficult to assess. This probably explains why most managements usually take a cautious approach when evaluating opportunity buys.

KEY WORDS AND CONCEPTS

Actual cost

AP price

The AP price and its influence on buyers

"As is, where is" condition

Barter group

Beginning inventory

Blanket orders

Blowout sale

Bottom-line, firm-price purchasing

Break point

Buyer fact sheets

Buyer pricing

Buyer profiles

Buyout sale

Cash discount

Cash rebate

Cherry picking

Closeout sale

Commodity

Commodity exchange

Competitive pressure

Conventional profit markup

Co-op purchasing

Cost-plus purchasing

Coupon refund

Credit terms

Daisy chain

Demonstration model

Derived demand

Direct bartering

Economic values

Economical packaging

Edible yield

Ending inventory

EP cost

Exchange bartering

Fixed-price contract

Forklift discount

Freight-damaged item

Futures contract

Hedging

How the AP price is determined

Introductory offer

Inventory available for the month

Itemized bill

Landed cost

Line-item purchasing

Long-term contract

Make-or-buy analysis

Menu price calculation

Monopolistic competition

Muzz-go list

Negotiations

Odd-hours delivery

Opportunity buy

Ordering cost

Panic buying

PD

PF

Precosting the menu

Product cost percentage

Product substitution

Profit markup

Promotional discount

Qualitative aspects of opportunity buys

Quality standard

Quantity discount

Sacred hours

Sales taxes

Salvage opportunity

Servable portion cost

Servable yield

Shopping around

Standard cost

Storage cost

Supplier services

Supplier's costs

Supply and demand

Target product cost percentage

Usable yield

Used merchandise

Use taxes

Variance

Volume discount

Wholesale club

REFERENCES

1. Patt Patterson, "Finding 'Bargains'—and Knowing How to Police Them," *Nation's Restaurant News,* April 5, 1993, p. 37.

2. Michael L. Facciola, "Supply & Dementia," *Food Arts,* May 1992, p. 112.

3. Marj Charlier, "Existing Distributors Are Being Squeezed by Brewers, Retailers," *The Wall Street Journal,* November 22, 1993, p. A6.

4. Warren Getler and Scott Kilman, "Cheddar Lovers May Take a Slice of These Futures," *The Wall Street Journal,* January 14, 1993, p. C1. See also, Scott Kilman, "Broilers May Return to Roost at Merc," *The Wall Street Journal,* November 19, 1990, p. C1; Leslie Scism, "Derivatives May Deliver Postal Savings," *The Wall Street Journal,* November 11, 1993, p. C1.

5. Patt Patterson, "Suppliers Offer Free Promo Help for the Asking," *Nation's Restaurant News,* March 2, 1992, p. 39. See also, Paul Moomaw, "Two Heads (and Two Pocketbooks) Are Better Than One," *Restaurants USA,* January, 1991, p. 12.

6. James W. Damitio and Raymond S. Schmidgall, "Bartering Practices in the Lodging Industry," *Hospitality Research Journal,* Vol. 17, No. 3, 1994, p. 101. See also, Mark Robichaux and Michael Selz, "Small Firms, Short on Cash, Turn to Barter," *The Wall Street Journal,* November 26, 1990, p. B1; Peter D. Meltzer, "Bartered Bucks," *Food Arts,* July/August 1993, p. 41; Michael Selz, "Health-Care Bartering Seen as a Money-Saver," *The Wall Street Journal,* December 23, 1993, p. B1; Sarah Hart Winchester, "Cutting Costs Without Cutting Quality," *Restaurants USA,* March 1995, p. 13.

7. Bob Ortega, "Swap the Sweat of Your Brow for a Suite Right on the Beach," *The Wall Street Journal,* June 16, 1995, p. B1.

8. Robert Liparulo, "Food as Currency," *Restaurants USA,* September 1993, p. 20.

9. Patt Patterson, "Review Purchasing List with Your DSR to Cut Costs," *Nation's Restaurant News,* October 11, 1993, p. 18.

QUESTIONS AND PROBLEMS

1. Assume that your EOQ is 500 cans. If you purchase 500 cans, you pay $343.50. If you buy 1,000 cans, you pay $650; 500 cans represents a three-month supply and 1,000 cans represents a six-month supply. Storage charges are 12 percent of inventory value per year. The cost of preparing one purchase order is $25.

    (a) Should you purchase 500 or 1,000 cans? Why?

    (b) Even if it is cheaper to purchase 1,000 cans, why might you reject such a huge order?

2. Consider the following problem data:

    EOQ = 500 pounds (one-month supply)

    Normal price = $1 per pound

    Storage cost = 24% per year, or 2% per month

    The product is ordered monthly. Cost of one purchase order = $20. You have an opportunity to purchase 1,000 pounds of this product this month at $.95 per pound. How much will you save if you purchase 1,000 pounds?

3. Assume that you normally purchase 60 cases of Canadian whiskey once every three months. The cost of the whiskey is $3,600. The distributor wants to sell you a six-month-supply, 120 cases, for $6,768. What do you suggest?

4. Explain how a buyer relates AP price to EP cost.

5. What are the four methods that suppliers use to determine their AP prices? As a buyer, which method would you prefer? Why? Which method would the supplier prefer? Why?

6. Review the various ways of reducing AP prices. In your opinion, which method is best? Why? Which is worst? Why?

7. What is the major objective of hedging?

8. Assume that you normally purchase 100 cases of Scotch per month at an AP price of $32.50 per case. You could purchase a two-month supply at an AP price of $30.00 per case. Your ordering cost is $25.00 per order and your storage cost is 24 percent per year. How much would you save if you purchased a two-month supply?

9. Briefly describe the concept of "derived demand."

10. What would be some major disadvantages of lowering your quality standard to reduce your costs?

11. What is the primary difference between a quantity discount and a volume discount?

12. List some advantages and disadvantages of exchange bartering.

13. Given the following data, determine the EP cost of each ingredient.

Ingredient	Edible Yield (%)	Serving Size	AP Price per Pound
Lettuce A	70	3 oz	$0.22
Lettuce B	80	3 oz	$0.29
Lettuce C	90	3 oz	$0.32

14. What are some advantages and disadvantages of purchasing used merchandise?

15. Define or briefly explain the following terms:

    (a) Blanket order

    (b) Cash discount

    (c) Introductory offer

    (d) Quantity discount

    (e) Break point

    (f) Move list

    (g) Promotional discount

    (h) Coupon refund

    (i) Sacred hours

    (j) Salvage buying

    (k) Buyer profile

    (l) Buyer pricing

    (m) PD

    (n) PF

    (o) Make-or-buy analysis

    (p) Direct bartering

16. Under what conditions would salvage buying be illegal?

17. Given the following data, compute the EP cost for a 6-ounce portion.

    Item: Prime rib

    AP price: $2.85 per pound

    Edible yield: 12 ounces per pound

18. What are the advantages and disadvantages of purchasing merchandise from a no-frills, wholesale club?

19. Under what conditions would management consider a product substitution strategy in order to reduce costs?

20. What are the major problems associated with the hedging strategy?

21. Given the following data, compute the standard cost for one seafood dinner.

Ingredient	Serving Size	Edible Yield (%)	AP Price per Pound
Fish	12 oz	75	$8.98
Rice	4 oz	100	$0.22
Beans	4 oz	90	$0.65

22. What is the name of the difference between the standard cost and the actual cost?

23. How could the actual cost be computed?

24. Given the data in Question 21, compute the suggested menu price for a seafood dinner, assuming that the target food cost percentage is 40 percent.

25. What could cause the actual cost to be greater than the standard cost? What could cause the standard cost to be greater than the actual cost?

CHAPTER 10

THE OPTIMAL PAYMENT POLICY

THE PURPOSE OF THIS CHAPTER

This chapter discusses:

- The major objective of a payment policy
- The cost of paying sooner than necessary
- The cost of paying too late
- The mechanics of bill paying

INTRODUCTION

Buyers usually have little influence on their company's payment procedures, unless they are, themselves, the owners who pay the bills. Usually the comptroller or some other financial officer is responsible for these decisions. But the buyer cannot be divorced entirely from this issue for at least four reasons. (1) Payment terms, cash discounts, opportunity buys, and so on, represent supplier services, and a buyer must consider them in value analyses. (2) At times these supplier services are negotiable, implying that the buyer needs at least some limited authority to bargain effectively. (3) Opportunity buys normally require quick payment. (4) Buyers must continue to work with suppliers who are sometimes "stalled" at bill-paying time. Such stalling tends to place the buyer in a relatively poor negotiating position in future dealings; hence, the buyer needs to be able to influence any such "stalling" decision. (See Figure 10.1.)

THE OBJECTIVE OF PAYMENT POLICY

The tenets of cash management are (1) keep your money as long as possible; (2) pay your bills at the correct time, neither too early nor too late; and (3) collect monies due as fast as you can.

While it is usually a good idea to hang onto its money as long as possible, sometimes the hospitality organization clings to its money too

PLEASE PAY FROM THIS INVOICE

Schulman
MEATS AND PROVISIONS
"OUR BEST TO YOU"
3010 VALLEY VIEW   LAS VEGAS, NEVADA 89102
364-5777
Federal Inspected Meat Plant Est. 6258

22058

IMPORTANT
MAIL REMITTANCE TO:
P.O. BOX 27707
LAS VEGAS, NV 89126

SOLD TO

ADDRESS

☐ C.O.D.   ☐ CASH   ☐ CHARGE   P.O. NO.   DATE   /   /

QUAN.	DESCRIPTION	WEIGHT	PRICE	AMOUNT
	PATTIES			
	PATTIES			

All claims must be made immediately upon receipt of goods. If any discrepancy, please call (702) 364-5777 otherwise late claims will not be allowed.

Received by

TOTAL →

Boxes _____   Pkgs. _____   Pcs. _____

All accounts are due the 10th of the month following date of purchase and after such date are past due accounts subject to an interest charge of 1¾% per month, which is **AN ANNUAL PERCENTAGE RATE OF 21%.** In the event legal proceedings are instituted to collect any sums due, the purchaser agrees to pay reasonable attorney's fee and costs.

I hereby certify that the above described product, which is offered for shipment in commerce has been U.S. inspected and passed by the U.S. Department of Agriculture, is so marked, and at this date is not adulterated or misbranded.

FIGURE 10.1. Some suppliers are reluctant to allow the hospitality operator to work with their money. Notice that this supplier exacts an interest penalty if the buyer's company fails to pay in the allotted period of time. (Courtesy Schulman Meats & Provisions.)

long, when, for example, there are financial incentives for paying earlier than you normally do. In the last chapter we considered the cash discount and the opportunity buy. In some cases, it could be costly to keep your money for 30 days if, by paying on the first day, you could receive a discount of 2 percent of your bill.

The specific aim, therefore, is to determine the optimal payment policy. Such a policy will dictate that you should pay your bills at that moment when you will receive the most benefit. To accomplish this, the buyer or accountant must balance the costs of paying money too early with the potential ill will created among suppliers who must wait too long for payment.

COST OF PAYING SOONER THAN NECESSARY

Theoretically, it is easy to calculate this cost. For example, if you pay $40,000 today instead of one week from today, and the bank in which you keep your money pays 5.5 percent simple interest per year on deposits, you would lose approximately $42.31.

$$\$40,000 \times .055 = \$2,200 \text{ Interest income per year}$$

$$\$2,200 \div 52 \text{ Weeks per year} = \$42.31 \text{ Interest income per week}$$

You also could invest your money in some type of marketable security for one week and perhaps earn a bit more interest income than the typical rates paid on bank deposits. From this interest income, you must subtract whatever it costs to engage in this type of investment-disinvestment routine. Whatever profit you have left over is an opportunity cost incurred by paying the bill today instead of one week from today.

Investing money in this fashion, though, is not typical of the vast majority of hospitality firms, especially since few of them have cash balances large enough to justify the time and effort needed to keep cash invested productively. For the most part, if you avoid paying your bills for one week, you immediately find another use for these funds in the business. For instance, you might decide to replace an oven and hope that this week's sales receipts will be sufficient to pay the current bills seven days from now. Or you might want to use the money to prepay an insurance policy. In other words, some sort of priority within the organization always awaits an application of cold, hard cash. Shuffling the priority list— borrowing from Peter to pay Paul—is often necessary in the hospitality industry.

Another potential cost of paying sooner than necessary is that such action can leave you cash starved and vulnerable to excessive financial risks. For example, if you needlessly drain your bank account too soon, you might be unable to take advantage of a once-in-a-lifetime opportunity buy. Or you might be in a precarious position if you suddenly need to pay cash to a serviceperson to make an emergency call to fix a refrigerator.

COST OF PAYING TOO LATE

Some hospitality operators attempt to preserve capital by stretching their accounts payable. Unfortunately, if you abuse the suppliers' normal credit period, you will incur several potential costs. For instance, a buyer's company could (1) gain a reputation as a slow payer; (2) jeopardize future credit potential; (3) damage credit ratings; (4) be put on a cash-on-delivery (COD) basis by all suppliers; (5) incur interest charges and/or penalty charges; (6) lose cash discounts or other favorable AP price reductions; (7) incur legal difficulties; (8) find that many suppliers will not do business with a poor credit risk; and/or (9) be able to purchase only from those suppliers who provide shoddy merchandise and poor supplier services.

WHAT'S THE BEST POLICY?

The best policy is probably the one that allows you to keep your money as long as possible, unless you have an incentive, like a cash discount, to pay early. Always keep in mind: The longer you can delay paying your bills, the more you operate with someone else's money.

Unfortunately, the average hospitality operation finds it impossible to negotiate specific payment terms. Most suppliers expect you to pay COD unless you have established credit, in which case you will normally be put on a monthly credit-term period.

The typical hospitality operation also tends to incur interest charges on any balances that are not paid off at the end of the 30-day period. For instance, it is not unusual for you to be able to pay a minimum monthly payment and let the remaining balance "ride" until the end of the next month. This "ride," though, is usually accompanied by a monthly percentage charge of about 1½ to 1¾ percent. In this situation, a buyer's company has some latitude in planning its payment schedule, since there is more time allowed by suppliers. However, at these high interest rates, it probably behooves us to pay our bills at the end of every month to avoid such charges.

Large hospitality organizations usually are able to negotiate a more favorable set of credit terms. Since they represent huge amounts of business, suppliers generally are willing to treat them more leniently and with more respect. In our experience, the typical large hospitality company generally seeks a 45-day credit-term period; that is, it expects to pay its bills every 45 days.

The small hospitality operator should try to set up a periodic payment schedule, perhaps setting aside one day a week to pay bills. Although this may not allow you to keep your money as long as you would like, it will at least systematize your payments. This systemized procedure is often more efficient in the long run than the juggling of bills and payment periods throughout the year. The only exception should be when there is some type of discount offered by suppliers in exchange for quick payment. In this situation, you should perform the appropriate opportunity buy analysis.

THE MECHANICS OF BILL PAYING

There are four bill-paying procedures that could be employed by hospitality operators.

PAID-OUTS

A method that is fairly popular with small hospitality operators is the paid-out. That is, when the delivery is received, assuming that everything is acceptable, the receiver reaches into the cash register and pulls out the appropriate amount of cash to pay the delivery driver. Instead of pulling out cash, the receiver could pull out a pre-prepared check and give it to the delivery driver. Either way, the emphasis is on paying cash on delivery.

This procedure does not allow you to work with the supplier's money, but it is very convenient. You avoid the need to plan for and execute periodic payments, you do not need to spend money for postage, and you avoid the printing cost of a check and other bank charges (assuming that you use cash).

Some suppliers will not allow their delivery drivers to accept paid-outs because of the fear of the drivers being robbed. It also is possible that it is illegal to pay COD for some purchases; for example, in some parts of the country, it is illegal to pay COD for liquor purchases. However, most suppliers will agree to the paid-out procedure as long as the amount of money involved is not too large.

INVOICES ON ACCOUNT

When a delivery is made, normally an invoice accompanies it. That is, you usually receive a written description of the delivery, noting such things as items delivered, prices paid, and so forth. (See Figure 10.1.)

The receiver normally is asked to sign the delivery driver's copy of the invoice, attesting to the fact that everything is acceptable. If there is a problem with the delivery—say, there is some damaged merchandise that must be sent back—the delivery driver may give the receiving agent a credit slip, or the hospitality operation will need to seek the appropriate credit directly from the supplier's main office.

Once the driver and receiver are satisfied, the driver leaves and the receiver arranges for storage of the shipment. No money changes hands at this point.

At the end of the credit period (e.g., at the end of the month, or at the end of the 45-day period), you will receive a statement listing all the invoice amounts delivered during the period, the previous balance, if any, that was left unpaid from the previous period, credits applied to your account, if any, and, if applicable, interest charges on last period's unpaid balance. You then need to reconcile this statement with your copies of invoices and credit slips accumulated during the period and report any discrepancies to the supplier.

Your copies of the invoices and credit slips may also be reconciled with your copies of purchase orders, or some similar order records, to ensure that all the merchandise received was in fact ordered by the hospitality operation.

After your reconciliation, you then send the supplier a check for the agreed-upon payment, or perhaps you will pay the entire balance.

CREDIT CARD PAYMENTS

Some hospitality operations, especially the small ones, prefer using a credit card to charge purchases and pay for them at the end of the credit period.[1] This is very similar to the invoices-on-account system described in the preceding section, though, with this procedure, the credit card company handles the billing instead of the suppliers.

When you use a credit card, suppliers must pay a fee to the credit card company. The fee is usually a percentage of the amount of money charged. The percentage amount usually depends on what type of credit card you use. For instance, a bank card, such as Visa or MasterCard, usually is less expensive than a travel and entertainment card, such as American Express.

While these fees increase the suppliers' costs of doing business, many suppliers may save money in the long run if they receive their payments quickly. For instance, if a buyer pays with a Visa credit card, the supplier should receive payment in about 2 to 3 days instead of waiting 30 to 45 days for its money. This gives the supplier the option of investing this money and earning a bit of interest income. Furthermore, since the credit card companies handle a good deal of the paperwork, suppliers will experience some administrative savings as well.

BILL-PAYING SERVICE

At times a hospitality operation might prefer depositing money into an escrow account and authorizing a bill-paying service to use this money to pay its accounts payable. For instance, if you hire a contractor to build an addition to your hotel, it is common practice for a bill-paying service to inspect the contractor's progress and pay off the project in stages—say, one-third of the price when the contractor begins work, one-third when the framing is up, and the final one-third when the addition is completed satisfactorily.

A bill-paying service will charge a fee, but in exchange will provide an extra margin of security. In addition to handling the paperwork and other assorted details, the service ensures that purchases meet buyers' specifications.

ANOTHER WORD ABOUT DISCOUNTS

Large hospitality operations tend to have more opportunity for discounts, especially promotional, volume, and quantity discounts—and, to a certain extent, cash discounts as well. Many chain operations can earn considerable income just by keeping track of the cash discount period, which is usually 10 days, and paying at the last possible moment before the end of this period. But discounts raise some problems.

First, you may become too intent on them and lose track of the real cost of purchases. Fortunately, keeping your books according to the *Uniform System of Accounts for Hotels and Restaurants* can separate for you the real cost from any discount.

Second, cash discounts may interfere with your normal accounts payable schedule. Unless you have several cash discounts, which is no longer likely, it may be too much trouble to pay bills on different days.

Third, you might stay with a "discounting" supplier longer than you should. For instance, if the supplier delivers slightly inferior foods from time to time, you may begin to overlook this in order to retain the discount.

Fourth, even if it is profitable to take advantage of a discount, it may be necessary to undergo a costly borrowing procedure to get the cash. The interest cost of such borrowing must be added to the cost of the purchase for decision purposes.

And fifth, if you are lucky enough to receive a cash discount, you need to know whether the payment due date is extended if you have to return the merchandise that is delivered and wait for two or three days for an acceptable replacement. Does the cash discount period start when the replacement arrives? Or does it start when the first, unacceptable delivery was made? This has caused many a strained relationship between buyers and sellers.

KEY WORDS AND CONCEPTS

Bank charges

Bill-paying service

Cash discount

Cash management

COD

Cost of paying too early

Cost of paying too late

Credit card payments

Credit period

Credit rating

Credit risk

Credit slip

Escrow account

Interest charge on unpaid balance

Invoices on account

The objective of a payment policy

Opportunity buy

Payment terms

Paid-out

Reconciling the supplier's end-of-period statement

Some problems with the acceptance of discounts

Stalling a supplier

Stretching the accounts payable

Supplier services

REFERENCE

1. Steven Lipin, "Office Supplies Are Battlefield for Credit Cards," *The Wall Street Journal,* July 22, 1993, p. B1.

QUESTIONS AND PROBLEMS

1. What is the main purpose of cash management?

2. How is cash management similar to inventory management? How do they differ?

3. If you pay a $10,000 bill today instead of two weeks from today when it is due, approximately how much money will you lose if you have to take the $10,000 out of a bank account that pays 2.75% simple interest per year?

4. What are the costs and benefits of "stalling" a supplier?

5. What should a manager do if he or she forecasts a temporary shortage of cash and will not be able to pay the bills on time next month?

6. What are some of the potential problems managers who accept discounts might experience?

7. Are there any advantages to paying your bills as early as possible? If so, what are they?

8. What are the major disadvantages of paying your bills too late?

9. What are some advantages of using paid-outs? What are some of the disadvantages?

10. Define or briefly explain the following terms:

    (a) COD

    (b) Credit terms

    (c) Optimal payment policy

    (d) Interest charge on the unpaid balance

    (e) Invoices on account

    (f) Credit rating

11. When should a hospitality operator request a credit slip from the supplier?

12. What are some advantages of using a bill-paying service? What are some disadvantages?

CHAPTER 11

Group:				Date: _____			REQUISITION SHEET	
Job Code: _____				Date Needed: _____				
Circle One:	DAIRY	DRY GOODS	PRODUCE		MEATS/SEAFOODS			

		Estimated						Actual	
Quan.	Unit	Unit Cost	Total Cost	Item Description		Quan.	Unit	Unit Cost	Total Cost

Received by: _____   Date: _____

Issued by: _____   Date: _____

THE OPTIMAL
SUPPLIER

THE PURPOSE OF THIS CHAPTER

This chapter discusses:

- Determining potential suppliers
- Determining a buying plan
- Supplier selection criteria
- Supplier-buyer relations
- Salesperson-buyer relations
- Evaluating suppliers and salespersons

INTRODUCTION

Buyers have a good deal more to do with selecting suppliers than fixing quality standards and economic values. The major exception to this rule occurs when some other company official insists that a buyer purchase from a certain supplier. This insistence usually means that some sort of reciprocal buying arrangement has been reached or that the owner/manager has prepared an approved supplier list without consulting the buyer.

THE INITIAL SURVEY

The first step in determining the optimal supplier is to compile a list of all possible suppliers, or at least a reasonable number of potential suppliers. Local suppliers' names can be gathered from the local telephone directories, local trade directories, local trade magazines, other similar publications, and other hospitality operators.

National suppliers' names can be obtained from similar sources. They also can be gathered from national buying guides (such as the *Thomas*

Food Industry Register or the annual *Buyer's Guide* published by *Restaurants & Institutions* magazine), visits to live trade shows and/or computer on-line "virtual" trade shows, and visits to industry trade centers.

National suppliers' names can also be obtained from computer on-line services. For instance, the National Restaurant Association (NRA) offers the Restaurant Association Network, which offers, among other things, supplier listings and commodity price indexes.[1] A comparable service is FoodNet, which links suppliers and food buyers interested in streamlining the selection and procurement process.[2]

National suppliers that are not on-line may offer the next best thing—CD-ROM catalogs.[3] They may publish their own CD-ROM catalogs or be joined in a cooperative venture, such as the *Nation's Restaurant News* Buyer's Advantage program or the *Hotel & Motel Management* Hotel Access CD.[4] These types of catalogs are especially useful for buyers seeking unique products.

The large corporations take the time to compile lengthy lists of suppliers. The procedure followed by most small operators is to seek out a more limited number of suppliers that carry most of the required items. In some cases, only one supplier may be contacted for a particular product line. This is true especially for such items as liquor and dairy products, since the middlemen dealing in these product lines usually have few competitors.

Whatever initial survey is undertaken, it can present three major problems. First, it may be difficult to determine which suppliers to include on the initial list. Many potential suppliers carry several product lines; consequently, the list can become larger than you would wish.

A second problem stems from the first. In their haste to shorten the potential supplier list, buyers may stop adding suppliers when they reach a certain number. The longer the list, the more time is required for interviewing, checking references, touring plants, and the other analytical work involved in culling the list. But indiscriminate culling can eliminate a good potential supplier. Furthermore, it tends to limit the pool of potential suppliers in the future if buyers stick with the original list. It can be costly to a hospitality firm to lock out a good supplier in this way.

The third problem is less common. It occurs when a buyer needs to purchase a unique item. In such situations, the search for a supplier can be extremely time-consuming.

TRIMMING THE INITIAL LIST

Buyers begin to narrow their initial list into an approved supplier list by looking closely at each supplier's product quality, AP price, and supplier services. (We assume that, at this stage, a buyer knows what types of products are wanted.) These factors help to separate acceptable suppliers from the initial list.

It is relatively easy to ascertain the quality standards and AP prices of suppliers. The major obstacle occurs when examining supplier services.

What is the best way to evaluate these supplier services? Basically, it becomes a matter of taste. But the important considerations come under the rubric of "performance." When evaluating performance, you should be interested in prompt deliveries, the number of rejected deliveries, how adjustments on rejected deliveries are handled, how well the supplier takes care of one or two trial orders, the capacity of a middleman's plant, and his or her technological know-how.

It might be easier to narrow a supplier list by trial and error. But a supplier's poor performance can leave you without a product and also with disgruntled customers demanding that particular product. It might be best, then, to accept the list-narrowing procedure as an essential aspect of purchasing.

THE RELATIONSHIP OF PURCHASING POLICY TO SUPPLIER SELECTION

Actually selecting the optimal supplier is the next logical step. It cannot be done, however, without buyers considering the type of procurement policies best for them. For instance, the buyer might want to work with one particular supplier and negotiate long-term contracts for some items. If this is the case, he or she must keep these requirements in mind when going over the approved supplier list. Some suppliers may wish to be accommodating; others may not.

Large corporations have a bit more latitude in formulating their preferred buying policies and then convincing suppliers to cooperate. Small operators have less discretion; that is, they may have to accept the buying procedures their suppliers prefer. But there are at least a few procurement policies available to any size operator. And, just as important, most suppliers are willing to adjust to more than one policy.

BUYING PLANS

Generally speaking, one finds in hospitality two basic buying plans: (1) the buyer selects a supplier first, and they work together to meet the buyer's needs, or (2) the buyer prepares relatively lengthy specifications for the items needed and then uses bid-buying procedures.

Selecting one or more suppliers to work with, the first plan, is not common. It usually occurs only when (1) there is a reciprocal buying policy; (2) only one supplier provides the type of item needed; (3) the buyer or owner-manager, for some reason, trusts the supplier's ability, integrity, or judgment; or (4) the buyer, for some reason, wants to establish a long-term relationship with a supplier. It is, however, somewhat more common in smaller operations where management, already spread thin with other operational problems, chooses to limit the number of suppliers, even in some cases to a single supplier for as many products as possible, a practice called "one-stop shopping," which we discuss shortly.

Bid buying is more common, particularly for items that are sold by several suppliers.[5] It works fairly well as long as buyers realize that all suppliers are not created equal. Also, buyers must keep in mind that obtaining the lowest bid may not ensure the lowest EP cost.

It is a matter of judgment as to which plan buyers should use. For some items, the first plan may be appropriate. For example, since the quality of fresh produce tends to vary significantly, a buyer may opt for the first plan; however, canned goods might be purchased strictly on a bid-buying basis.

Buyers who use bid buying generally take two approaches: (1) the "fixed bid" and (2) the "daily bid." The fixed bid typically is used for large quantities of products purchased over a reasonably long period of time. It is usually a very formal process.

The fixed-bid buying plan usually begins with the buyer sending a "Request for Bid" to prospective suppliers, asking them to submit bid prices on specific products or services. The request includes detailed specifications and outlines the process bidders need to follow as well as the process the buyer will use to award the contract.

Buyers send bid requests only to eligible, responsible bidders. An ineligible bidder is one who, by reason of financial instability, unsatisfactory reputation, poor history of performance, or other similar reasons, cannot meet the qualifications needed in order to be placed on the approved supplier list.

Responsible bidders usually need to send in sealed bids when participating in the fixed-bid process. A sealed bid is almost always required on major purchases to ensure fair competition among bidders.

After the sealed bids are opened, the buyer awards the business to the lowest responsible bidder. This bidder is awarded the contract because the unit price is lower, or the value per dollar bid is higher than that quoted by other bidders. Furthermore, the bid winner's reputation, past performance, and business and financial capabilities are judged best for satisfying the needs of the contract.

The daily bid is often used for fresh items, such as fresh produce. It is also used when purchasing a smaller amount—just enough to last for a few days or a week. (The daily bid method is sometimes referred to as "daily quotation buying," "call sheet buying," "open-market buying," or "market quote buying.") The daily bid usually follows a simple, informal procedure: (1) the suppliers that form a list of those you wish to do business with—the approved supplier list—are given copies of your specifications; (2) when it is time to order some items, you call these suppliers and ask for their bids; (3) you record the bids; and (4) the supplier selection usually is made by choosing the one with the lowest AP price quote.

Some sort of value analysis could be used here to determine the optimal plan to use, given the types of items being purchased. The optimal procedure, though, is not open to a pat formula because there are several good reasons for buyers to choose either plan. Convenience, degree of buyer skill, product availability, and so on, must be balanced when determining the optimal plan. In the final analysis, the plan used will result from examining several factors.

Regardless of the plan, or combination of plans, a buyer chooses, he or she must ascertain suppliers' willingness to participate in the plan. Most suppliers will jump at the chance to be a part of the first plan. Buyers, though, normally start with some type of bid-buying procedure, if only to determine which supplier they want to use all the time. Or, at the very least, buyers use bid buying in order to select the suppliers they plan to use for the next three, four, or six months.

Not all suppliers like to become involved with bid buying, especially if they feel that the other bidding suppliers are not in their league. These nonparticipating suppliers frequently balk at bid buying because their AP prices look high, due to the amount of supplier services they include. High AP prices usually do not win bids. Furthermore, the competing bidders may inflate their AP prices to just under those legitimately high AP prices. And the high-priced, reputable suppliers do not like to be party to this type of practice.

Many suppliers try to circumvent your desire to bid buy by offering various discounts, other opportunity buys, introductory offers, and so forth. In addition, they may try to become exclusive distributors for some items; if you want to purchase them you would have no choice in supplier selection.

OTHER SUPPLIER SELECTION CRITERIA

After determining a supplier's response to the two basic buying plans, a purchaser must assess the supplier's willingness to participate in additional aspects that are related to these two basic plans. Furthermore, there are several other related variables that must be evaluated when developing a list of acceptable suppliers. Some of the more common aspects and variables are discussed next.

COST-PLUS PURCHASING

The buyer might want to be charged whatever the supplier paid plus an agreed-upon profit markup. Recall from Chapter 9 the possibility of arranging this type of purchasing procedure. In this situation, you may be able to negotiate with suppliers for the agreed-upon profit markup percentage or set dollar amount to be added to the supplier's cost of obtaining the products. Larger hospitality firms are usually able to negotiate, whereas smaller operators may have to settle for a supplier's normal profit markup.

Suppliers are not always fond of cost-plus buying because it usually requires considerable work to alter AP prices. It also is necessary for the suppliers to share cost data with buyers, a practice that competitive businesspersons tend to frown upon. Large hospitality firms, though, tend to prefer cost-plus purchasing because experience suggests that it can reduce AP prices, reduce the buyer's administrative effort, increase the level of supplier services, and increase product quality. In short, cost-plus purchasing can increase value.

ONE-STOP SHOPPING

One-stop shopping (sometimes referred to as "sole-source procurement," "prime-vendor procurement," or "single-source procurement") appeals to many buyers because of its simplicity. A one-stop shopper tries to purchase as many things as possible from one supplier. The main advantage of this procedure is the reduction of the ordering cost. There is considerably less effort involved with fewer orders: less paperwork, less receiving activity, fewer deliveries, and less opportunity for error. Another advantage is the possibility of qualifying for a volume discount when you purchase a large dollar amount of merchandise; the one-stop buyer usually enters relatively large purchase orders and, hence, is more apt to qualify for a volume discount.[6]

Unfortunately, one-stop shopping does carry its share of disadvantages. One obvious disadvantage is the reduction in supplier selection flexibility. Another potential disadvantage with this setup is the possibility that your total dollars spent for purchases over the long run may be higher than if you shopped around a bit.

The reason for this second disadvantage is simple. Many suppliers carry reasonably large product lines, perhaps as many as 4,000 products under one roof. Some of these products are strong sellers, good-quality items that are competitively priced. Other products are not so good, nor are they as cheap as those comparable items carried by a competing supplier. As a result, although the one-stop supplier makes a minimum profit on some items, he or she typically makes up for it somewhere else, much the same as the food-service menu that carries several items, all with varying profit potentials. The idea of shopping around is to get the minimum profit items from each supplier, and to do this without spending more money, time, and effort than might be saved in AP prices.

No supplier can really provide complete one-stop service, as no one supplier can carry every item an operation needs. But some suppliers can and do carry much of what an operation needs. The fact that most suppliers cannot provide a broad range of products severely limits your pool of potential suppliers. If, for example, you want to use bid buying for most products, and you solicit bids from suppliers with the stipulation that the bidders must be prepared to provide all items you include on the bid, it is likely that only one supplier will be able to meet this requirement.

One-stop shopping may be more valuable for small operators. Although some AP prices may run a bit higher, chances are that the eventual costs of products used in production will be optimal. The AP price at the back door may be higher, but if your planned EP cost holds up with the additional time you can now spend in supervision and guest service, the eventual costs of products sold may be quite acceptable.

STOCKLESS PURCHASING

When the buyer purchases a large amount of product (for example, a three-month supply) and takes delivery of the entire shipment, the procedure is usually referred to as *forward buying.*[7]

When the buyer purchases a large amount of product, but arranges for the supplier to store it and deliver a little at a time, as needed, the procedure is called *stockless purchasing.* For instance, you might foresee the impending shortage of a 1990 vintage wine and, to offer this wine to your customers as long as possible, you might buy all the distributor has. Since your storage area might be limited, you ask that the wine distributor store your wine for you and deliver a bit at a time.

Stockless purchasing may also be used if the buyer suspects the AP prices for some items are about to increase drastically. This procedure is often used when purchasing such products as ashtrays, dinnerware, and flower vases, especially if the hospitality operation wants a particular logo on these items. A large purchase of personalized items usually results in a lower AP price per unit. But you may not be able to take advantage of this tradition if you have no place to store the items, unless, that is, the supplier will provide that supplier service.

CASH-AND-CARRY

The cash-and-carry procedure (sometimes referred to as "will-call purchasing") appears to be a marginal practice in the hospitality industry, as most buyers rely heavily on supplier services (especially delivery services) and are unwilling, or unable, to sacrifice them even though it may result in price concessions.[8] Some buyers, though, like this idea if it means a considerably lower AP price in exchange for providing their own delivery.

Some hospitality buyers are very dependent on the cash-and-carry option. For instance, off-premises caterers cannot always plan their purchases as carefully as local restaurateurs who enjoy more predictable business cycles. And small independent operators may not qualify for delivery or volume discounts.[9] Cash-and-carry then, is very important to these buyers.

Some suppliers resist cash-and-carry mainly because they have already invested heavily in the delivery function. Some do not want to deal with small buyers because of the inherent inefficiencies. Some, though, have set up one or more cash-and-carry locations (sometimes referred to as "wholesale clubs" or "warehouse wholesale clubs") to service small accounts. In fact, a few suppliers have aggressively pursued this type of business, seeking small accounts as well as the large corporate and institutional buyers.[10]

STANDING ORDERS

A standing order is an order placed with a supplier who repeatedly delivers just enough to bring the buyer's stock level up to par. A driver with a fully stocked truck shows up, takes inventory of what you have, drops off enough merchandise to bring you up to par, writes up an invoice, and leaves it with the bookkeeper. (The delivery drivers in this case are usually referred to as "route salespersons.")

Buyers like to use standing orders for items that have a standard usage pattern; milk and bread fit this description. Also, buyers sometimes like the convenience that standing orders provide. Buyers appreciate this method of purchasing even though some purchasing professionals suggest avoiding it because the procedure contradicts the basic principles of security and cost control.

With some products, like ice cream, standing orders are traditional. But where such orders are not traditional, the buyer is most likely unable to obtain this concession from suppliers, since most suppliers want some sort of minimum order before they schedule a delivery. They prefer a more precise order to justify sending a delivery truck.

COMPUTER HOOKUPS

The ordering that takes place when the buyer's computer talks to the supplier's computer is becoming more common in our industry, although it takes a considerable effort to establish this type of ordering procedure. Not all suppliers are as yet equipped with this innovation, so that if a buyer wants a supplier to participate in some sort of computer hookup, in some markets chances are the potential supplier pool will be limited.

Other forms of computerization are on the increase. For example, many suppliers have armed their salespersons with laptop computers with which to communicate a buyer's order directly to the supply house computer. This hastens the order procedure by shortening the lead time, eliminates inaccuracies, and provides an additional supplier service to the buyer.

Many suppliers also offer complimentary software and hardware to their larger customers that can be used to transmit electronically orders to the suppliers' distribution centers. This technology usually includes additional software packages that buyers can use to manage inventories, price menus, and calculate food costs.[11]

CO-OP PURCHASING

Recall that co-op purchasing is the banding together of several small operators in order to consolidate their buying power. A lower AP price is the major advantage. Few suppliers argue with the co-op concept. Many participate in this procedure as long as there are no glaring inefficiencies or inconveniences; that is, as long as the supplier makes one delivery to one location and receives one bill payment, he or she is willing to cooperate.

The major disadvantage of co-op purchasing is the cost of developing and operating the co-op. Someone must coordinate all members' needs and take on the challenge of supplier selection, negotiations, and so forth. A buyer also should realize that co-op purchasing may limit an individual member's influence in supplier selection. Each member surrenders a bit of flexibility as he or she goes along with the rest.

Co-op purchasing has recently enjoyed renewed popularity, primarily because it is seen as an effective way of reducing product costs.[12] In the past, when the co-op members had to do all the work, fewer buyers were interested in this type of buying plan. But, lately, several "buying services" (sometimes referred to as "buying clubs" or "contract houses") have emerged to streamline the process and make it more efficient.[13]

A buying service is a private company that buyers can join. For a fee, buyers can take advantage of the service's purchasing power as well as other subtle benefits, such as the service's willingness to share many profitable ideas with its members. In effect, the buying service is an easy way for small, independent operators to "hire" a highly skilled, professional purchasing executive.[14]

Each buyer or owner-manager has to make his or her own decision concerning the potential costs and benefits of co-op buying. The practice is, however, worth careful investigation. In some instances it can be a very profitable option.

LOCAL MERCHANT WHOLESALER OR NATIONAL SOURCE?

The small operator normally deals with local suppliers. But the larger ones sometimes bypass these middlemen and go directly to the primary source; this is especially common with equipment purchases. Large hospitality operations normally require national distribution so that all units in the chain organization can use the same type of products. Hence, they usually seek out the large suppliers who can provide this alternative.

The question of providing your own economic values, especially transportation and risk, must be addressed before you make a decision. And, as we have already pointed out, there are several advantages and disadvantages to be weighed here.

On a dollars-and-cents basis, small operations find it economical to purchase from local suppliers. Chains and other larger operations might, however, save money buying directly from the source. But the possible enmity engendered among the local suppliers must be considered here. Disgruntled locals are perhaps the biggest, though not immediately apparent, disadvantage associated with centralized buying and direct purchases. A buyer can expect little sympathy from bypassed local suppliers if he or she needs an emergency order or service on a piece of equipment.

A compromise is possible. For instance, a vice president of purchasing might go directly to the source and negotiate a long-term contract, say, for six months. Then he or she might "hire" local suppliers to take delivery from the sources and distribute the items to the local unit operations. Parceling out these end-user services is usually an acceptable and profitable compromise for all parties to the transaction.

DELIVERY SCHEDULE

We all have our preferences regarding the time of day and the day(s) of the week on which we would accept delivery from our suppliers. For instance, if we had our druthers, most of us would demand morning delivery.

Realistically, we often must make do with what we have available to us. However, this does not mean that we cannot swing our purchase dollars toward the supplier(s) who most closely matches our desired delivery schedule. This is a valued supplier service, and, although you often must expect to pay a little more for a preferred delivery routine, the overall effect may prove profitable for both you and the supplier.

ORDERING PROCEDURE REQUIRED BY SUPPLIER

As with the delivery schedule, buyers will be partial to those suppliers who most closely meet their needs. The suppliers who offer very convenient ordering procedures will most likely have a valuable competitive edge in the marketplace.

CREDIT TERMS

We are interested in the credit terms that are available from the various suppliers with which we might consider conducting business. It is important to note such things as the availability of cash discounts, quantity discounts, volume discounts, cash rebates, and promotional discounts; when payments are due (i.e., the credit period); the billing procedures; the amount of interest charges we may have to pay on the outstanding balance; and the overall installment payment procedure available, if any.

A preferred buying plan often will be bent to accommodate superior credit terms. That is, apparently hospitality operators are quite enamored with credit terms and will do what is necessary, within reason, to deal with those suppliers who offer generous credit terms. It is conceivable that this criterion could be the major consideration in supplier selection.

MINIMUM ORDER REQUIREMENT

Before a supplier will agree to providing you with "free delivery," normally you must order a certain minimum amount of merchandise. This is true even if you want to pick up the merchandise on a will-call basis, although the minimum order requirement usually dips a bit in this case.

Most buyers have little trouble in meeting minimum order requirements, so it is unlikely that such a criterion would be of concern. But the small operator might be very concerned with these stipulations, in which case this aspect becomes an important supplier selection standard.

VARIETY OF MERCHANDISE

This concept is related to the one-stop shopping opportunity discussed earlier. In general, a supplier may or may not have the one-stop shopping attraction for us, but he or she at least can offer a reasonable variety. There may be a variety of quality grades offered, brand names offered, and/or packers' brand names offered for the merchandise that is carried.

If a supplier specializes, for example, in fresh produce, he or she could offer tremendous variation within such a relatively narrow product line. A supplier who can offer us a variety of qualities of fresh produce may conceivably be more valuable than a one-stop supplier who carries only one quality level of fresh produce along with several other product lines.

LEAD TIME

The shorter the lead time, the more convenient it is for the buyer, since he or she can wait until the last possible moment before entering an order for delivery at a predetermined time. All other things being equal, you would probably want to deal with a purveyor who offers you the ability to call tonight for an order to be delivered tomorrow morning, rather than a supplier who requires two or three days of notice.

FREE SAMPLES

Suppliers will often give you one or two free samples for your evaluation, particularly if you represent a potentially large amount of business. However, some suppliers may not want to do this. And some buyers may not feel comfortable accepting free samples because it could compromise them.

RETURNS POLICY

This is a very sensitive issue and one that should be evaluated well before it ever becomes necessary to return merchandise and/or refuse to pay for goods or services. Needless to say, the more liberal the returns policy, the more you expect to pay in the long run.

A related issue is the return of prepayment for merchandise that you ordered but for some reason must refuse delivery. For instance, it often is necessary to put up a significant deposit for equipment purchases. If you decide that you do not want or need the item, what happens to your deposit? It would be prudent to iron out any potential problems early.

RECIPROCAL BUYING

You may one day want to initiate a reciprocal buying arrangement, that is, an arrangement whereby "you buy from me, and I'll buy from you." If so, you should inquire as early as possible about the suppliers' willingness to do this.

A related concept is the notion of doing business only with those who do business with you, or who send other business your way. In our experience, if you allow yourself to get entangled in a web such as this, replete with so many interlocking obligations, one little slip can cause the whole house of cards to tumble.

WILLINGNESS TO BARTER

As trading becomes more popular, you might decide to adopt it as part of your overall buying plan. If so, you must test the suppliers' desires to accommodate this request.

COOPERATION IN BID PROCEDURES

Most suppliers realize that you will want to shop around, at least occasionally. And most of them will respond to your request for bids and other related information. However, some suppliers are not particularly eager to spend this time or are so secretive about their price quotations that it becomes a burden for you to deal with them. These suppliers probably will not make your approved supplier list if you are a bid buyer.

SIZE OF FIRM

If you have a large amount of business, you must be assured that your suppliers are large enough to accommodate you. On the other hand, large suppliers may be too impersonal for you. Perhaps you would prefer dealing with the smaller firms, allowing you to talk to the owners regularly. If nothing else, dealing directly with an owner generally makes you feel that your concerns will be met consistently.

A related issue is the amount of time a supplier has been in business. Some buyers will consider suppliers only after they have established acceptable performance track records that indicate they can handle buyers' needs and will most likely be around for a while.

NUMBER OF BACK ORDERS

It seems to us that the supplier who has a history of excessive back orders will not be part of your approved supplier list. You can probably forgive a back order once in a while. But if it is a recurring problem, you cannot do business with such a purveyor. You want to do business with suppliers who have very high "fill rates." (A fill rate is a ratio calculated by dividing the number of items delivered by the number ordered. Ideally, it would always equal 100 percent.)

SUBSTITUTION CAPABILITY

On occasions when back orders cannot be avoided, it is nice if the supplier can provide a comparable substitute. Generally, though, the only suppliers capable of doing this are the ones who offer a one-stop shopping opportunity for you.

A related issue is the supplier who runs out of an item but who would be concerned enough about you personally to secure the products necessary to complete your order from another supplier or from one of your competitors. This type of purveyor is rare, but there may be one or two of them in your area.

BUYOUT POLICY

We can recall years ago when suppliers who wanted your business would agree to purchase your existing stock of competitors' merchandise. For instance, if a soap salesperson was soliciting your business, he or she might agree to buy out your existing stock so that you could begin immediately to use the new merchandise. This is an uncommon policy today, but it may exist somewhere. And if it does in your area, it represents one more criterion on which to judge a potential supplier.

A related issue is the willingness of a supplier to buy back outdated or obsolete merchandise. For instance, when purchasing replacement equipment, a major supplier selection factor would be the trade-in allowance offered by competing suppliers. All other things being equal, the supplier who has the most favorable policy is apt to have an edge over his or her competitors.

SUPPLIERS' FACILITIES

You should be especially concerned with a potential supplier's storage and handling facilities, the delivery facilities, and the facilities' sanitation. For instance, if the supplier uses old, dirty, and uncooled vans to deliver fresh produce, you may want to avoid that purveyor regardless of the AP price and other supplier services provided. Inadequate facilities will harm product quality, and this is intolerable.

LONG-TERM CONTRACTS

Some suppliers are unwilling or unable to enter into long-term contracts for AP price and/or for availability of the product during the contract period. If you prefer some type of long-term commitment, you may have to settle for a relatively short approved supplier list.

CASE PRICE

When you purchase a case of merchandise, say, a six-can case of tomatoes, you will pay a certain price for it, say, $12.00. If you wish to purchase one can of tomatoes, and you can purchase it for $2.00, you are receiving what is normally referred to as the "case price" for that can.

Few, if any, suppliers will give you a case price when you purchase less than a case. If you are lucky, a supplier will "bust" a case for you, but he or she will usually charge a premium to do this. Typically, either you purchase the whole case or you do business elsewhere.

When you purchase some items in small batches, it is important to deal with suppliers who understand your needs. In some situations, you cannot afford to purchase a whole case of, say, soup bases if you expect the contents to sit around for a period of time losing flavor and otherwise deteriorating.

BONDED SUPPLIERS

You are concerned about the capability of suppliers to cover the cost of any damage they might inflict on your property. Usually, before the appropriate government authority will issue a business license to a supplier, he or she must display adequate insurance coverage; that is, he or she must be bonded. However, what is adequate for the licensing bureau may not be adequate for you.

A related issue is the fact that you may inadvertently be dealing with an unlicensed supplier. You cannot do this because, if, say, one of your customers became ill from products provided by this supplier, you could become entangled in all sorts of litigation.

CONSULTING SERVICE PROVIDED

To a great extent, salespersons and suppliers in general are the primary sources of product, and related, information for the typical hospitality operator. Buyers are interested in data concerning product specifications, preparation and handling procedures, nutrition, merchandising techniques, and other similar types of advice.[15]

Smaller hospitality operators are especially loyal to suppliers and salespersons who willingly share their expertise. For example, the small caterer who is bidding for an unusually large banquet contract will appreciate the salesperson who takes the time to help prepare the proposal.

Formal consulting, though, is not something that every purveyor is able or willing to provide. For instance, when purchasing equipment, you may find that some dealers stock it, sell it, and deliver it, period. Other dealers provide some additional advice, say, they provide you with blueprints, or they seek the appropriate building permits for you. You pay more for this type of service, but you may be willing to do so. If such is the case, you must seek those suppliers who can provide for your needs.

DEPOSITS REQUIRED

For some products, you may need to put up a deposit. For example, if you purchase soda pop syrup, you may need to put up a cash deposit for the keg. Usually deposit requirements are not burdensome, but if they are, you probably will want to eliminate such a demanding supplier from your approved supplier list.

WILLINGNESS TO SELL STORAGE

Some suppliers will sell storage to you, which can be a tremendous service if, for example, you need space to house a large amount of merchandise that was purchased through a favorable opportunity buy.

A supplier who will sell storage probably is a rare find, but if you are fortunate enough to have one of them in your area, you must be certain to inquire not only about the fees for this service, but also about any other sort of requirements. For instance, to qualify to purchase storage, you may need to purchase $1,000 worth of merchandise per week. This may or may not be attractive to you, and you should be alert to these kinds of restrictions that could place you in an unprofitable position.

SUPPLIERS WHO OWN HOSPITALITY OPERATIONS

Some hospitality operations own commissaries and/or central distribution centers that will sell merchandise to other hospitality companies. For instance, many quick-service restaurants purchase Pepsi Cola products even though PepsiCo competes directly with these restaurants through its company-owned and franchised Pizza Huts, Taco Bells, and KFC outlets. The main issue, of course, is, could such a purchasing strategy be beneficial for the buyer?

At first glance, it would seem foolish to buy from a competitor. One would think that the competitor would learn too much about your business. Furthermore, would the competitor favor his or her hospitality units at your expense?[16]

On the other hand, there are some persons who feel that buying from another hospitality operator has its advantages. For example, the competitor understands the business much better than a conventional supplier and is much more conscious of the required supplier services.

SOCIALLY RESPONSIBLE SUPPLIERS

Some buyers prefer to work with suppliers who promote socially responsible agendas. For instance, some buyers will not purchase from suppliers that sell products manufactured by employees in foreign countries who do not receive a basic level of wages and/or benefits.[17] Some buyers will not purchase from suppliers carrying products whose processing causes damage to the earth's rain forests. And some buyers prefer to purchase from suppliers who employ minorities and deal with minority-owned subcontractors.[18]

Buyers can use subscription services to search for socially responsible firms. For instance, for an annual fee, a buyer can subscribe to referral services that list minority and/or female suppliers. Suppliers are typically listed by product category, and, with little more than a touch-tone phone and a few key words, buyers can quickly secure the information they need.[19]

REFERENCES

Usually a large part of your supplier selection work is devoted to obtaining personal references. This normally is an informal process, whereby you talk with your friends in the industry who may be able to provide you with meaningful input about certain suppliers. You might also consider contacting credit-rating firms to uncover a potential supplier's financial strength. Generally, though, if a friend whose opinion you trust has had a good experience with a particular supplier, you would want to do business with that firm.

It would appear that you are most anxious about a potential supplier's integrity and overall dependability. These are the characteristics you are trying to uncover when conversing with your friends. These factors can mean many things to many persons, but if a friend is impressed with a supplier's dependability and integrity, you probably want that supplier on your approved supplier list.

MOST IMPORTANT SUPPLIER SELECTION CRITERIA

No one can dictate the criteria that you should consider when selecting your suppliers. This is something that only you can judge for yourself. It is interesting, though, to note those criteria that are most important to members of our industry.

Generally speaking, most buyers are interested primarily in product quality. Suppliers must be able to provide consistently the quality needed, or else buyers cannot deal with them.

Supplier service generally is a close second to product quality. Dependability is critical. A supplier must ensure that buyers receive what they need when they need it.

The AP price seems to trail quality and supplier services in most buyer surveys. While this does not necessarily imply that buyers are unconcerned with product costs, it does emphasize the point that purchase decisions in the hospitality industry are not unduly influenced by AP prices.

The typical hospitality buyer seems to follow the supplier selection process adopted by Walt Disney World food services. When selecting its suppliers, Disney is concerned with product quality, supplier service, whether the purveyor is large enough to handle the account, and AP price.[20]

Regardless of the number and type of supplier selection criteria employed by the hospitality operation, the common thread running through them is one of consistency, dependability, loyalty, and trust.[21] If a supplier can render consistent value, chances are it will be on the approved supplier list of several hospitality operations. Furthermore, the suppliers who consistently provide acceptable value will continue to grow and prosper.

MAKE YOUR CHOICE

As you gradually complete your basic buying plan, you concomitantly reduce the potential supplier pool. Eventually common sense and company policy guide you toward the optimal suppliers. You do not want too many restrictions on your basic buying plan. On the other hand, you do not necessarily want to ignore all the suppliers' needs. You must strike a balance, within reason, so that both you and the seller feel confident that profit will result from the relationship. The best relationship is one in which both the buyer and the seller are satisfied.

SUPPLIER-BUYER RELATIONS

The buyer's principal contact with suppliers is through salespersons. In the initial stages of supplier selection, buyers may meet an officer of a supply house. But after this meeting, a supply house officer almost never usurps the salesperson's role. The top management of a supply house is never out of the picture, although it may be out of sight. Those officials work hard to improve business; some of their major activities include those discussed next.

SUPPLY HOUSE OFFICERS SET THE TONE OF THEIR BUSINESS

They normally set this tone by setting the quality standards of the items they carry, by determining the types of economic values and supplier services they provide, and by planning their advertising and promotion campaigns. While considering these aspects of the business, moreover, suppliers seek a balance between what they want to do and what their customers, the hospitality operations' buyers, need. (See Figure 11.1.)

SUPPLY HOUSE OFFICERS SET THE OVERALL SALES STRATEGIES

There are two basic sales strategies: (1) the "push strategy," in which suppliers urge their salespersons to do whatever is necessary to entice the buyer to purchase the product—the normal push is AP price discounts of one type or another—and (2) the "pull strategy," in which suppliers influence those who use the items purchased by the buyer. For example, a supplier may advertise heavily on TV, exhorting ultimate customers to demand his or her product in their favorite restaurant. If they do, the restaurant buyer has little choice but to purchase the product. In other words, the ultimate customer "pulls" the product through the channel; or if backdoor selling can be implemented successfully, a user in the company "pulls" the product through by influencing the buyer's purchasing decisions. (See Figure 11.2.)

You have undoubtedly seen many types of pull strategies. If, for example, a restaurant customer orders a Coke, which is a brand name, what

FIGURE 11.1. Some suppliers are willing to provide unique supplier services in an attempt to win your business. (Courtesy Stockpot Soups.)

"Perrier, please." *"Perrier, please."* "Perrier, please." "Perrier, please." "Perrier, please." *"Perrier, please."* "Perrier, please." *"Perrier, please."* "Perrier, please." "Perrier, please." *"Perrier, please."* "Perrier, please." *"Perrier, please."* "Perrier, please." *"Perrier, please."* "Perrier, please." *"Perrier, please."* "Perrier, please." "Perrier, please." *"Perrier, please."* "Perrier, please." *"Perrier, please."* "Perrier, please."

Today, people are more health-conscious than ever. Which is precisely why they're asking for pure beverages like Perrier. They trust that what's inside the "little green bottle" comes straight from the protected mineral spring in Vergeze, France. And, that it contains no salt, sugar, calories, caffeine, additives or preservatives.

Everywhere you turn, people are asking for Perrier. In restaurants, bars and clubs they're drinking America's most preferred nonalcoholic beverage.

Serve Perrier. It's preferred and profitable.

Perrier

For more information on the "Perrier, Please" Waitstaff Program, contact our Foodservice Department, The Perrier Group, 777 West Putnam Avenue, Greenwich, CT 06830

FIGURE 11.2. The pull strategy. (Courtesy The Perrier Group.)

choice does the buyer have? Likewise with catsup or hot sauce on the tables. Are not Heinz and Tabasco brands preferred by restaurant customers?

Of course, there are various shades and combinations of these two basic strategies, but, generally speaking, suppliers lean toward one. Or, at least, they lean toward one for some items and toward the other for their remaining items.

The pull strategy can be risky and extremely costly for suppliers to implement and maintain. But if it works, the rewards are fruitful indeed.

The pull strategy also is a major weapon suppliers use to steal business from one another.

SUPPLY HOUSE OFFICERS SPONSOR A GREAT DEAL OF PRODUCT AND MARKET RESEARCH

Suppliers also spend considerable time and effort evaluating the bids they make for buyers' business. Furthermore, they constantly prepare and revise files that contain information about current and potential customers. These information files are sometimes referred to as "buyer fact sheets" or "buyer profiles." They constitute a selling tool and contain as much or as little information as thought necessary to facilitate the sales effort.

The following pieces of information are usually found in these files:

1. Does the buyer have a favorable impression of the supplier's reputation? Generally speaking, a favorable impression makes it easier for a salesperson to get his or her foot in the door on the first sales visit.

2. What are the major characteristics of the ultimate customers of the buyer's company? (If the ultimate consumers are price conscious, the buyer will adopt a similar posture.)

3. Is the buyer concerned with AP prices?

4. Is the buyer concerned with fast and dependable deliveries?

5. Will the buyer take a chance on new products? Does he or she have the authority to suggest new products to the respective hospitality departments?

6. Does the buyer have a great deal of confidence in his or her purchasing skill? Or will second-guessing prevail?

7. Does the buyer have other duties? For example, is he or she a buyer and a user? Will these other duties minimize the time spent with salespersons?

8. Does the buyer insist on rigid quality control? Or will he or she accept certain exceptions or substitutions from time to time?

9. What is the possibility of setting up a reciprocal buying arrangement?

10. What is the payment history of the buyer's company?

11. How does the buyer treat suppliers and salespersons?

12. Are there any little things that irritate the buyer? For example, does he or she get annoyed if a salesperson is a few minutes late for an appointment?

SUPPLIERS TRAIN THEIR SALES STAFFS

In fact, they expend tremendous efforts in sales training, for both new salespersons and, continually, to educate the salespersons currently on the staff. Quite often the training materials are based on market research, new products, and buyer profiles.

SUPPLIERS KEEP THEIR SALESPERSONS' PROMISES

They must, for example, make sure that orders are handled properly and delivered on time.

SALESPERSON-BUYER RELATIONS

Salespersons (sometimes referred to as "distributor sales representatives" or "DSRs") are buyers' main contact with supplier firms. Buyers must usually meet several every week. Many of them are familiar faces; others are new. Establishing firm and fair business relations with them, and particularly setting the ground rules regarding sales visits, is essential to efficient procurement.

Buyers need to be aware of the sales tactics used by salespersons. Generally, on the first sales call, a salesperson might (1) make some attempt, however slight, at backdoor selling (i.e., he or she might try to interest a user in the supplier's wares); (2) attempt to use free samples and literature, in an effort to interest and possibly to obligate a buyer; (3) try to establish a justification for his or her presence; (4) try to talk a buyer away from the current supplier; or (5) try to be invited to return, thereby starting a nominal business relationship.

Sales professionals are usually adept at practicing what is usually referred to as "relationship marketing."[22] A salesperson after our business will bend over backward to start some type, any type, of business relationship. He or she will usually take any order, no matter how small, so that future sales visits are justified. Even if you purchase only one item once, he or she still feels, as "one of your suppliers," justified in dropping in periodically. It may seem ludicrous that a salesperson would hang around once you make it clear that you doubt that you will buy from him or her again. Also, you would think that supply house officers would prohibit salespersons from taking small orders. But you may not always be the buyer. The next buyer, or manager, may be more receptive. Today, it may be a small order; tomorrow, who knows? Hence, salespersons continue their efforts.

Small operators enamored of one-stop shopping like to avoid excessive contacts with salespersons and to minimize their ordering procedures. This desire turns them into house accounts. A house account is a regular, steady customer, for whom suppliers are not always motivated to provide generous supplier services. However, they may continue to provide exceptional supplier services in order to keep you happy.

This is a touchy issue. Dealing with many salespersons is time-consuming. But never seeing them at all is poor local public relations, shuts off good sources of information, and prevents them from helping you check inventories, production techniques, and any equipment they may have loaned you to use with their products. Good trade relations might dictate that you spread your orders out a bit more. But this too can be costly. Each operation must, therefore, balance the potential ill will with this loss of time and make the decision in the light of factors such as order size and management availability as well as public relations.

A full-time buyer for a large operation, though, is expected to spend a good deal of time with salespersons. The company pays the buyer to minimize the AP prices. In these larger organizations, other people are responsible for the steps the product follows from purchase to use. Someone watches for pilferage, shrinkage, and spoilage in storage. Someone is responsible for using cooking or other production techniques that avoid waste and shrinkage. Someone is responsible for avoiding overportioning of finished product. How these responsibilities are distributed is not relevant to the present point. Our point is that, in a large operation, the achievement of a good EP cost results not only from a good AP price but also from the proper working of a complex, skilled organization.

Several volumes have been written on sales tactics, strategies, and procedures. Buyers would be wise to read some of these materials, paying particular attention to such topics as (1) the personal characteristics of good salespersons, (2) types of salespersons, (3) things to avoid when dealing with salespersons, (4) things to do when dealing with salespersons, (5) types of sales tactics, and (6) techniques for evaluating salespersons.

We do not want to suggest that an adversarial relationship necessarily exists between buyers and salespersons. But buyers must expect salespersons to go to whatever ethical lengths they can to make sales. Salespersons come to sell, not to entertain. They want to meet your expectations, but for a price.

A good salesperson will never sell you something you do not need. But keep in mind that the main objective is to convert you into a regular customer, not by holding a gun to your head, but by providing you with satisfaction. Within reason, then, salespersons do what is necessary to make you a house account.

An alert buyer should be able to compete in the game of sales strategy and tactics. Objectivity helps a buyer, as does an understanding supervisor. In most cases, the buyer and salesperson work together for each other's benefit. Remember, though, business being business, buyers should never become too friendly with sales representatives.

EVALUATING SUPPLIERS AND SALESPERSONS

Suppliers and salespersons sometimes become such integral parts of a business that you start treating them as you would an employee. For this reason, you should periodically evaluate their performance and consider disciplining or rewarding them as necessary. The ultimate discipline is to switch to another source of supply. The ultimate reward is to become a house account. (This may be no reward for salespersons, though. Some supply houses pay no sales commissions on house account sales, the theory being that little effort has gone into making the sales. These salespersons may, however, receive a bonus when they do deliver a house account.) Obviously, there is a considerable range between these extremes and several discipline-reward combinations.

Most analysts agree that an operator should rate suppliers and their salespersons as part of the discipline-reward cycle. Few analysts agree on the criteria to use in these evaluations. For instance, some buyers are appreciative of the salespersons who take the time to listen to what the buyers have to say. Some buyers seek only those salespersons who can answer the buyers' questions completely and correctly. And some buyers are more enamored with effective and impressive sales presentations.

In any case, once again the common thread running throughout is consistency—consistent quality, consistent supplier services, and so forth. If suppliers and salespersons consistently fulfill their part of the bargain, whether made yesterday or last year, a buyer should have no complaint. Our suggestion, then, is to enumerate those factors on which you and the suppliers and salespersons agree and, from time to time, use a consistency yardstick to measure performance.

While you look for consistency, though, remember that a high AP price often accompanies high levels of consistency, especially consistent supplier services.

If you expect suppliers and their salespersons to be consistent, you must be consistent yourself. That is, you should never change your evaluation criteria unilaterally. Professional buyers generally try to be consistent, but users who also buy, in contrast to professional buyers, tend to be more subjective about the things they purchase as well as more abusive toward suppliers and salespersons. User-buyers, therefore, should be especially leery of finding these traits in themselves.

In the final analysis, evaluation here probably is a combination of art and science. Having evaluated consistency, you could examine other subjective factors. Resist being too hasty in this process. It is true that, unless you have a long-term contract, you can drop your supplier quite abruptly. But this may do more harm than good. If a supplier is deficient, allow a chance to improve, just as you would give a poor-performing employee a chance to improve. Never "fire" the supplier or salesperson without allowing a second chance. If you acquire a reputation for rash decisions, other suppliers or salespersons may become gun-shy, especially the ones who consider themselves fair and reputable performers. You do not want to be left with only the poorest supply choices.

A step short of cutting a supplier off completely that is often used is to cut him or her off for a week or so, just to make certain that this supplier realizes your business can be lost. This discipline supposedly helps keep suppliers in line. You want to be certain, though, that the supplier really did something to deserve this treatment and that the problem is not in your own operation rather than the supplier's.

GETTING COMFORTABLE

Supplier selection is not something to be done once and then forgotten. But small operators often seem to think it is, even when competing suppliers and salespersons bombard them with sales pitches.

Salespersons will fight to prevent you from settling in with one or two suppliers, unless they are among those you have selected. They do not want you to enter into the "comfort stage" of the supplier selection procedure. Their sales efforts will, in fact, become increasingly insistent. On the other hand, your current suppliers and salespersons will see to it that you are satisfied to the point that you will discourage the advances of other suppliers and salespersons. Of course, your current sources may get comfortable themselves and need to be brought up short now and then.

Many buyers and user-buyers become comfortable with a salesperson, but they at least remain aware of the need to examine alternate suppliers and to make a switch if necessary.

But flitting continually from one supplier to another involves a certain amount of emotional strain, broken loyalties, and disrupted business patterns. The switching becomes particularly difficult if your favorite salesperson goes to work for another supplier and you want to continue doing business with him or her. In effect, you allow this salesperson to carry your business to his or her new employer.

Generally, a supplier who takes good care of your needs deserves some type of reward. Suppliers and salespersons are, indeed, just like partners, or employees. Good employees are rewarded with continuous employment, a salary raise, or a bonus. Suppliers and salespersons should be treated with equal consideration. We are not sure whether it is always a good idea to become a house account, but we do believe that, at the very least, good suppliers and salespersons deserve first crack at your business, now and in the future. A restaurant manager once expressed this sentiment precisely when he remarked:

> We don't believe in getting locked into one supplier, because it would make us too vulnerable. But, on the other hand, we don't switch suppliers just to gain a few cents. We try to find suppliers who appreciate our dedication to quality and then stay with them. That doesn't mean we don't check the market every Monday and maintain a continuing check on prices. But we believe in commitment—on both sides.[23]

KEY WORDS AND CONCEPTS

AP price

Approved supplier

Approved supplier list

Back order

Barter

Bid-buying procedures

Bonded supplier

Bust a case

Buyer fact sheets

Buyer profiles

Buying clubs

Buying plans

Buying services

Buyout policy

Call sheet buying

Case price

Cash-and-carry

Cash discount

Cash rebate

CD-ROM catalog

Comfort stage of supplier selection

Computer hookup

Computerized data base

Computer on-line services

Consistency

Consulting service

Contract house

Co-op purchasing

Cost-plus purchasing

Credit period

Credit terms

Daily bid

Daily quotation buying

Delivery schedule

Deposits

DSRs

End-user services

Evaluating suppliers and salespersons

Fill rate

Firing a supplier

Fixed bid

Forward buying

Free samples

House account

Ineligible bidder

Lead time

Long-term contract

Market quote buying

Market research

Minimum order requirement

National distribution

One-stop shopping

Open-market buying

Ordering cost

Ordering procedures

Par stock

Potential supplier

Prime-vendor procurement

Product substitution

Profit markup

Promotional discount

Pull sales strategy

Push sales strategy

Quantity discount

Reciprocal buying

Relationship marketing

Request for bid

Responsible bidder

Returns policy

Route salesperson

Salesperson-buyer relations

Sealed bid

Single-source procurement

Size of a supplier firm

Socially responsible supplier

Sole-source procurement

Standing order

Stockless purchasing

Supplier-buyer relations

Supplier facilities

Supplier references

Supplier selection criteria

Supplier services

Suppliers who own hospitality operations

Trade center

Trade-in allowance

Value analysis

Volume discount

Warehouse wholesale club

Wholesale club

Will-call purchasing

REFERENCES

1. "NRA Goes On-Line," *F&B Business,* January/February 1995, p. 6.

2. "FoodNet Provides Ramp to Information Highway," *F&B Business,* January/February 1995, p. 18.

3. Patt Patterson, "Recession or No Recession, New Equipment Always Exists," *Nation's Restaurant News,* November 9, 1992. See also, William M. Bulkeley, "Publishers Deliver Reams of Data on CDs," *The Wall Street Journal,* February 22, 1993, p. B6.

4. *Nation's Restaurant News,* July 10, 1995, p. 90. See also, *Hotel & Motel Management,* September 18, 1995, p. 3.

5. Michael Guiffrida, "Saying What You Mean on Bids," *FoodService Director,* May 15, 1990, p. 78. See also, Patt Patterson, "Bid Buying Saves Time and Cuts Food Costs for Red's Seafood," *Nation's Restaurant News,* October 28, 1991, p. 58.

6. Patt Patterson, "Effective Purchasing in Recessionary Times," *Nation's Restaurant News,* February 4, 1991, p. 48. See also, Annie Stephenson, "Shopping Habits," *Hospitality,* April/May 1995, p. 20.

7. Patt Patterson, "Now May Be the Time for Distributors to Buy Ahead," *Nation's Restaurant News,* February 17, 1992, p. 24.

8. Patt Patterson, "Warehouse Clubs: A Foodservice Supply Source?" *Nation's Restaurant News,* December 14, 1992, p. 49.

9. Patt Patterson, "Back to Warehouse Clubs: Are They Good Supply Sources?" *Nation's Restaurant News,* February 8, 1993, p. 18.

10. Karen Blumenthal, "Shopping Clubs Ready for Battle in Texas Market," *The Wall Street Journal,* October 24, 1991, p. B1. See also, Bob Ortega, "Wal-Mart Sets Sights on Big Customers in Bid to Improve Warehouse-Club Unit," *The Wall Street Journal,* November 2, 1993, p. A4.

11. Bill Eacho, "Quality Service Through Strategic Foodservice Partnerships: A New Trend," *Hosteur,* Spring 1993, p. 28.

12. Peter D. Meltzer, "Bartered Bucks," *Food Arts,* July/August 1992, p. 42. See also, Timothy L. O'Brien, "Franchises Spearhead Renewed Popularity of Co-ops," *The Wall Street Journal,* November 29, 1993, p. B2.

13. Patt Patterson, "Purchasing Power: Getting a Little Help from HSG," *Nation's Restaurant News,* March 16, 1992, p. 46. See also, Patt Patterson, "A New Breed of Co-ops: Team Purchasing Can Work," *Nation's Restaurant News,* August 30, 1993, p. 20.

14. *Nation's Restaurant News,* May 15, 1995, p. 47.

15. Phil Roberts, "Looking for a Supplier 'Partner,' Not a Salesman," *Nation's Restaurant News,* September 9, 1991, p. 30. See also, Phil Roberts, "WholeSELLERS: Putting Wind in Our Sales," *Nation's Restaurant News,* September 21, 1992, p. 122. See also, Patt Patterson, "Commercial Electric Contest Can Spark Bright Ideas," *Nation's Restaurant News,* January 11, 1993, p. 18.

16. Ted Richman, "Suppliers' Demands Are Too High a Price to Pay," *Nation's Restaurant News,* December 19, 1994, p. 21. See also, Martha Brannigan, "Coke Is Victim of Hardball on Soft Drinks," *The Wall Street Journal,* March 15, 1991, p. B1.

17. G. Pascal Zachary, "Starbucks Asks Foreign Suppliers to Improve Working Conditions," *The Wall Street Journal,* October 23, 1995, p. B4.

18. Brett Pulley, "Culture of Racial Bias at Shoney's Underlies Chairman's Departure," *The Wall Street Journal,* December 21, 1992, p. A1.

19. Leon E. Wynter, "Supplying a Minority or Female Supplier," *The Wall Street Journal,* September 21, 1993, p. B1.

20. Stephen M. Fjellman, *Vinyl Leaves: Walt Disney World and America* (San Francisco: Westview Press, 1992), p. 390.

21. John R. Farquharson, "And These Doctors Make House Calls!" *Nation's Restaurant News,* September 21, 1992, p. 116. See also, Michael L. Facciola, "Supply & Dementia," *Food Arts,* May 1992, p. 113.

22. John Bowen, "Don't Imitate, Differentiate," *Nevada Hospitality,* July/August 1996, p. 20.

23. Patt Patterson, "Shere Sets High Standards for Coach and Six," *Nation's Restaurant News,* January 13, 1986, p. 4.

QUESTIONS AND PROBLEMS

1. What are the major problems associated with the initial survey stage of supplier selection? What would you suggest to alleviate these difficulties?

2. The buyer usually has a minor role in selecting equipment suppliers. What do you think is the usual role? Why would an owner-manager take the initiative in selecting equipment suppliers?

3. Identify the two basic buying plans. Suggest items that would be purchased under each plan.

4. Why do you think bid buying is so popular in our industry? What are the costs and benefits of this plan, as opposed to those of the other basic buying plan?

5. What are the advantages and disadvantages of one-stop shopping? Suggest the types of hospitality operations you feel would most likely benefit from one-stop shopping.

6. A buyer often takes a daily bid before placing a meat order. What does this procedure involve?

7. What are the major advantages and disadvantages of co-op purchasing?

8. What are some of the advantages of using a computer on-line service to search for potential suppliers? Does the CD-ROM technology offer the same advantages?

9. Assume that you are very happy with your current supplier, who has been supplying most of your needs for over a year. A new supplier comes along with what appears to be a better deal: a promise of lower AP prices along with the same quality and supplier services. What do you do? If possible, ask a hotel or restaurant manager to comment on your answer.

10. What is the difference between a formal bid procedure and an informal bid procedure?

11. What are the major advantages and disadvantages of will-call purchasing?

12. What are some advantages and disadvantages of purchasing only from socially responsible suppliers?

13. What is the difference between the "push" sales strategy and the "pull" sales strategy? Which strategy do you think a supplier prefers?

14. When is it appropriate for a buyer to use a fixed bid buying procedure?

15. Why might a supplier be reluctant to participate in a cost-plus purchasing procedure?

16. How could a buyer save money by using the stockless purchasing procedure?

17. What are some advantages and disadvantages of the standing-order purchasing procedure?

18. Why is it important to purchase merchandise only from licensed and bonded suppliers?

19. Develop a checklist that you would use to evaluate your suppliers. Assign degrees of importance to each item on the list. If possible, ask a hotel manager and/or a food buyer to comment on your list.

20. Define or briefly explain the following:

(a) Call sheet buying

(b) Approved supplier list

(c) Forward buying

(d) Cash rebate

(e) Comfort stage of supplier selection

(f) Credit period

(g) Buying club

(h) Direct purchase

(i) Credit terms

(j) Minimum order requirement

(k) Lead time

(l) Returns policy

(m) Buyout policy

(n) Case price

(o) Computerized data base

(p) Buyer fact sheet

(q) House account

(r) CD-ROM catalog

(s) National distribution

(t) Trade-in allowance

(u) Ineligible bidder

LIMITED PURCHASE ORDER
NOT VALID OVER $500.00

University of Nevada, Las Vegas
Federal Tax ID# 88-6000024
Business Center South • Las Vegas, NV 89154-1033
702-895-3521 • FAX 702-895-3859

PLEASE PRESS HARD

Date:_____

To: _____

Address: _____

City, State, Zip _____

Federal Tax ID No.: _____

Telephone: (____) ____-_____ Fax: (____) ____-_____

ORDER #: 2LPOB

Page 1 of _____ 26554

Agreement or Bid # _____

CONFIRMING ORDER?
☐ NO   ☐ YES
TO_____ ON _____

SHIPPING INFORMATION
UNLV/Receiving Department
Business Services Building
4505 Maryland Parkway
Las Vegas, NV 89154-1033
(No deliveries after 4:00 PM)

LINE #	QUANTITY	UNIT	COMPLETE DESCRIPTION	A/R	UNIT PRICE	TOTAL
001						
						TOTAL

Required Delivery Date:_____

Contact Name: _____

Phone Number: (702) _____FAX No: (702) _____

DEPARTMENT INFORMATION

Requesting Dept. Name: _____

Bldg: _____ Room: _____ Mail Code _____

Have items been received ☐ Yes ☐ No

INVOICE TO:
Business Center South
Disbursements
P.O. Box 71590
Las Vegas, NV 89170-1590

ACCOUNTING INFORMATION

LN	FUND	AREA	ORGN	SORG	OBJT	SOBJ	JOB #	TOTAL
01								
02								

COMMODITY CODE:_____

COMMODITY APPROVAL: _____

SIGNATURE AUTHORITY:_____

PRV1033-12/12-94 DISTRIBUTION: *White and Yellow*- Vendor, *Pink* - Purchasing, *Gold* - Department

NOTICE TO VENDOR
1.NO PARTIAL SHIPMENTS
  ACCEPTED.
2.DO NOT CHARGE SALES OR
  EXCISE TAX.
3.ORIGINAL INVOICE AND ONE
  COPY REQUIRED FOR
  PAYMENT.
4.PURCHASE ORDER # **MUST**
  APPEAR ON **LABEL, INVOICE**
  AND PACKING SLIP.

Source: University of Nevada, Las Vegas

TYPICAL ORDERING
PROCEDURES

THE PURPOSE OF THIS CHAPTER

This chapter discusses:

- The purchase requisition
- Ordering procedures
- The purchase order
- The change order
- Expediting
- Methods of streamlining the ordering procedures

INTRODUCTION

When actually engaged in buying products and services, a buyer is most concerned with obtaining the right amount and quality at the right time with the right supplier services for the right EP cost. In addition, he or she does not really complete the buying procedure, technically, until all products and services are properly received, stored, and issued to employees. In short, the buying responsibilities end only when the buyer turns these products and services over to those who will use them.

It is, of course, true that where the department head is a user-buyer, he or she may simply call in the order to an approved supplier. Similarly, many hospitality operations do not operate on a formal issues system. It is important to notice that even where there is an "open storeroom," someone still keeps a close eye on what has been removed from the storeroom by employees. In very large operations, and in many smaller clubs and hotels, however, the practice or requiring written issues, approved by the department head to draw food or supplies from a storeroom, is more common. The discussion that follows here describes the system found in those places using a formal issues system.

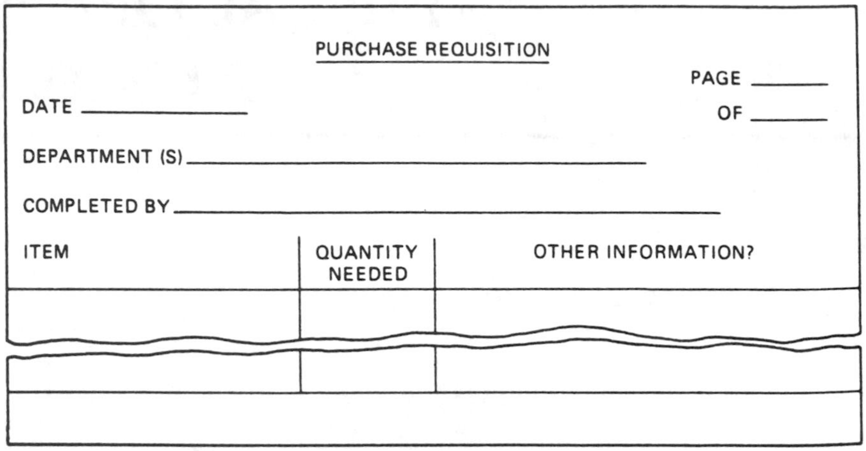

PURCHASE REQUISITION

PAGE ______
OF ______

DATE ______________

DEPARTMENT (S) ________________________________

COMPLETED BY ________________________________

ITEM	QUANTITY NEEDED	OTHER INFORMATION?

FIGURE 12.1. Purchase requisition.

PURCHASE REQUISITIONS

At times, before any orders are placed by the buyer, or coordinated by the unit manager, the department heads of the hospitality operation—for example, the chef, the executive housekeeper, the maître d'—prepare "purchase requisitions." These are forms that list those items or services needed by the particular department heads. (Figure 12.1 shows a typical purchase requisition.) Generally speaking, these requisitions grant the buyer the authority to go out into the marketplace and procure the items listed by the department heads.

A purchase requisition typically is used in the hospitality industry whenever a manager or supervisor needs an item that is not ordered regularly by the buyer. For instance, if a chef wants to try a convenience item, such as a frozen beef stew, and if this type of item is not regularly ordered, the chef must petition the buyer, and possibly other management people, for permission to use this product in production.

If an item is ordered regularly by the hospitality operation's buyer, then a purchase requisition is unnecessary. If the item is kept in a separate storage facility, the employee would need to complete a stock requisition and give it to the storeroom manager in exchange for the item. (See Chapter 14 for a discussion of stock requisitions and issuing procedures.) If there is no separate storage facility, such as in a typical restaurant unit, there may be no formal stock requisition system. However, usually an employee must obtain permission from a supervisor before he or she is allowed to take products, especially expensive products, from the shelves for use in production and service.

There are potential problems with the purchase requisition system. For one thing, it tends to dilute the selection and procurement function, in that too many people may be involved in deciding the types and qualities of products and services that should be purchased and used by the hospitality operation. Another problem is that the procedure tends to invite backdoor selling. Still another disadvantage is the time and effort required to implement and operate a purchase requisition system.

There are certain benefits associated with the purchase requisition. First, it can be a useful training device for those department heads who aspire to become full-time buyers. Second, it can relieve a buyer of responsibility for ordering mistakes; he or she can simply point out that so-and-so improperly completed the purchase requisition. Third, it can relieve the buyer of a good deal of paperwork. And, fourth, it is a way of controlling the use of the products and services in the various departments. This control can be easily accomplished by requiring additional information from the department head via the "other information" section shown in Figure 12.1. For example, the buyer may want to know how much product the department has on hand, how much was sold yesterday, how much waste was incurred during the past week, which supplier to contact, and so on. Requiring all this information does little to endear a buyer to the department heads, but this control mechanism is, nevertheless, one of the strongest aspects of the purchase requisition.

ORDERING PROCEDURES

Prior to placing an order, the buyer must determine the appropriate order size. The most common way to do this is to use the par stock approach, where the buyer or user-buyer must note what is on hand in the main storeroom areas and in the department areas (stock that is held by departments is normally referred to as the "in-process inventory"), subtract what is on hand from the par stock, and add in products needed for banquets or other special functions. The buyer then must prepare the appropriate purchase orders and send them to the suppliers or call them in, keeping one or more copies for his or her records. There may be interaction between department heads and buyers, but the full-time buyer normally relieves the department head of the major responsibilities associated with ordering.

In operations that have sophisticated computerized record-keeping and control systems, there is a greater tendency to use the Levinson approach to ordering (or some variation of it), which we discussed in Chapter 8.

These procedures are commonly used in both small operations and larger ones. The major differences between smaller and larger properties are the degree of formality and the presence or absence of a full-time buyer. In smaller properties, the user-buyer is more common.

The larger operations usually have at least one full-time buyer who is deeply involved in the purchasing function. In chain restaurants, for example, recall that there is usually a vice president of purchasing working in a home office, setting policies and procedures, while the unit manager handles only the paperwork for his or her particular store. Thus, the unit manager prepares the purchase orders based on the format and procedure designed by the corporate headquarters office. The unit manager then places the orders with designated suppliers, commissaries, or central distribution centers and sees to it that the products and services are properly received, stored, and issued to the respective departments.

The paperwork used in placing orders varies from one establishment to the next. But among those hospitality operations that do use various types of forms, the information in these forms is reasonably standard throughout the industry.

Once the various order sizes are determined, a buyer can place the order in one of several ways. The most common method is to give the order to the supplier's salesperson or distributor sales representative (DSR). You could phone in the order and leave it with a person who answers the telephone or leave it on voice mail. You also could phone in an order to the supplier's computer, or your computer could interact with the supplier's computer and, together, the computers can convey the necessary information.[1]

Another popular method is the use of the fax machine to convey ordering information. This is an inexpensive alternative to the computerized ordering process and, like the computer, allows the buyer to call in an order at any time. Unlike the computerized process, though, a buyer cannot verify his or her order with the fax procedure. If you talk to a computer, or to a person, you can obtain verification on the spot; that is, you know immediately whether the products you desire are available.

Management usually decides what ordering procedure to use, unless an approved supplier has a specific requirement. Small hospitality operations commonly follow one-stop shopping procedures and seek to minimize the ordering effort. Some larger organizations, though, especially the multiunit chain operations, normally contract to purchase large supplies of merchandise from several primary sources and/or intermediaries. Unit managers, therefore, may need to spend a bit more time when placing their orders if they must deal with several distributors.

THE PURCHASE ORDER

A purchase order can take many forms. At one extreme, an operation may not use one at all. At the other extreme, one may find a mind-boggling

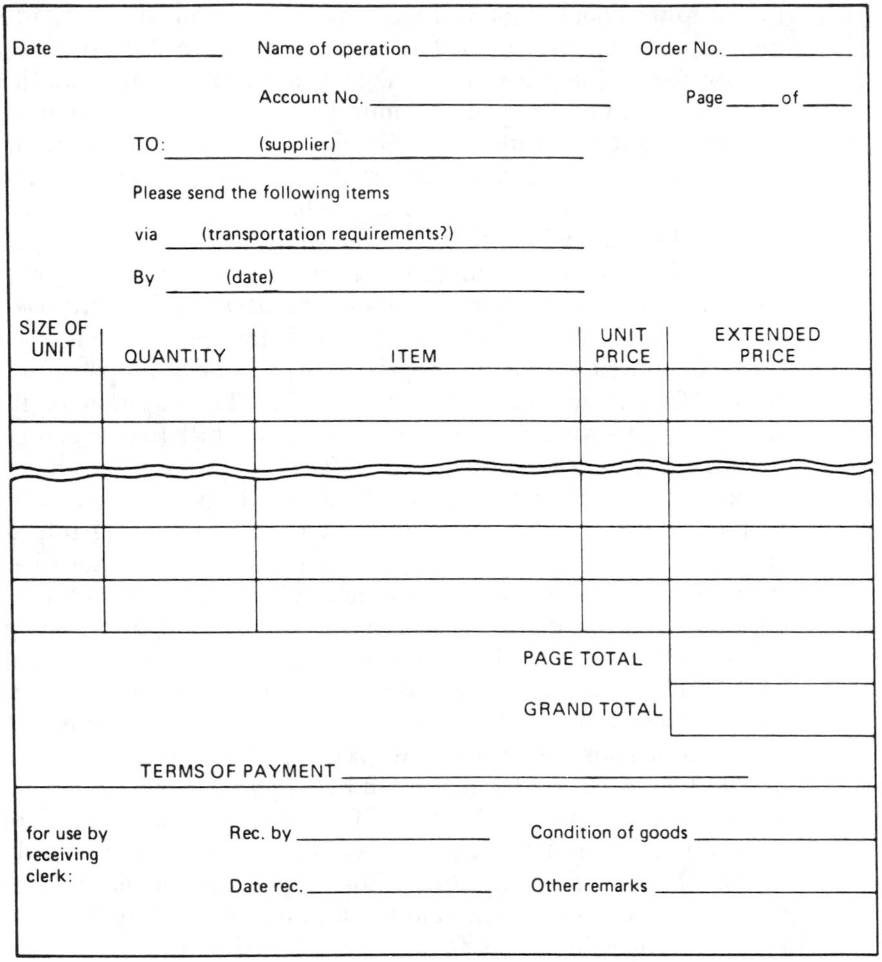

Date ______ Name of operation ______ Order No. ______

Account No. ______ Page ____ of ____

TO: (supplier) ______

Please send the following items

via (transportation requirements?) ______

By (date) ______

SIZE OF UNIT	QUANTITY	ITEM	UNIT PRICE	EXTENDED PRICE

PAGE TOTAL ______

GRAND TOTAL ______

TERMS OF PAYMENT ______

for use by receiving clerk: Rec. by ______ Condition of goods ______

Date rec. ______ Other remarks ______

FIGURE 12.2. Purchase order.

jumble of paper. Whatever shape it takes, a purchase order represents a request that a supplier deliver what you want, ideally at the time you want it. Figure 12.2 depicts a typical purchase order.

The typical purchase order resembles the purchase requisition. The date of the order is necessary to keep track of product usage patterns, as well as to suggest when to pay the bills. Some buyers may note the transportation requirement and packaging instructions. It is usual to indicate the desired receiving date, but, as a practical matter, you probably have only two choices: either take the supplier's predetermined delivery schedule or leave it. The quantity desired, the item type, the unit size (size of can, weight per unit, etc.), and the unit price and extended price (number of units times unit price)—all these entries are clear instructions to the supplier about what you want as well as your understanding of the pertinent AP price—either the current AP price or the AP price contracted for. Recording prices also makes it easier to keep track of the value of stock on hand and serves to remind a buyer that several thousands of dollars pass through his or her hands every year. The information to be used by the receiving clerk may or may not be included on the purchase order. But if a carbon copy of the purchase order is sent to the receiving clerk to be used when checking the delivery, it may be appropriate to include this information for the receiver. On the other hand, the receiving clerk may have a separate form he or she uses for this purpose.

Different operators have different opinions about the number of copies of the purchase order to prepare. It is possible to prepare and use eight copies. One copy goes to the supplier (1). The supplier might receive another copy, which he or she uses as the bill that accompanies the delivery of the various items or services (2). The supplier might receive yet a third copy, which is initialed and sent back to the buyer, indicating that he or she acknowledges the order and is entering into a binding contract (3). The buyer normally keeps a copy for his or her files to monitor usage patterns for future reference, as well as to keep track of which suppliers receive orders (4). The receiving clerk might get a copy so that he or she knows what deliveries to expect; he or she also might use this copy to check against the deliveries (5). The requisitioner, usually a department head, might like a copy for the department's files (6). The accountant or bookkeeper might want a copy to keep track of bills coming due and to compare this copy with the copy of the bill that accompanies the particular delivery (7). And, if there is a separate head office, the accounting office there may want a copy for its use and records (8).

Much more generally, only three copies are made: one for the supplier, one for the receiving clerk, and one for the buyer's records. (See Figure 12.3). A little less frequently, a fourth copy, which the supplier uses as the bill and sends back with the delivery, is prepared. The acknowledgement, requisitioner, accountant, and main office copies do not appear so frequently.

The decision on how many copies to use is, however, important. An essentially inescapable aspect of the buying procedure is the need to begin controlling the purchased products and services. In addition, control must be exercised from the moment an item is purchased until the time it is used in a productive capacity and the hospitality operation's customer pays for it. The objective is to control the cost and quality of all merchandise as it travels throughout the hospitality operation from one operating activity to another.

Purchased products normally follow the chain of operating activities noted in Figure 12.4. The control chain begins with buying; that is, it begins when the products and services legally become yours. To control these items, a great deal of record keeping may be essential. Keep in mind

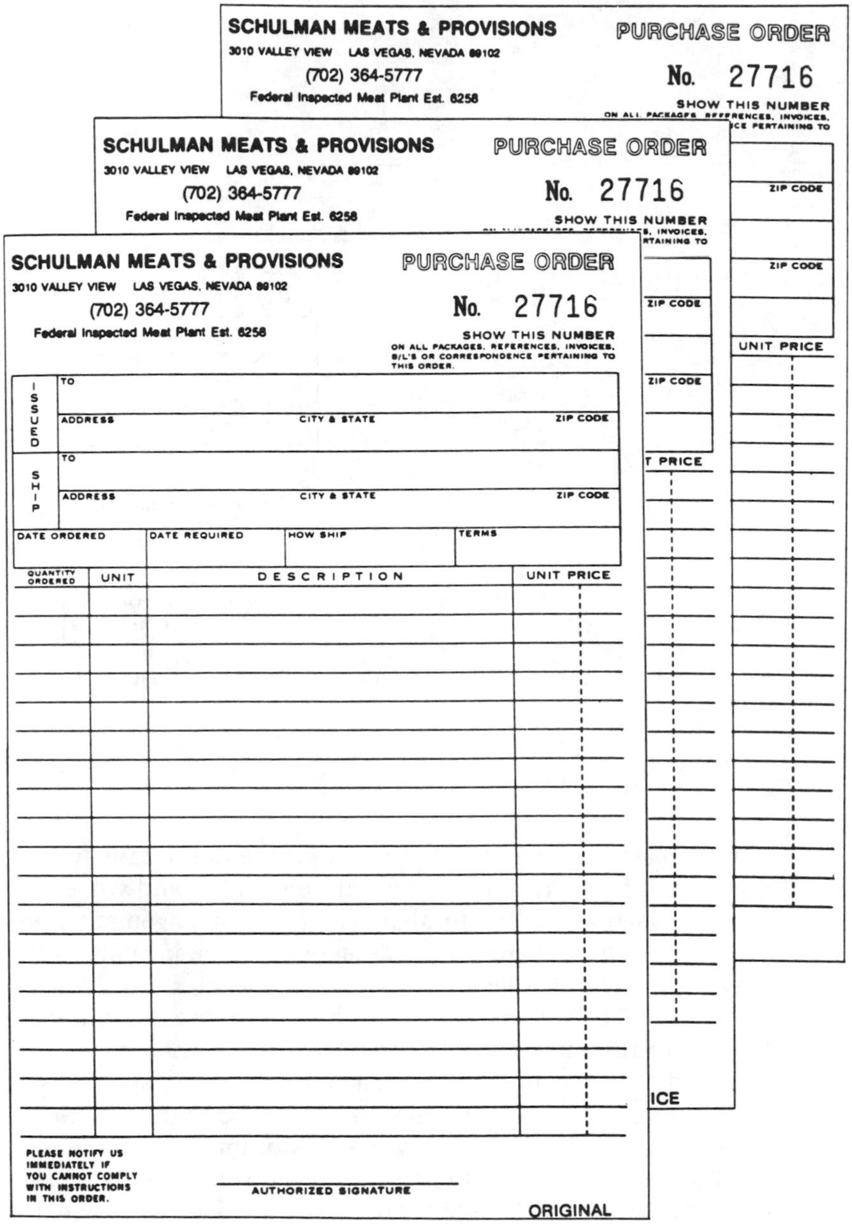

FIGURE 12.3. A three-part purchase order. (Courtesy Schulman Meats & Provisions.)

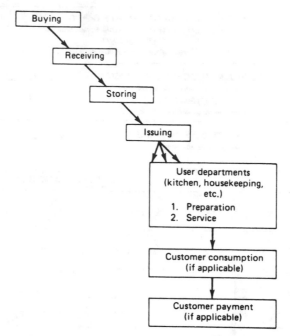

FIGURE 12.4. Typical operating activities in a hospitality operation.

that management may want to know where the item is within the chain, how much is at any one point within the chain, and whether the product is being used according to plan. The more management wants to know, the greater the potential record-keeping burden; hence, the greater the need for purchase order copies as well as the various other types of paperwork used. The sole reason for all this paper, or computerized records, is to control products and services. The greater the degree of control you want, the more complex a system you need. Consequently, at the very least, a purchase order record should exist so that deliveries can be compared with it. This is probably the minimum control you should have.

It is not our purpose to present a full discussion of control concepts; a good many excellent discussions of this subject already exist.[2] The best buying strategy in the world is worthless, however, if by the time the product is supposed to have reached the user department, some of it is spoiled, misplaced, stolen, or otherwise wasted. Larger firms can afford the paperwork burden or the computerized record-keeping procedures available in our industry. Fortunately, the smaller operator can minimize the paperwork and/or computerization as, generally speaking, he or she can substitute eyes and ears for these more formal controls.

CHANGE ORDER

At times it may be necessary to alter an original purchase order. Faced with this situation, a buyer normally calls the supplier and effects changes with little difficulty. But the original purchase order, if acknowledged by the supplier, is a legal contract, and the supplier could therefore sue the buyer's company if any unwarranted attempt is made to alter the contract. To be on the safe side, buyers should be sure to get it right the first time and not burden a busy supplier with change order requests.

EXPEDITING

Expediting is a buyer's effort to monitor the suppliers from day to day to ensure that products and services arrive at the right time and in acceptable condition. Expediting is not a common practice among most buyers unless there is a chance that a large order, required at a precise time, might be late in arriving. For instance, a banquet for 1,000 people tonight might depend on a delivery of 1,000 steaks this afternoon. In this situation, an extra phone call or a visit to the supplier is recommended.

Expediting is most often used, at least in the hospitality industry, when purchasing furniture, fixtures, and equipment (FFE). These items have a habit of showing up late, especially, for example, long after the planned grand opening of a new restaurant. In addition, purchased services may not always be performed at the exact time desired. In these situations, the buyer and probably even the senior management will certainly nag the suppliers.

STREAMLINING THE ORDERING PROCEDURE

Ordering is a time-consuming affair, and the paperwork and/or computerization can be costly. There are ways, though, of streamlining this process. Unfortunately, some of these ways force an operation to surrender a bit of control. We do not advocate dropping all paperwork and record keeping. We suppose that small hospitality operations could omit most, if not all, paperwork. But this drastic step would almost certainly encourage theft, waste, and overall employee carelessness. However, the point is well taken: if you can be in the hospitality operation at all times, you can use your eyes as a direct control system, instead of paperwork, an indirect control system.

Of course, larger organizations require some sort of an indirect control system. But even in these cases, there are some potential cost-cutting approaches.

BLANKET ORDER

One method of streamlining ordering procedures that we have already discussed deserves review here. Several items used by hospitality organizations have a low dollar value, and the time and effort involved in ordering them can sometimes be costly, especially if they are ordered frequently. Recall that a blanket order is one that includes a large amount of miscellaneous items—enough products to preclude, for example, weekly ordering. In other words, if a large par stock of miscellaneous items is set, the resultant order size usually saves ordering costs, but is not so valuable as to increase drastically the cost of storing them.

PURCHASE ORDER DRAFT SYSTEM

A purchase order with an attached check to cover the cost of the ordered items is called a *purchase order draft* and amounts to a prepaid order. This can, in some cases, save the buyer some money. For example, the supplier might be so glad to get the cash ahead of time that he or she grants a discount. Also, this system eliminates the need for a great deal of clerical work. Such a system, however, requires firm trust between supplier and buyer, especially in the sensitive area of returned merchandise and other adjustments that must be made—these always seem to be more difficult after you have paid your bill.

SUPPLIER'S FORMS

Some suppliers provide preprinted order forms. They may not be exactly what you would like, but they may be less expensive than your own. If your hospitality operation uses several expensive multipart forms, you could save a considerable amount of money by using a supplier's order blanks. Of course, the cost of all "free" things is recaptured somehow. The supplier, though, should be able to get these forms in huge quantities, thereby saving a little money, which, perhaps, is passed on to you.

STANDING ORDER

Recall that a standing order generally is a procedure whereby you set par stocks and the supplier's route salesperson, who perhaps comes to your place twice a week, leaves just enough product to bring you up to par. This procedure minimizes ordering costs and eliminates the need to prepare purchase orders.

COMPUTERIZATION

The cost of computerization has declined to the point where more and more hospitality operators can afford it. To some, it represents more of a cost than a benefit, but for others, the time saved, the increased accuracy, the reduction of paper-supplies cost and the labor saved have more than made up for the initial investment needed to adopt or add to a computerized record-keeping system. Furthermore, the reduction in lead time and the potential cost savings that are derived from linking your computer to the suppliers' computers eventually should result in minimum stockouts, minimum investment in inventories, and maximum customer satisfaction.

OTHER WAYS TO CUT COSTS

There are other potential cost-cutting procedures, but all are some variation of the five just noted. Essentially, management must decide what course to follow. For most hospitality organizations, control and a certain amount of costly paperwork go hand in hand. The most economical compromise between control and record keeping seems to be a four-part purchase order: one copy for whoever receives the deliveries, one for the buyer or user-buyer, one for the person who pays the bills, and one for the supplier. This is sufficient control at the initial stage of the cost control chain of operating activities. The receiver knows what to expect. The buyer and bill payer can compare the purchase order with the bill, or invoice, that accompanies the delivery. And the supplier has a copy for his or her records.

It now remains for us to explore how control is maintained throughout the receiving, storing, and issuing functions.

KEY WORDS AND CONCEPTS

Backdoor selling	Issuing
Blanket order	Levinson approach to ordering
Chain of operating activities	Methods of placing the order
Change order	Methods of streamlining the ordering procedure
Computerized ordering and record-keeping procedures	Open storeroom
DSR	Ordering procedures
Expediting	Par stock approach to ordering
Formal issues system	Purchase order
In-process inventory	Purchase order draft system

Purchase requisition	Storage
Receiving	Supplier's forms
Standing order	Variations of the Levinson approach to ordering
Stock requisition	

REFERENCES

1. Heidi Splete, "Paperless Processing," *F&B Business,* March/April 1995, p. 56. See also, Carol Casper, "DSRs and the New Technology," in *Hospitality in Review,* Michael M. Lefever, ed. (Dubuque, IA: Kendall/Hunt, 1996), p. 93.

2. See, for example, Paul R. Dittmer and Gerald G. Griffin, *Principles of Food, Beverage, and Labor Cost Controls,* 5th ed. (New York: VNR, 1994).

QUESTIONS AND PROBLEMS

1. What is the difference between a purchase requisition and a purchase order?

2. What information should you note on a purchase order? Why?

3. Call one or more suppliers in your area. Find out whether they provide their customers with order forms and, if so, how much, if anything, they charge for this supplier service.

4. Contact a buyer for a hospitality establishment and ask for an interview to discuss buying procedures. Some questions to ask follow:

    (a) How are order sizes determined?

    (b) Please explain the purchase order form in use.

    (c) List the information required by the purchase order and explain why that information is needed.

    (d) How many copies of a purchase order are prepared? Why?

    (e) What, do you suppose, is the cost of the ordering procedure?

    (f) How might that cost be reduced?

5. What is the purpose of expediting?

6. Describe the chain of operating activities for the typical hospitality operation.

7. What are some advantages and disadvantages of using a purchase requisitioning system?

8. What is the difference between a purchase requisition and a stock requisition?

9. How could a computerized ordering system save a buyer money and time?

10. Assume that a restaurant with an annual sales volume of $7,500,000 can computerize its ordering procedures at an initial investment in computers and other machinery of $14,500. What should you know about the current ordering procedures so that you can decide whether this initial cash outlay is economically feasible?

11. Briefly describe the purchase order draft system. Do you feel that this is an advantage or a disadvantage to the hospitality operator? Why? If possible, ask a food buyer to comment on your answer.

12. When would you be likely to prepare a change order document?

13. Specifically, how does a hospitality operator save money by using the standing order method of purchasing?

14. How might a buyer save money by using the blanket order procedure?

15. What are the advantages and disadvantages of the open storeroom form of issuing?

CHAPTER 13

Source: MGM Grand Hotel, Casino & Theme Park

TYPICAL RECEIVING PROCEDURES

THE PURPOSE OF THIS CHAPTER

This chapter discusses:

- The objectives of receiving
- The essentials for good receiving
- Invoice receiving techniques
- Other receiving techniques
- Good receiving practices
- Reducing receiving costs

INTRODUCTION

Someone once said, "Receiving is the proof of purchasing." It's at receiving that you determine what it is you actually got—not what you ordered but what you received. And there could be a lot of difference between the order you placed and the delivery you received. That's why receiving is so important to the proper control of purchasing.[1]

Receiving is the act of inspecting and either accepting or rejecting deliveries. It is an activity with many facets. In any particular hospitality operation, receiving can range anywhere from letting delivery truck drivers place your order in your storage facilities to having various receiving clerks waiting at the delivery entrance to check every single item to see that it meets the specifications set forth in the purchase order.

Although there are many varieties of practice, the variety of correct procedures, though subject to debate, is considerably less. For instance, many operations permit the bread route salesperson to come into the kitchen and storage areas, remove bread left over from the previous delivery, restock the operation, and leave the bill with someone. There are purists who could argue that this is poor practice on two counts: first, that the delivery agent could cheat on both returns and delivery and, moreover, that the delivery agent could steal other items while he or she was there.

Operators following this practice, however, would probably argue that the cost of a unit of product—a loaf of bread, for instance—is so small that the cost of a receiving clerk or management time to check physically returns and delivery is unwarranted. Moreover, the delivery agent in this case saves time. As to the theft issue, the delivery agent is no more likely to steal than are employees, as he or she is subject to the same controls they are. There are no hard-and-fast rules for a case like this. Each operator or company must weigh the advantages and disadvantages to arrive at a policy.

On the other hand, consider a situation in which a supplier supplies a very large portion of an operation's goods and offers, as a supplier service, to check the storeroom for all the items this supplier provides and determine what needs to be replenished. This might be done "to save the operator some time." Most people would argue, here, that not only the receiving but the purchasing function has been turned over to a supplier and allowing suppliers to do this is inappropriate.

THE OBJECTIVES OF RECEIVING

The objectives of receiving resemble the objectives of the purchasing function itself. Recall the main objectives: obtaining the correct amount and correct quality at the correct time with the correct supplier services for the correct EP cost. The main objectives of receiving are to check to see that the delivered order meets these criteria.

Another important objective of receiving is controlling these received products and services. Once the receiver accepts the items, whatever they are, they become the property of the hospitality organization. Thus, a cycle of control begins at this point.[2] For the most part, an owner-manager requires a certain amount of documentation during this receiving function in order to ascertain what was delivered and where the delivered items were sent within the organization. Keep in mind that this control activity can be simple or elaborate, depending on management's policy. At the risk of being redundant, though, we repeat that the best buying plan in the world is all for naught if someone or something goes awry during the cycle of control which causes a reduction in quality or an increase in costs.

In some large firms, additional control is exerted in the receiving function by placing receiving personnel under the direction of the accounting department. Thus, management minimizes the possibility of any fraudulent relationship between buyer and receiver. Small firms cannot afford this luxury.

On the other hand, some small units often use their very smallness—their lack of personnel—as an excuse to avoid receiving control. Although the small operator may not be able to afford the elaborate receiving department of a large hotel, he or she certainly can adapt the techniques used there to some degree. For instance, many small to medium-sized operations can designate a specific employee, perhaps a line cook, to act as receiver and the only person authorized to sign for received products. This person might warrant a modest salary increase for the added responsibility assumed. To make the task easier, he or she should be responsible for verifying counts and weights; quality evaluations can be left to some members of management.

ESSENTIALS FOR GOOD RECEIVING

To ensure that the receiving function is performed properly, several factors must be in place:

1. *Competent personnel* should be placed in charge of receiving activity. By "competent" we mean persons, full-time or part-time, who are reasonably intelligent, honest, interested in the job, and somewhat knowledgeable about the items to be received. Once this person is designated, it is necessary to train him or her to recognize acceptable and inferior products and services, though where the line cook-receiver combination is used, management usually needs to make quality checks and to supervise the receiving activity more closely.

    It is very important to provide the receiving agent with appropriate training. It can be a time-consuming, costly procedure, but one that is absolutely essential. The receiver must be able to recognize the various quality levels of merchandise that will be delivered to the hospitality operation. He or she must be able to handle the necessary paperwork and/or computerized record keeping adequately. And he or she must know what to do when something out of the ordinary arises. While the training costs may be considerable, they will be recovered many times over if the receiver is able to prevent merely one or two receiving mistakes per month.

2. *Proper receiving equipment* is a must. Since many deliveries must be weighed, accurate scales are perhaps the most important pieces of equipment in the receiving area. Temperature probes let receivers check the temperatures of refrigerated and frozen products. Rule measures are useful in checking trim, say, of fat on portion-cut steaks. Calculators are needed to verify costs. Cutting instruments, such as a produce knife, are handy when product sampling is part of the receiving process. Conveyor belts, hand trucks, and motorized forklift trucks can help transport the received items to the storage areas or, in some cases, directly to a production area. And, where applicable, receiving

agents must have the technology to read existing bar codes on product packaging in order to process shipments correctly. In short, the receiver should have enough of the proper equipment to do the most efficient, thorough job possible.

In a smaller operation, a reliable scale is a bare minimum. It is surprising how many small operations "save money" by purchasing an inexpensive scale that is often inaccurate. Then, because "it doesn't work anyway," they do not use it. This is the falsest of economies, since, even if you trust your supplier, unintentional errors can still occur.

3. *Proper receiving facilities* are necessary if you want a receiver to perform adequately. By "facilities" we refer to the entire receiving area. For example, the area should be well lit, big enough to work in properly, reasonably secure, and convenient for both delivery people and receivers.

In some older buildings, or in a hospitality operation built into another kind of building—for instance, an office building—you may not see exactly what we have described, but the closer management can move to this ideal, the better the receiver's job can be done.

4. *Appropriate receiving hours* should be scheduled. If possible, deliveries should be staggered so that a receiver is not rushed. Also, all delivery times should be relatively predictable so that a competent receiver is on hand and receiving is not left to whoever happens to be handy. Remember we mentioned that one of the biggest benefits of one-stop shopping is to minimize any difficulties and expense arising from too many deliveries. Perhaps now you can appreciate why many managers are unduly swayed by this potential benefit. It not only reduces the number of hours a receiver must work, but it also allows for a more secure back-door routine and, because of fewer transactions, minimal theft opportunities.

5. *A copy of all specifications* should be available to the receiver as a reference. This can help whenever ambiguity arises, as it sometimes will. When a supplier is out of your particular brand of soap, for example, he or she might deliver what is believed to be a comparable substitute. When this occurs, it becomes necessary for the deliverer and receiver to have a reference handy, unless the buyer insists on handling any substitutes personally, in which case the receiver will ask him or her to inspect the substitute. In many cases, though, drivers are not eager to wait for this decision; it is expensive for them to leave their trucks idle. As a result, decisions must often be made quickly, and a copy of the specifications can, therefore, be quite helpful.

6. *A copy of the purchase order* should be handy. Most hospitality operators feel that a receiver should know what is due to be delivered so that

he or she can be prepared. These purchase order copies are necessary to ensure this preparedness.

INVOICE RECEIVING

The most popular receiving technique is sometimes referred to as "invoice receiving." In this scheme of things, an invoice, or bill, accompanies the delivery. (See Figure 13.1) The invoice is an itemized statement of quantity, price, and other information that usually resembles the purchase order depicted in Chapter 12. The invoice may, in fact, be nothing more than a carbon copy of the original purchase order. The receiver uses the invoice to check against the quantity, quality, and prices of the items delivered. He or she may also compare the invoice with a copy of the original purchase order as a further check. The order is either accepted or rejected. If accepted, it is stored or delivered to a production department. Sometimes an invoice does not accompany the delivery. In these situations, the receiver normally fills out some type of form right there on the spot and treats this completed form as the invoice. The following paragraphs discuss the typical invoice receiving sequence in more detail.

DELIVERY ARRIVES

When arriving at a large operation, the delivery person must usually announce that he or she is there, sometimes by ringing a doorbell and asking the receiver for access. These procedures are, of course, less formal in a smaller operation, but they represent good security precautions.

The receiver opens the receiving area and, using the invoice and perhaps a copy of the original purchase order, checks first for the proper quantities. The receiver's first step, then, is to check each item's weight, count, or volume as quickly and efficiently as possible and compare these to the invoice and the original purchase order, or purchase record—the comparisons should match.

Next, where applicable, the receiver checks for the proper quality. Unfortunately, except when checking packers' brand names, this is the most difficult kind of check to make and, in some cases, is almost impossible to complete thoroughly. For example, it is difficult to determine the overall quality of lobster tails. Perhaps you can tell whether they have been refrozen. But we can never be sure if any particular tail is bad until it has been cooked—a bad lobster tail crumbles after it is cooked.

Some establishments expect the receiver to check only for quantities and to call someone else to inspect for quality. In these situations, the receiver calls the chef, housekeeper, maître d', or whatever department

Schulman

MEATS AND PROVISIONS
"OUR BEST TO YOU"
3010 VALLEY VIEW   LAS VEGAS, NEVADA 89102
364-5777
Federal Inspected Meat Plant Est. 6258

22058

IMPORTANT
MAIL REMITTANCE TO:
P.O. BOX 27707
LAS VEGAS, NV 89126

SOLD TO _____

ADDRESS _____

☐ C.O.D	☐ CASH	☐ CHARGE	P.O. NO.		DATE / /

QUAN	DESCRIPTION	WEIGHT	PRICE	AMOUNT
	PATTIES			
	PATTIES			
			TOTAL →	

All claims must be made immediately upon receipt of goods. If any discrepancy, please call (702) 364-5777 otherwise late claims will not be allowed.
Received by _____

Boxes _____   Pkgs. _____   Pcs. _____

All accounts are due the 10th of the month following date of purchase and after such date are past due accounts subject to an interest charge of 1¾% per month, which is **AN ANNUAL PERCENTAGE RATE OF 21%**. In the event legal proceedings are instituted to collect any sums due, the purchaser agrees to pay reasonable attorney's fee and costs.

I hereby certify that the above described product, which is offered for shipment in commerce has been U.S. inspected and passed by the U.S. Department of Agriculture, is so marked, and at this date is not adulterated or misbranded.

DUPLICATE

FIGURE 13.1. A typical invoice. (Courtesy Schulman Meats & Provisions.)

head is appropriate, to come check the quality of the items that will eventually be used in his or her department. The big drawback of this procedure is the potential time lag in waiting for the department head to arrive. Also, another problem is the possibility of the items, especially frozen ones, deteriorating while waiting for a quality check.

Large operations, particularly commissaries, usually engage quality control, or quality assurance, inspectors who check deliveries as well as the products prepared in the commissary. These inspectors do not normally work for the purchasing agent. In fact, they act as a check on the purchasing agent by keeping tabs on the quality that the purchasing agent procures.

If there is a quality discrepancy, the buyer should be notified as soon as possible, since it is his or her duty to deal with suppliers and salespersons. Moreover, the buyer may want occasionally to be on hand in order to gain a firsthand impression of the types of items that are actually delivered as compared with what was ordered.

After the quality inspection, and unless the entire order has been rejected, the receiver in some operations checks all prices and price extensions. (A price extension for a particular item on the invoice is the AP price per unit of that product times the number of units purchased.) The receiver might also check all sales taxes and other use taxes that are noted on the invoice to ensure accuracy. For instance, in most states, a hospitality operator must pay sales taxes for merchandise that he or she will not resell, such as cleaning soaps and chemicals, but not for products earmarked for resale to consumers, such as meats and produce.

Unfortunately, checking all these things can take too long, usually because a receiver must compare the prices on the invoice with those that were quoted by the supplier prior to ordering the merchandise. It is necessary to compare the invoice with the purchase order, or some other written purchase record, to check the prices in addition to noting whether the merchandise delivered actually was ordered in the first place. To save time, many operations have the accountant or bookkeeper check invoices later, before paying the bill.

It is probably a good idea to handle any AP price discrepancies as soon as possible. Waiting too long can produce confusion and distrust among business partners. Also, a supplier may be honest with you and would want to know immediately if, for instance, a delivery person has altered the prices on the invoice. The opposite can also be true; that is, the supplier, for example, may have quoted a much lower AP price over the phone than the one now written on the invoice. If so, you would want to notify the delivery person so that he or she will be a witness to this discrepancy.

REJECTION OF DELIVERY

In some cases, a receiver may note a discrepancy with prices and/or taxes noted on the invoice. Or he or she may have to reject all or part of an

NAME OF HOSPITALITY OPERATION

Request for Credit Memorandum

Date ____________ No. ____

To Supplier: Please credit our account because:

1. ______________________________

2. ______________________________

3. ______________________________

Return ordered by ______________________________

Invoice no. ______________

Date received ______________

____
Deliverer's signature

FIGURE 13.2. Request for Credit memorandum.

order. When this occurs, he or she might prepare a Request for Credit memorandum, which is a written statement attesting to the fact that the particular item or items did not meet quality, quantity, or price standards. Typical Request for Credit memoranda appear in Figures 13.2 and 13.3. The delivery person's signature shows that a representative of the supplier has agreed that the hospitality operation's account must be credited.

The objective of this memo is to ensure that your account is credited, that is, to ensure that all costs are accurate.

It also may be necessary to prepare a Request for Credit memo if you need to receive credit for product substitutions, as, for example, when a less expensive item than the one ordered is delivered. There also might be

"OUR BEST TO YOU"

Schulman Meats & Provisions

3010 Valley View
Las Vegas, Nevada 89102
876-1530 · Al Schulman · 876-1530
FEDERAL INSPECTED MEAT PLANT EST. 6258

2336
CREDIT REQUEST

DATE

P.O. NUMBER

INVOICE NUMBER	DATE	WEIGHT	ITEM	PRICE	CREDIT AMOUNT	REASON NUMBER

AUTHORIZATION

CODE KEY →

1 · REFUSED	5 · NOT ON TRUCK
2 · WRONG PRODUCT	6 · PRICE ERROR
3 · SPOILED	7 · INVOICE ERROR
4 · SHORT WEIGHT	8 · OTHER

FIGURE 13.3. A Request for Credit memorandum used by customers of Schulman Meats & Provisions. (Courtesy Schulman Meats & Provisions.)

arithmetic errors that require adjustment. And a back order may have been charged to you, in which case you might want to ensure that you do not pay for the items, thereby tying up your money unnecessarily, until you receive them.

When the accounting office pays the invoices, it will reduce the invoice amount by the amount indicated on the credit memorandum itself, which comes from the supplier after you send him or her a copy of the Request for Credit memo. Or the supplier will give you credit on your next delivery. Some operations eliminate credit memos if the supplier agrees to give his or her delivery people authority to reprice the invoice on the spot or if the supplier allows the delivery people to prepare a credit memorandum, or credit "slip," right then and there and give it to the receiver. However, if the shipment is delivered by a common carrier (i.e., an independent trucking firm), you must complete a Request for Credit memo as the driver will have no authority to alter the delivery.

When credit paperwork is prepared, the original copy is usually sent to the supplier. In addition, the receiver or buyer might call the supplier; this serves as a check on the delivery persons, who, for example, may have stolen the original item and substituted an inferior product. Another copy usually goes to whoever pays the bills. Some receivers might want to keep a copy as a reminder to be especially careful of any future deliveries from this particular supplier. In addition, the buyer may want a copy to keep up to date on the supplier's performance.

Whenever rejection is contemplated, the owner-manager must not act too hastily. It may not be a good idea to reject a product that deviates only slightly from your standard, for at least two reasons: (1) Suppliers may not like to do business with a customer who focuses on small detail, particularly one who sends back a reasonable substitute the supplier sent because the ordered item was unavailable, and (2) in many cases, a rejection leaves you short. It might be good business occasionally to accept some slight deviation, since the potential ill will generated among suppliers and your customers by hasty rejections may be detrimental.

RETURNING MERCHANDISE

The receiver may have something from a previous delivery that the delivery person must return to his or her company's warehouse. For example, there might have been an unintentional overbuy of canned pears last week that the buyer has arranged to send back. Usually in this situation, the supplier has given the delivery person a "Pick-Up" memorandum (Figure 13.4), authorizing him or her to take back the merchandise.

Whenever a belated return must be arranged, the delivery person will leave a copy of the Pick-Up memo with the receiver. This copy serves as a receipt for the returned goods. The supplier will issue a credit memo later on, once he or she inspects the returned merchandise and is satisfied that the return is justified.

ACCEPTANCE OF DELIVERY

When an order has been accepted, the receiver normally initials some paperwork attesting to the fact that everything is correct. The delivery person usually produces a delivery sheet or a copy of the invoice for the receiver to sign.

The receiver accepts most deliveries, unless the items are definitely substandard. Even if only part of a shipment is acceptable, the normal practice is to keep what is good and return the rest along with a Request

Schulman
MEATS AND PROVISIONS

"OUR BEST TO YOU"

3010 VALLEY VIEW BOULEVARD
LAS VEGAS, NEVADA 89102
(702) 364-5777

FEDERAL INSPECTED ESTABLISHMENT NO. 6258

CUSTOMER NAME

_____   **PICK-UP MEMO**

_____

_____

DATE		DRIVER		CUST NO			PICK UP MEMO NO	
QTY	GRADE	PROD CODE		DESCRIPTION			WEIGHT	PRICE

THIS IS NOT AN INVOICE OR CREDIT MEMO. IT IS A RECEIPT FOR MERCHANDISE RETURNED TO OUR PLANT FOR INSPECTION. YOU WILL BE ADVISED OF OUR FINDINGS AND DECISION AT THE COMPLETION OF THE INSPECTION.

DISPOSITION	DATE

FIGURE 13.4. A typical Pick-Up memorandum. (Courtesy Schulman Meats & Provisions.)

1. Date received _____
2. Received by _____
3. Prices checked by _____
4. Extensions checked by _____
5. Buyer's approval _____
6. Payment approval _____

FIGURE 13.5. Invoice stamp information.

for Credit memo. For the most part, an owner-manager is reluctant to send back everything because the resultant shortages can, as we said, lead to dissatisfied customers.

Upon acceptance of the deliveries, the receiver normally places the items in the proper storage location or, in some cases, delivers them to a production department.

To ensure that all pertinent checks have been made, the receiver normally applies an ink stamp with a predetermined format to the invoice. Figure 13.5 shows a typical invoice stamp format stamped on incoming invoices.

This format notes all checks that must be performed and provides a space for those responsible to affix their initials. The receiver normally initials the first three entries; the buyer, number 5; the accountant or bookkeeper, number 4; and the owner-manager, number 6.

After processing the invoice, the receiver may record the delivery on a "receiving sheet" or "receiving log." This sheet is nothing more than a running account of deliveries. Figure 13.6 depicts a typical receiving sheet.

To a certain extent, the receiving sheet is a redundant exercise: it contains a good deal of information already on the invoice or affixed to the invoice via one or more invoice stamps. Large hospitality operations traditionally use the sheet, but the whole process may be avoided without any significant loss of control by merely photocopying invoices for the buyer's and receiver's files.

One reason many operators like the receiving sheet is that it forces the receiver to record information, however redundant. Thus, mistakes previously overlooked sometimes come to light. Also, a copy of the receiving sheet usually stays in the receiver's files, which makes it handy for the receiver if he or she needs to consider a certain deliverer's past performance. Furthermore, the sheet is useful to cost accountants who prepare daily food, beverage, and nonfood cost reports. Since the receiving sheet notes the deliveries on one page, it is convenient. In addition, the "Other

DATE	TIME DELIVERED	QUANTITY	INVOICE NO.	PURVEYOR	DESCRIPTION OF ITEM (S)	UNIT PRICE	EXTENSION	DIRECT*			STORES†			OTHER INFORMATION ?
								FOOD	BEVERAGE	NONFOOD	FOOD	BEVERAGE	NONFOOD	

* The receiver notes in this column the amount of food, beverage, and non – food items that go directly to the production department, bypassing the main storage area. In other words, these items go directly into the in-process inventory.

† The receiver notes in this column the amount of food, beverage, and non – food items that go into main storage.

FIGURE 13.6. Receiving sheet.

Information" column can contain several comments not easily recorded on the incoming invoices. Such things as the delivery person's attitude and the cleanliness of the delivery truck may be important to the buyer in future negotiations with the particular supplier.

Another reason for some managements' continuing desire for the receiving sheet is that it can be treated as the receiver's daily report of activities. This type of report is particularly attractive to the accountant in a large hotel who is responsible for the receiver's actions.

On balance, however, it is far more economical to record all such information on the incoming invoices, or invoice copies, or attach a small post-in note to these invoices if space is insufficient, and then make a copy of this completed invoice for the receiver's files.

After making the necessary entries to the records, the receiver normally sends the incoming invoices, any credit slips, and a copy of the receiving sheet to the accountant or bookkeeper. If a bill of lading comes with the delivered items—a "bill of lading" is a piece of paper that represents title to the goods—he or she sends this along also.

If the storage areas are supervised and controlled by someone other than the receiver, this person may want a copy of the receiving sheet to compare what is on the sheet with what has been put in storage. This is yet another type of control serving as a check on the receiver, although the buyer's copy and the accountant's copy can serve as more than sufficient control.

At this point, the receiver normally has stored or delivered the items to production departments, completed the necessary paperwork, and sent the appropriate paperwork to the right office(s) along with any bills of lading that may have arrived at the receiving dock that day. He or she also keeps a copy of the receiving sheet.

ADDITIONAL RECEIVING DUTIES

As a general rule, the receiving procedure is now complete. But the receiver may have other, less routine duties to perform. He or she may have to do the following.

Date the Delivered Items

If it is too costly to do this dating, the usual compromise is to date the perishable items—the dating usually is done with colored tags or with an ink stamp. This can facilitate proper "stock rotation"—use of the older products first.

Price All Delivered Items

This pricing may also be too costly, but it can have such benefits as costing of inventories for accounting purposes and providing an easy cost reference. Some operators like to price the items for the psychological effect it supposedly provides. An item that has been priced is no longer just a piece of merchandise to employees, but an article of value to be treated accordingly.

Many properties use the "Dot System" to date and price inventories. These are color-coded, stick-on dots (usually a different color for each day) that have sufficient space to pencil in dates, times, and prices. Incidentally, this procedure is also used to identify and code prepreparedproducts produced by the kitchen staff; for instance, grated cheese to be used later on can be coded so that all cooks use the older merchandise first.

Create Bar Codes

In some large hospitality operations, the receiving agent may need to create bar codes and apply them to incoming products that do not have them on their package labels. This is usually done to enhance the inventory management and control process, in that it makes it very easy to track inventories and their AP prices throughout the operation. While it can be very expensive to invest in the technology needed to adopt this procedure, in the long run it could prove very cost-effective.

Apply "Meat Tags"

A meat tag contains information similar to the information on an invoice stamp. The major difference between the two is that the typical meat tag contains two duplicate parts (as shown in Figure 13.7). During the receiving procedure, one part of the tag is put on an item and the other part goes to the accountant or bookkeeper for control purposes. When an item moves from the storage area to production, the part on the item is removed and sent to the accountant or bookkeeper, who matches it with the other part and removes it from the inventory file. Specifically, meat tags are used as a check on the overall use of an item. For instance, comparisons are made between meat tags and stock requisitions (requests from a production department for items that are held in storage). Also, they are sometimes compared with the service department's record of guest services. For example, with steak items, the meat tags can be compared with the sales of steaks to customers, thus producing a check on waiters and waitresses. If everything goes right, all these comparisons will reveal that what was used from storage actually went to the paying customer with no loss of product along the way. The units recorded on the meat tags should correspond exactly to the amounts used in production and the amounts sold to customers.

The meat tag control is, however, cumbersome, and, like the receiving sheet, it tends to be redundant as well. If used, they tend to be used for

```
                                                    No. 100

        Date rec'd _____

        Item _____

        Grade _____

        Wt. _____

        Purveyor _____

        Date issued _____

        Date used _____

    — — — — — — — — — — — — — — — — —
                                                    No. 100

        Date rec'd _____

        Item _____

        Grade _____

        Wt. _____

        Purveyor _____

        Date issued _____

        Date used _____
```

FIGURE 13.7. Meat tag.

only high-cost products. Nevertheless, both meat tags and receiving sheets are used in operations that desire close control over the stock.

Housekeeping

Management usually requires the receiver to maintain a clean and efficient workplace. Also, he or she usually ensures that all equipment and facilities are kept in good working order.

Update AP Prices

Hospitality operations that use a computerized management information system normally maintain updated AP prices for all merchandise they buy. They also might maintain updated portion factors, portion dividers, and EP costs for all ingredients they currently serve as well as all ingredients they might serve in the future. Furthermore, computerized hospitality operations also tend to maintain costed recipes in a recipe file for those menu items that are currently being offered to customers, as well as those that may be offered at a future date.

A computerized system includes the necessary formulas and data bases to make the necessary calculations quickly. Since AP prices tend to vary from day to day in our industry, someone must continually "load the computer" with the new, current AP prices. In some operations, this task has fallen on the receiving agent. He or she, after performing the other required receiving duties, must follow the procedures needed to enter the new AP prices and remove the old, outdated AP prices. This task might just as easily be done by someone in the accounting department, but a receiving agent may be deemed the best person to do this work, especially if the task involves scanning bar codes of all incoming products.

Backhaul Recyclables

Some operations save their recyclables, such as corrugated cardboard, glass bottles, and metal cans, and hold them until a common carrier hired by a primary source to deliver a product shipment uses the emptied truck to "backhaul" the recyclables on the return trip. In this case, the receiving agent usually needs to help the driver load the truck and see to it that the driver has all the necessary paperwork and authorizations.

OTHER RECEIVING METHODS

We occasionally find other receiving procedures in use. For the most part, though, they are variations of invoice receiving. Some of these variations are described in the following paragraphs.

STANDING ORDER RECEIVING

This receiving procedure may not differ at all from invoice receiving. But there is a tendency to "relax" a bit when checking items received on a standing order basis. Also, delivery tickets instead of priced invoices may accompany the delivery, since the operation may make a regular, periodic payment to the supplier in exchange for the same amounts delivered at regular intervals.

It is really best to use invoice receiving to receive standing orders. Otherwise, delivery people, receivers, and bill payers can grow careless. In addition, deliveries may begin to "shrink" in both quantity and quality if strict receiving principles are not maintained.

BLIND RECEIVING

The only difference between blind receiving and invoice receiving is that the invoice accompanying the delivery contains no more than the names of the items delivered and no information about quantity and price. A duplicate invoice, which contains all necessary information, is usually sent to the accountant or bookkeeper one day before delivery.

Another form of blind receiving involves the need for the receiver to complete a "Goods Received Without Invoice" slip whenever a shipment comes in that does not have an invoice or delivery slip. For instance, a mailed delivery or shipment delivered by a messenger service may not have accompanying paperwork. If so, the receiver must check with management and, if the shipment is legitimate, inspect the products and complete the in-house invoice slip.

The whole idea behind blind receiving is to increase the margin of control. The receiver is forced to weigh and count everything and then record this information. Such a procedure effectively prohibits the receiver from purloining part of the delivery and altering the invoice. Also, the procedure precludes any fraudulent relationship between the receiver and the delivery person.

There seems to be a good deal of disagreement over the benefits of blind receiving. The general feeling in the industry is that the receiving agent should have some idea of what to expect, otherwise he or she might receive the wrong product, too much product, too little product, and so forth. Such unintentional errors can destroy an operation's production planning.

Blind receiving is a time-consuming, costly method of receiving and processing deliveries. Technology can be employed to speed up the process, but it normally is too expensive to be used for only a short period each day or in a small operation. Furthermore, drivers do not like to wait for a receiver to record every last detail of information.

Although we can appreciate the control benefits of blind receiving, we consider it an archaic method, similar to receiving sheets and meat tags. We know of few establishments that still use it. It is too expensive; besides, a receiver under suspicion can be checked with the accountant's copy of the original purchase order. The invoice should look just like the original purchase order, or else you had better look for a good explanation or a new receiver.

ODD-HOURS RECEIVING

The major difference with this receiving method is that the usual receiver is not on hand to receive the delivery. In most cases, an assistant manager is then entrusted with this duty. Although the invoice method may be applied during odd hours, an inadequate receiving job may result. The stand-in receiver usually has other pressing duties, and, as a result, the tendency is to rush the receiving process. The owner-manager normally recognizes this danger and tries to arrange for deliveries when the regular receiver is on duty. But some deliveries must be made at odd hours. As a result, it may be a good idea to print the regular receiving procedure on a poster that is hung in the receiving area to aid the stand-in receiver.

DROP-SHIPMENT RECEIVING

When a buyer purchases products from a primary source, usually he or she hires a common carrier to "drop ship" the merchandise to the hospitality operation. Recall that the common carrier is typically an independent trucker hired to provide only the transportation function.

When a common carrier delivers a shipment, the receiving procedure used is very similar to the standard invoice receiving process. The major difference, though, is the fact that the driver is not involved with any disputes that may arise between the buyer and the primary source, unless he or she is directly responsible for the problem. For instance, if the driver damages the goods along the way, the buyer must deal with driver or the driver's employer. But, as is more often the case, if the products do not meet the buyer's specifications, the shipment usually must be taken from the driver and held until the problems are rectified. The driver usually is not in a position to take back returned merchandise.

When disagreements arise between the buyer and the supplier in this case, it is a bit more difficult to resolve them. For instance, the buyer may have to arrange for another common carrier to return the shipment. Or he or she may have to wait for the supplier's representative to come out and check the items personally before a settlement can be reached. In addition, if the shipment is insured by an independent insurance company, its representative may need to inspect the claim and monitor the negotiations. When buying directly from primary sources, seemingly little problems can add a great deal of stress to the operation before they are cured.

MAILED DELIVERIES

When orders are delivered by mail, air freight, or United Parcel Service (UPS), the invoices that come with them are normally referred to as packing slips. These slips are treated like any other invoice. The major difference occurs when the order does not match the packing slip's description. In this instance, a Request for Credit memo, or some similar record, must be completed, but usually the management, not the receiver, does this. The receiver notes any discrepancy and then turns the shipment over to his or her supervisor.

COD DELIVERIES

Under this system, the receiver has the added duty of paying the delivery agent or, more commonly, sending the delivery agent to the office for the payment check. It is also possible that the receiver accompanies the delivery agent to the office so that he or she can attest to the adequacy of the delivered items.

GOOD RECEIVING PRACTICES

There are a number of sound procedures receivers should follow. Most of them fall loosely under the security category.

1. Beware of excess ice, watered-down products, wrapping paper, and packaging that can add dead weight to the delivered items. The receiver must subtract the amount of this dead weight (otherwise referred to as the "tare" weight) from the gross weight in order to compute the net weight of the merchandise.

2. Always check the quality under the top layer. Make sure that all succeeding layers are equal to the facing layer.

3. The packages should always be examined for leakage or other forms of water damage. This could indicate that the package contents are unusable. If the packages, especially cans, are swollen, the contents are probably spoiled and the shipment should be rejected.

4. If a package label carries an expiration date, the receiver should ensure that it is within acceptable limits. He or she should also ensure that dating codes are correct.

5. Do not weigh everything together. For example, separate hamburger from steak, and weigh each product by itself. If you weigh them together, you might begin to buy hamburger at a steak price.

6. Be wary of delivery persons eager to help you carry the delivered items to your storage areas. Trust is not the issue. The big problems with letting people on your premises are the distraction they cause among employees and the possibility that liability insurance premiums will increase.

7. Watch for incomplete shipments; watch for the delivery person who asks you to sign for a complete order after telling you that the rest of your order will arrive later. Later may never come.

8. Spot-check portioned products for portion weights. For instance, if you buy portioned sausage patties by the pound and sell them by the piece, a 2-ounce sausage patty that is consistently ¼ ounce overweight will inflate your food cost. But you will not reflect this in your sales, since your menu price will still reflect a 2-ounce portion. It is equally troubling if the sausage patties are underweight and you are purchasing them by the piece; a short weight of as little as ⅛ ounce can cost quite a bit of money in the long run.

9. Be careful of those closed shipping containers with preprinted dates, weights, counts, or quality standards. Someone may have repacked these cartons with inferior merchandise. It might be wise to weigh flour sacks, rice sacks, potato sacks, and the like, once in a while. Or even open a box of paper napkins to count them.

10. Be careful that you do not receive merchandise that has been refrozen. Also be on the lookout for supposedly fresh merchandise that actually is "slacked out" (i.e., has been frozen, thawed, and made to appear as if it is fresh).

11. At times, you may confuse brand names and/or packers' brand names. If you are in a hurry, this is easy to do.

12. When receiving some fresh merchandise, such as meats, fish and poultry, normally you give the suppliers a "shrink" allowance. For instance, it is possible that 25 pounds of fresh lobster today will be 24 pounds tomorrow because of dehydration. The product specification normally indicates the minimum weight per case that you will accept, but in some circumstances, you may not be able to judge the delivery as closely as you would like. When you weigh the shipment, it might be within your accepted tolerance; however, it is not easy to determine acceptability quickly when you are busy weighing several packages of various sizes. Delivery drivers know this, and, as such, some of them may be tempted to test your receiving skills to see how much shrink you are willing to accept.

13. In general, you are concerned about any product that you receive that does not live up to your specifications. In the final analysis, it is absolutely essential to prepare adequate specifications because this is the only way you can ensure that you have the appropriate standard upon which to judge incoming merchandise.

We do not intend to cast aspersions on suppliers or delivery agents. A good rule in business is to maintain a cautious optimism in receiving, but remember that it is possible to get "stung" in at least four ways: (1) the unintentional error; (2) the dishonest supplier with an honest delivery agent; (3) the honest supplier with a dishonest delivery agent; and (4) a dishonest supplier with a dishonest delivery agent. Keep in mind that once the receiver signs for the delivery, the items are yours. So verify that you receive the right quantity, quality, and AP price.

REDUCING RECEIVING COSTS

There are few ways to reduce receiving costs without losing a proportionate amount of control. Some common cost-saving methods that have been used are described next.

1. *Field inspectors* are sometimes used by larger firms, which saves some time for the receiver, since he or she need not check for quality and quantity as the inspector often seals the packages to be delivered. The overall cost, though, may not lessen; field inspectors, like receivers, must be paid.

2. *Computerized receiving* may save considerable time, though the initial cost of the technology needed to do this work may be prohibitive. Furthermore, our industry does not seem to have the degree of technical sophistication necessary to render this type of receiving commonplace.

3. *Night and early-morning deliveries* are often the rule in the downtown sections of many large cities to avoid daytime traffic congestion. With fewer distractions, delivery agents can make more deliveries, and part of the lower transportation cost per delivery may be passed on to you. A variation of this procedure is the "night drop," in which a delivery agent uses a key to get in, proceeds to place the items inside the door, locks up, and leaves. Opinion varies among operators regarding the degree of trust required for this practice.

4. *One-stop shopping* is perhaps the most common method of reducing receiving costs. Although some people are not enthusiastic about this buying method, all agree that it can reduce receiving costs.

In trying to reduce receiving costs, you must be careful that you do not just shift the costs around. For instance, lower receiving costs accompany one-stop shopping, but the saving from reducing the number of potential suppliers may be wiped out by higher AP prices from your single supplier.

Certain inescapable costs must be incurred if you expect to meet the objectives of the purchasing and receiving functions. It is absolutely essential not to negate the effective job the buyer may have done. In the final analysis, the receiving function affords few cost-cutting possibilities unless you are willing to give up a certain amount of control.

KEY WORDS AND CONCEPTS

Accepting a delivery

AP price

Backhaul

Bar codes

Bill of lading

Blind receiving

Checking the quantity, quality, AP price, sales and other use taxes

COD deliveries

Common carrier

Computerized receiving

Computerized record keeping

Credit memo

Credit slip

Cycle of control

Date and price delivered items

Delivery ticket

Dot system

Drop shipment

Early-morning deliveries

EP cost

Equal-to-facing layer

Essentials for good receiving

Expiration date

Field inspectors

Good receiving practices that should be followed

Goods Received Without Invoice slip

Gross weight

Handling an invoice discrepancy

Incomplete shipments

Invoice

Invoice receiving

Invoice stamp

Loading the computer with current AP prices

Mailed deliveries

Meat tags

Net weight

Night deliveries

Night drop

Odd-hours receiving

One-stop shopping

Packing slips

Pick-Up memo

Price extensions

Purchase order

Quality assurance

Quality control

Receiving objectives

Receiving sheet

Rejecting a delivery

Request for Credit memo

Returning merchandise

Route salesperson

Sales taxes

Shrink allowance

Slacked out

Specifications

Stock requisition

Standing order receiving

Stock rotation

Tare weight

Use taxes

Water damage

Ways to reduce receiving costs

REFERENCES

1. Patt Patterson, "Checks and Balances Prevent Disputes over Orders," *Nation's Restaurant News,* November 22, 1993, p. 82.
2. Robert B. Lane, "Food and Beverage Management," in *VNR's Encyclopedia of Hospitality and Tourism,* Mahmood Khan, ed. (New York: VNR, 1993), p. 39.

QUESTIONS AND PROBLEMS

1. You hear that your competitors are using a control device called "blind receiving." What is blind receiving? Under what conditions would you use this procedure?

2. Explain how one-stop shopping can reduce your overall receiving costs.

3. If possible, visit a local supplier and arrange to ride with a delivery person as he or she makes the rounds. Compare and contrast the receiving procedures you see in each hospitality operation. In addition, take the time to examine how the supplier processes his or her copy of the invoice.

4. If possible, arrange to spend one day in the receiving area of a hotel or restaurant. Evaluate the receiving procedures used by the receiver. In addition, try to follow the paperwork, from invoice processing, receiving sheet completion, and so on, up to the end of the receiver's paperwork duties. If management allows, pick out one invoice and stay with it as it travels from the receiving area to the accounting department. While in the accounting department, see whether you can determine how and when this particular invoice will be paid.

5. At ten o'clock in the morning on September 27, the following items were delivered by the A & H Foods Company:

Unit	Quantity	Description of item	Unit Price	Extension
Pound	80	T-bone steaks	$ 6.85	$ 548.00
Pound	18	Sliced bacon	2.80	50.40
Pound	20	Flank steak	4.25	85.00
Case	2	Floor wax, gallon cans	28.00	56.00
Case	2	Boston lettuce	16.50	33.00
Case	1	Canned green beans, no. 10 cans	17.50	17.50
Total				$ 789.90

Upon inspection, you determine that the sliced bacon is inferior and that you must return it to the supplier.

(a) Using Figure 13.2 as a guide, prepare a Request for Credit memo for the bacon.

(b) Using Figure 13.5 as a guide, complete the information on the invoice stamp that is commonly completed by the receiver.

(c) Using Figure 13.6 as a guide, transfer the acceptable items to the receiving sheet. *Note:* The flank steak goes directly into the in-process inventory.

6. What type of information would you like to have in the "Other Information" column of the receiving sheet? Why?

7. It is felt by many operators that the receiving sheet is useful in calculating daily food, beverage, and nonfood costs. How do you think the receiving sheet is helpful in this matter?

8. What should a receiving agent do if a question arises regarding the quality of merchandise received?

9. What should a receiving agent do if a delivery is made without an accompanying invoice?

10. A receiving agent will prepare a Request for Credit memo when

   (a) _____

   (b) _____

   (c) _____

11. List some objectives of the receiving function.

12. List the primary essentials that are needed for proper receiving.

13. What is the primary difference between invoice receiving and blind receiving?

14. Briefly describe the computation of price extensions.

15. Describe one purpose of using an invoice stamp.

16. What is the primary reason for using meat tags?

17. Briefly describe the concept of stock rotation.

18. What is a Bill of Lading?

19. What does it mean when we say that a food item has been "slacked out"?

20. Why should you separate meat items before weighing them?

21. What is the primary purpose of the Pick-Up memo?

22. Assume you must pay sales tax for all nonfood items you purchase. If the sales tax rate if 6 percent, recalculate the invoice total for Question 5.

23. What is the significance of the expiration date placed on the package label of some food products?

24. Assume you are checking in a shipment of canned goods. You notice some dried water spots on the bottom of one of the cases. You open the case and notice nothing leaking from the cans. Should you accept the shipment? Why?

25. What are the advantages and disadvantages of the standing order receiving procedure?

CHAPTER 14

TYPICAL STORAGE MANAGEMENT PROCEDURES

THE PURPOSE OF THIS CHAPTER

This chapter discusses:

- The objectives of storage
- The essentials needed to achieve the storage objectives
- Managing the storage facilities
- Suggested storage management techniques for the typical hospitality operator

INTRODUCTION

Storage is an activity typically performed in conjunction with receiving. As soon as the receiver inspects incoming merchandise, he or she places it in the proper storage facility. In some instances, the receiver may send some items directly to a production department. For example, prime ribs scheduled for tonight's banquet should go directly to the kitchen. (Items sent directly to the production departments are usually referred to as "direct purchases" or "directs" where an internal issues system is used.)

Often, the same person who receives also stores. Larger operations may divide this responsibility by assigning, for example, the receiving function to a receiving supervisor and the storage function to a storeroom manager. But the typical procedure is for the receiver and storeroom manager to be the same person. In small operations, the user-buyer or the chef might receive and store products and even manage the storage facilities. But good control implies some separation of responsibilities.

Regardless of the size of the hospitality operation, some attributes of good storage procedures prevail throughout the industry.

THE OBJECTIVES OF STORAGE

The basic goal of storage management is to prevent loss of merchandise due to (1) theft, (2) pilferage, and (3) spoilage.

Theft is premeditated burglary. It occurs when someone drives a truck up to the back door and steals all the expensive foods, beverages, and equipment. Generally, one does not design storage facilities to prevent this. One would need a citadel. Storage security is normally designed to discourage employee dishonesty by keeping honest employees honest. In some parts of the country, and the world, theft is common. Thus, a hospitality operator must see to it that the storage facilities are designed so as to make theft more difficult, generally by some combination of clear visibility of general access storage and very tight security on locked, limited-access storage located elsewhere. Locking storage areas when not in use and minimizing the number of persons who have access to the keys would appear to be good practices.

Pilferage is a serious problem in our industry, a problem that centers on the employee who sneaks off with a bottle of mustard or a couple of ashtrays. Eating on the job is another form of pilferage, unless the owner-manager allows it. Shoplifting also falls in this category.

Pilferage is sometimes referred to as "inventory shrinkage" or "skimming." The estimated dollar losses resulting from pilferage vary considerably, but industry experts feel that approximately 2 to 4 percent of every sales dollar is lost to employee and customer dishonesty. There are several potential ways of controlling pilferage, some of which we discuss in the next chapter. Unfortunately, in some cases the cure may be more expensive than the disease.

Spoilage can be controlled a little more easily than either theft or pilferage. Generally, spoilage can be minimized by adhering to rigid sanitation practices, rotating the stock so that older items are used first, and providing the proper environmental conditions for each item in storage. Rigid sanitation is, in fact, a must in all storage facilities. This involves two quite different kinds of steps. First, products that might induce spoilage in others through migration of odors or chemicals must be separated properly. To give two examples, fresh fish is not stored with butter, and cleaning agents are segregated from food products in storage.

A second and more obvious sanitation activity involves keeping the storage facility clean by, for instance, mopping it daily.

Any sanitation slipup not only hastens spoilage but also increases the risk of customer or employee sickness. Some states and local municipalities have legislation that requires hospitality management personnel to pass successfully some sort of a sanitation test or satisfactorily complete an approved sanitation course. There is also discussion suggesting that eventually all hospitality employees will have to pass some type of sanitation certification exam.

The proper environmental conditions for storage seem easy enough to achieve. But the expense of providing for all the various temperature and humidity requirements for an entire spectrum of food products can be burdensome for small restaurants. Nonfood storage is not so large a problem, but, even here, a good deal of valuable space may be required.

Freezers, separate produce, dairy, and meat refrigerators, and separate dry storage areas for groceries, beverages, and cleaning supplies can all add up to a large investment, so large that smaller operations often try to make do with outdated facilities, which can get them into difficulty with the local health department.

The benefits of proper environmental conditions are definite but sometimes not readily apparent. The prevention of food-borne illness does not carry a price tag. Moreover, improper storage can cause a significant loss of nutritional value and taste. The value here is difficult to quantify. Lost nutrition does not necessarily concern restaurant customers, but school food-service operations might consider this loss unacceptable. Fortunately, even though you may maintain an old, erratic refrigerator, proper stock rotation and a reasonably quick stock turnover can minimize quality loss.

It would probably be enlightening for operators to monitor the losses attributable directly to improper environmental conditions. For example, how much cheese has to be discarded because it absorbed onion flavors? How much of your flour attracts excessive moisture? Most operations experience some losses due to complete spoilage or due to the fact that products, while technically not spoiled, have passed their peak of culinary quality and are not suitable for guest service. But when these losses are compared with the cost associated with providing the proper environment, they may seem insignificant.

They are not insignificant, however, if you go beyond mere dollars and cents. You must be very concerned, for example, with the loss of your operation's reputation should a customer get sick after eating in your establishment. How do you compare this reputation loss with the cost of proper environmental conditions?

There is an old saying in hospitality: "The most important asset a hospitality company has is its reputation." And this asset should be protected first. Clearly, a few thousand dollars pales in comparison with a loss of goodwill. But how many operators are able to make this connection? We see the few thousand dollars easily. But we do not necessarily see the loss of goodwill as the primary concern.

WHAT IS NEEDED TO ACHIEVE THESE OBJECTIVES?

The major factors needed to achieve the storage objectives are discussed next.

ADEQUATE SPACE

Of all requirements, this is probably the hardest for hospitality operators to comply with. Usually, you must accept what you have to work with unless you are willing to remodel or add more floor space to the building.

If you are constructing the building from the ground up, designers can plan for optimal space, for now and for the future. But when building costs must be cut somewhere, the storage area is vulnerable. This is too bad, for it not only hampers current storage demands, but also limits the types of products you can store in the future. And this more or less permanently limits what you can offer your customers.

Generally, the space needed for all storage is between 5 square feet per dining room seat and 15 square feet per hotel room, depending on the amount of sales, types of items sold, the quantity of nonfood items carried in storage, and the local health district space requirements. A well-managed facility usually allocates about 10 to 12 percent of the total property for the storage function.[1] Typically, an owner-manager tries to minimize the storage space so that he or she can add more dining room seats or rooms. Real estate is expensive, and no one can blame you if you prefer tables and chairs that generate sales to storage shelves whose direct relation to sales is not so clear. But the smaller the storage space is today, usually the more limited are your offerings tomorrow.

ADEQUATE TEMPERATURE AND HUMIDITY

A hospitality operation that houses one or more food-service facilities will need to follow its local health district temperature requirements and space requirements. Generally speaking, the health district mandates that all potentially hazardous food—such as meats, seafood, and poultry—must be stored at 40°F, or below, or at 140°F, or above. Nonhazardous food and nonfood items usually have no temperature requirements. Furthermore, they usually have no mandated humidity requirements.

A local health district typically mandates certain space requirements so that good housekeeping practices can be performed. For instance, usually merchandise must be stored about 4 inches from the walls, ceiling, and floor. Food items usually must be stored on shelving that is not solid, so that proper air circulation can be maintained. Food cannot be stored under any exposed or unprotected sewer lines or water lines, or in rooms with toilet or garbage facilities. Furthermore, material such as soaps, chemicals, and pest-control supplies must be stored in a separate storage area so that it can neither contaminate food and beverage products nor be picked up by accident by someone obtaining food supplies.

While health district requirements are important, they represent *minimum* standards of sanitation and wholesomeness. The wise hospitality operator will go beyond these requirements in order to ensure that the shelf life of all stored merchandise is maximized. (See Figures 14.1, 14.2,

Food	Recommended Temperatures (°F/°C)	Maximum Storage Periods	Comments
Meat			
Roasts, steaks, chops	32–36/0–2.2	3 to 5 days	Wrap loosely
Ground and stewing	32–36/0–2.2	1 to 2 days	Wrap loosely
Variety meats	32–36/0–2.2	1 to 2 days	Wrap loosely
Whole ham	32–36/0–2.2	7 days	May wrap tightly
Half ham	32–36/0–2.2	3 to 5 days	May wrap tightly
Ham slices	32–36/0–2.2	3 to 5 days	May wrap tightly
Canned ham	32–36/0–2.2	1 year	Keep in can
Frankfurters	32–36/0–2.2	1 week	Original wrapping
Bacon	32–36/0–2.2	1 week	May wrap tightly
Luncheon meats	32–36/0–2.2	3 to 5 days	Wrap tightly when opened
Leftover Cooked Meats	32–36/0–2.2	1 to 2 days	Wrap or cover tightly
Gravy, Broth	32–36/0–2.2	1 to 2 days	Highly perishable
Poultry			
Whole chicken, turkey, duck, goose	32–36/0–2.2	1 to 2 days	Wrap loosely
Giblets	32–36/0–2.2	1 to 2 days	Wrap separate from bird
Stuffing	32–36/0–2.2	1 to 2 days	Covered container separate from bird
Cut-up cooked poultry	32–36/0–2.2	1 to 2 days	Cover

FIGURE 14.1. Shelf lives of some refrigerated foods. (Reprinted with permission from *Applied Foodservice Sanitation Certification Coursebook*, Fourth Edition. Copyright 1992 by the Educational Foundation of the National Restaurant Association. All rights reserved.)

Food	Recommended Temperatures (°F/°C)	Maximum Storage Periods	Comments
Fish			
Fatty fish	30–34/−1.1–1.1	1 to 2 days	Wrap loosely
Fish—not iced	30–34/−1.1–1.1	1 to 2 days	Wrap loosely
Fish—iced	32/0	3 days	Do not bruise with ice
Shellfish	30–34/−1.1–1.1	1 to 2 days	Covered container
Eggs			
Eggs in shell	40/4.4	1 week	Do not wash. Remove from container
Leftover yolks/whites	40–45/4.4–7.2	2 days	Cover yolks with water
Dried eggs	40–45/4.4–7.2	1 year	Cover tightly
Reconstituted eggs	40–45/4.4–7.2	1 week	Same treatment as eggs in shell
Cooked Dishes with Eggs, Meat, Milk, Fish, Poultry	32–36/0–2.2	Serve day prepared	Highly perishable
Cream-Filled Pastries	32–36/0–2.2	Serve day prepared	Highly perishable
Dairy Products			
Fluid milk	38–39/3.3–3.9	5 to 7 days after date on carton	Keep covered and in original container
Butter	38–40/3.3–4.4	2 weeks	Waxed cartons
Hard cheese (Cheddar, Parmesan, Romano)	38–40/3.3–4.4	6 months	Cover tightly to preserve moisture

FIGURE 14.1. Continued

Food	Recommended Temperatures (°F/°C)	Maximum Storage Periods	Comments
Soft cheese			
Cottage cheese	38–40/3.3–4.4	3 days	Cover tightly
Other soft cheeses	38–40/3.3–4.4	7 days	Cover tightly
Evaporated milk	50–70/10–21.1	1 year unopened	Refrigerate after opening
Dry milk (nonfat)	50–70/10–21.1	1 year unopened	Refrigerate after opening
Reconstituted dry milk	38–40/3.3–4.4	1 week	Treat as fluid milk
Fruit			
Apples	40–45/4.4–7.2	2 weeks	Room temperature till ripe
Avocados	40–45/4.4–7.2	3 to 5 days	Room temperature till ripe
Bananas	40–45/4.4–7.2	3 to 5 days	Room temperature till ripe
Berries, cherries	40–45/4.4–7.2	2 to 5 days	Do not wash before refrigerating
Citrus	40–45/4.4–7.2	1 month	Original container
Cranberries	40–45/4.4–7.2	1 week	
Grapes	40–45/4.4–7.2	3 to 5 days	Room temperature till ripe
Pears	40–45/4.4–7.2	3 to 5 days	Room temperature till ripe
Pineapples	40–45/4.4–7.2	3 to 5 days	Refrigerate (lightly covered) after cutting
Plums	40–45/4.4–7.2	1 week	Do not wash before refrigerating

FIGURE 14.1. Continued

Food	Recommended Temperatures (°F/°C)	Maximum Storage Periods	Comments
Vegetables			
Sweet potatoes, mature onions, hard-rind squashes, rutabagas	60/15.6	1 to 2 weeks at room temp. 3 months at 60°F	Ventilated containers for onions
Potatoes	45–50/7.2–10	30 days	Ventilated containers
All other vegetables	40–45/4.4–7.2	5 days maximum for most; 2 weeks for cabbage, root vegetables	Unwashed for storage

FIGURE 14.1. Continued

and 14.3.) You can accomplish this objective by following the temperature and humidity guidelines presented by the Educational Foundation of the National Restaurant Association (NRA).[2] Its recommendations are:

• Meat and Poultry: 32° to 40°F; 75 to 85 percent relative humidity

• Fish: 30° to 34°F; 75 to 85 percent relative humidity

• Live shellfish: 35° to 45°F; 75 to 85 percent relative humidity

• Eggs: 38° to 40°F; 75 to 85 percent relative humidity

• Dairy products: 38° to 40°F; 75 to 85 percent relative humidity

• Most fruits and vegetables: 40° to 45°F; 85 to 95 percent relative humidity

• Nonrefrigerated, dry storage: 50°F (ideal); 60° to 70°F (adequate); 50 to 60 percent relative humidity

• Freezer storage: 0°F, or below

To maintain these suggested temperature and humidity requirements, the hospitality operator must invest in a considerable amount of expensive storage facilities. For instance, in large hotels, it is common to find several walk-in refrigerators and freezers, each one serving a particular environmental need. The typical hospitality operator cannot afford this

Food	Maximum Storage Period at −10° to 0°F (−23.3° to −17.7°C)
Meat	
Beef, roasts and steaks	6 months
Beef, ground and stewing	3 to 4 months
Pork, roasts and chops	4 to 8 months
Pork, ground	1 to 3 months
Lamb, roasts and chops	6 to 8 months
Lamb, ground	3 to 5 months
Veal	8 to 12 months
Variety meats (liver, tongue)	3 to 4 months
Ham, frankfurters, bacon, luncheon meats	2 weeks (freezing not generally recommended)
Leftover cooked meats	2 to 3 months
Gravy, broth	2 to 3 months
Sandwiches with meat filling	1 to 2 months
Poultry	
Whole chicken, turkey, duck, goose	12 months
Giblets	3 months
Cut-up cooked poultry	4 months
Fish	
Fatty fish (mackerel, salmon)	3 months
Other fish	6 months
Shellfish	3 to 4 months
Ice Cream	3 months. Original container. Quality maintained better at 10°F (−12.2°C).
Fruit	8 to 12 months
Fruit Juice	8 to 12 months
Vegetables	8 months
French-Fried Potatoes	2 to 6 months
Precooked Combination Dishes	2 to 6 months
Baked Goods	
Cakes, prebaked	4 to 9 months
Cake batters	3 to 4 months
Fruit pies, baked or unbaked	3 to 4 months
Pie shells, baked or unbaked	1½ to 2 months
Cookies	6 to 12 months
Yeast breads and rolls, prebaked	3 to 9 months
Yeast breads and rolls, dough	1 to 1½ months

FIGURE 14.2. Shelf lives of some frozen foods. (Reprinted with permission from *Applied Foodservice Sanitation Certification Coursebook*, Fourth Edition. Copyright 1992 by the Educational Foundation of the National Restaurant Association. All rights reserved.)

Food	Recommended Maximum Storage Period If Unopened
Baking Materials	
Baking powder	8 to 12 months
Chocolate, baking	6 to 12 months
Chocolate, sweetened	2 years
Cornstarch	2 to 3 years
Tapioca	1 year
Yeast, dry	18 months
Baking soda	8 to 12 months
Beverages	
Coffee, ground, vacuum packed	7 to 12 months
Coffe, ground, not vacuum packed	2 weeks
Coffee, instant	8 to 12 months
Tea, leaves	12 to 18 months
Tea, instant	8 to 12 months
Carbonated beverages	Indefinitely
Canned Goods	
Fruits (in general)	1 year
Fruits, acidic (citrus, berries, sour cherries)	6 to 12 months
Fruit juices	6 to 9 months
Seafood (in general)	1 year
Pickled fish	4 months
Soups	1 year
Vegetables (in general)	1 year
Vegetables, acidic (tomatoes, sauerkraut)	7 to 12 months
Dairy Foods	
Cream, powdered	4 months
Milk, condensed	1 year
Milk, evaporated	1 year

FIGURE 14.3. Shelf lives of some dry storage foods. (Reprinted with permission from *Applied Foodservice Sanitation Certification Coursebook*, Fourth Edition. Copyright 1992 by the Educational Foundation of the National Restaurant Association. All rights reserved.)

Food	Recommended Maximum Storage Period If Unopened
Fats and Oils	
Mayonnaise	2 months
Salad dressings	2 months
Salad oil	6 to 9 months
Vegetable shortenings	2 to 4 months
Grains and Grain Products	
Cereal grains for cooked cereal	8 months
Cereals, ready-to-eat	6 months
Flour, bleached	9 to 12 months
Macaroni, spaghetti, and other noodles	3 months
Prepared mixes	6 months
Rice, parboiled	9 to 12 months
Rice, brown or wild	Should be refrigerated
Seasonings	
Flavoring extracts	Indefinite
Monosodium glutamate	Indefinite
Mustard, prepared	2 to 6 months
Salt	Indefinite
Sauces (steak, soy, etc.)	2 years
Spices and herbs (whole)	2 years to indefinite
Paprika, chili powder, cayenne	1 year
Seasoning salts	1 year
Vinegar	2 years
Sweeteners	
Sugar, granulated	Indefinite
Sugar, confectioners	Indefinite
Sugar, brown	Should be refrigerated
Syrups, corn, honey, molasses, sugar	1 year
Miscellaneous	
Dried beans	1 to 2 years
Cookies, crackers	1 to 6 months
Dried fruits	6 to 8 months
Gelatin	2 to 3 years
Dried prunes	Should be refrigerated
Jams, jellies	1 year
Nuts	1 year
Pickles, relishes	1 year
Potato chips	1 month

FIGURE 14.3. Continued

investment. Consequently, he or she must ensure rapid inventory turnover so that product quality does not deteriorate to the extent that customer dissatisfaction would result.

ADEQUATE EQUIPMENT

A proper storage area requires at least three major types of equipment: shelving/racks; trucks; and covered containers. Shelving, wall racks, and floor racks (sometimes referred to as "dunnage racks" or "pallets") are essential, because you cannot store anything directly on the floor. Motorized and/or nonmotorized trucks are needed to transport products in and out of storage. And covered containers, such as see-through plastic buckets and pans, are needed to hold products (such as cored lettuce) you may want to remove from shipping crates before placing into storage.

PROXIMITY OF STORAGE AREA TO RECEIVING AND PRODUCTION AREAS

To the extent possible, you should install the storage facilities close to the receiving dock and to the production departments. In addition, it is desirable to place the receiving, storage, and production areas on the same floor level. This saves time and also ensures that products are not out of their storage environments for excessive periods.

ACCESS TO PROPER MAINTENANCE IS ESSENTIAL

Depending on the size of the operation, there can be thousands, tens of thousands, even hundreds of thousands of dollars worth of inventory on hand at any one time. One freezer breakdown can ruin a considerable amount of frozen food. A leaking water pipe can damage huge amounts of food in the dry storage areas.

A maintenance contract is, therefore, useful, though it carries no guarantee that the service person can get there precisely when needed. Some operations hire maintenance personnel to ensure that service is available at a moment's notice. Unfortunately, smaller operations cannot afford this luxury. Their best bet is to purchase good equipment in the first place.

PROPER SECURITY IS A MUST

Chapter 15 contains a discussion of relevant security considerations, not only for storage, but also for other aspects of the selection and procurement function.

COMPETENT PERSONNEL ARE NEEDED TO SUPERVISE AND MANAGE THE STORAGE FUNCTION

Typically, one person receives, stores, and issues items to production departments. It is even more common for one person to buy, receive, store, and eventually use the items in production. A working chef, for example, may do all this.

Large firms usually impose some separation of responsibility; small firms often have to rely on whoever is available at the time to receive and store incoming merchandise. And when a production department needs an item, quite often someone just goes into an unsecured storage area to get it.

It is often asserted that the savings from good receiving, storage, and issuing can be quantified; some experts put the potential savings at 2 percent of a hospitality operation's sales, although others would opt for the lower figure of 2 percent of its purchases. Since no actual cost studies are available to back up either figure, it is hard to assert a hard-and-fast rule beyond saying that good procedures in this area of logistics are important, involving potential savings of perhaps as much as 2 percent of sales.

Any savings you achieve in this area will correlate highly with the competence of the person(s) performing these functions. It is one thing to have a rule that nothing leaves the storeroom without permission; it is something else again to implement and enforce this rule. Hence, the ability of people working in these areas is critical. The best-designed receiving and storage facilities and receiving, storing, and issuing procedures are all for naught if the right person is not on the job.

Finally, we have to realize that ideal circumstances do not always occur. Sales volume may not be large enough to permit the operation to "follow the book" and have people available for all functions. Conversely, volume may be large enough to afford proper support staff, but the labor market may be too tight and the kind of people you want for this function may be unavailable. It is challenging to develop ways of securing goods under these less than ideal conditions.

SUFFICIENT TIME TO PERFORM THE NECESSARY DUTIES IS ALMOST ALWAYS MISSING

Adequate time is just as important as employee talent. There is more to receiving, storing, and issuing than just weighing food and putting it into storage. There are many other things to do, like monitoring the necessary control procedures, maintaining sanitation, rotating the stock, keeping track of usage patterns, and so on.

Small operations cannot always afford the time to do all these things. But even the larger companies tend to load down the receiver-storeroom clerk with such extraneous duties as sorting mail.

It is unfortunate when hotels, restaurants, institutions, and clubs go to the expense of hiring good people and designing excellent receiving, storing, and issuing procedures, but then stop short at providing enough time to discharge these functions adequately.

STOREROOM REGULATIONS ARE AN ABSOLUTE MUST, FOR BOTH CONTROL AND PREDICTABILITY

Regulations dictate who is allowed to enter the storage areas and who is allowed to obtain items from storage. Also specified is the required procedure to use to obtain these items. In some cases, the senior management determines these guidelines. But larger firms that set broad guidelines often expect the storeroom manager to work out the day-to-day details necessary for a smooth-running operation.

MANAGING THE STORAGE FACILITIES

Small operations usually hope that the storage facilities will manage themselves. An idle food server, for example, might be sent into the storeroom now and then to clean up. Or the chef may have a few moments to rotate the stock. Often, though, the storage areas of small operations are not managed systematically.

The one exception seems to be the liquor storeroom. An owner-manager keeps this area locked at the very least. In addition, he or she may personally receive these items. And since the liquor control commission requires bars to maintain records of their liquor purchases, considerably more bookkeeping and record keeping is done here than elsewhere. Liquor storage tends, then, to be well organized almost everywhere, but the same cannot be said for soap, paper towels, and light bulbs. The food storage area falls between these two extremes, but the degree of attention here varies dramatically from one operation to another. For instance, in some places, food servers enter the storeroom at will to retrieve salt, pepper, catsup, and so on. In others, only a predetermined number of hours during the day are set aside for issuing supplies of any sort.

Larger operations that can afford the luxury of a receiver-storeroom manager assign him or her several activities. The major ones are discussed next.

1. Inventories must be classified and organized in a systematic fashion. This procedure simplifies general control and also helps with the preparation of reports that deal with inventories and their costs.

    Some storeroom managers label the shelf location with the name of the item that occupies that spot; they take this step in dry, refrigerated, and frozen storage. Furthermore, a diagram of a storage facility, complete with a guide noting where each particular item can be found, is often displayed on the doorway of the facility. Other operators, however, take a considerably more flexible approach to control the use of storage space.

It is important for operators to organize and classify their inventories in a manner that satisfies the local legal requirements. For instance, normally the local health district stipulates that toxic materials must be housed in a separate storage facility and that this location must be locked unless it is necessary to enter it. It is conceivable that in your locale alcoholic beverages must be kept in a separate area because underage employees must not be exposed to this merchandise.

2. Usage rates must be determined for all inventories. The storeroom manager must keep track of the usage patterns so that he or she can revise and help improve ordering procedures and par stock levels. In addition, this information can help determine the optimal reorder point.

3. The storeroom manager must occasionally make an emergency order or travel to the supplier's location to pick up extra items, particularly if a stockout threatens. The storeroom manager may also need to pick up an order right away rather than wait for the scheduled delivery. This is sometimes necessary when a supplier must alter his or her normal delivery schedule.

4. The storeroom manager also keeps track of accumulating surpluses. The chef may fail to inform the buyer that certain items have been removed from the menu. This communication breakdown happens now and then. It is more liable to occur in the largest operations—those that have two or more dining facilities and two or more food production areas.

5. The storeroom manager may be responsible for disposing of items that are no longer used by the hospitality operation. The buyer may want to do this personally, but often the storeroom manager may arrange to return merchandise to the supplier, trade it, or otherwise get rid of it.

6. The storeroom manager may need to effect transfers of merchandise to other company outlets. For instance, if another unit in the restaurant chain needs frozen french fries, you may need to send it some of yours. You might also do this if you are overstocked and another unit is understocked. Whatever the case, when doing this, the storeroom manager usually must complete a Transfer Slip (which is similar to an invoice) so that the stock is controlled and accounted for properly.

7. The storeroom manager may keep track of all inventories and their corresponding dollar value. This is an important and time-consuming duty. Some companies want to keep a perpetual inventory system. That is, they want to know what is on hand in the storeroom at all times. These firms might even keep track of all in-process inventories in addition to the storeroom inventories. As a rule, however,

Perpetual inventory for period _____

Name of item _____

1	2	3	4	5	6	7	8
Date Delivered	No. of Units	Unit Price	Date Issued	No. of Units	To Whom Issued	Returns to Storeroom	Balance

FIGURE 14.4. Bin Card.

this kind of control requires a considerable amount of computer technology.

Sometimes such a system is used without a computer for only a few items, since it costs a good deal of time and money. In this case, it is generally used for the most expensive items. And, to a great extent, it is used for most liquor.

Since you must keep records of liquor purchases, it is only a bit more trouble to keep a perpetual inventory by keeping a "bin card" next to each type of liquor in storage. (See Figure 14.4.)

A bin card is a record of all liquor, or other items, delivered, all liquor sent to the production areas—bars, kitchen, service areas—and, in some cases, all liquor sent back to storage from the production areas.

At one time, several large hotels and clubs kept no inventories in the production areas when these areas were closed. That is, at the beginning of a shift, a bartender, for example, would pick up and sign for a complete par stock of all the items needed during the shift. Any necessary replenishment was usually handled by an assistant manager. At the end of the shift, the bartender would send everything back to storage. The storeroom manager then would determine what had been used during the shift, and this amount had to correspond to the bar sales amount. This type of procedure is no longer in widespread use in our industry, but it is still followed for banquet bars.

Such a procedure is time-consuming and also requires someone in the storeroom to set up the par stocks for each user. But it does eliminate the need for stock requisitions—a concept we address in our discussion of issuing later in this chapter. Some operations do insist that at least the more expensive items be treated this way. For instance, the chef may follow this procedure with meat and fish. And the bartender may have to do it for some liquors. In other words, the storeroom manager monitors closely the costly items and requires the users to pick up and return them; it is unacceptable to keep any of them in the in-process inventory except during working hours.

The perpetual inventory has some advantages, such as providing for a tight degree of control. Moreover, many operators believe that if they constantly monitor inventory levels, they will remain close to the optimal levels because they will have accurate par stocks.

The cost of maintaining a perpetual inventory "by hand" for more than a few items today is virtually prohibitive. Not only does the labor cost of accomplishing it loom large, but experience teaches that hand-posted records often contain a good deal of human error, often to the point of making their value questionable. Consequently, the greatest use of perpetual inventory for a total inventory is found in hospitality operations in which all departments are integrated into a computerized management information system.

Operators who once swore by the perpetual inventory system now tend to take a complete physical inventory once every week, every 10 days, semimonthly, or monthly. In this way they keep track of their overall performance.

A physical inventory, in contrast to a perpetual inventory, is an actual counting and valuing of all items in storage and, in some cases, of all items in the in-process inventory. There are three good reasons for taking a physical inventory. (1) It is useful to have this information before calculating order sizes and preparing purchase orders. (2) It is necessary for accountants who must calculate product costs.* For example, they might want to compute the actual food cost for the month (as shown in Figure 14.5). (3) Assuming some type of perpetual inventory is used, the physical inventory count can be compared with the "theoretical" inventory count shown on bin card records. In this case, the actual inventory should equal the theoretical inventory, or else there may be an inventory control problem.

---

* Some small operations take a physical inventory perhaps only once a month, usually because they have too little time to do it more often. But they can still get some idea of product costs just by keeping track of purchases. Although this is not entirely accurate, in the long run, the amount of food purchases, for example, for the month, comes close to the actual food cost for that month.

   Large operations might also compare food purchases with food costs for the same period. Eventually, there should be some relationship between the two. And this relationship should remain somewhat constant, or else something might be wrong.

The cost equations are:

$$BI + P - EI = C$$

$$C \div S = C\%$$

where BI = beginning inventory

P = purchases for the month

EI = ending inventory

S = sales

C = food cost

C% = food cost percentage

Note that in the example below, some operations may make other adjustments, such as granting a credit for employee meals, in order to determine the actual food cost for food sold to guests.

BI (which is last month's EI). $12,000

P. . . . . +20,000

EI. . . . . −14,000

Credit for employee meals . . . . − 2,000

C. $16,000

If S = $49,000, C% = $16,000/$49,000 = 32.6%

FIGURE 14.5. Calculation of this month's actual food cost.

Taking a physical inventory can be very time-consuming, especially if every item, including the inventory of goods in production, is counted. It is not, however, so time-consuming as maintaining a perpetual inventory.

Regardless of the amount of time needed to perform a physical inventory, usually the hospitality operation must do it at least once a month. The monthly profit and loss statement for the operation must be prepared, and it cannot be done unless you know your cost of goods sold expense. And you cannot compute this expense unless you take a physical inventory.

There are several ways of taking the inventory. One method requires two persons, one calling and the other writing. Usually when this or any other procedure is used, the storage facilities are laid out in some predetermined pattern, such as alphabetically. The inventory sheets are preprinted with the items' names and spaces where the writer can record the numerical entries. In a computerized installation, the sheets can be printed by the computer. Those without computers must prepare these sheets in some other way.

Another inventory-taking method that may eventually become popular in the hospitality industry is to use a hand-held bar code scanner to record stock levels. In a hospitality operation that has a fully integrated, computerized management information system, such a procedure is a natural addition to the overall inventory management process.

Operators who do not have access to the latest computer technology can adopt shortcuts that speed the inventory-taking process with only minor sacrifices of accuracy. Some of these shortcuts follow. (1) They count everything in the storage areas and then add on a certain predetermined percentage to represent the amount of items in the in-process inventory. (2) They count only full-case equivalents. That is, they do not add in a half can of baking powder; they just count full cases, boxes, or cans. (3) They combine inventory taking with the ordering procedure. If the storage manager's count is sufficiently accurate, correct purchase orders can be prepared. This does have the drawback of offering the storeroom manager the opportunity to manipulate the count, a risk that must be judged acceptable if this procedure is to be followed. (4) They use a tape recorder to recite units and dollar values, and someone later on transcribes the information. (5) They may use a hand-held computer device to encode their inventories, and later on, this electronically gathered information can be processed and printed.

Some operators do not want their storeroom manager taking inventory, at least not all the time. They would rather have someone else do it periodically to serve as a check on the storeroom manager. For instance, the storeroom manager may keep some type of perpetual inventory, and an accounting department representative, for example, takes a physical inventory once or twice a month to check on the storeroom manager's accuracy as well as to calculate various product costs so that financial statements and reports can be prepared.

Small operators sometimes do something similar. For example, they might ask the head bartender to take a physical inventory of the food storage areas while the chef, or head housekeeper, inventories the liquor. Each of these user-buyer-storeroom managers may keep some type of perpetual inventory system while deferring the actual physical counting to another department head. Or the owner-manager might do the actual physical counting once or twice a month while the department heads keep some sort of a perpetual inventory for some or all items. Finally, some member of management who is not attached to any one department may assist the department representative with this inventory.

In extreme cases, an owner-manager may hire an outside service to take a physical inventory periodically. This is sometimes done to get an absolutely unbiased inventory report. It is also traditionally done by someone who wants to buy the business, as part of the audit of the entire operation.

EXERCISING TIGHT CONTROL OVER THE STOCK

Tight control exists when only a few persons are authorized to withdraw items from the storeroom. It also exists when effective and efficient security precautions prevail.

These control and security aspects are perhaps the most important parts of the storeroom manager's job. Unfortunately, many operations neglect them. It is also true that many operations do not have storeroom managers. In some of these operations, this represents a wildly uncontrolled situation. On the other hand, this is not always true.

Some operations with no specific storeroom person manage to produce excellent product costs with open storerooms. These forms, however, limit who may enter the storeroom to persons who are under close, continuous supervision. Commonly, these firms also maintain minimal stocks so that pilferage is more noticeable to supervisors. In some cases, only small "working storerooms" are open to employees and larger storerooms that are used to stock the working storerooms are accessible only to a limited number of management personnel.

Ideally, when a storeroom manager is present, he or she issues items only to authorized persons and only when they present an official stock requisition. A stock requisition (see Figures 14.6, 14.7, and 14.8) is a formal request made by a user for the items needed to carry out necessary tasks. The primary purposes of the stock requisition are to control who gets the items and to record how much of an item is issued and when it is issued.

The control is not over the storage stock alone but also extends, to some degree, to the in-process inventories. For instance, if the requisitioner (the user) had to note how much of an item is currently held in the in-process inventory (as in Figure 14.6), he or she would hesitate to requisition too much, thereby preventing in-process items from slipping to the back of the shelf, eventually to spoil.

The accountant or bookkeeper might use the requisitions to calculate product costs. For example, he or she might merely add up all the food requisitions and direct purchases for the week and use this computation as the week's food cost. This procedure can be reasonably accurate, especially if you set strict par stocks on all items in the in-process inventory. (But this approach may be impractical, especially for liquor. After all, how do you issue a half bottle of liquor?)

No. 873

Date_____   Page_____   of_____

Department_____

Requested by_____

1	2	3	4	5
Item	Amount Requested (in units)	Unit Cost	Extended Value	Other Information
			col. 2 X col. 3	such as: how much of the item is in process? what's the forecasted usage of the item?

Signature of
requisitioner_____

Requisition
filled by_____

FIGURE 14.6. Stock requisition.

Some operators hold the accountant responsible for issues, not only for the purpose of calculating product costs, but also for serving as an additional check on the receiver or storeroom manager. This approach is impractical for smaller firms, even though it is theoretically sound to have a separate person responsible for each operating activity.

The issuing activity is, as you can imagine, time-consuming, especially if requisitioners can drop in any time. Some operations allow the storeroom to issue only at certain times during the day. In some operations, the requisitioners must prepare their requisitions in the morning, send them electronically to the storeroom manager's computer terminal or

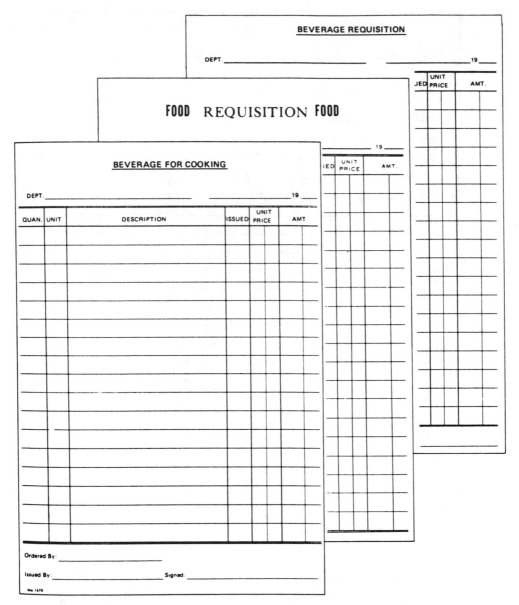

FIGURE 14.7. Large hospitality operations tend to have a variety of stock requisitions. In this example, food is separate from beverage, and beverage used for cooking warrants its own stock requisition slip. (Courtesy Las Vegas Hilton.)

WORLD'S LARGEST HOTEL. CASINO & THEME PARK

WAREHOUSE REQUISITION

Department: _____   Date: _____

Cast Member: _____   Extension: _____

Remarks: _____

Item Number	Item Description	Quantity

Approval: _____

WHS0600 (10/93)   White - Originator   Yellow - Warehouse

FIGURE 14.8. An all-purpose stock requisition. (Courtesy MGM Grand Hotel, Casino & Theme Park.)

put them in the storeroom manager's mailbox, and then wait for the store-room manager to deliver the items on a predetermined schedule. If users run out of items during their shift, some member of management may enter the locked storage facilities, complete a stock requisition, time permitting, and take the necessary items to the user. If time is precious, he or she may complete the necessary forms a little later.

In the rare situation in which each user picks up a complete par stock from the storeroom manager at the beginning of the shift and then returns what is left at the end of the shift, the time spent filling out and processing forms might be reduced considerably.

Additional control is obtained if the storeroom manager issues exact amounts of ingredients needed for one day, or one shift. For instance, a storeroom employee may weigh out the ingredients according to the recipes to be prepared during the shift. (When this is done, the storeroom usually houses an area referred to as the "ingredient room" to do this type of work.)

A VALUE ANALYSIS OF STORAGE MANAGEMENT PROCEDURES

Proper storage management has never been a hallmark of our industry. This has resulted in needless merchandise loss. Nevertheless, we can sympathize with managers faced with potentially large storage management costs.

It costs a great deal of money, time, and effort to manage inventories adequately. In most large operations, it is a full-time job to receive and inspect incoming merchandise, to store it, to keep track of it, and to issue it properly. The benefits supposedly consist of the traditional 2 percent saving mentioned earlier. But when one compares an easily noticed cost with a relatively hazy benefit, it is no wonder that most operators have forgone systematic storage management techniques. The issue becomes more cloudy when we add the possibility of customer dissatisfaction that can arise because of stale or spoiled products resulting from improper storage management.

Large operations have more to gain by employing a full-time receiver-storeroom manager. They can usually afford more personnel, and that 2 percent translates into many dollars for them.

The small operator, by contrast, faces a bigger dilemma. None of us can really blame him or her for refusing to spend several hundred dollars per month managing the storage function. Clearly, this operator needs control as much as anyone, but what is needed is some sort of truncated method of storage management that is reasonably effective yet fairly economical.

Our suggestions for these small operators follow. (1) Use one-stop shopping to reduce significantly the number of deliveries. (2) Have the owner-manager, or assistant, receive and inspect all incoming merchandise; send expensive* items to the main storage facilities and less expensive items to the production areas, that is, to the in-process inventory. (3) Have the owner-manager, or assistant, issue par stocks of the expensive items to the users—the cooks, housekeepers, bartenders, servers—at the beginning of their shift. (4) Lock the main storage facilities. (5) If additional expensive items are needed during the shift, have the owner-manager, or assistant, retrieve them. (6) At the end of the shift, have the owner-manager, or assistant, open the main storage facilities to accept the expensive items that were not used during the shift. (7) Have the owner-manager, or assistant, record the number of expensive items used during the shift and pass this information along to the bookkeeper, who will compare what was used during the shift with what was sold. (This comparison procedure is sometimes referred to as a "critical item inventory analysis." It is also sometimes referred to as auditing the "inventory sales," that is, the amount of sales that should have been recorded and collected for based on the amount of inventory that is missing.) If the comparison reveals a significant variance between what is missing and what was sold, the owner-manager, or assistant, must diagnose the cause(s) of this problem and correct it as soon as possible.

In a sense, we are asking the small operators to repeat history, since this procedure was a bit more popular in the past. Operators began to turn away from it when they discovered that cooks and bartenders did not have enough time to pursue it, especially as these users began to assume many other responsibilities. But we think that this system can be just as applicable today as it once was, assuming that top management supports and enforces it. Moreover, we see no reason that it would not work for every operator. It should grant the small operator an additional element of control, as it is certainly a constructive alternative to leaving storage facilities open and unattended most of the time.

There are, of course, a couple of disadvantages to this system: (1) it takes a bit more time to complete, and (2) there is a need to have enough physical space, refrigerators, and freezers to hold in-process inventories; otherwise the owner-manager must run back and forth to the locked storage facilities too frequently. This running gets tiring, so that, in time, he or she may leave the main storeroom open.

We have not directly addressed the cost-benefit analysis of storage management procedures. But any such analysis ultimately rests upon the analyst's interpretation of relevant costs and benefits, as does every other

---

* Expensive items usually are all meat, fish, poultry, desserts, liquor, and some nonfood items; all other items can be controlled less stringently.

economic analysis. The 2 percent argument is too vague; it fails to incorporate such noncash benefits as smooth operations and a no-nonsense image that investors and employees appreciate. After all is said and done, management must decide the appropriateness of accepted storage management principles. It is not an easy decision, but few important managerial decisions are.

KEY WORDS AND CONCEPTS

A typical issuing procedure

Auditing the "inventory sales"

Bin card

Computerized management information system

Controlling only the most expensive merchandise

Critical item inventory analysis

Direct purchase

Disposing of merchandise no longer required

Educational Foundation of the NRA

Factors needed to achieve the storage objectives

Food cost = beginning inventory + purchases − ending inventory − other credit

Health district storage requirements

Ingredient room

In-process inventory

Inventory classification

Inventory control and security

Inventory shrinkage

Inventory usage rates

Managing the storage facilities

NRA

One-stop shopping

Open storeroom

Par stocks

Perpetual inventory

Physical inventory

Pilferage

Purposes of taking a physical inventory

Skimming

Speeding up the inventory-taking process

Spoilage

Stock requisition

Storage objectives

Storage space

Storage temperature and humidity

Storeroom layout

Storeroom manager

Theft

Theoretical inventory value

Transfer Slip

Working storeroom

REFERENCES

1. M. C. Warfel and Marion L. Cremer, *Purchasing for Food Service Managers,* 2d ed. (Berkeley, CA: McCutchan Publishing Corporation, 1990), p. 144.

2. *Applied Foodservice Sanitation,* 4th ed. (Chicago: The Educational Foundation of the National Restaurant Association, 1992), pp. 121–124.

QUESTIONS AND PROBLEMS

1. List the objectives of storage management. What is normally needed to achieve these objectives?

2. What are the typical storeroom manager's activities? Which one do you feel is most important? Why?

3. Briefly describe how a perpetual inventory system works.

4. In most operations it is too expensive to maintain a perpetual inventory for all items. However, it may be beneficial for some items. Which items would you like to keep on a perpetual inventory basis? Why?

5. What is one of the main purposes of taking a month-end physical inventory?

6. If possible, contact a hotel manager and ask permission to observe a physical inventory procedure. Try to follow up the inventory procedure to determine its purposes and to see the uses for this information. Ask the manager to discuss the inventory-taking process.

7. What are some ways of shortening the inventory-taking procedure? Which seems best? Worst? Why?

8. Assume that you own a table-service restaurant. Annual sales are approximately $1,200,000. Should you hire a receiver-storeroom manager? What are the potential costs and benefits? If you think that this person might be too expensive, could you assign additional tasks to the person's job description to justify the expense? If yes, what would some of them be? Why? If possible, ask an independent restaurateur to comment on your answer.

9. Assume that a storeroom manager notices that a shipment received by the receiving agent had an accompanying invoice with the notation "Direct Purchase" stamped on it. What should the storeroom manager do with this shipment?

10. What is the main difference between "theft" and "pilferage"?

11. Given the following data, compute the food cost percentage.

   Total sales: $500,000
   Food sales: 75% of total sales
   Beverage sales: 25% of total sales
   Beginning food inventory: $25,000
   Ending food inventory: $30,000
   Total food purchases: $200,000
   Employee meal cost: $6,000

12. Briefly describe the temperature and humidity guidelines suggested by the Educational Foundation of the National Restaurant Association.

13. What are the advantages and disadvantages of computerized inventory-management procedures?

14. If the food beginning inventory is $12,500, the food purchases are $40,000, and the food cost is $47,500, what is the food ending inventory (dollar amount)?

15. Define or briefly explain the following terms:

(a) Skimming

(b) Bin card

(c) Theoretical inventory value

(d) Full-case inventory-taking procedure

(e) Stock requisition

(f) Ingredient room

(g) Inventory sales

(h) Shoplifting

(i) Working storeroom

(j) Health district storage requirements

(k) In-process inventory

(l) Credit for employee meals

(m) Open storeroom

(n) Par stocks

(o) Authorized access to storage areas

(p) Critical item inventory analysis

SECURITY IN THE PURCHASING FUNCTION

THE PURPOSE OF THIS CHAPTER

This chapter discusses:

- Security problems associated with the purchasing function
- Preventing security problems

INTRODUCTION

Several years ago, many hospitality operators considered theft and pilferage manageable costs of doing business and routinely added a slight markup to menu and room prices to compensate for these losses. In fact, credit card companies supposedly continue these practices today. But because of increased competitive pressure and shrinking profit margins, the hospitality industry has become more concerned about these problems.

This concern with security should come as no surprise. After all, "the U.S. Department of Commerce (DOC) found that employees steal approximately $120 billion from their employers each year. Almost as shocking, the DOC estimates that one-third of employees steal from their companies at least once a year."[1] "The Insurance Institute of America indicates that 65 to 75 percent of all merchandise losses are the result of inside stealing."[2] Furthermore, an industry expert estimates that "the foodservice industry loses approximately $20 billion a year to theft and cash mishandling; approximately 5% to 8% of gross sales is lost to internal theft; 75% of all missing inventory is from theft; [and] the majority of employees caught stealing have worked for an operation for an average of five to seven years."[3]

It would appear that this heightened interest in security can be attributed to at least four factors: (1) hospitality operators find it increasingly difficult to pass on security losses to the consumer in the form of higher menu and room prices, (2) the public in general has become more security conscious, (3) the cost of insurance coverage has skyrocketed, and (4) a good deal of unfavorable publicity has focused on the hospitality purchasing function.

Much of this unfavorable publicity centers on the willingness of purchasing agents to accept gifts and other economic favors. The president of Rax Restaurants resigned after an internal investigation indicated "improprieties in supplier relations," such as the fact that some supply contracts were awarded without competitive bidding.[4] The president of Whataburger Inc. resigned amid allegations of supplier kickbacks.[5] A buyer for J. C. Penney Co. admittedly "supplemented his salary with as much as $1.5 million in bribes and kickbacks."[6] Some dairy companies admitted that they schemed "to fix milk prices at an artificially high level by colluding on bids to supply milk for school lunch programs."[7] "More than 30 Louisiana chefs, restaurateurs and fishermen were arrested on charges of buying and selling banned fish."[8] And in case you think today's employees are the only ones who steal, two well-known celebrities of the nineteenth century, Cesar Ritz (said to be the greatest hotelman ever) and Auguste Escoffier (said to be the "king of chefs, and the chef to kings"), "were sacked for stealing from the hotel larder and taking kickbacks from food purveyors, to the tune of roughly $20,000."[9]

There is probably no more theft or pilferage today than there has been in the past, but what there is has certainly been more widely publicized. This notoriety has forced hospitality operators to reexamine their attitudes toward security. Management is no longer willing to ignore theft, fraud, pilferage, and shoplifting as minor problems.

Security has, of course, always been important in the hospitality business. But it can be difficult to provide adequate security, particularly in the service areas and areas frequented by customers, because physical facilities are not always designed with security in mind. Security can be more of a consideration during the designing of storage areas, but it often must take a back seat in dining rooms, lounges, front offices, and other public areas.

In many respects, however, a buyer can enforce a good measure of security in his or her realm of responsibility. The activities and duties of buyers, receivers, storeroom managers, and so on are hidden from public view. If desired, then, management can set policies that go so far as to effect an armed camp atmosphere in the receiving and storage areas of the hospitality operation.

SECURITY PROBLEMS

Several potential security problems arise in connection with purchasing, receiving, storing, and issuing, and an owner-manager must be on guard against them. The major ones are discussed next.

KICKBACKS

A buyer, or user-buyer, could easily collude with a supplier, salesperson, or delivery agent. The operation could thus receive inferior merchandise, paying for a superior product, while the buyer and accomplices pocket the difference in the AP price. (This difference is referred to as a "kickback.")

Sometimes two or more conspirators "pad an invoice," that is, add on a phony charge. This is a form of kickback that requires the cooperative efforts of at least two thieves.

A form of kickback also occurs when a conspirator sends an invoice that has already been paid through to the bookkeeper, who pays it again. The thieves then pocket the payment.[10]

Another form of kickback happens when supposedly defective incoming merchandise is "returned" (returned to the thieves, that is, who hope that the bookkeeper will forget or ignore this transaction).

Much the same thing occurs when "short orders" are delivered or when half an order is delivered in the morning, with the other half promised in the afternoon—the afternoon that never comes. Again, the thieves depend on the bookkeeper or management to overlook the shortage.

Perhaps the most common type of kickback happens when the buyer agrees to pay a slightly higher AP price and, unknown to the owner-manager, receives an under-the-table payment from the supplier. The payment sometimes comes as merchandise—silverware, sound systems, cameras, and so on. This collusion is extremely difficult to detect, especially when, overall, the product costs appear to be in line.

The thing to keep in mind about kickbacks is that although the hospitality operator sometimes loses, the honest supplier always loses if his or her salespersons or delivery agents conspire with receivers, buyers, or bookkeepers. It is difficult, however, for continuing theft to go undetected if the supplier is honest, because he or she usually is constantly alert to these practices. Thus, the supplier's management and the buyer's management have the same interests at heart.

INVOICE SCAMS

A problem related to kickbacks occurs when someone diverts a bill payment to a fictitious company or a fictitious account. The conspirators then pocket the payment. Similarly, someone might present a fictitious invoice to the bookkeeper, which the bookkeeper pays, the payment going directly to the thief's post office box.

At first glance, it would seem difficult for a buyer to set up an invoice scam. However, even the largest hospitality companies are not immune to this type of fraud. For instance, a buyer for Marriott Corporation pleaded guilty to stealing more than $1.4 million from the company over a 14-year period by altering invoice copies and having them paid into a dummy bank account that he controlled. He admitted doing it because, at first, he needed the money. But as time went on, he continued the scam because "it just seemed so easy after it got started."[11]

SUPPLIER AND RECEIVER ERROR

Incoming invoices must be checked for arithmetic errors. It is surprising how many unintentional mistakes occur. These could be a form of kick-back. Either way, the loss is the same.

Several other more or less unintentional mistakes can occur. Most of them are relatively minor. But, in the long run, little losses add up. Some of the typical ones are (a) losing credit for container deposits or returned merchandise, (b) receiving a substitute item of a slightly lower quality than that ordered and failing to issue a Request for Credit memo or other-wise to ensure that the cost difference is corrected, (c) receiving the wrong items unintentionally (such as receiving bulk butter instead of butter pats), and (d) weighing items with an inaccurate scale.

INVENTORY THEFT

Restrict access to all storage areas and receiving facilities. Only autho-rized persons should be allowed to enter these areas. Furthermore, these areas should be locked when not in use.

The most common type of "inventory shrinkage" is pilferage by em-ployees. Restricted access can reduce pilferage opportunities. Adequate supervision in the production and service areas of the hospitality opera-tion also can reduce or eliminate pilferage and shoplifting opportunities.

INVENTORY PADDING

Recall from Chapter 14 our discussion of the physical inventory-taking process, and that one of the reasons for doing this was to compute various product costs. The formula used to compute, for example, the actual food cost for the month is:

$$
\begin{array}{l}
 \text{Beginning inventory} \\
\underline{+\ \text{Purchases}} \\
=\ \text{Food available for sale} \\
-\ \text{Ending inventory} \\
\underline{-\ \text{Other credit (e.g., food used for employee meals)}} \\
=\ \text{Cost of food sold}
\end{array}
$$

If our beginning inventory is $12,000, our purchases are $20,000, the ending inventory is $14,000, and the other credit is $2,000, the actual food cost is $16,000 ($12,000 + $20,000 − $14,000 − $2,000 = $16,000).

Let us assume that a food supervisor wants to reduce this food cost figure in order to earn a greater performance bonus. An easy way, albeit illegal way, is to increase the ending inventory amount, that is, "pad" the inventory so that top management is led to believe that the supervisor produced a highly favorable food cost for the month. (Notice that, in this example, if the ending inventory is artificially inflated to $15,000, the cost of food sold drops to $15,000 from $16,000). Unless management supervises the inventories very carefully, a person could easily steal the merchandise, alter the inventory records, and no one would ever uncover the fraud unless an independent audit was conducted.[12]

INVENTORY SUBSTITUTIONS

In those hospitality operations that have an open-storeroom policy, it is relatively easy for an employee to remove high-quality merchandise and substitute inferior goods. The stolen merchandise can be consumed, or it can be sold on the black market. This potential security problem is similar to inventory padding, in that an independent audit may be needed to uncover it.

TELEPHONE SALES SCAMS

All companies are susceptible to telephone solicitors who use illegal tactics and high-pressure selling techniques to defraud buyers. These salespersons, sometimes referred to as "WATS-line hustlers," rarely deal with the authorized purchasing agent. They usually attempt backdoor selling and will offer free gifts and other inducements to clinch a sale.

It would appear that the most common type of telephone fraud involves offers of sweet deals on replacement toner used for copying machines and laser printers.[13] These telephone solicitors, sometimes referred to as "toner-phoners," typically portray themselves as representing major supply houses offering once-in-a-lifetime low prices, though the unsuspecting buyer usually receives watered-down merchandise and high service charges.

A related problem occurs whenever an unauthorized and unordered shipment arrives at your doorstep. If you mistakenly pay for this shipment, it is unlikely that you will ever get your money back.

INABILITY TO SEGREGATE OPERATING ACTIVITIES

Ideally, a hospitality operation would separate the buying, receiving, storing, and bill-paying procedures. Usually a separate person pays the bills, but this is not the case with the other operating activities.

The most common potential problem is the buyer, or user-buyer, who receives the products he or she orders. There is nothing inherently wrong with this practice, but it can allow a buyer to order one thing and receive another—perhaps an inferior product. Worse yet, the buyer can substitute inferior merchandise for the ordered products, converting the better products to his or her own use.

Nevertheless, buyers who receive are common in our industry normally because (1) they are the only ones who can recognize the various product quality standards (this is especially true of buyers who command an expertise in an area in which the rest of the staff has little knowledge, such as wine stewards); (2) the buyer must do other things to justify his or her job (buying may not be enough work); and (3) management just cannot afford to hire a separate receiver.

SUSPICIOUS BEHAVIOR

A variety of employee behaviors call for management scrutiny. The owner-manager should be wary of employees who (1) seem unduly friendly with suppliers, salespersons, or delivery agents; (2) hang around storage areas needlessly; (3) needlessly handle keys or locks; (4) make too many trips to the garbage area, bathroom, locker room, or parking lot (perhaps to move stolen merchandise); (5) requisition abnormally large amounts of supplies; (6) make frequent trips to the storage areas for no apparent good reason; (7) have relatives working for your suppliers; (8) stray from their assigned work stations too frequently; (9) are seen passing packages to guests; (10) are seen stuffing boxes or packages under a couch in a public area, which may later be picked up by a confederate; (11) permit delivery agents to loiter in unauthorized areas; and (12) have visitors on the work site. The list could go on. Since many employees cannot be restricted to one work area, theft and pilferage opportunities are always a part of the workplace.

PREVENTING SECURITY PROBLEMS

In general, an owner-manager can do three main things to prevent security breaches: (1) select honest suppliers, (2) employ honest employees, and (3) design the physical facilities so that tight, effective security conditions can be maintained.

It is difficult to assess the honesty of potential suppliers. Even if they are willing to talk about dishonesty, the most that they usually say is, "We don't do anything like that." The more dishonest the suppliers, the salespersons, or the delivery agents, the less likely they would be to admit it. It is useful, though, to ask other hospitality operators for their advice. Whatever report you receive on a supplier, you must remember that bad practices may have been corrected. As with so much else, in the final analysis, management's own informed judgment must be the guide.

Assuring employee honesty is no simple matter. Hospitality operators have trouble with pilferage for two reasons. First, the products we use are easily converted into cash. Second, few hospitality operators do more than just fire a dishonest employee. Having petty thieves arrested is still uncommon, and, as a result, a thief has little to lose if caught.

Lately, more employers have begun to prosecute dishonest employees and dishonest customers. If it becomes the rule, swift stern action of this type should help minimize the number of dishonest people who are employed by hospitality enterprises.

An effective personnel recruiting and selection procedure is a hospitality operator's main weapon in the fight against employee theft and pilferage. One aspect of personnel selection that represents a highly controversial issue is the use of background investigations, particularly the investigation involving the use of "integrity" (that is, "honesty") tests or other similar reference-checking techniques. It is thought that these tests are the most effective weapon in the war against theft and pilferage.[14]

Integrity testing has become more popular in the past few years primarily because employers cannot use polygraph machines or other similar devices to determine employee honesty during the recruiting and hiring stages. Any type of honesty testing, though, will be controversial because these types of tests are not completely accurate. Furthermore, there is the feeling among many persons that these tests, as well as pre-employment drug tests, are an invasion of privacy.

Being certain that a new employee is honest is no simple or sure matter. Reference checks can tell what a previous employer knows—or what he or she wants to tell us—about past behavior. But stresses and strains could convert an honest employee to a dishonest one. Probably the best rule, here, is a cautious optimism about people, combined with a set of controls that make dishonesty difficult to engage in and relatively easy to check.

Designing the physical facilities to ensure proper security is relatively easy in back-of-the-house storage facilities, that is, easy if the operation is being built from the ground up, or if it is undergoing extensive remodeling, and if the owner-manager can spare the necessary funds. Unfortunately, many existing operations have flaws that prevent tight security. These flaws are often impossible to correct or, if correctable, require large expenditures.

In most cases, then, hospitality operators fall short in attempting to arm themselves with the previously cited three basic weapons in the fight against crime and must learn to work, instead, with the resources available. Nevertheless, all operators can take several specific steps to prevent theft and pilferage:

1. Document cash paid-outs carefully. Be certain that the delivery person receiving them initials your copy of the invoice properly. A canceled check always is your preferred receipt, but the convenience of paid-outs is important to many smaller operators. Nevertheless, you must be certain that your accounts are credited properly.

2. Never pay an invoice that shows a post office box number as the supplier's address without checking further. For that matter, do not pay a bill unless you are familiar with the supplier's name and address. But it is the box number that is more suspicious. If employees are trying to cheat by sending fraudulent invoices to the bookkeeper, a box number can be the tip-off.

3. Those who buy should never pay the bills. A buyer who pays may be tempted to pay himself or herself once in a while.[15] Most companies require the manager to verify all invoices for payment and then forward them to the accounting office or to company headquarters. Someone at headquarters then pays. Smaller firms can copy this practice to some degree by separating the buying and paying functions.

4. Cancel paperwork on all completed transactions. At the very least, you should mark an invoice paid as soon as you pay it so that this same invoice will not be paid again. Sometimes a type of perforating machine is used to punch a series of holes in the invoice, indicating that payment has been made.

   In addition to canceling all documentation, make sure it has been completed. For example, if part of a delivery must be returned, see to it that a Request for Credit memo is prepared or that you have otherwise received credit for the return.

   As an added precaution, the bill payer should compare the invoice with the original purchase order or other ordering record to ensure that he or she does not pay for nonexistent merchandise. If there are no purchase order copies, take steps to remedy this situation; it is just too easy to pay a fraudulent or padded invoice, particularly if the amount involved is relatively small.

   Furthermore, be especially careful to compare the AP prices noted on the invoice with those that were quoted to you earlier. You would be surprised at the number of times the quotations are less than the prices noted on the invoices. In most instances, this probably represents an innocent mistake (e.g., perhaps the computer at the supplier's warehouse was not programmed correctly). However, if you are not diligent in your comparisons, an unscrupulous supplier can earn a bit of extra income by saying one thing and charging another.

5. It would be a good idea to arrange, now and then, for an independent audit of the hospitality organization's operating procedures. If done on a random, unannounced basis, an audit can be an excellent deterrent to theft and pilferage. The independent auditor should (1) analyze invoices and payment checks to determine their accuracy, completeness, and consistency; (2) check the receiving routine and equipment; (3) inspect the storage facilities, taking a physical inventory and noting how consistent it is with the inventory figures recorded on accounting records; the physical inventory should also be

consistent with the sales volume and purchase expenditures; (4) check receiving sheets and stock requisitions for consistency with invoices, purchase orders, and payment checks; and (5) check consumption against reported units of sales—for example, compare the stock requisitions of steaks with guest checks in the dining room and the in-process inventory in the kitchen.

Surprise audits are used successfully in such other enterprises as banks, in which the audit team enters the premises, shuts down some teller windows, and begins the audit procedure. One cannot always shut down a hospitality facility, but there are slow periods when a surprise audit can be performed.

The surprise audit is undoubtedly a powerful control on theft and pilferage. It can easily have the same effect on employees as a surprise integrity test. And it is not unduly expensive. Most operations can easily afford such audits.

6. Hospitality employers do not use undercover agents as a rule in the back of the house. But spotters, or "shoppers," are occasionally used in the front of the house.[16] For instance, many bars pay a shopping service to send someone around periodically who, posing as a customer, observes all pertinent activities. This person then prepares a report for management, commenting on such things as product quality, service, whether anyone appeared to pocket cash illegally, and so on. A shopping service is relatively inexpensive and, like the surprise audit, represents a powerful crime deterrent.

7. Related to the surprise audit is the use of integrity tests and drug tests. These tests are relatively inexpensive. However, they may not be 100 percent accurate. In the hands of a competent evaluator, though, they may be a fair evaluation of employee honesty.

Some hospitality operations do not like to use any sort of honesty or drug-testing program. They do not wish to use something that may not always be accurate. Nor do they want to invade a person's privacy, which could hinder the development of a favorable employer/employee relationship.

8. If an operator does not relish preemployment testing, and is not satisfied with a surprise audit now and then, he or she can resort to a fidelity bonding company. A "bonding company" insures a hospitality operator against employee theft of cash. Not all employees are bonded, but cashiers usually are. Since the bonding company performs a thorough background check of all employees it insures, however, you could conceivably bond everyone for the sole purpose of investigating each applicant, though this might prove a fairly expensive way of getting thorough background checks. In lieu of bonding, an operator could employ a less-expensive background-checking firm (sometimes referred to as a "résumé-checking" service) as an alternative.[17]

Bonding is expensive. In addition, it tells you only about the past, not the future. And if a thief has never been caught, he or she will obviously receive a clean bill of health from the bonding company. Moreover, you must first determine the legality of this activity. Some states and municipalities may restrict background investigations of this type.

9. An owner-manager might consider investing in a trash compactor. A lot of stolen items are removed from the operation in trash cans, to be retrieved later by an off-duty employee or an accomplice. A compactor minimizes this opportunity.

10. Whenever possible, employees should be allowed to enter or leave the premises through only one door. And this door should not be used to receive deliveries, unless there is some sure way of guarding and controlling access to it. If necessary, it is better to insist that employees use the front door, the same door used by customers. As irritating as this requirement might sound, it helps to minimize theft and pilferage.

11. Employees should not be allowed to park their cars close to the building or near a doorway or large window that can be opened. This prevents them from sneaking out quickly with merchandise, stashing it in the car, and returning to the workplace.

    A related difficulty involves an outside area replete with such hiding places as tall shrubs, storage or garbage bins, and other nooks and crannies. Whenever possible, eliminate these potential repositories or limit employee access to them.

12. If possible, keep employee locker rooms and rest rooms within a reasonable distance so that you can check them once in a while. But they should not be too close. An employee can use either complete isolation or quick access to hide stolen items.

    If you cannot place these facilities in an optimal place in the building, the next best thing is to equip the employee lockers with heavy see-through screens instead of solid doors, as this eliminates an attractive hiding place for stolen items. Also, these facilities should not be too close to an exit or large window that can be opened.

13. Delivery agents should not be allowed to enter the premises or loiter in unauthorized areas unless their presence is necessary for such things as standing orders. Some of them merely want to be helpful by putting items in storage. But some may have sticky fingers. Furthermore, they tend to distract employees.

    A lot of socializing goes on in the receiving and storing areas. The owner-manager must make the decision concerning this and any related activities.

14. Receivers should not be rushed. They should take their time and inspect all deliveries adequately, keeping in mind some of the common receiving problems we discussed in Chapter 13.

15. As much as possible, let no one remain in the back of the house who has no business there. Friends of employees should be kept out of these areas. Salespersons and delivery agents cannot always be barred, but they can be restricted to certain places in the back of the house.

    You should restrict these people because, not only do they distract employees, they also might try to establish some sort of pilfering arrangement with an unscrupulous employee. Moreover, the seeds of backdoor selling could find fertile ground.

16. The owner-manager should invest in some cost-effective physical barriers. These include (1) time locks that can be opened only at certain times by certain persons; Marlock computerized locking systems (or equivalent) are excellent choices as they will print out reports noting who accessed the system (and whether such persons were authorized to do so) as well as access times; (2) heavy-duty locks that are rotated occasionally, with the keys or key cards entrusted only to those who absolutely must have them; Modeco locks (or equivalent) are preferred as they are considered the most secure;[18] (3) adequate lighting in the storage areas so that thieves cannot hide; (4) reasonably priced closed-circuit television (CCTV), which can be an excellent deterrent to theft; (5) uniformed guards, who may inspect employees, their packages, and their time cards when they leave work; (6) see-through screens on all storage facility doors—heavy screens can keep thieves out, while allowing a supervisor to spot-check the storage areas quickly; and (7) perimeter and interior alarm systems; a sound control system is especially useful for areas in the property that are not continuously open.

17. An owner-manager should try to remove collusion opportunities by separating the buying receiving, storing, and issuing activities. He or she might even go as far as to separate the bookkeeping and bill-paying functions. This is good control, but it may be impractical for all but the largest firms.

    But some separation is possible. For example, an owner-manager might order an assistant manager to help the receiver–storeroom manager or the chef-buyer-receiver to inspect incoming merchandise. In addition, a surprise audit can go a long way toward achieving the type of control a complete separation of these operating activities usually affords.

18. An owner-manager should compare what he or she is paying current suppliers with AP prices available from other suppliers for the same

type of merchandise. It would, of course, be more reliable to compare EP costs whenever possible, as a premium AP price can be, as we have said, entirely justifiable under certain circumstances. But managers must make the effort to compare AP prices periodically, since it is just too easy for buyers, or user-buyers, to pay a bit more for a little kickback. This practice is extremely hard to discover, but it is essential not to overlook this all too tempting opportunity within the reach of most buyers.

19. If possible, try not to hire employees who have relatives working for suppliers. Better to eliminate this and other similar conflicts of interest from the start.

20. Make sure that whoever pays the bills checks them over carefully. Sometimes a phony invoice gets slipped in. (This is especially true with bills for regularly scheduled periodic services, such as waste removal.) Or you might run into the problem of receiving a solicitation from a company, but the solicitation looks just like an invoice. If you are not careful, someone might honor the solicitation, thinking that it is just another bill that must be paid.

   If possible you should develop an approved payee list (i.e., a list of names of individuals or companies eligible to receive a check from you). If a bill pops up and the supplier's name is not on the approved payee list, it should not be paid unless management personally approves.

21. As much as possible (and without compromising quality), take everything out of its shipping container before storing it. This practice minimizes the problem of "inventory shrinkage" before you even open the case.

   In addition, when you take a physical inventory, actually lift a few containers; that is, make sure there is something in the container. It is possible for someone to take a full one and leave an empty one, or substitute an inferior product, in its place.

22. Be leery of putting up cash deposits. It is possible that a supplier or, more commonly, someone who does remodeling work or other types of service, will request a deposit for one reason or another. Be careful that this person does not take your deposit and skip town on you. It does not happen too often in our industry, but it does occur now and then with people who, for example, do some remodeling work for you and need some cash up front to buy their materials. Also, you could get stung if you send away for something advertised in a trade paper; the sales advertisement may be disguising some sort of sham operation. Unless you know your suppliers and other vendors, you probably should avoid paying anything until you receive your purchase.

23. It might be worthwhile to become a house account for one or more suppliers whose integrity you trust completely. Although being a

house account usually increases the AP prices you must pay, at least for some items, you do have the assurance that your friends will not conspire with others to defraud your establishment.

24. Management must develop a procedure to prevent the possibility of unrecorded merchandise getting into the storage facilities or into the in-process inventory. For instance, nothing should be received unless it is accompanied by an invoice or unless the receiver records it somehow. If this is not done, there will be more stock in inventory than that recorded. And, as a result, this excess inventory could be pilfered by employees somehow and no one will be able to detect the problem. An old bartender's trick is to deliver his or her own personal bottles to the establishment and later sell drinks made with the contents of these bottles and pocket the cash.

25. When ordering merchandise, make certain that you are not rushed into purchasing inadequate products. For instance, it is possible that a telephone salesperson can call you unexpectedly, offering what at first might appear to be sterling goods. Some phone solicitors may resort to deceptive practices to sell.

    You also might misinterpret, say, an advertisement, and end up ordering something through the mail that you do not want. For instance, you might mistakenly order an off-brand artificial sweetener packaged in blue-colored, individual packets, assuming the product is the nationally recognized Equal brand merchandise.

26. You should develop an approved supplier list and instruct all persons who have ordering responsibilities to use the suppliers on the list. Of course, there are exceptions to any rule, but management must be informed if, for example, someone in the operation wishes to purchase something from an unfamiliar supplier. You would want to investigate this supplier, utilizing the procedures discussed in Chapter 11, and then make the final decision regarding the admissibility of this supplier to your approved supplier list.

    It would appear that using an approved supplier list is one of the most effective controls for things such as kickbacks and other forms of skullduggery. It is a practice that is followed by the vast majority of large hospitality operations.

27. The hospitality operator should avoid purchasing merchandise in small, single-service packages. These items are very easy to pilfer, though their convenience for customer service may override the need for greater security.

28. One of the most effective deterrents to theft and pilferage is to restrict access to all high-cost products. While it is not always feasible to lock up everything, management must maintain close control over those items that represent the bulk of the purchase dollar.

29. You should maintain close tabs on all expensive items throughout the production and service cycles. For instance, each day a manager should conduct a critical item inventory analysis; that is, he or she should balance the use of key, expensive ingredients with the stock requisitions and guest checks. There should be no difference between the actual usage of these items and their expected (i.e., "standard") usage.

30. If affordable, management should adopt computer technology available to calculate the theoretical inventory value (sometimes referred to as the inventory "book" value) so that it can be compared with the value determined by a physical inventory count. Unlike hand-posted records, the computer allows a quick, convenient compilation of bin card balances that, when compared with the physical inventory count, will immediately highlight inventory control problems.

31. Management must ensure that access to all records is restricted to only those individuals who are authorized to make entries in those records, or to those persons who must analyze them.

32. There are additional security precautions for an owner-manager to recognize. But we have discussed the principal ones associated with the back of the house, that is, those that are pertinent to the purchasing function. Several security considerations are, of course, relevant to the front of the house. You should take the time to peruse some of the excellent materials dealing with these concerns.[19]

Control and security have become popular terms in the hospitality industry. They are increasingly the subjects of books, seminars, newspaper features, and magazine articles. But some of these often omit a crucial factor: employee supervision.

The best systems fail without proper supervision. Physical barriers, audits, separation of responsibilities, and so on are the machines, but supervision is the grease. Without it, security cannot operate. The owner-manager has two eyes: they should be used instead of depending too much on indirect control and security systems.

An owner-manager may well slip into one of two camps: (1) security will become a mania, and he or she will use everything possible to protect the property; or (2) security will occupy a low position on the priority list—visiting with guests, for instance, may be more important to some managers than overseeing production.

Control, security, and supervision go hand in hand. Successful operators find the time to supervise properly. Unfortunately, these operators seem to be in short supply; otherwise, the losses due to employee theft and pilferage would not increase as they seem to do every year.

The glamour of the hospitality industry sometimes tempts us to forget the mundane aspects of employee supervision and motivation. Buyers are no different. They would much rather write specifications, test new food products, and bargain with salespersons than supervise employees. Effective supervision may not guarantee success, but inadequate supervisory attention practically guarantees failure.

WHO CHECKS THE CHECKER?

Who watches over the manager, especially if you are an absentee owner? Also, who watches the chef while he or she is watching someone else? We have to draw the line somewhere and eventually trust someone. It is virtually impossible to have a complete set of checks and balances. An adequate management information system, however, should help you monitor your operating results in a way that will indicate where, if at all, there may be problems in the purchasing-receiving-storage cycle.

KEY WORDS AND CONCEPTS

Accepting gifts

Actual product cost calculation

Actual usage

Alarm system

Approved payee list

Approved supplier list

Backdoor selling

Background investigations

Background-checking firm

Bonding company

Bribery

Cancel transactions appropriately

Cash deposits

CCTV

Compare bid AP prices with those listed on invoice

Critical item inventory analysis

Document paid-outs

Fictitious invoices

Honest, unintentional mistakes

House account

Independent surprise audits

Indirect control system

Integrity test

Inventory book value

Inventory padding

Inventory shrinkage

Inventory substitutions

Inventory theft

Invoice padding

Invoice scams

Kickbacks

Marlock system

Modeco locks

Physical barriers

Physical inventory

Reference checks

Restricted access

Résumé-checking service

"Returned" merchandise

Security problems

Selecting honest suppliers and
  employees

Segregate operating activities

Separate buyer from bill payer

Shoppers

Short orders

Standard usage

Stock requisition

Supplier and receiver error

Suspicious behavior

Telephone sales scams

Theoretical inventory value

Toner-phoners

Undercover agents

WATS-line hustlers

REFERENCES

1. Gregory Goussak, "Employee Theft and Fraud in the Food Service Industry," *The Bottomline,* October/November 1993, p. 20.

2. Donald E. Lundberg and John R. Walker, *The Restaurant: From Concept to Operation,* 2d ed. (New York: John Wiley & Sons, 1993), p. 101.

3. Beth Lorenzini, "Internal Security," in *Winning Foodservice Ideas.* Michael Bartlett, ed. (New York: John Wiley & Sons, 1994), p. 242.

4. Carolyn Walkup, "Former Rax Prexy to Pay $400K," *Nation's Restaurant News,* January 6, 1992, p. 1.

5. Ron Ruggless, "Whataburger Prexy Jim Peterson Resigns," *Nation's Restaurant News,* January 17, 1994, p. 1. See also, Rick Van Warner, "Kickbacks Can Trip Up a Company: Set Honesty as the Only Policy," *Nation's Restaurant News,* January 24, 1994, p. 19.

6. Andrea Gerlin, "How a Penney Buyer Made up to $1.5 Million on Vendors' Kickbacks," *The Wall Street Journal,* February 7, 1995, p. A1.

7. "Milk Price-Fixing Case Yields Guilty Plea, Prosecutors Say," *The Wall Street Journal,* August 27, 1991, p. B5. See also, Stephen Chapman: "Fixing Milk Prices: Crime, Blessing or Both?" *Las Vegas Review Journal,* September 13, 1991, p. 11B; "Mrs. Baird's Bakeries Found Guilty of Fixing Bread Prices in Texas," *The Wall Street Journal,* February 15, 1996, p. B5.

8. "Louisiana Chefs Arrested in Illegal-Fish Sting," *Nation's Restaurant News,* May 1, 1995, p. 2.

9. Paul Levy, "Skimming at the Savoy: Britain's Foodiegate," *The Wall Street Journal,* May 30, 1985, p. 28.

10. Howard Schultz, "Washing Away the Sin of Overpayment," *The Wall Street Journal,* August 9, 1993, p. A12. See also, Pat DiDomenico, "Don't Get Scammed," *Restaurants USA,* June/July 1992, p. 18.

11. Michael York, "Ex-Marriott Official Pleads Guilty in Theft," *The Washington Post,* August 29, 1992, p. C7.

12. Lee Berton, "Inventory Chicanery Tempts More Firms, Fools More Auditors," *The Wall Street Journal,* December 14, 1992, p. A1.

13. Timothy L. O'Brien, "Copier-Toner Phone Scams Are Targeting Small Firms," *The Wall Street Journal,* July 16, 1993, p. B2. See also, "Beware of the Scam," *Nevada State Purchasing Newsletter,* June 1995.

14. Terry Franklin, "Honesty Tests Are Best Weapon Vs. Theft," *Nation's Restaurant News,* May 1, 1995, p. 26. See also, Gilbert Fuchsberg, "Integrity-Test Firms Fear Report Card by Congress," *The Wall Street Journal,* September 20, 1990, p. B1.

15. "For a U. of California Campus, a Purchasing Agent Seemed the Ideal Employee— Until He Got Caught," *The Chronicle of Higher Education,* April 10, 1991, p. A26.

16. John Stefanelli, "Using Mystery Shoppers to Maintain Hospitality Company Service Standards," *Hospitality & Tourism Educator,* Winter 1994, p. 17.

17. Eugene Carlson, "Business of Background Checking Comes to the Fore," *The Wall Street Journal,* August 31, 1993, p. B2. See also, Phillip M. Perry, "StopThief," *Restaurants USA,* November 1995, p. 13; Jenny Hedden, "Sorting Out the Bad Eggs," *Restaurants USA,* February 1996, p. 13.

18. Jim W. Moffa, "50 Ways to Increase Restaurant Security, Safety," *Nation's Restaurant News,* January 17, 1994, p. 18.

19. See, for example, Russell Bintliff, *Crimeproofing Your Business: 301 Low-Cost, No-Cost Ways to Protect Your Office, Store, or Business* (New York: McGraw-Hill, 1994); Rudolph Kimiecik, *Loss Prevention Guide for Retail Businesses* (New York: John Wiley & Sons, 1995); and Robert L. O'Block, *Security and Crime Prevention,* 2d ed. (Boston: Butterworth-Heinemann, 1991). See also, *Security Management,* American Society for Industrial Security, 1655 North Fort Myer Drive, Suite 1200, Arlington, VA, 22209.

QUESTIONS AND PROBLEMS

1. What security problems do you risk when you allow the buyer to receive deliveries? When you allow the buyer to pay for the items he or she orders?

2. Assuming that it is legal, should a hospitality operator use an integrity test in employee selection? Why? What are the potential advantages and disadvantages of the test? If possible, speak to an operator who likes to use it and one who does not. Compare and contrast their thoughts.

3. Is employee supervision the best deterrent to theft and pilferage? Why? If possible, ask a hotel manager or restaurant manager to comment on your answer.

4. What are some of the relatively inexpensive physical barriers that an owner-manager can use to deter theft and pilferage?

5. Are there any benefits associated with independent, random audits? Do you think they would be worth the time and expense? If possible, ask an accounting firm what it would charge for such a service. Also ask a representative of this company to comment on the costs and benefits of surprise audits.

6. Assume that you do not want to use an integrity test. How would you check a job applicant's honesty?

7. Why is an owner-manager generally reluctant to put up a cash deposit?

8. Why is paying with a check preferable to using a cash paid-out?

9. List three examples of kickbacks.

10. Why does a buyer often double as the receiving agent? Give at least two reasons.

11. What is the primary purpose of using an approved payee list as part of the overall bill-paying procedure?

12. The approved supplier list represents a major security precaution that is popular among large hospitality companies. Give some of the reasons for its popularity.

13. Why would a hospitality operator use a shopping service?

14. Why would a hospitality operator require employees to be bonded?

15. What is "check padding?" What can you do to avoid it?

16. What are the major advantages of becoming a house account?

17. What are the major disadvantages of becoming a house account?

18. What is the primary reason for not hiring an employee who has a relative working for one of your suppliers?

19. Why would you be reluctant to purchase an item from a telephone salesperson?

20. What is the most common type of kickback arrangement?

21. What could a hospitality operator do to protect the company from being defrauded by an invoice scam?

22. What is "inventory padding"? What can you do to prevent it?

23. Assume that your buyer is purchasing all meat items from one purveyor. You note that other meat purveyors offer the same type of meat products, and that their AP prices are consistently 2 to 3 percent lower than what you are paying. You decide to talk to the buyer about this situation. What questions would you ask? Why? If possible, ask a hotel or restaurant manager to comment on your answer.

24. When should a hospitality operator use undercover agents in his or her operation?

25. What are "inventory substitutions"? What can you do to prevent them?

CHAPTER 16

COMPUTER TECHNOLOGY APPLICATIONS IN PURCHASING*

THE PURPOSE OF THIS CHAPTER

This chapter discusses:

- Distributor applications
- Buyer applications

INTRODUCTION

As noted in Chapter 3, technological applications in the selection and procurement function have evolved rapidly over the years. There currently are many forms of computer technology available to assist primary sources, intermediaries, and hospitality buyers. The cycle of purchasing, distribution, receiving, storage, issuing, and product usage can be streamlined considerably for those who can afford the necessary technological tools.

DISTRIBUTOR APPLICATIONS

Distributors can use computer software applications to track and analyze many business functions. For instance, they typically use specialized, customized software to build customer data bases that can be utilized to predict customer behavior. This type of software can also be used to estimate the number and types of hospitality operations that might open in a particular area.

* By Andy Feinstein, The Pennsylvania State University.

Suppliers also use software applications to facilitate the sales process. For instance, some suppliers have all inventories counted, costed, organized, and stored on computerized product data bases. This information allows them to manage and price their products quickly and easily. It is much more convenient for everyone than is the traditional method, whereby buyers receive product lists from distributors that note product names, manufacturers, identification numbers, and other descriptive information but, unfortunately, do not note product availability status. Product status must be obtained by calling the sales representative or by calling the distributor directly. The buyer then must call in the order or place it with the sales representative. This traditional method is still widely used, though many buyers use the fax machine to communicate instead of the phone.

Some distributors have further streamlined the sales process and have taken it to the technological forefront by developing extensive on-line ordering systems. Through a system of this type, a buyer's computer can communicate with a distributor's computer via a modem. This line of communication allows buyers to order products directly on the computer and receive instant feedback on pricing and availability. Such systems also minimize the ordering function and the paper trail for distributors. In many cases, distributors provide free-to-use computer hardware and software if the buyers purchase a sufficient amount of merchandise from them.

Some distributors use sophisticated software applications to outline the routing sequences their drivers must follow when delivering products. A distributor can enter into the computer all locations drivers need to visit the following day (by typing an address or placing a marker on a digital map). Using a routing model, the computer develops the most efficient route to take and indicates the optimal number of delivery trucks to use.

Routing software is often integrated with time efficiency programs. A time efficiency program estimates driver downtime and the amount of product that should be delivered per hour, by taking into account street traffic flow, various times of day, and the expected time spent in loading and unloading shipments. It can also compare these estimates with actual results. In addition, the software can provide further feedback, such as what streets to take and what time of day they should be avoided in order to reduce delays caused by traffic or highway construction. Related software can be integrated with a time efficiency program to track delivery errors, discrepancies, and complaints or comments by customers, receiving agents, and/or salespersons.

All of these software programs are usually integrated to form one cohesive process. This process enables the distributor to minimize order placing and delivery costs and to resolve problems quickly.

BUYER APPLICATIONS

Over the past few years, many technological products have been developed to streamline the selection and procurement process and make life easier for the hospitality buyer who can afford to use them. Hospitality operators have generally been eager to adopt labor- and time-saving electronic equipment to enhance the purchasing function and the overall inventory control process.

FAX MACHINE

The recent introduction of a cost-effective fax machine has revolutionized the order-taking and receiving process. It allows buyers to check off on a piece of paper those items they want to purchase and submit this information instantaneously over the telephone lines. This process significantly reduces the confusion and mistakes sometimes associated with verbal orders. Furthermore, since a fax machine's printed output can be stored for historical records, it can be used to verify orders, prove they were sent, and establish usage patterns.

PERSONAL COMPUTER

The personal computer, discussed throughout this chapter, is by far the most powerful and useful tool a hospitality owner-manager can have, even if it is a stand-alone machine with only a few features. With the invention of the first spreadsheet software program in the late 1970s, operators were given the ability to analyze huge amounts of data and to manage inventories more effectively. Previously, the majority of inventory costing and counting was done by persons armed with calculators, paper, and pencils.

Personal computers have also made it possible for hospitality operators to base purchasing decisions on current data, thus minimizing the need to guess about such things as current food costs and menu item popularity.

COMPUTERIZED POINT-OF-SALE (POS) SYSTEM

Before the introduction of the computerized POS system, it was very difficult to track sold menu items and the ingredients needed to make them. The gear-driven cash register merely stores cash and provides some limited sales information on printed receipts. Today, POS systems are very much like personal computers. They have built-in microprocessors that can tabulate and organize tremendous amounts of sales data very quickly.

More advanced POS systems feature touch-screen technology. They also allow users to "86" (i.e., delete) menu items, track employee activity, analyze worker productivity, and force order modifiers (e.g., when a food server enters a steak order, the computer asks, "What temperature?" or if the food server enters a baked potato order, the computer asks, "Butter and sour cream with that?"). Some even allow a server to carry a wireless ordering system to the table; orders entered this way are automatically sent to the display screen in the bar and/or kitchen.

In large hospitality operations, POS systems are networked and communicate with a central computer (sometimes referred to as a "server"). This server can track sales from the connected computers (sometimes referred to as "nodes" or "workstations") in all departments or areas within the hospitality operation and instantly provide vital information to managers. For instance, more advanced POS systems have inventory-tracking systems that automatically delete from inventory the standard amount of each ingredient that is used to make each menu item, thereby giving the manager a theoretical inventory usage figure that can later be compared with actual physical counts. Furthermore, some POS systems allow purchase orders to be drafted directly to the distributors, based on sales and inventory reduction information.

BAR CODE SCANNER

Some hospitality operations place universal product code (UPC)-labels on their inventory items (or use those applied by the suppliers) to streamline the inventory control process. The physical count then usually consists of scanning each product in the storeroom with a hand-held scanner. There is no need to spend time locating a product on a lengthy printed inventory list and recording, by hand, the total number of units in inventory at the end of the month. Instead, the data are gathered quickly with the hand-held scanner and down-loaded to the computer for instant analysis.

The hand-held scanner can also be used to count in-process inventories. For instance, each type of alcohol in a lounge can be bar coded to streamline the beverage inventory procedure. Without bar codes, the typical procedure in beverage operations is to estimate, by sight, the amount of beverage remaining in a container to the nearest tenth. This is a very tedious, time-consuming process that often yields inaccurate results. Using a hand-held scanner and a programmable small scale, the operator merely scans the bar code and then places the container on the scale. By reading the code, the computerized scale recognizes the type and container size of beverage, computes the total weight, and subtracts the container weight and, if necessary, the weight of the attached pourer. It then calculates the residual weight and converts it to fluid ounces. This precise measurement system provides an incredible amount of cost control in the beverage area, because it immediately highlights discrepancies between the amount of beverage the POS system indicates should have been used and the actual usage computed with the bar code scanner.

PRODUCT IDENTIFICATION AND SPECIFICATIONS

Buyers have many options available to "spec out" products for their hospitality operations. Traditional forms include buyers guides, such as the National Association of Meat Purveyors' (NAMP) *The Meat Buyers Guide.* This printed guidebook notes specific product information and is illustrated with many full-color photos. Computer technology, though, allows printed guidebooks to be converted to digital formats. For instance, publications such as *The Meat Buyers Guide* will eventually be available on a CD-ROM disk. (The CD-ROM is a digital form of a printed publication.) In this case, it will enhance the buyer's ability to select meat products very efficiently. The buyer will no longer have to flip through hundreds of pages to find a specific cut of meat. He or she will be able to search and find a suitable product in a few seconds. Furthermore, this technology will allow the buyer to view the exact location on a meat carcass from which a specific retail cut of meat originates. This retail cut of meat can then be linked to software that will suggest appropriate recipes and cooking techniques.

There are other CD-ROM products on the market that can also streamline the product identification and specification process. These software packages allow users to search data base indexes listing thousands of product categories and locate information about the suppliers who sell them. These CD-ROMs contain an endless amount of information. If a product is made somewhere in the world and is distributed by someone, chances are it can be found on one of these disks.

PRODUCT ORDERING

Some distributors have developed sophisticated software and hardware packages that allow buyers to order products directly from a personal computer. An example of this technology is the Alliant-LINK DIRECT™ Information System available from Alliant Foodservice.

Alliant Foodservice (formerly Kraft Foodservice), a national distribution company generating $4.5 billion per year in sales, wanted to develop a method whereby a distributor could streamline and minimize the buyer's ordering procedure, thereby creating a value-added service for the buyer. At the same time, when buyers use this ordering system, they streamline the order-taking process at the distributor's end. Previously, a distributor had to enter a buyer's order from a fax, phone call, or written purchase order, but through the new system this inefficient "multiple ordering" process is eliminated. Instead, the order is entered directly into the distributor's computer system by the buyer. This process will reduce labor costs and time on the buyer's end and on the distributor's end. Another distributor benefit of the process is the likelihood that users of this ordering system will become house or "prime vendor" accounts.

Alliant Foodservice developed a national system that communicates to a large bank of computers in a central location. This central location (in Phoenix, AZ) stores a massive amount of information on data bases. These data bases contain Alliant's product costs and pricing, product availability, buyer profiles, and so forth.

Individual personal computers located in hospitality operations throughout the country can access this central location to seek product information or to place orders. Utilizing a modem, special software provided by Alliant, a user name, and a password, hospitality operators can link their computers to the central bank. These computers can be used by buyers to price and order from a digital list of products Alliant sells in their own geographic areas.

The system allows product information to be retrieved in several ways, unlike the typical printed catalog in which everything is listed alphabetically and/or by product categories. For instance, electronic data bases compiled by Alliant Foodservice allow users to search for and evaluate all types of hot dogs Alliant sells. Buyers can view hot dogs by size, types of ingredients, and packers' brands. The user can also narrow the search, for example, to 4:1 (four hot dogs per pound), pure-beef hot dogs, Oscar Mayer brand. From this narrow list, the user can then choose the desired product or continue to refine and narrow the search. Once the desired product is found, the hospitality operator can then "tag," or choose, products he or she wants to buy.

At the end of the selection procedure, the hospitality operator can acquire product pricing information. Buyers can also find out which master cases Alliant is willing to bust.

If everything is acceptable to the buyer, the order can be transmitted right on the computer. The buyer can also tell the computer what products to substitute if there are any out of stock. The central computer then takes the order and communicates this information to the local Alliant Foodservice distribution center, which delivers the products the following day.

Alliant-LINK DIRECT also has software modules that can analyze the hospitality operation's inventory (including products not bought from Alliant), provide historical purchasing and invoice information, and analyze and cost recipes.

INVENTORY TRACKING AND STORAGE MANAGEMENT

If product orders have been made through an on-line ordering system, this information can also be used in a number of different ways. For instance, it can be linked to other software and used in the equations and formulas noted in Chapters 8, 9, and 14.

Today many hospitality operators use some type of computer application to increase their inventory and cost control efforts. For instance, some operators develop elaborate spreadsheets using generic spreadsheet software, such as Lotus 123® or Microsoft Excel®, where they list all their products in inventory and then develop mathematical formulas to calculate costs and usage. On the last day of each month, they physically count their storeroom and in-process inventories and enter this information on the spreadsheet. They also enter all product costs, which usually come from typing in invoice receipts for the month or from directly downloading the information from an electronic ordering system they are using. The information currently entered is the ending inventory, and the information entered the previous month is the beginning inventory. Once the major variables have been entered (beginning inventory, ending inventory, purchases, and other end-of-month adjustments), the computer can easily calculate the monthly cost of goods sold.

Some hospitality operators use "off-the-shelf" software packages and services that are specifically designed to manage inventory in a hospitality environment. These software packages can streamline the back-of-the-house hospitality operation. Many of them can be linked to an operator's POS system. These packages can also cost recipes, analyze a recipe's nutritional information, calculate food and beverage costs, evaluate a food item's sales history, forecast sales, develop audit trails, allow instant stock level information, and enhance menu planning efforts. In addition, many of them can track employee work schedules, attendance patterns, and work-hour accumulations.

When generic spreadsheet programs or off-the-shelf software does not meet a hospitality operator's needs, he or she might hire a software consulting firm that specializes in the hospitality industry. A specialist can develop customized software applications to satisfy almost any need. Furthermore, the developers of some off-the-shelf software products can customize some or all of their software packages.

INTERNET

The Internet is rapidly changing the way hospitality operations select and procure products. It can streamline operations and minimize costs for suppliers and buyers. The Internet also allows buyers and sellers to communicate information relatively quickly. Furthermore, it allows buyers and suppliers to acquire information from a wide variety of worldwide sources.

Although many forward-looking hospitality and food-service distributors are already developing Internet applications, content related to the purchasing activity is currently in its infancy. However, there is a vast amount of information that can be accessed by anyone who can afford the time, money, and effort needed to enter the "Information Superhighway." Over the next few years, it is estimated that the Internet will become more useful and more user-friendly, which will cause the selection and procurement process to evolve into a highly technical, mechanical process.

The Internet is a worldwide network of computers. Its name derives from "internetworking," the original description of computers and networks linked together. It all began in the late 1960s at the Advanced Research Projects Agency of the U.S. Department of Defense. Its original name was ARPANET, and its original intention was to allow scientists a way of communicating directly with one another while simultaneously exchanging information with all persons having access to the system.

The first system consisted of computers located at Stanford University, the University of California at Los Angeles (UCLA), the University of California at Santa Barbara (UCSB), and the University of Utah. Computers linked to the Internet typically communicate via phone line transmission, although cable, wireless, and optical communications are also in use.

This worldwide network offers many benefits to the hospitality buyer. The major ones are described in the following paragraphs.

Electronic Mail (E-mail)

E-mail allows hospitality buyers to communicate with primary sources, intermediaries, colleagues, and any other person who has an E-mail address. It allows buyers to send information or documents to other individuals. For instance, a buyer can compose a letter to a distributor, soliciting competitive bid data. However, instead of sending the letter through the postal system, he or she can send it electronically to that distributor's E-mail address.

The E-mail address consists of a person's user name and the host providing access to the Internet at that location. A buyer can also send the same letter simultaneously to all persons on a mailing list. For instance, he or she can request pricing information from many suppliers with merely a few keystrokes. If all relevant suppliers are on the mailing list, the buyer will be more productive.

E-mail also allows the sender to include files and documents with the original communication. For those who want the full range of capability, there is Multimedia E-mail, a system that allows the sender to add graphics, animation, and sound bytes to the message.

Newsgroups

A newsgroup is an electronic bulletin board used by many persons who share a common interest. (Newsgroups are sometimes referred to as "interest groups" or "discussion groups.") Each newsgroup specializes in a particular topic. People with similar interests can "post" messages to a newsgroup, and other subscribers to the group can read and respond to them. Newsgroups are typically part of the USENET news system, which was developed in 1979.

Newsgroups are a great way to keep current in the foodservice industry. They also allow individuals to obtain specific information and input very quickly. For instance, a buyer can compose a short message soliciting supplier references, the feasibility of forming a purchasing co-op, or the availability of a unique product, send it to a newsgroup, such as rec.food.restaurants, and receive relevant information without the normal time delay inherent in other forms of communication. Some popular food-related newsgroups are sci.bio.food-science, rec.food.restaurants, rec.food.baking, alt.food.low-fat, alt.cooking-chat, and rec.food.cooking.

Mailing lists are very similar to newsgroups. However, rather than people posting messages to an electronic bulletin board, they communicate by sending messages through E-mail to an entire group. Subscribers to a particular mailing list can read and respond to E-mail messages that have been sent to the whole group. Some mailing lists are moderated (these are usually referred to as "manual" lists), whereas some route messages automatically to all members (these are usually referred to as "LISTRSERVs").

World Wide Web (WWW)

Probably the most active part of the Internet is the World Wide Web (WWW). The "web" is a graphical interface that allows information to be connected through "hyperlinks." Hyperlinks allow users to select a word or image and connect to more information about the topic. Users who have graphical browser software on their systems can easily locate and view all pertinent information about any topic on the web.

Information is located on various web "sites." A site, or site "location," is referred to as a Uniform Resource Locator (URL). Information can be found by entering the site URL or by using one of the many search engines that are designed to locate information based on key words or associations.

The web portion of the Internet has many sites useful to the selection and procurement function. Many of these sites provide detailed, current information and can include text, graphics, photographs, sound bytes, animation, full-motion video, and interactivity.

There is much information on the Internet to assist the hospitality buyer. For instance, sites range from those providing daily news about the hospitality industry to those specializing in unique cookware and equipment, and just about anything in between. The amount of information, already rather huge, nevertheless continues to grow each day.

An example of the use of this dynamic technology is the University of Florida Agricultural Department's web site. A portion of this site is dedicated to information about fresh produce farming and distribution within the United States. This site allows users to view current information about products currently grown and harvested in certain geographic regions. It also contains information about standardized shipping costs per case.

Although this information may seem too detailed for the average hospitality operator, it can be useful in certain situations. For instance, this site provides information about the seasonality of specific fresh produce items and the current weather in their growing regions. While a buyer's printed produce specification guide might note that, for example, the growing season of asparagus is over, data on this web site might indicate that, in fact, the growing season has been extended for several weeks due to unseasonably good weather. Moreover, if a buyer wants to know why lettuce AP prices have increased, he or she might find that recent flooding in the lettuce-growing region has caused considerable crop damage, thereby inflating prices.

Other web sites can help buyers spec out products. For instance, there are many food marketing boards in the United States that have been organized to provide information about a particular product to interested persons. For example, the California Avocado Commission has the responsibility of promoting the sale and purchase of avocados. This board, as well as many others, such as the California Walnut Board, the Ontario Pork Producers' Marketing Board, and the California Cherry Advisory Board, have web sites that include information about their products, for instance, suggested recipes, current crop reports, and variety and grade specifications. These sites also allow viewers to engage in question/answer activity with the board administrators.

Information on food web sites can help the buyer make key decisions about the type, variety, and quality of product that should be ordered. The buyer can find recipe suggestions and consult with experts about a particular product. Although the buyer's local suppliers are usually very knowledgeable about their products, the food sites, especially those maintained by the marketing boards, have the ability to gather immediately vast amounts of current information from growers, processors, and manufacturers (primarily because these suppliers are paying to maintain these associations and their web sites).

Many national premium brands also have web sites. For instance, well-known brands such as Nabisco, Land O'Lakes, Ragu, BirdsEye, McCormick, Butterball, and Indian Harvest are just a few keystrokes and/or mouse clicks away.

WHAT LIES AHEAD?

It is hard to believe that the use of computer technology in the selection and procurement function is only in its infancy. In the future, technology will bring more ideas, more tools, and more information to hospitality operators. And it cannot come too soon, since hospitality operators will continue to experience more competitive markets, slimmer profit margins, and a shrinking labor force. Technology will help operators overcome these obstacles and help them succeed.

In a competitive environment, hospitality operators have less time to make key managerial decisions. Making the correct decision quickly can be done, but only if operators have access to the necessary technological tools.

Suppliers in the future will probably bear more of the burden of providing hospitality operators with the proper technology to suit a more technical, mechanical selection and procurement process, as well as the burden of helping operators control their businesses more efficiently. Since hospitality businesses are the suppliers' customers, it is in their best interest to ensure that these companies make the correct purchasing and other key management decisions. Suppliers, therefore, will be more actively involved with their customers, helping them to develop and evaluate new menus, substitution possibilities, inventory management procedures, and marketing strategies and to streamline the business process through the use of electronic commerce.

In the future, it is thought that the distinguishing factors between suppliers will not be so much the products they sell (the major products are already very close in quality and cost), but the supplier services they provide and the technology they use and can share with hospitality operators. In addition, because of time constraints, competition, and economies of scale, many industry experts feel that more hospitality operators will practice one-stop shopping, thereby teaming with prime vendors to enhance their competitive positions.

KEY WORDS AND CONCEPTS

Actual inventory usage

The Alliant-LINK DIRECT Information System

Bar code scanner

CD-ROM

Central computer

Cost control

Customized software

Data base

Down-load

E-mail

Fax machine

Free-to-use computer

Graphical browser software

House account

Hyperlink

Interest group

Internet

Inventory control

LISTSERVs

Mailing list

Manual list

Marketing boards

Modem

Multimedia E-mail

Newsgroup

Node

Off-the-shelf software

One-stop shopping

On-line ordering system

Order modifier

Personal computer

POS system

Posting messages

Prime vendor account

Product identification

Product status

Routing software

Search engine

Server

Specifications

Spreadsheet software

Theoretical inventory usage

Time efficiency program

Touch-screen technology

Uniform resource locator (URL)

USENET system

Virtual discussion group

Web site

Wireless ordering system

World Wide Web (WWW)

SUGGESTED EXERCISES

1. Plan a field trip to a full-line distributor (such as Alliant) to view the computerized ordering, routing, delivering, and invoicing system.

2. Plan a field trip to a hospitality operation that uses an on-line ordering system. (It is recommended that you visit the supplier before visiting the hospitality operation in order to obtain the best possible perspectives on these interactive computerized systems.)

3. Visit the web site that has been developed by John Wiley & Sons, Inc., to accompany this text. The address is:

   http://www.wiley.com

   Ideally, the first visit to this site will be done in a computer lab where the lab instructor can guide viewers through the site's highlights. After this introduction, viewers should spend as much time as possible visiting areas of interest, as well as the interactive exercises designed to sharpen selection and procurement skills.

SELECTION
AND PROCUREMENT
OF THE ITEMS

CHAPTER 17

FRESH PRODUCE

THE PURPOSE OF THIS CHAPTER

This chapter discusses:

- The selection factors for fresh produce
- Purchasing, receiving, storing, and issuing fresh produce
- The in-process fresh produce inventory

INTRODUCTION

The purchasing of fresh produce calls for a great deal of skill and knowledge. When you buy fresh, natural food products, several variations within the same product line can appear daily.

Take, for example, variations in quality. At times, all available lettuce is of poor quality. The real mark of an amateur is to insist on top quality when there just is not any to be had or to accept poor quality when he or she should know good quality is available. The U.S. Department of Agriculture publishes information on both price and quality in the *Daily Fruit and Vegetable Report,* available by written request from the U.S. Department of Agriculture, Washington, DC. Other subscription services, such as *The Packer: The National Weekly Newspaper of the Fruit & Vegetable Industry,* and *Produce Planner: The Price & Availability Report for the Foodservice Industry,* are additional sources of current fresh produce data.

Throughout the growing season, different varieties of produce grown in different areas come to market. Usually, as areas closer to you are harvested, product quality improves. Quality differences can be traced, too, to the fact that different areas favor different plant varieties.

This natural variation in quality presents considerable difficulty. But your troubles do not necessarily stop here. Another major problem that may face the buyer is lack of acceptable sources of supply for fresh produce. Also, at times, it is impossible to get the quality you want, the quantity you need, or both.

Another related problem is the obvious variation in AP price that accompanies the variation and availability of quality and quantity. You must expect AP price variation throughout the year for produce, both within a given grade and among grades. For this reason, a single year-round price is unrealistic.

Still another difficulty is the availability of a tremendous number of varieties of merchandise. There are several hundred varieties of fresh produce items regularly available at one time or another from various primary sources and intermediaries. Some supply sources stock more than 500 varieties of fresh produce.[1] Without research, it is difficult to decide which variety to use for a particular purpose.

Storage conditions throughout the fresh produce channel of distribution affect culinary quality and availability of produce. For instance, controlled atmosphere storage of apples extends the product's life. Unfortunately, apples that have been stored in this way should be used quickly because their shelf life is very short once removed from the gases used in the controlled atmosphere. Unless your supplier tells you that your apples have been stored in such a manner, excessive spoilage could result if you buy a week's supply at a time.

Fresh produce buyers, especially those who work for supply houses, are, as you might expect, extremely well paid. This fact alone indicates the difficulty and huge responsibility associated with the job. Even the assistant fresh produce buyer for a supply house requires about two years of on-the-job training before being allowed to make major purchasing decisions.

Next to fresh meat buying, fresh produce buying is perhaps the most difficult purchasing task faced by the hospitality buyer.[2] In fact, it can be so difficult that some operators hire professional produce buyers to select and procure these products for them.[3]

SELECTION FACTORS

The owner-manager usually specifies the quality levels of fresh produce desired. The buyer normally carries out these specifications, as much as possible.

Management personnel, often in cooperation with other persons in the hospitality operation, usually consider one or more of the following fresh produce selection factors when determining the quality standards as well as the preferred supplier(s).

INTENDED USE

As with any product or service you intend to purchase, it is very important to identify exactly its performance requirement or intended use. This could save money in the long run because you will not purchase, say, a superb-quality product to be used for a menu item if a lower-quality, hence, lower-price, product will suffice. For instance, apples that must be on display on a buffet line should be very attractive, and you would probably pay a premium price for this appearance. But if apples were to be used in a fruit cup, where their appearance would be camouflaged to some degree, perhaps a lesser quality would be adequate, inasmuch as looks and taste are not always the same.

EXACT NAME

The fresh produce market is full of confusing terminology, increasingly so since agribusiness has developed so many new types and varieties of fruit and vegetables. A buyer cannot order merely a type of fresh produce, say, lettuce. He or she must be sure to specify the variety of lettuce required, such as romaine lettuce, leaf lettuce, or iceberg lettuce. He or she must specify Burbank russet or Norgold russet potatoes; Jonathan, Winesap, Golden Delicious, or McIntosh apples; and so forth. Adding to the confusion is the recent introduction of genetically altered fresh produce items that have been developed to increase product shelf life.[4]

Each variety serves a specific culinary purpose; therefore, a buyer must stay carefully and closely in tune with the needs of the hospitality operation. And he or she must find a supplier who is almost equally aware. Keeping track of the types, varieties, and styles of fresh produce can be a taxing task. But it is an absolutely necessary one for hospitality operations that prepare many menu items from raw ingredients.

U.S. GOVERNMENT GRADES (OR EQUIVALENT)

USDA's Agricultural Marketing Service (AMS), through its Fruit and Vegetables Division, establishes grade standards for fresh fruit, vegetables, and nuts under authority of the Agricultural Marketing Act of 1946. The first grade standard for fresh produce was established for potatoes in 1917. U.S. No. 1 was the term given the highest grade. It covered the majority of the crop and meant that the product was of good quality. U.S. No. 2 represented the remainder of the crop that was worth packing for sale under normal marketing conditions. Currently, the USDA has grading standards for approximately 150 types of fruits, vegetables, and nuts.

Although government grades are used as a quality guideline, the buyer should be aware that each vegetable or fruit may have a different grading schedule. For example, the grades for grapefruit are U.S. Fancy, U.S. No. 1, U.S. No. 2, U.S. Combination, and U.S. No. 3; the grades for carrots are U.S. Extra No. 1, U.S. No. 1, U.S. No. 1 Jumbo, and U.S. No. 2; and apples are graded as U.S. Extra Fancy, U.S. Fancy, U.S. No. 1, and U.S. Utility. (See Figure 17.1.)

Since most specifications for fresh produce include some reference to federal grades, you need to know where to find this information. Grading

FIGURE 17.1. Federal grade stamp used for fresh produce.

data can be obtained from the USDA. They also can be found in *The Produce Marketing Association Fresh Produce Reference Manual for Food Service.* (See Figure 17.2.)

The U.S. government grader considers several factors when grading fresh produce, but appearance is the most important factor. The critical appearance factors include size and size uniformity, maturity, shape, color, texture, and freedom from disease, decay, cuts, and bruises. Other factors sometimes come into play. For example, if the grader knows that the fresh produce will be shipped a long distance, say, from California to Chicago, he or she may grade it more stringently, since he or she wants to ensure that the produce will represent that stated grade in Chicago, not just in California. The wise buyer will insist that the fresh produce must meet the specified grade at the time of delivery, not at the time the products were shipped from the supplier's warehouse.

There are several grading terms in the marketplace for fresh produce products. The most commonly used terminology for fresh fruit, vegetables, and nuts are as follows:

- Fancy—the top quality produced, represents about 1 percent of all produce
- No. 1—the bulk of the products produced, the grade that most retailers purchase
- Commercial—slightly less quality than U.S. No. 1
- No. 2—much less quality than U.S. No. 1, but very superior to U.S. No. 3
- Combination—usually a mixture of U.S. No. 1 and U.S. No. 2 products
- No. 3—low-quality products just barely acceptable for packing under normal packing conditions
- Field run—ungraded products

CAULIFLOWER

SEASONS

	% OF TOT. PROD.	J	F	M	A	M	J	J	A	S	O	N	D
ARIZONA	13%												
CALIFORNIA	79%												

▒▒ — PEAK SEASON

VARIETY DESCRIPTIONS

Although there are several varieties, cauliflower is not generally ordered by variety. In addition to white cauliflower, a purple variety is also available. Generally available in whole heads, pre-trimmed heads and florets. **Recommendation:** PRE-TRIMMED/FLORETS - Excellent. (Pre-trimmed heads and florets decrease preparation/labor time.) WHOLE HEADS - Good. PURPLE CAULIFLOWER - Excellent for salad bar use. Because purple cauliflower turns white when cooked, it should be used raw.

RECEIVING & INSPECTING

Good quality cauliflower should have a creamy white or purple curd with bright green, fresh-looking leaves. While size of head does not indicate quality, it is very important in terms of yield. Avoid cauliflower with significantly discolored or dried-looking curd.

STORING & HANDLING

Ideal Storage Temperature/Atmosphere: 32-35°F./85-90% relative humidity.
Storing Tips: Do not wash before storing.
Handling Tips: Because of its coloring and texture, cauliflower shows damage easily. To prevent damage to curd, handle with care; do not drop shipping containers on floor. Avoid excess handling as oils from skin darken curds.

ORDERING SPECIFICATIONS

PACKAGING:
☐ 40 to 60-lb. bulk crates
☐ 18 to 25-lb. cartons holding counts of 9, 12, 16
☐ 9, 6, 12 & 16-count cartons holding pre-trimmed heads
☐ 10 to 20-lb. bags loose or vacuum-packed florets

GRADES:
☐ U.S. No. 1
☐ U.S. Commercial
Differences between grades are based primarily on external appearance.

SIZE/YIELD:
☐ 6 count
☐ 9 count
☐ 12 count
☐ 16 count

☐ 1 medium head = 6 cups raw florets
                = 3-1/2 cups cooked florets

FIGURE 17.2. Example of the type of product information noted in *The Produce Marketing Association Fresh Produce Reference Manual for Food Service*. (Courtesy Produce Marketing Association.)

The grades most commonly used in food service are the top grades, since the low grades yield less, require additional labor for trimming, and often have a shorter shelf life. Thus, they are not generally a good buy, even at a lower price.

The grade that is most often ordered is the high end of U.S. No. 1, or the equivalent. Clubs, hotels, and restaurants normally order the high end of U.S. No. 1 or the U.S. Fancy grade; the low end of U.S. No. 1 normally is reserved for the supermarkets and grocery stores. The few items that fall into the lower-grade categories may not make it to market in any form, although part or all of them could find their way to some of the food-processing firms that produce juices, jams, and generic-branded canned fruit and vegetables.

Generally, if you tell purveyors you are interested in U.S. No. 1, they will know what you are talking about and what you want. If you bid buy, and U.S. grades are a major criterion on your specifications, be sure you use the appropriate grade terms.

The use of government grades in buying fresh produce typically is not the sole selection criterion. They are noted, of course, but buyers usually do not base their purchase strictly on a grade, as there are considerable problems with variation in quality due to several seasonal factors. The grade, then, is but one factor.

Sometimes grades are unavailable for some fresh produce, because (1) the suppliers refuse to have it graded, (2) you may be purchasing an item for which there is no grading standard, or (3), more commonly, the produce may come from a foreign country that does not necessarily carry a grade, though it must be inspected before it is allowed to enter this country.

PACKERS' BRANDS (OR EQUIVALENT)

Most of us are not so familiar with branded fresh produce as we are with branded canned and frozen goods. Perhaps the most familiar brands are the Sunkist brand used for citrus fruits and the Blue Goose brand used for several high-quality fruits and vegetables.

With fresh produce, a packer's brand may also indicate that a particular packing process has been used or that a particular cleaning and cooling process has been followed in the field. (See Figure 17.3.) U.S. grades may or may not indicate these attributes, depending on the area of the country from which the products come.

Consistency, which should be a hallmark of packers' brands, can be particularly important with fresh produce. For instance, such consistency can produce a much more predictable EP cost, which is always difficult to calculate for fresh produce in the best of situations. For example, many products, like whole lettuce, are sold by the case. Some are firm and weighty; others have a lot of space between the leaves. Citrus fruit varies

FIGURE 17.3. A packer's brand is a useful selection factor when the buyer wants to purchase precut fresh produce. (Courtesy Fresh Western Marketing Inc.)

in juice content from one crop to the next; those carrying a packer's brand may be more consistent. Asparagus may be old and woody or young and pleasantly crisp, but a packer's brand usually is consistently sound.

Even though a packer may not purchase the U.S. government grading service, he or she must still undergo the inspection procedure, which consists of random visits by a government inspector. In addition, if the packer wants to use a brand name, most states require that this name be registered with the state's department of agriculture.

There are packers' brands for many varieties of fresh produce. Packers' fresh produce brands that do not include some reference to federal grades make up only a small portion of the fresh produce business, and they are not widely known in most parts of the country. In most cases, the packer uses the brand name in conjunction with the U.S. grade designation. Or he or she may just stencil on the box the designation "No. 1." This sign indicates that the product is not under continual government inspection, nor has it been graded, but that, in the opinion of the packer, the product meets all U.S. requirements for the U.S. No. 1 graded products.

A major problem found with packers' brands for produce is that packers sometimes put out two categories of the same brand. For example, some packers have been accused of putting the same brand name on demonstrably different qualities of the same product—and further trying to imply that both qualities are the same, since they both carry the same name—for instance, on a high U.S. No. 1 and on a low U.S. No. 1. The high 1 comes to us, the hospitality operation; the low 1 goes to the supermarkets. The possibility of a switch should disturb and alert hospitality buyers.

We have known buyers who use both U.S. government grades and packers' brands when developing their fresh produce buying procedures. Some buyers go one step further to specify a particular supply house when purchasing these products.

PRODUCT SIZE

A buyer does not merely order a box of lemons but indicates the size of the lemon wanted by specifying the count per box. The lower the count, the larger the lemon. Many other fresh fruits are sold this way. Still another common way, especially for tomatoes, is to indicate how many tomatoes a buyer wants in one layer of the "lug," or box. For example, a "4 by 5" specification indicates a certain tomato size because the buyer is ordering a layer of tomatoes with 4 on one side and 5 on the other, or 20 tomatoes per layer. Some products carry a unique nomenclature; for instance, onions are sometimes sized by the packer into the four product sizes of prepack, large medium, jumbo, and colossal. Furthermore, you may find that some produce in your area is sized according to the approximate number of pieces per pound; for example, a "3 to 1" item size indicates that there are approximately three items per pound.

In our experience, indicating the appropriate size is something that is easily forgotten, especially by the novice buyer. Most of us are unaware of the many sizes available, and so we tend to overlook this selection factor. However, agribusiness has advanced to the point where there are several sizes within narrow product lines; for instance, Idaho potatoes come in 12 sizes, ranging from 4 to 18 ounces apiece.

Product size is a very critical selection factor for at least two reasons. First, it would be embarrassing to serve guests items of varying sizes. And second, if the products are sold by the piece rather than by weight, it would be impossible to achieve effective cost control if varying sizes are served.

SIZE OF CONTAINER

Whenever possible, we like to purchase the size of container that is consistent with our needs. For instance, if we do not sell very much of a particular product, we appreciate being able to purchase it in small containers so that waste and spoilage do not occur.

As with many other types of foods and beverages, though, there are uniform container sizes in the fresh produce product line. For instance, avocados typically come in a "flat" (one layer of product) or a "lug" (two layers of product). While some suppliers may be willing to "bust" a case, chances are you will need to pay for this added supplier service.

As a general rule, most fresh produce items are packed in at least two or more container sizes. Usually the hospitality buyer will find one of these sizes suitable for the operation's needs.

TYPE OF PACKAGING MATERIAL

While there are several standardized types of packaging materials available in the fresh produce product line, our experience tells us that there is quite a variation in the quality of materials available. For instance, high-quality fiberboard certainly will cost more than thin brown paper wrappings, but with the former, you will protect the merchandise, whereas with the latter, you probably will lose some of it because of damage in shipping and handling. The AP price variation for some fresh produce is related solely to the quality of packaging, with less expensive merchandise wrapped in inadequate packaging and more expensive product wrapped in high-quality packaging.

PACKAGING PROCEDURE

Packing generally has two styles: layered merchandise and slab-packed merchandise. With the former, the product is layered nicely, usually between sheets of paper or cardboard. With the latter, product is tossed into the container and the lid is slammed shut. If it is important to preserve the edible yield of an item, then you probably should opt for better packaging arrangements, or the savings associated with slab-packing will be illusory.

For some product, you can request each item to be individually wrapped and layered in the case. You may also be able to purchase products that are layered in a "cell pack," that is, a cardboard or plastic sheet that has depressions in it so that the items can sit in them and not touch each other. For instance, some apples are packed this way. These procedures are expensive, but if it is necessary to preserve the appearance of the apple, there probably is no better way to accomplish your goal than to insist that they be used.

MINIMUM WEIGHT PER CASE

Since so much fresh produce is purchased by the case, or by the container, we should note the minimum weight we will accept. For instance, whole iceberg lettuce weights vary considerably, which implies that the bid price for it will vary quite a few dollars per case.

Fresh produce also tends to shrink, that is, dehydrate, while in transit. Specifying a minimum weight allows you to receive the appropriate amount while simultaneously giving suppliers some shrink allowance.

In some cases the buyer might indicate a "decay allowance" on a fresh produce product specification. For instance, when purchasing ripe plums, slab packed, there are bound to be a few unusable ones in the lot. The buyer and supplier should agree on the number of bad pieces that will be acceptable.

Another dimension of this selection factor is the possibility that you might wish to indicate a weight range per case of produce you order. This gives suppliers a bit more flexibility and ensures that, once in a while, you might receive more weight, hence, more usable servings of product, than you would if you indicated on your specification merely a minimum weight required.

PRODUCT YIELD

Some fresh produce we purchase will be subject to a certain amount of unavoidable waste (trim). For example, when purchasing whole, fresh turnips, you should note on the product specification the minimum edible yield expected or, alternatively, the maximum amount of acceptable trim loss.

POINT OF ORIGIN

If you shop around, you must be careful that you understand the differences in quality, texture, appearance, and/or taste that will accompany products that come from different areas of the country or the world. If you do business with only one or two purveyors, generally they will try to provide fresh produce that is somewhat consistent in these characteristics. But such is not the case if you wish to deal with several purveyors.

Another dimension of this selection factor is the problem associated with noting on your menu the point of origin for certain menu offerings. For instance, if you indicate that you serve Idaho potatoes, you must be certain that your potatoes actually come from Idaho, or you will be in violation of truth-in-advertising legislation.

COLOR

If necessary, you must specify the color preferred. For example, there are red peppers and green ones. Generally, when you specify the type or variety of merchandise desired, you will have indicated color. If not, you must be sure to do so if it is relevant.

PRODUCT FORM

Fresh produce can be purchased in many forms, that is, with varying degrees of economic "form" value added. At one extreme are whole products that have no value added, and at the other extreme are ready-to-serve products.

Many operators today prefer purchasing value-added "precut" fresh produce that has been subjected to additional cleaning, chopping, and so forth. For instance, you can purchase peeled and sliced onions, potatoes, and similar items. These are more expensive, but in the long run are typically more economical than whole products that require considerable labor and handling prior to service.[5]

DEGREE OF RIPENESS

Some fresh produce can be purchased at varying stages of ripeness. Usually the hospitality buyer will purchase mature, fully ripened produce. However, immature, green produce can also be found. For some items, such as bananas and tomatoes, there are several stages of ripening that can be ordered; these options may be quite suitable for the operation that wishes to ripen some of its own fresh produce so that it is at its peak of quality when served.

RIPENING PROCESS USED

Some merchandise is ripened naturally, on the plant. This produce is a bit more expensive because of the difficulty of handling and the loss experienced by producers who often end up with some rotting merchandise in their fields. The taste of the item, though, may be so desirable to you that you would be willing to pay for it.

Some produce is ripened in a "ripening room." It is picked when it is green and then is placed in a room, or train car, or truck. Ethylene gas then is introduced into the "room." When some produce ripens naturally, it emits ethylene gas, so the introduction of this gas into the "room" merely speeds up the ripening process. Unfortunately, if the process is hastened too rapidly, the fresh produce item, say, bananas, will turn bright yellow, but the fruit under the skin will not have kept pace (i.e., it will not be very flavorful because it has not ripened fully even though the skin color would lead us to think that it has).

PRESERVATION METHOD

Some fresh produce is refrigerated throughout the channel of distribution, but this type of preservation is not required by the federal government. Fresh produce is not considered a potentially hazardous food; consequently, it can be left unrefrigerated. It is necessary to note on your specification your refrigeration requirement, if any.

For some items, such as potatoes, bananas, and most onions, refrigeration is unnecessary. However, they still should be kept in a cool environment so that they do not overripen.

Refrigeration is expensive, so expect to pay more for refrigerated fresh produce. But unrefrigerated (or uncooled) merchandise goes bad so quickly that your EP cost for such produce will usually be much greater than the EP cost associated with refrigerated produce.

If you are purchasing precut, convenience fresh produce, refrigeration is mandatory. The supplier must preserve the appropriate "pulp" temperature, or else the produce will deteriorate rapidly. For instance, chopped salad greens should be delivered at a pulp temperature of approximately 34 to 36°F in order to preserve its culinary quality.

Some products are preserved by waxing them. For instance, Mother Nature uses this process for such foods as peppers and cucumbers. Producers are also allowed to apply wax to some items, especially when the natural wax is removed by them during the cleaning of the product. The wax prevents moisture loss and also contributes to the appearance of the produce. There are some items that are traditionally waxed, and you will receive them in this state unless you specify otherwise. Fresh produce items most likely to be waxed by producers are apples, avocados, bell peppers, cantaloupes, cucumbers, eggplant, grapefruit, lemons, limes, melons, oranges, parsnips, passion fruit, peaches, pineapples, pumpkins, rutabagas, squash, sweet potatoes, tomatoes, and turnips.

Some fresh produce is preserved in controlled atmosphere storage. The produce is put into a room, and the room then is sealed. Oxygen is removed, and a variety of other gases are introduced. Without oxygen, the produce will not spoil—it will remain as is for a considerable period of time. Unfortunately, when it is removed from this environment, it deteriorates very rapidly. Generally, suppliers do not sell this type of merchandise to hospitality operators; rather, they sell it to supermarkets and grocery stores. But when you shop around, you would be wise to note on your specification that you prefer merchandise that has not been stored in a controlled environment.

Some of the fresh produce that comes to market has been chemically treated with pesticides in order to preserve its shelf life and palatability. If the buyer does not want this type of merchandise, he or she can opt to purchase fresh produce that has been "organically" grown, that is, grown without the use of synthetic chemicals and fertilizers.[6] You also could purchase fresh produce that has been grown in nutrient-rich water instead of chemically treated soil. This "hydroponic" fresh produce is especially popular with fine-dining establishments because it can be grown in the food-service operation and served almost immediately after harvest. If you purchase organic and/or hydroponic merchandise, you must expect to pay a premium AP price.

TRUSTING THE SUPPLIER

Specifying U.S. grades, packers' brands, and one particular supplier makes you a "house account" of the highest order, which may or may not be in accord with company policy. Fresh produce buying does not lend itself easily to bid buying, simply because there are so many things to consider; and, in some parts of the country, there are not many suppliers to bid for your business. Consequently, this is an area in which you may wish to rely on your supplier's highly developed expertise.

There are several things to control. For instance, just because you specify Sunkist and U.S. No. 1, there is no guarantee that you will receive them. The box might note U.S. No. 1, but it can easily have been repacked with lower-quality product.

The delivery schedules, seasonal changes, weather factors, the supplier's buying capabilities, the transportation and storage facilities, the speed with which the supplier rotates products—all are factors crucial to your operation. There is some slack with processed items, but with fresh products of any kind, you must be assured of the quality you need and want—assured that it will be as good on your table as it was in the field. If you do not work closely with a fresh produce supplier, you take some risks.

PURCHASING FRESH PRODUCE

Your first step in purchasing fresh produce is to obtain *The Produce Marketing Association Fresh Produce Reference Manual for Food Service.*

Red delicious apples Used for fruit plate item U.S. Fancy Washington State 72 count 30- to 42-pound crate Moisture-proof fiberboard Layered arrangement, cell carton Whole apples Fresh, refrigerated Fully ripened	Cauliflower, white Used for side dish for all entrées U.S. No. 1 (high) 12 count 18- to 25-pound carton Moisture-proof fiberboard Loose pack (slab pack) Pretrimmed heads Fresh, refrigerated Fully ripened
Sweet Spanish, yellow globe onion Used for onion rings U.S. No. 1 (high) Jumbo size 50-pound plastic mesh bag Whole onions Fresh, unrefrigerated Fully ripened	Iceberg lettuce Used for tossed salad U.S. No. 1 (high) 10-pound poly bag Loose pack (slab pack) Chopped lettuce Fresh, refrigerated Fully ripened

FIGURE 17.4. Example of fresh produce product specifications.

This unique publication contains very detailed specifications for many fresh produce items. It also includes information on receiving, storing, and handling techniques.

Your next step is to decide on the exact type of produce and quality you want. A buyer may not make this decision unless he or she is a user-buyer or owner-user-buyer. Once you settle on the type and quality, you should prepare specifications for each item. These specifications should be as complete as is needed. They should include all pertinent information, especially if you intend to engage in bid buying. Follow the guidelines noted in Chapter 7, and examine Figure 17.4 for example product specifications. See, also, Figure 17.5 for an example product specification outline for fresh produce.

After you prepare your specifications, your next step is to consider the suppliers likely to satisfy your needs. Here, again, you can become a house account, use bid buying, or settle on some procedure in between.

Over the years, several fresh produce buying groups and trade associations have evolved. This, in turn, has made such merchandise more readily available in all local markets. Generally, though, it is difficult to find more than one or two consistently capable full-line, fresh-produce suppliers. While you may find several suppliers handling a few fresh produce

Intended use:

Exact name:

U.S. grade (or equivalent):

Packer's brand name (or equivalent):

Product size:

Size of container:

Type of packaging material:

Packaging procedure:

Minimum weight per case:

Product yield:

Point of origin:

Color:

Product form:

Degree of ripeness:

Ripening process used:

Preservation method:

FIGURE 17.5. Example of product specification outline for fresh produce.

items as a sideline to their regular business of canned goods, frozen foods, and various nonfood items, overall, the lack of several full-line fresh produce suppliers makes it difficult if you want to engage in bid buying.

An added attraction in the fresh produce area is the independent farmer, who will occasionally want to sell you his or her "farm-fresh produce." These individual farmers typically are small business persons who gather together one or two days a week in what is referred to as a "farmer's market." Some of them may sell on the roadside. And some of them may allow customers to come in and "pick their own." Over the years, farmers' markets have become more visible, numerous, and popular.

In some instances, the small local farmer will be a wise choice. For example, as part of a college project, we once required some students to compare an independent farmer's AP prices and supplier services purchased by a restaurant with a high-priced menu with the same products and supplier services offered by other fresh produce suppliers. We found that the restaurant's management was paying the farmer about 7 percent more per month. But his fresh produce, in our opinion, was unusually excellent. In addition, the farmer delivered daily. Unfortunately, he could not supply all the needs of this restaurant. But, for what he did supply, in our opinion, he certainly provided the best overall value.

But reliable independent farmers are hard to find. Our experience has also taught us that some of these "farmers" purchase their products from supermarket suppliers, and then give the impression that the produce is home grown.

Another problem that might concern a buyer is the fact that the farmer's facilities and products are not likely to be inspected by either the state or the federal government.

Adventurous operators might consider developing their own fresh produce gardens. Lately several restaurant chefs have taken this unique step.[7] Gardens located on the premises will ensure freshness. They can also be excellent marketing and promotional tools used to attract guests.

Normally, the independent hospitality operator attempts to establish specifications. Then he or she moves around from one supplier to the next until the specifications are most closely met. Bid buying is not as prevalent in the fresh produce trade as it is for processed foods and nonfoods.

RECEIVING FRESH PRODUCE

When you receive fresh produce, try to resist the temptation to examine only the printing on the containers and cartons and to look only at the top layer of merchandise. Some receivers may merely look at the box of lettuce, read "24 heads," and take it for granted that there are 24 heads of lettuce in the carton.

We are not suggesting that you break open every carton to see whether it really contains full count, because the damage to fragile fruit and vegetables is extensive when they are unpacked, especially if they are packaged in special protective films that extend the shelf life of the vegetable or fruit. A visual inspection of the top layer plus the weight of the entire carton will give the buyer a quick and accurate idea of the quantity and quality of the produce received. This should be combined with sampling of a proportion of containers in which the buyer carefully unpacks a box of produce to check the count, size, and quality throughout the box. A good place for this inspection is in refrigerated quarters, such as a walk-in refrigerator, so that the produce does not become warm, thus decreasing its shelf life. (See Figures 17.6 and 17.7 for signs of acceptable and unacceptable quality in some fresh produce items.)

Unless you trust your supplier and your buyer completely, you would do well continually to review your receiving practices very carefully. At the very least, you should check to see that the quality is equal throughout and try to satisfy yourself that if repacking has been done, the merchandise is acceptable to you. Then weigh the container. After checking quality and quantity, check the prices and complete the appropriate accounting documents.

	Signs of Good Quality	Signs of Bad Quality, Spoilage
Apples	Firmness; crispness; bright color	Softness; bruises. (Irregularly shaped brown or tan areas do not usually affect quality.)
Apricots	Bright, uniform color; plumpness	Dull color; shriveled appearance
Bananas	Firmness; brightness of color	Grayish or dull appearance (indicates exposure to cold and inability to ripen properly)
Blueberries	Dark blue color with silvery bloom	Moist berries
Cantaloupes (Muskmelons)	Stem should be gone; netting or veining should be coarse; skin should be yellow-gray or pale yellow	Bright yellow color; mold; large bruises
Cherries	Very dark color; plumpness	Dry stems; soft flesh; gray mold
Cranberries	Plumpness; firmness. Ripe cranberries should bounce	Leaky berries
Grapefruit	Should be heavy for its size	Soft areas; dull color
Grapes	Should be firmly attached to stems. Bright color and plumpness are good signs	Drying stems; leaking berries
Honeydew melon	Soft skin; faint aroma; yellowish white to creamy rind color	White or greenish color; bruises or water-soaked areas; cuts or punctures in rind

FIGURE 17.6. Signs of acceptable and unacceptable quality in some fresh fruit items. (Reprinted with permission from *Applied Foodservice Sanitation Certification Coursebook*, Fourth Edition. Copyright 1992 by the Educational Foundation of the National Restaurant Association. All rights reserved.)

	Signs of Good Quality	Signs of Bad Quality, Spoilage
Lemons	Firmness; heaviness. Should have rich yellow color	Dull color; shriveled skin
Limes	Glossy skin; heavy weight	Dry skin; molds
Oranges	Firmness; heaviness; bright color	Dry skin; spongy texture; blue mold
Peaches	Slightly soft flesh	A pale tan spot (indicates beginning of decay); very hard or very soft flesh
Pears	Firmness	Dull skin; shriveling; spots on the sides
Pineapples	"Spike" at top should separate easily from flesh	Mold; large bruises; unpleasant odor; brown leaves
Plums	Fairly firm to slightly soft flesh	Leaking; brownish discoloration
Raspberries, Boysenberries	Stem caps should be absent; flesh should be plump and tender	Mushiness; wet spots on containers (sign of possible decay of berries)
Strawberries	Stem cap should be attached; berries should have rich red color	Gray mold; large uncolored areas
Tangerines	Bright orange or deep yellow color; loose skin	Punctured skin; mold
Watermelon	Smooth surface; creamy underside; bright red flesh	Stringy or mealy flesh (spoilage difficult to see on outside)

FIGURE 17.6. Continued

STORING FRESH PRODUCE

Fresh produce must be stored immediately at the proper temperature and humidity. Figure 17.8 notes these requirements for some vegetables. The larger food-service operations usually have a separate cool area or refrig-

	Signs of Good Quality	Signs of Poor Quality, Spoilage
Artichokes	Plumpness; green scales; clinging leaves	Brown scales; grayish-black discoloration; mold
Asparagus	Closed tips; round spears	Spread-out tips; spears with ridges; spears that are not round
Beans (snap)	Firm, crisp pods	Extensive discoloration; tough pods
Beets	Firmness; roundness; deep red color	Gray mold; wilting; flabbiness
Brussels sprouts	Bright color; tight-fitting leaves	Loose, yellow-green outer leaves; ragged leaves (may indicate worm damage)
Cabbage	Firmness; heaviness for size	Wilted or decayed outer leaves (Leaves should not separate easily from base.)
Carrots	Smoothness; firmness	Soft spots
Cauliflower	Clean, white curd; bright green leaves	Speckled curd; severe wilting; loose flower clusters
Celery	Firmness; crispness; smooth stems	Flabby leaves; brown-black interior discoloration
Cucumber	Green color; firmness	Yellowish color; softness
Eggplant	Uniform, dark purple color	Softness; irregular dark brown spots
Greens	Tender leaves free of blemishes	Yellow-green leaves; evidence of insect decay

FIGURE 17.7 Signs of acceptable and unacceptable quality in some fresh vegetable items. (Reprinted with permission from *Applied Foodservice Sanitation Certification Coursebook*, Fourth Edition. Copyright 1992 by the Educational Foundation of the National Restaurant Association. All rights reserved.)

	Signs of Good Quality	Signs of Bad Quality, Spoilage
Lettuce	Crisp leaves; bright color	Tip burn on edges of leaves (slight discoloration of outer leaves is not harmful)
Mushrooms	White, creamy, or tan color on tops of caps	Dark color on underside of cap; withering veil
Onions	Hardness; firmness; small necks; papery outer scales	Wet or soft necks
Onions (green)	Crisp, green tops; white portion two to three inches in length	Yellowing; wilting
Peppers (green)	Glossy appearance; dark green color	Thin walls; cuts, punctures
Potatoes	Firmness; relative smoothness	Green rot or mold; large cuts; sprouts
Radishes	Plumpness; roundness; red color	Yellowing of tops (sign of aging); softness
Squash (summer)	Glossy skin	Dull appearance; tough surface
Squash (winter)	Hard rind	Mold; softness
Sweet potatoes	Bright skins	Wetness; shriveling; sunken and discolored areas on sides of potato (Sweet potatoes are extremely susceptible to decay.)
Tomatoes	Smoothness; redness. (Tomatoes that are pink or slightly green will ripen in a warm place.)	Bruises; deep cracks around the stem scar
Watercress	Crispness; bright green color	Yellowing, wilting, decaying of leaves

FIGURE 17.7. Continued

USDA Recommended Storage Requirements for Vegetables

Commodity	Storage Temperature	Relative Humidity	Maximum Total Storage Period*
Asparagus	32–36F	95%	2–3 weeks
Broccoli	32–35	90–95	10–14 days
Carrots (topped)	32–35	90–95	4–5 months
Cauliflower	32–35	90–95	2–4 weeks
Celery	32–35	90–95	2–3 months
Lettuce	32–34	95	2–3 weeks
Onions, green (scallions)	32–35	90–95	—

* This maximum storage includes commercial storage of produce before it is delivered to your loading dock. If you intend holding fruits and vegetables in your walk-in for any length of time, consult your produce house or distributor to determine how long you can safely store produce that has already been in storage.

FIGURE 17.8. Recommended storage requirements for some fresh vegetables. (Courtesy *Restaurants & Institutions* magazine, a Cahners publication.)

erator for these items. But any cool temperature is better than none at all. Avoid all delays: Most fresh produce deteriorates considerably when it is left at room temperature. For example, fresh corn loses about 50 percent of its sugar in the first 24 hours after it is picked, but proper refrigeration can slow this deterioration. In fact, most fully ripened produce becomes inedible quite quickly if it is held in the wrong storage environment.

To extend the shelf life of fresh produce, the buyer must research the best possible storage environment for each fruit or vegetable. This must include knowledge of how the produce is packaged. Some packages are designed to extend the shelf life of the product, and these items are best stored by keeping them in their box, carton, or cello wrap, and merely placing them in the refrigerator. On the other hand, some vegetables arrive in crates that are not designed to extend their shelf life. Celery, for example, usually arrives in a crate and rapidly loses moisture and becomes limp if not repacked; cello bags or plastic, reusable, see-through tubs are excellent for repacking. Contrary to popular opinion, produce should not be washed before it is stored. Moisture enhances the growth of soft rot microorganisms and invariably decreases the shelf life of the fruit or vegetable. Washing may also remove protective wax coating designed to extend the shelf life of vegetables such as green peppers and cucumbers.

You also should expect to extend fresh produce shelf life if you practice proper fresh produce handling techniques. The techniques are, in fact, quite simple. The general rule is to handle the merchandise only when it is absolutely necessary. Do not pick it up, move it around, bend it, or bounce it, because this will cause unnecessary bruising that will manifest itself in excessive spoilage and waste.

Improper storage not only reduces quality but may reduce nutritional value as well. If you are nutrition conscious, bear in mind that you may be losing some nutritional value if you neglect proper storage procedures.

If you can arrange for frequent deliveries from your fresh produce supplier and move your produce rapidly through production, you can be a little more flexible with your storage duties. But, as many suppliers are unwilling to provide daily delivery, you should plan for a suitable storage facility.

ISSUING FRESH PRODUCE

Fresh produce purchases often bypass the central storage facility and go directly to the food production department. If you first move the fresh produce to a central storage facility and issue it later to the food production department, you may want to issue these items as ready-to-go. That is, you may consider issuing cleaned, chopped onions instead of whole onions; sliced tomatoes instead of whole tomatoes; or topped, peeled, and cut carrots instead of whole carrots. (Figure 17.9 notes preparation waste of some fresh fruit and vegetables.) By doing this, you may be able to effect a labor cost savings or extract better value from higher-paid cooks and chefs.

You should follow proper stock rotation when issuing produce. (Figures 17.8 and 17.10 note storage times for some fresh produce items.) And since these items spoil quickly, make sure that the requisitioner takes no more than necessary. It may be wise to ask him or her to note the in-process inventory before asking for more stock.

IN-PROCESS INVENTORIES

The buyer is relieved of responsibility for fresh produce when it is issued to a user. But since we direct this book toward managers who need a more panoramic view of the hospitality industry, we should comment on the use of these purchased items by the production and service staffs.

You will discover, if you have not already, that control of purchasing, receiving, storing, and issuing fresh produce is easier than is control of produce production and service. A great deal of supervision is required to ensure that salad greens, for example, do not sit out at room temperature too long.

	Raw Weight	Approximate Edible Yield	Approximate Waste (%)
Apples	1 lb	13 oz	19%
Apricots	1 lb	12 oz	25%
Asparagus	1 lb	9 oz	44%
Avocado	1 lb	12 oz	25%
Bananas	1 lb	13 oz	19%
Beans, green	1 lb	14 oz	13%
Broccoli, whole head	1 lb	10 oz	38%
Brussels sprouts	1 lb	16 oz	0%
Cabbage	1 lb	13 oz	19%
Cantaloupe	1 lb	11 oz	31%
Carrots, no tops	1 lb	12 oz	25%
Cauliflower, trimmed	1 lb	16 oz	0%
Celery, whole stalk	1 lb	12 oz	25%
Cranberries	1 lb	16 oz	0%
Cucumbers	1 lb	14 oz	13%
Eggplant, whole	1 lb	13 oz	19%
Grapefruit	1 lb	11 oz	31%
Lemons	1 lb	11 oz	31%
Limes	1 lb	11 oz	31%
Lettuce, untrimmed	1 lb	12 oz	25%
Melon, honeydew	1 lb	11 oz	31%
Mushrooms	1 lb	16 oz	0%
Onions	1 lb	14 oz	13%
Oranges	1 lb	11 oz	31%
Pears	1 lb	13 oz	19%
Peppers, green	1 lb	13 oz	19%
Potatoes, sweet	1 lb	11 oz	31%
Potatoes, white	1 lb	12 oz	25%
Squash, summer	1 lb	14 oz	13%
Strawberries	1 lb	14 oz	13%
Tangerines	1 lb	11 oz	31%
Tomatoes	1 lb	14 oz	13%
Turnips	1 lb	12 oz	25%

FIGURE 17.9. Preparation waste of some fresh produce items.

We have known several restaurants that undertook considerable expense to purchase fresh produce efficiently, only to see the savings disappear because an inexperienced manager did not, or could not, supervise its use. Many operations protect the AP price, or back-door cost, very well, but the EP cost, or front-door cost, does not often enjoy equal consid-

STORAGE TIMES FOR FRUITS AND VEGETABLES

APPLES, Fresh Store in fruit or vegetable box three weeks to a month. Inspect daily to remove rotten fruit so that the balance will not be contaminated. Watch for blue mold or black rot.

APRICOTS Easily stored for one to two weeks.

ASPARAGUS Can be kept for two weeks but must be crated with the heels packed in moss.

AVOCADO May be kept in refrigerator one week after ripening.

BANANAS May be kept at 50 to 60 degrees and used within two to three days after ripening. Do not store in the cooler at any time.

BERRIES All fresh berries can be kept for a week to 10 days. However, it is recommended that these be used as quickly as possible for best flavor.

BROCCOLI Can be stored for 8 to 10 days.

CABBAGE EARLY VARIETY will keep about two weeks. LATE VARIETY is much sturdier—will last two months.

CANTALOUPE Inspect daily for ripeness. When ripe, may be held in the cooler for one week.

CARROTS If in good condition, they may be kept in the storeroom for a few days. Under refrigeration, they will last three months.

CAULIFLOWER May be kept for two weeks if the leaves are not cut away. After the leaves are removed, it deteriorates rapidly.

CELERY Should not be kept longer than a few days. If it is wilted, placing in water will freshen it.

CORN Corn is one of the most sensitive of vegetables and should be used within 24 hours after arrival.

CRANBERRIES May be stored in a vegetable box for as long as two months.

CUCUMBERS These are not sturdy and should be used within a week.

EGGPLANT Should not remain in storage more than a week.

GARLIC Can be kept for about two months at temperatures from 55 to 65 degrees. In a vegetable cooler at temperatures 32 to 36 degrees, garlic will last four months.

GRAPEFRUIT Will last six weeks at 32 to 36 degrees.

GRAPES White seedless or red Tokay grapes will keep for four weeks. Red Emperor, obtainable in late fall, will keep for two months.

KALE In temperatures from 32 to 36 degrees, kale will remain in good condition for three weeks.

LEMONS May be kept from one to two months at 50 to 60 degrees.

LETTUCE, Iceberg If in good condition and inspected regularly, iceberg lettuce may be kept for four weeks. The leaves should not be removed until the lettuce is to be used, unless they have begun to rot. However, to obtain a maximum quality, lettuce should be used as soon as possible after arrival.

LIMES Will not last in storage over two weeks.

MELONS May be stored a maximum of three weeks. However, it is recommended that they be used as soon as the proper degree of softness is achieved.

MUSHROOMS Fresh, should not be kept more than one or two days.

ONIONS, Green If kept under refrigeration, they will last a week or 10 days.

ONIONS, Yellow If stored in a cool, dry place, unrefrigerated, they will last three months.

ORANGES Should be used within a week if possible. If necessary, they may be held in a reasonably good condition for a month or six weeks.

PARSNIPS Can be stored two to three months at 32 to 36 degrees.

PARSLEY A week is about the time limit for parsley. Keep it well iced.

PEACHES Most varieties will last about a week; the yellow cling variety about two weeks. Peaches must be inspected and sorted each day.

FIGURE 17.10. Storage times for some fresh produce items. (Reprinted from *Lodging* magazine.)

PEARS	Summer or Bartlett variety—before ripening, they may be kept three weeks at 65 to 75 degrees. After ripening, they must be refrigerated and used within a few days. They require gentle handling to prevent bruising and must be sorted every 5 days. Bosc or Comice variety—may be kept six weeks before ripening if sorted weekly. After ripening, must be used within a few days. Winter Anjou or Winter Nelis variety—will keep eight to ten weeks before ripening.	PUMPKIN	Can last for a month at temperatures from 50 to 60 degrees. However, it is better to buy the canned variety.
		RADISHES	Should not be kept longer than a week, and it is wiser to use them within a few days. The leaves should be removed as soon as possible.
		RHUBARB	May be kept for a week, but since it loses flavor after a short time, it should be used as soon as possible.
PEPPERS	May be held for about three weeks.	ROMAINE	Will generally last about 10 days.
		SPINACH	Must be properly iced to last any time at all. Even then, one week is its time limit.
PINEAPPLES	May be kept as long as two weeks on a ripening table at temperatures from 65 to 75 degrees. Once ripe, they should be used within 2 or 3 days.	SQUASH, Summer	Will last only two weeks
		SQUASH, Winter	Can be held at 50 to 60 degrees for three months
		STRAWBERRIES	Must not be kept longer than 2 days and require a temperature from 32 to 36 degrees.
PLUMS	Green Gage or red—will keep for two weeks but after ripening must be used within a few days.	TOMATOES	Should not be kept over a week after ripening. They require daily sorting for ripeness.
POTATOES, White	May last four months in cool, dry, well-ventilated place that is refrigerated. New potatoes, however, should not be kept for more than five or six weeks.	TURNIPS	White—they will keep about 10 days or two weeks without refrigeration. Under light refrigeration, they will last three months.
POTATOES, Sweet	These do not have the staying power of white potatoes. They require a cool place, 50 to 60 degrees, and should not be kept for more than a week. They will last for three or four weeks if the air is extremely dry.	WATERMELON	May be held a week or 10 days, but no longer.

FIGURE 17.10. Continued

eration. Figure 17.9 shows that there is considerable unavoidable loss with fresh produce; the chances for excessive loss increase if proper supervision is absent.

KEY WORDS AND CONCEPTS

AMS

AP price

Approximate waste percentages

Bust a case

Cell pack

Color

Controlled atmosphere storage

Decay allowance

Degree of ripeness

Difference between two levels of U.S. No. 1

EP cost

Ethylene gas

Exact name

Farmer's market

Field run

Flat

Form value

Genetically altered fresh produce

Grading factors

Hydroponic fresh produce

Independent farmer

In-process inventories

Intended use

Layered packaging

Lug

Minimum weight per case

Organic fresh produce

Packaging material

Packaging procedure

Packers' brands

Point of origin

Precut fresh produce

Preservation method

Produce Marketing Association

Product form

Product size

Product yield

Pulp temperature

Purchasing, receiving, storing, and issuing fresh produce

Ready-to-serve produce

Reference books that can be used when preparing specifications

Ripening process used

Ripening room

Shelf life

Shrink allowance

Size of container

Slab packed

Storage requirements for fresh produce

Trim

Trusting the supplier

Type of product

USDA

U.S. grades

Value-added products

Variety of products

REFERENCES

1. Kathleen Deveny, "America's Heartland Acquires Global Tastes," *The Wall Street Journal,* October 11, 1995, p. B1.

2. Patt Patterson, "A Hard Sell: Buying Produce Is No Day in the Park," *Nation's Restaurant News,* January 25, 1993, p. 23.

3. Thomas M. Burton, "Buying Fine Produce for Finicky Chefs Is No Bowl of Cherries," *The Wall Street Journal,* August 6, 1991, p. A1.

4. Scott McMurray, "New Calgene Tomato Might Have Tasted Just as Good Without Genetic Alteration," *The Wall Street Journal,* January 12, 1993, p. B1.

5. Elizabeth Schneider, "Veggies in Volume: Beating the Buffet and Banquet Blahs," *Food Arts,* November 1991, p. 76. See also, Patt Patterson, "Fresh-Cut Vs. Raw Produce: Where's the Value"? *Nations Restaurant News,* September 13, 1993, p. 95.

6. Charles Thienpont, "More Growers Plant Organic Crops—See Prices 50% Below Last Year," *FoodService Director,* April 15, 1990, p. 58. See also, Diane Welland,

"Chefs Consider Organic Produce," *Restaurants USA*, September 1991, p. 26; and David Belman, "The Time Is Ripe for Organics," *Restaurants USA*, August 1995, p. 18.

7. Jennifer Batty, "Restaurants with Farms Start a Blooming Revolution," *Restaurants USA*, August 1992, p. 30.

QUESTIONS AND PROBLEMS

1. Name the U.S. grades for fresh produce.
2. What is the most frequently ordered grade of fresh produce in our industry?
3. A product specification for fresh lemons could include the following information:
   (a) _____
   (b) _____
   (c) _____
   (d) _____
   (e) _____
4. Why does the hospitality operator normally not care for fresh produce that has been in controlled atmosphere storage?
5. Why should we note on our specifications for fresh produce the minimum weight per case?
6. Why is the point of origin for fresh produce very important?
7. What is an appropriate intended use for green tomatoes?
8. When would you use a packer's brand in lieu of a U.S. grade when preparing a product specification for fresh tomatoes?
9. When would you purchase fresh produce from a farmer's market?
10. Why might it be difficult to engage in bid buying when purchasing fresh produce? When would you bid buy? Why? If possible, ask a school food-service director to comment on your answer.
11. Outline the specific procedures you would use to purchase, receive, store, and issue salad greens—lettuce, red cabbage, and carrots—and baking potatoes. Assume that these products will be used in a steak house. If possible, ask a steak house manager to comment on your answer.
12. Prepare product specifications for the products noted in Question 11.
13. Assume that you manage a cafeteria and that you have run out of salad greens at 7:30 on a Saturday night. What do you do? If possible, ask a cafeteria manager to comment on your answer.
14. Supplier A offers lettuce at $16.75 per case. B offers at $18.50 per case. Yield for A is 88 percent; for B it is 94 percent. A expects COD payment; B gives seven days' credit terms. Which supplier would you purchase from? Why?

15. Why is it important to note the exact variety of fresh produce desired, instead of merely noting the type of item needed?

16. What is an appropriate intended use for U.S. No. 2 grade tomatoes?

17. What does the notation "3 to 1" indicate to the buyer?

18. Precut fresh produce usually carries an AP price that is much higher than that of raw fresh produce. Note some of the reasons for this difference.

19. What are some of the methods fresh produce suppliers can use to extend the shelf life of fruits and vegetables?

20. When would you specify organically grown fresh produce on a product specification for fresh produce?

21. What is a "decay allowance"?

22. What critical information is missing from the following product specification for onions?

Onions
Used to make onion rings
U.S. No. 1 Grade (or equivalent)
Packed in 50-pound mesh bags

23. What is the advantage of purchasing genetically altered fresh tomatoes?

24. What is an appropriate intended use for "field run" fresh produce?

25. For what types of products is "pulp temperature" an important selection factor?

CHAPTER **18**

CALIFORNIA CLING PEACHES · FRUIT MIXES · U.S.A. BARTLETT PEARS

Source: Canned Fruit Promotion Service

PROCESSED PRODUCE AND OTHER GROCERY ITEMS

THE PURPOSE OF THIS CHAPTER

This chapter discusses:

- The management considerations surrounding the selection and procurement of processed produce and other grocery items
- The selection factors for processed produce and other grocery items
- Purchasing, receiving, storing, and issuing processed produce and other grocery items
- The in-process inventory of processed produce and other grocery items

INTRODUCTION

The purchasing procedures for convenience items, such as processed fruit, vegetables, and such other grocery items as pastas, fats and oils, and spices, are more routine than those required for fresh products. In general, the qualities are more predictable, and the AP prices do not fluctuate so widely as those for fresh products.

Lest you think that this area of purchasing does not present difficulties, we point out that purchasing processed items requires several management considerations. As is almost always the case, these considerations center on the determination of what you want, what type of product is best suited for your needs, and which supplier to use to accommodate these needs.

MANAGEMENT CONSIDERATIONS

Many processed products and grocery items, once thawed, or opened, or heated, have extremely short in-process shelf lives. In addition, reheating or reusing many of these items usually results in inferior finished products, a problem that processed produce shares with most convenience products.

One of the ironies about processed produce is that most produce items are processed in the first place to reduce their perishability in their fresh state. Consequently, when we mishandle these items in the food-service operation, we defeat one of the main reasons that they were fabricated under controlled conditions.

Food processors process produce for many other reasons as well, not merely to preserve them. These primary sources in the channels of distribution also seek to smooth out seasonal fluctuations and to capture an item at its peak of flavor; in doing so, they transfer some work from your kitchen to the food processing plant.

A major management decision involving processed produce items, then, is whether to use them at all. (An operation usually has little choice for other grocery items, although some properties make their own pasta, render their own fat, and blend their own condiments.) In light of the considerable current interest in "natural, whole foods," this decision cannot be taken lightly. Some operations make a point to remind their patrons that all vegetables on their menus are cooked from the fresh state. Whether this approach has marketing value may be a matter of opinion.

It is probably impractical to imagine any storeroom without a few cans of tomatoes on its shelves. Thus, the decision here is not an either/or proposition. It is more a question of which products should be fresh and which should be processed. Moreover, some of the methods we use to cook certain fruits and vegetables do not produce food that tastes substantially different from its processed counterpart. For example, a tomato sauce made with canned tomatoes may taste about the same as one made with fresh tomatoes. And, finally, you can combine some fresh products with some processed ones. For instance, a tomato and green bean casserole can be made with fresh tomatoes and canned or frozen beans, or with fresh beans and canned tomatoes.

Once you realize that you must use at least some processed produce and other grocery items, you face the question of which processing method to choose.

For some products, there is little choice. For example, if you must purchase plain pasta, it is a dried product, though some fresh refrigerated and some precooked frozen pastas are available. There are other processing techniques, like pickling and other kinds of fermentation. Foods processed in these ways are purchased almost exclusively for the taste the processing imparts and not necessarily for convenience, AP price considerations, or other reasons. Also, some other preservation methods, such as adding chemical preservatives and refrigerating some soup bases, have become standard; unless you specify otherwise, you will receive the product this way.

If you opt for canned goods or shelf-stable products packed in aseptic packaging, you receive the benefits of standardized packaging, longer shelf life, and cheaper storage costs. But you also get a distinctive "canned" taste. For some items, for example, tomato sauce, cans or aseptic packages are the normal choices. For others, such as white asparagus spears, they may be the only choices.

If you choose frozen processing, you have the benefit of fresher flavor, or at least a taste as close as possible to natural flavor. Moreover, purveyors claim that only products picked at their peak of flavor are frozen. Unfortunately, frozen fruit and vegetable packaging is not quite so standardized as can packaging. You also take greater risks with frozen items—the chances of thawing and refreezing, a freezer breakdown, and freezer burn. The shelf life of many frozen items is not so long as that of canned and bottled items. The AP prices tend to be higher, and there is a higher storage cost associated with frozen products. (One of the biggest difficulties with any frozen product is the possibility of thawing more than you need. The excess cannot be refrozen without a considerable diminution of quality. Usually, the item then is wasted entirely. But frozen products are just too costly to throw out; consequently, you may try to work them into the menu somehow at the risk of alienating customers.)

Some processed items usually are sold only in the frozen state. For example, corn on the cob and french fries are normally available only fresh or fresh frozen.

When choosing dried products, you are obviously going to save on storage and, if you care for them properly, they will have a long shelf life. Also, since the food is lightweight and does not require refrigeration, its transportation costs remain low, which in turn reduces the AP prices. On the other hand, though, the AP prices of many dried items stay high because of the amount of time and/or energy used to process them.

Unfortunately, you cannot purchase very many food items in a dried state, and many of those that you can buy are expensive. For instance, dried fruit requires very ripe, hence, costly, fruit with a lot of natural sugar. These qualities make such fruit particularly desirable, for example, in upside down cakes. Thus, the AP price for dried pineapple rings will probably exceed that of the canned counterpart. But the taste is different—dried pineapple is extremely sweet and strong.

A major difficulty with dried items is the need to reconstitute them. A mistake here, even a tiny one, can ruin the product. Another difficulty is the style of packaging. For instance, macaroni products come in all sorts of packaging materials and package sizes. Dried fruit is sometimes nicely layered on waxed paper and lined up neatly in a box. But it may also be slab packed (e.g., tossed in randomly and pushed together so that by the time you get it, much of it may be damaged).

Some processed items are, however, usually sold only in a dried state. Instant mashed potatoes, dried onion flakes, and dried spices are three examples.

Your selection of a processing method, then, is affected by (1) food quality, (2) AP price, and (3) the need for convenience. Although the standards of quality vary within each processing method, by and large, the taste, AP prices, and convenience are predetermined by the processing method itself.

Yet another major management decision regarding processed products centers on the question of substitution. For example, a recipe for mixed vegetables could include some fresh product, to use leftovers; some frozen product, bought at bargain prices; and some dried product, to take advantage of the excess sweetness. But consider the problem of inertia: since these purchases do not usually represent a large percentage of the purchase dollar, few operators devote much effort to determining the cheapest recipe unless they have access to a computerized management information system. Although there may not seem to be a great deal of money-saving potential in this area, some money can, nevertheless, be saved.

When you purchase processed food, you usually can get what you want. You name it, and somebody will make it if, of course, your purchase volume is large enough. For instance, fats and oils can be manufactured almost according to individual specifications, but one must, naturally, pay for this service. Nevertheless, when you purchase these products, it is nice to know that you can get what you need.

Here are some other management considerations involving processed food that occur now and then.

1. Some buyers tend to neglect generally accepted purchasing principles when it comes to some processed produce and grocery items, probably because usually a small amount of the total purchase dollar is involved—the majority, of course, going toward meat, fish, poultry, alcoholic beverages, and desserts. For example, the temptation is strong to set the par stock for condiments and let it go at that. This tendency is further fostered by manufacturers or suppliers who rely heavily on "pull strategies" for some of these items. Products like Heinz catsup and A-1 steak sauce that grace a dining room table seem almost traditional. To a lesser extent, other condiments, such as olives, pickles, and relishes, fall into this category.

2. The neglect we mentioned may also be nurtured by the cavalier attitude with which some employees approach inventory. For instance, some managers allow service personnel to bypass the normal issuing system when they need steak sauce, hot sauce, or similar condiments. In many small operations, they walk into the storeroom and take what

they need. And if a bottle or two spills or disappears, few supervisors get upset.

3. Numerous "impulse" purchases flood the market. For example, you can buy devices to drain near-empty catsup bottles; you can buy a device to check the pressure in canned goods; and you can buy an implement that can reveal whether a product has been thawed and refrozen.

4. For one reason or another, several new products are introduced each year in grocery product lines. Of course, there really are not many new food products, just new combinations of existing foodstuffs. For example, you can find all sorts of new vegetable combinations and sauce variations. The same is true for rice and pasta concoctions. Taking the time to examine all these "new" ideas can finally force you to neglect other more important business.

5. Sometimes buying one processed item entails buying something else. For instance, if you buy semolina flour to make your own pasta, you must also buy the pasta machine. Or if you buy corn flour to make your own tortillas and taco shells, you may need a special basket to hold the tortillas in your french fryer.

6. Processed foods present several "opportunity buys," such as introductory offers, quantity discounts, volume discounts, salvage buys,* and going-out-of-business sales by other hospitality operations. For those operators who control a lot of purchase money, long-term contracts may also be available. These opportunities usually mean a bit of extra analysis. You must decide whether you are going to buy these items on a day-to-day basis or whether you are going to succumb to a salesperson who comes in with a flamboyant special offer.

7. You must decide which container size you should buy. Smaller packages have higher AP prices per unit, but they sometimes provide the best EP cost. There is a related concern: should you buy individual, filled catsup bottles or should you keep the empty bottles and refill them from a No. 10 can of catsup or from some other bulk-pack catsup. The latter choice may entail some waste, but it may also produce the best EP cost.

8. A final major consideration relates to (6): you may be offered a bargain in canned green beans, but—and here is the problem—you normally use frozen green beans. Should you nibble on the offer? Do not take this temptation lightly. When profits run a little low for your business or you are just naturally conservative with money, you would be sur-

---

* Recall that these purchases may be outlawed by local health authorities—at any rate, these are questionable opportunities, because you cannot be sure that the products have not been exposed to prolonged heat, chemicals, or other contamination.

prised how big a few pennies can look. (This problem is also related to introductory offers or other types of "push strategies." Suppliers often try to switch a buyer from one item to another by manipulating temporarily the AP price.)

SELECTION FACTORS

It is management, either alone or in conjunction with others, that decides the quality, type, and style of food wanted for each processed item. During this decision-making process, the owner-manager should evaluate the selection factors in the following paragraphs.

INTENDED USE

As always, you want to determine exactly the intended use of the item so that you will be able to prepare the appropriate, relevant specification. For instance, canned fruit used in a recipe that has several ingredients need not be as attractive as one to be used as an appetizer.

EXACT NAME

Confusing terminology clutters the market, especially the processed produce market. For instance, you cannot order just pickles; you order Polish pickles, Kosher pickles, sweet pickles, and so on. You cannot order canned pears; you order canned Bartlett pear halves. You must order extra virgin olive oil if you want olive oil with the lowest possible acidity.

The list of these designations can grow incredibly long, but you must become familiar with the market terminology, and not just for the items we consider in this chapter. There do seem to be, however, more esoteric terms in the area of processed produce and other grocery items than in most other areas.

The federal government has provided some assistance to the buyer who is responsible for ordering many processed foods. Recall from Chapter 3 that it has issued several "standards of identity" that essentially establish what a food product is—for example, what a food product must be to be labeled "Strawberry Preserves." Some standards, in addition, set specific processing requirements, such as cooking and other procedures, to assure wholesomeness and safety of the finished product. For instance, an "organic" food, such as canned organic vegetables, must contain at least 90 percent organic ingredients, that is, ingredients that are grown without added hormones, pesticides, herbicides, or synthetic fertilizers.

These types of standards, however, do not keep different companies from making distinctive recipes. For example, the USDA content requirement for beef stew specifies only the minimum percentage of beef (25 percent) that the stew must contain. It does not prevent a manufacturer from using combinations of other ingredients or increasing the amount of beef to make the product unique. Hence, all brands of stew probably will taste somewhat different, which makes it risky to rely only on standards of identity when selecting processed produce and other grocery items in addition to some meat, dairy, fish, and poultry items.

There are standards of identity available for approximately 235 items if you care to use them. The USDA has set standards for meat and poultry products, and the FDA has set them for cacao products; cereal, flour, and related products; macaroni and noodle products; bakery products; milk and cream products; cheese and cheese products; frozen desserts; sweeteners and table syrups; food flavorings; dressings for food; canned fruits and fruit juices; fruit butters; jellies; preserves and related products; soda water; canned and frozen fish and shellfish; eggs and egg products; oleomargarine; nut products; canned and frozen vegetables; and tomato products.

For some items, you may be able to make do with only a standard of identity. For instance, although all types and brands of orange juice are not the same, most of them are close. Likewise with other juices. Thus, you might be governed primarily by the AP price for these products.

U.S. GOVERNMENT GRADES (OR EQUIVALENT)

The FDA or USDA's Agricultural Marketing Service (AMS) Fruits and Vegetables Division inspects processed produce and other grocery items. If any meat is incorporated in the product, the USDA's Food Safety and Quality Service (FSQS) takes responsibility for it. Recall that there is continuous federal inspection or equivalent state inspection for any type of meat product that is sold. If no meat is involved, the inspector inspects only once in a while, maybe two or three times a year, as a check for wholesomeness. Of course, some state and local inspection may also come into play. These inspections are mandatory, but the U.S. grading service is voluntary and must be purchased by the food processor. A processor can pay for continuous inspection and can get continuous inspection with or without a grade.

Federal grades have been established for canned or bottled, frozen, and dried fruit and vegetables and other grocery items. (See Figure 18.1.)

Grading factors for canned and bottled foods include color, uniformity of size and shape, the number of defects and blemishes, and the "character" (meaning texture, tenderness, and aroma). Other grading factors come into play, depending on the item being graded. For instance, the quality of the packing medium—the water or syrup—may be important for some products. Also, for some items, such as canned, whole tomatoes, the "drained weight," that is, the servable weight that remains after the juice is removed, is considered by the grader when evaluating the total score.

FIGURE 18.1. Federal grade and inspection stamps used for processed produce and other grocery items.

Grading factors for frozen food include maturity, uniformity of size and shape, quality, color, and defects and blemishes.

Grading factors for dried foods include uniformity of size and shape, color, blemishes and defects, moisture content,* and how the products are packed (are they carefully layered or packed tightly together in a container, thus destroying their natural shape?).

As with fresh produce, there is no neat categorization of grading nomenclature. As a matter of convenience, you could rely on the following grading categories for canned or bottled and frozen items:

1. A—the very best product with excellent color, uniform size, weight, and shape, and few blemishes
2. B—slightly less perfect than grade A
3. C—may contain some broken and uneven pieces, perhaps some odd-shaped pieces; the flavor usually falls below grades A and B, and the color is not so attractive

* There is no federal standard for moisture content. The usual dried item has at least 75 percent of its moisture removed, but this is not enough to make the product last a long time. The term "sun-dried" implies a high moisture residual, about 25 percent, whereas foods dehydrated in other ways usually contain 5 percent or less of moisture.

Again, for convenience, you could rely on the same nomenclature for dried foods:

1. A—the most attractive and most flavorful product
2. B—not quite so attractive as grade A
3. C—more variations in taste and appearance, and usually broken pieces

Although this convenient grading system we note for canned or bottled, frozen, and dried products might be ideal, it is not reality. Not all these types of foods use the grading system A, B, and C. For example, canned mushrooms carry grades A, B, and Substandard. Frozen apples carry the same grades. Frozen apricots carry the grades A, B, C, and Substandard. And several dried foods carry the grades A, B, and Substandard.

Sometimes you hear the terms "Fancy," "Choice," or "Extrastandard." These are alternate terms for U.S. grades that are used by several people in the channel of distribution. For example, many buyers use the following U.S. grade designations when purchasing canned fruit and canned vegetables:

Canned Fruit	Canned Vegetables
Fancy	Fancy
Choice	Extrastandard
Standard	Standard

A further confusion in this area is the fact that some processed items carry two grade designations, some carry three, and the rest carry four.

Still another difficulty: Some products might contain the notation "Grade A." But if the notation does not say "U.S. Grade A," the products have not been graded by a federal inspector. The government allows a packer to say "Grade A" if these products would grade out at grade A if a government inspector were to grade them.

As a general rule, in many channels of distribution, for several product lines, an item could carry the same type of grading nomenclature used by the federal government, even if the appropriate government agency did not grade the product. As long as a nongovernment graded item does not carry the "U.S." prefix, food fabricators are allowed to use "Grade" on their labels. It behooves the buyer to note carefully whether a purchased item has "U.S. Grade A" or "Grade A" listed on the package label; there is quite a difference between the two terms.

It would not serve the purpose of our discussion to drag you through every grade. But you must be aware of the potential confusion that meets the buyer in this area. As we noted in Chapter 17, you usually can communicate with the purveyor and make your desires known. Of course, if you are a bid buyer, you must seek out the relevant grading standards if you want them on your specification.

Since many specifications for processed produce and other grocery items include some reference to federal grades, you need to know where to find this information. Probably the most complete and most convenient sources of grading information are the *ComSource Canned Goods Specifications Manual* and the *ComSource Frozen Food Specifications Manual.*

Many buyers will include federal government grades on their specifications primarily because they want to ensure that the products are produced and packed under continuous government inspection. However, if there is any meat included with the item, or if there is any egg breaking necessary in the fabrication of the item, the federal government mandates continuous inspection even though the food processor does not want to purchase the grading service. Also, a buyer could specify that the products desired must carry the federal government shield that notes that the product was "packed under continuous inspection of the U.S. Dept. of Agriculture." The USDA will provide this service, for a fee, to those primary sources who want inspection only, and who do not want to purchase the federal government grading service.

PACKERS' BRANDS (OR EQUIVALENT)

We have noted in Chapter 11 that a bit of "pull strategy" is inherent in these product lines. Hence, buyers can sometimes be "coerced" into purchasing Heinz catsup, A-1 steak sauce, Del Monte relish, and so on.

In addition, many processed items come and go. Thus, if you want a particularly esoteric combination of fruit, you might find only one producer who handles it.

Also, since packaging can be unstandardized, you may seek out the brands that meet your particular packaging requirements. (Recall that a brand normally implies more than just product quality.)

For some items, particularly something like frozen peas in cream sauce, a packer's brand may be your most important indication of quality and flavor. The quality of a fruit or vegetable varies from year to year and from place to place. The top-of-the-line brands make an effort to smooth out these annual fluctuations.

Packers' brands may be desirable, therefore, if only because subtle differences occur between, for example, tomato packers. Canned tomatoes can, after all, vary tremendously, not only in appearance, but in taste as well. Consequently, some buyers may be wary about trading Heinz for Del Monte simply because they detect a slightly different flavor.

There is a tremendous variety of brands available to the buyer. For instance, some companies package only the best quality merchandise and will pack lower-quality products only if these items carry some other brand name. These firms refer to themselves as "premium" brands. Recall from Chapter 7 that some companies prepare several qualities under the same brand-name heading; that is, they carry several "packers' grades" (i.e., packers' brands) in their sales kits. For instance, you sometimes can purchase a specific producer's brand of carrots, but you will notice that there are different-colored labels for each quality of carrots packed by that specific producer. These different-colored labels represent the packer's "grades" produced by the company.

A buyer also could opt for generic brands. They are not as plentiful in the wholesale distribution channels as they are in the retail grocery stores and supermarkets, probably because if we desire this type of quality, there already exists a packer's brand to satisfy our needs. If you insist on purchasing generic brands, you probably will need to shop at the numerous warehouse wholesale clubs that cater to small businesses.

The generic brands can be very economical. Generally speaking, they typically are offered at very low AP prices for at least three reasons: (1) lower, or nonexistent, selling and advertising costs; (2) lower packaging costs; and (3) in some cases, lower quality. Lower quality, though, does not necessarily imply lower nutritional value. Also, buyers are apt to receive a more uniform quality when ordering single-ingredient generic-brand food. For instance, canned sliced peaches would tend to have better and more consistent quality than, say, mayonnaise, which includes several ingredients and involves relatively complicated processing.

PRODUCT SIZE

A very important consideration is the question of size, or count. For example, when you order pitted green olives in a No. 10 can, you should also indicate the olive size you want. You can do this by stating a specific count, which in turn implies a number, or count, of olives in a particular can. The higher the count, the more in the can and the smaller the olive. Sometimes, too, you can specify the approximate number of product pieces you would like in a can. You will, however, usually find yourself limited in the count that you can have. There are only a few choices. (See Figure 18.2.)

In lieu of specifying the count, the buyer could use other marketing terms that essentially serve the same purpose. For instance, while it is true that olive sizes can be indicated by stating the count desired, you could use terms such as "large," "extra large," "jumbo," or another appropriate marketing term to convey the necessary size information to your suppliers.

A buyer also may want to know how many cups he or she can get from a can or a frozen pack. Although these volume measurements appear on consumer products' package labels, you must be careful with volumes listed on commercial labels. They are sometimes misleading. For instance, on an instant mashed potato can label, there could be a recon-

FIGURE 18.2. Typical product sizes for peach and pear halves. (Courtesy Canned Fruit Promotion Service.)

stituted, or ready-to-serve, volume of 3 gallons stated—a volume attainable only if you whip the potatoes long enough to incorporate a great deal of air.

SIZE OF CONTAINER

You must indicate on your specification the exact size of the container that you wish to buy. (See Figure 18.3.) To do this, you should determine whether the size of each package meets your needs. It costs more per ounce to buy dried oregano in a little bottle than in a much larger container. But if you do not use much dried oregano, some product in your big container will go to waste. So the EP cost becomes your main consideration when you evaluate appropriate container sizes.

TYPE OF PACKAGING MATERIAL

For frozen and dried products, especially frozen, the packaging materials are not nearly so standardized as are those for cans and bottles. If you buy large amounts of these products, say, an annual supply, you should examine the packaging very carefully. Will it hold up for a few weeks or a few months in the freezer? Can moisture seep into the dried containers?

Another packaging consideration that emerges occasionally is ease of opening. Can you reclose the package tightly enough to save the rest of the contents for later? Sometimes an item comes in an inconvenient package, which can lead to waste. In this case, the EP cost goes up. A more convenient package generally costs more. But as long as the EP cost is acceptable, it may be worth it.

We should address the need to use environmentally safe packaging whenever possible. When we purchase cans or bottles, they may not be as convenient as, say, plastic pouches or aseptic containers. However, at least we can recycle them. This helps protect our environment and, in some parts of the country, we may even be able to earn a small amount of income from recycling plants who purchase these materials.

Another packaging consideration is the issue of "personalized" packaging. (See Figure 18.4.) For some processed items, such as sugar packets, a buyer could order packaging that contains the hospitality operation's logo or another form of advertisement. Sometimes these options will increase the AP price of the underlying food item; however, the advertising value may more than offset the added expense.

PACKAGING PROCEDURE

This is an important consideration for some processed produce and other grocery items. As a general rule, packing usually has two styles: slab-packed merchandise and layered merchandise. Most processed produce and other grocery items are necessarily slab packed, that is, they are

A Guide to Common Can Sizes

6 oz.	Approximately ¾ cup 6 fl. oz.	Used for frozen concentrated juices and individual servings of single strength juices.
8 oz.	Approximately 1 cup 8 oz. (7¾ fl. oz.)	Used mainly in metropolitan areas for most fruits, vegetables and specialty items.
No. 1 (Picnic)	Approximately 1¼ cups 10½ oz. (9½ fl. oz.)	Used for condensed soups, some fruits, vegetables, meat and fish products.
No. 300	Approximately 1¾ cups 15½ oz. (13½ fl. oz.)	For specialty items, such as beans with pork, spaghetti, macaroni, chili con carne, date and nut bread—also a variety of fruits, including cranberry sauce and blueberries.
No. 303	Approximately 2 cups 1 lb. (15 fl. oz.)	Used extensively for vegetables; plus fruits, such as sweet and sour cherries, fruit cocktail, apple sauce.
No. 2	Approximately 2½ cups 1 lb. 4 oz. (1 pt. 2 fl. oz.)	Used for vegetables, many fruits and juices.
No. 2½	Approximately 3½ cups 1 lb. 13 oz. (1 pt. 10 fl. oz.)	Used principally for fruits, such as peaches, pears, plums and fruit cocktail; plus vegetables, such as tomatoes, sauerkraut and pumpkin.
46 oz.	Approximately 5¾ cups 46 oz. (1 qt. 14 fl. oz.)	Used almost exclusively for juices, also for whole chicken.
No. 10	Approximately 12 cups 6 lbs. 9 oz. (3 qts.)	So-called "institutional" or "restaurant" size container, for most fruits and vegetables. Stocked by some retail stores.

FIGURE 18.3. Average can sizes. (Courtesy American Can Company, Greenwich, CT.)

FIGURE 18.4. Example of personalized packaging. (Courtesy Lady Luck Casino Hotel, Las Vegas, NV, and Caesars Palace, Las Vegas, NV.)

poured into the container and then the container is sealed. Some products, though, such as dried fruit, can be slab packed, or they can be neatly layered between sheets of paper or cardboard. Furthermore, some layered merchandise, such as frozen, double-baked, stuffed potatoes might be individually wrapped.

As usual, the layered and/or individually wrapped products will cost you more, at least in terms of higher AP prices. However, when you consider the fact that better packaging, and a more careful packing style, minimize product breakage and other forms of product loss, the resulting EP costs may be quite acceptable.

DRAINED WEIGHT (SERVABLE WEIGHT)

It is usually a good idea to consider weights instead of volumes. The weight of the contents of a can can vary. It is good practice to perform a cutting test to determine "drained weight" (servable weight) when purchasing canned items, that is, the weight of the product less its juice. (This is computed by draining the product in a specific sieve for a certain amount of time.) Some packers' brands offer a lot of fruit and little juice. Another brand could have more juice and less fruit. You must be concerned with portions per can and drained weights—with EP cost—to be sure.

Recall that food processors need to note on consumer package labels the serving size and number of servings in the package. They may eventually be required to list the weight of the fruit and, separately, the weight of the juice, water, or syrup. To a certain extent, we can estimate the amount of juice by the absence or presence of the words "heavy pack" or "solid pack." If these words do not appear, expect a lot of liquid—for example, about 5½ ounces of liquid in the typical 16-ounce can of fruit. The term "solid pack" means no juice added; "heavy pack" means some juice added, but not much.

Best of all, however, the drained weight is what you should measure. It is more reliable than estimating weights by looking at the can's label.

When you compare the weights of two or more packers' brands of frozen products, you should thaw frozen fruit, and cook frozen vegetables from the frozen state, before weighing them. Do the same with dried products: weigh them only after you have reconstituted them.

Be wary of buying anything after considering only the volume. Remember from Chapter 3 the standard of fill, which protects us from the packer who fills a can only halfway and pretends to give a lot for the money. Remember, too, the possibility that an unscrupulous supplier may pump air into a product or lower the specific gravity of a product (by decreasing the product's density he or she makes it lighter). Some possible examples here include ready-to-serve potato puffs. (Should you buy them by count or by weight?) Tomato puree can vary in density. It can weigh about as much as an equal amount of water, which has specific gravity of 1.00. Or it can have a specific gravity of 1.06 or even a little more, hence greater weight.

TYPE OF PROCESSING

You must indicate the type of processing desired. The type of processing implies certain flavor and texture characteristics, as well as specific product-preservation techniques. Generally, you will purchase canned, bottled, frozen, and/or dried merchandise.

COLOR

In some cases, you will need to specify the color preferred. For instance, there are canned red apple rings and there are green ones. The same choices are available for bottled maraschino cherries. Generally, when you specify the exact name of the item wanted, you will indicate the color required. If your exact name does not include this notation, you must be sure to point it out elsewhere on the specification if it is relevant.

PRODUCT FORM

You will need to indicate at times the specialized form of the merchandise that you want. Usually this is not necessary if you are purchasing the common, ordinary processed produce and grocery items. But if you are purchasing, say, a particular vegetable casserole, you may want to note the amounts and types of vegetables desired. Or you may find it necessary to point out that you want a minimum amount of almonds in the frozen green beans you want to procure for your establishment.

PACKING MEDIUM

For some products, there are several packing mediums available. For example, for canned fruit, you could select fruit packed in water, in syrup, or with no added medium. You also can specify the syrup density desired by noting the minimum "Brix" level. Thick syrup has a higher Brix (i.e., more sugar) than light syrup. The federal government sets minimum Brix levels for some products, but you may want higher levels. For instance, a higher Brix carries a higher AP price, but since fruits packed in heavy syrup do not break easily, the resulting EP cost may be quite satisfactory.

When purchasing vegetable products, you may be able to specify the type and amount of sauce desired. For instance, frozen broccoli could be packed with butter sauce, cheese sauce, or some other specialized sauce.

THE USE OF ADDITIVES AND PRESERVATIVES

The concern shown by some with the issue of preservatives in canned, bottled, frozen, and dried items appears to be less than for dairy and meat products. We could not get the products we need if we had to settle for "fresh" produce all the time. Moreover, we could not store fresh produce efficiently and would probably waste much of it. But some companies are more discreet with their additives and preservatives than others.

If the thought of additives and preservatives bothers you, you may have difficulty weeding out the offending packers' brands. Furthermore, you will find "organic," "whole," "natural" foods to be expensive. Why? For one thing, you have entered a market with few suppliers. Also, shelf life is reduced, resulting in greater handling costs and subsequently greater spoilage loss.

OTHER INFORMATION THAT MAY APPEAR ON A PACKAGE LABEL

The federal government requires a great deal of information to be displayed on consumer product labels. However, required label information aside, the typical hospitality operator would be much more interested in other kinds of information that may or may not appear on a package label.

Many operators would like to see packing dates, freshness dates (or shelf lives), and serving cost data noted on package labels. Many also would like to see the lot number on a package label. (Since the quality of product shifts, it would be nice to be able to reorder, for instance, corn of not only the same packer's brand but also from the same batch that previously ordered corn was obtained.) School food-service buyers seek out products that carry Child Nutrition (CN) labels, that is, labels that indicate how the products conform to the nutritional requirements of the USDA. When food processors put these details on their package labels, you must expect to pay a bit for this added information value.

ONE-STOP SHOPPING OPPORTUNITIES

Smaller operations tend to prefer one-stop shopping for many items, including processed products. Some manufacturers try to encourage this habit by joining some sort of distribution co-op. For instance, the Continental Organization of Distributor Enterprises, Inc. (CODE) is a group that food processors can join. The group members then use the CODE label, which permits the CODE group to market and distribute an extensive line of products. This procedure permits the operator to use the one-stop shopping strategy.

Some national corporations also carry extensive lines of processed produce and other grocery items and compete directly with local and regional distributors. For instance, General Mills, Green Giant, Pillsbury, and Schilling produce, market, and distribute wide varieties of processed products. These companies normally offer only one level of product quality, and they usually control all aspects of production and distribution. As a result, their products are often referred to as "controlled brands."

Some national corporations carry extensive lines as well as extensive qualities of processed produce and other grocery items. For instance, S.E. Rykoff & Co. distributes many types of products, and it distributes many different "packer's grades" (i.e., packer's brands) in most product lines. Some of the qualities the company offers carry the names "Golden Rey" brand and "S.E.R." brand. (See Figure 7.5.)

As the typical hospitality operation grows, it shows less and less of a tendency to use one-stop shopping for processed produce. There are too many opportunity buys and long-term contracts at a good savings available, but they can usually be exploited only if one shops around. The larger firms usually have the time to do this shopping around. In addition, as the menu gets larger and incorporates more variety, an operation has less opportunity to satisfy its needs with the one-stop shopping method.

There is, however, a subtle advantage to one-stop shopping for processed produce, other grocery items, and also for meat products. Shortages sometimes occur for these items, and being a good customer may ensure you a continual supply. In fact, some suppliers "allocate" certain product lines; that is, they predetermine how much a buyer can purchase. This amount is referred to as the buyer's "allocation."

AP PRICE

The EP cost is the only relevant concern for a purchaser. The EP cost includes not only the cost of the product but, indirectly, the cost of the labor it takes to prepare and serve it and the cost of energy needed to work with it, as well as other overhead expenses. It is difficult to make these judgments. But you must force yourself to look beyond, for example, the drained weight of canned mushrooms.

Since there are an interminable number of varieties, styles, and packaging methods for processed foods, there are correspondingly different AP prices. It is not easy to tell whether it is advantageous to take a C grade instead of a B grade for a savings of perhaps 5 cents a can. The trade-off here would in most cases be a matter of opinion. Since lower grades are perfectly acceptable in some recipes, lower qualities can save money without reducing a recipe's acceptability.

For similar items, you could pay similar AP prices. But some suppliers may give better quantity discounts and volume discounts than others. And, typically, these discounts are quite lucrative. Therefore, bid buying can save money, but only if you are willing to accept a large supply, put the cash up front, and make your buy at new pack times, that is, when packers' produce this year's products.

Unfortunately, there may not be enough bidders for your business, especially if your local supplier cannot find enough of a product to satisfy your requirements. But even if you find only one supplier, a large buy can be valuable—a substantial savings may be yours if you can store and protect a large supply. (Here are subtle disadvantages: If you are "locked in" for a year, your menu is somewhat set; also, if AP prices for similar items fall, you cannot easily take advantage of them when your storage area is full.)

SUPPLIER SERVICES

Normally, canned products require only nominal supplier service. Most of these items are not readily perishable, so you are not likely to be concerned with how quickly the supplier moves them. But this cannot be said of frozen items. If you doubt the capability of a supplier to maintain at least 0°F, you should avoid this person. Frozen food costs more because it maintains a better culinary quality, but this quality rapidly deteriorates if storage temperatures are above zero or if they fluctuate; in addition, these problems reduce shelf life drastically.

You may occasionally want to obtain a stockless purchasing deal, in which you protect an AP price for six months to a year. This tactic rarely saves as much as traditional forward buying, in which you take delivery of a large amount. But now and then it can produce a reasonable saving.

You would also like to receive reasonable "break points." You do not want to buy 100 cases before you get a price break, or quantity discount. Fifty cases are preferable. We have noticed that break points are somewhat standard among suppliers.

Sometimes an AP price shoots up drastically, and purchasers like to be warned about this beforehand, if possible. (If you use bid buying exclusively, you may not receive that warning. If you are a house account, chances are you will.)

Together with fluctuating AP prices, which really are not so common with processed products as they are for fresh foods, comes the shortage potential. A rainstorm can reduce the canned peaches supply. Are you on the list of those slated to get some of that supply? (Again, the bid buyer may be left behind. Indeed, he or she always takes a chance that nobody will answer the solicitations for bids. The house account may be better serviced.)

Here is another supplier service to consider: If you want a low grade, can you get it? Low-grade products generally are not in plentiful supply. (Here again, house accounts find themselves in a better position than bid buyers.)

Yet another service is the delivery schedule. Realistically, though, most of us can live with one delivery every week, or even one every two weeks. If, however, you have only a limited storage area, you might want other arrangements.

LOCAL SUPPLIER OR NATIONAL SOURCE?

You can easily go to the primary source for a direct purchase and have the carload of canned tomatoes "drop shipped" to you (i.e., delivered straight to your back door). You can also buy direct and arrange for a local supplier to distribute the merchandise.

You already know our views on buying directly and bypassing your local supplier. Still, you must do what you believe is best under given circumstances.

PURCHASING PROCESSED PRODUCE AND OTHER GROCERY ITEMS

Your first step in purchasing processed produce and other grocery items is to obtain copies of reference materials that contain useful information that you can use to prepare specifications. Most suppliers publish several in-house materials, particularly individual brochures that detail their major product lines. Also, probably the most complete and most convenient general publications are the *ComSource Canned Goods Specifications Manual* and the *ComSource Frozen Food Specifications Manual*. These references include considerable product information as well as detailed descriptions of grading factors used by U.S. government graders.

Your next step is to determine precisely what you want. This may not be an easy task, since there are several management decisions involved. Some items are traditionally purchased canned or bottled, frozen, or dried. But the tradition does not hold true for all products.

Once you know what you want, you can make the actual purchase simple or difficult. It will be relatively simple if you buy on a day-to-day

Pineapple slices Used for salad bar Dole brand (or equivalent) 66 count No. 10 can Unsweetened clarified pineapple juice	White cake mix Used to prepare cupcakes Pillsbury Food Service brand 5 pounds Cardboard box
Whole canned onions Used for plate garnish U.S. Fancy 350 count No. 10 can Water pack	Confectioners powdered sugar Used for baking C & H brand 1 lb. cardboard box Packed 24 lb. per case

FIGURE 18.5. Example processed produce and other grocery items product specifications.

basis. If you become dissatisfied with a particular packer's brand, you can switch to another. It is, however, a little more adventurous to enter the bid-buying route, especially when you seek to lock up a six-month or one-year supply.

If you enter into a long-term contract on a bid basis, you will need detailed specifications. You may find it beneficial to prepare these detailed specs even if you do not use bid buying; it is good discipline to place your ideas on paper before you actually commit yourself to any type of purchase. Figure 18.5 shows some example product specifications. Figure 18.6 notes an example product specification outline for processed produce and other grocery items.

If you enter the long-term route, usually available in this product area even for smaller operations, you have a bit of work ahead of you. Before you put your name on a long-term contract, you should examine the bidders' products very carefully. A mistake in this area can be extremely costly, and unintentional mistakes happen easily. For example, you may examine three brands of canned tomatoes. You may perform all sorts of tests—comparing drained weights, looking for tomato skins, noting the clearness of juice—but you may discover too late that one brand has slightly less acid. These tests, mentioned earlier, are called "can cutting tests." If competing salespersons or suppliers are in attendance, the testing is sometimes referred to as "holding court." The purchaser usually completes a checklist for each brand and then compares each brand's scores. (See Figures 18.7 and 18.8.) If you are buying for large commissary

Intended use:

Exact name:

U.S. grade (or equivalent):

Packer's brand name (or equivalent):

Product size:

Size of container:

Type of packaging material:

Packaging procedure:

Drained weight:

Type of processing:

Color:

Product form:

Packing medium:

FIGURE 18.6. Example product specification outline for processed produce and other grocery items.

production, a little oversight like too much acid in a recipe can impair significantly the culinary quality of the finished product.

Another problem can occur through purchasing errors. How do you return a year's supply of canned tomatoes to a supplier if you make an error? And here is a related problem: If you buy a year's supply, and you later notice that the product is not quite so good as what you contracted for, you must protect yourself by retaining a few unopened packages that were available for your cutting test just prior to signing the contract; then you have on hand a standard of quality you can use to prove you actually contracted for something better.

Here are more suggestions for cutting tests. (1) Always check frozen fruit after it has thawed, and, in particular, check the fruit's texture, which tends to suffer in the freezing process. (2) Be sure to cook frozen vegetables from the frozen state before testing them. (3) Check all canned goods immediately after opening them, and check especially the odor. Canned products are cooked during the canning process to kill harmful bacteria so that the product will stay wholesome and not deteriorate. Thus they are ready to eat. And (4) make your tests of dried and concentrated products, such as soup, on the reconstituted product.

Generally, then, make your tests on the products after they have been prepared for customer service. In some instances, you may even want to prepare a full recipe with each one of the competing bidder's products and then perform your tests.

SAMPLE	1	2	3
Vendor/brand			
Drained weight			
Color			
Size			
Uniformity of size			
Defects			
Clearness of syrup			
Grade			
Flavor			
Case price			
Unit price			
Serving size			
EP cost/serving			

FIGURE 18.7. Checklist for canned sliced peaches.

These tests can take time and effort, unless you are invited to a supplier's headquarters for some type of product introduction or abbreviated cutting test. But it is normal practice in large organizations to spend a great deal of effort when considering a quantity buy.

Once you enter into a long-term contract, either a stockless purchase or a forward buy, the latter being common only in large operations or those that have a commissary or central distribution center, you will still undoubtedly be approached by salespersons carrying similar products. For instance, each competing supplier with its new brand of spaghetti sauce will bring it to your attention. Or, thanks to backdoor selling, a cook may urge you to buy a new type of soup base.

	Cling Peaches	Bartlett Pears	Fruit Cocktail
Color:			
Grade B:	Reasonably bright, possibly slight discoloration.	Reasonably uniform in color, may show tint of pink, appear translucent.	Fairly clear liquid and distinct color.
Grade C:	Reasonably bright, yellow-orange, possibly greenish-yellow.	May vary noticeably, appearance could be either white or brown.	
Texture/Character			
Grade B:	Reasonably good texture, no more than 10% of fruit being mushy.	Reasonably tender, may possess moderate graininess.	Texture of fruits may vary, from firm to soft.
Grade C:	Fairly good texture.	Texture may vary noticeably, with soft or frayed edges.	
Defects			
Grade B:	Reasonably free of pit material, not more than 5% crushed or broken.	Major defects may not exceed 10% of fruit and minor defects by 20%.	Refer to USDA guidelines for acceptable defects for each individual fruit in fruit cocktail.
Grade C:	Fairly free of pit material, less than 20% of fruit may be blemished.	Major defects may not exceed 20% of fruit and minor defects by 30%.	
Uniformity			
Grade B:	Largest unit may not exceed smallest unit by more than 60%.	Largest unit may not exceed smallest unit by more than 75%.	No more than 20% of fruit may vary substantially in size.

FIGURE 18.8. Guidelines for examining some canned fruit products. (*Source:* USDA.)

	Cling Peaches	Bartlett Pears	Fruit Cocktail
Grade C:	Largest unit may not exceed smallest unit by more than 100%.	Largest unit may not exceed smallest unit by more than 100%.	
Smell:	No offensive odors should be present in fruit or liquid of any grade.		
Taste:	Distinct and fruity.	Similar to mature pears.	Ability to detect flavor of individual fruits.
Sample Size:	#10 can equals 30 halves or 100 slices.	#10 can equals 30 halves or 100 slices.	#10 can
Pack Ratio:	N/A	N/A	Peaches 30%–50% Pears 25%–45% Grapes 6%–20% Pineapple 48 pieces Cherries 24 halves

FIGURE 18.8. Continued

Actually, you will not see too many revolutionary products. But you may see subtle changes, such as different packaging. For instance, you may buy a new packer's brand of soup base if it is similar to the one you now use, simply because it comes in a 30-pound pack instead of the 1-pound packs you currently purchase. If you buy the new product, your old supplier may come out with a 22-pound pack, and so testing tends to be a continuing process.

A very complicated test arises when you want to evaluate canned peas and frozen peas by using each in two versions of the same recipe, or if you want to try other combinations of canned, frozen, and dried. For instance, one stew recipe might be made three ways—with frozen onions, canned onions, and fresh onions. Which meets your criteria the best?

We have not seen very many local small producers in the processed produce area. But let us say somebody in the family has won a state fair blue ribbon for his or her canned pears and now wants to sell them. We do not consider it a good idea to buy these items. Indeed, recall that most states prohibit the use of home-cooked products in food-service operations, because they come from unapproved sources.

Having struggled successfully with all these details, your task becomes, at last, relatively easy. The ordering procedures themselves rarely present any burdensome difficulties.

RECEIVING PROCESSED PRODUCE AND OTHER GROCERY ITEMS

Generally accepted procedures for inspecting the quality of delivered processed produce and other grocery items have been established:

1. *Canned and bottled products.* Check the containers for any swelling, leaks, rust, dents, or broken seals. These characteristics (especially swelling) indicate contamination problems. Refuse damaged containers as well as those that are dirty, greasy, or generally unkempt.

2. *Dried products.* Check the condition of the containers. If you can see the dried foods, look for mold, broken pieces, and odd appearance.

3. *Frozen products.* Check the condition of the container, looking for any indication of thawing and refreezing—stained packaging indicates this. Check the food temperature. You want to see $-10°F$, but $0°F$ is acceptable. If you can see the frozen foods, check for "freezer burn," the excessive, often brownish dryness that occurs if the food has not been protected properly in frozen storage.

Occasional problems occur with quantity checks. Most of these processed products come in cases, and when the case is full, you may assume that they are full of exactly what you ordered. Repacking is rare, but it can happen. In any event, you ought to open at least some cases when receiving these items. This is particularly true when receiving a large quantity.

Make sure that you carefully check incoming products against the invoice and a copy of the purchase order. Some packers' brands resemble one another. Also, be careful of supplier substitutions, which can occur from time to time, especially for these types of products.

Quality checks are not always easy, mainly because you are limited in what you can actually see. Rarely will a chef, for example, come to the receiving dock to check the quality of processed products, unless a large quantity is being delivered.

After checking the quality and quantity, check the prices, and complete the appropriate accounting documents.

STORING PROCESSED PRODUCE
AND OTHER GROCERY ITEMS

Generally accepted procedures for storing processed products have also been established:

1. *Canned and bottled products.* Store these products in a dry area at approximately 50 to 70°F. You should avoid any wide fluctuation in temperature and humidity. Heat can be especially damaging. For instance, it robs spices of their flavor; it hastens the oxidation of frying fats, which means that these fats will not retain flavor, nor will they last as long in the french fryer; and it hastens the chemical changes in canned items, which means taste changes. You also need to avoid dampness, which causes rust and attracts dust and dirt. In hot climates you might consider refrigerating such items as spices and fats. Keep all canned and bottled products tightly covered, opening only what is necessary; otherwise, they will lose some shelf life.

2. *Dried products.* Be especially careful of dampness, as it can hasten the growth of mold, thereby ruining the products. Try to keep these products a little cooler than canned items so that insects are not attracted to them.

3. *Frozen products.* If at all possible, store these products at −10°F or lower. At this temperature you will preserve the maximum flavor, especially if the other distribution channel members have maintained this temperature. Be careful not to damage any packages, as this will eventually lead to freezer burn. Also, avoid fluctuations in temperature, which reduce shelf life drastically.

Perhaps the most unfortunate thing about storing processed produce and other grocery items is that so many of them require slightly different storage environments. As a practical matter, we can hardly satisfy each requirement, so we try to reach a happy medium by paying especially close attention to proper stock rotation.

It is not, however, always easy to ensure proper rotation because many employees grow complacent in their handling of processed items, thinking they will hold forever. Theoretically, canned, bottled, and dried food will last a long time, but no one would try to keep them very long. Nor will frozen food last forever; freezing merely slows, but does not eliminate, deterioration.

Other storage considerations include (1) keeping the items off the floor where they can attract dirt, and (2) when filling flour bins, and other such storage bins, trying not to mix the new flour or sugar with old. (If possible, use bins that load from the top and let you unload from the bottom.)

ISSUING PROCESSED PRODUCE AND OTHER GROCERY ITEMS

One often finds a good deal of neglect for many processed items. Such products as individual containers of catsup, salt, and sugar—usually food that goes to the service personnel stations—are not always controlled closely. The best way to avoid this waste is to ensure that there are written stock requisitions for every item and that no requisitioner asks for more than necessary. You can control a requisitioner by asking him or her to take note of the in-process inventory prior to asking for additional stock.

Think for a moment how you would issue half-cans or some similar amount. The fact is, if this problem arises frequently, you might be better off with smaller containers.

Finally, the EP cost is more vulnerable to attack in the area of in-process inventories. And here, as elsewhere, supervision is the key. Without effective and efficient supervision, it is futile to spend time and effort to save money in purchasing.

KEY WORDS AND CONCEPTS

Additives and preservatives

Advantages and disadvantages of the various processing methods

Allocation

AMS

AP price

Aseptic packaging

Break points

Brix

Can cutting test

CN label

Color

Common can sizes

Controlled brands

Drained weight

Drop shipment

Environmentally safe packaging

EP cost

Exact name

FDA

Forward buying

Freezer burn

Freshness dates

FSQS

Generic brands

Going-out-of-business sales

Grading factors

Heavy pack

Holding court

Impulse purchase

In-process inventories

Institutional can size

Intended use

Layered packaging

Lot number

Management considerations when
purchasing processed produce and
other grocery items

New pack time

One-stop shopping

Opportunity buys

Organic, whole, natural foods

Packaging material

Packaging procedure

Packed under continuous government
inspection

Packers' brands (grades)

Packing dates

Packing medium

Personalized packaging

Premium brands

Product form

Product size

Product testing factors

Pull strategy

Purchasing, receiving, storing, and
issuing processed produce and other
grocery items

Push strategy

Quantity discount

Recommended storage procedures

Reference books that can be used
when preparing specifications

Salvage buys

Shelf life

Shelf-stable products

Single-ingredient generic-brand food

Size of container

Slab packed

Solid pack

Specific gravity

Standard of identity

Stock rotation

Sun-dried versus other drying methods

Supplier services

Type of processing

USDA

U.S. grades

U.S. Grade A versus Grade A

Volume discount

Warehouse wholesale club

QUESTIONS AND PROBLEMS

1. What are the U.S. grades for canned, bottled, frozen, and dried items?

2. Give an example of optional information a packer could note on a package
   label.

3. Assume that you own a small coffee shop and that you have no franchise
   affiliation. Your annual volume (open 24 hours, every day) is $825,000.
   You sell hamburgers, and you are currently using Heinz individual catsup
   bottles. You can save about 8 percent of your $438-a-year catsup expense,
   (i.e., $0.08 \times \$438 = \$35.04$ per year) if you buy bulk-pack catsup and
   plastic containers and fill these containers from the pack. What course do

you recommend? If possible, ask a coffee shop manager, or owner-manager, to comment on your answer.

4. What is an appropriate intended use for canned peas?

5. Give an example of the "pull strategy" in the processed produce and other grocery items channel of distribution.

6. What is the primary difference between U.S. Grade B and U.S. Grade C products?

7. What are the grading factors for canned and bottled products?

8. What are the grading factors for frozen products?

9. What are the grading factors for dried products?

10. What critical information is missing from the following product specification for canned peach halves?

Peach halves
Packed in light syrup
CODE brand, red label (or equivalent)
Packed in No. 10 cans, 6 cans per case

11. Why is organic food more expensive than nonorganic processed produce products?

12. Note three examples of grocery products that you have seen in a restaurant operation that carry personalized packaging. What are some of the advantages and disadvantages of personalized packaging?

13. Assume that you normally purchase 1,200 cases of canned peaches every three months. (You order once every three months.) The AP price per case is $8.75. Your supplier offers you a one-year supply for $8.60 per case, COD. (You currently have 30 days in which to pay your invoices from this supplier.) Assume you are the purchasing director for a 400-room hotel that does excellent restaurant and banquet business. What course of action do you suggest? If possible, ask the manager of a comparable property to comment on your answer.

14. What is an appropriate intended use for dried apricots?

15. Assume that you are the purchasing director for a university food service with 15 dormitories, 8 snack bars, and an unpredictable banquet business. Currently, you operate a central commissary and a central distribution center. Outline the specific procedures you would use for the purchasing, receiving, storing, and issuing of canned peach halves. If possible, ask a university food-service purchasing director to comment on your answer.

16. Your supplier calls to say that the price of tomato paste is due to rise soon. It is suggested that you purchase at least 2,500 cases immediately. Assuming that you find your supplier completely trustworthy, what specifically should you consider before making your decision about this potential purchase?

17. What are the recommended storage temperatures for canned and bottled products and for frozen products?

18. Assume that you manage a steak house. You have been using individually wrapped ¹/₂-ounce portions of catsup. On a Saturday afternoon you notice that you have very few of these packets left, as last night's business was especially brisk. At first glance, you do not believe you can get a delivery from the commissary—the steak house is part of a national chain—until Monday morning. But you are open tonight until 9 P.M. and all day tomorrow, 11 A.M. to 9 P.M. What course of action do you take? If possible, ask a steak house manager to comment on your answer.

19. Assume that you manage a college food-service facility. You want to purchase your annual requirement of canned tomatoes. There are four brands of tomatoes, three reasonably well-known brands and one generic brand. The AP prices vary only slightly among the three name brands, but there is a 22 percent savings with the generic brand. Unfortunately, the generic brand contains mostly broken pieces and has a drained weight that is 15 percent less than the name-brand merchandise. In addition, the supplier warns you that the quality of the generic brand is not predictable from year to year. Which type of merchandise would you purchase? Why? If possible, ask a college food-service manager to comment on your answer.

20. A product specification for frozen corn could include the following information:

    (a) _____

    (b) _____

    (c) _____

    (d) _____

    (e) _____

21. The choice of which food processing method a buyer selects is usually affected by three major criteria. What are these three criteria?

22. Why would a canned tomato puree with a high specific gravity usually be more expensive than one with a lower specific gravity?

23. What is the difference between the designations, "U.S. Grade A" and "Grade A"?

24. What is an appropriate intended use for frozen asparagus spears?

25. Define or explain the following terms:

    (a) AMS

    (b) CN label

    (c) Standard of identity

    (d) Stock rotation

    (e) Break point

    (f) Drained weight

(g) Heavy pack

(h) Specific gravity

(i) New pack time

(j) Can cutting test

(k) Holding court

(l) Freezer burn

(m) Solid pack

(n) Premium brand

(o) Generic brand

(p) Packer's "grade"

CHAPTER 19

Source: Alliant Foodservice

DAIRY PRODUCTS

THE PURPOSE OF THIS CHAPTER

This chapter discusses:

- The selection factors for dairy products
- Purchasing, receiving, storing, and issuing dairy products
- The in-process dairy products inventory

INTRODUCTION

The typical food-service operation can use one supplier for its dairy products—a sort of built-in one-stop buying strategy. Alternatively, a purchaser can take the time to evaluate the wide variety of suppliers available for each type of dairy product.

A purchaser can invest time in yet another way: evaluating substitution possibilities. For instance, will it be butter or margarine? Will it be a nondairy coffee cream or half-and-half? Or will you purchase natural cheese or cheese that has vegetable fat instead of butterfat? Since butterfat is a very expensive fat, the owner-manager could evaluate the types of substitution possibilities that may save money. But substitution cannot usually be done without some flavor and nutrition alteration. Also, the type of food-service operation you have minimizes the number of substitution possibilities; for example, you probably would not want to serve margarine chips in a gourmet dinner house. In addition, you must be careful not to serve one product and imply that it is another; for example, you cannot serve half-and-half and imply it is cream (a richer product that has more butterfat and is more expensive). Truth-in-menu legislation in some parts of the country prohibits this, and common sense suggests we should not attempt it elsewhere.

The purchaser faces another series of substitution issues: one dairy item may be substituted for another in food production recipes. For example, one does not have to use sour cream for the baked potato; there are at least two alternatives: a cultured dressing, which is like a low-fat sour

1 cup butter	1 cup margarine $^7/_8$ to 1 cup hydrogenated fat plus $^1/_2$ teaspoon salt $^7/_8$ cup lard plus $^1/_2$ teaspoon salt $^7/_8$ cup rendered fat plus $^1/_2$ teaspoon salt
1 cup coffee cream (20 percent)	3 tablespoons butter plus about $^7/_8$ cup milk
1 cup heavy cream (40 percent)	$^1/_3$ cup butter plus about $^3/_4$ cup milk
1 cup whole milk	1 cup reconstituted nonfat dry milk plus $2^1/_2$ teaspoons butter or margarine $^1/_2$ cup evaporated milk plus $^1/_2$ cup water $^1/_4$ cup sifted dry whole milk powder plus $^7/_8$ cup water
1 cup milk	3 tablespoons sifted nonfat dry milk powder plus 1 cup water 6 tablespoons sifted nonfat dry milk crystals plus 1 cup water
1 cup buttermilk or sour milk	1 tablespoon vinegar or lemon juice plus enough sweet milk to make 1 cup (let stand 5 minutes) $1^3/_4$ teaspoons cream of tartar plus 1 cup sweet milk

FIGURE 19.1. Some dairy product substitutions.

cream, or an artificial nondairy product. Since butterfat content is almost directly related to the AP price of a dairy item, these types of substitutions can be cost-effective. However, again there will necessarily be some flavor and nutrition alteration in the final product.

To a certain extent, it is a matter of opinion whether these flavors are different. So it may be to your benefit to experiment. Whenever you combine two or more ingredients in a recipe, the possibility of recipe change always exists. More possibilities exist for dairy products than for other ingredients because anytime you have fat, you have at least one substitution possibility: yogurt for sour cream, skim milk for whole milk, pasteurized process cheese for natural cheese, and so on. Figure 19.1 notes some dairy product substitutions.

Once you decide, in general, what dairy products you want, you must next determine the exact products and supplier(s) you would like to use. What is the difference between one whole milk brand and another? There should be little, as most dairies use fairly standardized management techniques. But they may vary somewhat in their quality control programs and their processing methods, so that perhaps a taste comparison between dairies is not wasted effort. There will be slight flavor variations if the type of feed differs among dairies and if the dairy herds are in different stages of lactation, that is, if there is a seasonal variation.

Chances are that even though there may be little difference in flavor between one brand of whole milk and another, the same cannot be said of things like ice cream and cheese. For these items, there is a good possibility that you will unconsciously become a house account. Once you settle on a particular brand of cheese, for example, you may find it difficult to discontinue it in favor of another, especially if the cheese is served alone. Your customers probably would notice any change. The taste of many dairy products, especially cheese, tends to be unique to each producer.

Small operators prefer one-stop shopping for the majority of their dairy products. But the one supplier may not have everything needed. Consequently, the decision sometimes involves a choice between one or two suppliers, and fewer deliveries, who may not always have exactly what you want versus several suppliers, and more frequent deliveries, who carry what you need.

It is not easy to decide which choice to make. On the one hand, dairy products do not usually represent a great deal of the purchase dollar. Hence, you could argue that there is little potential gain associated with evaluating every available brand and supplier. On the other hand, the substitution possibilities can be lucrative. But the only sure way of knowing whether you have examined all the substitution possibilities is to plow through every available brand and supplier. To complicate matters, a lot of new products come and go.

In some cases, it is preferable if you can get exactly the dairy products you want from one or two suppliers. But in many instances, a more careful search of the possibilities pays for itself.

SELECTION FACTORS

Management personnel usually determine the varieties and qualities of dairy products they want to include on the menu and may or may not work in cooperation with other company personnel in making these decisions. Regardless, many of the following selection factors are normally considered.

INTENDED USE

As always, you want to determine exactly the intended use of the item so that you will be able to prepare the appropriate, relevant specification. For instance, if a cheese is needed primarily for flavor and only secondarily for appearance, the specification should reflect this.

EXACT NAME

It is very important to note the exact, specific name of the item that you want because the majority of dairy products carry a standard of identity

Item	Minimum Percentage Fat
Cheddar cheese	30.5%
Cottage cheese, creamed	4.0%
Cottage cheese, dry curd	.5% (Maximum)
Cottage cheese, low fat	.5% to 2.0%
Cream cheese	33.0%
Ice cream	10.0%
Ice milk	2.0% to 7.0%
Milk, evaporated	7.9%
Milk, low fat	1.0% to 2.0%
Milk, skim	0.1% to 0.5%
Milk, whole	3.25%
Mozzarella cheese	18.0% to 21.6%
Mozzarella cheese, part skim	12.0% to 18.0%
Neufchatel cheese	20.0% to 33.0%
Pasteurized process American cheese	26.8%
Pasteurized process American cheese food	23.0%
Pasteurized process American cheese spread	20.0%
Ricotta cheese	11.0%
Ricotta cheese, part skim	6.0% to 11.0%
Sour cream	18.0%
Whipping cream	30.0%

FIGURE 19.2. Some dairy products' legally defined minimum fat contents.

set by the federal government. The standard is based primarily on the minimum amount of butterfat content the product must carry in order to be called by a certain name. For some products, the standards of identity also prescribe minimum or maximum amounts of milk solids allowed. Figure 19.2 notes some dairy products' legally defined minimum fat contents.

If your operation can use these minimum governmental standards, you may find bid buying the easiest procedure. Assuming that everything else is equal, you could write your specifications with just the words, for example, "vanilla-flavored ice milk." Thus, assuming that every bidder meets the required standard, you could save money when one supplier bids lower than the rest.

U.S. GOVERNMENT GRADES (OR EQUIVALENT)

The Agricultural Marketing Service (AMS) of the USDA, Poultry and Dairy Division, has set federal grading standards for poultry, eggs, and

FIGURE 19.3. Federal grade and inspection stamps used for dairy products.

dairy products. U.S. grades, however, do not exist for every type of dairy product. But milk, which is the base for all natural dairy products, usually is graded. As is true with most commodities, grading of milk and milk products is voluntary; however, many states require milk to be graded by the federal government. (See Figure 19.3.)

Most states and local municipalities have stringent health codes covering milk production. Like most foods high in protein, milk is a good medium for harmful bacteria. Consequently, it must be produced and bottled under government-prescribed conditions. The U.S. Public Health Service's Milk Ordinance and Code contains provisions covering such activities as the approved care and feeding of the dairy cows, the handling of the milk, the pasteurization* requirement, and the holding temperature of the milk.

Dairies have little to say about milk production. They do have the option of homogenization, that is, dividing the butterfat globules so that they stay in the milk as a permanent emulsion and do not rise to the top. And, of course, they can dictate what to do with their milk: sell it to ice cream makers, sell it to dry milk producers, market it to households, and so on.

Fluid milk grades are based primarily on the finished product's bacte-

---

* Heating the milk to kill disease-causing (but not spoilage) bacteria. Milk that is not pasteurized is referred to as "raw milk." Hospitality operators usually are not allowed to serve raw milk to their customers.

rial count. There are two federal government grading designations for fluid milk:

1. Grade A—milk considered by the government to be the fluid milk sold in retail stores and delivered to consumers.
2. Manufacturing Grade, sometimes called Grade B—milk in which more bacteria are allowed than in Grade A; this is milk used for manufacturing milk products, such as butter, cheese, and ice cream.

Some persons discuss a third grade of milk, a certified grade. This refers to milk that has very little bacteria and can be used for infants and sick persons; technically, certified is not classified as a grade, but some buyers treat it as such.

There are always some spoilage bacteria in pasteurized milk, but these bacteria are harmless. In addition to the number of bacteria, the grader also considers the milk's odor, taste, and appearance.

Milk can be fortified with vitamins A and D, and some states allow other types of nutrient additives.

As we noted previously, few dairy products are graded; this is primarily because the fluid milk used to produce them is usually graded and produced under continuous government inspection. Furthermore, the federal government has not set grading standards for most dairy products. In addition to fluid milk, U.S. grading standards have been set for dry milk, Cheddar, Swiss, Colby, and Monterey Jack cheeses, and butter.

The federal grades for dry nonfat milk are:

1. Extra
2. Standard

The federal grades for dry whole milk are:

1. Premium
2. Extra
3. Standard

The grading factors for dry milk evaluated by the grader include the product's color, odor, flavor, and bacterial counts, how scorched the milk is, how lumpy it is, how well it will go into solution, and how much moisture it contains.

The federal grades for Cheddar, Swiss, Colby, and Monterey Jack cheeses are:

1. AA
2. A

3. B

4. C

The grading factors for cheeses evaluated by the grader include the product's appearance, flavor, texture, odor, color, finish, and plasticity (i.e., body).

The federal grades for butter are:

1. AA

2. A

3. B

The grading factors for butter evaluated by the grader include the product's flavor, odor, freshness, texture, and plasticity.

Some states use their own grading systems. For example, Wisconsin imposes grades for cheese. Also, the "U.S. Grade A" designation on a package label indicates that the federal government graded the dairy product, whereas the notation "Grade A" on the package label signifies that the dairy product meets specific criteria established by a state, county, and/or local government agency.

Additional terminology sometimes appears in the dairy products market, but this terminology does not necessarily represent governmental grades. Instead, these tend to be terms and designations that, for one reason or another, have become popular. For example, ice cream carries several designations. It can be called "premium," "regular," or "competitive" (premium has 15 to 18 percent butterfat, regular has about 12 percent, and competitive has 10 percent). Or ice cream might be called "French," which means that eggs have been used as a thickening agent.

Another very common type of terminology that is especially prevalent on dairy product package labels is dating information. In some states, "pull" dates must be listed on the dairy products' package labels. These dates tell supermarket managers, suppliers, and consumers the last day that the products can be sold. If states do not require pull dates to be listed, they usually require some sort of coded dates, or "blind" dates, to be noted on the package labels.

Typically, hospitality buyers opt for Grade A milk and a comparable quality for all the other dairy products. Since several dairy products differ in taste as one goes from one supplier to the next, however, it is not difficult to understand why U.S. grades, and even local government grades, are not the major selection criterion.

PACKERS' BRANDS (OR EQUIVALENT)

The difference in taste between one supplier and another can be remarkable for cheese, yogurt, ice cream, sherbet, and dry milk. It is, in fact, amazing how different the taste can be between two brands of apparently equal merchandise.

Consequently, brand names tend to become important to buyers. Food-service managers cannot be easily persuaded to drop their current ice cream for competing products. Of course, the bid buyer, or the buyer who has the time, checks out different brands of dairy products now and then. New dairy items enter the market periodically. Some of these new products could save you a bit of money. Or something new might be a good substitute.

PRODUCT SIZE

A few dairy products will require size designations. For instance, butter could be ordered in one-pound prints, 50-pound slabs, or one or more "chip" sizes. Cheese slices usually come in two or more sizes; for example, you might order a one-ounce size for the cheeseburger platter, and a two-ounce size for the grilled cheese sandwich plate.

SIZE OF CONTAINER

Experience shows that the size of the container is very important for dairy products. These items are very perishable, so you must do whatever you can to minimize leftovers.

There usually are various package sizes from which to choose. Naturally, the smaller the package size unit—for example, half-pint milk containers in contrast to half-gallons—the higher the AP price. The EP cost could, however, be lower. For instance, bartenders use cream in some drinks. A small package could carry a premium AP price, but if the cream drink volume is low, you may waste cream if you use large containers. In this case, the EP cost would jump to an unacceptable level.

Not every supplier carries the package sizes you want. For instance, if you are satisfied with a particular brand, but you would like individual portion packs, you may not be able to get them.

TYPE OF PACKAGING MATERIAL

Dairy products packaging materials generally are quite standardized throughout the industry. One of the major reasons for this is that dairy regulations usually specify minimum packaging requirements that will protect the culinary quality and wholesomeness of the products.

The buyer usually can select from among a wide variety of packaging materials. There are plastic, fiberboard, metal, glass, and aseptic containers. But while dairy products are usually packaged in rather standardized materials, typically there are two or more choices available for many products.

There also are personalized packaging materials available for some dairy products. For instance, some dairies will include your operation's name and/or logo on individual half-pint containers of milk, individually wrapped butter chips, and single-serve creamers. Of course, you must be prepared to pay a bit more in exchange for this added value.

PACKAGING PROCEDURE

This can be an important consideration, especially for the single-serve dairy product items purchased by many restaurant operators. For instance, you can purchase butter chips that are layered in a five-pound container and separated by pieces of waxed paper. Or you can obtain individually wrapped butter chips (which, by the way, may be required by your local health district in order to protect the wholesomeness and cleanliness of the butter).

As you undoubtedly know by now, the layered, and/or individually wrapped dairy products, will carry premium AP prices. But, as we also know, the end result, that is, the EP costs, may be quite acceptable if we purchase premium packaging and packaging procedures that tend to protect the shelf life of the merchandise.

PRODUCT YIELD

For some dairy products, it may be necessary to indicate the maximum waste you will accept (or alternatively, the minimum yield acceptable). For instance, you would need to indicate whether you will accept rind on the cheese you want to buy. Or you should note on your specification that you will not accept more than two broken cheese slices per hundred.

PRODUCT FORM

For some dairy items, you may need to note the exact form of the product. For instance, you will need to note sliced, whole, grated, shredded, or crumbled cheese. Or you need to note whipped butter, if applicable, instead of butter.

PRESERVATION METHOD

Most dairy items are kept under continuous refrigeration. Some, such as perhaps a few cheeses, are not; however, if you require refrigeration, then you would need to note this on the specification.

Some dairy items are frozen. The obvious ones are the ice creams and the ice milks. However, there are suppliers who freeze the cheeses and butter they sell. If you do not want frozen dairy items, you may have to specify this for some items that you purchase.

A few dairy items are traditionally canned. For instance, evaporated milk, sweetened condensed milk, and canned, whole milk are usually marketed in metal containers. Whole milk also comes in aseptic packages and can be kept at room temperature for months. This "shelf-stable" product is "ultra-pasteurized" (UP), and its taste is very similar to fresh, refrigerated, whole, fluid milk. However, it would appear that it is not very popular in the United States.

When considering preservation methods, the wise buyer also takes the time to specify the maximum pull date allowed at time of delivery. If stored correctly, dairy products will remain safe to consume for a few days after the pull date; however, their culinary quality could be compromised to the point where we would not want to serve them to our guests.

BUTTERFAT CONTENT

In general, as the butterfat increases, so does the AP price; but more butterfat also makes for a better product. Moreover, dairy products with a high butterfat content tend to be treated with more respect by the producer. A premium ice cream typically contains high-quality flavorings—fresh fruits rather than fruit syrups, for example.

If you are satisfied with the amount of butterfat mandated by the U.S. government's standard of identity, you can ignore this selection factor. However, if you wish a product that is more or less "creamy," you must note this requirement on your specification.

MILK SOLIDS CONTENT

The federal government also mandates the maximum amount of nonfat, dried milk solids that some dairy products can have. If these standards are acceptable to you, this selection factor is irrelevant. However, if you desire fewer solids than the maximum allowed, you must indicate your exact requirement on the specification.

OVERRUN

The amount of air in a frozen dairy product is referred to as "overrun." Most people in our industry consider overrun to be the amount of air incorporated into any type of dairy product.

Some dairy products contain a good deal of air. If you whip butterfat, you incorporate air. And butterfat holds the air for quite a while, even longer if the product is frozen or if it contains some added emulsifiers.

The air content is crucial to the flavor of such items as ready whipped cream in an aerosol can, ice cream, and ice milk.

Whipped cream is usually sold by the number of ounces in the can. But not always. It can be sold by volume, which is a typical measure of quantity for all ice types of products. If you start to compare AP prices on the basis of volume, keep in mind that air costs nothing. You could be buying more volume but less solid product.

The federal government standard of identity for ice cream dictates that 1 gallon must weigh at least 4½ pounds and contain at least 1.6 pounds of total food solids, so for this type of product, you are protected to some extent. But this is not the case for such items as whipped topping. For these types of items, you must be ever mindful of the exact value of the purchase.

CHEMICAL ADDITIVES

A few dairy products contain chemical additives that stabilize, emulsify, and preserve them. At times the dairy industry has been unjustly criticized for this. We suppose it is easy to assume that dairy items include several chemical additives. But such just is not the case. Because milk is a food for babies, it has been kept natural for many decades. The products that typically contain chemicals are the nondairy items. All in all, dairy products in their natural form, processed or relatively unprocessed (pasteurized), have significantly fewer chemical additives than other processed foods.

UNTREATED COWS

In this age of biotechnology, dairies are able to treat their herds with synthetic hormones designed to increase milk production. Some buyers, though, may not want to purchase products made from this type of milk. If so, they would need to note on their specifications that they will accept only products coming from cows that have not been treated this way.

HOW THE PRODUCT IS PROCESSED

Dairy processing methods usually fall under government inspection. But these inspections only ensure wholesomeness, not flavor, convenience, or packaging.

The type of processing can be very important for some dairy products. For example, all Swiss cheeses are a bit different. Although they all meet a minimum standard of identity, there can be substantial differences in aging methods and aging times. The packer's brand usually indicates these processes.

A purchaser may want to know whether or not the process is "natural." For example, some cottage cheeses contain an absolute minimum of additives; others may contain extra acid, such as phosphoric acid to set the curd, and artificial flavorings. If you want all dairy items to be natural, you will have to search out the appropriate brand.

NONDAIRY PRODUCTS

Many operators may use nondairy items for several reasons, such as (1) AP prices may be lower; (2) nondairy products, being less perishable, save on storage costs and reduce waste; and (3) weight watchers and those people who cannot tolerate lactose (milk sugar) may represent a clientele worth accommodating.

Unfortunately, most artificial items contain some chemical additives and usually are not nutritionally equivalent to the products they imitate; consequently, some customers may refuse to use them. The fat substitutes being marketed today do not impress many nutritionists, who doubt very much that these products will make people healthier or slimmer. Furthermore, the nondairy products may not work in some recipes that call for dairy ingredients.

AP PRICE

In a free market area, there may be some opportunities to reduce the AP price. In a controlled state, legally you must pay at least the minimum AP price.

Most states have a variety of price control and credit control policies; that is, the price and the type and amount of credit a dairy can extend to its customers is regulated by the local governments. Every now and then, someone starts a drive to eliminate the local government's and the federal government's power in this area, but the price and credit controls seem to weather these attacks very well.

Dairy products provide few quantity buy opportunities, although there may be money-saving long-term contracts for some items if it is legally possible.

Also, some dairy products, especially cheese, are imported. Import taxes tend to add up, thereby increasing AP prices.

ONE-STOP SHOPPING

Most hospitality operators like one-stop dairy shopping because of the standing order they can bargain for and dairy suppliers typically provide. If a purchaser can get the supplier to bring his or her current stock of dairy items just up to par, this supplier service is an added plus. However, the supplier then controls the inventory level; but since dairies often provide frequent deliveries, this reduces the amount of inventory of perishable items one must carry.

One-stop shopping tends to entail a higher AP price. To receive the convenience we noted, however, one may be willing to pay more.

PURCHASING DAIRY PRODUCTS

Your first step in purchasing dairy products is to determine precisely what you want and then determine the delivery schedule you feel will be appropriate. Daily delivery is preferred. Most dairy products are, after all, very perishable. Hence, any purchasing tactic or supplier service that helps control the quality of these items should be followed and bargained for.

Preparing elaborate specifications for dairy products is usually not necessary unless you are a bid buyer or if you expect to enter into some long-term contractual arrangement with a supplier. As always, though, it might be good discipline to reduce your ideas to detailed written specifications before you commit yourself to purchasing any item. Figure 19.4 shows some example product specifications. Figure 19.5 notes an example product specification outline for dairy products.

If you use the ordinary types of dairy products and if you are in a noncontrolled state, bid buying might be profitable, although, as a percentage of your total purchase dollar, these savings are liable to be small. There are, of course, many suppliers and packers' brands. If you can live with some variations, your savings can add up.

Butter Used for customer service U.S. Grade AA Butter chips 90 count Layered arrangement, easily separated 5-pound box Waxed, moisture-proof, vapor-proof Refrigerated	Nondairy coffee whitener, liquid Used for customer service House brand $3/8$-ounce portion, single serve 400 servings per case Loose pack (slab pack) Moisture-proof carton Unrefrigerated
Bleu cheese Used for tossed salad Frigo brand Crumbles 5-pound poly bag 4 bags per case Moisture-proof, vapor-proof Frozen	Half-and-half Used for customer service U.S. Grade A $3/8$-ounce portion, single serve 400 servings per case Loose pack (slab pack) Moisture-proof carton Refrigerated

FIGURE 19.4. Example of dairy product specifications.

Intended use:

Exact name:

U.S. grade (or equivalent):

Packer's brand name (or equivalent):

Product size:

Size of container:

Type of packaging material:

Packaging procedure:

Product yield:

Product form:

Preservation method:

FIGURE 19.5. Example of product specification outline for dairy products.

Sometimes independent farmers seek to do business with you. It might be best to avoid these people no matter how "natural" their products may seem or how good the deals they offer. The products might not come under the rigid quality control standards set by the federal and state governments.

If you purchase a large quantity of dairy products, you should take the time to evaluate some of the substitution possibilities. Several products are capable of providing comparable culinary quality in a recipe, and a few minutes of cost calculation could indicate that a particular recipe is much less expensive to produce than comparable ones. For instance, if you use a lot of fresh milk to prepare breads, a switch to dry milk may yield a comparable-quality finished product at a lower EP cost.

RECEIVING DAIRY PRODUCTS

When you receive dairy products, take the time to examine them carefully for dirt, broken containers, and faulty wrapping. Milk cartons can get dented, and cheese wrappings sometimes crack or split. Since these products deteriorate quickly, you should be reluctant to accept anything that does not look clean and properly packaged.

You must check to see that you receive everything you have ordered. This check can be difficult for at least two reasons. First, with so many dairy items on one invoice, either you or the supplier may miss something. Second, some dairy items are delivered on a standing order basis. This is typical with ice cream and sherbet, and it may allow the delivery agent to work alone stocking your freezers. When leaving, he or she may present an invoice for you to sign. If you are busy, you may not make a thorough check on what has been delivered. Or an unscrupulous delivery agent may tell you that a container that already was in the dairy box was delivered today.

A related problem centers on supplier substitutions. For instance, the supplier may be out of Roquefort cheese and send you bleu cheese instead, not wanting to see you operate without at least a similar item. But some substitutes in the dairy line do not always match well, especially for cheeses.

You should take the time to make planned but random taste tests, though these are not often done. If you buy a proprietary brand, you have some assurance of quality.

Since most dairy items are perishable, you might consider moving everything into a refrigerated area before you make your inspection. After checking qualities and quantities, check the invoice arithmetic and complete the appropriate accounting procedures.

STORING DAIRY PRODUCTS

Most dairy products should be stored in a refrigerator or freezer as soon as possible. Dried, canned and bottled items can go to the storeroom, as can, possibly, some of the nondairy products.

If you are going to serve, for example, a cheese platter tonight, you might leave the cheese out at room temperature. This is the correct temperature at which cheese should be served. If you are going to serve it later in the week, though, keep it refrigerated, as room temperatures cause most cheeses to age, which means they quickly change in odor, flavor, and appearance.

Most dairy items readily pick up odors. Therefore, we suggest that you maintain a separate dairy refrigerator. If that is impossible, keep these items tightly covered.

As much as possible, keep dairy products, and particularly cheeses, in their original packaging. And when you store them, try not to nick or cut the packaging. This is easy to do and hastens spoilage and waste.

When storing dairy products, take a bit of extra time to ensure that you rotate the products on the shelves properly. You cannot take a chance that a customer will get sour milk. It is not easy to tell whether the food is rotated properly unless you take extra time to check the pull dates many dairies put on their products. Dairy products are not like lettuce: if a head of lettuce is bad, you know it, but whole milk in individual half-pints is harder to monitor.

ISSUING DAIRY PRODUCTS

You should issue the older dairy products first. Many of these items, especially ice cream, go straight from receiving to a production area. If they are issued from a central storeroom, make sure that the requisitioner receives the correct product. For example, if the requisitioner wants milk for a cake recipe, make sure that he or she gets the appropriate dry milk.

Since most dairy products deteriorate rapidly, try not to handle them any more than you have to. Also, make sure that the requisitioners do not take more than they need for any one particular work shift or job. You might consider asking the requisitioner to make a note of the in-process inventory before asking for most stock.

IN-PROCESS INVENTORIES

Dairy products fall victim to spoilage, waste, and pilferage whenever they stay in-process for any extended period. They spoil because butter, cheese slices, and coffee cream, for example, are often left at room temperature too long. Or employees waste dairy products, for example, by failing to empty completely milk containers and cans of whipped cream. Pilferage is particularly common. For instance, employees may help themselves to a quick glass of milk once in a while.

As usual, supervision is the key. It helps both to head off waste and pilferage and to avoid, as well, such embarrassing situations as a customer tasting curdled coffee cream or rancid butter.

KEY WORDS AND CONCEPTS

AMS	EP cost
AP price	Exact name
Blind dates	Fortified milk
Butterfat content	Grading factors
Chemical additives	Homogenization
Disease-causing bacteria	In-process inventories

Intended use

Lactose

Manufacturing grade

Milk solids content

Nondairy products

One-stop shopping

Overrun

Packaging material

Packaging procedure

Packers' brands

Pasteurization

Personalized packaging

Preservation method

Price and credit controls

Processing method

Product form

Product size

Product yield

Pull dates

Purchasing, receiving, storing, and
    issuing dairy products

Raw milk

Shelf-stable products

Size of container

Spoilage bacteria

Standard of identity

Substitution possibilities

Synthetic hormones

Truth-in-menu legislation

Ultra-pasteurized (UP)

U.S. grades

U.S. Grade A versus Grade A

U.S. Public Health Service's Milk
    Ordinance and Code

Vitamins A and D

QUESTIONS AND PROBLEMS

1. What are the U.S. grades for fresh fluid milk?

2. What are the U.S. grades for butter?

3. What is the minimum weight of a gallon of ice cream?

4. What is the minimum butterfat content for ice cream?

5. What is an appropriate intended use for ice milk?

6. What is an appropriate intended use for margarine?

7. What is an appropriate intended use for dry nonfat milk?

8. Assume that you operate the food service in a minimum security prison. You serve approximately 500 inmates and 120 civilian staff members a day—three meals as well as various snacks. You have a severely tight food budget. Outline the specific procedures you might use to purchase, receive, store, and issue whole, fluid milk for use in cooking and as a beverage. *Note:* The prisoners are your workers. If possible, ask a prison food-service official to comment on your answer.

9. What is the primary purpose of pasteurization?

10. What is the primary purpose of homogenization?

11. What are the U.S. grades for dry nonfat milk?

12. What are the grading factors for Cheddar, Swiss, Colby, and Monterey Jack cheese U.S. grades?

13. What critical information is missing from the following product specification for milk?

Milk, fluid
U.S. Grade A
Used for cooking and baking
Bulk container

14. What is the primary difference between "premium" ice cream and "competitive" ice cream?

15. What is an appropriate intended use for nondairy coffee creamer?

16. Explain why dairy products should not be stored with fresh produce.

17. A product specification for an ice cream bar could include the following information:

(a) _____

(b) _____

(c) _____

(d) _____

(e) _____

18. One-stop dairy product shopping is especially popular among small operators. Why do you think this is the case? What advantages are there? Disadvantages?

19. Why do most government jurisdictions prohibit restaurants from serving raw milk?

20. Define or explain the following terms:

(a) Pull dates

(b) Certified milk

(c) Fortified milk

(d) Lactose

(e) Minimum butterfat content

(f) Overrun

(g) Controlled AP prices.

(h) Ultra-pasteurized

(i) Personalized packaging

(j) Product form

(k) Aseptic container

(l) Nondairy products

(m) Product yield

(n) Standard of identity

(o) U.S. Grade A versus Grade A

CHAPTER 20

Source: American Egg Board

EGGS

THE PURPOSE OF THIS CHAPTER

This chapter discusses:

- The selection factors for eggs
- Purchasing, receiving, storing, and issuing eggs
- The in-process egg inventory

INTRODUCTION

Purchasing fresh shell eggs is a relatively easy task. Buying processed eggs—frozen eggs, imitation eggs, dried eggs, and other pre-prepared egg items—can, however, present problems. In general, the most important egg purchasing considerations center on determining what you want and what type of product is best suited to your needs.

SELECTION FACTORS

As with all products, management personnel normally decide in advance the quality of eggs the operation needs. Either alone or in cooperation with other employees, they usually evaluate the following selection factors when determining the standards of egg quality and, to a certain extent, fresh and processed egg suppliers.

INTENDED USE

As always, you want to determine exactly the intended use of the item so that you will be able to prepare the appropriate, relevant specification. For instance, an egg product may be needed primarily for flavor and only secondarily for appearance. If so, the specification should reflect this.

EXACT NAME

Generally, this selection factor causes very little difficulty. Fresh eggs are chicken eggs, so if you use the term "eggs," this is what you will receive.

The term "fresh" shell eggs also implies that they are less than four weeks old. Shell eggs older than four weeks are referred to as "storage" eggs. Shell eggs kept under refrigeration, or in a controlled atmosphere, for long periods of time may be unacceptable to you. However, if your spec notes "shell eggs" or "eggs" instead of "fresh shell eggs" you may be disappointed with your purchase.

There may be a bit more consideration of this selection factor when you order processed egg products. In this case, you must be absolutely certain that you indicate the exact name of the item you want lest you receive an unacceptable product.

U.S. GOVERNMENT GRADES (OR EQUIVALENT)

The Food Safety and Quality Service (FSQS) of the USDA employs inspectors to check eggs for wholesomeness, and, while federal shell egg inspection is a voluntary program, in most states a producer must submit to either this inspection or one operated by the state itself. These inspectors also examine the condition of the laying hens, their environment, and their feed.

Under the Egg Products Inspection Act of 1972, plants that break and further process fresh eggs must submit to continuous government inspection. The concern of the states was the original impetus for this rule, as well as the rule of continuous government inspection for many dairy products; the states' major concern is the contamination risk present with these items. In these states, the federal and state agencies often work together to perform the necessary inspections.

Egg producers, or egg farmers, can elect to purchase the USDA's egg grading service. In some states, they have no choice—the state requires them to have their eggs graded by a federal inspector. If the eggs are graded, they must be produced under continuous government inspection.

Thus, the government consumer grades have become familiar quality guidelines. (See Figure 20.1a–d.) There are three consumer grades for fresh shell eggs:

1. AA—the top quality produced. Only the freshest products will earn this grade. The grade is very hard to obtain because once an egg is about one week old, its quality deteriorates to Grade A.

2. A—indicative of slightly lower quality. A fresh egg older than about one week usually falls into this grade category. The product's egg white and egg yolk are not quite as firm as those found in Grade AA merchandise. However, both A and AA eggs are generally suitable for all finished menu products where appearance is important.

FIGURE 20.1a. Federal grade and inspection stamps used for eggs.

3. B—there are considerable appearance problems with this grade. The egg white will be very watery and the egg yolk will be very flat and susceptible to breaking under even the slightest pressure. Grade B merchandise is suitable only for finished menu products that will disguise the egg's appearance.

Within these grade categories, an egg can be rated high, medium, or low. Thus, there are nine possible grades.

Fresh eggs are graded mainly on interior quality and exterior quality factors. Interior quality, such as the firmness of the egg yolk and egg white, is determined primarily by freshness; exterior quality factors, such as shape, cleanliness, and soundness, are determined by age of the hen, feed eaten, and general management of the flock and of the egg-laying facilities. The fresher an egg, the better it is, assuming that the laying hen is the right age (from 6 months to 1½ years old), is eating a proper diet, and is living in an appropriate environment.

The grader uses a process called "candling" to check the interior quality of fresh eggs, passing the egg over a light source, which reveals the yolk (dead center implies freshness), the size of the air space (which gets larger as the egg becomes older), impurities, and cracks. The grader may also crack open a few randomly selected eggs to determine the height and firmness of the egg white.

FIGURE 20.1b. Conveyors move the eggs while they are brushed and washed.

The grader might also evaluate the condition of the shell, especially if the laying hens are relatively old. Older hens produce eggs that have rougher shells as well as thinner shells.

The use of U.S. grades for fresh egg purchasing is widespread, even though a wide tolerance exists between egg grades. A major advantage of graded shell eggs is that they have been produced under continuous government inspection. It is a good idea to insist on this type of inspection, because shell eggs are on the FDA's list of potentially hazardous foods. Fresh shell eggs, even those that appear to be sound, can be contaminated with salmonella bacteria by the hens. Continuous government inspection, as well as insisting on constant refrigeration, should help mitigate this problem.

Hospitality buyers usually purchase Grade A eggs. The AA grade is difficult to obtain. In addition, the A grade normally suffices, particularly for fried and scrambled eggs and omelettes.

PACKERS' BRANDS (OR EQUIVALENT)

Some supermarkets pack their own eggs; hence, these eggs carry a packer's brand. But among hospitality buyers, one does not find a great deal of brand loyalty for fresh shell eggs. The federal grade is the most common quality indicator.

But packers' brands can be extremely important when purchasing

FIGURE 20.1c. Federal inspector checking the temperature of liquid eggs.

processed eggs, such as imitation egg whites and low-cholesterol shell eggs. Processed eggs, while produced under continuous government inspection, do not have established grading standards. Hence, in almost every instance, brand names are the only reliable indication of quality.

PRODUCT SIZE

Buyers are normally interested in the size and uniformity of the shell eggs they purchase. The U.S. government helps in this area by requiring egg producers to indicate the size of the fresh eggs somewhere on the container if the eggs inside have been graded by a federal inspector. There are six sizes for shell eggs:

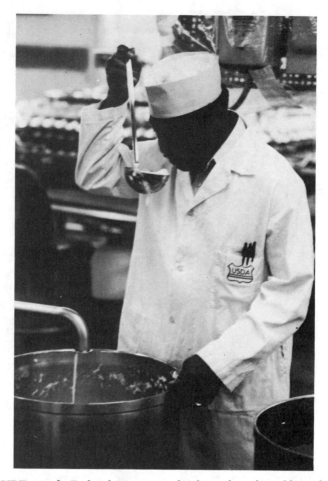

FIGURE 20.1d. Federal inspector checking the odor of liquid eggs.

1. Peewee—15 ounces per dozen
2. Small—18 ounces per dozen.
3. Medium—21 ounces per dozen.
4. Large—24 ounces per dozen
5. Extra large—27 ounces per dozen
6. Jumbo—30 ounces per dozen

Peewee eggs, sometimes called "pullet eggs," come from younger hens, usually at the beginning of their laying life. Jumbo eggs come from relatively older hens, usually at the end of their laying life. These extreme sizes are not common in the fresh egg trade. If you want these sizes, normally you must visit a farmer with very young and very old hens in the flock.

When choosing eggs to be fried, scrambled, poached, or prepared in omelettes, purchasers usually prefer the large size. These eggs have a very acceptable appearance and show up well on the plate. Also, those who purchase fresh eggs for use in cake, batter, or drink recipes tend to use the large egg because most quantity recipes, as well as recipes found in most cookbooks, assume a 2-ounce egg.

A buyer who keeps close track of the AP prices for each size might be able to save a few pennies when purchasing fresh shell eggs. For instance, in a recipe calling for eggs by weight, if large eggs cost $0.90 per dozen and medium eggs cost $0.80 per dozen, you could determine the best price per ounce in the following manner:

$$\$0.90 \text{ per dozen} \div 24 \text{ oz. per dozen} = \$0.0375 \text{ per ounce}$$
$$\$0.80 \text{ per dozen} \div 21 \text{ oz. per dozen} = \$0.0381 \text{ per ounce}$$

Hence, the large eggs represent a slightly better buy.

We do not normally see buyers use this procedure; it is probably more useful to the homemaker than to a commercial buyer often restricted to the large-size egg. But if a buyer wants to purchase a large volume of eggs for use in various recipes, and the labor is available to process them, such a procedure might save money.

SIZE OF CONTAINER

For shell eggs, the normal package size is a 15-dozen or 30-dozen crate. At times, you might order one or more "flats" (a flat contains 2½ dozen fresh eggs). It is unusual to purchase eggs in 1-dozen or 1½-dozen containers.

Processed eggs offer a bit more variety in package sizes, so you must be prepared to note on your specification exactly the one that suits your needs best.

TYPE OF PACKAGING MATERIAL

For fresh shell eggs, the packaging is standardized. You probably will not need to consider this selection factor if you order only fresh eggs.

The same may not be true with processed eggs, though. For these products, there can be a considerable variation in packaging quality. Improperly packaged products can support tremendous bacterial multiplication. Hence, you must be concerned with this selection factor. This is especially true if you must store the processed egg products on your premises for a reasonably long period of time.

Frozen egg products normally are packaged in moisture-proof, vapor-proof containers. In most instances, a processed product, such as frozen, precooked scrambled eggs, normally is packaged in a heavy plastic pouch;

these pouches are sometimes referred to as Cryovac bags, or Cryovac packaging. (Cryovac is a brand name. It is the company that developed the "shrink-wrap" technology that allows food fabricators to store products for considerable lengths of time.)

Some frozen items may be packaged in metal containers. For instance, frozen eggs, or frozen eggs yolks, typically are packaged in 30-gallon cans.

Dried egg products normally are packaged in metal containers. Some are also available in aseptic containers. For instance, dried egg whites typically are available in cans, but there are some processors who package them in airtight, plastic-lined bags.

PACKAGING PROCEDURE

This will not be a concern for most egg products purchased by the typical hospitality buyer. The types of packaging and packaging procedures for fresh shell eggs are very standardized. Likewise with most processed products.

In a few instances, the buyer may need to specify a desired packaging procedure. For example, if you want to purchase frozen, precooked, plain omelettes, you could purchase them individually wrapped and stacked neatly in the case, or you could purchase them in a layered arrangement, where they are separated by sheets of waxed paper. In some cases then, it is possible to specify a combination of inner wrapping and outer wrapping that meets your needs.

COLOR

In some parts of the country, customers prefer the brown shell egg, and buyers must keep this preference in mind. There may be a price difference between brown and white shell eggs, but no difference in flavor and nutrition has been proved. Perhaps consumers perceive some psychological difference. Be that as it may, the buyer who once worked in Chicago and now works in New England may have to contend with the brown color preferences in this new area.

PRODUCT FORM

In some instances, you may wish to purchase one or more convenience egg products. For instance, you may want to buy precooked, refrigerated, whole, peeled eggs and use them to garnish your salad bar offerings. Or you might wish to purchase cheese-stuffed, frozen, precooked omelettes. As always, the added from value will increase the AP prices, but the ultimate EP costs may be quite affordable.

PRESERVATION METHOD

A buyer should know how fresh and processed eggs are preserved so that he or she can make additional judgments concerning their quality. The most common preservation methods are discussed in the following paragraphs.

Refrigeration

This is the most common preservation method for fresh shell eggs. As fresh eggs get older, they lose quality: moisture dissipates, the white gets thinner, and the yolk becomes weaker. Refrigeration is the best deterrent to this quality loss. The FDA recommends that state and local health districts require fresh shell eggs to be received and stored at 40°F or less in order to minimize food-borne illness that can result if the eggs are contaminated with small amounts of salmonella bacteria. There is, however, no federal law requiring refrigeration. The wise buyer does not jump to the conclusion that the fresh shell eggs purchased have been kept under constant refrigeration.

Oil Spraying

Some producers preserve their fresh eggs by spraying them with oil. Oil spraying is not quite as effective as refrigeration, though it is a reasonably effective alternative.

Oil Dipping

Oil spraying and oil dipping theoretically are similar, but dipping is, nevertheless, not as effective. Oil-dipped eggs tend to experience more weight loss than do oil-sprayed eggs.

Overwrapping

To retard moisture loss and the tendency for its yolk and white to thin, an egg can be doubly wrapped in heavy plastic film. If wrapped correctly, this method is superior to oiling eggs.

Controlled Atmosphere Storage

Some producers hold eggs in an oxygen-free environment. The oxygen is removed and is replaced by carbon dioxide. As an egg ages, it loses moisture and carbon dioxide. The carbon dioxide in the environment acts as a counterpressure, thus preventing the loss of carbon dioxide and keeping the egg white firm. This is an expensive method, but it is used by producers who wish or need to hold shell eggs for a while.

As a general rule, suppliers do not sell controlled-environment eggs to food-service operators. They are intended for supermarket and grocery store distribution. As with fresh produce, once eggs are removed from the controlled atmosphere, their quality deteriorates very rapidly; hospitality operators cannot tolerate this problem.

The Processing Method

When you buy processed eggs, you are actually purchasing an egg that has been preserved in a manner other than in its shell. Among the most common forms of processed eggs are frozen eggs, frozen egg yolks, and frozen egg whites. These are normally used by large bakeries. There are some labor savings associated with these products, since no one in the operation has to process them. But there are problems too. First, if they have not been frozen correctly and if sugar or glycerine was not added to them before freezing, the yolks will be rubbery. Second, thawing frozen eggs is a tricky process. If they are thawed at room temperature, harmful bacteria can multiply rapidly. If they are thawed in the refrigerator, unsupervised employees may not be patient enough to wait out this relatively long thawing procedure. (Allow three to five days in the refrigerator for thawing a 30-pound can.)

Another familiar form of processed eggs is dried eggs, dried egg yolks, and dried egg whites. These also are used by large bakeries. They normally are not used for scrambled eggs; rather, they tend to work better in recipes that call for eggs because a cook can measure them easily. About the only problem associated with dried eggs, other than their reconstitution, is the possibility that some of the product may be scorched during the drying process, but this is much less of a problem today than it used to be. Spray drying—spraying the liquid egg mixture into a heated environment—is a superior method. Freeze-drying—freezing liquid eggs and going from the frozen state directly to the dried state—is also successful.

You can purchase other types of processed egg products. For instance, you can order frozen deviled eggs and frozen, cooked scrambled eggs. These items are expensive because of the convenience that they represent, but the labor saving you should experience with them might more than offset the high AP price.

TRUST THE SUPPLIER

You will rarely go wrong if you stipulate U.S. grades for fresh shell eggs or if you settle on a particularly desirable brand name for a processed egg product. You may need to check, though, that the egg supplier maintains the specific storage environment you expect. A buyer usually demands that fresh eggs be refrigerated.

The buyer must also consider the other obvious supplier services. The problem with buying eggs is not so much selecting the quality as making sure that the supplier can make adequate deliveries and moves only fresh product. Since suppliers abound in the egg trade, the choice can be wide. Again, bid buying or becoming a house account both have their advantages and disadvantages: You must make your choice.

PURCHASING EGGS

As usual, the first step in egg purchasing is to determine precisely what you want. As we noted earlier, fresh shell eggs present few problems: the most widely used quality is U.S. Grade A, and the normal size is large. Considerably more combinations of qualities and sizes are available, and management, alone or in conjunction with other key employees, must determine the efficacy and usefulness of these other combinations as they relate to a particular operation.

The qualities and styles of processed eggs are not so easily chosen. If you buy these items, your best bet is to consider brand names. Since there are no federal quality standards for processed egg products (although you could specify that the processed product be prepared with fresh eggs of a certain U.S. grade), the convenience and reliability of the packer's brand name eventually become the overriding factors.

Once you know what you want, prepare a complete specification that includes all pertinent information, whether or not you use it in bid buying. If nothing else, the discipline of preparing this document will help to ensure that you have considered all relevant factors and are, indeed, purchasing the egg product that suits your needs. Figure 20.2 shows some example product specifications. Figure 20.3 notes an example product specification outline for egg products.

After determining what you need and when you need it, you must evaluate potential suppliers. You will find in the fresh egg trade a reasonable number of potential suppliers, good news for those who like the bid-buying strategy. The biggest problem in supplier selection probably comes in determining which supplier provides the freshest eggs. U.S. Grade A on the box is no guarantee of the quality of the eggs inside.

The processed egg trade does not offer so many suppliers or brands to consider. If you want dried eggs, you may be surprised at the meager number of purveyors in this area. And if you want imitation eggs, you may find even fewer suppliers. Likewise, not too many producers carry such speciality items as frozen deviled eggs.

As we found with fresh produce, the independent farmer is very active in the fresh egg trade. But be wary of these independents. Keep in

Fresh shell eggs
Used for fried, poached, scrambled
  eggs
U.S. Grade A (high)
Large size
30 dozen (full case)
Moisture-proof carton
12 flats per case, 2½ dozen per flat
White shell
Refrigerated
	Scrambled egg mix
	Used for scrambled eggs on buffet
	Scrambleez brand
	5-pound container
	Moisture-proof, vapor-proof con-
	  tainer
	6, 5-pound plastic pouches (Cryo-
	  vac bags) per case
	Frozen

Meringue powder Used to prepare dessert topping R & H brand 6-pound container Plastic, resealable container Unrefrigerated	Frozen, whole, shelled eggs Used to prepare bakery products McAnally brand 30-pound container Metal can

FIGURE 20.2. Example of egg product specifications.

mind that they can purchase eggs from someone else and then resell them to you, implying that the eggs are from their own farms.

Moreover, these farmers may not be checked by government inspectors. Also, their flocks may be too young or too old, and the hens may not be well managed.

Intended use: Exact name: U.S. grade (or equivalent): Packer's brand name (or equivalent): Product size: Size of container: Type of packaging material: Packaging procedure: Color: Product form: Preservation method:

FIGURE 20.3. Example of product specification outline for egg products.

One potential advantage of the independent farmer is that he or she may be able to get shell eggs to you one or two days after laying. In a typical supply house, you can expect to receive eggs that are almost a week old. But if the farmer does not provide refrigerated storage, the older egg may be a better buy, because an unrefrigerated two-day egg has less quality than a refrigerated seven-day egg.

Another potential advantage might be the willingness of the independent farmer to bargain for an AP price based on an agreed-upon markup of the wholesale egg market price. This might represent a reasonable savings. Most suppliers usually are not eager to use this type of pricing technique for any but the largest customer.

Before purchasing any egg product, take some time to evaluate the substitution possibilities. Several processed items substitute nicely for fresh eggs, and vice versa. If you buy a lot of eggs, it may pay to have recipes printed several ways to include various forms of eggs and egg substitutions. For instance, cake recipes might be written to incorporate fresh eggs, dried eggs, or frozen eggs. If the AP prices vary favorably, a few minutes of cost calculation might signal that one of these recipes is demonstrably more economical than the others.

RECEIVING EGGS

When receiving fresh shell eggs, take the time to examine them carefully for cracks, dirt, and lack of uniformity. Check the temperature to see if they meet your refrigeration requirements. Also make sure that all the eggs are there. You do not always have to believe what is written on the side of the container. Weighing the containers might be the easiest quantity check.

It is difficult for receiving personnel to determine the age of fresh eggs. You could hold them up to the light: a really fresh egg should have the yolk dead center. Or you can see whether they float in water. (If they do, they are old.) The delivery agent may think that you have lost your mind if you expect him or her to wait around while you conduct this ritual. But a little skepticism never hurt a purchaser.

Processed eggs usually require other sorts of inspection. Assuming that all the products you ordered have been delivered, you need to assess the quality. This is not very easy. You can check frozen egg products to see whether any crystallization has occurred—an indication of refreezing. You might use a temperature probe to test frozen egg products.

You can check the can pressure of any canned dried egg products; there are devices on the market you can use in making this quick, simple test. An abnormally high pressure could indicate that the contents are contaminated.

If you do not take the time to check quality or if you do not have the time, you must trust your supplier and delivery agent. And because processed egg quality is always difficult to determine, we suppose that a certain degree of trust is inherent here in any case.

After checking the quality and quantity, check the prices and complete the appropriate accounting procedures.

STORING EGGS

Fresh eggs should be refrigerated as soon as possible. In addition, since these items pick up odors quickly, consider keeping them in their original containers or placing them in some other type of covered container. Some large operations maintain a dairy refrigerator to keep fresh eggs away from the particularly odorous products like peeled onions.

Processed eggs also require the definite storage environment, either frozen or dry storage, suggested by the form in which they come.

ISSUING EGGS

You should rotate the stock properly so that the oldest items are issued first. This may be accomplished by dating containers as received. In some cases, the egg purchases go straight into production. If you issue eggs from a central storeroom, make sure, for example, that the requisitioner who wants eggs for a cake recipe gets the frozen or dried eggs, if applicable.

Because fresh shell eggs deteriorate rapidly once they leave refrigeration, make sure that the requisitioners take no more than they need for any one particular work shift or job. You might consider asking the requisitioner to take note of the in-process inventory before asking for additional stock.

IN-PROCESS INVENTORIES

The benefit of good purchasing effectiveness can be immediately offset if one does not supervise in-process inventories. If breakfast cooks leave fresh shell eggs out at room temperature all day, their quality could drop a grade. The same can be true with processed eggs. As always, supervision is the key. Without it, there is little sense in taking care to purchase the proper items for the production staff. The best thing a supervisor can do is insist that all eggs be kept in the recommended environment at all times and removed from this environment only when necessary.

KEY WORDS AND CONCEPTS

AP price

Candling

Color

Controlled atmosphere storage

Cost per ounce of fresh shell eggs

Cryovac

Egg Products Inspection Act

EP cost

Exact name

Fresh egg flat

Fresh shell eggs

FSQS

Grading factors

Independent farmer

In-process inventories

Intended use

Large egg, most typical size purchased

Packaging material

Packaging procedure

Packers' brands

Potentially hazardous food

Preservation method

Processed eggs

Processing method

Product form

Product size

Purchasing, receiving, storing, and issuing eggs

Shrink wrap

Size of container

Storage eggs

USDA

U.S. grades

QUESTIONS AND PROBLEMS

1. What are the U.S. grades for fresh shell eggs?

2. List the sizes for fresh shell eggs.

3. What procedure can you follow to determine the freshness of shell eggs?

4. What will be the AP price per ounce of a large shell egg at $1.25 per dozen?

5. Outline the specific procedures you would use for the purchasing, receiving, storing, and issuing of fresh shell eggs that will be used for three-minute eggs. Assume that you are the manager of an employee food service. If possible, ask an employee food-service manager to comment on your answer.

6. Assume that your buffet brunch has another hour to run and that you have just run out of fresh eggs. You were preparing omelettes and scrambled eggs for use on the buffet line. You have a couple of cans of dried eggs and one can of frozen eggs in storage. Could you use these processed eggs to tide you over? If not, what do you suggest? If possible, ask a food-service manager to comment on your answer.

7. An independent farmer calls on your country club to solicit its fresh egg business. The following offer is made: daily delivery, eggs no more than one day old, AP price 2 cents higher than the daily market quotation listed in *The Wall Street Journal,* which is higher than the AP prices charged by other suppliers. What do you suggest? (*Hint:* Eggs that are too fresh should not be used for hard boiled eggs, as the shells are difficult to peel; otherwise, we know of no problems with very fresh eggs.) If possible, ask a country club manager to comment on your answer.

8. Assume that you are the kitchen supervisor for a resort hotel. Your Sunday brunch normally includes scrambled eggs. Your cooks have been preparing them in a steamer and serving them in a chafing dish—customers then help themselves. The quality of this product is not as good as you would like it to be, but the alternative of scrambling a few eggs at a time to order is not viable. You could purchase frozen, scrambled eggs packed in 5-pound Cryovac bags. They only need to be steam heated for 20 minutes. The quality, in your opinion, is superb. But the AP price is very high—approximately three times the price of fresh eggs. What do you suggest? If possible, ask a resort hotel's food and beverage director or kitchen supervisor to comment on your answer.

9. What is an appropriate intended use for frozen whole shelled eggs?

10. What is an appropriate intended use for dried egg whites?

11. A product specification for dried eggs could include the following information:
    (a) _____
    (b) _____
    (c) _____
    (d) _____
    (e) _____

12. The food-service buyer normally specifies the large-size fresh egg because
    (a) _____
    (b) _____

13. What are the two typical package sizes for fresh shell eggs?

14. Fresh shell eggs can be preserved in the following ways:
    (a) _____
    (b) _____
    (c) _____

15. What happens to a fresh shell egg as it becomes older?

16. What is the preferred preservation method for fresh shell eggs?

17. When is a fresh shell egg at its highest quality?

18. A "flat" contains _____ dozen fresh shell eggs.

19. What are the primary grading factors for fresh shell egg grades?

20. What is the primary indication of quality of a processed egg product?

21. What is the difference between the designations "U.S. Grade A" and "Grade A"?

22. When would you purchase imitation egg products?

23. A product specification for frozen omelettes could include the following information:

    (a) _____

    (b) _____

    (c) _____

    (d) _____

    (e) _____

24. What is an appropriate intended use for U.S. Grade B shell eggs?

25. What critical information is missing from the following product specification for frozen egg mix?

Frozen egg mix
Used for low-fat entrées
EggBeaters brand

CHAPTER 21

Source: Alliant Foodservice

POULTRY

THE PURPOSE OF THIS CHAPTER

This chapter discusses:

- The selection factors for poultry
- Purchasing, receiving, storing, and issuing poultry
- The in-process poultry inventory

INTRODUCTION

Poultry is a term applied to all domesticated birds used for food. Poultry is not an especially difficult item to purchase, unless you are in the market for certain types of processed items. Generally, raw poultry is still considered to be a "commodity," which means the typical buyer does not perceive a great deal of difference between one frying chicken and another.

The poultry that food services typically buy are chicken, turkey, and duckling. On occasion some might also purchase goose, squab, and Cornish hen. For the most part, a particular class of bird is raised the same way all over the country. For example, frying chickens are raised in about eight weeks. They consume a relatively standardized diet—standardized, at least, according to nutritional needs—and are slaughtered, cleaned, and packed with similar production line techniques. In short, raising any bird these days is a standard, scientific undertaking. You find very few small-scale producers, though a few independent farmers here and there may seek your business.

As with other products, the major problem is deciding exactly what it is you want. If you want fresh or fresh frozen poultry, you will have several suppliers from which to choose. And unless you include packers' brands of fresh poultry, the AP price will be about the same among the suppliers, provided, of course, that the quality and supplier services are also the same among these suppliers.

If you want other types of processed poultry, you obviously face the question of the degree of convenience you would like built into your product. You can usually purchase whole, dressed birds (it is not easy to purchase live birds these days); cut-up birds; and precooked, prebreaded, presliced, and prerolled poultry. There are numerous processed poultry products, as well as some imitation items, available.

Some types of processing are undertaken by only a few food fabricators. But unlike other processed foods, this is not the case for the entire spectrum of poultry products. For instance, cut-up frying chickens can be purchased from a variety of sources. But canned, cooked whole chickens can be purchased from only a few suppliers.

In general, you will encounter little difficulty when purchasing these items. There are numerous suppliers. And there are numerous styles of poultry items available in the market.

SELECTION FACTORS

As with all products, the owner-manager normally decides the quality, type, and style of poultry products desired.

Either alone or in cooperation with other employees, the owner-manager usually evaluates the following selection factors when determining the desired standards of quality and, to a certain degree, the supplier for poultry items.

INTENDED USE

As always, you want to determine exactly the intended use of the item so that you will be able to prepare the appropriate, relevant specification. For example, poultry used for soup will differ from that needed for a deep-fried menu item.

You may want to select a poultry item you can use for two or three purposes. This approach is not ordinarily recommended because each item has one best use. Poultry has a short shelf life, especially if it is fresh. Consequently, fresh poultry should be turned quickly. One way to do this is to use the poultry you buy in several different dishes.

If you buy a lot of poultry, you should examine the substitution possibilities because bargains may await you. You might, for instance, substitute turkey rolls for turkey breasts or for whole turkeys. You could substitute canned poultry for fresh; you could purchase precooked, chopped chicken pieces if the intended use is for chicken salad; and you could use precooked sliced turkey breast instead of cooking your own.

Substitutions can disrupt the production and service functions. And, of course, you must keep track of the distinctive culinary differences between these items. The culinary quality varies for at least two reasons: (1) for different menu items, food processors use poultry of different ages, and (2) the processing method itself could rob or add favorable qualities.

A major issue with any processed product centers on the substitution possibilities and on how much convenience you want built into it. Whatever type of processing you want, you have a generous number of suppliers from which to choose, which gives you additional flexibility. Poultry products encourage the bid buyer.

EXACT NAME

This is an important consideration because the federal government has established standards of identity for many poultry items. For instance, some fresh products are standardized according to age at time of slaughter and/or sex of the bird. (See Figure 21.1.)

Age can affect the intended use of the poultry. Poultry to be cooked with dry heat should be young if you wish to have a tender product. (As poultry ages, it becomes less tender. But it also develops more fat, which carries flavor.)

If you want to simmer a chicken for chicken soup, you would proba-

---

CHICKEN

Young (tender) birds
Broiler/fryer—9 to 12 weeks old; 1½ to 3½ pounds; either sex

Roaster—3 to 5 months old; 3½ to 6 pounds; either sex

Capon—less than 8 months old; 6 to 10 pounds; desexed male bird

Cornish game hen—5 to 7 weeks old; 1 to 1½ pounds; immature bird

Old (less tender) birds
Stewing hen—over 10 months old; 3 to 7 pounds; mature female bird
Stag—over 10 months old; 3 to 7 pounds; mature male bird

TURKEY
Fryer/roaster—less than 16 weeks old; 4 to 8 pounds; either sex

Young hen—5 to 7 months old; 8 to 14 pounds; female bird

Young tom—5 to 7 months old; over 12 pounds; male bird

Yearling hen—under 15 months old; up to 30 pounds; mature female bird

Yearling tom—under 15 months old; up to 30 pounds; mature male bird

DUCK
Duckling—under 8 weeks old; under 4 pounds; either sex
Duck—over 16 weeks old; 4 to 6 pounds; either sex

FIGURE 21.1. Definitions of some poultry products.

bly opt for an older bird. It will have more flavor, and moist heat will ensure tenderness. As a bonus, the bird tends to have a higher conversion weight (i.e., a greater edible yield). If it gets too old, though, much of the weight begins to collect in the abdominal fat. This fat can be collected and used for, let us say, a roux for cream of chicken soup. But the yield of cooked meat per pound of raw chicken may be less than expected because of the extra fat.

Sex is not particularly important for young birds, but, in older birds, the difference in taste, texture, and yield diverges dramatically between the sexes. Females tend to be tastier, juicier, and have higher conversion weights. So, if you purchase mature poultry, take note of the sex, especially if you are bid buying.

As with other product lines, occasionally a buyer encounters market terminology that defines very specifically what a poultry product is. For instance, "free-range" chickens are allowed to roam free instead of spending their lives in cages. "Kosher" chickens, prepared according to Jewish dietary laws, are also allowed to roam free, are usually a stronger breed, tend to be a little older at time of slaughter in order to promote flavor development, and are free of hormones and other chemicals and artificial ingredients. Since these types of poultry products are usually much more expensive than those raised in the typical way, the buyer must not use this terminology carelessly.

If you purchase processed poultry products, it may not be enough to note merely the exact name, because even though there are standards of identity for things such as chicken pot pies, the producers of these items need to meet only some minimum standard. Also, even though you may not be averse to a producer's particular formula, keep in mind that, with the chicken pot pie example, there are several onion varieties and potato varieties. If you are dealing with fresh poultry, either whole birds or standardized parts, the use of the exact name usually is adequate because these fresh items are more consistent among producers. But the same cannot be said for processed products. These items can and will vary significantly among producers, so overreliance on standards of identity for them can be a bit chancy.

U.S. GOVERNMENT GRADES (OR EQUIVALENT)

Inspection of poultry became mandatory with the 1957 Poultry Products Inspection Act. This law applies to all raw poultry sold in interstate commerce as well as to processed products such as canned and frozen items.

Some states conduct their own poultry inspection programs, and the 1968 Wholesome Poultry Products Act requires the state program to be at least equal to the federal inspection program. Poultry inspected under a state program, however, can be sold only within that state. Any poultry

FIGURE 21.2. Federal inspection stamp used for poultry items. The number appearing in the stamp identifies the poultry plant where the bird was processed and inspected.

product transported across state lines or exported to another country must be produced under continuous federal inspection. In states not conducting inspection programs, all plants are required to be under continuous federal government inspection. (See Figures 21.2 and 21.3.)

Federal inspection for wholesomeness and federal grading are performed by the Food Safety and Quality Service (FSQS) of the USDA. Assuming that the product is wholesome, a poultry producer can elect to purchase the grading service.

Some states leave no choice: the poultry producers must have their products federally graded after they are inspected. As a practical matter, most poultry product specifications contain a U.S. grade designation. Consequently, producers have little choice no matter how you look at it.

Poultry is graded by federal inspectors according to several grading factors. The grader considers (1) conformation (Does the bird have good form?); (2) fleshing (Does the bird have a well-developed covering of flesh?); (3) fat covering (Is there any flesh showing through the skin; that is, is it a "thin-skinned" bird?); and (4) other factors (Are there bruises on the bird? excessive pin feathers left after cleaning? broken bones? missing parts? discoloration?).

Several poultry grades exist. The consumer grades are as follows:

1. A—This is the top poultry quality produced. It indicates a full-fleshed bird that is well finished and has an attractive appearance.

2. B—This bird usually has some dressing defects, such as a torn skin. Also, it is generally less attractive. For example, it might be slightly lacking in fleshing, and the breast bone may be very visible.

3. C—This bird resembles Grade B, but it lacks even more in appearance. Also, it might have parts of its carcass missing.

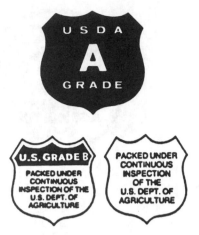

FIGURE 21.3. Federal grade and inspection stamps used for poultry products.

In addition to consumer grades, the federal government also offers a "procurement" grading system. There are two procurement grades: I and II. These grades, which are intended for use by noncommercial "institutional" food services, are based almost entirely on the amount of edible yield the poultry products contain. Appearance of the birds is deemphasized.

Some state and local markets use these three commercial grades: Extra, Standard, and No Grade. They are similar to the procurement grades, although the tolerances between these grades are wider than those of the consumer and procurement grades.

A specification for poultry products generally contains some grade reference. This is especially true if the buyer is purchasing fresh, refrigerated, or fresh, frozen whole birds or parts. If the buyer is purchasing processed products, such as prebreaded, precooked chicken patties, he or she is more apt to rely on a packer's brand name to specify the desired quality.

The use of U.S. grades for poultry, especially the consumer grades, is very popular in the food-service industry. Buyers usually opt for U.S. Grade A products when appearance is very important. For instance, a fried chicken entrée would most often be prepared with the highest-quality raw products. Lower grades are usually sold to food processors. They are often referred to as "manufacturing grades," in that they are not usually intended for food-service operations unless they undergo some sort of processing that will alter their appearance and culinary quality. If appearance is not so important to the hospitality operation, as when raw poultry is used to prepare chicken salads, turkey casseroles, or pot pies in the operation's kitchen, the lesser grades may be adequate.

PACKERS' BRANDS (OR EQUIVALENT)

For fresh, refrigerated and fresh, frozen poultry, brand loyalty rarely comes into play. There seems to be a little more reliance on specific brands of raw turkey or duck. But this does not seem to be the case for chicken.

Some manufacturers attempt to take poultry out of the commodity class and instill brand loyalty in consumers. There are several brand names from which to choose. For instance, Perdue, Tyson, and Foster Farms are some of the brand labels a buyer could specify for fresh, refrigerated chicken.

There is some value, as well as a higher AP price, associated with proprietary chicken brand names. For example, the producers generally slow down the assembly line to use a "soft-scald" procedure, which removes feathers at a lower temperature, thereby increasing significantly the tenderness of the bird. Some producers use a "chill pack" preservation procedure for their finished products. This maintains the chicken's temperature at about 28 to 29°F (it freezes at about 27 to 28°F), thereby increasing the product's shelf life without freezing it. Furthermore, these brand name items usually are produced in exceptionally clean and sanitary environments. Very high levels of sanitation will increase a product's shelf life because the shelf life is related directly to the numbers of bacteria found on the skin of the bird.

The brand-name campaign seems aimed primarily at the homemaker. Hospitality operations that list a lot of poultry signature items on their menus strive to ensure that their customers identify such poultry with the operations that prepare it, and not with a particular packer's brand name. Generally, packers' brands are important to the hospitality buyer only when he or she is purchasing processed poultry products.

PRODUCT SIZE

When purchasing raw poultry products, the buyer usually cannot specify an exact product size. Rather, he or she must indicate the acceptable weight range. For example, it is necessary to indicate a weight range for whole birds and, to some extent, for raw poultry parts, such as chicken thighs and turkey breasts.

As a general rule, the larger bird, the higher its edible yield. For instance, an interesting fact about turkey is that the bird's bone structure stops developing when it reaches about 20 pounds. Turkeys over 20 pounds will have more fat and a bit more meat on the same skeleton. If the intended use allows, you should purchase large birds as they may be the most economical choice.

The buyer also must note the product size of any processed products that the operation needs. Fortunately, he or she normally can specify an exact size for these items and does not have to rely on weight ranges.

There are many sizes available for things such as precooked, breaded chicken breasts, chicken patties, turkey pot pies, and so forth.

PRODUCT YIELD

For some poultry products, say frozen, breaded chicken patties, you may want to indicate the maximum yield, or the minimum trim, expected. For example, you may want to note on the specification that you will accept no more than 2 broken pieces in a 48-piece container of chicken patties.

SIZE OF CONTAINER

As always, you must indicate the size of the package that you prefer. If necessary, you would need to note the size of any inner packs. For instance, you may want a 30-pound case of frozen chicken chow mein, with six 5-pound plastic pouches per case.

TYPE OF PACKAGING MATERIAL

There is a reasonable variety of packaging quality, so you would do well to consider this selection factor when preparing your specifications. The variety is considerable for fresh product—for instance, fresh poultry may arrive at your back door wrapped in butcher paper, or packed in cardboard, wooden crates, or in large, reusable plastic containers that the suppliers will pick up when they deliver the next shipment. The relatively short shelf life of fresh items makes it necessary for you to reject packaging that would do anything to shorten this life drastically.

When you purchase several types of processed products, you will experience a greater variety of packaging qualities. Usually processed items that we use in our industry are packed in moisture-proof, vapor-proof materials that are designed to withstand freezer temperatures. Be certain that the items you purchase in this manner are packaged properly so that you avoid any unnecessary loss of product.

PACKAGING PROCEDURE

As with most products, poultry is packaged in many different ways. For instance, most raw, refrigerated items are slab packed, while their frozen counterparts are usually layered. Whole birds typically are individually wrapped if they are frozen, whereas the fresh, refrigerated ones may not be; in fact, the fresh items will normally be slab packed with crushed ice covering them. (This is sometimes referred to as an "ice-pack" procedure.)

Fresh or frozen boneless poultry products are sometimes packaged in "cello packs." Products packed this way usually come in a 5-pound box that has six cello-wrapped portions containing approximately two to four poultry pieces in each wrap.

Fresh poultry birds or bird parts may also come in a "gas-flushed pack." In this arrangement, the poultry is placed in plastic bags, and the air is "flushed" out of the bag and replaced with carbon dioxide. This packaging procedure (a type of controlled atmosphere packaging) is done primarily to extend the fresh poultry's shelf life.

Some fresh, refrigerated product can be purchased in a "marinade pack." For instance, some suppliers will pack individual poultry parts, say chicken wings, in a reusable plastic tub, and pour a specific marinade solution over the products. The chicken wings will absorb the required flavor as they journey through the channel of distribution, so that by the time they are delivered to the hospitality operation's back door, they can be put directly into production.

Most processed poultry products purchased by the typical hospitality operation will be frozen and layered. These items are usually referred to as "individually quick frozen," or IQF. This indicates that the products are flash frozen and layered in the case.* In some instances, they may even be individually wrapped.

PRODUCT FORM

One of the amazing things about the poultry trade is the seemingly endless number of products available and the forms in which they can be purchased. On one extreme are the raw products, while at the other extreme we find several artificial meat items, such as "ham" and "hot dogs," that are produced with poultry.

If you purchase whole birds, you will have the option of purchasing them whole, or you can request that they be cut into a certain number of pieces. You also may be able to specify a particular cutting pattern that you desire, although the standards of identity set by the federal government address this issue fairly well; hence, it is often unnecessary to dwell on this aspect.

If you purchase whole birds, you will have the option of whether you want the variety meats included or excluded. These variety meats are the organ meats, such as liver and heart. They are not usually included with whole birds intended for use by food-service establishments, so if you want them, you normally will need to indicate this desire on your specification. Usually, if a food-service operator needs to purchase variety meats, he or she will purchase them separately; for instance, chicken livers are normally purchased separately, packed in a 5-pound Cryovac bag.

Sometimes raw poultry, especially raw poultry parts, includes a bit of

---

* This is sometimes referred to as a "snap pack" or "shatter pack." When you remove a layer of frozen items from the case and drop it onto a tabletop, the IQF portions should snap apart easily. If they do not come apart easily, it usually means that they have been thawed a bit and refrozen.

cutting and trimming that adds to the AP price of the items, but enhances their convenience. For instance, we can order boneless, skinless chicken breasts. This convenience, while initially a costly alternative, could, in the long run, result in the most economic EP costs.

If you need to purchase a good deal of highly processed poultry products, such as precooked turkey rolls or frozen, pre-prepared chicken stew, and if you are not satisfied with the federal government minimum standards of identity, you will need to do something to indicate the particular type of formula you want. For example, you may find it necessary to specify in great detail a chicken patty's proportion of white and dark meat, the amount and type of breading, and so forth. You might be able to utilize a packer's brand, one that resembles what you want, but this convenience may not always be available.

PRESERVATION METHOD

Most poultry purchased for use in the hospitality industry is preserved in one of two ways: refrigerated or frozen. Much of the refrigerated product is packed at the chill-pack temperatures. If a supplier does not provide the chill-pack alternative, usually he or she will provide the ice-pack method, which tends to accomplish the same purpose of the chill pack, namely, the reduction of the storage temperature to just above freezing. (Both chill pack and ice pack are used to maintain temperatures of about 28 to 29°F.)

The food-service operation that strives for a good poultry reputation usually purchases fresh, ice-packed, or chill-packed, poultry. For instance, if fried chicken is the signature item, it is very unlikely that a frozen item would be used. Frozen poultry birds and parts cause several problems. For instance, it is very easy for them to thaw just a bit during the receiving cycle and become freezer burned when they refreeze in storage. You also will get a red tinge around the bones when they are cooked. Furthermore, these items will lose flavor and moisture if they are thawed too long before cooking, or thawed too much.

Some fresh poultry (as well as fresh meat, fish, and produce) may be preserved with irradiation. Irradiation removes almost all traces of harmful bacteria in meat and fish, and spoilage bacteria in fresh produce. However, many critics maintain that nutrients are lost during the irradiation process and that not enough information is known about the safety of this procedure. Hence, many food services are not eager to embrace this technology.

Processed poultry products generally are purchased in the frozen state. There are some canned products, but they are seldom used by the typical hospitality operation. For instance, you could purchase frozen chicken noodle soup, or a canned alternative. The canned item is usually less expensive, but many food-service operators will opt for the frozen variety because the culinary quality is superior.

AP PRICE

Raw poultry products offer little spread in AP price from one supplier to another. The distance that a finished poultry item must travel to get to your back door, though, does make a difference. For example, Long Island duckling usually costs more than a duckling raised closer to home. But given the same style of poultry, the same quality, and the same supplier services, the AP prices are pretty much the same.

In addition, AP prices for raw products tend to be more predictable because poultry can be produced by farmers much more easily and quickly than many other foods. For instance, it takes about two years to bring a steer from birth to the dining room table. With frying chicken, it takes only a few weeks. Also, the fresh poultry AP prices reflect the standardized, scientific management used in raising poultry. For instance, the suppliers use pretty much the same feeding formulas and environments so that the poultry looks the same, tastes the same, and has the same conversion weight.

Since the AP prices vary little, the EP costs, theoretically, should also be similar between competing suppliers' raw products.

The AP prices vary quite a bit for processed items, and this requires you to estimate EP costs as well as customer acceptance of these processed products.

If you buy a lot of chicken, consider entering into long-term contracts or, at least, the hedging technique we discussed in Chapter 9. You may be able to maintain an AP price that you can live with by hedging in the commodity futures market. In addition, quantity buys offer reasonably good savings.

TRUST THE SUPPLIER

No matter what type of poultry you buy—fresh or processed—you can find several potential suppliers in the marketplace. There is no need to become a house account unless you want to.

The AP prices of raw poultry do not vary significantly among suppliers. Consequently, bid buying these items may not be so profitable as it is for processed products, unless, of course, you can get some additional service. For instance, if you buy fresh poultry, you will want it kept at least about 30 to 35°F. Also, you might want the supplier or processor to cut it up and put it into a marinade of some sort. Or you might want a whole chicken cut into eight, nine, or ten parts, depending on the intended use. Not every supplier can do these things. But if two or three have these capabilities, you might consider bidding out your business once in a while.

In our experience, a purchaser tends eventually to become a fresh poultry house account; that is, he or she tends to purchase from one trusted supplier. This product requires at least a 30 to 35°F temperature environment as well as one that is very sanitary. We have known buyers whose only evaluation of a fresh poultry supplier centered on the odor emanating from his or her poultry storage refrigerator. A clean refrigerator, to them, meant a reliable supplier.

Several suppliers sell various processed poultry items. The exact one you want, though, may be available from only one purveyor.

If you are very particular, you may find that you have to cast your lot with one supplier. If you are satisfied with a variety of choices, bid buying and extra negotiating might generate rewards.

PURCHASING POULTRY

As always, the first step in purchasing is to decide on the quality and type of product you want. For fresh poultry, and even for some processed poultry, you may find few suppliers who can give you exactly what you want, particularly if you have special requirements. As we have noted, though, there are usually enough potential suppliers to satisfy the bid buyer.

The normal quality purchasers use for poultry is U.S. Grade A, especially when appearance is important. Of course, you can buy several combinations if other grades are available. However, you cannot always assume that Grade B is available for every item since most producers strive to achieve the A grade.

Once you know what you want, it is usually beneficial to prepare a complete specification. It should include all pertinent information, whether or not you use it in bid buying, simply because the discipline of preparing this written document helps to ensure that you have considered all relevant factors and are, indeed, purchasing the right quality and quantity. Figure 21.4 shows some example product specifications. Figure 21.5 notes an example product specification outline for poultry products.

After preparing your specs, you then must evaluate the potential suppliers. Keep in mind that for raw poultry, since quality and AP prices usually vary only a little, the important consideration probably is supplier services. Consider such matters as freshness, delivery capabilities, temperature control, and plant appearance.

One can find many processed poultry product suppliers, but not so very many if you have strict requirements. For instance, if you want turkey or chicken cold cuts, there are not many suppliers.

As in the fresh produce and egg trade, the independent farmer can probably supply poultry. We do not recommend this unless the farmer's products and plant are under continuous inspection.

Broiler/fryer, raw
Used for fried chicken lunch entrée
U.S. Grade A
Quarter chicken parts, cut from
   whole birds weighing between
   $2\frac{1}{2}$ to $3\frac{1}{4}$ lb. dressed weight
No variety meats
Ice packed in reusable plastic tubs
Approximately 30 lb. per tub
	Boneless chicken breast, raw
	Used for dinner entrée
	Tyson brand
	4-oz portions
	48, 4-oz. portions packed per case
	Moisture-proof, vapor-proof case
	   with plastic "cell-pack" inserts;
	   products layered in cell packs
	Frozen

Chicken base Used to prepare soups and sauces Minor's brand 16-oz. resealable plastic containers 12 containers packed per case Refrigerated	Turkey breast, raw Used for sandwiches U.S. Grade A Bone in, skin on Under 8 pounds Wrapped in Cryovac (or equivalent) Refrigerated

FIGURE 21.4. Example of poultry product specifications.

Intended use:

Exact name:

U.S. grade (or equivalent):

Packer's brand name (or equivalent):

Product size:

Product yield:

Size of container:

Type of packaging material:

Packaging procedure:

Product form:

Preservation method:

FIGURE 21.5. Example of product specification outline for poultry products.

RECEIVING POULTRY

First, make the normal quality and quantity checks. Because harmful bacteria can multiply rapidly on poultry, especially at room temperatures, many operations receive and inspect poultry in refrigerated storage. The delivery agent and the receiver go straight to this area.

The raw poultry quality check is not difficult to make. The grade shield is usually displayed prominently on the carton, and with whole poultry, on the wing of each bird. (But be careful that the boxes have not been repacked. You can never be quite sure of what is in the box, regardless of the grade noted on the carton. A trustworthy supplier is the best insurance.)

The quality check can cause some trouble if you are concerned with the age of the poultry. For instance, you might purchase hens to get the flavorful meat. But how do you know whether the hen is as old as it should be? You can look at its size and the amount of abdominal fat. To the trained eye, this check is routine. But some receiving agents lack this skill.

Processed products normally require other types of quality checks. The normal check of frozen products—looking for proper temperature, signs of thawing and refreezing, and inadequate packaging—and of canned products—leaks, rust, and swollen cans—must be performed.

After satisfying yourself of the quality, you must check the quantity. You normally buy poultry by the pound or by the bird. Also, some poultry comes packed in ice. This tends to make weighing difficult. You might have to weigh enough birds to see whether they are within the weight range you have specified. Hence, you may have to dig around in the ice a little. Or you may have to weigh the poultry with the ice on it, but preferably with the ice temporarily removed. Or you might weigh the packer's brand prepackaged chill-pack chicken to compare it with the weight stated on the label.

You also need to check the types of parts, variety meats, and processed items you receive, if you have purchased these products. Sometimes you order legs and you get wings. Or you order chicken livers and you get gizzards. Or you order chicken franks and the supplier delivers turkey franks. These are usually honest mistakes, but they can ruin a production schedule.

It is possible to streamline the poultry receiving process by using the USDA's Acceptance Service. This service is popular among large food-service operators for meat and poultry items. Remember that you can hire an inspector to help you write specifications. Also, under the Acceptance Service, the federal inspector, or the state counterpart, will accept or reject the product according to what you specify.

After making quality and quantity checks, check the prices and complete the appropriate accounting procedures.

STORING POULTRY

Fresh and frozen poultry should be stored immediately and at the proper temperatures and humidity. It should be stored in the environment its form suggests.

Fresh poultry has a short shelf life. This shelf life can be extended from three to four days to up to a week if proper storage practices are followed. If the chickens are received in an ice pack, they should be stored as is, but in such a way that melted ice runs from the storage package and does not soak into the birds. As ice melts, additional ice should be added, usually no more than every other day. When poultry items are received packed without ice, the shelf life is extended by placing them in a perforated pan, layering in ice, and refrigerating them. This maintains the temperature at approximately 28 to 29°F.

Some operations may wish to marinate their poultry. This also lengthens the shelf life and imparts a distinctive flavor. You can also extend poultry's shelf life by precooking it, though this could hamper your standard production schedule.

Whatever storage procedures you follow, do not handle poultry any more than is absolutely necessary. If improperly handled, it will become contaminated.

Since poultry is expensive, you might consider keeping a perpetual inventory of it. If so, you will need to enter the appropriate information on bin cards or into the computerized inventory management system.

ISSUING POULTRY

If you use a perpetual inventory system, you will need to deduct the quantity issued.

If applicable, you will need to make the following decision: Should you issue the item as is? Or should you issue it as ready to go (for example, cut up and breaded, or precut)? Recall that there are several advantages and disadvantages, regardless of what choice you make.

You should follow proper stock rotation when issuing these items. Also, since these products, especially the fresh ones, deteriorate rapidly and are expensive, make sure that the requisitioner does not take more than is absolutely necessary. If you can, force this person to note the in-process inventory before asking for more poultry.

IN-PROCESS INVENTORIES

Depending on the type of poultry product, there are several degrees of potential waste. For example, it is easy to burn a breaded poultry item on the outside while failing to cook it thoroughly on the inside. Or if you are carving a whole roast turkey, a lot of usable meat can stick to the bones. Or leaving it too long under a glow lamp can make a once beautiful roast turkey collapse into a heap of rubble.

If you use several types of poultry, make sure you keep them straight. For example, a cook might unknowingly use the chopped, cooked chicken slated for chicken salad in the soup.

Probably the biggest consideration with in-process poultry inventory is the sanitation problem. Staphylococcus and salmonella bacteria should not be present on cooked poultry products. However, if contaminated after cooking, usually by a human handler or by placing on a contaminated surface, bacteria grow very quickly at warm temperatures (40 to 120°F). For example, a finished chicken à la king kept in a warm steam table, instead of a hot one, for four or five hours can become sufficiently contaminated to cause an outbreak of food-borne illness.

KEY WORDS AND CONCEPTS

Age of bird at time of slaughter
AP price
Cello pack
Chill pack
Commodity
Contamination problems
Conversion weight
EP cost
Exact name
Free-range chicken
FSQS
Gas-flushed pack
Grading factors
Ice pack
Independent farmer
In-process inventories
Intended use
IQF
Irradiation

Kosher chicken
Manufacturing grade
Marinade pack
Material used in processed products
Number of pieces per bird
Packaging procedure
Packers' brands
Poultry Products Inspection Act
Poultry used for more than one menu item
Preservation method
Procurement grades
Product form
Product size
Product yield
Purchasing, receiving, storing, and issuing poultry products
Sex of bird
Shatter pack

Shelf life

Signature item

Snap pack

Size of container

Standard of identity

State grades

Substitution possibilities

Trust the supplier

Type of packaging material

USDA Acceptance Service

U.S. grades

Variety meats

Weight range

Wholesome Poultry Products Act

QUESTIONS AND PROBLEMS

1. What are the U.S. consumer grades for poultry?

2. Why is the age of a bird at time of slaughter an important selection factor?

3. Why do hen turkeys generally have a higher AP price than tom turkeys?

4. What is an appropriate intended use for a broiler-fryer?

5. The primary grading factor for the poultry grades "Procurement I" and "Procurement II" is _____.

6. What are the lower-quality poultry products generally used for?

7. Outline the specific procedures you would use for purchasing, receiving, storing, and issuing frozen, prebreaded broiler-fryer parts. Assume that these parts will be used in a school food service or in a hospital food service. If possible, ask a school food-service director or a hospital dietitian to comment on your answer.

8. What type of poultry product would you purchase if you were planning to prepare chicken and dumplings and you wanted to use fresh chicken? Why?

9. If you serve turkey and dressing, you could use fresh turkey or a processed product, such as a turkey roll. What are the potential advantages and disadvantages of using the fresh product? What are the potential advantages and disadvantages of using the processed product?

10. What is another name for the term "conversion weight?"

11. What is the primary difference between the poultry grades U.S. Grade A and U.S. Grade B?

12. Why is the weight range of a fresh, whole bird an important selection factor?

13. What critical information is missing from the following product specification for sliced, cooked chicken breast?

Sliced, cooked chicken breast

Used for deli sandwiches

Country Pride brand (or equivalent)

Packed in Cryovac bags

Refrigerated

14. Describe the necessary storage conditions for fresh and processed poultry.

15. Prepare a product specification for the product noted in Question 8.

16. Why are free-range and kosher chickens more expensive than chickens raised in the typical way?

17. Why are frozen chicken parts, such as breasts and thighs, unacceptable to many food-service operators?

18. What method can you use to extend the shelf life of fresh poultry?

19. Explain why we call a chicken a "commodity" item.

20. Assume that you manage an employee food service. You serve lunch only—5,000 lunches per day, five days a week. A poultry purveyor calls to tell you he is going out of business. He has about 7,500 pounds of frozen, cut-up broiler-fryers. He will sell you this for 50 percent of today's current AP price. You have to let him know your decision tomorrow. What do you suggest? If possible, ask an employee food-service manager to comment on your answer.

21. A product specification for turkey franks could include the following information:

    (a) _____

    (b) _____

    (c) _____

    (d) _____

    (e) _____

22. What are the major advantages of the chill-pack procedure?

23. When would you substitute a processed chicken patty for a boneless, skinless chicken breast?

24. Prepare a product specification for the following poultry products:

    (a) Chicken wing

    (b) Turkey ham

    (c) Chicken egg roll

    (d) Duckling

    (e) Chicken patty

25. What is the difference between the ice-pack procedure and the marinade-pack procedure?

C H A P T E R 22

Source: Alliant Foodservice

FISH

THE PURPOSE OF THIS CHAPTER

This chapter discusses:

- The selection factors for fish
- Purchasing, receiving, storing, and issuing fish
- The in-process fish inventory

INTRODUCTION

Buying fresh fish can be one of the most frustrating jobs in all purchasing. Processed—that is canned, salted, and frozen—fish is easier to buy. With fresh items, not only will you find very few suppliers, but you may also have to take whatever fresh fish is available. If you want fresh fish on the menu, you might have to offer whatever your supplier has in stock. And at times, your supplier may have nothing.

It is very difficult to obtain a wide variety of fresh fish unless you are willing to deal with all potential suppliers. It also is very difficult to maintain consistent culinary quality unless you have a working relationship with all of them. It is not unusual for a food-service operator to purchase only one type of fresh fish from as many seafood suppliers as possible in order to obtain a steady supply and consistent quality.

One nice thing about fish is that you can usually get by with processed products, unless you want to advertise fresh items. If you insist on fresh fish, it is not particularly difficult to buy something fresh; it is just that there are, as we said, few suppliers from which to choose. Moreover, unless you are close to a large body of water, the "fresh" fish can be in tired condition; its AP prices can fluctuate, which can force you to price your menu almost every day; once you get the fish, the production employees may not be able to handle it properly unless they are highly skilled in this area; and some choice items, like Dover sole, Maine lobster, or Alaska king crab, cannot always be purchased fresh. Unless you can obtain a reasonably steady supply, you might reconsider any decision to feature fresh fish on the menu.

Some companies take the guesswork and the difficulty out of the selection and procurement of fresh fish by "growing their own," or by purchasing products that are grown by suppliers under controlled conditions. For instance, large restaurant companies that own commissaries can practice "aquaculture," that is, fish farming, which serves to produce fish products of consistent size and culinary quality. Any food-service operation, though, can purchase farm-raised fish from the suppliers who provide this option.

Aquaculture is not a new development; in fact, it traces its roots to China, where the Chinese people have farmed fish since before the birth of Christ. However, it has only been in the last few years that the procedures have become very popular.

Many buyers are fond of farm-raised fish because it eliminates a lot of the risk from the fish purchasing process. It also ensures stable quality and a consistent supply.

Each year there is an increase in the amount of farm-raised fish purchased in the United States. According to the National Restaurant Association (NRA), farm-raised catfish is the largest segment of the aquaculture industry. Other popular farm-raised fish are trout, tilapia, salmon, oysters, mussels, clams, scallops, abalone, crawfish, and shrimp. While aquaculture technically can be expanded to include other fish species, such as halibut and flounder, the technology needed to do it effectively and efficiently is still being refined.

The fresh fish buyer must be very knowledgeable about the fish products he or she purchases. These products are not very standardized, and, unlike other fresh products, such as fresh produce and fresh meats, there are not many market guidelines available except for only a handful of items. Hence, if you are charged with the responsibility of purchasing fresh fish products, you can never know too much about them.

SELECTION FACTORS

Management must determine the varieties and qualities of fish wanted on the menu. Again, this type of decision usually is made in cooperation with other company personnel. Several of the following selection factors are usually considered.

INTENDED USE

As always, you want to determine exactly the intended use of the item so that you will be able to prepare the appropriate, relevant specification. For example, a broiled whitefish needs a more attractive appearance than does whitefish that will be used in breaded fish patties.

SALTWATER SPECIES	FRESHWATER SPECIES
Cod	Catfish
Flounder	Lake perch
Haddock	Lake trout
Halibut	Pike
Mackerel	Rainbow trout
Mahi Mahi (Dolphin)	Smelt
Monkfish	Tilapia
Ocean catfish	Whitefish
Ocean perch	
Pollock	**SHELLFISH SPECIES**
Salmon	Abalone
Sea bass	Clam
Sea trout	Crab
Snapper	Crawfish
Sole	Lobster
Swordfish	Mussel
Tuna	Oyster
Turbot	Scallop
Whiting	Shrimp

FIGURE 22.1. Popular varieties of fish products used by the food-service industry.

EXACT NAME

There are many varieties of fish in the world. In the United States, more than 200 varieties are sold. Suffice it to say, you must be especially careful and indicate the precise name of the item you want. Figure 22.1 notes some of the more popular varieties of fish product used by the food-service industry.

Unfortunately, even if you indicate an exact name, you could receive an unwanted item because the fish industry is fond of renaming fish. For example, on the East Coast of the United States the name "lemon sole" refers to a particular size of flounder, whereas on the West Coast and in Europe it refers to other fish species. A similar problem occurs with the name "snapper." It seems that almost everything under the sun is called snapper.

The federal government actually encourages this renaming of fish because it would like to see the public eat products that are quite good, yet suffer from an image problem because they have unappealing names. Many perfectly delicious and nutritious fish species abound primarily because they are protected by repugnant names. Lately, though, several "trash" fish have become more popular.

Renaming fish also is done in an attempt to increase its marketability and profitability. For example, we recall that years ago there was a product called "Slimeheads" or "Australian Perch." There was little demand

Block—a solid cube of raw fish; usually skinless; normally weighs about 10 to 20 pounds.

Breaded/battered—fish product coated with a seasoned crumb or batter mixture.

Butterfly fillet—two small fillets held together by a small, thin piece of skin.

Chunk—cross section of a large, dressed fish. It contains the cross section of the backbone. It is similar to a bone-in beef pot roast.

Drawn—whole fish that has been eviscerated, i.e., the entrails have been removed.

Dressed—a completely clean fish; usually has the head attached; can be cooked as is or processed into steaks, fillets, portions, etc.

Fillet—boneless fish, cut away from the backbone.

Fin fish—fish that has fins and a backbone. There are "fat" fin fish and "lean" fin fish. There are saltwater and freshwater species.

Green, headless—usually refers to a raw, unprocessed shrimp.

Peeled and deveined (P&D)—a shrimp without its shell or black vein.

Portion—a piece of fish cut from a block of fish. It is similar to a fillet, but does not meet the exact definition of the fillet.

Shellfish—fish products that are completely or partially covered by a shell. There are crustaceans, whose shells are soft (e.g., shrimp), and mollusks, which have hard shells (e.g., oysters).

Shucked—fish that has been removed from its shell. Normally used when ordering shell-less mollusks.

Steak—a cross section of a large fish that has been cut from a dressed fish carcass.

Stick—a small piece of fish usually cut from a fish block.

Whole (round)—fish right out of the water; nothing has been done to it.

FIGURE 22.2. Common marketing terms for fish products.

for it. However, once the Australians renamed it "Orange Roughy," sales skyrocketed. And, we might add, so did its price.

Renaming fish is a particularly sensitive issue in our industry. We must be careful to receive only those products that we actually order. If our customers are more adventurous and would accept the more exotic species, then we will order them. If not, we must be certain to select only those suppliers who will help us achieve our purchase objectives.

In addition to the exact name of the product, you must be certain that, where applicable, you use the appropriate market terminology in your particular area that further identifies what you want. While there are some common market terms, each growing and harvesting area tends to adopt its own peculiar nomenclature to identify some items. Figure 22.2 notes some of the most common marketing terms.

There are a few fish products that have federal government standards of identity. For instance, a "lightly breaded" shrimp product must contain at least 65 percent shrimp, whereas a "breaded" shrimp product must contain at least 50 percent shrimp. As with all standards of identity, though, they represent minimal requirements. Furthermore, in the fish trade, only a handful of processed products are subject to the standard of identity regulations. Consequently, the wise buyer usually does not rely on standards of identity when preparing specifications for fish products.

U.S. GOVERNMENT GRADES (OR EQUIVALENT)

The U.S. Department of Commerce's (USDC) National Marine Fisheries Service provides grade standards and grading services for fishery products similar to those provided by the USDA for other foods. The Commerce Department's grading program also provides official inspection for edibility and wholesomeness of fishery products, and many of its grade standards specify the amount of fish component required in a processed product.

Few fish items are graded by the U.S. government. The products that have had grading standards established for them are processed products, such as breaded and/or precooked items.

Fish grades are based on several grading factors. The grader normally will evaluate the appearance, odor, size, uniformity, color, defects, flavor, texture, and the product's point of origin. The federal grades for fish products are:

1. A—This is the best quality produced. The appearance and culinary quality are superior. Grade A products have a uniform appearance and are practically devoid of blemishes or other defects.
2. B—This is good quality, generally suitable for many food-service applications. It has significantly more blemishes and/or defects than does Grade A product.
3. C—This grade resembles Grade B, but it is lacking in appearance. It is suitable only for finished menu items, such as soups and casseroles, where appearance is not critical.

If a buyer uses U.S. grades as one of his or her selection factors, normally only the U.S. Grade A designation is specified. (See Figure 22.3.) The lower grades usually do not carry a federal grade shield; rather, these manufacturing grades are left unmarked and are usually sold to food fabricators who will process them into several types of convenience fish products.

PACKED UNDER FEDERAL INSPECTION (PUFI) SEAL

Recall from Chapter 3 that fish products are not subject to mandatory continuous federal government inspection. The Food and Drug Adminis-

FIGURE 22.3. Federal grade stamps used for fish.

tration (FDA) provides periodic inspections for all food-fabricating plants, monitors imported and interstate fish shipments, and requires fish processors to adopt the HACCP system to increase food safety. There also is a cooperative agreement between federal and state agencies that monitors the farm beds where oysters, clams, and mussels are raised. However, these inspections fall far short of those used by the U.S. Department of Agriculture (USDA) to monitor meat-packing, poultry-packing, and egg-breaking plants.

Fish are cold-blooded animals; hence, the diseases afflicting them supposedly do not threaten the humans who eat them. However, fish can be exposed to many toxins, bacteria, and parasites that can be harmful to humans. While properly prepared and served seafood causes no more health problems than do meat products, and fewer problems than do poultry items, nevertheless, fish buyers seem to be reluctant to purchase fish that has not been produced under continuous government inspection.

One way to ensure continuous government inspection is to demand that all fish products you purchase carry a U.S. grade designation. Fish products that are produced and graded under the U.S. Department of Commerce inspection program may carry the USDC "Federal Inspection" mark or the U.S. grade shield. Unfortunately, grading designations, as mentioned earlier, are available only for a few fish items. Another problem is that only fish produced in the United States can carry the federal government's grade or inspection shield; according to the National Restaurant Association (NRA), about two-thirds of the fish consumed in the United States comes from approximately 120 other countries.

An alternative is to purchase only those fish products that are produced under the continuous inspection of a state or local government agency. However, these agencies normally do not provide an extensive array of inspection services. And the ones they do provide usually are not very comprehensive.

The only sure way of obtaining fish items that are produced under continuous government inspection is to demand that any fish product you purchase carry the Packed Under Federal Inspection (PUFI) seal. (See

FIGURE 22.4. This seal signifies that the fish product is clean, safe, and whole-some and has been produced in an acceptable establishment with appropriate equipment under the supervision of federal inspectors.

Figure 22.4.) The seal indicates that the product is clean, safe, and whole-some and that it has been produced in an establishment that meets all sanitary guidelines of the USDC's National Marine Fisheries Service. The product is not graded for quality, but it meets acceptable commercial quality standards set by the federal inspection agency.

If you specify that all fish you buy must carry the PUFI seal, it proba-bly will reduce significantly the potential number of suppliers who can bid for your business. Continuous fish inspection is a voluntary program, and not many fish processing plants participate. Furthermore, time-consuming inspection is not easily adaptable to many fish suppliers who sell fresh fish products; in many instances, the products are caught in the morning and sent via air express to the food-service operation, where they will be used on the menu that evening.

PACKERS' BRANDS (OR EQUIVALENT)

Most fresh fish does not carry a brand name; hence, this criterion is not a useful selection factor for fresh items. But packers' brands for processed fish items, especially canned fish, abound. In fact, a brand name, as well as the reputation of the product's producer and distributing suppliers, is very important to many buyers. For instance, we probably could safely assume that Star Kist and Chicken of the Sea brands instill a good deal of confidence in the marketplace.

In some instances, a brand name may be the only guide to seafood consistency. In addition, the type of processed product you want may be available only from one company. (For example, there are not too many firms producing marinated baby sardines.)

Few beginning purchasers are familiar with the brand names in the seafood area. As a result, these brands may not be very useful, at least until you study the brands and experiment with them.

Some brand-name processed fish products carry the U.S. Grade A designation. Things such as fish sticks and raw breaded shrimp usually carry this type of grading mark. The brand is indicative of a certain culinary quality, and the grade shield assures wholesomeness.

PRODUCT SIZE

As usual, size information is a very important selection factor. Fish products come in so many sizes that a specification without this type of information is seriously deficient.

Some shellfish items, such as crab legs and lobster tails, are usually sized by count. For these two products, the count will be based on 10 pounds. For instance, if lobster tails are sized "10/12," there are approximately 10 to 12 pieces in a 10-pound lot.

For many fresh fish products, you may only be able to specify a weight range. For example, if you are purchasing large salmon fillets, the supplier may be unable to accommodate an exact size.

If you are purchasing whole fish products, you also will need to settle for a weight range. For instance, you cannot specify an exact size for whole lobsters. You must be satisfied with one of the five traditional sizes available: "chickens" (approximately 1 pound), "quarters" (1 to 1¼ pounds), "selects" (1½ to 2½ pounds), "jumbos" (2½ to 5 pounds), and "monsters" (over 5 pounds).

For processed products, you normally are able to indicate the exact desired weight per item. For instance, when purchasing breaded fish sticks, you normally can choose among several available sizes.

The sizing system is an informal procedure that has developed over the years. There are no federal government standards dealing with this issue. Furthermore, there probably are producers who have their own type of size designation that they attach to their items. If this is the case in your area, you will need to determine the exact nomenclature so that your specifications are adequate.

PRODUCT YIELD

You may need to indicate the minimum yield you will accept, or the maximum trim you will allow, for the fish products you receive. For instance, you could note on your specification that you will accept no more than, say, 2 percent broken fish sticks in every 20-pound case you buy. Or you will accept no more than 2 percent dead oysters for each barrel purchased.

SIZE OF CONTAINER

When considering the size of the individual fish products you purchase, you also must give some thought to the size of the container you would prefer. There is sufficient variation in container sizes to satisfy most buyer preferences. Generally speaking, the size and type of packages available for fish products are very similar to those used to package poultry products.

TYPE OF PACKAGING MATERIAL

Fresh fish often is delivered in reusable plastic tubs. The products normally also are packed in crushed ice, that is, fresh product is often "ice packed."

Processed fish items usually are packaged in cans, bottles, or moisture-proof, vapor-proof materials that are designed to withstand freezer temperatures.

Live-in-shell fish items usually are packaged in moisture-proof materials. These products also may be packed in seaweed, or some other similar material designed to prevent dehydration. Usually these products are not packed in ice or in fresh water because these packing media will reduce the products' shelf lives.

As mentioned, generally fish products are packaged in the same type and variety of materials used to package poultry products. The buyer therefore, has several choices.

PACKAGING PROCEDURE

Once again, we note the similarity between poultry and fish products. As with poultry, fish items are slab packed, layered, chill packed, ice packed, cello packed, and individually quick frozen (IQF). Some items are also available in a marinade pack; for instance, you may be able to purchase Cajun-seasoned sole fillets.

Fresh shellfish typically are slab packed. Fresh fin fish normally are ice packed in order to preserve culinary quality and extend the shipment's shelf life. Some fresh fin fish are placed in "modified atmosphere packaging" (MAP), a type of controlled atmosphere packaging, which involves chilling freshly harvested fish, placing it in plastic wrap, and pumping into the wrap a combination of carbon dioxide, oxygen, and nitrogen. The shelf life of fresh fish packaged this way can be as long as three weeks.

Fresh frozen fish products are usually trimmed, cut, IQF, and packaged on board a fish-factory ship. These items are often cello wrapped and placed in moisture-proof, vapor-proof containers.

Processed frozen fish items are most often processed, IQF, layered on plastic or waxed sheets or plastic "cell packs," and placed in moisture-proof, vapor-proof containers. As with similarly processed frozen poultry products, this type of packaging procedure is sometimes referred to as a "snap pack" or "shatter pack."

PRODUCT FORM

Fish is processed into many forms. The food-service operation that strives for a high-quality seafood reputation normally needs to use dressed fresh fish and, if further processing is necessary, to perform these tasks in the operation's kitchen. However, there usually are several high-quality processed convenience items available. For instance, breaded/battered, portion-control products are very popular, as are portion-control stuffed, marinated, and other preseasoned fish products.

There are many unique types of convenience fish products available. For instance, there are "flaked and reformed" "shrimp" items, which consist of odd scraps of shrimp material shaped to look like whole shrimp. And there are several imitation fish products—such as imitation shrimp and seafood salad—that are made with a fish-based paste called "surimi." Surimi is also used to produce various "meat" products—such as imitation frankfurters and bacon bits. While these products do not necessarily provide the same health benefits as do the real things, some of these low-cost substitutes are very attractive to budget-conscious restaurant operators.

If you purchase a good deal of processed fish, you may need to rely exclusively on packers' brands as your indication of quality and other desired product characteristics. If you do not use brand name identification, and you are purchasing, say, a frozen fish patty, you would need to note on your specification the types of fish and other food matter that must be used to prepare these items. You also would need to note the proportion of these materials desired. If you do not note these characteristics, and you do not wish to specify a particular packer's brand name, you cannot expect to maintain quality control. While there are federal standards of identity for some fish products, we cannot rely on them exclusively because they represent only minimum guidelines to which the commercial fish processor must adhere.

Usually the major issues that need to be resolved when contemplating the purchase of processed fish products are (1) what are the substitution possibilities and (2) what degree of convenience do you want?

There are several substitution possibilities. Processed fish products come in many forms. For instance, you can substitute fillets for steaks, butterfly shrimp for headless shrimp, or imitation crab for the real thing. The alternatives are limited because, as you go from one item to the next, the culinary quality changes. The manager must not risk alienating his or her customers.

The degree of convenience desired usually is related to the labor skill, equipment, and utensils available to produce menu items, and the size of the kitchen and storage facilities. The economics of the food-service industry these days tend to favor the use of many convenience products, and so long as the culinary quality is acceptable, the manager will seriously consider using them.

Whatever degree of processing you desire, you will typically have more than one supplier from which to choose. Fresh fish may be scarce, but there usually are two or more brands of processed fish from which to choose. This makes it nice for those buyers who like to shop around and bid buy. It also makes it nice if you want to move fish items around on your menu. It gives you much more flexibility.

PRESERVATION METHOD

Fish is preserved in many ways: frozen, dried, smoked, refrigerated, ice packed, cello packed, chill packed, live, live-in-shell, and canned.

The operation that offers fish signature menu items prefers live, live-in-shell, and/or ice-packed or chill-packed dressed fresh fish. If fresh product is unavailable, the frozen item is normally the preferred alternative, as at least it ensures a steady, year-round supply.

For some products, canned is the preferred choice. For instance, snails, tuna, and sardines normally are purchased in cans or bottles. Indeed, Americans buy more canned fish than any other type, fresh or processed.

PACKING MEDIUM

In some instances, you will need to indicate the specific packing medium desired. For example, canned tuna is packed with water or with several varieties of oil. The same is true for other canned fish products. Since the packing medium will affect significantly a product's culinary quality, the buyer must be careful to include this selection factor on the specification.

POINT OF ORIGIN

A lobster is not a lobster. If the product comes from Maine, it is not the same lobster as those that come from Australia. Likewise with any other type of fish, fresh or processed; the area it comes from influences its distinctive character, flavor, and texture. Hence, buyers sometimes carefully specify the origin of the fish they buy, especially if they purchase a great deal of fresh fish.

Many food-service operators note on their menus the points of origin for some menu offerings. This seems to be very popular for fish products. For instance, it is quite common to see menus that advertise Lake Superior whitefish, Alaskan salmon and crab legs. Australian lobster tails, and Chilean sea bass. (See Figure 22.5.) This menu nomenclature forces the buyer to purchase fish products that originate from these locales. Substi-

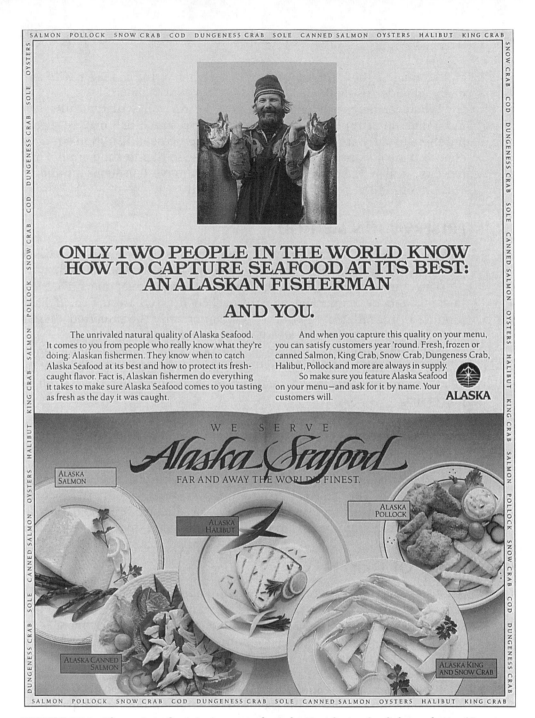

FIGURE 22.5. The point of origin is a popular selection factor for fish products. (Courtesy Alaska Seafood Marketing Institute.)

tute items cheat the customer. And in some parts of the country, any substitutes would violate truth-in-menu legislation.

TRUST THE SUPPLIER

If you use a great deal of fresh fish, you may have to cast your lot with one primary supplier, assuming that you are satisfied with his or her capability. Together, you and the supplier take what you can get from several sources, usually dictated by season, from the various seafood-producing areas of the country or the world.

For instance, if you buy fresh, live-in-shell lobster, the typical scenario may go something like this. You go through a local supplier, or you buy directly from the East Coast, and order what you want for the next two or three days. The lobster is shipped air freight. At the airport in your city, or a nearby city, the lobster is put into a taxicab, or your local supplier's van, and is brought right to your back door. You pay the cabbie and send a check to the fish producer, paying the going rate for that day, usually on a cost-plus basis. Or you pay the local supplier, and he or she takes care of paying the initial source. This scenario often takes place for other types of fresh fish as well. Only with other types, you may need to accept what is available.

When you buy fresh fish products, you often set a different menu price every day or every week. In the live lobster example, a typical price-setting strategy is as follows: Pay for the lobsters. Throw out any dead ones, perhaps 2 out of 24. Divide the total AP price plus any freight cost by 22. Add a markup to cover labor, overhead, and profit, and use this figure as the live lobster menu price for today or for however long it takes to sell this batch of lobster.

It is a good idea to deal consistently with trusted suppliers when you purchase a great deal of fresh fish. The items are not standardized, the quality is variable, the supply is erratic, and the prices change constantly. You need the supplier's expertise. And you must be confident that he or she will charge the correct market price for the items and not try to take advantage of your inability to track the fresh seafood market on a daily basis. Furthermore, you must ensure that the products you purchase are wholesome and safe for human consumption. Fresh fish are very difficult items to move successfully through the distribution channels. There are several contamination opportunities. The competent fresh-fish supplier deserves your respect.

When you buy processed fish, there is no need to become a house account. Processed fish buying, like most processed food purchasing, lends itself nicely to bid buying. You learn, in time, the qualities associated with particular brand names. You can also learn to specify the type of processing you want and the area where the fish is to come from.

Bear in mind, too, that there is a "new pack" time for canned fish, similar to the new pack time for canned fruit and vegetables. If you have the money and the expertise, and large firms often have both, bid buying for a six-month or one-year supply can be rewarding.

PURCHASING FISH

Your first step in purchasing fish is to acquire some of the indispensable reference materials available. For instance, the fish buyer should have a copy of *The New Fresh Seafood Buyer's Guide,* published by VNR, New York. He or she should consult some of the leading trade journals, such as *The Seafood Leader;* the March/April annual buyer's guide issue is especially useful. The buyer should also consider subscribing to the *Seafood Price-Current.* This report contains twice-weekly market prices for many fish products from various regions of the United States.

Your next step is to contact the FDA Office of Seafood Safety and ask for a list of approved interstate fish suppliers operating in your area. Your local health district can supply a list of suppliers who operate only in your local market.

Next you need to decide the exact type of product and quality you want. Once you decide what you want to include on the menu and what quality you want, you should take the time to prepare a specification for each product. We do not think that specs are very valuable for fresh fish, since you usually have to take what is available or go someplace else. You might prepare a statement of quality, give it to your supplier, who then might call you when something meeting your standard comes in. A statement of quality might include the area the fish is to come from, its size, form, and preservation method, and if the fish is grown under controlled conditions, you might be able to specify its feed and nurturing techniques.

If you buy processed fish, you should prepare detailed specifications so that you compile your ideas of exactly what you want. They must include all pertinent information, especially if you will use them in bid buying. Figure 22.6 shows some example product specifications. Figure 22.7 notes an example product specification outline for fish products.

If you buy processed fish in quantity, it might be worth a little trouble to shop around. For instance, buying a lot of frozen fish, say a six-month supply, can save you a bit of money, as long as your storage costs are reasonable. (Many frozen fish suppliers will set up a stockless purchase plan for you. Or they will provide the same type of supplier service for a slight carrying charge.)

Another interesting aspect of buying processed fish is the reasonable spread in the AP prices between one brand name and another. Naturally, when the AP price is lower, you usually suspect a lower quality. Although

Tuna, solid white, albacore Used to prepare tuna salad Chicken of the Sea brand Water pack 66.5-ounce can 6 cans per case Moisture-proof case	Australian lobster tails Used for dinner entrée U.S. Grade A (or equivalent) 16/20 count 25-pound moisture-proof, vapor- proof container Layered pack Frozen
Seafood Newburg Used for banquet service Overhill brand 6-ounce individual portion pack 48 portions per case Packaged in moisture-proof, vapor- proof material To be reconstituted in its package Frozen	Clam juice (ocean) Used for beverage service Nugget brand 46-ounce can 12 cans per case Moisture-proof case

FIGURE 22.6. Example of fish product specifications.

Intended use:

Exact name:

U.S. grade (or equivalent):

PUFI seal:

Packer's brand name (or equivalent):

Product size:

Product yield:

Size of container:

Type of packaging material:

Packaging procedure:

Product form:

Preservation method:

Packing medium:

Point of origin:

FIGURE 22.7. Example of product specification outline for fish products.

this conclusion is typically true when you purchase other processed products, especially canned fruit and vegetables, it is not always the case with processed fish. For example, you will find a big difference in AP price between canned dark-meat tuna and tuna that is white. Some people care very little about this color differential. Another example is the processed fish stick: a little more cod and a little less haddock may yield a fine-tasting product at a more economical AP price. Different formulas for fish patties, fish stews, and other processed entrées can yield substantially different AP prices while maintaining acceptable quality standards.

Minimum order requirements may trouble you. If you do buy fresh fish, but only a little, you might find that a high-minimum-order requirement and freight cost hinder your desire to serve a high-quality fish entrée.

Sometimes you may be tempted to buy fish from your neighbor who has just returned from a fishing trip. There is no mandatory federal inspection requirement for your neighbor, and the fish may be perfectly good. Your state or local health district, however, may have some regulations prohibiting the sale of this fish. In our opinion, you should avoid this practice, since you never really know where the fish comes from or how it has been handled.

Since fish availability can be somewhat unpredictable, sometimes a buyer can find real seafood bargains. The supplier may have some merchandise on a "move list." Or perhaps more shrimp has suddenly shown up on the market and its AP price has gone down. Or the tuna industry has a larger promotional effort. Before you jump at these bargains, though, consider four things. (1) Can your employees handle the new item, if it is a new item to them, properly? (2) Do you have the proper equipment to prepare and serve it? (3) If it is an item currently on your menu, should you drop your menu price? And (4) should you use this bargain as a loss leader on your menu? That is, would you be willing, for instance, to serve a bargain shrimp in your lounge at a very inexpensive menu price to attract customers who supposedly will then order more profitable merchandise from you later on during their visit to the restaurant? This type of promotion may establish a trend whereby you would be forced to continue it well after the AP price of shrimp soars.

Management and the buyer must decide what fish they want. Then they must engage the supplier that can handle their needs. For processed fish, bid buying may be the answer, but this is not always possible when purchasing fresh merchandise.

RECEIVING FISH

When a fish shipment is delivered, the first step is to check its quality. If you examine fresh fin fish, or fresh, shucked shellfish, the product should have a mild scent, not fishy. Its flesh should be firm; it should spring back when slight pressure is applied. There should be no slime on the product. Gills should be bright pink or red. If the head is attached, the eyes should be clear and bright. And to ensure quality and maximum shelf life, the product should be ice-packed or chill-packed.

Sometimes suppliers will send "slacked out" fish (i.e., thawed frozen fish) instead of the fresh product ordered. Usually this product looks a little dry, or it has "ice spots" (i.e., dried areas) on its flesh.

When examining live fish, you should see a product that is very active. You do not want live fish that seem sluggish or tired. Also, the product should be heavy for its size.

Live-in-shell crustaceans, upon examination, should also be very active and feel heavy for their size.

If you are evaluating live-in-shell mollusks, the shells should be closed, or they should close when tapped with your fingers. Open shells indicate that the products are dead and are past their peak of culinary quality. They also should feel heavy for their size.

Frozen fish should be frozen solid. They should be packaged in moisture-proof, vapor-proof material. There should be no signs of thawing or refreezing (such as crystallization, dryness, items stuck together, or water damage on the carton). And, if applicable, there should not be an excessive amount of "glaze" on the items (i.e., a protective coating of ice on the frozen products added by the producer to prevent dehydration).

Canned merchandise should show no signs of rust, dents, dirt, or swelling. Canned fish is especially dangerous if it is contaminated, so the receiving agent can never be too careful when evaluating the containers.

One problem with checking the quality of fresh fish is knowing whether you have received the right species—the item you ordered. Many fish products look similar to the untrained eye. For example, it is not easy to distinguish bay scallops from shark meat cubes, red snapper from Pacific rockfish, or cod fillets from haddock fillets.

Here is a corollary problem: What represents good quality to one nose may be offensive to another. We have seen receivers try to send back fresh fish items because they did not "look right." They had to be convinced that the slipperiness or ocean aroma was natural.

Another problem with receiving fresh fish arises when you must return it. Suppose that the delivery person made a mistake. If he or she takes it back, chances are that the product will go bad before the supplier can resell it. You are also left without a fresh fish item you may need that very night. Consequently, you might keep it and use it if the quality is acceptable in spite of its being the wrong variety. You then would complete a Request for Credit memorandum or make some mutually agreeable settlement.

An unfortunate problem with some processed fish is that it is hard to tell whether they will be acceptable once they are prepared for customer service. For instance, you may not know whether a frozen lobster tail is bad until you cook it and it falls apart. With a fresh lobster tail, the experienced cook can usually judge its quality before cooking it.

After satisfying your nose and eyes, you should go on to weigh, preferably without the ice, or count the merchandise and then get it into the proper storage environment as quickly as possible. Fresh fish will deteriorate right before your eyes if you fail to keep it refrigerated. Whatever you do, do not let fresh and frozen fish stay on the receiving platform any longer than is absolutely necessary. (Some companies put scales and checking equipment in the walk-in refrigerator to receive fish, poultry, and meat. Or they may roll the scale into the refrigerator temporarily.)

If you are receiving a shipment of shellfish from a supplier on the FDA's Interstate Certified Shellfish Shippers List, there will be a tag in the container noting the number of the bed where the shellfish were grown and harvested. You are required to keep this tag on file for 90 days (if the products are fresh) or two years (if they are frozen). If an outbreak of foodborne illness is traced to the shellfish, health officials must be able to determine the lot number of the offending products so that they can be removed from the channel of distribution.

In some areas, there may be other tags accompanying a fish shipment. For instance, some parts of the country do not allow the importation of fish from other areas unless they carry identifying tags. These tags usually are issued to indicate that the products are acceptable to the local Fish and Game office and the local health district, and that they have not been purchased from unapproved, local sources.

After making quality and quantity checks, check the prices and complete the appropriate accounting documents.

STORING FISH

Fresh fin fish and fresh, shucked shellfish should be maintained at approximately 32°F and at no less than 65 percent relative humidity. These products are best stored on a bed of crushed ice and covered with waxed paper to prevent dehydration. If you cannot use crushed ice, the products should be wrapped tightly in plastic wrap, aluminum foil, or some other suitable container and stored in the coldest part of the refrigerator. The maximum shelf life for these items is about two days.

Live fin fish must be stored in storage tanks specifically designed to hold the particular types of products you buy. Live-in-shell fish can also be stored in these water tanks, though they could be kept in their original containers and covered with damp cloths. As a general rule, these items should not be stored in fresh water or crushed ice. This is especially true for mollusks, because the fresh water can kill them.

Frozen fish should be stored at 0°F. Ideally you would store them at −10 to −15°F because these temperatures are conducive to maximum shelf life (about three months). If the products have the correct amount of glaze on them, they could maintain acceptable culinary quality for up to one year.

Canned or bottled fish products should be kept in a dry storeroom. The ideal temperature of this storeroom would be 50°F, though 70°F is acceptable. The storeroom's relative humidity should not exceed 60 percent.

ISSUING FISH

Most fresh fish goes directly into production. But if fish enters an issue-controlled storage area, you will need to prepare issue documents when it goes to production.

As when you issue most items, again you face the choice: Should you issue the product as is? Or should you issue it as ready to go? For example, oysters could be shucked ahead of time; escargot can be preprepared; or someone might portion the fresh snapper, put it in pie pans, and season it, so that all the broiler cook has to do is pop it into the oven

Try to avoid the temptation of prepreparing the snapper and then storing the portions in a freezer. On the one hand, this practice allows the broiler cook to take the preprepared snapper out of the in-process freezer and put it in the oven. This is convenient; it also mitigates against leftovers, which usually go straight into the garbage can. On the other hand, some of the flavor is lost by freezing fish this way. Besides, if you have fresh fish on your menu, you have to risk some loss; you will also have to price these menu items so as to take into account the probable losses.

Of course, it is absolutely essential to follow proper stock rotation when issuing the product. Also, since these items deteriorate rapidly and are expensive, make sure that the requisitioner does not take more than absolutely necessary. Ask him or her to note the in-process inventory before requisitioning more fish.

IN-PROCESS INVENTORIES

A great deal of risk—spoilage, especially—is associated with fish, particularly fresh fish. And the risk increases dramatically if it is not handled properly at this step. Merely placing fish on the menu probably places you in a higher "risk category."

Try to reduce losses in the in-process inventories; typically there is some loss, particularly if you carry several fresh fish items on the menu.

But two things are paramount: (1) Do not handle the product needlessly, as this spreads bacteria and hastens the deterioration of fish quality. And (2) do not preprep any more fish than you can use during the shift. Conservative prepreparing can cause production problems later on if you get an unexpected rush, but it is necessary if you want to avoid excessive leftovers.

KEY WORDS AND CONCEPTS

AP price

Aquaculture

Cello pack

Chill pack

Crustacean

Exact name

FDA Office Of Seafood Safety

Fin fish

Fish and Game office requirements

Fish "frankfurter"

Flaked and reformed fish products

Glaze

Grading factors

Health district requirements

HACCP system

Ice pack

Ice spots

In-process inventories

Intended use

Interstate Certified Shellfish Shippers List

IQF

Live

Live-in-shell

Loss leader

Lot number

Manufacturing grade

MAP

Marinade pack

Marketing terms for fish products

Mollusk

Move list

National Marine Fisheries Service

New pack time

Packaging procedure

Packers' brands

Packing medium

Point of origin

Popular varieties of fish products

Preservation method

Processed fish

Product form

Product size

Product yield

PUFI seal

Purchasing, receiving, storing, and issuing fish products

Renaming fish

Shatter pack

Shelf life

Shellfish

Shucked fish

Size of container

Slacked out

Standard of identity

Statement of quality

Stockless purchase plan

Substitution possibilities

Surimi   Type of packaging material
Tagged fish   USDA
Trash fish   USDC
Trust the supplier   U.S. grades
Truth-in-menu legislation   Voluntary inspection

QUESTIONS AND PROBLEMS

1. List the U.S. grades for fish.
2. A product specification for frozen, breaded shrimp could include the following information:
    (a) _____
    (b) _____
    (c) _____
    (d) _____
    (e) _____
3. Briefly describe the necessary storage environments for fresh fish products.
4. The delivery agent arrives at 5 P.M. with 20 pounds of fresh whitefish. You ordered 20 pounds of fresh snapper. The supplier was out of snapper and sent whitefish. He tried to call you earlier about it, but could not get through to you. What would you do in this situation? If possible, ask a food-service manager to comment on your answer.
5. Outline the specific procedures you would use for purchasing, receiving, storing, and issuing frozen lobster tails. Assume that the tails will be used in a steak house for a steak and lobster tail entrée. If possible, ask a steak house manager to comment on your answer.
6. What is an appropriate intended use for canned, dark-meat tuna?
7. What does the acronym PUFI stand for?
8. What are the differences between fin fish and shellfish?
9. What are the two main types of shellfish?
10. What is the difference between a fish fillet and a fish portion?
11. KWG enterprises sells a frozen, breaded shrimp, 8 to a pound, for $7.69 per pound. Its fresh, raw shrimp, 14 to a pound, sell for $6.24 per pound. You normally sell about 24 orders of fried shrimp each day. Which product would you buy? Why? If possible, ask a food-service manager to comment on your answer.
12. Why is the point of origin of a fish product an important selection factor?
13. What does the term "14/16 crab legs" indicate to the food-service buyer?
14. What is the primary difference between "round" fish and "drawn" fish?

15. Your supplier calls to tell you that he has just gotten a good buy on frozen ocean perch. You have never used this item before on your menu, but, with the low AP price quoted by your supplier, you are tempted. You have to buy 500 pounds, but this does not seem too troublesome. Assume that you operate a family-style restaurant. What would you do? Why? If possible, ask a family-style restaurant manager to comment on your answer.

16. What critical information is missing from the following product specification for shrimp?

Whole, raw, headless shrimp
Used for shrimp scampi
U.S. Grade A (or equivalent)
Packed in 5-pound laminated cardboard containers

17. List the grading factors for fish products.

18. Under what conditions would you purchase an imitation fish product?

19. What is the purpose of the tagging system that is in effect for shellfish products?

20. When would you purchase a flaked and reformed fish product?

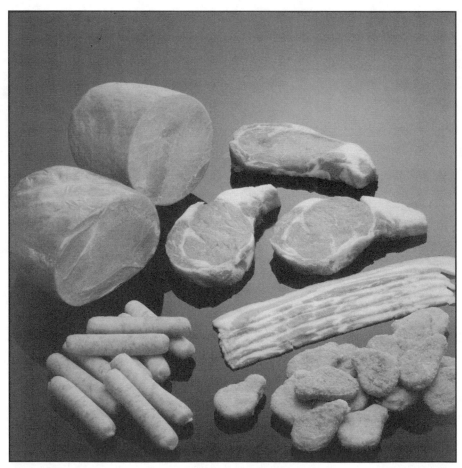

CHAPTER 23

Source: Alliant Foodservice

MEAT

THE PURPOSE OF THIS CHAPTER

This chapter discusses:

- Some management considerations surrounding the selection and procurement of meat
- The selection factors for meat
- Purchasing, receiving, storing, and issuing meat
- The in-process meat inventory

INTRODUCTION

Meat probably represents the major portion of the food-service purchase dollar. And, as you might expect, purchasers have a tendency to be especially careful when making meat-buying decisions. The meat industry and the federal government have made these purchases a little easier by providing many convenient guidelines. But this help has not relieved us entirely. Buying meat can still be a time-consuming experience.

TYPES OF MEAT ITEMS PURCHASED

Most operations purchase some type of beef or pork item in addition to many types of cold cuts and sausages. To a lesser extent, some operations use lamb, veal, perhaps some preprepared meat entrées such as beef stew, and other less familiar products. Figure 23.1 notes some of the more popular types of meat products used by the food-service industry.

MANAGEMENT CONSIDERATIONS

As a rule, operations lack no supervision in the purchasing, receiving, storing, and issuing of meat. Nor is there any lack in the supervision of its

BEEF	LAMB
Brisket	Breast
Bottom sirloin butt	Hotel rack
Butt steak	Leg
Chicken fried steak	Loin
Chuck	Loin chop
Cubed steak	Rib chop
Eye of round	Shoulder
Ground beef	
Inside round	**PORK**
Outside round	Back rib
Porterhouse steak	Boston butt
Rib	Center-cut chop
Ribeye roll	Cutlet
Ribeye steak	Fresh ham
Short loin	Ground pork
Skirt steak	Loin
Strip loin steak	Loin chop
T-bone steak	Rib chop
Tenderloin	Spare rib
Tenderloin steak	Tenderloin
Top sirloin butt	
Top sirloin steak	**VARIETY MEAT**
	Calf liver
CURED MEAT AND SAUSAGE	Steer liver
Bacon	Sweetbread
Bologna	
Bratwurst	**VEAL**
Breakfast sausage	Breast
Corned beef	Cubed steak
Frankfurter	Cutlet
Ham	Hotel rack
Italian sausage	Ground veal
Knockwurst	Leg
Luncheon meat	Loin chop
Pepperoni	Rib chop
Polish sausage	Shank
Salami	Tenderloin

FIGURE 23.1. Popular types of meat products used by the food-service industry.

use in production. But deciding on the quality you want and the cuts you prefer is not easy. Moreover, you also must seek out suppliers who can provide what you want on a continuous basis. And, except for standard types of meat items, this is no simple task either, as those who are responsible for the ordering, expediting, and receiving of meat products will attest.

Some of the major managerial meat-purchasing decisions are discussed in the following paragraphs.

SHOULD YOU OFFER MEAT ON THE MENU?

Or should you minimize the amount of meat items that you offer? Realistically, most of us need some meat entrées on the menu, though some operations, such as vegetarian restaurants, can do without them. The question usually is, how tied do we want to be to meat? How much of our image do we want to be associated with it?

In many cases, meat on the menu is the "signature item." If you are tied to this concept, your image is difficult to alter. You must stay with your specialty regardless of AP price increases and availability.

Sometimes meat items make their way onto the menu in very discreet ways: as leftovers from last night, which might become the luncheon chef's special; as the trimmings from a large piece of meat recast as meat loaf or beef stew; and those added to the menu based on customer request. What we intended to serve once sometimes blossoms into an unwieldy number of meat-related menu items, usually because we want to use every scrap and ounce of leftovers. We may not mind throwing out the scraps from other food, but this is not usually the case with meat because of its high cost.

SUBSTITUTION POSSIBILITIES

We can substitute fish or poultry for meat. We can experiment with different grades of meat. (For instance, if we use a moist cooking method, we can get by with a lower meat grade from an older, tougher, but more flavorful animal. Or we could purchase lower grades and tenderize them artificially.) We could use some artificial products, such as soybean extender in hamburger meat and meat loaf. We could take a chance on more exotic types of meat dishes, such as buffalo, the hybrid "beefalo," or venison.

The list of meat substitution possibilities is virtually endless. But some of these substitutions are visible to the consumer, such as a low-quality steak that has been mechanically or chemically tenderized for a naturally tender steak of higher quality. Meat recipes that contain several ingredients make good candidates for some lower-cost substitution. Meat loaves, stews, and casseroles can be manipulated by including or excluding certain fats, meat qualities, and fillers.

You always take a chance when you substitute, especially if your customers are accustomed to one item and suddenly taste another product they detect as completely unfamiliar.

THE QUALITY DESIRED

We can take a lot of time in determining the quality of the product we want. But you cannot always get the meat you want as readily as you might think.

As always, the quality you need reflects the intended use of the product and the image you wish to project. But since a lot of meat comes fresh, you tend to have quality variations, just as you have with fresh produce. Most raisers of meat animals have standardized the care and feeding of animals to minimize quality variations. Also, meat that is processed, especially pork that is cured for ham and bacon, offers a great deal of predictability. But we do buy a lot of fresh meat; consequently, what we want may not always be available.

Shortages of certain meat items thwart our plans in other ways as well. For instance, we cannot always get the meat of highest quality because it is usually in short supply. This forces a purchaser to rethink his or her strategy. On the other hand, we cannot always get the low-quality products we might want either.

Because of the problems associated with finding consistent quality and a continuous supply of meat, one does not see a great deal of shifting from one supplier to the next. As we show later, there is a limited amount of bid buying, and the bids that are made and accepted often cover a long period. There is a tendency to stay with one supplier, perhaps badgering him or her on occasion to meet a competitor's proposed deal.

TYPE OF PROCESSING

Frozen meat is not always popular with hospitality operators, although a lot of places must use frozen meat—hamburger patties, for example—to operate efficiently. Also, if you buy in large quantities, you might need to buy it frozen. You probably sacrifice some taste with a frozen product, although proper freezing, thawing, and cooking methods can make the difference almost imperceptible. The taste of frozen versus fresh meat has become mostly a matter of opinion. Indeed, with modern freezing technology, freezing does not really harm the product, and you can even cook most items successfully directly from the frozen state. Quality problems with frozen foods usually are caused by inadequate handling, not by freezing.

Some meat items are processed; most of us would not have it any other way. Bacon, ham, and bologna are rarely made in-house from scratch. We also tend to purchase fresh meat items that have already been to some extent butchered. One can buy a beef "side" (fully half the animal) or a preportioned sirloin steak, and just about any variation in between.

You will, of course, have to decide what type and amount of processing is most economical for you. But the prospects grow particularly interesting when you begin to consider portion-cut meat, that is, meat that needs nothing more than some cooking or heating. One finds quite a spread between the AP price per pound for ready-to-cook sirloin steak and the AP price per pound for the whole loin, which is a "wholesale cut" of beef from which some sirloin steaks are cut. Likewise, one finds an even greater AP price per pound spread between a portion-cut steak and the side of beef.

As we have noted earlier, it is usually more economical to let suppliers wield the cutting tools, as long as they are interested in doing so. Some hospitality operations can provide this economic value cheaper than can a middleman. These companies also hope to increase quality control of meat products by performing a great deal of fabrication in-house. But over the years, more and more hospitality operations have moved toward purchasing prefabricated meat products. Many restaurants, for instance, concentrate on devoting as much space as possible to the revenue-generating dining room and lounge. For them it is too expensive to utilize a great deal of space for a butcher shop.

It is generally thought that in-house meat fabrication presents four major problems:

1. It requires more labor hours and increased labor skill. These commodities are expensive. Furthermore, they tend to be in short supply.
2. This practice tends to increase the level of pilferage.
3. Avoidable waste also tends to increase whenever you engage in major production efforts.
4. Your sanitation needs increase substantially. Meat production creates a considerable amount of "working" dirt and waste products which must be removed constantly to avoid meat contamination. The typical restaurant kitchen does not have the equipment, time, and skill needed to perform these duties adequately.

On the other hand, there are some disadvantages to purchasing portion-cut meats. For instance: (1) They are usually the same weight, but you may have to pay more if you want the same shape and thickness. This uniformity might be very useful to relatively inexperienced cooks. (2) Smaller cuts of meat may be easier to steal. (3) Sometimes a case of precut steaks contains one or two steaks of demonstrably lower quality. Can you catch this problem in time? Can the cook notice the difference in time?

Convenience entrées, such products as frozen fajitas, baked and sliced meat loaf, and stuffed peppers, are not very popular with many hospitality operations. But college, hospital, and other institutional food services use these products readily. Some other hospitality operations occasionally use them as backup reserve, for large banquets, or for employee meals.

REDUCING THE AP PRICE AND THE EP COST

Meat purchasers can find all sorts of ways to reduce the AP price while keeping the EP cost, profit margins, and dollar profits acceptable.

Some opt for substitutions, such as using fish for steak, offering casseroles instead of sandwich steaks, and widening the menu to include lower-cost products. (This latter tactic reduces AP prices but also menu prices. Your cost of food as a percentage of menu sales prices might fall, but your dollar sales volume might also decline and cut into the number of dollars you have left to cover labor, overhead, and profits.)

You can also substitute meat of lower quality and tenderize it. You can buy some of the formed meat products: cheaper meat that has been "flaked," then re-formed and sliced to resemble a steak. Or you can add soybean extenders as long as you follow the legal requirements. (For example, soybean-extended ground beef cannot be called hamburger.)

Another way of reducing the AP price and the EP cost is to shrink portion sizes. Or, instead of including the baked potato with the steak, charge customers a little extra for it. (This reduces the EP cost of the steak dinner, not the EP cost of the steak itself.) Or, instead of including tossed salad with the dinner menu price, substitute cole slaw. These substitution strategies, tried from time to time, always carry a certain amount of risk.

A way to protect the AP price and EP cost, if only for a while, is to enter into some sort of long-term contract. By permitting you to retain your standards of quality, this arrangement can considerably reduce the risk of blurring your image and annoying your customers that accompanies the other cost-cutting strategies we just noted.

You may make a saving if you contract for perhaps a six-month supply of beef. Of course, you have to have a lot of money to buy the huge quantities that are necessary to interest a supplier. Consequently, only large chains regularly follow this method.

Not everyone, though, thinks you can save money this way. For instance, the daily cash price for meat may drop considerably tomorrow. However, you would at least have the item available.

The hedging procedure (see Chapter 9) may be a viable way of maintaining a relatively stable AP price. Large food-service companies that have the money and skill needed to practice this procedure might save money in the long run.

As a practical matter, the smaller operator might have to make do on a day-to-day basis. If he or she tries to spend too much time concentrating on the AP price, the EP cost might be neglected. It may be better for the small operator to concentrate on the EP cost, and especially concentrate on ways of reducing it that represent little or no risk—for instance, he or she should ensure that there is minimal waste in production and service, minimal shrinkage, zero pilferage, and so forth.

Every once in a while a purchaser might find a bargain. Unfortunately, most bargains come from new suppliers in the form of temporary introductory offers. Or bargains may force a purchaser to buy a new convenience entrée at a special AP price or to take fresh frozen meat in lieu of fresh refrigerated.

Normal quantity buy opportunities do appear. But, aside form products on a move list, fewer meat bargains are available than one finds in other product areas. Nor do you find buyers shifting suppliers or meat specifications too quickly. Meat is a major purchase. Hence, discretion is more widely practiced among meat buyers.

SELECTION FACTORS

As with all products, management decides on the quality and style of meat desired. Then, either alone or in cooperation with other personnel, management evaluates several of the following selection factors when determining standards of quality desired and suppliers.

INTENDED USE

As always, you want to determine exactly the intended use of the item so that you will be able to prepare the appropriate, relevant specification. For instance, bacon used on the breakfast menu will be cut differently from bacon that will be cooked and crumbled and used as a salad topping.

EXACT NAME

As with all products, it is very important to note the exact name of the item you want lest you receive something that will not suit your needs. To some extent, identifying the exact product that you prefer is a bit easier in this channel of distribution than it is in some of the other product lines. There has evolved over the years a great deal of standardization, which has been spurred by the meat industry, meat users, and the USDA.

For instance, the federal government has set several standards of identity for meat products. If you specify that you want hamburger, you will get a mixture that is 70 percent lean meat and 30 percent fat. Of course, as with all standards of identity, the producer is free to improve upon the government definition. In this example, the producer can use beef from just about any part of the animal; if you expect to receive a specific type of meat in your hamburger, you must include this information on your specification.

Using standards of identity, therefore, is a bit risky unless you further illustrate on your specification additional appropriate information. You will be able to reduce the additional amount of information considerably

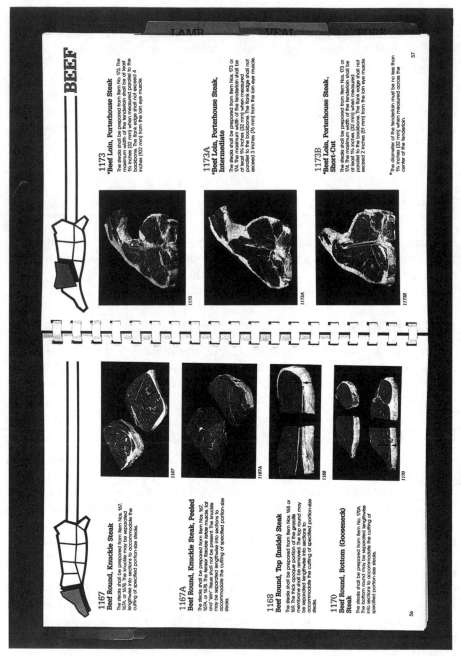

FIGURE 23.2. IMPS numbers for some meat products. (Reprinted from *The Meat Buyers Guide*. Author and publisher: The National Association of Meat Purveyors, 8365-B Greensboro Drive, McLean, VA 22102–3585. First printing, August 1988. Copyright 1988. All rights reserved.)

if you utilize in your specification the IMPS numbering system for meat items. The acronym IMPS stands for Institutional Meat Purchase Specifications. These numbers take the place of part of a meat specification. For instance, if you order a 1112 ribeye steak, you get a particular style and trim.

The IMPS numbers evolved from a cooperative effort by the National Association of Meat Purveyors (NAMP), the National Live Stock and Meat Board, food-service purchasing agents, and the USDA's Agricultural Marketing Service Livestock division. These numbers are included in *The Meat Buyers Guide,* published by the NAMP. In addition to the numbers, there is a description and picture of each item. This is very desirable to buyers who can then "order by the numbers" and be assured of receiving the exact cut of meat they want.

The IMPS numbers, sometimes referred to as the IMPS/NAMP numbers, or the MBG (*Meat Buyers Guide*) numbers, provide a considerable degree of convenience. The typical buyer would never think of preparing meat product specifications without first consulting this major reference book.

The IMPS numbers are indexed from the 100 series to the 1400 series. The first digit of the number refers to the type of product; the remaining digits indicate a specific cut and trim. Figure 23.2 notes the IMPS numbers for some meat cuts. And Figure 23.3 notes *The Meat Buyers Guide* Table of Contents.

Series 100	Beef, standardized cuts*
Series 200	Lamb, standardized cuts
Series 300	Veal, standardized cuts
Series 400	Pork, standardized cuts
Series 500	Cured, cured and smoked, and fully cooked pork products
Series 600	Cured, dried, cooked, and smoked beef products
Series 700	Edible by-products**
Series 800	Sausage products
Series 1000	Beef, portion cuts***
Series 1200	Lamb, portion cuts
Series 1300	Veal, portion cuts
Series 1400	Pork, portion cuts

* Standardized cuts are sometimes referred to as "wholesale cuts."
** Edible by-products are sometimes referred to as "variety meats."
*** Portion cuts are sometimes referred to as "retail cuts."

FIGURE 23.3. *The Meat Buyers Guide* Table of Contents. (Reprinted from *The Meat Buyers Guide.* Author and publisher: The National Association of Meat Purveyors, 8365-B Greensboro Drive, McLean, VA 22102–3585. First printing, August 1988. Copyright 1988. All rights reserved.)

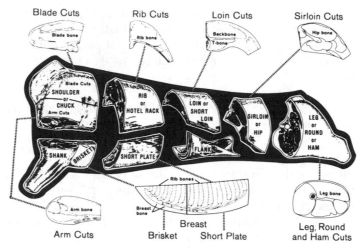

FIGURE 23.4. Basic cuts of meat. (Courtesy National Live Stock and Meat Board.)

If for some reason you do not wish to use the IMPS numbers when preparing specifications, you must at least be able to indicate the exact cut of meat you want or the exact type of processed item you need. Fresh meat comes in four basic cuts: (1) the whole carcass; (2) a side, essentially half a carcass; (3) a wholesale, or primal, cut; and (4) a retail cut. Figure 23.4 shows the basic cuts of meat. There are numerous other cutting terms, such as hotel-sliced bacon, Spencer-cut prime rib of beef, and square-cut chuck. It is the buyer's responsibility to become familiar with these cuts and related terminology, especially if he or she decides to forgo the use of IMPS numbers.

In addition to cuts of meat, you need to know about other terms used in the trade. Two major ones are "variety meats," such organs as liver, tongue, and heart, and "sausages," the preserved, usually dried or salted, chunked or chopped meat and spices shaped into tubes. Some sausages have skins; some do not. Some are cooked; some are not.

Sometimes the federal government undertakes either to add more terminology or to include definitions of the terms it uses in its grading practices and in its list of grading standards. It would be wise to stay abreast of these changes if you purchase a great deal of meat.

If you purchase a great deal of processed products, you must be concerned with the exact name as well as the specific form and culinary quality of the items. Again, there are standards of identity for many things. For instance, there is a minimum formula for preprepared beef stew. Generally, though, these identity formulas are not very useful as a major selection factor for processed meat products.

U.S. GOVERNMENT GRADES (OR EQUIVALENT)

Inspection of meat for wholesomeness has been mandatory since passage of the Federal Meat Inspection Act in 1907. The law applies to all raw meat sold in interstate commerce as well as to processed products such as sausages, frozen dinners, canned meats, and soups made with meat.

Some states conduct their own meat inspection programs, and the 1967 Wholesome Meat Act requires these programs to be at least equal to the federal inspection programs. Meat inspected under a state program, however, can be sold only within that state. Any meat carcass or processed product transported across state lines or exported to another country must be inspected by the Food Safety and Quality Service (FSQS) of the USDA. In states not conducting inspection programs, all meat plants are required to be federally inspected.

The inspection program begins with approval of plans for a slaughtering or processing plant to ensure that the facilities, equipment, and procedures are adequate to provide for safe and sanitary operations. Facilities and equipment in plants must be easy to clean and to keep clean. The floor plan, water supply, waste disposal methods, and lighting must be approved for each plant facility. Each day before operations begin, the inspector checks the plant and continues the inspection throughout the day to ensure that sanitary conditions are maintained. If at any time the equipment is not properly cleaned or an unsanitary condition is discovered, slaughtering or processing operations are stopped until corrective steps have been taken.

Inspection of animals is done both before and after slaughtering. Before slaughter, all livestock are examined by USDA inspectors for signs of disease, and any animal appearing sick undergoes a special examination. No already dead or dying animal is allowed in the slaughtering plant.

After slaughter, each carcass and its internal organs are examined for signs of disease or contamination that would make all or part of the carcass unfit as human food. (See Figure 23.5.) To ensure uniformity in the inspection process, veterinary supervisors regularly monitor the procedures and work of the inspectors.

Rabbit meat is not required to be federally inspected. The rabbit industry has a voluntary program that requires rabbit meat packers to pay for inspection.

Meat that passes the rigorous USDA inspection is marked with a federal inspection stamp. (See Figure 23.6.) This stamp notes the number of the meat processing plant where the meat was slaughtered and packed. The stamp does not appear on all meat cuts. Usually it is visible only on the wholesale cuts of meat. Some retail cuts, though, may include remnants of an inspection stamp unless it is completely removed during the cutting and trimming process.

FIGURE 23.5. Federal inspector checking a beef carcass.

The inspection program provided by the USDA is the most trusted inspection program available. The program used by the military to inspect its meat products before use in troop feeding is equal to the USDA's procedures. There are several types of inspection programs, though, that are not the same as USDA inspection for wholesomeness. For instance, religious inspections are performed in some meat plants. These inspections certify only that the meat items satisfy the religious codes, not that they have met a certain standard of quality.

In addition to its meat inspections, the federal government also prepares guidelines on such topics as humane slaughter techniques, animal husbandry, and transportation techniques.

After the meat has been inspected and passed, it may be graded for

FIGURE 23.6. Federal inspection stamps used for meat products. The number appearing in the stamp identifies the meat plant where the meat was processed and inspected.

quality under the FSQS's voluntary quality grading program. Quality grades exist for beef, lamb, pork, and veal. There also is a voluntary yield-grading system available for beef and lamb. While there is no formal yield-grading system for pork, these items' quality grades are based primarily on yield; other culinary characteristics play a lesser role. Veal is not graded for yield.

The grading programs are conducted under the authority of the Agricultural Marketing Act. The grades are published by the Agricultural Marketing Service (AMS) Live Stock & Feed Division. The standards provide an objective evaluation of the culinary quality and edible yield of fresh meat items. (See Figure 23.7.)

Meat packers and other meat middlemen, not necessarily the packer, can purchase the USDA's meat grading services. Voluntary grading, which has been offered since 1927, must be paid for by the meat packer or whoever requests it.

It is quite common for buyers to use government grades as one selection factor when they purchase meat. This procedure is popular with many manufacturers, middlemen, and retailers, but not all. Some cattle breeders and meat packers feel that grading is too capricious and inconsistent. And some persons are not happy with the changes and proposed changes (usually done for health and nutrition concerns) in the grading systems that have occurred over the years. Nevertheless, approximately 50 percent of the meat sold in this country is graded for quality.

All in all, several problems have been associated with federal grades.

FIGURE 23.7. Federal grade stamps used for meat items.

But this has not deterred buyers from using them. They may not rely so heavily on the grades as they once did, but most meat specifications contain some reference to a U.S. grade.

Beef quality grades are based on several grading factors. The primary grading factor is the amount of "marbling" present in the flesh. (Marbling refers to the little streams of fat that run through the meat.) Other grading factors evaluated by the federal grader include the age of the animal at time of slaughter; sex of the animal; color of the flesh; firmness and texture of the flesh and fat; shape and form of the carcass; and amount of defects and blemishes.

U.S. quality grades for beef also are subject to several limiting rules. Some are strictly defined by the USDA, while others grant some discretion to the federal grader. The most severe limiting rule, and the one that normally causes a great deal of anxiety among meat producers, is the one associated with the beef animal's "maturity class." These animals are divided into five maturity classes:

Class A—Age at time of slaughter is 9 to 30 months.

Class B—Age at time of slaughter is 30 to 42 months.

Classes C, D, E—Age at time of slaughter is greater than 42 months.

It is the grader's responsibility to determine the animal's physiological age at the time of slaughter. He or she does this by examining the color and texture of the lean meat, the condition of the bones, and the amount of hardening (i.e., ossification) of the cartilage.

Beef animals' quality grades are affected by their maturity class. For instance, regardless of the quality present in Class C cattle, it cannot be graded prime. In general, any beef animal greater than 42 months of age at time of slaughter cannot receive the highest quality grade regardless of its score received on the other factors considered by the grader. Figure 23.8 shows this relationship.

The federal quality grades for beef are:

1. Prime—Best product available. Tender and very juicy. Contains 8 to 10 percent fat. Usually the animal has been grain fed for at least 180 days in order to develop the exceptionally large amount of firm, white fat. Extremely flavorful.

2. Choice—Contains at least 5 percent fat. There are three levels: high, medium, and low. High Choice is similar to Prime, though the animal has been grain fed for only about 150 days. Medium Choice indicates that the animal has been grain fed about 120 days. And Low Choice results when the animal has been grain fed about 90 days. Food-service operators normally purchase High and Medium Choice; Low Choice is typically sold through supermarkets and grocery stores.

3. Select—A very lean product. It contains 4 percent fat. Sometimes referred to as "grass-fed" beef. The fat on this product is usually not very white, nor is it very firm. This grade is becoming very popular in supermarkets. It is a low-cost item and is more healthful than the higher-quality grades. However, it lacks flavor.

4. Standard—Similar to Select. It lacks even more in juiciness and tenderness. It has a very mild flavor. This product also tends to be referred to as "grass-fed" beef.

5. Commercial—Beef from older cattle. It is especially lacking in tenderness. Usually dairy cows receive this quality grade. Because of its age at time of slaughter, some of this meat may be quite flavorful.

6. Utility, Cutter, and Canner—Quality grades assigned to very old cattle. Old breeding stock usually is classified into one of these three quality grade categories. Generally, these products are not available as fresh meat. Rather, these manufacturing grades are intended for use by commercial food processors.

Lamb quality grades are based primarily on the color, texture, and firmness of the flesh; quality and firmness of the "finish" (i.e., the fat cover on the carcass); the proportion of meat to bone; and the amount and quality of the "feathering" (i.e., the fat streaking in the ribs and the fat streaking in the inside flank muscles).

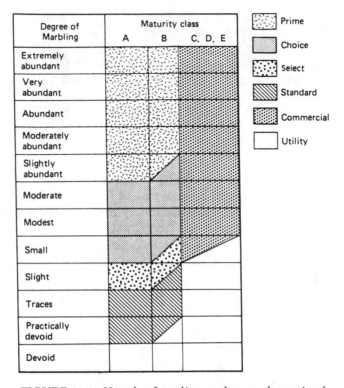

FIGURE 23.8. How beef quality grades are determined.

The federal quality grades for lamb are:

1. Prime
2. Choice
3. Good
4. Utility

If a food-service operation offers fresh lamb on the menu, the Prime and Choice quality grades are normally used. The lower-graded products are not intended for use as fresh meat items. As is typically the case in our industry, these manufacturing grades are used primarily by commercial food processors to prepare convenience food items.

Pork quality grades are based almost exclusively on yield. The most important consideration is the amount of finish. Pork quality, though, also is related to the color, firmness, and texture of the finish and the feathering. Grain-fed pork animals will produce better-quality products, far superior to those produced by animals fed other types of feeds.

The federal quality grades for pork are:

1. No. 1
2. No. 2
3. No. 3
4. No. 4
5. Utility

Most pork is used by commercial food processors to fabricate a variety of convenience items, such as ham and bacon. Because of this, and the fact that most pork is separated into smaller cuts before it leaves the meat-packing plant, very few pork carcasses are graded for quality. Meat packers and purchasing agents rely on the various packers' brands (i.e., packers' "grades") available.

If fresh pork is used on the menu, the typical food-service operation necessarily must use the No. 1 or No. 2 quality grade, or equivalent packers' brands. The lower-quality items will shrink too much during the cooking process, thereby resulting in an unacceptable finished menu item.

Veal quality grades are based on the color, texture, and firmness of the flesh; the proportion of meat to bone; quality and firmness of the finish; and the amount and quality of the feathering. High-quality veal will have a pink color and smooth flesh.

The federal quality grades for veal are:

1. Prime
2. Choice
3. Good
4. Standard
5. Utility
6. Cull

The Prime and Choice quality grades are intended for use as fresh products. The lower-quality products tend to be tough and, therefore, are more commonly used to fabricate convenience items.

PRODUCT YIELD

The federal government provides a voluntary yield-grading service for beef and lamb. There is no formal yield-grading system available for pork and veal. However, recall that the U.S. quality grades for pork are based primarily on yield. The pork grades are sometimes referred to as "yield standards." The U.S. No. 1 pork grade represents the leanest, meatiest

FIGURE 23.9. Federal yield grade stamp used to indicate yield of a carcass.

product, whereas U.S. No. 4 product has about twice as much fat and one-third less meat.

Yield grades are based on the (1) amount of external fat; (2) size of the ribeye muscle; (3) quantity of kidney, pelvic, and heart fat; and (4) carcass weight.

Yield grades range from 1 to 5, 1 indicating greatest yield, 5 the least. Some limiting rules apply. For instance, a USDA Prime beef cannot earn a 1 or 2 yield grade, as Prime beef has a great deal of fat (hence, flavor), which reduces considerably its usable lean. USDA Choice beef cannot earn a 1 yield. To a certain extent then, quality and yield grades affect one another.

Buyers who purchase large cuts of beef, such as beef sides, quarters, or wholesale cuts, often specify a desired yield grade. In some instances, they are unable to specify an exact yield grade; instead, they are able to denote only a yield range. For instance, a buyer may purchase a USDA Commercial beef brisket, with a U.S. yield grade of 1–2 (or its equivalent). (See Figures 23.9 and 23.10.)

If a buyer purchases only retail cuts, he or she still could use the federal government yield-grading standards. For example, a buyer could insist that a sirloin strip steak be cut from a beef carcass that carries U.S. yield grade No. 1 (or its equivalent).

If you use the IMPS system and/or the USDA yield grades, you can be assured of standardized edible yields for the fresh products you purchase. If you do not utilize these procedures, you will need to indicate on your specification the minimum yield, or the maximum trim, you will accept.

PACKERS' BRANDS (OR EQUIVALENT)

Some fresh meat producers do not agree with the need for quality grading and have assigned their own brands to their fresh meat, sometimes re-

FIGURE 23.10. Federal inspectors checking the quality and yield of beef carcasses.

ferred to as packers' grades. Packers' grades, although similar to the federal grades, may not reflect an objective viewpoint.

Many meat producers have developed packers' grades. For instance, Armour sells "Star Deluxe," "Star," "Quality," and "Banquet." Several other companies have similar packers' branding systems in place. A significant number of food-service buyers find this procedure quite acceptable.

A few meat producers sell organic products. If their animals are raised on organically grown grass and feed, the package labels can note "certified organic food" or some similar notation. Furthermore, if the producers' organic production methods are certified by the USDA, they can note this on the package labels and include it in their brand names.

Any type of processed meat, other than fresh frozen or portion cut, is often purchased on the strength of a brand name. Most pork products, particularly those that are cured, are purchased this way. In almost every instance, these brand names are the only indication of quality. We have seen few specifications for cold cuts, for example, that did not rely on a brand name or its equivalent. (It is possible to detail the material used in these items. For a product like breakfast sausage it would be easy to specify the amount of pork, fat, seasonings, water, and type of grind. For most other types of products in this area, though, it would not be this easy.)

Packers' brands are sometimes used when purchasing portion-cut meats, though not usually so often as in purchasing other processed items. First, although portion-cut items have a standardized weight, not all packers necessarily supply the same shape. Second, the packaging can differ drastically; steaks may be individually wrapped and neatly stacked, or tossed together in a box. Third, although all the items are of equal weight, some may be sloppily cut, with excess nicks and tears.

There are other forms of brand name identification that exist in the meat channel of distribution. For instance, there are the SYSCO brand Supreme Angus Beef products that include only young beef of predominantly Angus breed that fall within the upper two-thirds of the USDA Choice grade. There is also the popular Certified Angus Beef Program. If a meat packer's products meet the quality standards mandated by this program, they are allowed to carry the certification seal. The program, developed by the American Angus Association, stipulates that a beef product must have at least modest marbling, be in the youngest maturity class, and qualify for U.S. yield grade 1, 2, or 3.

PRODUCT SIZE

Invariably you must indicate the size of the particular piece of meat you order. This task is made easy due to the fact that *The Meat Buyers Guide* notes weight ranges for wholesale cuts of meat, as well as standardized portion sizes for retail cuts. For instance, all large cuts are categorized into

four weight ranges: A, B, C, and D. The smaller retail cuts can be purchased in several sizes. The IMPS regulations stipulate that portion cuts
specified between 6 to 11 ounces must be accurate within ½ ounce; those
specified between 12 to 17 ounces must be accurate within ¾ of an ounce;
and those specified 18 ounces must be accurate within 1 ounce.

If you purchase processed convenience items, such as frozen, pre-
prepared stuffed peppers, a size indication may also be required. Usually
a particular packer's brand carries only one size, so if you consistently
specify the same brand on your specification, you will not need to specify
product size information.

SIZE OF CONTAINER

Container sizes are standardized in the meat channel of distribution. Processed products come in package sizes that normally range from about 5
pounds to over 50 pounds. For instance, frozen, prepranked beef stew
may be packed in a 5-pound Cryovac bag, packed six bags to a case. The
stew also may be packed in a 5-pound oven-ready, foil tray (sometimes
referred to as a "steam-table" pack), packed six trays to a case.

Fresh, portion-cut meat products, usually are packed in 10-pound
cases. Some, such as ground beef, normally come in 5-pound and 10-
pound Cryovac bags. Fresh, wholesale cuts of meat normally are packed
in a container that is big enough to accommodate them. For instance, if
you order beef rib, IMPS number 109, weight range C (18 to 22 pounds
each), they will usually be packed three to a case. In this instance, you
would not specify the size of the container if an accurate size could not be
determined. Or you might be able to specify a "catch weight" (approximate weight) of 60 pounds per case.

If you purchase canned or bottled merchandise, the appropriate can
number, or volume designation, must be specified. For instance, canned
chili can be purchased in a No. 10 can. And beef jerky often is packed in a
one-gallon jar.

TYPE OF PACKAGING MATERIAL

The typical packaging materials used in the industry are moisture-proof,
vapor-proof materials. Cryovac plastic, or its equivalent, is especially
popular because it is ideal when a meat packer wants to "shrink wrap" the
product (i.e., pack the meat in plastic and pull a vacuum through it so that
air is removed and the wrapping collapses to fit snugly around the product).

Packaging quality has a significant effect on the meat product's AP
price. Most suppliers adhere to the standardized materials. However, a
supplier who seeks to undercut his or her competitor could easily do so
by using inferior packaging materials. This is false economy because the

buyer must be concerned with protecting meat properly, especially if it is or will be frozen.

PACKAGING PROCEDURE

Large cuts of meat are necessarily slab packed in containers that are big enough to hold them. Portion cuts are usually layered; if you prefer, the packer will wrap each portion cut individually and then layer them in the case. Not every supplier will do this because it adds to his or her costs of doing business. However, most will accommodate your needs if you are willing to pay them for these services.

It is not unusual to have a wide choice of packaging procedures for a meat item. For instance, bacon comes in a "shingle pack" (i.e., the way you normally find it in the supermarket), "layout pack" (i.e., several bacon strips are placed on oven paper; the cook can conveniently place a layer of this bacon on a sheet pan and pop it into the oven), or "bulk pack" (i.e., produced by a type of slab-packing procedure).

The packaging procedure for meat items parallels those used in the poultry and fish channels of distribution. While the ice-pack method is, to our knowledge, nonexistent for meat products, all other procedures are available from at least one supplier.

PRODUCT FORM

Once again we note the usefulness of *The Meat Buyers Guide*. If you use the IMPS numbers when specifying meat cuts, the meat will be cut and trimmed according to the standards that exist for those items.

If you are purchasing processed items, you can rely to some extent on *The Meat Buyers Guide* because it does contain IMPS numbers for several convenience items. However, there are many more items available in the meat channel of distribution that are not noted in this reference book. You must be very careful to indicate the exact product desired; usually the best way to ensure that you obtain a suitable convenience product is to rely on a packer's brand name.

PRESERVATION METHOD

Most meat products purchased by food-service buyers are preserved in one of two ways: refrigerated or frozen. Canned and bottled merchandise are also available. For instance, you could purchase canned soups and canned chili products; however, many operators tend to favor the frozen varieties.

Meat is also preserved by curing it and/or smoking it. Curing is accomplished when the meat is subjected to a combination of salt, sugar, sodium nitrite, and other ingredients. Smoking preserves the meat and, in most instances, cooks it as well. Many cured items are also smoked.

We purchase a good deal of cured and/or smoked products. We are primarily concerned with the unique flavor, texture, and aroma created by these preservation methods. Usually these products are refrigerated when delivered to the hospitality operation, though many of them could be frozen. For instance, bacon, which is a cured and smoked product, may be refrigerated or frozen.

There has been a great deal of controversy in our industry concerning the use of nitrites. Sodium nitrite combines with certain amino acids to form nitrosamine, a carcinogenic substance. Nitrites continue to be used, though in lesser amounts than before, because of their superior preservation qualities and also because they can control the growth of *Clostridium botulinum,* the deadly bacterium that causes botulism food poisoning. Nitrites also are responsible for the characteristic color and flavor of cured meat products.

If an operator uses cured and/or smoked products, he or she must ensure consistent culinary quality by specifying very clearly the types of products desired. Usually the only way to obtain consistency is to specify a particular packer's brand. The many combinations of curing and/or smoking procedures that can be used almost forces the buyer to select one desired packer's brand for each item purchased. Product substitutions are inadvisable because customers would notice them very quickly.

TENDERIZATION PROCEDURE

If you buy meat to be used for steaks and chops—meat that will be broiled or fried—it has to have a certain degree of tenderness. Meats of higher quality come with a good measure of natural tenderness. In other cases, though, it may be necessary for someone in the channel of distribution to introduce a bit of "artificial" tenderization. And, usually, a primary source or a middleman contributes this effort.

The natural tenderization process is referred to as "aging" the meat. Beef and lamb can be aged. Pork and veal usually are not. There is dry aging, in which the meat is held for about 14 days in carefully controlled temperature and humidity. Dry aging tenderizes the meat and also adds flavor. A very old animal would be flavorful, but no amount of aging would tenderize it. Hence, young meat that is aged a little really goes through a rushed maturation process. A couple weeks of dry aging might produce as much flavor as an extra year of life.

Not all meat qualifies for the dry-aging procedure. Only the higher-quality grades can be dry aged successfully. For instance, only USDA Prime beef and USDA Choice beef (high Choice and medium Choice—not low Choice) are good candidates for dry aging.

Dry aging is, however, expensive. Since the meat loses moisture, it weighs less after aging, which forces up its AP price. Also, dry aging forces extra investment in facilities and inventories, which in turn forces up the AP price even more.

In the late 1970s, the FDA approved a new aging process for beef. It involves spraying meat with a mold. (Mold naturally forms during dry aging; the new process just hurries it up.) It is claimed that this new process accomplishes in 48 hours what it used to take 2 weeks or more to accomplish under the conventional dry-aging method.

You should never assume that the meat you purchase has been dry aged. This expensive procedure must be requested, and you must be prepared to pay for it.

Another type of aging done in the trade is called "Cryovac aging." This method involves wrapping the meat cuts in heavy plastic vacuum packs, sealing it tightly, and keeping it refrigerated for about 10 days to 2 weeks. The wrapped meat can be in transit, aging itself while it is trucked to your back door. This process is less expensive than dry aging and causes no weight loss. Unfortunately, Cryovac aging causes very little flavor development. If you do not specify a tenderization procedure, you can expect that the fresh meat you purchase will undergo this Cryovac aging process. This is the most common form of aging available.

Aging usually provides a good meat product. Its biggest disadvantage is that the meat cooks to the well-done state too quickly. Also, the Cryovac-aged meat seems to be much drier than dry-aged meat if it is cooked past the medium state.

Some people are under the impression that they can purchase unaged meat (sometimes referred to as "green" meat) and successfully age the product themselves in the refrigerator or freezer. Certainly the temptation exists for purchasing green meat, because the AP price would be significantly lower than the one for a properly aged product. Unfortunately, meat will not age in the typical refrigerator. It also will not age if it is frozen, or once it is cooked. It will age properly only if its storage environment has the required temperature and humidity.

If you are going to roast large wholesale cuts, you can do a bit of aging yourself. By cooking these items in a slow oven, say, at between 200 and 225°F, you actually simulate aging. You do not add much flavor, but at these temperatures the meat tenderizes somewhat while it cooks.

Another type of tenderization procedure that can be used on beef animals is a process called beef electrification. This was introduced in 1978. It consists of subjecting a beef carcass to three 15-minute 600-volt electric shocks. This process allows meat to be aged for only about two-thirds of the normal aging procedure. In addition, the electrification process not only reduces the aging time but increases tenderization by about 50 percent.

Two other types of tenderization methods are in use, "chemical" and "mechanical." Chemical tenderizing occurs when an enzyme is added to the meat to tenderize it. Meat packers can inject enzymes into live animals just before slaughter. They also can give postmortem injections. Or, after dressing the meat, and usually after cutting it into no more than ½-inch thick pieces, packers can dip the meat into an enzyme solution and allow it to remain in solution for about 30 minutes. (This dipping method, however, keeps the enzyme from penetrating the muscles too deeply.)

Restaurants themselves may use the dipping tenderization procedure in their own kitchens when they offer a low-priced steak dinner. The steak probably comes from a lower-quality animal. The operation wants it tender, though, and chemical aging is a way of getting it tender.

The chemical procedures are not as popular today as they once were in our industry. A major problem concerns the possibility that the enzymes used will continue to attack the muscles and connective tissues of the meat if the meat product is kept at a temperature range of approximately 120 to 140°F. This could easily result in a product that is very mushy and, hence, unacceptable to the guest.

Mechanical methods can also be used, some of which are considered preferable to chemicals, which, if not applied properly, can ruin the product. The familiar mechanical tenderizing methods are grinding and cubing. These alter the shape of the product, but not the taste.

Another common tenderization procedure is the "needling" method, which involves submitting a wholesale cut to a machine with several tiny needles. The needles penetrate the meat, tenderizing it without altering its shape. You have to look carefully for the needle marks, and, once the meat is cooked, you cannot see them. This method can be used on boneless or bone-in wholesale cuts. It is most often used on wholesale cuts to be used for steaks or roasts.

There is a flaking and reforming process used to tenderize inexpensive, tough pieces of meat. These pieces are flaked, not ground, and then pressed together to resemble, say, a loin of beef. "Steaks" are then cut from this "loin."

You can accomplish mechanical tenderization yourself; you can even buy a needling machine if you wish. For that matter, you can age your own meat and apply a dipping chemical bath. The question is: Who can provide these services less expensively—you or your supplier?

The tenderization question usually arises only when you are purchasing fresh beef products. If tenderized at all, the mechanical method is used on veal. More typically, it is roasted very slowly. There is rarely a tenderness problem with pork. Lamb is aged, but only about half as long as beef.

POINT OF ORIGIN

Occasionally a food-service operator notes on the menu the point of origin for a meat entrée. For instance, you may see "Iowa Corn-Fed Beef," "West Virginia Ham," "Wisconsin Veal," or "Belgian Blue Cattle" (a rare, costly, imported breed that is exceptionally low in fat and calories) listed on a menu. If you want to use this form of advertising, you must purchase the appropriate product or else you will violate any relevant truth-in-menu legislation.

INSPECTION?

We noted earlier that rabbit meat production is not required to be federally inspected for wholesomeness. If inspection of this item is important to you, it is necessary to indicate it on your specification.

If you purchase meat that comes from another country, its inspection for wholesomeness may not be as demanding as the one U.S. meat producers must undergo. For instance, many food-service operations purchase a great deal of cow meat from foreign countries. This product must be inspected by the federal government before it is allowed to enter the United States, but the inspection is hampered somewhat because some exporting countries use additives and chemicals that are not covered by U.S. regulations. As far as we can determine, this has not caused any health hazards. But, again, if you are very concerned with product safety, you should indicate on your specification that you want considerably more inspection than that normally provided.

Some buyers may be concerned with the various chemicals and additives that can be used to enhance meat production. If so, they should seek out the meat producers who do not use these methods. Alternatively, private inspectors, such as the USDA's Acceptance Service, can be hired to ensure that the meat products meet their standards. The USDA also has an inspection program buyers can contract for that ensures the meat they purchase is free of pesticides and pesticide residues.

ARTIFICIAL/IMITATION MEAT PRODUCTS

Several artificial meat products are available. For instance, soybean and oat bran can be used as meat extenders. Or they can be used to create such items as "bacon bits."

Many meat producers sell "ham," "hot dogs," and other similar items that are made with chicken, fish, and/or turkey.

Some food-service operators like artificial/imitation meat products because they usually have less fat; hence, they have less cholesterol and may even have fewer calories than the real thing. This generally translates into a lower AP price, though at times a low-fat product may be much more expensive than the traditional item.

These products seem to be very popular in the institutional segment of the food-service industry. However, there is no reason that they cannot enjoy success in any type of food-service operation. If you introduce them as a new menu item, they might sell briskly. Obviously, if you substitute them for a current menu item, you could be taking a chance.

ONE-STOP SHOPPING OPPORTUNITY

Not every meat supplier carries all the meat products you need, especially if you occasionally purchase some unusual items or convenience entrées. In general, the more processing you want, the more suppliers you need to deal with. One-stop shopping opportunities are not the rule in meat buying unless your shopping list contains only the ordinary items. Your decision is: Should I tailor my menu around one or two suppliers? Or should I write the menu and take my chances with a lot of suppliers? This is not an issue to be taken lightly. On the one hand, purchasers like to make deals and bid buy because of the potential savings. On the other hand, purchasers do not enjoy taking risks with signature items.

AP PRICE

The AP price varies for meat items, as well as for the packaging and other economic values added, in a rather predictable way. Several companies keep statistics on these AP prices and on the availability of meat supplies. If you have adequate cash reserves, you might do well with quantity buys once or twice a year for fresh meat and many processed meat items. On the cash market, buying day to day, you take your chances. (Recall, though, that not everyone agrees that large contracts, the futures market, and other such strategies are profitable ventures.)

There is concern among some buyers in the meat industry with the way contract prices may be set. In some cases, large meat contracts are prepared in such a way that the eventual AP price you must pay is not known until the day you take delivery. On that day, the price reported in the "Green Sheet," or in some comparable market pricing report, may be the one you must pay to your supplier.

The Green Sheet is the nickname for the *HRI Meat Price Report.* It is a weekly guide to current AP prices being paid to U.S. meat producers for beef, lamb, pork, veal, and poultry, as well as for several types of processed meat items. Some buyers do not wish to gamble on this type of pricing mechanism. While it is true the eventual AP price may be lower than expected, it could also be much higher. It is a risk some buyers do not want to take. Or it may be a risk that some hospitality firms forbid their buyers to take.

We want very much to reduce the AP price and EP cost of meat, since it represents such a large part of our purchase dollar. But the sword also cuts the other way: While a good deal represents potentially great savings, miscalculation represents potentially high losses.

One way of keeping AP prices down is to bid buy among acceptable suppliers. The time involved, as well as the inconvenience, may be worthwhile. We have known good savings to accrue by this method. But switching suppliers indiscriminately, especially for your signature items, can be risky. Different delivery times, supplier capabilities, and product form may be trivial concerns for other items, but for meat they usually are crucial.

PURCHASING MEAT

Your first step in purchasing meat is to obtain a copy of *The Meat Buyers Guide.* This unique publication is an indispensable reference source that every meat buyer should have. There are other good meat reference books, but *The Meat Buyers Guide* is the only source that addresses exclusively the purchasing function.

Your next step is to determine precisely what meat you want. As we noted earlier, fresh meats are usually selected on the basis of U.S. grades and IMPS numbers. And processed convenience items typically are selected on the basis of packers' brands. Supplier selection may be based on more subjective criteria.

Once you know what is wanted, it is wise to prepare specifications for each item. As always, the specifications should include all pertinent information, whether or not you use them in bid buying. Figure 23.11 shows some example product specifications. And Figure 23.12 notes an example product specification outline for meat products.

After determining what meats you need, you must evaluate potential suppliers, determine your order sizes, fix your order times, and so on. There are, as we said, many suppliers in the fresh and processed meat area. Most parts of the country are a bid buyer's paradise. Purchasing meat, therefore, can be as easy or as difficult as you want to make it. In fact, as long as you avoid esoteric meat items, you can often find one-stop shopping opportunities. Conversely, you can shop around or practice trade relations.

Even though meat buying is a bid buyer's dream, most buyers approach it cautiously. You might see some long-term contract bidding, perhaps three or six months, but you rarely see indiscriminate shopping around. Most meat buyers seem to be concerned with supplier services, especially dependability. A good reputation helps a meat supplier tremendously. After all, his or her customers must have their signature items. And stockouts are intolerable to them. A purchaser must have the correct item at the right time.

Cautious buyer attitudes naturally make it difficult for new meat suppliers to establish themselves. For the same grade and cut of meat there

New York strip steak Used for dinner entrée IMPS number 1180 USDA Choice (high choice) Cut from USDA Yield Grade 2 carcass Dry aged 14 to 21 days 12-ounce portion cut Individually wrapped in plastic film Layered pack 10- to 12-pound case Refrigerated	Flank steak Used for London broil entrée IMPS number 193 Sipco brand Weight range B (1 to 2 pounds) Packed eight pieces per Cryovac bag Packed 6 bags per case Case weight, approximately 70 pounds (catch weight) Refrigerated
Beef base Used to prepare soups and sauces LeGout brand 16-oz. resealable plastic containers 12 containers packed per case Refrigerated	Vegetable beef soup Used for lunch appetizer Campbell brand 51-oz. can Packed 12 cans per case Unrefrigerated

FIGURE 23.11. Example of meat product specifications.

Intended use:

Exact name:

U.S. grade (or equivalent):

Product yield:

Packer's brand name (or equivalent):

Product size:

Size of container:

Type of packaging material:

Packaging procedure:

Product form:

Preservation method:

Tenderization procedure:

Point of origin:

FIGURE 23.12. Example of product specification outline for meat products.

should, in theory, be no difference in items. But the way in which an item is handled, the delivery service, and the supplier's dependability tend to overshadow this fact. Consequently, new suppliers must resort either to offering low AP prices, at least on an introductory basis, or to offering exceptionally attractive supplier services.

The quality and style of processed meat items are not easily decided. Thus, packers' brands and supplier trust tend to weigh heavily in these decisions. The owner-manager, either alone or in consultation with others, determines the requirements. Of course, if you need esoteric meats, you will have more trouble finding suppliers. Packers' bands are important guides, but the brand you want may not be available in the local community. Or, more likely, only one supplier stocks it. We have often noticed such items available on a cost-plus basis only.

Of course, there is the ever-present independent farmer. Some farmers sell fresh meat, but many like to sell products like homemade sausage. We suggest staying away from all uninspected meat.

Before buying any meat item, and usually before or during the writing of specifications, take the time to evaluate the multitude of substitution possibilities.

Meat buying does not have to be difficult, but it is certainly not easy, especially if you are responsible for procuring a wide variety of meat products. In general, the minimum knowledge the buyer needs can be summarized as follows: the different types of meat, the U.S. grades and appropriate brand names, the various cuts, and the intended uses for the meat items. (See Figures 23.13 through 23.16.)

RECEIVING MEAT

When meat products reach an operation, many owner-managers insist that all inspection be done in the walk-in refrigerator. This practice minimizes spoilage opportunities, but it may be too cautious for some. However, it drives home the fact that you cannot take chances with meat—it is too expensive to treat carelessly.

The quality check may be handled by the chef or by someone in your operation who knows meat quality. Did you receive what you ordered? For instance, you might have ordered top round, High Choice, and received bottom round, High Choice—an innocent mistake that could lead to a stockout and a disgruntled customer at the dinner hour.

You should check the condition of the meat. If, for example, fresh beef is not a bright, cherry red, it could be old. Or it could just be packaged too tightly, such as the Cryovac-packaged meat, so that it has not had enough oxygen to give it the bright, cherry red color, or "bloom," as it is some-

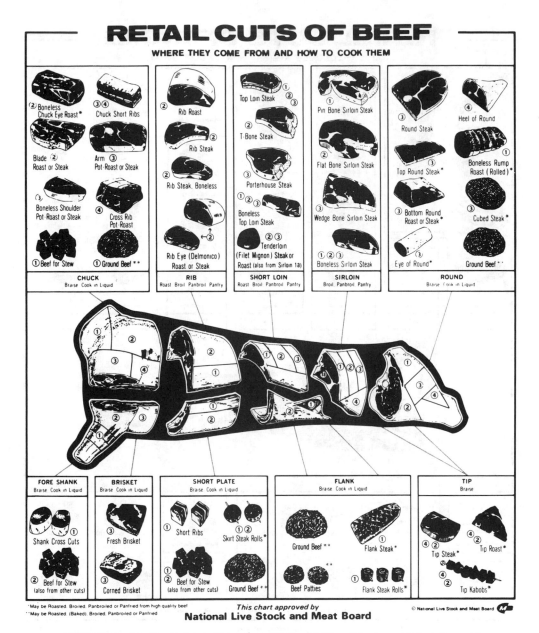

FIGURE 23.13. Beef chart. (Courtesy National Live Stock and Meat Board.)

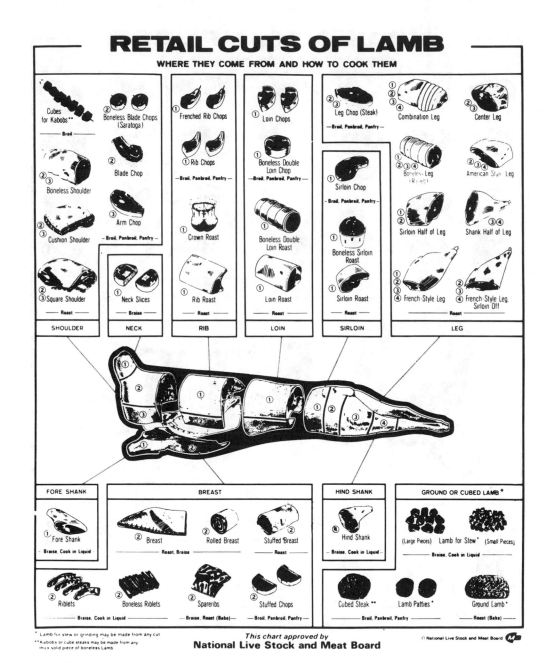

FIGURE 23.14. Lamb chart. (Courtesy National Live Stock and Meat Board.)

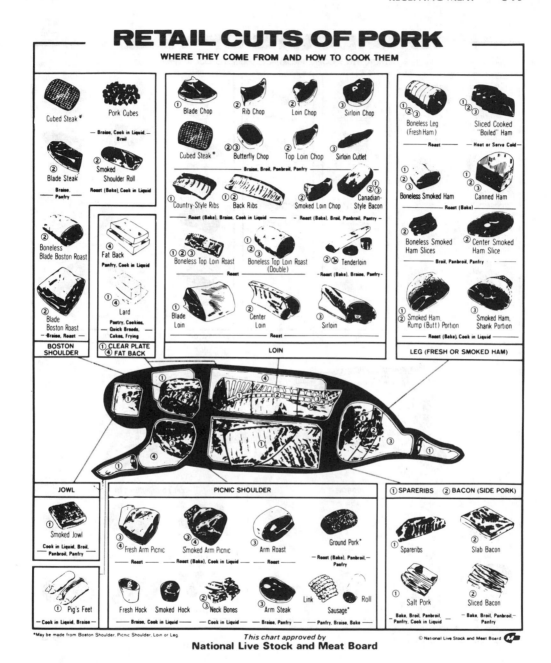

FIGURE 23.15. Pork chart. (Courtesy National Live Stock and Meat Board.)

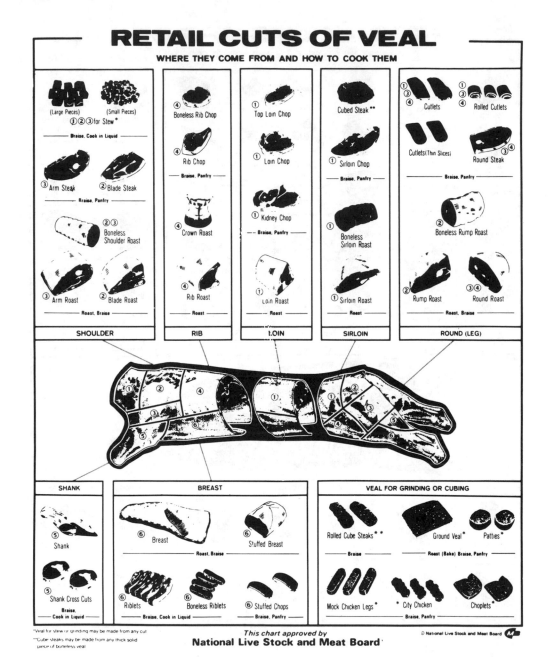

FIGURE 23.16. Veal chart. (Courtesy National Live Stock and Meat Board.)

times called. All meats have a characteristic color. If the color is not right, you should double-check the meat.

Odor is another sign. If meat has an unpleasant odor, refuse it. (Fresh pork is difficult to check for odor because it deteriorates from the inside out, not the outside in.)

If meat products have a slimy look and are slimy to the touch, refuse them. This slime consists of spoilage bacteria.

Another condition to check is the packaging. It should be more than adequate, especially for frozen meats.

The temperature of the item should also be checked. You want about 40°F, minimum, for refrigerated meat and 0°F, minimum, for frozen meat. Other processed items, those that are preserved with chemicals, like some sausages, could be less chilled. But you should not make a habit of receiving even these products when warm, as it could imply a certain degree of general carelessness on the part of your supplier or a willingness on your part to relax standards.

Making these kinds of checks on fresh meat and some processed items is not difficult. For frozen meat, though, it can be a little more difficult. Spoilage, for example, is more difficult to detect in frozen items.

Next you should check quantities. Look for such specifications as weight, count, and sizes. If all the meat you ordered is in one container, you should segregate and weigh the contents separately. Also make sure to deduct the weight of the carton and packaging.

Do not rely completely on what is printed on the meat packages. Repacking is not impossible for an unscrupulous supplier or a larcenous employee.

After checking the quality and quantity, move next to the prices. Recording the deliveries should also receive a reasonable amount of your attention. Receiving sheets, bin cards, and meat tags are all commonly used methods for protecting expensive meat items. As you might imagine, meat entails a greater emphasis on record keeping than other foods. And most purchasers express considerable concern with ironing out any potential problems with suppliers ahead of time. Most of them quickly agree on the policies regarding returns, credit terms, and substitute meat items a supplier might deliver because he or she is out of your regular order.

It is possible to streamline the meat receiving process by using the USDA's Acceptance Service. This practice is popular in meat purchasing, even though it is expensive. Using this service, a hospitality operator can pay a meat expert to write meat specifications and to ensure that the specified products are actually delivered. Acceptance buying is sometimes referred to in the meat trade as "certified buying" or "certification." (see Figures 23.17 and 23.18.)

Also of interest to the meat buyer is a related program offered by the USDA called the "Product Examination Service." This service entails the inspection of purchased meat by a federal inspector while the products

FIGURE 23.17. Federal stamps used to indicate that a meat product meets the buyer's specifications under USDA Acceptance purchasing.

FIGURE 23.18. Federal inspector applying the USDA Acceptance stamp to a wholesale cut of meat.

are in transit. The primary purpose of this service is to ensure that the products do not suffer quality deterioration during shipment.

STORING MEAT

Fresh meat must be stored in the correct environment. It must be kept clean and cold. And the stock must be rotated properly.

Keeping the products clean and sanitary is the biggest challenge. Meat products are susceptible to bacterial contamination, so it is important to perform the necessary housekeeping chores in order to minimize contamination. Mandatory government inspection ensures that most meat is very clean when it is delivered. More commonly, it is a dirty storage refrigerator that contaminates good meat.

The meat should be stored in a separate meat refrigerator if you have one. Try not to store it with cooked meat items. But if you must, put the cooked items above the raw ones, so that the drippings from the raw meat cannot contaminate the cooked food. Try to store fresh meat at 35 to 40°F.

You should not wrap fresh meat too tightly, nor should you stack it too tightly. Both of these actions tend to cut down on the beneficial cold air circulation around the pieces of meat.

If the product is frozen, try to store it at −10°F or lower. If you must freeze some chilled meat, be careful to wrap it correctly and to store it in a freezer only as long as suggested. (It is not a good idea for you to freeze meat, because the typical hospitality operation's freezer is designed to hold frozen foods, not to freeze fresh products.)

ISSUING MEAT

You should rotate the stock properly so that the oldest items are issued first. Meat is rarely received and sent straight to production; an employee typically needs a stock requisition to get it. There tends to be more control of meat items at the requisition stage. In many cases, a perpetual inventory has been started when the meat delivery was made. And the stock requisition is commonplace. The requisitioner should return any unused meat at the end of his or her shift. The meat consumed should be consistent with the guest checks, that is, the amount of meat items sold during that shift. This control may be somewhat time-consuming, but it is quite common in hospitality operations for meat and other expensive items.

By all means, make sure the requisitioner gets the right item and the right quantity, and make sure that the in-process inventory does not get large enough to encourage waste or pilferage.

IN-PROCESS INVENTORIES

Surprisingly, in-process meats cause relatively little trouble. These items receive the bulk of the supervisory efforts; moreover, the penalties for pilferage and waste are normally quite severe.

Some employees will make "mistakes" (burn a steak, accidentally on purpose, and give it to a friend or eat it themselves). You can reduce this practice by demanding that the mistake be turned in to the storeroom, along with the rest of the leftover meat, at the end of the shift so that it can be accounted for at that time.

Meat also provides some opportunity for shortchanging the customer. For example, a server might slice the beef a little thin and keep the extra few ounces handy to trade for a few ounces of gin saved in a similar fashion by the bartender. As is usually the case, effective supervision is the best answer.

KEY WORDS AND CONCEPTS

Advantages and disadvantages of portion-cut meat

Agricultural Marketing Act

American Angus Association

AMS Live Stock & Feed Division

AP price

Artificial meat products

Beef electrification

Botulism

Bulk pack

Carcass

Catch weight

Certified Angus Beef Program

Certified buying

Chemical tenderization

Cryovac aging

Curing

Dry aging

Edible by-product

EP cost

Exact name

Feathering

Federal Meat Inspection Act

Finish

Flaked and reformed meat products

FSQS

Grading factors

Grass-fed beef

Green meat

Green Sheet

Has meat been subjected to USDA, or equivalent, inspection?

Hedging

Imitation meat products

IMPS numbers

IMPS/NAMP numbers

In-process inventories

Intended use

Layout pack

Limiting rule

Long-term contract

Management considerations when purchasing meat

Manufacturing grade

Marbling

Maturity class

MBG numbers

Mechanical tenderization

NAMP

National Live Stock and Meat Board

Needling procedure

One-stop shopping

Packaging procedure

Packers' brands

Point of origin

Popular types of meat products

Portion-cut meat

Prefabricated meat

Preservation method

Primal cut

Product form

Product size

Product yield

Purchasing, receiving, storing, and
  issuing meat products

Reluctance to change meat suppliers

Retail cut

Sausage

Shingle pack

Shrink wrap

Side

Signature item

Size of container

Smoking

Sodium nitrite

Standard of identity

Standardized cut

Steam-table pack

Substitution possibilities

SYSCO brand Supreme Angus Beef

Tenderization procedure

The Meat Buyers Guide

Truth-in-menu legislation

Type of packaging material

USDA

USDA Acceptance Service

USDA Agricultural Marketing Service

USDA Product Examination Service

U.S. quality grades

U.S. yield grades

Variety meat

Voluntary inspection for rabbit meat

Weight range

Wholesale cut

Wholesale Meat Act

QUESTIONS AND PROBLEMS

1. What are the quality grades for beef primarily based on?
2. All meat must be inspected during production in the United States except _____ meat.
3. What are the USDA quality grades for beef?
4. What are the USDA quality grades for pork?
5. What are the USDA quality grades for veal?
6. What are the USDA quality grades for lamb?
7. Assume that you manage a high-check-average, full-service club, with annual food and beverage sales of $1.8 million. Your normal purchase

order size of T-bone steaks, per week, is approximately 1,200 pounds. The current AP price is $6.80 per pound, which will probably hold steady for the next six months. Your current supplier is a long-time good friend, and you are his biggest account. He has carried you during lean times in the past, and you have never had any problems with him. He is dependable and delivers twice a week, in the morning. Down the street is the ABC Corporation's central distribution center, whose management is after your T-bone steak business. Their deal is a six-month contract, AP price of $6.55 per pound, same quality, cut, yield, and packaging of T-bone, with deliveries in the afternoon twice a week. What do you suggest?

8. What are lower-quality grades of meat typically used for?

9. What is the primary reason the food buyer uses the IMPS numbering system when preparing meat specifications?

10. You notice that your delivery of 500 portion-cut steaks is not up to your normal standard, the only problem being they each weigh 10 ounces instead of your normal 12. It is Friday, 4 P.M., and these steaks are for use this weekend. Your meat purveyor normally is closed on the weekends. What would you do? If possible, ask the owner of a specialty restaurant to discuss this problem with you.

11. What are the USDA yield grades primarily based on?

12. A product specification for fresh pork chops could include the following information:

   (a) _____

   (b) _____

   (c) _____

   (d) _____

   (e) _____

13. Label the wholesale cuts of this side of beef.

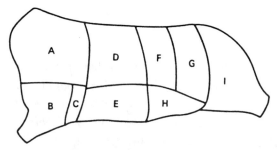

14. It is painfully evident to you that meat prices are constantly rising with no relief in sight. But this inflationary spiral has not been enough to encourage you to purchase large quantities and invest in freezer storage facilities. Just recently, your meat purveyor has indicated that he intends to go out of business. This supplier calls you and asks whether you wish to purchase

his large inventory of meat products at distress prices. Obviously, you are overwhelmed at the possibility of tremendous cost savings.

(a) What must you know before making an intelligent decision concerning the purchase of this huge inventory?

(b) Assume that you wish to purchase this inventory. Must you also purchase a freezer? Why?

(c) Under what conditions would it be advisable to purchase a freezer?

15. Briefly describe the maturity classes for beef.

16. What is the primary purpose of using the USDA's Product Examination Service?

17. What critical information is missing from the following product specification for lamb, loin chops?

Lamb, loin chops
Used for dinner entrée
IMPS number 1232
6-ounce portion cut
Packed in 10- to 12-pound containers

18. Assume that you manage a full-service country club. Wesson Brothers, purveyors of fine meats, has been your main source of meat supply for a considerable period. Recently, Wesson proposed to its customers a rather interesting "trade-off." Wesson would like to get out of the transportation business and is seriously considering allowing all its customers to pick up their own orders; in return for picking up, the AP price will be reduced 8 percent. Wesson is asking its customers for their opinions. If at least 50 percent of its existing customers perform the transportation function for themselves, Wesson will expect all other customers to do likewise.

(a) Would you like to perform the transportation function? Why?

(b) If Wesson introduces this proposed policy, how much would you want the AP price of your purchases to decrease? Is 8 percent enough? Do you think the EP cost of the proposed method would equal that of the current method? Why?

(c) Assume that Wesson introduces the policy. Further assume that you do not wish to perform the transportation function. In addition, assume that Wesson has a monopoly for certain products that you must have. What do you suggest? If possible, ask a country club manager to comment on your answer.

19. Assume that you manage a hospital food service. Currently, it costs about $42 per day to feed one patient, including food, labor, and direct operating supplies. You expect meat prices to increase next year by approximately 7 percent, but the hospital administration will not increase your food budget. You must make do with the $42 for all next year. Currently, you are serving meat at least two times a day on the average. You do not want to reduce

this frequency, but you must cut meat costs somewhere. You ask the steward (food buyer) for some suggestions. What do you think the steward would propose? Why? If possible, ask a hospital food-service director to comment on your answer.

20. List some differences between dry aging and Cryovac aging.

21. Give an appropriate intended use for hamburger that has been extended with soybean.

22. Why are meat buyers reluctant to shop indiscriminately for their meat items?

23. The AP price of lean hamburger is $1.89 per pound. The AP price of regular hamburger is $1.09 per pound. The lean shrinks 10 percent when cooked; the regular shrinks 30 percent.

    (a) At what AP price must the lean sell to make it equal in value to the regular?

    (b) Assume that the EP cost of both lean and regular is equal. What other specific considerations should you examine before purchasing either the lean or the regular?

24. Prepare a product specification for the following meat products:

    (a) Veal cutlet

    (b) Skirt steak

    (c) Prepared chili with beans

    (d) Breakfast sausage

    (e) Ham

25. When would you purchase an imitation meat product?

26. When would you purchase a flaked and reformed meat product?

27. What benefit would a restaurant owner gain if he or she noted on the menu the point of origin for the meat menu offerings?

28. Briefly describe one type of meat product you might purchase that would be a good candidate for the needling tenderization procedure.

29. What are the quality grading factors for veal and lamb?

30. Define or explain briefly the following terms:

    (a) Variety meat

    (b) Wholesale cut

    (c) Retail cut

    (d) Marbling

    (e) FSQS

    (f) NAMP

    (g) Curing

(h) Feathering

(i) Certified buying

(j) Layout pack

(k) Bloom

(l) Beef electrification

(m) Green Sheet

(n) Shrink wrap

(o) Manufacturing grade

CHAPTER 24

ALCOHOLIC AND NONALCOHOLIC BEVERAGES

THE PURPOSE OF THIS CHAPTER

This chapter discusses:

- The major management considerations surrounding the selection and procurement of alcoholic beverages
- The selection factors for alcoholic beverages
- Purchasing, receiving, storing, and issuing alcoholic beverages
- The in-process alcoholic beverage inventory
- The major management considerations surrounding the selection and procurement of nonalcoholic beverages
- The selection factors for nonalcoholic beverages
- Purchasing, receiving, storing, and issuing nonalcoholic beverages
- The in-process nonalcoholic beverage inventory

ALCOHOLIC BEVERAGES

As a general rule, alcoholic beverages are the easiest items a food-service buyer can purchase. For one thing, they are very standardized products that are manufactured under controlled conditions. Unlike many food products, the quality of alcoholic beverages is very consistent.

Most alcoholic beverages will not spoil. Draft beer will spoil if it is not consumed within three to four weeks. And some other items, such as canned and bottled beer, and a few wines, will tend to lose their culinary quality over a long period of time. But, as a general rule, the buyer does not have to worry about an oversupply of alcoholic beverages spoiling before it can be served to customers.

Another nice thing about alcoholic beverages is that many customers tend to order a favored brand name. For instance, the typical customer would not ask the restaurant operator for Heinz catsup; he or she would take the one offered by the establishment and not give it a second thought.

However, this customer would more often than not specify an exact brand name when ordering a favorite alcoholic beverage. The buyer's job is made much easier because of this type of "pull" strategy that exists in the alcoholic beverage channel of distribution. Some brands are so popular that the bar owner must carry them.

In some instances, these favorite brands are carried by only one supplier in your market area. Some suppliers are exclusive distributors for one or more products. If the bar operator wants these brands, he or she has only one source of supply for them. Since there are several exclusive distributorships in the alcoholic beverage trade, the buyer does not need to shop around very much.

In the extreme case, the state is the only supplier of every brand. There are 18 "control" states. (See Figure 24.1.) The buyers in control states must follow the states' specific ordering and bill-paying procedures. This makes the buying job much easier; however, the excessive regulation found in these states tends to increase significantly the EP costs of alcoholic beverages.

In "license" states, there are also several government regulations that make the buyer's job easier. For instance, there is a certain amount of

---

Alabama

Idaho

Iowa

Maine

Michigan

Mississippi (wholesale only)

Montana

New Hampshire

North Carolina

Ohio

Oregon

Pennsylvania

Utah

Vermont

Virginia

Washington

West Virginia

Wyoming (wholesale only)

FIGURE 24.1. Control states.

price control in some areas; that is, the state or local government agency stipulates that alcoholic beverages must be sold for minimum wholesale prices and minimum retail prices. While there are AP price discount opportunities, and other sorts of "deals" available in license states, there are not that many for the buyer to evaluate; fewer opportunities imply less work for the buyer.

License states are a bit more liberal than control states in terms of liquor-ordering and bill-paying procedures. For instance, licensed distributors are able to deliver products, whereas in control states, usually the buyer must pick up his or her order at the state liquor warehouse. They also are allowed to offer credit terms, whereas in control states, usually the buyer must pay cash when he or she picks up the order. The license state, though, does not grant carte blanche to its liquor distributors; these suppliers are restricted much more than are other types of suppliers.

License states tend to restrict the amount and types of supplier services that can be provided. Consequently, even in a state where two or more suppliers carry some of the same brands, the buyer may not be able to exploit the situation.

MANAGEMENT CONSIDERATIONS

The problems associated with alcoholic beverages rarely center on purchasing procedures. The more fundamental questions follow here.

SHOULD WE OFFER ALCOHOLIC BEVERAGE SERVICE TO OUR GUESTS?

This is not an easy decision, especially for hospitality operations that cultivate a family image. On the one hand, liquor sales are very profitable; they are much more profitable than food sales, and such items are easier to produce and serve to the guest. However, on the other hand, liquor consumption has steadily declined in the United States over the years due to health and nutrition concerns, tougher DWI laws, laws prohibiting happy hours, and social pressures created by such groups as Mothers Against Drunk Driving (MADD).

Many food-service operations rely on alcoholic beverage sales to make ends meet. They cannot easily make the required profit merely by selling food. However, even if an operator wanted to serve liquor, he or she may not be able to secure a retail liquor license from the appropriate government agency, either because none are available or because the price tag is exorbitant. It is a trying procedure to get a license, and the paperwork, legal proceedings, and hearings can quickly drain your resources. The procedure usually is not so difficult, however, if you want to serve only beer and wine.

In most parts of the country, liquor licenses are restricted in number. For instance, usually there is no more than one liquor license available for every 2,000 to 3,000 residents. Thus, if no license is available from the appropriate government entity, you must purchase it from an individual who has one. This can be very expensive, particularly if the demand for these licenses far exceeds the restricted supply.

There are other major expenses associated with liquor service—expenses that the nonliquor establishment does not incur. For instance, there are increased liability insurance premiums and license renewal costs. Operating expenses also may increase substantially if you need to hire floorpersons to restrict minors, participate in a safe-driver program and/or a designated-driver program, and comply with government-mandated record-keeping procedures.

Some hospitality operations are trying to maintain their beverage profit margins by altering their marketing policies to exploit the consumer trend toward drinking more wine, beer, and nonalcoholic beverages. For instance, where state law allows, several bar operators have "brew pubs" (i.e., combination of food service and a small, in-house mini-brewery). Some operators offer wine bars. And there are even some food-service operations that publish a wine list and a water list.

WHAT QUALITY OF LIQUOR SHOULD WE SERVE?

An age-old argument centers on the worth of premium brands versus lesser known brands. This decision is further complicated because operations usually serve "well brands" and "call brands." Well liquor, sometimes called the "house brand," is served when a patron asks, for instance, for a shot of Scotch without specifying a particular brand. Call liquor refers to specific brand names, as when a patron asks for a shot of Cutty Sark.

Generally, the AP price difference at wholesale between premium brands and lesser known brands is not significant. But if you sell a considerable quantity of liquor, the savings from even a modest difference can amount to a considerable sum. The question then becomes, should we save a few pennies on each drink or should we impress our customers by pouring only recognized brand names?

This issue should not be taken too lightly, since it generates wildly differing opinions. Part of this controversy has to do with yet another difference between seemingly comparable liquor brands—the "proof," or alcoholic strength. The proof number, as in "100 proof," refers to the alcoholic content of a liquor; it is twice the percentage of alcohol present in the liquor. Thus, "100 proof" bourbon contains 50 percent alcohol.

Some equally well known brands have different proofs. Some have

80, some 86, some 90, and others have 100 or more. If you decide on a lower-quality brand with a lower proof, you may not be able to dilute it so much in a mixed drink. Thus, the premium brand advocates point out that the EP cost per serving, sometimes referred to in bars as the "pouring cost," for the lower-proof brands may not be significantly less than the pouring cost of a higher-proof brand.

Many food-service and bar operations serve premium brands as their well brands. This is sometimes referred to as the "premium well." Apparently, these operators are willing to forgo a few pennies of extra profit per drink to satisfy customers, impress them, and hope that this will have an overall favorable impact on the net profit of the entire hospitality operation.

SHOULD WE SERVE DRAFT BEER, BOTTLED BEER, OR BOTH?

Many guests prefer draft beer. It is something they cannot normally get at home. Unfortunately, draft beer is difficult to serve properly. You must keep the lines clean, monitor the tap pressure, tap new kegs, and be alert to sanitation. Nevertheless, draft beer is a good merchandising tool, and it can attract considerable business. Also, draft beer can yield a lower pouring cost than bottled beer, even taking into account the additional labor and other costs involved.

Even if you want draft beer, however, you may not be able to get the brand you prefer. Beer distributors sometimes want to restrict the number of retail outlets for their product. This is especially true of the small regional brewery seeking exclusivity for its products.

WHICH WINES SHOULD WE SERVE?

Which wine should we use as our "house wine"? (House wine, like well liquor, is served when someone orders a glass or carafe of wine without specifying any particular brand or vintage.)

Buying wines is trickier than buying other alcoholic beverages. Wines require of the buyer or the owner-manager considerable product knowledge, especially since the restaurant patron does not always have one or two preferred brands in mind as he or she does for beer and distilled spirits. Thus, service personnel may have to suggest wines, and it is important that they provide correct choices that will complement the dining experience. This requires both solid training and knowledgeable supervision.

Perhaps the major wine issue is how many varieties and types to carry. If you offer several wines, you must put up with several operational difficulties: (1) wine is difficult to store properly; (2) it requires considerable storage space; (3) it may languish in storage a long time before it sells;

(4) service personnel must be trained to sell and serve it correctly; and (5) a variety of wines may require several suppliers. A substantial wine inventory can also mean tying up large amounts of capital. The capital costs—interest on borrowed money or loss of interest on alternate investments, that is, an opportunity cost—of a large wine cellar can be a major consideration in wine list design.

The potential advantages of a well-stocked wine cellar, though, can be many. The main ones include (1) prestige, (2) indulging and pleasing the patrons, (3) a marketing edge, and (4) higher profits.

On the other hand, a wine emphasis could be a waste of money and effort in many operations. Some operations are in between. A steak house, for instance, could have a minimal wine list or a broad one, depending on the clientele.

Some operators like to speculate in wine. They like to buy wine and wait for it to increase greatly in value so that they can sell it at a high profit. Wine speculating, for them, is a little like playing the stock market. This sort of "investing" passes beyond the responsibility of the ordinary purchaser.

HOW MANY BRANDS OF DISTILLED SPIRITS AND BEER SHOULD WE CARRY?

Few patrons expect a wide choice of beers, unless you offer several brands as a promotion. But guests can be miffed if they cannot get their favorite brand of distilled spirit. However, if you opt for a wide variety of brands, you incur the same difficulties and potential advantages we noted for wine.

The decision is not easy. You do not want to stock everything, but you want to know where to draw the line. In our experience, the added investment between a restricted stock and more variety is not great, especially when you consider how much you have invested in the hospitality operation in the first place. For example, it costs more than $100,000 to erect one first-class hotel room. What, then, are a few more bottles of liquor and the space needed to store them? Nevertheless, in striking a balance, the costs and benefits of holding inventory discussed earlier in this text cannot be ignored.

THE APPROPRIATE MENU PRICE FOR ALCOHOLIC BEVERAGES

Your customers are very sensitive to menu prices for these products because they typically have a good idea of the retail price of these items in the local liquor store. Hence, there is a greater need, as a bar operator, to emphasize your service and other intangible features of your operation. If you offer a fine dining and/or drinking experience, you should have more flexibility in your menu-pricing procedures. But if your hospitality operation is rather plain, offering no unique experience to the guest, your pricing system must take this into account.

Many customers today are switching from hard liquor to wine, beer, and nonalcoholic beverages. Thus, the operator must price these menu items just as high as the hard liquor menu items, lest there be a tremendous loss of net profit. This is why it is so common to see a glass of water priced for as much as a Scotch and soda—the operation cannot survive unless it achieves a certain profit margin per drink, regardless of the type of drink a customer demands.

The issue of menu pricing, as with many marketing decisions, is replete with opinions and "gut feelings," which seem to be more prolific with liquor than with other menu items, thus making this area of your business a bit more difficult to handle.

SELECTION FACTORS

For the purposes of our discussion, we assume that your hospitality operation has a full liquor license and is allowed to serve beer, distilled spirits, and wine. As we mentioned earlier, generally it is easier to purchase alcoholic beverages than it is to purchase other food and nonfood items. But a few selection factors must be considered. We discuss these factors next.

INTENDED USE

As always, you want to determine exactly the intended use of the item so that you will be able to prepare the appropriate, relevant specification. For example, a house wine may be packaged differently from wines that will be sold by the bottle.

EXACT NAME

You must ensure that you note the exact name of the item you want, or else you risk receiving something that will not suit your needs. Usually this selection factor presents no difficulty, because over the years, a great deal of standardization has developed in this channel of distribution. Figure 24.2 notes some of the more popular varieties of alcoholic beverage products used by the beverage service industry.

The liquor- and wine-producing countries and states typically define several of the alcoholic products made within their borders, as well as part or all of the production processes. There are also standards of identity for many items. For example, bourbon must meet a certain formula, as

BEER
Ale

Bock beer

Lite beer

Malt liquor

Pilsner

Premium beer

DISTILLED SPIRITS
Bourbon whiskey

Brandy

Canadian whisky

Cordial

Corn whiskey

Gin

Irish whisky

Liqueur

Rum

Rye whiskey

Scotch whisky

Tequila

Vodka

WINE
Aromatized wine

Dessert wine

Sparkling wine

Specialty wine

Table wine

FIGURE 24.2. Popular types of alcoholic beverages used by the beverage service industry.

must Tennessee whiskey. And vintners who grow their own grapes typically must follow certain pruning processes on the vines; this is especially true in Europe.

BRAND NAME (OR EQUIVALENT)

Brand name is the most fundamental selection factor. For the vast majority of alcoholic beverages, brand name tends to be the only characteristic a patron considers. This is especially true for call liquors your guests expect you to have on hand.

It would be difficult to utilize in your operation an "equivalent" brand name if patrons insist that they be served the name of distilled spirit, wine, or beer specified. But you may be able to do this if, for example, guests are not so demanding, say, those who are banquet guests. Or it may be possible to convince a customer to try a different brand of beer or wine in lieu of the preferred one.

Where the law allows, some hospitality operators purchase alcoholic beverages that carry customized brand labels. This is especially true with wines. For instance, it is common for hotel guests to find the hotel's name on a bottle of wine located inside the in-room minibar refrigerator. This strategy enhances the hotel's advertising and promotion program. It also makes it difficult for guests to compare the hotel's price with comparable wine prices at the local liquor store.

VINTAGE

The year of production is an important wine selection factor. Some wine companies decline to indicate a production year. For most fine wines, however, the production year ("vintage") is important. Skilled wine buyers consider the year as well as the manufacturer of the wine.

The year or date of production is also important when purchasing products that could lose culinary quality. For instance, a buyer should consider these dates when purchasing beer. He or she should also check them when purchasing nonalcoholic beer; freshness is important, because alcohol acts as a preservative, suggesting that older products would not have a satisfying taste.

ALCOHOL CONTENT

Alcoholic beverages have varying levels of alcohol content. As a general rule, beer products contain approximately 3.2 percent to more than 6 percent alcohol; wines contain approximately 12 percent to as much as 20 percent alcohol; and most distilled spirits contain anywhere from about 56 proof (i.e., 28 percent alcohol) to 151 proof (i.e., 75.5 percent alcohol).

Usually the state or local government agency restricts the alcohol content of these beverages. For instance, some areas prohibit the sale of any distilled spirit that exceeds 100 proof. This is one reason that many breweries, wineries, and distilleries manufacture products with different alcoholic strengths.

Since there are several bands that contain different alcoholic strengths, the buyer must ensure that he or she orders and receives the correct item. For example, it is not uncommon for a distiller to sell an 80-proof bourbon and an 86-proof bourbon, both bourbons carrying the same brand name. There also are "light" distilled spirits, that is, items that are about 54 proof, or approximately one-third less alcohol than the standard 80-proof spirit. Furthermore, there are nonalcoholic spirits, beers, and wines available. You must be very careful to avoid ordering a product you cannot use.

Some buyers are concerned primarily with the alcohol content of the beverage. For instance, brandies for use in flaming dishes should carry a high alcohol content. Brand name need not be a consideration if the guest is not likely to see it.

Alcohol content may also be considered when one compares various brands of the same liquor. For example, having decided on a well Scotch, you might opt for a higher proof, even though the brand name may be unfamiliar. Some people believe that obscure brands of liquor with proofs equal to or greater than premium brands, are attractive products that are not significantly different in taste from the premium brands. If it is cheaper, therefore, it should at least be considered.

SIZE OF CONTAINER

Package sizes are very standardized in this channel of distribution. Hence, there should be little difficulty with this selection factor. (See Figure 24.3.)

Of course, you must determine the appropriate size to fit your needs. For example, the larger the size, generally the less per milliliter or ounce you will pay for the product. However, you may not want to invest in a larger package size if the item purchased is a slow mover or is subject to spoilage.

TYPE OF CONTAINER

Packaging materials are also very standardized in the alcoholic beverage distribution channel. Generally, products come in glass or plastic bottles, cans, or kegs. Some products, such as a few wines, are packed in aseptic "bag-in-the-box" packages (i.e., bulk wine packed in a plastic liner and then placed into a cardboard box—similar to the bulk milk containers used in milk-dispensing machines).

It is possible that a company manufactures a product, such as table wine, and packages it in corked bottles and also in bottles with screw-top lids. Usually there is some distinction in the exact name that indicates this type of packaging difference. However, the buyer must ensure that he or she does not accidentally purchase a product that the hospitality operation cannot use.

There are some opportunities available to personalize your beverage containers. Recall that a buyer might consider purchasing alcoholic beverages from a supplier who is willing to include the hospitality operation's

BEER
12-ounce bottle
Keg (15.5 gallons)
Keg (13.2 gallons)
$\frac{1}{2}$ keg (7.75 gallons)
$\frac{1}{4}$ keg (3.88 gallons)

DISTILLED SPIRITS
750-ml bottle
1-liter bottle
1.75-liter bottle

WINE
187-ml bottle
375-ml bottle
750-ml bottle
1-liter bottle
1.5-liter bottle
3-liter bottle
4-liter bottle
5-liter container
18-liter container

FIGURE 24.3. Popular container sizes for alcoholic beverages used by the beverage service industry.

name and logo on the package label, thereby creating a more impressive merchandising effect and customer experience. Personalized packaging for liquor products is especially popular in hotels that use these products for room service and catered events. They also make excellent additions to complimentary fruit baskets in guest rooms.

Some suppliers also will number your liquor containers, or otherwise code them, so that it will be easier for you to control their use in the operation. For instance, it is sometimes very easy for a bartender to bring his or her personal liquor bottle to work, sell the contents, and pocket the receipts. With coded containers, the supervisor would quickly notice the unauthorized bottle.

POINT OF ORIGIN

This is a very important selection factor for wines. The point of origin implies taste variations. In some cases, as with imported wines, the point of origin denotes the type of government inspection to which the products were submitted.

PRESERVATION METHOD

Wines should always be maintained at cool temperatures. Red wines are normally served at about 60°F; white, rosé, and sparkling wines should be served at refrigerated temperatures, about 40°F.

Canned and bottled beers also should be kept cool. The distributor should ensure that they do not become too warm while in transit.

Draft beer must be kept refrigerated. It has the shortest shelf life of all alcoholic beverages and tends to lose its culinary quality very rapidly if it is not kept under constant refrigeration.

Distilled spirits can be kept at any temperature, though excessive heat will tend to cause them to evaporate a bit. Also, the products with considerable sugar in them could sour under extreme heat conditions. Generally, though, since distilled spirits are inert products, their shelf lives are virtually unlimited.

It is usually not too difficult for the licensed distributor to maintain the proper temperatures, but this is not the case in the control states where buyers must pick up their orders from the state liquor store warehouses. Unless you have an appropriate vehicle, or can hire one, your liquor items will not receive the best possible in-transit storage environment.

AP PRICE

You must, normally, pay the going price for the liquor items you stock. The price is controlled either directly, as in a control state, or indirectly, as in a state that requires minimum wholesale prices. Price maintenance for alcoholic beverages is not as restrictive today as it once was. Liquor purveyors and liquor retailers in some states have more flexibility in setting their prices. But since the largest part of the price represents tax, we may never see a completely free market in alcoholic beverages.

Quantity buys are available, though, as with most products we purchase. And we can expect to achieve a quantity discount. Beware, though, that the potential savings do not require you to invest in considerably more of a product than you might be able to use within a reasonable time.

You can also save on liquor—about 10 percent—by purchasing the largest containers, such as the 1.75 liter bottle of distilled spirits. These are clumsy, but they are acceptable or even preferable if you have an automatic bar, that is, a bar that, with a push of a button, automatically dispenses a portion-controlled amount into a glass.

Distributors are sometimes permitted by the state to offer a price discount. (These are sometimes referred to as "post-offs" in control states.)

These discounts can be granted by the distributor and usually are. They normally do not require you to do anything special to obtain them, except, perhaps, purchase a little bigger order size to achieve a substantial savings.

The discount does not always take the form of money. Sometimes a buyer receives, for example, a free bottle of liquor for every case or two that he or she purchases at the regular AP price.

Price is sometimes a major concern when purchasing imported products. These products may carry considerable import taxes and/or other tariffs. Some imported products have lower tariffs than others; consequently, there may be a considerable price differential between several similar items. For well items, a purchaser has an opportunity to at least weigh the AP price differences when making a decision in this area.

SUPPLIER SERVICES

Liquor distributors do what they can to provide some supplier services. Unfortunately, they are severely restricted by law in what they can do for their customers.

One supplier service that a distributor provides is simplification of clerical routines; for example, he or she may be able to give you paperwork forms to use, such as blank purchase orders, bin cards, and the like. These forms can save you some money, and since you are required to maintain records of your purchases of alcoholic beverages, the forms represent indeed a worthwhile supplier service.

Other supplier services that distributors sometimes provide include menu planning help, especially for wines. Most hospitality operators are reluctant to let a supplier plan their food menus. But the wine list preparation is a different matter, particularly if the operator is not very familiar with wines. The distributor can also provide a timely delivery schedule; personnel training, especially in wine service; new recipes; some sales and merchandising suggestions; reasonable minimum order requirements, which is important when you have to buy one or two bottles of a slow-moving liquor; assistance in understanding and complying with local liquor codes; and, for those whose operations can use them, a few trinkets, such as clocks, can openers, and calendars.

Those buyers with extensive wine lists are eager to receive as much product as possible from the best wineries. Since these primary sources tend to "allocate" product among the various buyers, you would appreciate as large an allocation as possible. In this case, the size of the allocation is a much-prized supplier service.

Federal, state, and local governments severely limit the types of supplier services a distributor can give, because the governments worry about kickbacks and various other illegal temptations these supplier services invite.

For well brands, management has a choice about which brands to use; hence, the AP price might be important for these items. But since differences in AP price among the major brands is slight, supplier services may be more important.

PURCHASING ALCOHOLIC BEVERAGES

Once you have determined the types of beverages you want, the purchasing procedure follows a fairly routine pattern. Ordering and delivery schedules become precise; you rarely have any control over them.

The list of potential suppliers normally is listed in a liquor industry publication that notes products, distributors, and AP prices; for instance, in Nevada, there is a monthly publication entitled *Nevada Beverage Analyst* that contains this information.

Many distributors issue their own publications in hard copy or online formats. For instance, in southern Nevada, the DeLuca Liquor & Wine Ltd., Nevada Liquor & Wine, Ltd., Eagle Vineyards, Ltd., and Coors of Las Vegas companies issue a quarterly publication entitled *The Spirit of Southern Nevada* that contains AP price information for the products they distribute.

In most cases, payment schedules are also predetermined. If you buy in a control state, you have no choice about how to buy. You usually order once a week and pay cash when you pick up your order. In a license state there are limited credit terms available.

Probably the largest decision faced by the buyer is how much to order. The typical par stock is set for one week; slow-moving items may be ordered once a month or less often.

Minimum order requirements occasionally present problems, because you probably would not want to order a case of something that takes you a year to sell. Here the choice may be to take it or leave it. However, most distributors allow you to combine odd-sized orders into a case lot. For instance, you can often buy two bottles each of six different brandies and receive a "case price," which is considerably lower than if you purchased each bottle separately. Normally, the buyer purchases in case lots, but the supplier who lets you "bust" cases and still receive the favorable price may be providing an attractive supplier service.

Buyers often face two other major decision points when purchasing alcoholic beverages: (1) the post-off opportunity discussed earlier and (2) the need, perhaps, to purchase a very large supply of one brand. For example, there is only so much Ferrari Carano vintage Merlot to go around. If your customers like this wine, you might consider buying as much as possible to ensure that you can offer it as long as possible. But such a large purchase might require a stockless purchase, which requires

Brandy Used for drink service at main bar E & J brand (Original Extra Smooth) 80 proof 750-ml bottle	Alcohol-free White Zinfandel Used for wine list in main dining room Sutter Home Fré brand Less than 0.5% alcohol by volume 750-ml bottle Delivered at cool temperature
London Dry Gin Used for drink service at main bar Gilbey's brand 80 proof 750-ml bottle	Vodka Used for drink service at service bar Smirnoff brand 80 proof 1.75-l bottle

FIGURE 24.4. Example of alcoholic beverage product specifications.

you to pay now for the large order and ask the distributor to send you a little at a time.

Once you know what you need, it is a good idea to prepare specifications for each liquor product. Figure 24.4 shows some example product specifications. And Figure 24.5 notes an example product specification outline for alcoholic beverage products.

There is a tendency to downplay the use of specifications in liquor purchasing, primarily because there are very few bid-buying opportunities. Also, there are times when the buyer has the opportunity to

Intended use: Exact name: Brand name (or equivalent): Vintage: Alcohol content: Size of container: Type of container: Point of origin: Preservation method:

FIGURE 24.5. Example of product specification outline for alcoholic beverage products.

evaluate only the products available in the local area. This is especially true for fine wines and other specialty products.

It is possible to contract today with a winery, brewery, or distiller to prepare products according to your precise formulas. Some large hospitality organizations may consider offering to its customers these house brands. As is the case with personalized packaging, the added prestige and merchandising value may more than compensate for the extra cost and effort expended to secure these products.

RECEIVING ALCOHOLIC BEVERAGES

Because of its high cost and extreme exposure to theft, hospitality operators spend much care and effort receiving alcohol. Generally, the receiver is a supervisor, an owner-manager, or an assistant manager—much less frequently a receiving clerk.

If you have a large wine list, it is traditional, even necessary, to employ a wine steward. This employee usually does it all: he or she buys, receives, stores, and sells the wine in the dining room. This procedure flies in the face of generally accepted control activities. But, again, few staff people are sufficiently knowledgeable about wines. The wine steward, then, in an operation with a complex wine list, is necessary because he or she has a complicated expertise.

Whoever receives the product typically follows the procedures we noted in Chapter 13. He or she checks the quantity, sometimes by weighing unopened cases, and compares invoices with the purchase orders as well as with the labels on the beverages. It is crucial to check some labels very carefully; for example, some liqueurs are made with a brandy base and some are made with a neutral spirits base—the label indicates this, but these labels may be unclear to the uninitiated receiver. Also, the 750-milliliter bottle may be mistaken for the liter bottle.

Beer kegs can present some receiving difficulty. Some delivery agents want to attach the kegs in your refrigerator, or at least deliver them to the refrigerator, which may be against company policy. Another problem is that the kegs may be jostled too much at the receiving area, which could cause quality deterioration.

The receiver must also be alert to compute the exact amount of deposits that must be put up for bottles and kegs. He or she must be certain that these deposits are correct and that the company receives the appropriate credit for those kegs and bottles being returned to the distributor.

After examining the merchandise and being satisfied that everything is correct, the receiver completes any required paperwork. It is important to keep in mind that the federal government requires you to maintain liquor invoices and bill-paying records. The state and local government agencies may have similar requirements.

STORING ALCOHOLIC BEVERAGES

Storing alcoholic beverages is easier than storing many other food products. The typical procedure is to set aside a separate storage facility just for alcoholic beverages. Several operations also maintain separate storage facilities for beer and wine, although this is not a common practice; usually all alcoholic beverages are stored within the same general area.

These items must be secured better than other food and nonfood items mainly because they are easy to steal and convert to cash. The storage facility must be kept locked, with as few persons as possible having access to the keys. For example, the keys to a well-stocked wine cellar might be restricted to the wine steward and perhaps one or two other service personnel.

It is common to add the amount of new product placed in the storeroom to a bin card or enter it into a computerized inventory-management system. As we mentioned previously, many operators maintain a perpetual inventory of most alcoholic beverages.

Most operators take the bottles out of their shipping containers. This extra security precaution, although not so popular for bottled beer, eliminates the possibility of later discovering an empty bottle, or no bottle, in the liquor case.

Distilled spirits, wine, and beer all have somewhat unique storage requirements. They are as follows.

DISTILLED SPIRITS

This liquor requires little care, and its storage life is usually long. It should be placed in a dry storage facility devoid of direct sunlight and excessive heat. Some people believe that distilled spirits improve in flavor if they age a while, but this is not true once they are put in the bottle. In addition, if some bottles are even slightly open, evaporation can occur. And spirits that contain sugar should not be stored long once they have been opened; not only do they evaporate, they also develop offensive odors.

WINE

Wines are harder to store. They require specific temperature and humidity conditions. Generally, red wines are kept in a cool area. White wines and sparkling wines are usually kept under refrigeration because they are served cold.

Most wine bottles are stored on their side, to keep the cork moist so that it can be removed easily. If this type of wine is stored standing up for a protracted period, the cork may dry out. A dry cork permits more air to pass through it, and this air causes wines to change gradually in flavor and eventually to turn to a form of vinegar. You do not need to follow this procedure for fortified wines, that is, wines to which brandy has been added to raise the alcohol content—sherry, port, and madeira are common fortified wines. Nor would you follow it for wines that come in screw-top, capped bottles. A final reason for storing wine bottles on their side relates to old wines that contain sediment. If properly stored, the sediment collects in the bottle neck to be more easily removed at the time of service.

You should avoid subjecting wine to excessive heat as well as to widely fluctuating temperatures. Both can cause wine to turn to a form of vinegar. Consequently, you should avoid displaying wines in the dining areas for long periods. You also should not jostle the wine bottles as this will cause settled sediment to go back into solution.

In contrast to distilled spirits, some wines improve in flavor as they age in the bottle. In fact, wine has a life cycle: birth, adolescence, maturation, adulthood, and death. Red wines have longer lives than white wines. At times you may have to buy wine that is immature and wait for it to mature before you can serve it.

Most wine sold in large bag-in-the-box bulk containers is sometimes referred to as "jug wine." It is often used for the house wine. Although this type of wine does not improve in flavor as it ages, and it has a relatively long shelf life, it can spoil if you keep it too long after opening it.

If you wish to serve leftover wine, or if you want to serve fine wines by the glass, you should consider purchasing a wine-dispensing unit specifically designed to store opened bottles of wine. You can open a wine bottle, serve one glass, and put the opened bottle in this unit where its quality will be maintained. The unit uses a nitrogen-flushing process to eliminate oxygen (which causes quality deterioration); it also maintains the proper storage environment. This unit is very expensive; however, if an operation wishes to offer a "wine bar," it is an essential piece of equipment.

If you do not have a wine-dispensing unit of this type, you still could save opened wine and serve it later. To do this, you must reseal the bottle tightly, refrigerate it, and try to serve it as soon as possible. There is a bottle seal device on the market that allows you to reseal an opened bottle, attach a hand pump, and physically pump out as much air from the bottle as possible. You then should store this leftover product in the refrigerator. By pumping out most of the air, you extend the leftover wine's shelf life.

If it is impossible, or undesirable, to save opened wine, perhaps it can be used for cooking purposes. It could also be used to make vinegar; for instance, there is a vinegar-starter kit you can purchase, to which you add wine and perhaps one or more other ingredients. Eventually, the wine vinegar can be used for salad dressings and other vinegar-based food items.

BEER

Keg beer is not pasteurized; therefore, it must be kept under refrigeration at approximately 36 to 38°F. If not, the active yeasts continue to work, to manufacture more alcohol and CO_2 gas. If this process continues long enough, eventually it sours the beer. It could also cause the keg to explode.

Kegs should not be kept more than two weeks. By this time the quality and fresh taste have vanished, and patrons are sure to complain if you try to serve it. Plan, therefore, to rotate the kegs properly and, if possible, to arrange for weekly deliveries at the very least.

Beer kegs are usually stored in a walk-in refrigerator that is very close to the bar. They are tapped in place, and the beer travels through the lines to the bar. If you have more than one bar, you might find it necessary to have a refrigerator for each one.

Be careful of freezing beer. If it freezes and then thaws, you will find that a quantity of flakes settles and refuses to go back into solution, and the solution, therefore, changes. This beer must be discarded.

Most canned and bottled beers are pasteurized. They, therefore, have longer life than keg beer. Under refrigeration, canned beer has a storage life of approximately four months; bottled beer one of approximately six months. Without refrigeration, these lives shrink to less than three months. By no means will canned and bottled beer retain their quality and fresh taste indefinitely.

Canned and bottled beer often are delivered in unrefrigerated trucks. Thus, some quality deterioration has already begun, though if you then place it in a refrigerator, you can slow it somewhat. The life of canned and bottled beer is similar to that of fresh eggs: time and warm and fluctuating temperatures are the greatest foes.

Once beer is opened and poured, there is no way you can save it for later. Some recipes can use it, like fritter batter and welsh rarebit, but even here, you would prefer fresh beer. Consequently, if the beer is not consumed, there is little you can do to preserve it for later.

ISSUING ALCOHOLIC BEVERAGES

Unlike most other food and nonfood items, alcoholic beverages occasion the strict scrutiny of owners and managers. In fact, some sort of perpetual inventory implemented in conjunction with tight security on the physical storage facilities is the rule rather than the exception.

In many operations, the food and nonfood storage facilities may be left unattended and unguarded, but not in the case of alcoholic beverages. Even if no full- or part-time storeroom manager is on hand, the owner-manager, assistant manager, or head bartender normally assumes this task. Rarely do employees have the authority to get their own alcoholic beverages.

Typically, a requisitioner prepares a stock requisition. In addition, the requisitioner also may be required to turn in an empty bottle for every full one requisitioned, though technically this might be illegal, as some states require us to break the empties as soon as they are drained.

Management also should set fairly strict par stocks for most if not all alcoholic beverages. This makes it easier for bartenders to requisition only what they need. It also ensures that excess stock does not accumulate around the bar areas.

In operations that demand the strictest control, or in those that have several banquet bars or temporary bars, one might encounter a little different form of issuing. In these places, it is possible that the head bartender or assistant manager stocks each bar; that is, he or she brings it up to par. During the shift, if more product is needed, it is obtained from the head bartender or assistant manager. At the end of the shift, the employee either returns all the remaining stock to the storeroom or locks it up at his or her station. The head bartender or assistant manager counts what is left and determines the liquor usage. This quantity expressed in sales should jibe with the amount of sales as recorded on the cash register and with the amount of cash and/or drink tickets collected from guests. This control procedure represents a little more work, but it seems to us to be a worthwhile procedure.

Before issuing alcoholic beverages, especially distilled spirits, management may want to code the bottles with a number or with some sort of marking that can only be seen with an infrared light. As noted earlier, coding is done so that dishonest employees cannot slip in their own bottles, sell their own beverage to the guest, take the money, and pocket it without ringing up a sale.

If your operation maintains an extensive wine list, you might consider allowing the wine steward free access to the wine storage facilities while he or she is selling it in the dining room. This may sound like poor management, but it can work out well if you keep track of what the wine steward buys and what he or she sells in the dining room. A physical inventory, performed regularly, can also help to uncover any inexplainable shortages or other problems attributable to the wine steward.

Operations that have an extensive automatic bar system can simplify the issuing process and, in some cases, eliminate it for many beverage items. For example, in a major hotel, there could be several bar areas throughout the property connected to a central liquor dispensing room. This room holds all the liquor, which is fed through lines that end at the dispensing heads located at each bar. Bartenders, therefore, do not have to requisition these alcoholic beverages, since someone, usually an employee of the food and beverage control office, loads the beverages on the system and is responsible for maintaining a constant supply.

IN-PROCESS INVENTORIES

Purchasing, receiving, storing, and issuing alcoholic beverages are not difficult tasks, though selecting and procuring a list of fine wines can be. The real difficulties await you in the preparation and service of these products. The general feeling in the industry seems to be that when you deal with food, you must be primarily concerned with quality and product control—for example, with meat shrinkage and excessive trimming losses. But, since alcoholic beverages do not incur these problems, your primary concern is personnel control.

Certainly some problems can be associated with product control, but they are minimal: basically, a bit of over- or underpour, spillage, and an occasional mistake. These problems are easily controlled and generate much less alarm than can an overcooked prime rib or a salty clam chowder.

Security considerations are the real problem in bars. Bartenders may begin to pour free drinks for other employees or their friends. They may take it upon themselves to pour drinks "on the house." They may overpour for their friends and make up the difference by underpouring for other patrons or by replenishing the liquor supply with water. (This method is a form of inventory padding.) Or they may charge their friends for less than they actually consumed, making up the difference by overcharging a guest who is not fully aware of what he or she actually purchased. (This is sometimes referred to as check padding; that is, an unsuspecting patron's guest check is padded with overcharges.) Some bar operators employ a mystery shopping service to help prevent these problems.

There are so many opportunities for dishonesty in the bar business that it can be tiring just to enumerate them. But you cannot ignore them. You must practice tight security procedures. And when you do, take note of the most important security measure of all: supervision. Since our primary concern in bars is personnel control, it stands to reason that our most effective tool is employee supervision.

NONALCOHOLIC BEVERAGES

In many respects, the purchasing of nonalcoholic beverages parallels that of alcoholic beverages. Of course, one has more freedom here mainly because patrons do not seem to have the same brand loyalties as they do for alcoholic beverages. For instance, if you do not serve Coke, only a few customers will balk at Pepsi.

On the other hand, some soft drink companies are very active in enforcing their rights under copyright law, and so, in listing soft drinks, as on a menu or drink list, care must be taken to be accurate. The terms Coca-Cola and Coke are proprietary brand names and can be used only when Coca-Cola is served.

MANAGEMENT CONSIDERATIONS

Management must decide several things about nonalcoholic beverages, but the three most important are, (1) How many varieties to carry? You could offer several types of soft drinks, juices, and mixers. One brand of coffee, tea, and milk is sufficient, but soft drinks, for example, represent a major area of decision. (2) Should you use soft drinks in the bottle and can, or should you use dispensing machines that mix concentrate, water, and carbon dioxide? There is less profit with canned and bottled, but more convenience. Customers seem to prefer soft drinks in a glass or disposable container, with ice, because the beverage stays fresher and colder. (3) How important is the choice of a coffee supplier? *Very* important. This is a lesson that most seasoned hospitality operators learn quite early in their careers. A coffee and tea that are appropriate for the type of hospitality operation are selected very carefully, and it is not without a great deal of handwringing that a hospitality operator decides to take a chance with a product that will "save money." The portion cost of these items is insignificant when compared with the impression they leave with customers. So, as in the selection of a meat supplier, it is unusual for operators to switch suppliers capriciously.

SELECTION FACTORS

Despite the relative purchasing freedom nonalcoholic beverages permit, the selection factors must be considered quite carefully before deciding what to buy. Once you know what you want, the buying is easy, especially since the same type of exclusive wholesale distributorship system exists for many nonalcoholic beverages as exists for alcoholic beverages. The major selection factors are discussed next.

INTENDED USE

As always, you want to determine exactly the intended use of the item so that you will be able to prepare the appropriate, relevant specification.

For instance, a soda used in an alcoholic punch recipe may be of lower quality than one that will be served straight.

EXACT NAME

Some nonalcoholic beverages have minimum standards of identity set by the federal government. For instance, the word "juice" implies that the product is 100 percent derived from the fruit or vegetable—no water is added.

This is not true for all products, though. For instance, there are several types of "drinks" on the market, and one needs to examine these items very carefully for taste, color, and so forth before determining their suitability.

To some extent, there are trade association standards that are followed and adhered to by certain types of nonalcoholic beverage producers. For instance, the New York Coffee and Sugar Exchange sets minimum standards for coffee products.

U.S. GOVERNMENT GRADES (OR EQUIVALENT)

There are grades for fruit and vegetable juices, as noted in Chapter 18. Green tea also has a grade standard, as does milk. But the remaining nonalcoholic beverages carry no grades, though some things, such as coffee and tea, can receive an endorsement from one or more institutes.

BRAND NAME (OR EQUIVALENT)

Brand names are important to buyers. Like all of us, they have been conditioned to rely on certain products through habit and advertising. But many customers are indifferent to brands. One thing about brand names to keep in mind is the fact that you may be able to promote a certain brand and thereby enhance your business. Some suppliers help you by granting some type of promotional discount.

You are not tied to a brand. You can shop around, and if the quality and customer acceptance between brands are similar, you have a reasonable choice. Keep in mind, though, what we said earlier about copyright laws and proprietary rights of suppliers in regard to brand names.

SIZE OF CONTAINER

A fairly wide array of package sizes is available to the purchaser of nonalcoholic beverages. Sizes normally range from 6-ounce single-serve containers to 5-gallon kegs of syrup. In general, in the soda pop trade, the sizes are not so numerous as they are in, say, the fruit and vegetable juices line. Nevertheless, it is very important to select and procure the package size that suits your needs.

TYPE OF CONTAINER

There are several packaging materials from which to select. The quality of these materials is very standardized, so the major decision is determining which type of material suits your needs best. For some products, such as soda pop syrup, your choices usually are limited to bottles, kegs, and bag-in-the-box containers. But with an item such as ready-to-serve soda pop, more options are available.

Some suppliers offer unique types of containers, though usually these can be used only in the dispensing equipment that they provide. For instance, some Vitality brand juices can be purchased in an Express Pak® that fits snugly into the Vitality dispenser. The dispenser releases a programmed portion size at the push of a button.

You might be interested in personalized packaging for some of your nonalcoholic beverages. For instance, some dairies will personalize the single-serve containers of milk that you purchase. A corollary might be the willingness of a soft drink company to personalize the disposable drink cups sold to you, along with the soda pop syrup.

Some hospitality companies purchase some nonalcoholic beverages that are not packaged. For instance, some soda pop suppliers can pump syrup from their trucks into your reusable tanks attached to the pop dispensing machine. This may be a convenient alternative. It also can reduce packaging needs and contribute to a cleaner environment.

PRODUCT FORM

Generally, you can purchase "premix" beverages or "postmix" beverages. Premix products are ready to serve. You can purchase them in bottles, plastic cartons, waxed cartons, cans, kegs, or bag-in-the-box containers.

Postmix products require some additional preparation by someone on the staff of the hospitality operation. You can purchase these products in much the same type of containers in which premix products are packed.

With postmix products, you anticipate saving a few dollars because you are purchasing concentrates—frozen, dried, or liquid—and are providing the reconstitution needed to bring the item up to service. For instance, most soda pop dispensing units are set up in such a way that you must hook up a water supply line, a container of concentrate, and a cylinder of carbon dioxide gas. When a customer orders a soda pop drink, the ingredients are mixed as they flow through the lines into the glass or disposable drink cup. This procedure also provides a freshly mixed finished product, which is pleasing to the customer.

You will need to consider other product characteristics when purchasing nonalcoholic beverages; for instance, the type of grind desired for coffee; whether the coffee is regular or decaffeinated; the size and type of crystals for instant coffee; whether the cola is diet or regular; and so on. Furthermore, there are enough "low-fat," "low-sodium," and "low-something-or-other" to confuse even the most knowledgeable hospitality buyer.

Most nonalcoholic beverages can be purchased with varying degrees of form value. The more convenient the form, the more you generally must pay for the item. But a high AP price means nothing if the EP cost and overall value are acceptable. If you are concerned about the AP price, though, it would appear that you can reduce it considerably by accepting less form value.

PRESERVATION METHOD

Premix products generally are delivered at room temperature, though there is no reason that you cannot insist that the supplier maintain refrigerated temperatures while the items are in transit. Some specialty products, such as "natural" apple juice, tend to be kept under constant refrigeration by suppliers in order to preserve their quality and extend their shelf lives.

Postmix products will be preserved at dry storage, refrigerated, or freezer temperatures, depending on the type of item. For instance, powders will be kept at dry storage temperatures; liquid coffee concentrate will normally be kept at refrigerated temperatures; and liquid juice concentrates normally are delivered at freezer temperatures.

For some products, such as ground coffee or whole coffee beans, the products normally will be kept at dry storage temperatures unless you specify something different. Since refrigerated and freezer temperatures tend to extend these products' shelf lives, the buyer may want to consider dealing only with those suppliers who provide them.

AP PRICE

Quality and AP price seem to go hand in hand; the higher quality seems to imply, within reason, a higher AP price. This may not always be the case, especially when a certain soft drink company tries to gain a foothold by reducing prices temporarily. But the straight-line relationship between AP price and quality holds up reasonably well. For example, a less expensive premix soft drink implies that the flavorings are artificial; in addition, these products do not hold the carbon dioxide gas very long once they are opened. Thus, their overall value is seriously undermined.

EP cost can also rise disproportionately for some nonalcoholic beverages. For instance, several coffees taste somewhat similar, but the type of grind and the type of bean can make a difference in how much coffee you need to use to brew a pot.

Many nonalcoholic beverages present opportunity buys, such as quantity and promotional discounts. For example, Coke may help you defray your menu printing costs if you include its brand name on the menu. Also, price wars can occasionally erupt between the major soft drink companies.

You can save money by continually going from one soft drink brand to another. Pepsi and Coke constantly strive for your business. If you own your own refrigeration and dispensing and ice-making machinery, the switch is easy. If the supplier owns this equipment, it is not convenient to change, even though it may be economical. Another problem: You cannot sell Pepsi if Coke is advertised on your menu.

Sometimes the AP price is irrelevant. For instance, some states require wholesale price maintenance for milk; some even require retail price maintenance for milk. While the purveyor or retailer can charge more than the minimum required under the law, the minimum requirement is the price that is usually charged to all buyers.

SUPPLIER SERVICES

Supplier services are crucial when you purchase nonalcoholic beverages. If you have two relatively similar brands from which to choose, you tend to choose the one that carries with it more supplier services. Some distributors give away things—anything from menu decals to refrigerators—as long as you continue to buy from them. In general, however, you are not interested in such trinkets as clocks. But your interest surely will be piqued when a "free" refrigerator awaits you. The fact that this refrigerator can be used for items other than those you purchase from that distributor makes such a "gift" useful indeed.

Some suppliers also give you the free use of brewing equipment, dispensing equipment, coffee pots, and so forth when you purchase their beverage products. Or the company will charge you a token amount for the use of the equipment. These "equipment programs" are popular in our industry. You tend to pay more for the beverage products when you participate in this program, but the convenience may be worthwhile. Also, if you really want a particular beverage product, you might as well take the equipment program because unless you are a very large hospitality company with a great deal of purchasing power, it is unlikely that you will receive a discount if you do not take it.

The type of delivery schedule, ordering procedures, and minimum order requirements also are important. Moreover, if you are participating in an equipment program, you must ascertain how well the distributor will maintain the equipment.

PURCHASING NONALCOHOLIC BEVERAGES

Once you have decided on the types of beverages you want, your purchasing procedure follows a fairly routine pattern.

Ordering and delivery schedules are pretty well set, though they are not so solid as those for alcoholic beverages. In addition, you have more payment freedom; the credit terms are subject to more negotiation possibilities than are those for alcoholic beverages.

As with alcoholic beverages, the primary decision is how much to order. The par stock for these items usually varies quite a bit from one operation to the next. A three-day stock for soft drinks is typical; one for coffee and frozen beverages might run a week or more. A perishable product, such as milk, should be purchased, where possible, on a day-to-day, standing-order basis.

When purchasing soft drinks, it is normal for a route salesperson to call on you and "bring you up to par." Usually you can obtain a standing-order procedure for these types of items.

Some suppliers stipulate minimum order requirements. But these rarely present difficulty, as they might with alcoholic beverages, because it is unlikely that you would carry an exceptionally slow-moving nonalcoholic beverage.

Like alcoholic beverages, nonalcoholic beverages encourage an operator to follow the par stock approach entirely and to deal with several distributors to obtain the desired variety of beverages. Some distributors carry wide lines of beverages, but most carry only one or two varieties of nonalcoholic beverages.

Except for the normal quantity and volume discounts, other opportunity buys are infrequent. Those available normally take the form of introductory offers or, most commonly, promotional discounts. Promotional discounts normally take the form of menu printing and the provision of other signs. Introductory offers and free samples pop up sporadically, whenever soft drink firms make an extended effort to steal business away from each other. It is generally possible to obtain a cash discount if you pay the route salesperson COD.

As with alcoholic beverages, though, detailed specifications are not usually prepared for these items, as brand-name merchandise that can fit your peculiar storage and dispensing machinery tends to be the major consideration. However, some large hospitality enterprises with the resources to shop around might prepare detailed specs for such products as tea, coffee, and juices. Figure 24.6 shows some example product specifications. And Figure 24.7 notes an example product specification outline for nonalcoholic beverage products.

RECEIVING NONALCOHOLIC BEVERAGES

The suggested receiving principles noted in Chapter 13 should be used. Unfortunately, though, the care exercised in receiving alcoholic beverages dissipates when it comes to nonalcoholic beverages.

Receivers normally check the quantity, AP prices, and condition of

Coffee Used for drink service at main bar and at dining room side stands Yorkshire brand Ground, decaffeinated 12-oz. packets, vacuum packed Packed 24 packets per case	Tomato juice Used for drink service at main bar Campbell brand (or equivalent) 46-oz. can Packed 12 cans per case
Cola Used for drink service at main bar and at dining room side stands Pepsi brand 5-gal. bag-in-the-box Syrup Postmix	Orange juice Used for breakfast beverage Sunkist brand (or equivalent) U.S. Grade A (or equivalent) Concentrate (3 to 1) 32-oz. can Packed 12 cans per case Frozen

FIGURE 24.6. Example of nonalcoholic beverage product specifications.

the delivered goods. Refrozen merchandise, split packages, and broken glass are the major quality checks, along with a careful examination of the labels to see whether the correct product has been delivered. The best quality check would be to note the effective age of the product, but this is difficult. For example, time is an enemy of coffee quality; unfortunately, it is hard to tell how old the coffee is when you receive it unless there is some type of dating on the package. Some companies, such as PepsiCo, put freshness dates on some of their products; for instance, Diet Pepsi package labels contain a "best if consumed by" date.

Intended use: Exact name: U.S. grade (or equivalent): Brand name (or equivalent): Size of container: Type of container: Product form: Preservation method:

FIGURE 24.7. Example of product specification outline for nonalcoholic beverage products.

Receivers must also be careful to account properly for any returned merchandise, especially empty returnable containers. Since you may have to pay bottle and keg deposits, you should ensure that you receive the appropriate credit when you return the empties. And after examining the merchandise and being satisfied that everything is correct, a receiver must complete any necessary paperwork.

STORING NONALCOHOLIC BEVERAGES

Storing nonalcoholic beverages in the correct environment can retard quality deterioration. Coffee quality, for example, rapidly fades in heat. Many operators keep ground and whole-bean coffee under refrigeration or even in the freezer.

Canned and bottled beverages do best in a refrigerator, although some products, like canned tomato juice, keep well in a dry storeroom.

Frozen items must be stored in a freezer and should not be thawed in advance. For instance, frozen juice concentrate should not be thawed prior to preparation; it should be mixed with water while it is frozen and be allowed to thaw in this manner. Ideally, you would have a dispensing unit that is programmed to mix one glass of juice at a time, using the frozen concentrate stored in the unit. This ensures a high-quality finished product and a satisfied guest.

With frozen beverages, take the time to check, periodically, the condition of their containers, as they have a tendency to crack and split.

ISSUING NONALCOHOLIC BEVERAGES

As we implied, some operators do not extend a great deal of control over nonalcoholic beverages. The fact that many of these products go directly to a production department, or sometimes even to self-service dispensing units in the dining room, mitigates against a strict accounting. Ideally, they should be controlled as much as any other product. But, since they rarely represent a great portion of the total purchase dollar, they tend to be taken for granted.

In operations that do a lot of bar business, the bartenders may also be responsible for their mixers—the soft drinks, cream, and juices used in the preparation of cocktails. In this situation, the mixers might receive as much attention as that accorded the alcoholic beverages.

There are three major reasons that managers and owners slight nonalcoholic beverage control. First, the cost of controlling these items may be much higher than any potential savings. Second, many operators allow employees to drink soft drinks, milk, and coffee for free, or for a modest "drink fee" deducted from their paychecks; if so, why would they steal them (although they might give them away to preferred customers)? And third, these items may get shifted back and forth between the bar, the kitchen, room service, and poolside service, which makes monitoring difficult.

IN-PROCESS INVENTORIES

Many problems with nonalcoholic beverages center on the pre-preparation, preparation, and service functions: (1) How much do you let employees drink on the job? (2) Who makes the coffee? an idle warewasher? a server who is not busy at the time? (3) Who refills the milk dispenser? (4) Who retrieves the single-service cans of tomato juice? (5) How much coffee should you make at one time? how much iced tea?

Here again, supervision is the key. Waste can be a problem in this area, and a reasonable savings can accrue to the operator who monitors and controls the use of these items carefully.

KEY WORDS AND CONCEPTS

Alcohol content

Allocation

AP price

Appropriate menu price for alcohol

Aseptic package

Automatic bar

Brand name

Brew pub

Call brand

Capital costs

Case price

Check padding

Control state

Drink fee

EP cost

Equipment program

Exact name

Exclusive distributorship

Freshness dates

House brand

House wine

Importance of the coffee supplier

In-process inventories

Intended use

Inventory padding

Inventory sales control procedure

Jug wine

License state

Light liquor

Liquor industry publications

Liquor license

MADD

Management considerations when
   purchasing beverages

Nitrogen flush

Perpetual inventory

Personalized packaging

Point of origin

Popular types of alcoholic beverage
products

Postmix

Post-off

Pouring cost

Premium well

Premix

Preservation method

Price maintenance

Product form

Proof

Pull strategy

Purchasing, receiving, storing, and
issuing beverage products

Route salesperson

Size of container

Standard of identity

Stockless purchase

Supplier services

Type of container

U.S. grades

Vintage

Well brand

Wine-dispensing unit

Wine speculating

QUESTIONS AND PROBLEMS

1. What type of hospitality operation would be most inclined to use a premium well brand? Why?

2. What is the alcoholic content of a spirit of 100 proof?

3. What is the recommended storage procedure for white wines?

4. What is the recommended storage procedure for keg beer?

5. An owner-manager would be interested in a soft drink company's equipment program because he or she could achieve several advantages from this program. What are some of these advantages?

6. Note one major disadvantage of an equipment program.

7. Assume that you own a small neighborhood tavern. You employ one bartender and one barback (i.e., someone who assists the bartender). You also tend bar. Who should order the items? Why? Who should receive and store them? Why?

8. What are the major advantages and disadvantages of providing your guests with a well-stocked wine cellar?

9. What is the major selection factor for alcoholic beverages?

10. The selection factor "point of origin" is an important consideration for _____ products.

11. A product specification for fruit juice could include the following information:

    (a) _____

(b) _____

(c) _____

(d) _____

(e) _____

12. Assume you are a country club manager. You are choosing the well brand you want to use for Scotch. One brand is 86 proof. Its AP price is $12.40 per liter. Another brand, with the same proof, has an AP price of $11.50 per liter. The former brand is fairly well known and is thought to be a respectable product. The latter brand is rather obscure. Which brand would you select? Why? If possible, ask a country club manager to comment on your answer.

13. What is the primary difference between a premix beverage and a postmix beverage?

14. Why are detailed specifications not often prepared for alcoholic beverage products?

15. Is it a good idea to let a wine steward purchase, receive, store, and sell the wines? Why? Assume that you allow this practice. How would you exercise control over the wine steward? If possible, ask a hotel food and beverage director to comment on your answer.

16. What critical information is missing from the following product specification for beer?

Beer

Used for bar service

Packaged in 12-ounce, nonreturnable bottles

Packed 24 bottles per case

17. What are some of the differences between a license state and a control state?

18. The consumption of alcohol in the United States has declined over the past few years. What are some of the reasons for this decline?

19. When would you specify personalized packaging for a beverage product?

20. Define or explain briefly the following terms:

(a) Liquor license

(b) Aseptic package

(c) Pull strategy

(d) Pouring cost

(e) House wine

(f) Jug wine

(g) Post-off

(h) Case price

(i) House brand
(j) Wine steward
(k) Check padding
(l) Price maintenance
(m) Wine speculation
(n) Perpetual inventory
(o) Inventory padding

CHAPTER 25

Tabletop Made Easy

We've started a service revolution. Acquired by Vitro, S.A., makers of Crisa glassware, we combine our 150 years of foodservice marketing experience with the vast financial and technological resources of one of the world's largest glassware makers. As WorldCrisa, formerly World Tableware International, we now offer more products and service support from one supplier than you've ever seen.

For more information, contact WorldCrisa at 203-265-8000.

WorldCrisa delivers tailored programs to fit your needs:
- Glassware
- Dinnerware
- Buffet and Holloware
- Flatware
- Candles
- Tabletop accessories

We can match existing items you have in service or custom coordinate your entire tabletop. In fact, we can do things for your business that you never dreamed possible.

Source: World Crisa Corporation

NONFOOD
EXPENSE ITEMS

THE PURPOSE OF THIS CHAPTER

This chapter discusses:

- The major management considerations surrounding the selection and procurement of nonfood expense items
- The major selection factors for cleaning supplies, cleaning tools, maintenance supplies, permanent ware, single-service disposable ware, preparation and service utensils, fabrics, other paper products, and miscellaneous items

INTRODUCTION

Some operations devote a great amount of money to nonfood expense items, which are sometimes referred to as "operating supplies." (An expense item is one that can be written off in the current year's income statement; that is, it is not a "capital" item in that it does not have to be depreciated over a period of years.) But the attention that is lavished on food and beverage items typically is greater than that devoted to these types of purchases.

Buying nonfood items is sometimes a highly routinized activity. The buyer usually sets the major guidelines, and the department heads are held responsible for ensuring an orderly flow of cleaning agents, stationery, glassware, and so forth. In these instances at least some minimal attention is paid to the purchasing decision.

Smaller operations unfortunately tend to view these purchases as nuisances and may try to consummate them as speedily as possible. But this can be a serious mistake. Although these purchases often represent a comparatively small portion of the total purchasing dollar, a considerable number of managerial concerns surround these purchases—concerns that can, upon closer examination, dramatize the need for careful nonfood procurement procedures.

MANAGEMENT CONSIDERATIONS

Buying nonfood expense items sometimes presents difficult decisions. The quality of mop you purchase will probably not influence your sales volume, but the quality of your guest cleaning supplies—things like individually wrapped or liquid soap, and paper or linen towels in the rest rooms—definitely help to shape your image. Consequently, you should not make purchasing decisions on these items lightly. Some of the considerations that can affect these decisions are discussed next.

PERSONALIZATION OF NONFOOD ITEMS

The degree of personalization that you want in a nonfood item is related to the image you wish to create. How customized do you want your nonfood products to be? Will any old paper napkin do? Or should it have your name on it? Or some other type of advertising or insignia? In some cases, nonfood items become advertisements in disguise and should be treated accordingly. (Chapter 26 contains a discussion of advertising services.) This fact makes it difficult for a purchaser to evaluate the price of nonfood items. Generally, the more personalized these items become, the higher their price.

When we consider the price of a matchbook, for example, we have to divide it into two components: the advertising component and the functional component. We can note the price for plain matchbooks, to which any increment in price would represent an advertising expenditure.

Sometimes a purchaser forms the habit of staying with a certain style of nonfood guest supplies. Salespersons know this, so that it is only natural for them to sell you one item—say, a personalized napkin—for a very reasonable price. The idea might be for you to work the item into your business, for your customers to become enamored of it, and then the salesperson urges you to buy similar additional nonfood expense items for perhaps a little higher price.

The process may not operate quite like this, but image is crucial to the sale of nonfood items, and salespersons know this. They constantly remind you of this. By so doing, they can place a purchaser accustomed exclusively to food buying on the defensive.

The image phenomenon does complicate some nonfood purchases. Moreover, once you have decided what you want, it may be hard to turn back, since you cannot necessarily go to another supplier and get exactly the same product.

It is not that you will be stuck for life with a certain type of napkin, but you may hesitate to change styles too abruptly. One does not make major changes without incurring some risk. For instance, customers really notice when a food service moves from high-quality guest supplies to a lower quality. You should make sure, then, that several of your nonfood items will serve your needs for a long time.

NONFOOD PRODUCT VARIETY

Another major concern is the many nonfood items available on the market and the numerous suppliers who carry items of this type. This situation favors the bid buyer. But it can cause confusion and anxiety for the typical owner-manager, who may seek relief with a sympathetic one-stop supplier. Because many of these selection and procurement decisions may influence your image for quite some time, however, it may be wise to take more time and give bid buying a try.

Bid buying offers a bit more potential benefit in the nonfood area because, if you purchase in large quantities, you can often get favorable bids from several competing suppliers. And since you may not need to go through the time-consuming bidding procedures too often, the little bit you do endure can bring impressive savings. Finally, because these items are not perishable, there is no spoilage; hence, their as-used cost is much more predictable, unless, of course, you fail to exert proper supervision over in-process inventory use.

If you buy a lot of standard nonfood items, such as plain napkins, ordinary flatware, and standard drinking glasses, bid buying may be less beneficial. These standard items typically present a smaller spread in price, quality, and supplier services among suppliers. The wider spreads normally occur when you buy personalized items and have varying quality requirements.

DEGREE OF PRODUCT CONVENIENCE

An interesting managerial issue is the degree of convenience to specify in certain nonfood items. For example, do you want one all-purpose cleaner, which, according to some people, does not exist? Or do you want to spend time selecting individual cleaning agents for specific uses?

Form economic value appears once again in this situation. Obviously, the greater the convenience, the greater the form value; hence, you can expect a higher AP price.

Perhaps the touchiest issue associated with nonfood convenience centers on disposable versus reusable items—for example, linen napkins and place mats versus their paper or plastic counterparts. The permanent versus disposable argument that surrounds permanent dish and silverware and disposables is especially acute. Several studies "prove" the economics of permanent ware. But, as you can imagine, a lot of people consider disposables the wisest choice. Complicating the issue further is the negative environmental impact associated with disposable ware, though some buyers overcome this by purchasing items made with recycled materials.

For some types of hospitality operations, permanent ware is necessary to maintain the appropriate image. But any operation can work in at least a few disposables, and most customers accept some, if only paper towels in the rest room. And the convenience of using them is certainly something we cannot argue with.

In our opinion, permanent ware is the logical choice if you are concerned with cost saving. With reusable items, you avoid the cost of solid waste disposal. Moreover, disposable ware is not only expensive but a waste of our natural resources unless we take the time to send them to a recycling plant after use.

NONFOOD IMPULSE PURCHASING

A subtle problem in buying nonfood expense items is the impulse purchase. At times a buyer might purchase a nonfood item on the spur of the moment. A lot of little things, such as coin rolling devices and vegetable cutters, enter the operation and perhaps are used very seldom if at all. The lesson here is: Do not purchase anything unless you are absolutely certain it is needed.

SUPERVISING NONFOOD ITEMS

Another problem associated with nonfood items is the tendency to neglect the supervision of employees when they use them. Although few of these items represent a large portion of the purchase dollar, their continual disappearance and misuse can increase significantly the overall operating costs. All too often, for instance, a cook who delimes the steam table pours in a half-gallon of delimer solution instead of the recommended half-quart. Or he or she might toss out a dirty mop head instead of sending it to the laundry.

The examples of waste are numerous and expensive. Thus, the supervisor should strictly monitor the usage of these nonfood items. Larger operations take this need for supervision as a given. But they too can become lax at times. For example, during a rush period, who stops to make sure that there is only one paper doily, instead of two or three, under the shrimp cocktail boat?

Even the large operations have a tendency to set flexible par stocks for the nonfood items and then allow the department head to monitor the usage rates and order replacement items he or she deems necessary. In these situations, it is possible that there could be frequent stockouts of these items, since these purchases may not be monitored so closely.

QUANTITY AND VOLUME DISCOUNTS

Whenever possible, you should make every attempt to purchase large amounts of these products. In our experience, there is a very good savings associated with this practice. The discounts available in the nonfood channel of distribution are quite attractive, and if you have the money and the storage space necessary to participate in this practice, the as-used costs for the supplies usually will be considerably less than those obtained with small order sizes.

NONFOOD PACKERS' BRANDS

The use of packers' brands as a selection factor does not seem to be so prevalent for nonfood expense items as it is for food and beverages. You might rely on a specific producer, especially for personalized items, but not for standard, everyday items. There are so many producers and varieties of standardized nonfood expense items that the buyer often is encouraged to shop around.

SYSTEMS SALE

A systems sale occurs when you purchase a particular product, say, a specific type of cash register, which can accept only paper guest checks and/or paper cash register tapes that are manufactured by one company, usually the company that also manufactures the cash register.

There is a type of trade-off that must be considered by the owner-manager whenever the opportunity arises to participate in a systems sale. On the one hand, the salesperson of the main item, say, the cash register, might be willing to sell the register for a very low price. But, when you need the paper products, parts, and so forth, for its operation, you could be staring at expensive prices with no available alternative.

OPERATING SUPPLIES SCHEMES

For one reason or another, we are more vulnerable to ripoff artists in the nonfood expense items, capital equipment items, and services channels of distribution. The care and diligence we exercise in our food and beverage purchasing somehow appear to wane a bit when we buy nonfood products.

For instance, there is a tendency to order these kinds of items from a catalog, or from some other type of advertised solicitation, say, one that shows up in a trade magazine. It is possible that the item ordered in such a way does not satisfy us because the catalog description may be misleading.

Another problem encountered by many businesspersons is the office supply telephone salesperson. These "WATS-line hustlers" or "toner-phoners" offer what appear to be tremendous bargains, but unfortunately the merchandise delivered is inadequate. The Better Business Bureaus (BBB) throughout the country probably have thick files listing all sorts of scams like this.

It is important to follow rigorous selection and procurement procedures for all products and services you must purchase. For instance, in our recent examples, you could not get hurt if you followed an approved supplier list that restricted the buyer's purchasing authority.

SAFETY CONSIDERATIONS

Some nonfood expense items may present a safety hazard. For instance, you must be concerned with toxic chemicals, cleaners that impart distasteful odors, and cleaners and similar products that, while safe in and of themselves, could, through mishandling, become dangerous.

We cannot always refuse to purchase something because it represents a possible danger. But we should be well prepared to store and use such items properly. The local health districts normally require stringent storage procedures for toxic materials. We must supplement these legal requirements with stringent operating procedures of our own to ensure that no harm comes to us or our guests.

Some hospitality operators would rather eliminate the need to store and to use toxic products by purchasing a service to do the work for them. For example, instead of purchasing, storing, and using pest control materials, it might be preferable to hire a pest control company to perform this function.

NEW VERSUS USED

Some nonfood expense items can be purchased in a used condition. Such things as china, glass, and silver often are available from secondhand dealers, at auctions, or from other hospitality companies that are liquidating their assets.

In our experience, you can save a tremendous amount of money if you are lucky enough to stumble onto a good deal. As with any type of used item, though, you must be willing to take your chances. Furthermore, you must be willing to spend considerable time and effort to locate this type of merchandise.

EQUIPMENT PROGRAM

It is possible to purchase a nonfood expense item and concomitantly obtain from the supplier the equipment needed to use it. For instance, if you purchase a certain amount of dishwasher machine chemicals, it is possible to rent the machine from the chemical supplier at a very favorable rate. It also may be possible to receive the use of a dishwasher machine and all the chemicals you need while paying a certain amount for each rack of soiled tableware you run through the machine.

These equipment programs are similar to the ones we noted for non-alcoholic beverages in the previous chapter. The same advantages and disadvantages are applicable here. Owner-managers, though, seem to prefer some sort of equipment program because it eliminates the need to invest in the equipment and the equipment generally is maintained free of charge. In the long run, it probably costs more to operate in this fashion; however, in the short run, such a strategy can enhance the hospitality company's cash flow.

LIFETIME COST

Some nonfood expense items have a long life. They are not used once and discarded, but will remain with the business for a reasonable period of time. Consequently, when computing their as-used costs, it is important to consider additional factors.

For long-life items, we must be interested in the original AP price of the product. We must also be aware of any operating costs that will be associated with the use of these items. For instance, a cleaning tool must be wielded by someone who receives a wage. And if the cleaning tool is less expensive than another one, but requires more time to wield, in the long run we do ourselves a financial disservice if we purchase such an item.

Likewise, we must consider the potential salvage value of the long-life item. For instance, somewhere down the line, we might be able to trade in a cleaning tool for a new model and receive a very generous trade-in allowance.

This concept probably is best understood by using a "new car" example. A very expensive new car can easily cost less to operate and can retain its value much longer than can an automobile that has a much lower sticker price.

CREDIT TERMS

Sometimes you must purchase a large amount of these items. You should consider shopping around for the best credit terms if this option is available. You should be especially discerning of the amount, if any, of deposit you must put up before you are allowed to place an order for something that must be customized. Furthermore, if you change your mind about the item later on (i.e., you do not wish to purchase the product even though you ordered it), find out ahead of time what happens to your deposit—do you lose all of it or only part of it?

PURCHASING NONFOOD EXPENSE ITEMS

There are several ways to purchase nonfood expense items, though there are fewer ways to buy them than to buy food. But perhaps because nonfood expense items are not perishable, the various alternatives available can be quite viable and represent a few cost-saving opportunities. Many of these items can be purchased on a day-to-day basis. Or they can be purchased as far in advance as your storage permits.

The major problems are, what is the proper par stock, and who is the appropriate supplier? These are not easy questions because there are several quantity and volume discount variations among suppliers. And, since these products are not perishable, most suppliers will try to accommodate your needs.

Typically, the par stocks are large. And if you want any sort of personalization, usually you must purchase in huge quantities from one supplier. Also, it is common to find some sort of stockless purchase arrangement.

Multiunit operations save the most when they exercise their quantity buying power. Franchisees also tend to purchase from the company commissary, as this usually represents the lowest possible price to them.

The principal step in buying nonfood expense items is deciding exactly what you need. This is not necessarily an easy task because there are many potential suppliers and many varieties of items available. For some products, such as cleaning supplies, the quality and as-used cost differences between them may not be readily apparent.

Irish coffee mug Used for bar service Standard restaurant logo on white background Libbey brand (or equivalent) 8.5-oz. mug Packed 24 per case	Disposable foam cup Used for hot drinks Plain white color CODE brand (or equivalent) 6-oz. cup size 25 cups per plastic sleeve Packed 40 sleeves per case

Bar straw
Used for bar service
House brand (or least expensive
   brand)
Red color
$7^{3}/_{4}$-in. straw
500 straws per box
Packed 10 boxes per case
	Liquid chlorine bleach
	Used for general cleaning purposes
	House brand (or least expensive
	   product)
	1-gal. plastic container with screw-
	   top cap
	Packed 4 to 6 gallons per case

FIGURE 25.1. Example of nonfood expense item specifications.

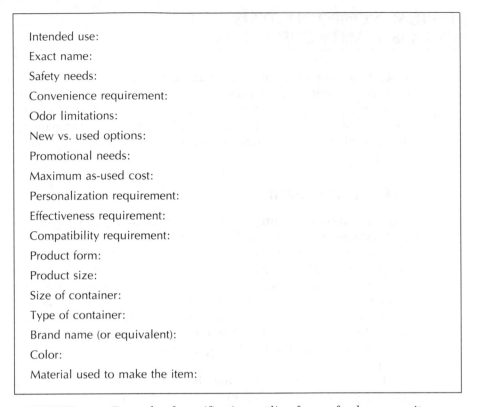

Intended use:

Exact name:

Safety needs:

Convenience requirement:

Odor limitations:

New vs. used options:

Promotional needs:

Maximum as-used cost:

Personalization requirement:

Effectiveness requirement:

Compatibility requirement:

Product form:

Product size:

Size of container:

Type of container:

Brand name (or equivalent):

Color:

Material used to make the item:

FIGURE 25.2. Example of specification outline for nonfood expense items.

Once you know what products will suit your needs, it is a good idea to prepare specifications for them. Figure 25.1 shows some example specifications. And Figure 25.2 notes an example specification outline for nonfood expense items.

As with liquor, there is a tendency to deemphasize the use of specifications when buying nonfood expense items. Many times when we need these products, we go to the supplier and examine them personally before placing an order. Alternatively, it is common for salespersons to demonstrate and/or show these products to potential buyers before soliciting purchase orders.

Purchasing nonfood expense items can be as easy or as difficult as you want to make it. As we have already noted, it may be to your benefit to expend a lot of effort to select and procure these products because your work may be rewarded with lower AP prices and, it is hoped, lower as-used costs. Realistically, we find that many hospitality operations use one-stop shopping; perhaps for these operations, the number of dollars saved do not compensate for the extra purchasing efforts.

TYPICAL NONFOOD ITEMS USED BY HOSPITALITY OPERATORS

Hospitality operators typically purchase in the following nine nonfood expense categories: (1) cleaning supplies, (2) cleaning tools, (3) maintenance supplies, (4) permanent ware, (5) single-service disposable ware, (6) preparation and service utensils, (7) fabrics, (8) other paper products, and (9) miscellaneous items. We discuss each of them in the next paragraphs.

CLEANING SUPPLIES

Several types of cleaning supplies are normally purchased in the hospitality industry: guest supplies, such as moisturizing cream; chemical cleaners; soaps; detergents; bleach; and polishes and waxes. The guest supplies usually represent as much advertising as guest convenience. For instance, the individually wrapped soap, shampoo, and shoe polish placed in guest rooms normally carry some type of advertising.

When purchasing guest supplies, you might be able to bargain for a promotional discount. For example, will Procter & Gamble give you a price reduction if you use its soap in your guest rooms, guest rest rooms, and poolside showers?

Cleaning supplies, other than those purchased for customer needs, are usually selected on the basis of the following factors:

- *As-Used Cost.* A buyer is concerned with the efficiency of the cleaning agent. Efficiency is especially critical because in addition to the cost of the cleaner, you must consider the cost of labor and energy needed to use it. For example, the buyer is concerned with the cost of cleaning a square foot of floor or a square foot of tile. When examining various samples of these cleaners, then, the buyer often must make several cost computations, but this is necessary if one is concerned with efficiency.

- *Product Effectiveness.* Can the product you are considering actually get the job done? Or are there one or more exaggerated claims?

- *Adaptability.* Can the cleaner be adapted to other cleaning needs? That is, can we use one cleaner instead of two or more? There is a controversy regarding this issue: Many people do not believe that there is one all-purpose cleaner. Besides, they point out that, even if you do find one, your total stock of cleaning agents will not be any less. Although this may be true, it is more convenient to purchase one variety instead of several. And it is possible that the AP price of all-purpose cleaners may be less than the combined AP prices of seldom used one-purpose cleaners.

- *Product Safety.* Will the product harm the item being cleaned? Can it harm the person using it? Does it have the potential to harm the environment? If so, you should consider hiring a professional service instead of using it yourself.

- *Ease of Use.* Is the product easy to use, or do employees have to undergo extensive training or briefing to master it?

- *Odor.* Does the cleaner have a strong, lingering odor sufficient to cause guest and employee discomfort?

- *Container Size.* Do you have to buy the cleaner only in very large containers? Although they are cheaper per unit than smaller containers, large containers are harder to handle and can cause waste due to spillage.

- *Supplier Services.* Examine the supplier services and the product information carefully. For instance, you may require personal instruction for things like dishwashing machine chemicals and silver polish usage. And, at times, you may encounter some difficulty when using the products; it would be nice to be able to call the supplier or salesperson and ask him or her to help you at a moment's notice.

    A very popular service is the 24-hour maintenance and troubleshooting service that such chemical companies as Eco-Lab provide to their customers. In some cases, this service can be more important to you than the products themselves.

Purchasing cleaning supplies is not particularly difficult once you select the suppliers you wish to deal with. Likewise, receiving these products poses no more than the run-of-the-mill problems.

Storage, though, can present some difficulty. These supplies must be stored away from foods and beverages to avoid contamination. You most likely will be in violation of your local health department's sanitation regulations if you do not segregate the storage of these products.

CLEANING TOOLS

Food services and lodging operations purchase several types of cleaning tools, such as brooms, mops, buckets, pot brushes, and squeegees. Several selection factors affect the purchasing decision here, for example:

- *Cost.* It is not easy to determine the long-term cost of a broom because you never know how long a broom will last. Nor do you always know who is going to push the broom—someone you pay specifically to push it or an idle employee whose salary remains the same regardless of his or her activity behind a broom. Consequently, most buyers consider the purchase price a minor selection factor. The general feeling seems to be that it pays to purchase high-quality hand tools because (1) they withstand the tough punishment normally meted out by busy employees, (2) the product cost pales in comparison with the cost of the labor needed to wield these tools—high-quality tools should be more efficient, and

(3) since high-quality tools generally last longer, the as-used cost should be minimal.

- *Employee Skill.* Consider the skill of the people using the tools. Low-skill (low-cost) employees usually need better products and perhaps more convenient products to work with.
- *Material Used to Make the Item.* Brushes and brooms, to cite two examples, are manufactured from a variety of raw materials. Sponges and scouring pads also come in various materials. It is important to identify the type of material that best suits your needs and your budget.
- *Used Tools.* It is possible to purchase used tools at a salvage sale, going-out-of-business sale, auction, or used products stores. The savings normally are considerable. You agree to take the items on an as-is, where-is basis. Although the savings may be attractive, the quality of the tools may be quite low. In addition, you must take the time to shop around for these types of deals. And usually you must provide your own delivery.

The cleaning tool procurement procedures are fairly routine. As usual, you first either bid buy or find the suppliers who understand what you need and are willing to work with you. You often find impulse purchasing in this area. Moreover, many of us are sometimes tempted to buy some type of gadget that may carry an exaggerated claim.

Receiving and storing cleaning tools poses no more than the ordinary problems. Their in-process storage and use can, however, create problems. Keeping the tools maintained—that is, the mop heads clean, mop buckets empty when not in use—can be difficult. High-quality tools should minimize these difficulties and make cleaning easier and more efficient.

MAINTENANCE SUPPLIES

Hospitality operations purchase several types of maintenance supplies: light bulbs, fuses, plumbing parts, and other similar items. The supplies purchased usually depend on the type of service or maintenance contracts you might have with a professional service. Generally, for most repair and maintenance needs, you contact a professional service who provides the necessary parts and labor.

But all operations buy at least some maintenance supplies. The small operation may buy only light bulbs and a few other things. But larger operations, especially the big hotels, may stock everything from light bulbs to water pipes. Purchasers use several factors for selecting these items, and we discuss them next.

- *Cost.* The price of maintenance supplies may or may not be relevant. When you purchase things like water pipes or fuses, you must purchase good-quality merchandise. There is not an inferior quality, since many of these items must pass safety and other building code standards set by federal and local governmental agencies.

If you do have a choice among a variety of qualities, you need to consider the life of the replacement part. If you do not want to change light bulbs every other month, you will need a higher-quality, more expensive bulb.

You also need to consider the length of time you will remain in your particular operation. If, for example, you intend to sell your business next year, you may not want to splurge for the best maintenance parts; perhaps a lower-quality, less expensive item will do.

- *Labor Availability.* You should consider the labor you have available to do the maintenance. If you have only a few labor hours for maintenance, you should consider purchasing easy-to-use replacement parts or long-life parts or engaging in a maintenance contract with a professional service. This trade-off is one that operators contemplate quite often. When you purchase replacement parts, you also have to think about providing the labor. Labor is quite expensive, and you want to reduce it; hence, many small operators learn how to "fix the ice machine" themselves.

- *Used Supplies.* Should you ever purchase used maintenance supplies? As in saving the old spark plugs from your car and using them in the power lawn mower, the possibilities exist if you care to trouble yourself.

- *Sizes.* Maintenance supplies come in various sizes, shapes, model numbers, and the like. You must be very certain that you purchase the exact product or else it will not serve your needs. For instance, an air-conditioning filter of the wrong size can be used in your air-conditioning system only at the risk of damage to the machinery.

- *Capitalizing Expenses.* If you get tired of replacing parts and maintaining equipment, you can "capitalize" these expenses; that is, you can buy more expensive capital equipment that does not need much maintenance work. But this decision represents a major capital equipment decision and is typically made only by the owner-manager, not by the buyer.

The procurement procedure for these supplies is reasonably straightforward, and receiving and storing present no more than the average problems. Two unique problems we do notice with these items are, first, a tendency to carry a lot of these supplies in stock. This tendency is understandable, as an owner-manager gets annoyed very quickly if there are no light bulbs to replace the burned out pool lights. If you work at it, you might be able to reduce the stock level, although only you can decide how much of a stockout potential you are willing to accept.

Second, maintenance schedules can be a headache. For example, should you replace the light bulbs as they burn out, or should you estimate the average life of the bulbs and change all of them at once, thereby saving some labor cost?

PERMANENT WARE

Your initial investment in permanent ware is actually a capital expenditure, in that it must be depreciated on the income statement. But, once you purchase your original stock, the replacements you buy every so often—or have delivered, if you are on a stockless purchase plan—are generally considered "costs of doing business," expenses that will be written off on this year's income statement.

Several types of permanent ware enter the typical food-service operation: plates, silver (or other flatware), glasses, ashtrays, vases, salt and pepper shakers, creamers, sugar bowls, and so forth. You may, however, have the option of using disposables, depending on your type of hospitality operation.

There are comparatively few selection factors for permanent ware, but they are very critical. We discuss them next.

- *What Permanent Ware Do You Need?* You must decide exactly what you want. If you want standardized items, you could go to just about any supplier and buy them. For run-of-the-mill products, you will find very little spread between prices. Determining exactly what you want depends on how much impact you think these items have on your image. The more personalization required, the more these products cost and, typically, the fewer suppliers you have to choose from. In addition, the greater the degree of personalization, usually the larger the quantity you must buy, or guarantee to buy, to make it economical for you and the supplier.

- *AP Price.* The AP price for these items may be a marginal consideration if you purchase highly personalized products. But for standardized products, you could reduce the price by opting for lower quality.

  It is also possible to reduce the price of certain personalized items. For example, manufacturers will produce standard shapes, to which you can ask them to apply certain lettering or other pictorial designs. Typically you receive only a few options, but they may be enough to satisfy your taste and budget.

- *The Need to Match.* How well does the plate you select go with the salt and pepper shaker set, or with the general decor? The tendency is to select all the permanent items together, as one set, to ensure compatibility and a standard design and image throughout. Operations that have mismatched permanent ware risk developing a poor image.

- *Source of Supply.* Should you buy these items directly or from local suppliers? As with all direct purchases, you must be able to provide the missing economic values, which, in most cases, is best left to the professionals. If we buy directly, we probably cannot obtain a stockless purchase plan, which is something of great value to most operations that have limited storage facilities.

- *Material Used to Make the Item.* There is a seemingly endless variety of materials used to manufacture permanent ware. Vitrified china, cut crystal, plastic, and so forth are available. Prices will vary with the type of material, as will the image you create.

- *Sizes.* You must note the specific size of product you require. For instance, the volume of glasses, the shape of plateware, and so forth must be considered.

- *Length of Service.* To a certain extent, there is a trade-off between price and durability. But durability is not the same as the life of a product in this case, since theft is a constant problem faced by all hospitality operators; shoplifting in particular is a major concern. So, although we may pay for higher quality and durability, ironically, we may make these items more attractive to thieves.

- *Used Permanent Ware.* Again, you could purchase used items and incur the advantages and disadvantages we noted earlier.

The major purchasing concern, of course, is deciding what products you need and want. Once you decide, you should shop around a little, at least initially. When you settle on a supplier—and you normally settle on one, especially if you purchase highly personalized items—the rest falls easily into place because you stay with this supplier for your replacements. Similarly, receiving and storing are not major problems with permanent ware items.

But difficulties can occur with the in-process inventory. Waste, breakage, and pilferage take their toll. When they do, operations may be tempted to replace the original item with a cheaper imitation. This practice works for some, but it could hurt the image of most operations. The decision to reduce quality must always be considered very carefully.

SINGLE-SERVICE DISPOSABLE WARE

As we noted earlier in this chapter, the major decision in this area is whether to use disposable ware exclusively, permanent ware exclusively, or some combination of the two. In some states and local municipalities, the disposables purchase decision is restricted considerably. For instance, some areas outlaw the use of any type of disposable product unless it is biodegradable. Some areas also mandate the use of paper goods made with unbleached materials; for instance, instead of purchasing white paper coffee filters, you may be restricted to the brown, unbleached alternative. It may also be necessary to purchase products made from recycled materials.

Several types of disposable ware are available from a multitude of suppliers. For instance, you can buy single-service plates, platters, bowls, cups, glasses, knives, forks, spoons, and ashtrays. The selection factors for these items are similar to those for permanent ware, with the addition of the following:

- *What Do You Need?* The decision on precisely what you want and need is a critical one. There are a variety of items available, numerous quality variations, and several possible substitutions you might make for permanent ware.

  You can find just about what you want, too. You can usually select from among several acceptable degrees of personalization and from among several price and quality combinations. You can find exceptionally strong, attractive items, or you can buy very inexpensive, standard items. Once you decide what you want, though, the number of potential suppliers diminishes in proportion to the amount of personalization you want.

- *Packaging.* You can buy some disposable ware packaged together. For example, you can get a single-service package that includes a fork, knife, spoon, napkin, and salt and pepper individuals. These packets are expensive, but they are very convenient in some applications, for instance, for take-out dinners.

  To save money, and to help protect the environment, many operations try to minimize these packaging alternatives. For instance, they may purchase recyclable, single-service cups packed in cases without dividers. The paper saved this way not only helps the environment, it can also mean long-term AP price reductions.

Some operations, like fast-food restaurants with brisk carry-out business, use a good deal of disposable ware. Some would never consider these products. The multitude of restaurants that fall between these two extremes must do some serious decision making. It is possible to include at least some disposable ware. This can be costly, since the price of these items, many of which are petroleum-based products, is high. But their convenience cannot be denied; nor can we forget that the cost of dishwashing machines, their space requirements, and their operation, can be costly as well—not usually so expensive as disposable ware in the long run, but, in the short term, disposable ware may be the logical alternative.

When you decide what you want in the way of disposable ware, it is typical, as we noted for some other nonfood expense items, to settle on one supplier. You must certainly do so if you want a high degree of personalization.

Once you have selected your supplier(s), the procurement procedures, receiving, and storing then follow a fairly routine pattern.

Issuing and the in-process inventory of disposable ware present few problems, mainly because most places that use them keep track of their usage as an extra control measure. For example, many fast-food operators keep track of the number of single-service cups used during the shift. If 100 are missing, management takes it to mean that 100 drinks were sold. The missing inventory of beverage and the cash taken in should be consistent with the missing 100 cups.

Finally, waste can become a problem if you let customers help themselves to disposable ware or permit employees to make indiscriminate use of these items.

PREPARATION AND SERVICE UTENSILS

Your initial purchase of these items, say, when you first go into business, is treated as a capital investment. That is, the initial purchase is depreciated. But replacement items can be treated as a current expense.

A hospitality operation must normally keep several items of this type on the premises: pots, pans, service trays, dish racks, carts, salad dressing holders, and so on.

Generally, the selection factors noted for permanent ware are the same for preparation and service utensils. There are two additional concerns, though. First, you must be alert to any safety hazards and any unusual sanitation difficulties with such things as knives and other utensils. And, second, the material used to make the item is an important consideration. For instance, aluminum, copper, cast iron, stainless steel, and so forth can be used to make pots, but each material serves a different purpose and carries a different AP price.

In some instances, you might consider replacing some of these products with their disposable counterparts. For instance, you can purchase single-use steam table pans, which are used for cooking or reheating food and then holding it in a hot steam table for service.

Purchasers generally do not have to be especially concerned with the image aspect of these items. The procurement procedure for such products parallels that for permanent ware in that the owner-manager tends to settle on a particular supplier.

Some utensils lend themselves to only one or two choices of suppliers. Such items as dish racks and refrigerator trays may have to be purchased from the equipment dealer who sold you the dishwasher and the refrigerator. Fortunately, a reasonable amount of standardization exists between most equipment, so that you can avoid this potential problem.

The in-process usage of these items must be supervised closely. Our experience suggests that these utensils will yield years of acceptable service if they are not abused—once abused, they tend to deteriorate rapidly.

FABRICS

Hospitality operations may purchase several types of fabrics: uniforms, bed linen, costumes, drapes, curtains, and so on. There are three ways to procure them: buy, lease, or use disposables. If you buy or lease permanent fabrics, you then must decide whether you will clean and maintain them yourself or whether you will use some type of laundry service. (See the discussion of laundry and linen supply service in Chapter 26.)

It is possible to buy disposable fabrics, such as aprons and hats. Even uniforms and costumes can be purchased that are completely disposable.

If you care to, you can buy uniforms and let the employees clean and maintain them. Or you can even let the employees buy their own uniforms and costumes, as well as clean and maintain them. If you do this, you must be sure that you do not violate the federal and/or state Department of Labor's regulations governing employee compensation.

As with all nonfood expense items, you must decide precisely what you want. And with fabrics, you must be prepared to like what you select, since you cannot easily change your mind without incurring some extraordinary added expense.

Many of the concerns relevant to permanent ware are applicable as well to fabrics, especially the concern about image. There are, however, a few additional considerations, and we discuss them next.

- *Length of Service.* You must decide how long you want your fabrics to last. In addition to being more costly, long-life fabrics may outlast an image and may have to be discarded if you remodel the facilities, even though they may still be functional.

- *Maintenance.* You must determine a maintenance schedule for your fabrics. Large hotels usually employ laundry and seamstress workers who keep these items in good repair. Smaller hospitality operations must usually decide whether they want to provide these services for themselves or to purchase a professional laundry and linen supply service that will take over these duties. Generally, the smaller operations opt for the professional service.

- *Who Chooses?* Who should choose the fabrics and fix their specifications? This might be an emotional issue. For example, the owner-manager may buy dust-catching draperies, leaving the housekeeper to clean and maintain them. Perhaps it might be best to have a group of employees involved in the selection process, because once the draperies are installed, those responsible for their maintenance will be aware of the reasons for their selection.

  If you expect the employees to keep their own uniforms cleaned and maintained, you should bear this in mind when selecting them. A little advice from the users will go a long way toward promoting harmonious relations in the future.

- *Fabric Types.* Should you consider easy-care, wash-and-wear types of fabrics? At one time these items looked poor, but their appearance has now improved significantly. The good ones are very expensive, though, and they have shorter life spans than alternative fabrics. You must balance these disadvantages with the convenience and the savings associated with less care and maintenance and, if applicable, the savings you realize by not investing in ironing equipment.

Once you determine the fabrics you want, as well as how you want to have them cleaned and maintained, their purchase is not particularly difficult. In general, you will not have a large number of suppliers from which to choose, especially if you decide to purchase a laundry and linen supply service.

When selecting a supplier, keep in mind that some of them will help you select uniform styles and give related advice regarding other types of fabrics you need.

Fabric receiving and storage are not particularly difficult, although you might have some receiving problems if you are using a professional laundry and linen supply service. There is some difficulty with services of this type because, when they deliver, they also pick up soiled items; sometimes there are items missing that should be in the soiled batch and this can cause some confusion and delay. It is also costly, as many laundry and linen supply operators require you to pay for lost items.

In-process care and maintenance can cause some difficulties. Large hotels usually do a good job when taking care of these items; there are linen rooms in these operations, which are analogous to the food storeroom with all the proper controls. But the smaller operations cannot afford this luxury. Nor are they so likely to clean and maintain their fabrics on schedule, which, if not done, will shorten their useful life.

OTHER PAPER PRODUCTS

Several types of paper, other than paper cups, plates, and napkins, appear in hospitality operations. These include guest checks, cash register tape, tissues, doilies, scratch pads, stationery, and purchase order forms and other accounting documents. These items are usually selected according to the following factors:

- *Image.* Once again, the image of the operation must be considered. Most of these paper products will be seen by patrons, suppliers, and the general public.
- *Special Requirements.* Your product needs might inadvertently restrict the number of potential suppliers from which to choose. For instance, you may require a special type of guest check to fit the cash register you

have; the tissue must fit the tissue dispenser; and the purchase order records must fit your filing system.

- *Personalization.* Some of these products may have to be personalized to your operation. A personalization requirement may reduce the number of suppliers from which you can choose. Of course, you can always get what you want, but if you resist a standardized format, you might have to go to specialized suppliers.

- *AP Price.* The price of many of these items is important, in that you often encounter considerable waste in usage. Effective supervision can minimize this problem; and it can be an expensive problem, especially if you misuse the expensive multipart forms.

  Some suppliers, as a supplier service, might provide complimentary forms of one type or another. Even though you may pay for these in the long run, chances are that your supplier can get these much cheaper than you because of his or her quantity purchasing power.

  It is possible that you may be able to get a promotional discount. For instance, paper towels or tissues may carry a brand name, which may justify a lower purchase price for you.

- *Minimum Order Requirements.* Generally, it is not uncommon to see a large order size requirement for some of these items; this saves you quite a bit of money, but you could encounter unforeseeable storage costs. You might get a stockless purchase plan for things like personalized stationery or calling cards. Or if you accept a standard type of product that differs only in that it has your name on it instead of someone else's, perhaps you do not have to buy so much at one time.

Once you decide what you want, the purchasing, receiving, and storing of these products rarely present any particularly troublesome problems. Typically, management sets par stocks, and the users order up to par level as needed or as dictated by management.

The in-process inventory may generate some waste. It probably is impossible to avoid it entirely, although good supervision can keep it down to acceptable levels. There is, however, some inevitable waste with paper products, if only because it is not cost effective to monitor consistently the paper napkins or paper towels customers take; nor can you eliminate completely employee mistakes.

MISCELLANEOUS ITEMS

Such products as flowers, pest control supplies, and plant food fall into this category. For many of these things, especially insecticides, we suggest you avoid purchasing and storing them on your premises. Kept on the premises, these materials could contaminate food and injure guests and employees. It is best to hire a professional service to handle these dangerous products.

As with all nonfood expense items, we are sure that the same selection factors and managerial concerns apply: image is a major factor for many of them. And depending on the miscellaneous product you are evaluating, most of the other criteria noted in this chapter will dictate the selection and procurement process.

KEY WORDS AND CONCEPTS

AP price

As-used cost

Bid buying

Capital item

Capitalizing expenses

Credit terms

Depreciation

Disposable versus reusable

Employee skill

Equipment program

Exact name

Expense item

Image

Impulse purchase

In-process inventories

Intended use

Labor availability

Labor skill

Length of service

Lifetime cost

Management considerations when
purchasing nonfood expense items

Material used to make the item

Minimum order requirement

New versus used

Operating supplies

Operating supplies schemes

Packers' brands

Personalization

Product color

Product compatibility

Product convenience

Product effectiveness

Product form

Product odor

Product safety

Product size

Promotional discount

Promotional needs

Purchasing, receiving, storing, and
issuing nonfood expense items

Quantity discount

Size of container

Stockless purchase

Supplier services

Systems sale

Toner-phoners

Type of container

Typical nonfood expense items

Volume discount

WATS-line hustlers

QUESTIONS AND PROBLEMS

1. Five typical nonfood expense items that we might purchase are

(a) _____

(b) _____

(c) _____

(d) _____

(e) _____

2. A product specification for permanent ware could include the following information:

    (a) _____

    (b) _____

    (c) _____

    (d) _____

    (e) _____

3. To stock your coffee shop fully with new preparation and service utensils, you will have to pay about $4,000. After scanning the newspaper classifieds and calling equipment dealers, you estimate that you could get everything you need in a used, as-is condition for about $1,200. What do you suggest? If possible, ask a coffee shop manager to comment on your answer.

4. What is the primary difference between a nonfood expense item and a nonfood capital item?

5. When considering the lifetime cost of some nonfood expense items, you should compute the

    (a) _____

    (b) _____

    (c) _____

6. What are the primary advantages and disadvantages of purchasing used nonfood expense items?

7. What critical information is missing from the following product specification for dinner plates?

Dinner plates
Used for entrées and some desserts
Permanent, vitrified china
House brand (or least expensive items)
Bulk packed

8. Assume the following facts: Cleaning agent A costs $1 per quart; cleaning agent B costs $1 per pint; both agents will do the same cleaning job. What other information would you like to have before deciding which one to buy?

9. Outline the specific procedures you would use to purchase, receive, store, and issue disposable ware. Assume that these items are to be used in a catering operation. If possible, ask a caterer to comment on your answer.

10. Assume that you operate the food service in a 500-bed hospital. You currently use permanent ware; own a dishwashing machine and dishes;

and employ seven full-time (40 hours per week) dishwashers with an average wage, including fringe benefits, of $12.65 per hour. You are exploring the possibility of converting to disposable ware. Preliminary estimates are $18,500 per-month expense for the type and amount of disposable ware you need. What do you suggest? If possible, ask a registered dietitian (RD) to comment on your answer.

11. The concept of image is central to the selection of many nonfood expense items. Why is this true? What types of operations do you think must be most concerned with this issue? Which the least concerned? Why?

12. The "color" selection factor would be an important consideration for the following nonfood expense items:

    (a) _____

    (b) _____

    (c) _____

13. Briefly describe the concept of "capitalizing" an expense.

14. Briefly describe the "systems sale" concept.

15. Safety is an important consideration when preparing a product specification for the following nonfood expense items:

    (a) _____

    (b) _____

    (c) _____

16. Prepare a specification for the following nonfood expense items:
    (a) Water glass
    (b) Silver polish
    (c) Plastic fork
    (d) Mop
    (e) Ounce scale

17. Determine what type(s) of disposable products, if any, are outlawed in your local market area. If one or more items are banned, what does the typical food-service operation use instead?

18. Why is the selection factor "employee skill" an important consideration when purchasing cleaning supplies and cleaning tools?

19. Given the following data, determine the most economical product.

	Cleaner A	Cleaner B
AP price	$3.25/qt	$4.15/liter
Amount of cleaning solution yield per container	4 qt	4½ liters
Amount of area cleaned per container	100 ft²	125 ft²

20. What are some advantages of hiring a professional pest control operator in lieu of handling your own pest control work? What are some of the disadvantages?

CHAPTER 26

Source: MGM Grand Hotel, Casino & Theme Park

SERVICES

THE PURPOSE OF THIS CHAPTER

This chapter discusses:

- The major management considerations surrounding the selection and procurement of services
- The general procedures used when purchasing services
- The selection factors for waste removal, financial, groundskeeping, pest control, advertising, consulting, decorating and remodeling, maintenance, vending machine, insurance, laundry and linen supply, and cleaning services

INTRODUCTION

In most hospitality operations, the manager purchases the services needed. The purchasing directors of large corporations may contract for some services. Or a department head might purchase one specifically for his or her department. But as a general rule, since many services are provided primarily by local suppliers, the unit manager, whether employed by an independent operation or part of a chain, tends to have a great deal of input in the selection and procurement process.

MANAGEMENT CONSIDERATIONS

When managers buy services, many of them assume that service costs are fixed costs. That is, they assume that they must spend a certain number of dollars per year for services and that they cannot get along without these services.

It is true that some services represent unavoidable costs of doing business. Expenditures for items such as legal, accounting and bookkeeping, and insurance services are necessary, although the range in cost and quality can vary considerably. Some other services, though, are more or less discretionary. For example, you do not necessarily have to purchase menu design services or cleaning services; in many cases, operators are perfectly capable of doing these things themselves.

Thus, one of the main things to remember about services is that they are not all fixed costs. You do have some discretion. Consequently, you should consider spending as much purchasing time and effort on them as you would on food, beverages, and supplies.

Perhaps you should even spend a little extra time. If you receive a bad load of tomatoes, you can correct the mistake or change suppliers without too much difficulty. But if you purchase a service that turns out to be poor, you have additional problems. First, you may not know it is poor until the job is completed. Moreover, if you buy a poor service, it is poor—period. There is no such thing as an in-between service. You may be able to salvage a few good tomatoes from the bad load delivered to you. But such partial value is usually not the case with services.

As you can already guess, then, it may be difficult to judge the quality of a service in advance. For instance, it is difficult to judge the carpenter's ability unless you have samples of work available; but, even then, you have no guarantee that he or she will replicate past performance. Only when the work is finished will you really know, but at that point it may be difficult to do much about it if major alterations are needed.

Faced with this problem of evaluating service performance, it is easy to neglect inspecting the service provider's performance. Managers who never think of receiving a food item without inspecting it just assume that the maintenance crew that comes around once a month performs its assigned tasks.

We once purchased a chimney-cleaning service. The crew came in one night every six weeks to clean the chimney directly over the open-pit charcoal broiler. None of us ever checked to see what was being accomplished, as we assumed the crew to be conscientious. One night we had a good-sized fire in this chimney. Sure enough, the fire marshal quickly discovered that the chimney had not been cleaned for months and was coated on the inside with several inches of grease.

Thus, another concern with services is whether they are hard to monitor and inspect. An inability or unwillingness to inspect can easily lead to poor performance completely overlooked by the manager or department head.

Another major service concern is, Should I buy the service or should I do it myself? In many cases, the same considerations that determine whether you cut your own steaks or purchase portion-cut steaks enter the picture here. Moreover, the same emotional arguments usually surface. One of the major differences, though, is that some services do, in fact, require experts. For example, it is unlikely that you can provide your own legal and insurance services.

A cost-benefit analysis of doing your own service work will probably indicate which pattern is best. Your decision to provide your own economic values and supplier services when you purchase products can be based on previous experience, but there is no clear-cut historical pattern to guide your decision in this case. In some instances, it is cheaper to wash your own windows; in some cases it is not. Contrast this to the readily compiled evidence that shows, for example, that cutting their own steaks from a side of beef usually is too expensive for most hospitality operators.

Thus, you normally have a little more flexibility when pondering the question of whether to provide some of your own services. A great deal of tradition, however, suggests that operators buy some services while providing others on their own. As you might imagine, traditionally hospitality operators purchase a service when it is either impossible (e.g., it might require a complicated expertise), too expensive (e.g., it might require costly equipment), or very inconvenient to provide it themselves.

Lately it has become more common for managers to practice what is referred to as "outsourcing." Oursourcing involves identifying work that is not central to the hospitality company's primary mission and contracting with a service provider to do it. For instance, payroll processing is necessary, but it is something our guests will never encounter. Hence, it may be a good candidate for outsourcing.

The number and types of outsourcing opportunities in our industry have exploded over the past few years. Hospitality managers have become more focused on their core businesses and do not wish to be distracted by noncore activities. It is thought that at least 70 percent of all companies in the United States outsource one or more functions.

If the hospitality operator is leasing his or her real estate facilities, certain services may be provided by the landlord as part of the lease contract. For instance, tenants in a shopping center normally pay a monthly rental fee plus a common area maintenance (CAM) fee. The CAM fee is used by the landlord to defray the costs of parking lot maintenance, window cleaning, waste removal, rest room maintenance, and other expenses related to the general upkeep of the shopping center's common areas. Usually the CAM fee is not as negotiable as is the monthly rental payment schedule.

In this situation, the landlord shoulders the burden of selecting and procuring the necessary services. On the one hand, this relieves tenants of this time-consuming activity; however, on the other hand, they relinquish the opportunity to do the work themselves or to shop for the best possible prices.

Examining a service provider's background and abilities is another major management consideration. It is necessary, at times, to contact current and/or previous customers and solicit their advice. It is a good idea to inquire from the business license bureau such particulars as the service provider's status, whether he or she carries the proper insurance coverage, and whether customer complaints have been lodged against that service provider. It is also a good idea to contact the local Better Business Bureau (BBB) and ask to examine the file that might exist on the service provider.

Avoid unlicensed, uninsured service providers. Their mistakes can cost you a great deal of money. They have no insurance to handle any claims for damages you may sustain. Also, if they install, say, some electrical wiring incorrectly, and this leads to a fire, your insurance company may not honor any claims you make for damages.

Some unlicensed and uninsured service providers are moonlighters, but not all moonlighters are uninsured and/or unlicensed. Unfortunately, moonlighters cannot always provide you service exactly when you need it. Consequently, even though a moonlighter may be a less expensive choice, whether you can tolerate the delays in service is a major management concern. In some cases, delays are no problem, but they can be devastating at other times.

To recap, at least five major concerns come into play when one purchases services: (1) services are not fixed costs, (2) it can be difficult to evaluate a service provider's performance, (3) you must decide whether to provide your own service or buy it, (4) it is necessary to examine a service provider's background and abilities, and (5) you must consider the advantages and disadvantages of using moonlighters.

There are other less worrisome concerns, although they may become very important under certain circumstances: (1) you may have to allow strangers on your premises, (2) you may have to allow strangers access to personal and confidential information, and (3) you may have to give a third party direct control over some aspect of your business.

GENERAL PROCEDURES IN SERVICE PURCHASING

Once you decide which services you intend to purchase, you should prepare a specification for each one, detailing as much as possible the desired criteria. Figure 26.1 notes an example specification outline for services.

It is not particularly difficult to prepare some type of specification. You usually can include what you want accomplished and when you want the work completed. Your inspection procedures are not as easy to detail. However, complete specifications are *absolutely essential* if you intend to use a bid-buying strategy.

Bid buying services is just as risky as it is in the products areas. But bid buying services can produce a potentially greater monetary reward, as prices for services tend to vary considerably from one provider to another. And, in many cases, the lowest-price service will still provide acceptable

Intended use:

Exact name of service required:

Quality of materials that must be used:

Quality of the finished work:

Completion time:

Required work schedule:

Amount and type of experience required:

Business license:

Other licenses required:

References:
    BBB:
    Licensing division(s):
    Current customers:
    Former customers:
    Other:

Insurance coverage (bonded) for:
    Security:
    Property damage:
    Liability:
    Incomplete work:
    Deposits:
    Other:

Moonlighting restrictions:

Priority restrictions:

Guarantee(s):

Desired bill-paying procedure:

Inspection procedure(s):

FIGURE 26.1. Example of specification outline for services.

quality. This is true because service providers are more eager to reduce their prices when business is slow; since most service providers are small firms, if they do not work at that particular service, they do not have sales of other service or product lines to support them until business picks up. A lower price may be accompanied by a less acceptable standard of quality. But, assuming you can inspect and monitor the service provider's performance, you should be able to extract maximum value.

    Bid buying, negotiating with service providers, and monitoring the actual work—all this can be time-consuming. Although it is commendable to get the most for your purchase dollar, you must get the results you need. Thus, your service-purchasing strategy has to be constructed with this in mind: It is worthless to save a dollar only to find out that the chimney is still dirty. Although we do not condone careless spending, you must keep in mind that if you pay too much, all you really lose is money. But if you fail to get the service results you want, you have lost whatever you paid and have received very little in return. If the canned goods are unsatisfactory, you can quickly rectify the error. If a service is unsatisfactory, you are less likely to be as forgiving and are more apt to dismiss the offending service provider and contact someone else. In addition, the delays associated with an inadequate service can be bothersome.

We do not intend to suggest that bid buying is ineffective. But bid buying always carries inherent dangers, particularly if you do not have the time to do it correctly. You must do what you feel is best, but, really, the only relevant aspect of service purchasing is to get what you want. And perhaps the best way to get it is to settle with one service provider and, together, determine what you need, when you need it, how much it costs to do the job correctly, and what payment arrangements will ensure that you receive the quality of service necessary. While discussing your needs, you should also evaluate the service provider's past performance by asking for and calling his or her references—the people he or she has served or is servicing currently.

These are general guidelines about service purchasing. Emphases change a little as we go from one particular service to another. For instance, it seems more appropriate to bid buy a contract cleaning service than to bid buy a lawyer's service. Following the discussion of the services normally purchased, you can probably make an intelligent decision about the buying strategy best for you.

TYPICAL SERVICES PURCHASED BY HOSPITALITY OPERATORS

Hospitality operators typically use the following services: (1) waste removal, (2) financial, (3) groundskeeping, (4) pest control, (5) advertising, (6) consulting, (7) decorating and remodeling, (8) maintenance, (9) vending machine, (10) insurance, (11) laundry and linen supply, and (12) cleaning. We will discuss these services in turn in the following paragraphs.

WASTE REMOVAL

You will probably need to purchase your own disposal service, as few cities and towns provide a tax-supported service for hospitality operations. If you are located in a shopping center or office park, perhaps part of your CAM fee covers the cost of waste removal.

There are many small operators in this area—the person who buys a truck and goes into business is typical. Sometimes these small operators are efficient; sometimes they are not.

Whomever you hire, you should make sure that they (1) provide on-time collection; (2) do not mangle and destroy the containers; (3) do not mangle the containers' enclosed housing area (if any); (4) remove all refuse piled on the ground; (5) replace the containers in the proper locations; (6) provide suitably large and strong containers for your type of business; (7) if necessary, provide containers with locks in order to prevent others from dumping on your premises; and (8) charge a competitive price.

The main purpose of waste disposal is to keep a neat and sanitary garbage area. Find someone who will maintain this area in the way that is appropriate for your type of business.

Another detail is the pickup schedule. You do not want a refuse service driving through the parking lot in the middle of the lunch or dinner hour. Also, if the truck looks unkempt, you probably should shy away from that service, though, realistically, you may not have a large selection of potential suppliers in your vicinity from which to choose.

If you have a grease trap that must be cleaned periodically, it would be convenient to use the waste removal firm that can provide this additional service. You may be willing to pay a bit more for this one-stop shopping opportunity.

In a few parts of the country, the local government may be the only waste removal service available. Or it might mandate that all businesses must use a specific waste removal company. Hence, you cannot shop around for the best deal; you must agree to the legislated terms and conditions.

Some waste removal companies may pay you for your waste. For example, there are some recycling firms, such as grease salvers and metal salvers, who will pay a modest amount for recyclable waste. However, to take advantage of this other-income opportunity, you generally need to take the time to segregate your wastes. And in some instances, you may need to deliver the waste to the recycling plant.

FINANCIAL

There is no greater fallacy than to think that you have no flexibility when you shop for loan capital, checking services, or for other types of financial services. Many people think that all banks, for example, charge the same rates and provide equal services. Since financial institutions are regulated by law, many of us assume that one is a good as the other. However, these institutions do have some discretion within the law. And the intangible "supplier services" they provide more than likely vary considerably.

You need bankers who will provide you with checking accounts,

petty cash accounts, payroll accounts, loans, cash management techniques, computer services, and perhaps benefit packages for your employees. In most cases, the accountant, bookkeeper, or owner-manager negotiates for a banker's services, either with banks or, for some services, other
types of financial institutions.

In too many instances, we hesitate to negotiate. In these situations, we
often become a house account, particularly in those areas of the country
where few financial institutions exist.

Financial institutions are like any other supplier; they want your business and they want you to become a house account. They strive to make it
very inconvenient for you to purchase one service from them and other
services from their competitors.

Some banks, for instance, might offer a better rate of interest on a loan
if you keep a savings or payroll account with them or if you allow them to
make a bit of income by processing your payroll checks. Or some bank
charge card services may be more timely and more convenient.

The typical hospitality operation usually has little time available to
evaluate several financial institutions when purchasing these services.
Often an operator tends to "grow up" with a local banker, the banker who
was there to encourage and nurse along the operator during the business's
early days. As long as this banker can consistently provide a wide range of
services, the grateful operator will tend to remain a house account. And in
some situations, such an arrangement is mutually beneficial.

It would be very unusual for large hospitality operations to use one-
stop shopping for financial services. These firms usually have more time
and skill available to examine the combination of services and service
providers most favorable to them. Moreover, the amount of cash turnover
a large company deals with gives it a stronger bargaining position. Like
corporate purchasing directors who have the time, ability, and responsibility to seek out the better deals, corporate accountants and treasurers
have the same capabilities. For the smaller operator who uses one-stop
shopping for other items, it is probably best to use the same purchasing
procedure when buying financial services.

GROUNDSKEEPING

Few operators, other than large lodging facilities, are able to provide their
own landscaping, snow removal, or parking lot maintenance services. It is
typical to purchase these services from reputable service providers. It also
is common to find these services provided by a landlord as part of the
CAM-fee arrangement.

Probably the most difficult groundskeeping service to purchase is the
landscaping service. Small firms are particularly prominent in the landscaping business. Anyone with a rake or a shovel can easily enter the

business. You should avoid anyone who does not have a demonstrated knowledge of this trade.

Landscapers usually undertake snow removal in the winter months to supplement their income and to keep busy all year long. Thus, it is possible to contract with one firm to handle all your ground maintenance.

Again, your objective is clear: you want an attractive exterior. Rather than negotiate a low price, you might economize by minimizing the number of plants, trees, and lawns you nurture, assuming that you are more interested in a price you can afford than in an extravagant outdoor display. (Some of these service providers also maintain your inside plants, although you often must go to another source if you want to purchase or rent house plants.)

When you purchase a landscaping service, be specific about what you want done and when you want it done. Resist the temptation to say, "Cut the grass when necessary." Ambivalent instructions like these can lead to conflicts later on. Say, instead, something like, "Cut and edge the lawn, and clean up afterward, every Thursday afternoon after four o'clock."

These landscape services often have a firm rate schedule, unless you happen to find one whose business is slow. Keep in mind, though, that a landscaper with few customers may be a poor choice. The good ones often have more business than they can handle.

Another possible difficulty is that neighborhood children, and other similar groups, may pester you to let them perform these tasks so that they can earn a little spending money. As with all amateur work, there usually is something that could have been done better. On the other hand, though, assuming there are no potential liability problems, you might build some good community relations by doing this.

PEST CONTROL

Pest control is one of the trickiest control areas in all hospitality. It is easy for some to feel that they are pest control experts, as spraying chemicals appears to be the only thing necessary. But pest control is a difficult service to perform, and some chemicals are so dangerous that only licensed pest control operators (PCO) can legally handle them.

Probably the best strategy is to contract for a weekly or monthly visit as well as a price to be charged for emergencies, like an unanticipated infestation. Calling a pest control service only when an obvious problem arises is bad business. A great deal of damage to your building, as well as to your reputation, may have already occurred.

Purchasing the service is generally preferable to providing it yourself. When you purchase it, you need not store poisonous chemicals on your premises—always a risky practice.

Your purchasing objective here is obvious: no pests. You must determine what pest control services charge, and you should check their performance by conferring with their customers. Normally, prices among these firms are very competitive. The pest control company that can provide the best service schedule, solid advice on how to correct building problems that invite infestation, and direction regarding the appropriate sanitation procedures your employees should follow probably is your first choice.

A few national pest control companies exist. Large chain operations might consider negotiating one contract at a lower price to include every unit in the chain.

The cost of pest control service is small indeed compared with the problems it can solve and the expenses it can save. This is no place to be a stickler on a few cents difference between service providers.

ADVERTISING

Most operations use some sort of advertising—newspaper, magazine, radio, television, or some combination thereof. Printed brochures, flyers, and menus all serve as advertising media. In addition, several in-house promotion kits are on the market.

When evaluating advertising purchases, an important element to keep in mind is the audience you intend to reach with your message. You must select the advertising medium, or media, that will reach that audience. You should not, for example, buy a newspaper ad strictly on the basis of its low price. When purchasing advertising, it is usually best to opt for quality over quantity.

In most instances, the amount you must pay is directly related to the size of the intended audience. You will need to ensure that the advertising medium consistently delivers the guaranteed audience size by checking periodically independent rating services' reports detailing these statistics. Reputable advertising media will issue "make-goods," which is free advertising time granted to buyers if the actual intended audience size was less than the guaranteed one.

When you choose advertising, a major concern is the cost per potential customer reached by the ad or the cost per potential customer influenced by the ad. The cost is difficult to compute, but the media buyer, or the medium, usually can come up with a reasonably accurate figure.

Another important consideration is the ability to trade your products or services for advertising. One problem with this kind of advertising is that if the ads are not to your liking, you may have less influence than a cash-paying customer. By the same token, a station manager can complain about your products or services, though he or she can hardly complain if you pay cash.

Another question to ponder is the use of soft drink company signs and printing. Coke, for instance, often shares the cost of menu printing and sign preparation as long as its logo is prominently displayed. You must decide, as with all promotional discounts, whether you want to be closely identified with this particular supplier.

Still another consideration is sponsoring local athletic teams and advertising in local high school and college newspapers. As far as we can determine, no studies have been done to evaluate the efficacy of these types of advertising. Many companies, though, feel that these methods contribute to good and profitable public relations.

You could go through an advertising agency or other media-buying service rather than deal with the various advertising media personally. When you select an agency, you normally discuss what you want and how much you can afford. The agency develops an overall advertising strategy and selects the various media to use. You pay the cost of the advertisements, and the agency often takes a percentage, or commission, of these expenditures as its fee. Normally the agency is paid on a sliding-percentage scale. However, it could receive a flat rate. Or it might be paid on "merits"; that is, its income could be directly related to the sales success generated by the advertised product or service.

Many experienced hospitality operators prefer using an intermediary when purchasing advertising services. They consider it more convenient and efficient as well as less costly in the long run. Some buyers think that, as in purchasing food, it may be cheaper to purchase directly from the primary source. However, typically that is not true in the advertising channel of distribution. Furthermore, a qualified media-buying service will see to it that your advertisements are located and displayed correctly, and at the right time.

Newspaper Ads

Typically, commercial restaurants purchase newspaper ads; and they normally purchase an ad on a run-of-the-press basis, which means that the ad will be put any place in the paper at the discretion of the advertising editor, though you can specify in a very general way what you want and do not want.

A trick of the newspaper advertising business is for the salesperson to offer you a story on your operation. Be careful here, because salespersons can deliver on this promise only if they control the paper's editorial department. An article, though, often has much more influence on the consumer than does one ad.

If you decide to purchase a newspaper ad, you will probably see it featured in the local restaurant section. Indeed, it may cost you more to put it elsewhere in the newspaper. You can usually save money by contracting for an ad space over a period of time, such as an ad that is printed once a week for 25 weeks. Over the long run, the cost of each of these ads should be less than the cost of individual ads purchased once in a while. As with all purchases, there are quantity discounts available.

The cost and benefits of newspaper advertising are hard to calculate accurately. It is especially hard to compute them when, for example, you buy an ad in the local high school newspaper. If you use newspaper ads to recruit employees, you probably can assess their value a little more easily. Also, you can count the number of coupons that customers tear out of your ad in response to, for instance, a special-price promotion.

Newspaper ads do serve as good reminders to your customers. They keep your name in the public eye.

Radio Ads

Radio ads are charged on a different basis from newspaper ads. They are sold on a space-available basis, sometimes referred to as run-of-the-station. Depending on the station, length of the ad, and the time of day desired, the price varies considerably.

Radio stations can usually tell you with reasonable accuracy who is listening. Newspapers and magazines cannot be so accurate because these pieces may be read by more than just the original purchaser before eventually being discarded.

Unlike other advertising media, radio tends to build business slowly over the long run. Consequently, you must be patient. You will usually have to run radio spots for quite some time before you experience significant results. However, although it takes time for a radio campaign to generate results, radio is an efficient medium because specific audiences are fairly easy to target.

TV Ads

Network television is usually too expensive for hospitality operations except at the regional or national chain level. Most operations, though, can afford it if they agree to run commercial messages during nonprime time, or on local independent stations.

If you opt for TV advertising, you usually need the help of a professional advertising agency or other media-buying service.

It is not a good idea to begin television advertising unless you can sustain it. The costs are prohibitive for a one-shot ad. For production of a few commercials, you might pay, for example, exclusive of the cost of airing the commercials, several thousand dollars.

It is common for radio, newspaper publishers, publishers of playbills and other types of programs, and outdoor billboard companies to trade their services for food, beverage, and rooms. This type of exchange bartering, usually referred to as "trade outs" or "due bills," can save you a great deal of money by reducing your out-of-pocket expenses. Many television stations, though, are reluctant to trade air time.

Magazine Ads

Magazine advertising has to be used selectively. Some magazines of the gourmet, airline, and tourist variety may reach your market, especially if your operation tends to attract people from a wide geographical area. There also are magazines published to meet the tourism needs of a single city, and many hospitality operators find advertising in these periodicals profitable. Some trade magazines and travel indexes can be useful, especially to lodging operations that want to advertise to and solicit business from business travelers, travel agents, and companies seeking conventions and meetings facilities.

Magazine ads are excellent sources to use for recruiting management employees. The trade papers are especially useful here.

Telephone Directories

The prices of most directory advertising are fixed. The main decision is whether to buy an illustrated ad or accept the one- or two-line notations most operations choose. Some places like the bigger, illustrated ads, as this allows them to depict a map, prices, services available, hours of operation, and so on—additional information that is useful to the out-of-town visitor. These larger ads, though, are fairly expensive.

The most common directory used by hospitality operators is the Yellow Pages directory. However, there are many others available. A recent survey concluded that there are approximately 6,000 directories published in the United States each year.

When selecting a directory, you should consider cost, number of years it has been published, target audience, and how it is distributed to readers.

Some computer on-line services provide directory services that you can purchase or otherwise acquire. These are especially popular and useful in tourist destination locations.

Printed Brochures, Matchbooks, and Menus

Brochures and flyers are quite useful in some circumstances and for some operations. Their publication rates are usually fairly standard in the industry, and they vary according to the number of colors you want, the quality of the paper or other materials, the printing style, and so on. In addition, printers often offer generous break points, that is, very attractive quantity discounts; this may be a curse, though, if you cannot use them all, which might be the case with printed menus.

You may wish to hire a graphic artist to design a logo or pictorial layout, and an editor to develop the wording style. This naturally adds somewhat to the expense, but it is often worthwhile in the long run to have a professionally completed document.

Most operations purchase matchbooks, swizzle sticks, napkins, and so forth emblazoned with their logo. These items, too, keep your name before the public. In fact, bars usually must rely on this form of advertising and internal promotion, since they usually cannot advertise on radio or television.

Outdoor Ads

Billboards are especially useful if you have continuing messages to display. For example, if you book entertainment and if the entertainers change weekly, a billboard can convey this message to several thousand people effectively and cheaply. Billboards are also a good choice when you want to build awareness.

Operations along the side of a highway, or near a highway, often use billboards and signs to guide travelers. The use of these media along highways, though, is strictly regulated by law.

The main disadvantage to outdoor ads is the community's concern for visual pollution. Billboards and signs have come under heavy attack in some areas. These areas severely restrict the amount and type of outdoor advertising one can display. In some states, such as Hawaii, billboard advertising is prohibited.

The rates for outdoor advertising are fairly well established and, to a certain extent, are influenced by the type you want, how much of it you are willing to contract for, and other similar considerations. There are numerous options available. For instance, you can spend a minimum amount by arranging for a joint promotion with some related firm, such as a soft drink company; or perhaps you might splurge on an expensive sign linked to a computer that can change messages quickly and easily. The range between these two extremes is considerable.

Direct-Mail Advertising

Many hospitality operations use periodic mailings to current and/or prospective customers promoting some sort of special price, event, or other form of offering. If you have a reasonably updated mailing list, or can purchase a useful one, it merely remains for you to design the appropriate flyer, stamp it, and mail it.

It could be expensive to purchase a mailing list. Most lodging operations maintain a guest history, whereas food-service operations usually do not. However, the cost of the list, the printing, postage, and so forth must be compared with the expected increase in net income that the direct-mail campaign will produce.

The nicest thing about direct mail is that you usually can develop something whose effectiveness can be tested very easily. If, for instance, you include a response option for the customer (such as a coupon), you can determine very quickly the success rate of the direct-mail campaign. If the campaign is deemed unsuccessful, it is very easy to alter the direct-mail literature and schedule a remailing.

Another dimension of the direct-mail campaign is the phone solicitation effort. Generally, instead of mailing the information, you would hire someone to solicit prospective business by telephone. This can be very effective, say, for banquet business, where the telephone solicitor makes every effort to arrange for an appointment for you to meet with a prospective catering, meeting, or convention customer.

CONSULTING

Consultants abound in our industry. Some of the most typical include (1) designers, (2) feasibility researchers, (3) lawyers, (4) accountants and bookkeepers, (5) operations planners and counselors, (6) energy advisers, (7) employee trainers, (8) architects, (9) building contractors, (10) property appraisers, (11) engineers, (12) real estate advisers, (13) business brokers, (14) fire and safety inspectors, (15) data processors, (16) printers, (17) equipment rental firms, and (18) computer specialists.

Some trade publications publish lists of consultants in some of their issues. For instance, the trade paper *Hotel and Motel Management* normally publishes a list once or twice a year. This list usually includes national consultants, those who work in more than one part of the country. But, as a rule, most consulting work, like most services, is provided by local firms.

Generally, one tends to purchase a consultant's service whenever the task to be performed is relatively complicated and highly technical and is not part of the owner-manager's daily routine. For instance, accounting and bookkeeping, design, legal, and computer consulting services are the types of things you may not be able to do for yourself very well.

Some other types of consulting can be performed in-house by a member of the company. Such tasks as menu design, certain feasibility studies, and the like, can easily be done by many operators. An operator may not do so well with menu design as a professional menu designer, but he or she can probably do reasonably well.

Large organizations often hire in-house consultants as permanent staff members to handle these functions. Usually these specialists are required to travel from one unit operation to another, solving problems, doing research, and performing several other related activities.

The need for consulting service is normally determined either by a user somewhere in the organization or by the owner-manager. Purchasing this service can be tricky. In some cases, you can map out exactly what you want, thereby occupying a relatively good position for evaluating various consultants. But for the most part, you will be dealing with professionals, some of whose work you may not completely understand.

There is a certain type of bid buying you can use when purchasing this kind of service. Essentially, this would require you to describe the problem you have and the results you would like. Then you might ask two or more consultants to prepare a proposal for you. The proposal would typically include such considerations as the objectives of the job, what will be done to achieve them, what the final results will be, what approach the consultant will take, time constraints, and the fee for the consulting service. Your job would then be to evaluate the proposals and select one.

A nice thing about these proposals is that they rarely cost you anything. In addition, during proposal preparation, the consultant may help you define more clearly just what it is you need.

Some consultants assume the buyer's role by engaging in what is sometimes referred to as "negative selling." They tell you how severe your problem is, that they have a very busy schedule, but that they have to see what they can do to help you since you definitely need help quickly. You may find yourself begging the consultant to save you; that is, you try to sell him or her on taking the job and your money.

If you use the proposal approach, try to negotiate a firm contract; unfortunately, some consultants have a strong incentive for milking the job. A fixed-fee contract will protect you from this tendency.

Our suggestion is to examine a consultant's references. Be watchful of negative selling. If you can, ask one to perform a "trial job," an inexpensive job you need done, which can be an excellent test of future work habits and of overall competence.

We would try to negotiate on price, but we would be careful not to rush the work. We might make a bonus offer for early completion or some other incentive for good, quick work. We would also make sure that the fee is not completely determined by how much potential money we can save, because, per the recommendation, we might have to invest a lot in order to save a little.

The objective is, in short, to complete the job satisfactorily. As a result, cost considerations might sometimes be a secondary concern.

You must sometimes use trust as your sole criterion in selecting consultants because the consultants often direct some of your money to other people. For instance, when discussing a consulting job possibility with a professional consulting firm, you will probably talk to one of the partners, usually a seasoned veteran in his or her field. Although this partner will retain limited supervision of the job, the work might be done by one or more junior members of the consulting firm; or the work might be subcontracted to another party. This is sometimes done in feasibility studies and real estate appraisals.

The key to developing an excellent working relationship with a consultant is to be very clear about what you need. You must be willing to spend as much time as necessary with the consultant so that he or she can obtain the information needed to do the job properly. And, while you certainly must maintain your privacy, you cannot expect positive results if you treat the consultant as an outsider.

Before purchasing a consulting service, you might try to get it free. For instance, if your problem relates to energy, the public utilities companies might do a free energy audit and recommend ways of conserving precious fuel. Your trade association might have a staff member who can help you design a menu. Suppliers and salespersons often stand ready to offer valuable advice. And the federal government's Small Business Administration (SBA) sponsors consulting, and other similar programs, for qualified small businesses.

DECORATING AND REMODELING

These services are almost always purchased, and small contractors dominate in these fields. Be wary of them and be careful if the persons you hire are moonlighters. The smaller the contractor, the less likely he or she is to be able to afford the equipment necessary to do an excellent job. And a moonlighter, although perhaps good, may have trouble meeting a time deadline. You should take the time to solicit competitive bids from established contractors who can provide several references and are licensed, insured, and familiar with your needs.

When evaluating these services, you may be concerned more with time than with money. That is, you certainly do not want to pay outrageous prices, but you must first see to it that you are not unduly inconvenienced or closed down too long. Since time is money, you may be willing to pay a bit more to get the work completed earlier.

It is probably a good idea to see, in person, examples of the work before you contract for it. Go to a place where the workers have hung wallpaper and see whether you like the job. This is the nicest thing about purchasing these types of services: you can always see what has been done in the past, and the past work serves as a continuing standard of quality for the contractor to maintain in his or her future work. (Watch, though, that you do not visit only the best work, while the skeletons remain safely in the closet.)

When purchasing this type of service, it would appear that the buyer is very concerned and quite fearful about the possibility of incomplete work or work that is shoddy and cannot, or will not, be repaired by the service provider. It would be well worth the extra expense of forcing the service provider to purchase a performance bond (i.e., an insurance policy guaranteeing satisfactory completion of all work).

A related problem with this type of work is the lien-sale type of contract that these service providers normally want you to sign. This contract stipulates that the service provider can attach a lien to the entire property if you fail to pay him or her for the work performed. The logic in this contract suggests that the service provider can hardly "take back" an improvement to your property and that this improvement by itself is worthless. Hence, the service provider must be able to take over the entire property to gain satisfaction. To counteract this problem, you must insist that you will make installment payments that correspond with the major stages of the project, and that you will pay only when a stage is completed satisfactorily. Once you pay for the entire project, the service provider must agree to sign an unconditional lien release, verifying that he or she has been paid in full. This can be a difficult and inconvenient process if there are several persons working on your place, but it is necessary to avoid any possible loss of your entire property.

MAINTENANCE

There would appear to be in our industry an almost endless variety of repair and maintenance services. Some of the more typical ones are (1) security; (2) fire and intrusion alarm; (3) locksmith; (4) dishwashing machine; (5) knife sharpening; (6) plumbing; (7) electrical; (8) refrigeration; (9) heating, ventilation, and air conditioning (HVAC); (10) beverage dispensing equipment; (11) elevator; (12) sign; (13) water systems; (14) office machines; (15) cooking equipment; (16) computers and (17) transportation services.

The typical hospitality operator tends to purchase one or more maintenance contracts to supplement the service agreements that normally accompany new equipment purchases. Although the terms "maintenance contract" and "service agreement" are often used interchangeably (along with the more generic term, "service contract"), they are different. Whereas a service agreement covers equipment defects and malfunctions during the warranty period, a maintenance contract is much more detailed. Usually, for a consistent monthly fee, the maintenance contractor provides routine maintenance, such as periodically changing filters and lubing mechanical parts. Most contracts also cover emergency service when you need it, such as when a freezer suddenly breaks down.

Most new mechanical equipment you purchase generally comes with some sort of warranty or service agreement. During the guarantee period, usually only major repair problems are covered; you are responsible for routine maintenance. Many equipment dealers, though, sell "extended" warranty coverage in the form of a maintenance contract, designed to relieve you of all repair and maintenance responsibilities. Also, after this period expires, the dealers usually are willing, for a price, to extend your coverage once again.

Some operators do not wish to purchase maintenance contracts. They would rather wait until they need service, and then pay only for what they need. This may be a good idea, because maintenance contracts, especially those sold by equipment dealers and manufacturers, tend to be very lucrative for these primary sources and intermediaries. However, many operators like the "insurance" that maintenance contracts provide and are willing to pay for peace of mind.

Buying a contract is not an easy decision. First, you are generally asked to pay up front for the next year's service. Also, the price usually is not negotiable. Another major difficulty is the possibility that the servicepersons will take care of cash customers before taking care of any of your emergency needs; that is, now that they have your money, they may not be eager to be as punctual as they might be for cash customers, though they should be equally as concerned about your future business once the initial contract expires.

There is one thing you must always do before signing a maintenance contract: You must be certain that the service is available as advertised. For example, if the service is supposedly available 24 hours a day, 7 days a week, you should make sure that this is always the case. For example, you might call the serviceperson at 3 A.M. If there is no answer, forget that maintenance contractor.

VENDING MACHINE

Some operations use coin-operated vending machines for both customer and employee convenience. The machines dispense cigarettes, candy, soft drinks, food, video games, virtual reality entertainment, telephone access, music, and many other items.

In many cases, these machines come with set agreements: the company puts them in your operation, you agree to provide adequate space and necessary utilities to power the machines, the company takes full responsibility for the maintenance and restocking of the machines, and you get to keep some percentage of the gross sales of the machines.

A major purchasing consideration is whether or not you want these machines on your property.

Another major concern is the potential quality differences between competing companies' machines and the products in these machines. Also, one company may service its machines much better than the others, as well as restock them more regularly.

Of course, you must be concerned with the commission split the company agrees to. You also are interested in the "user" discounts provided, that is, can you use these machines personally at no cost, or at a reduced cost? These financial considerations, along with the services provided, are normally the deciding factors when you shop for vending machine service.

Another major consideration is whether you want to buy your own machines and do all the work yourself. You can make a good profit with them, but the initial cost and the ongoing maintenance costs can be exorbitant. If the sales volume is large, you might do very well with your own machines. However, you may not want to add these responsibilities to your already long list of responsibilities; the work can be tedious, especially the maintenance aspects, which requires you to have a highly trained repair person, someone the large vending machine companies have.

A large hospitality operation could contract with an intermediary who will oversee the vending machine program in effect for all the company's individual locations across the country. For instance, there are intermediaries that will take on the responsibility of ensuring that all locations have the latest, state-of-the-art equipment, receive the appropriate service, and earn the maximum commission split. Usually these intermediaries set national contracts with the hospitality operations. This is very convenient, for it means that a hospitality operation will receive one report and one commission check each period. It also eliminates the need for unit managers to deal with several local vending machine companies on a day-to-day basis.

INSURANCE

Unfortunately, there is no one all-inclusive insurance policy a hospitality operator can buy. He or she must purchase more than one. The typical policies, often dictated by state and local laws and codes, by lenders, and by landlords, include (1) fire and extended property damage; (2) storekeeper's liability; (3) business interruption insurance; (4) crime coverage for burglary and robbery; (5) personal injury insurance, with protection for libel, slander, defamation, or false arrest; (6) glass insurance; (7) product liability; (8) vehicle insurance; (9) fidelity bonds for those employees who handle money; (10) third-party liability insurance for bars; (11) workers' compensation; and (12) comprehensive insurance to protect against an employee's dishonesty toward customers.

There are several additional insurance policies an operator can purchase at his or her discretion. Some of these include (1) health or life insurance for company personnel, (2) other types of policies to be used as employee benefits, such as disability insurance, and (3) extra insurance on expensive antiques, works of art, and furnishings.

Generally speaking, when evaluating insurance coverage, you should consider three major factors: (1) extent of the coverage, that is, the amount of deductible you must pay; (2) reimbursable losses, that is, the types of exclusions for which you cannot collect damages; and (3) the conditions you must satisfy before you can collect.

Before contracting with an insurance company, the buyer should also determine the quality and ability of the persons handling the claims.

Some discreet conversations with other customers of the insurer(s) you are thinking of dealing with can give you a sense of the promptness and fairness of claims adjustments.

Another major consideration when selecting an insurer is the number of policies you can obtain from one source. The more you can receive under one roof, so to speak, the fewer the number of insurers you need to deal with. Thus, it is common to go to one independent insurance broker and secure all your insurance needs through one person. Brokers work for the buyer. They deal with insurance agents and insurance companies when putting together an insurance package that will meet their clients' needs.

If you prefer, you can buy insurance direct. That is, you can buy from a company that sells directly to the insured. This is cheaper because you save the agent middleman's fee; however, you do not get the advice and counsel of this middleman. Companies that sell directly are sometimes referred to as direct writers. Automobile and life insurance can easily be purchased direct.

The buyer also can purchase insurance from an exclusive insurance agent. However, this type of agent represents only one insurance company. Consequently, if you need some unique insurance coverage, you may have to deal with several exclusive agents.

If available, you should consider joining a risk-purchasing group. This is a type of co-op purchasing arrangement that essentially allows individuals to become part of a larger group and, thereby, reduce insurance costs for all group members. Hospitality chain organizations can easily qualify for these plans. The independent operator might consider joining a group, such as those maintained by most restaurant and hotel associations, that buys insurance for its members. Group plans are always less expensive.

It is reasonably easy to evaluate an insurance company's performance, as most states keep records of their dealings with the various companies. Also, a buyer can check an insurance company's rating in one of the several rating agency publications, such as *Best's Insurance Reports.* This is an annual publication that notes each insurance company's history, financial performance, and other related data. The sound companies are rated A or A+.

Insurance is often highly technical, and it is appropriate to consult legal counsel before making a decision. Some busy managers leave much of the dealing with insurance companies to their attorneys, but this is an expensive move, as attorneys charge by the hour and happily interview anyone you send them. As with so many other complex decisions, it may be best to determine what coverage you want and then negotiate the price with a limited number of reliable bidders, in this case having your judgment backed up by your attorney. And it is usually to your advantage to shop and compare insurance policies. Our experience shows that there is a wide spread in prices for essentially equal coverage.

LAUNDRY AND LINEN SUPPLY

No service generates as much disagreement as does laundry and linen supply. It seems that some persons have a good experience with these suppliers and other people just are not satisfied.

If you use linens and uniforms you may (1) buy your own and purchase a laundry service, (2) purchase the laundry service and rent the fabrics, or (3) purchase your own fabrics and laundry machines and do your own work.

The first two options require less work on your part than the third, in that you just order what you need, receive it, store it, and use it. And there is only a minor amount of effort you can expend to shop around, since there are normally only two or three laundry and linen supply services in your area from which to choose.

Larger operations are more interested in the third option. They often own an in-house laundry system and apparently are happy with it. Smaller operations might experiment with their own laundry machinery. However, it would appear that the cost of the space needed to house the machinery, labor cost, cost of cleaning chemicals, and other overhead costs are usually too expensive for these properties.

Some operations have gone so far as to eliminate linens and uniforms altogether; they use disposable linens and give their employees a uniform allowance so that they can provide their own uniforms.

Renting a laundry and linen supply service is more convenient, and you receive professional service. If you erect your own laundry, be prepared for more responsibility to accompany the savings you may realize. If you eliminate permanent fabrics, be prepared for the high cost of disposables and, possibly, customer resistance to disposable napkins, tablecloths, and bed linens.

If you decide to rent linen and laundry service, you should evaluate each potential supplier on the following factors: (1) length of contract; (2) service schedule; (3) how seasonal fluctuations are handled; (4) variety of products offered; (5) overall cost of the service; and (6) cost of lost, damaged, or stolen products for which you are responsible.

It is possible to have your own laundry and your own dish and pot washing system managed in your establishment by an outside management contractor. There are independent contractors that supply laundry and steward services. In some cases, they might provide the least expensive alternative.

CLEANING

There are several specialized contract cleaning services. Some of the more typical ones include (1) exhaust hood, (2) degreasing, (3) window, (4) carpet and upholstery, and (5) concrete cleaning services.

Unlike many services, cleaning is one that the typical hospitality operation conceivably could perform on its own. Consequently, using contract cleaners tends to generate a good deal of discussion, which usually centers on the crucial question: Should I purchase this service or should I do it myself?

It is probably better to do some cleaning tasks yourself, particularly the ones that must be done every day. The weekly or monthly cleaning tasks that require a great deal of specialized equipment should probably become the responsibility of a contract cleaner. Unfortunately, the distinction between these two types of tasks is not always clear.

We find many an operation that contracts for an outside firm to take care of virtually all the cleaning. Hospitals often use these services, and some housekeeping contractors try to sell complete services to hotel properties.

For such heavy cleaning as carpet shampooing, it seems best to purchase this service. You eliminate the need for expensive equipment, the need to store expensive shampoo, and the need for expensive labor.

The disadvantages of contract cleaners must, of course, be considered. The major one is the lack of complete control over the workers. Also, the cost may be quite expensive, although it is unlikely you could provide many of these services more cheaply.

Contract cleaners are numerous. But, like decorators, contract cleaners are relatively easy to evaluate. You can contact references and ask to examine the work.

If a contractor does a poor job, there are usually several to take his or her place. The number of competitors in the field helps keep their prices within reasonable limits and their service timely.

The biggest problem we have noticed with contract cleaners is the laxity with which hospitality operators examine and inspect the work done in their establishments. (Recall our chimney story earlier in this chapter.)

A secondary problem is the tendency sometimes to use friends, neighbors, or high school students. It may be convenient and neighborly to let these amateurs earn a few dollars, but the quality of their work probably is not very professional or competent. Nor is it wise to expose yourself to potential liability.

A final concern is the problems that some contract cleaners have in maintaining a complete staff themselves. They are frequently shorthanded and may, as a result, provide you with poor service. In addition, when you inspect work that they have done for someone else, you do not know whether the same people working today for the contract cleaner were the ones responsible for the job you are examining.

ANOTHER WORD ABOUT SECURITY WHEN BUYING SERVICES

There are always shady characters ready to sell you a nonexistent product or service or to pretend that they have a real bargain for you—a bargain that never materializes. Hospitality operators do not usually buy questionable bargains that are advertised.

However, services invite all sorts of ingenious tricks. For instance, purchasing an ad in a soon-to-be-published directory can be costly—the directory may never be printed. Also, donating money to buy ad space in a charitable association's publication may be costly and a waste unless you have verified that the charity is a bona fide operation.

Invoices for services usually go directly to the bookkeeper, who might pay them routinely. Therefore, you should check these bills and initial them, because a dishonest company may send an invoice that resembles the ones your bookkeeper always pays.

Dishonest people may also try to slip in their own invoice for the waste removal service or for any other service you pay for on a regular, periodic basis. Again, if the bookkeeper does not check the bills carefully, you might pay for the same service twice.

Another insidious problem, to which small operators are particularly vulnerable, is the contractor who demands a deposit before beginning work, but who then never returns. For example, suppose that you want someone to install new cabinets in the room service area of the hotel. You are told that he needs $400 to procure the materials needed to complete the job. You give him the money, and you never see this contractor again.

Admittedly, this problem occurs more with homemakers than with commercial businesses. But this can happen to us if we deal with moonlighters and other contractors who are not licensed by the state or city. If you have any doubts about a contractor, you could contact the Better Business Bureau (BBB). Or you might put your deposit money in an escrow account, which the materials supplier can receive only after delivery of the materials. Or you can pay the materials supplier directly without giving any money to the contractor. Finally, you might consider working strictly with your friends or strictly with those with whom you have had previous positive business dealings, or with those who are members of the local chamber of commerce or other similar civic groups.

In Chapter 15, we discussed the major security problems associated with purchasing, receiving, storing, and issuing. The problems we noted there seem to multiply exponentially when you buy several services, especially services that are difficult to monitor and are paid for on a regularly scheduled basis.

Small businesses, rather than large, are usually the targets for dishonest persons who realize that small operators have less time to examine every detail. But, as we noted in Chapter 15, you must force yourself to be careful. Dishonest acts are just too common and too easily perpetrated.

KEY WORDS AND CONCEPTS

Advertising service

BBB

Best's Insurance Reports

Bid buying

Bonding

Business license

CAM fee

Cleaning service

Completion time

Consulting proposal

Consulting service

Decorating and remodeling service

Direct writer

Due bill

Either a service is good, or it is bad—
there is no in-between

Exact name

Exclusive insurance agent

Experience requirement

Extended warranty coverage

Financial service

Groundskeeping service

Guarantee

Inspection procedures

Insurance broker

Insurance service

Intended use

Laundry and linen supply service

Lien-sale contract

Maintenance contract

Maintenance service

Make-goods

Management considerations when
purchasing services

Media-buying service

Merits

Moonlighter

Negative selling

Outsourcing

PCO

Performance bond

Pest control service

Promotional discount

Purchasing services

Quality of the finished work

Quality of the materials used

References

Required work schedule

Risk-purchasing group

Run-of-the-press

Run-of-the-station

SBA

Security problems

Service agreement

Should you perform the work yourself
or hire a service?

Some services must be purchased

Trade out

Types of advertising services

Types of cleaning services

Types of consultants

Types of insurance coverage

Types of maintenance services

Unconditional lien release

User discount

Vending machine service

Warranty

Waste removal service

QUESTIONS AND PROBLEMS

1. A specification for pest control service could include the following information:

   (a) _____

   (b) _____

   (c) _____

   (d) _____

   (e) _____

2. What is the major disadvantage of hiring a moonlighter to provide a service to your hospitality operation?

3. List some disadvantages of hiring an unlicensed service provider.

4. Assume you manage a full-service restaurant. Your linen service is mediocre. You are paying $48,000 a year for the service. An in-house laundry setup would cost $20,000. The costs of operating the in-house laundry would be $22,000 per year. What do you suggest? Also, what does the $22,000 include? If possible, ask the owner-manager of a full-service restaurant to comment on your answer.

5. Why is completion time a very important selection factor when evaluating potential repair and maintenance service providers?

6. What is the difference between run-of-the-press and run-of-the station?

7. Should you trade your products for advertising services, or should you pay cash? Why?

8. Assume you are the owner-operator of a fast-food hamburger operation with an annual sales volume of $850,000. What services would you consider purchasing? Why? If possible, ask an owner-operator of such an operation to comment on your answer.

9. A specification for vending machine service could include the following information:

   (a) _____

   (b) _____

   (c) _____

   (d) _____

   (e) _____

10. List some advantages of purchasing a cleaning service.

11. List some disadvantages of purchasing a cleaning service.

12. Assume that you run a school food service serving 500 elementary students, lunch only, five days a week. Currently, you use no pest control service, having opted to let the school custodian spray the necessary chemicals. Lately, though, you feel that the insect problem could be han-

dled much better by an outside service. Prepare a specification for this service. If possible, ask a school food-service manager to comment on your answer.

13. What is the major disadvantage, to the purchaser, of a lien-sale type of contract?

14. What is the major disadvantage of purchasing your insurance from a direct writer?

15. Assume that you own a small, 30-room motel. You have no food service. You wish to expand to 50 rooms, but you need to research the market to determine whether there is a demand for more rooms. Should you do the research yourself, or should you hire a consultant? If possible, ask the owner-manager of such an operation to comment on your answer. Assume that you want to hire a consultant to do this work. How would you go about selecting one?

16. Briefly describe the concept of "negative selling."

17. What are some of the costs and benefits of operating your own laundry machinery and purchasing your own linens?

18. What is the primary purpose of purchasing a fidelity bond?

19. List some advantages and disadvantages of purchasing a maintenance contract.

20. What is the difference between a service agreement and a maintenance contract?

21. A specification for financial services could include the following information:

    (a) _____

    (b) _____

    (c) _____

    (d) _____

    (e) _____

22. Assume that your real estate lease contract requires you to pay a monthly CAM fee. What is the purpose of this fee?

23. A recycling operator contacts you and offers the following deal: If you save your aluminum and cardboard and bring it to her plant, she will give you $0.45 per pound for the metal and $0.08 per pound for the cardboard. How much money would you want to earn each month before you would be interested in this deal? If possible, ask a restaurant manager to comment on your answer.

24. When would you expect an advertising medium to issue "make-goods" to its customers?

25. Briefly describe how a buyer could use an escrow account as part of a bill-paying schedule used to pay a remodeling contractor.

CHAPTER 27

Source: Vulcan-Hart

FURNITURE, FIXTURES, AND EQUIPMENT

THE PURPOSE OF THIS CHAPTER

This chapter discusses:

- The major management considerations surrounding the selection and procurement of furniture, fixtures, and equipment
- The general procedures used when purchasing furniture, fixtures, and equipment
- The selection factors for furniture, fixtures, and equipment
- Financing the purchase of furniture, fixtures, and equipment

INTRODUCTION

Furniture, fixtures, and equipment (FFE) are sometimes referred to as capital items. A capital item is a depreciable asset. Unlike the cost of the nonfood expense items discussed in Chapter 25, under most circumstances the cost of these FFE items cannot be used as tax deductions in the year in which they were purchased. Instead, the hospitality operator must depreciate their value over a period of years (i.e., only a part of the purchase price can be taken as a tax deduction in one year).

A capital item is a long-life item. It is anticipated that it will last in service for more than 1 year, perhaps as long as 20 years, given proper repair and maintenance. While its value may be depreciated over, say, a 3-year period, it conceivably can remain useful and productive for a much longer period of time under normal operating conditions.

The selection and procurement procedure for these items generally involves the typical principles enumerated in Part 2 of this text. Of course, there is an added dimension, namely, that FFE stays around a long time. Consequently, you are very conscious of the least potential for error. If you receive a poor batch of tomatoes, it is relatively easy to rectify this problem. But if you select and procure an inappropriate fax machine, you may have to live with this white elephant longer than you care to.

MANAGEMENT CONSIDERATIONS

On the surface, it would appear relatively easy to determine the types of FFE you need. Basically, the types of products you sell—menu items, quality of rooms, guest transportation to the airport, and so forth—usually dictate the types and qualities of FFE you must have to operate your business sufficiently. Unfortunately, this is only the first step in determining the FFE requirements.

A major concern is the effect that any future plans might have on your need for FFE. For instance, you might want to alter your menu. Or you might wish to add extra banquet rooms. Should you select FFE today in anticipation of tomorrow's needs? Or should you take care of today only and worry about tomorrow when it comes?

We all have growth aspirations. And we all should be concerned about tomorrow because, these days, FFE can become obsolete quickly. If we do not have some foresight, conceivably our hospitality operation could become dated almost overnight. You must balance today's budget demands with tomorrow's requirements if you expect to withstand the ebb and flow of the competitive pressure in the hospitality industry.

Another major FFE concern you must face is the issue of capitalizing an operating expense. To capitalize an expense is to reduce a current expense, say, the energy expense, by investing today in machinery that is expensive yet will reduce energy consumption. The added investment in higher-quality equipment will lead to operational savings later on. But at what point is this trade-off economically advisable?

In our industry, it would appear to us that most hospitality operators are willing to invest one dollar today if they can recoup that one dollar in two to three years. That is, if the operational savings are such that the original investment is paid back in two or three years, generally most hospitality owner-managers will consider capitalizing an expense.

The prediction of savings is difficult. The credibility of your estimates must be acceptable before you trade dollars today for perceived savings tomorrow. You can never be 100 percent certain of your predictions. And you can never tell when operational costs will level off, drop, or suddenly rise dramatically. For instance, in some properties, the initial investment in computerization is much more than the amount of labor savings that can be experienced over a two- to three-year period. Labor may be the least expensive alternative for today. But what about tomorrow?

Several other related problems arise whenever you contemplate the capitalization of expenses. And these problems almost always involve future considerations and your inability to predict them adequately. The fact that you cannot foresee the future completely puts you in somewhat of a ticklish position.

Deciding on the person or persons who should select and procure the FFE items is another major managerial concern. When planning FFE choices, four categories of persons typically are involved: (1) user(s), (2) owner-manager(s), (3) buyer(s), and (4) consultant(s).

The user sometimes is involved in the process because his or her performance on the job may be directly related to the equipment used. And since the user's job performance evaluation is critical to his or her success in the company, it generally is a good idea to invite user input. The user sometimes is also involved as the instigator of an FFE purchase. For instance, he or she may suggest to a supervisor that a dated meat slicer should be replaced with a more modern piece.

The final decision regarding any FFE purchase belongs with the owner-manager. He or she must take the ultimate responsibility for any FFE purchase, so it is logical that this purchase decision be made by the owner-manager.

The owner-manager probably will set the quality standards, note the preferred supplier, and oversee the receiving and installation of the items. He or she normally will be more actively involved in the purchase of FFE than in the purchase of other products. Since these items are expensive and remain a part of the hospitality operation for quite some time, the owner-manager is motivated to be very careful.

If the hospitality firm employs a full-time buyer, he or she typically would be involved as a technical resource person, answering such questions as, Is the desired quality available? What type of payment plans are available? How long will it take to receive the merchandise? and so on.

Depending on the magnitude of the FFE purchase, you may seek the assistance of one or more consultants. For instance, an accountant may be asked to prepare various installment payment options for your review. Or, if you are considering firing someone and replacing him or her with a machine, an accountant might be employed to prepare an estimate of future savings.

If a major remodeling job is contemplated, you might consider using a designer or architect to assist your efforts. These types of individuals normally are employed when building a new facility. They also are typically employed by the multiunit hospitality companies.

Consultants often are worth the added cost you must pay to procure their services. They can detail the FFE needed as well as determine the most effective and efficient layout and design for your specific type of operation. Furthermore, they will see to it that your FFE are installed according to existing fire, health and safety, and building codes.

Since these consultants normally deal in a highly technical area, you probably cannot get too far without their help. They do not come cheap, but the efficiency they may be able to build into your design can take care of their fee and leave you a bit of savings besides.

Some consultants or consulting advice can often be obtained from FFE dealers. That is, you can do business with a "design/build" dealer who is prepared to provide free of charge all the advice and assistance you need as long as you purchase all your FFE from that dealer. This is a one-stop arrangement, and you become a house account. The disadvantages of this, however, can be offset by better supplier services as well as by a decrease in the amount of "downtime" you might need to incur (i.e., the amount of time during which you cannot profitably conduct business because you are still waiting for some FFE to be delivered and installed).

Determining from whom to buy is another major managerial concern. For most hospitality operators, the decision is simple: they usually satisfy their needs by selecting a reputable FFE dealer, or dealers. This is especially true if a reasonably large purchase is contemplated and supplier services represent a major requirement.

There are other sources of supply, though. For instance, you may be able to procure FFE through contract supply houses, a sort of co-op arrangement available in the lodging trade; food and beverage suppliers who deal in FFE as a sideline; mail-order catalogs; the primary sources; other types of local co-ops; chain headquarters that may offer to their affiliates the opportunity to purchase FFE; consultants, such as designers and contractors, who may sell FFE; leasing companies that can provide some items to you; firms that deal in used merchandise, repossessed merchandise, and the like that may be available in your area; warehouse clubs; and auctioneers, who sometimes are instrumental in liquidating FFE. Usually, you must balance convenience, reputation of the supplier, and so forth with the purchase price, installation costs, and other related costs when making your decision.

With so many choices and options available, it may be difficult to locate those who are knowledgeable and prepared to offer the necessary level of service. The optimal supplier is critical for FFE, since to drop that person in favor of someone else can cause tremendous problems, especially time-delay problems. In our experience, the amount of supplier service the supplier will provide, as well as its quality, is a major consideration in most instances.

Another major managerial concern with FFE is the question of reconditioning versus replacing these items, where such a choice is possible. In some cases, it might be economically attractive to recondition, remodel, and/or rebuild some items instead of purchasing new ones. The cost of making do with an existing item may be much less than the purchase price for a new replacement.

But while the reconditioning cost may be quite attractive initially, there may be other problems. For instance, it would appear that reconditioned machinery does not have the long expected life that a new replacement has, so the long-term cost of reconditioning may not be beneficial at all. Another problem might be the downtime experienced during the rebuilding stage for, say, a walk-in refrigerator—typically, it takes longer to recondition, rebuild, and/or remodel than it does to provide a new installation.

In the short run, rebuilding can be the best answer, but in the long run, it may not satisfy your needs. You should, though, at least consider the potential of reconditioning because you do not want to spend any more money than necessary to accomplish your goals.

A final concern to management that we have witnessed in our experience is the impulsive purchase of certain types of FFE items. For instance, many purchase decisions for furnishings are impulsive. An owner-manager may return from a vacation trip with an antique clock in tow that will "be perfect for the lobby." Or he or she visits another restaurant and falls in love with the wall coverings in that establishment, prompting him or her to do a bit of remodeling.

GENERAL PROCEDURES IN FFE PURCHASING

It is not particularly difficult to prepare some type of specification for FFE. Often formal specifications are not prepared for replacement FFE because most operators will "look around," say, at trade shows, in competitors' operations, and in catalogs, trade papers, and so forth before forming an opinion. These operators usually have a very good idea of the type of FFE required before they actually sit down to negotiate with one or more FFE suppliers.

An operator normally has past experience to guide him or her in formulating the appropriate purchasing strategy for replacement FFE. Generally, if the operator has had a good experience with the current items, he or she is most likely to replace them with the same brand, or equivalent. This dependence on yesterday makes it difficult for new manufacturers to gain a foothold unless they offer something unique. But you may be reluctant to try something new and unproven unless you are willing to prepare a relatively detailed specification.

Hospitality operators normally examine replacement FFE very closely before making their purchase decisions. For instance, many of them like to attend the trade shows that cater to our industry because usually there are several FFE dealers in attendance who have demonstration models available for inspection. It would appear that attending a trade show is preferred to visiting a dealer's showroom. It offers a less threatening atmosphere as well as the opportunity to compare and contrast several alternatives.

Visitors to trade shows normally preplan their activities in order to maximize the use of their time. Since time is limited, buyers are able to evaluate only a few FFE selection factors or else they will get bogged down at one dealer's booth display. Trade show visitors want to view many alternatives. To do this, generally they should evaluate only a few major factors, such as the item's functionality, its quality of construction, warranties, its total cost (e.g., AP price plus delivery and installation charges), and the supplier's depth of knowledge and amount of service that can be provided.

When a major FFE purchase is contemplated, normally specifications are necessary. Chances are you will need to finance this type of purchase through a lender, and this person normally requires you to obtain competitive bids for the project that will represent collateral for the loan.

The FFE specification will include many of the selection factors we will note later in this chapter. For all intents and purposes, these specifications are similar in scope to those you prepare for food and beverage items. They do tend, though, to be purchase specifications rather than product specifications, since the required supplier services, which are not a part of the product specification, are very important when a major FFE purchase is planned.

In addition to the major types of supplier services you will require, the FFE purchase specification normally will include further information. It often will include:

1. *Instructions to bidders.* This is the where, when, and how to submit a competitive bid. Included in the specification is all pertinent information, of which the bidder should be cognizant, that will indicate how the project will be awarded and what criteria, such as lowest cost, fastest completion time, and so forth, will be used to make the award decision.

2. *General conditions.* You must note several contingencies in this section of the specification. For instance, you could detail (a) code requirements, (b) access rights (e.g., will the community allow the transportation of heavy equipment on the roadways, or must the equipment be delivered in pieces?), (c) royalties that must be paid, (d) other local ordinances, (e) provisions for modifications, (f) the treatment of cost overruns, (g) the treatment of delays, and (h) liability coverage needed by the supplier.

3. *Specific conditions.* In addition to the list of FFE needed, and their desired characteristics, you also must note delivery dates and procedures, installation dates and procedures, and other related details.

4. *Detailed drawings.* This probably is the major distinction of FFE specifications. For a major purchase, you typically include architectural drawings of all custom equipment as well as any pertinent layout and design plans. These drawings aid bidders. They also help to avoid ambiguity.

Once specifications have been prepared, you should make a list of potential suppliers and, from that list, develop an approved supplier list. After selecting the best supplier, you may need to modify the specifications, monitor FFE orders and delivery, monitor any subcontracting that may be necessary, and obtain the training and other start-up help needed.

SELECTION FACTORS

There are several selection factors for FFE items. You would expect this to be the case since the purchase of FFE is a major decision—one that cannot be performed hastily. Fortunately, we do not need to purchase these items very often. But when we do, our procedures must be planned very carefully. The major selection factors are as follows.

INTENDED USE

As is the case with all things we purchase, we must identify the intended use of the item so that we can detail the appropriate, relevant specification. This is a bit more difficult to do in the FFE area, primarily since so many of the items must be used to satisfy several production and service requirements. But difficult or not, we cannot proceed very far until we isolate the intended use of the FFE needed.

EXACT NAME

There are times when this selection factor can cause a bit of confusion. For instance, it is insufficient to note on your specification the term "oven." Rather, you must be careful to detail the specific type of oven you need. For instance, there is a great deal of difference between a standard convection oven and a convection-steam oven.

Another dimension of the exact name is the model numbers that manufacturers use to distinguish similar types of equipment items. When comparing different brands of the same type of item, it is important to determine the comparable model numbers.

LIFETIME COST

The FFE purchase decision is a long-term process. You sometimes must plan one or more years in advance of your actual purchase. And the items you are buying are expected to have a reasonably long operating life. Consequently, it is impractical to consider only the initial AP price of the FFE since there are so many other expenses associated with them over their normal life span.

Besides the AP price, it is imperative that you consider:

1. Trade-in value of your old FFE
2. Delivery costs
3. Installation and testing costs
4. Relevant operating costs
5. Potential operating savings
6. Trade-in value of the new FFE when you decide to replace it or liquidate it

The related costs can add up very quickly. The inexperienced buyer may not realize this. For instance, delivery, installation, and testing costs can easily be 10 percent, or more, of a walk-in refrigerator's AP price. When soliciting competitive bids, the wise buyer always asks the suppliers to quote the "installed, ready-to-operate" purchase price.

If the initial AP price exceeds your budget, the general tendency is to forgo the purchase or to settle for less quality, hence less expensive, FFE. This may or may not be an appropriate strategy. On the one hand, a new piece of equipment might improve worker productivity significantly. But, if you are struggling under a heavy debt load, it may be unwise to risk bankruptcy.

Sometimes an operator can save money by setting up a personal "equipment rental" firm and purchasing all of the FFE through this firm. For instance, you can call yourself "XYZ" rentals, send a purchase order direct to the manufacturer, and usually obtain the lowest-possible AP prices. Manufacturers usually quote their lowest prices to customers who will lease or resell the merchandise, as they do not need the extra supplier services required by the typical hospitality buyers.

In some cases, an operator might be swayed by a low AP price only to get stung later with high operating costs. For instance, an equipment dealer might quote a low AP price, knowing full well that you will need to purchase his or her expensive parts, supplies, and so forth because there are no other alternatives. You should be skeptical of any unusually low AP price quotations. If it sounds too good to be true, you might be getting hit with a lowball bid.

A lowball bid can take many forms. For example, some salespersons might justify their equipment by pointing out to you its labor-saving potential. Labor saving in our industry is very difficult to achieve, and quite often it is illusory. You might save two work hours per shift if you purchase a floorwashing machine, but if you must fire a full-time employee to save these two hours, chances are you will not do this because you may have a hard time replacing the other six work hours per shift needed to perform other necessary duties. Likewise, even if you fire a full-time person, before you know it, you have hired a part-time employee; and eventually that person is converted into a full-time employee. Result: less labor savings than originally anticipated.

Other lowball possibilities to consider are the following:

1. Equipment loans or sample test periods may spoil the user. Sometimes once you order an item and you take a loan or test period, this gives the salesperson an excuse to drop in a lot, thereby allowing him or her to convince the user that he or she should have some expensive attachments. So, what is economical to start with may become quite expensive in the long run.

2. The new equipment may not be compatible with what you now have; therefore, you may need to purchase expensive adaptors to make it work.

3. If you get a stripped-down model, the user may persuade you to obtain expensive options.

4. The supplier might be discontinuing that particular line of equipment; where will you get replacement parts?

5. The supplier may put in several exceptions on any warranty or guarantee (e.g., you may have to pay the first $500 of any service call for the first year).

6. You may find out too late that you are required to purchase a large inventory of spare parts right now. (This could be an illegal tying agreement, though.)

Generally, the issue with any capital expenditure is not what it costs initially, but what it is worth over its lifetime. Judging FFE on the AP price alone is usually a mistake. You must force yourself to consider its lifetime cost. However, if you plan to be out of business one or two years from now, then an overreliance on AP price might be appropriate.

POTENTIAL OPERATING SAVINGS

Quite often, a piece of equipment is purchased primarily to effect a savings in operating expenses. That is, the decision is made to capitalize an operating expense by investing in something today that will cause some of your expenses to decrease in the future. (See Figures 27.1 and 27.2.)

Management can control several operating expenses that are good candidates for possible future reduction. For instance, the cost of merchandise, labor, energy, taxes, water, waste removal, and so forth might all be reduced if we proceed to invest in something today.

There are several mathematical models available that we can use to test the feasibility of buying equipment based on its potential operating savings. A typical formula that operators use to guide the capital investment decision is the *payback period* formula. The payback period refers

FIGURE 27.1. Equipment sometimes is purchased because of its product-saving potential. (Courtesy Winston Industries.)

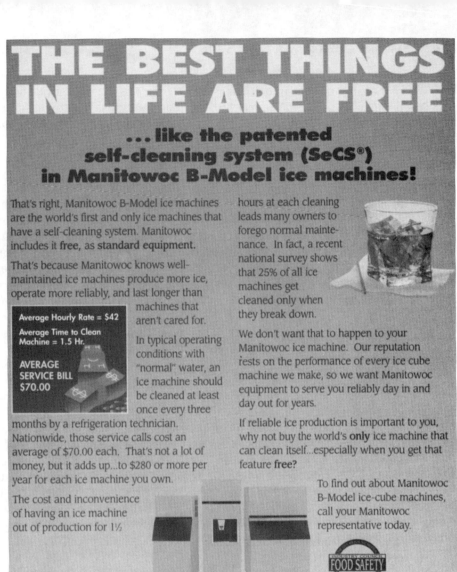

FIGURE 27.2. Equipment sometimes is purchased because of its labor-saving potential. (Courtesy Manitowac Equipment Works.)

to the amount of time it takes to recoup the original investment. For instance, if you must invest $5,500 in an energy-saving oven today, how long will it take, say, how many years will it take, for you to save $5,500 of energy costs? If it takes more than three years to recoup the initial investment, the typical operator will not purchase the oven.

Probably it is most useful to use the *net present value* procedure, which takes into account the time value of money (i.e., the fact that a dollar saved next year is worth considerably less than a dollar saved today). The net present value procedure requires you, first, to compute the present value of the future savings. To do this, estimate the savings and then discount them to take into account the fact that the longer you must wait to receive these savings, the less they are worth today. Furthermore, the longer you must wait, the risk of losing the savings becomes greater and greater, which implies that the future savings are worth even less today.

Second, the net present value procedure requires you to subtract from the present value of predicted savings the amount of the initial investment you must make today. If the answer is greater than zero (i.e., if the present value of the predicted savings is greater than the amount of money you must invest today), the investment today is economically attractive.

Several other types of formulas have been developed for specialized applications. For instance, some tell you in what year a piece of equipment should be replaced and some tell you when to perform maintenance.

The formulas are useful, but they do require numbers. And the answers are only as good as the numbers you provide. Consequently, the use of the formulas is anticlimactic. The real challenge is to come up with the proper number estimates. Knowing the formula is useful only if you can come up with reasonably accurate numbers. And herein lies the challenge to management.

In many cases, it is very difficult to predict future operating savings. For instance, let us consider the potential to save time and possibly increase the overall productivity of the hospitality operation. If you own a cafeteria, you might consider purchasing a computerized cash register because you might get customers through the line faster. Well, some salespersons might tell you, "If you get the customers through faster, you can serve more customers." Hence, the new cash register causes an increase in customers. But wait. How does this all connect? Do patrons eat in your place because of this speed? Maybe yes, maybe no.

You might also hear the same argument with a faster dishwashing machine. For instance, if you wash dishes faster, you can serve more meals, since you get back the dishes faster. Again, this is an illusory argument because you could always increase your stock of dishes. Likewise, it is unlikely that customers visit you because you have a fast dishwasher.

Be careful of other productivity arguments. For example, it is not advantageous to own a 400-slices-per-hour toaster if you sell considerably less toast.

Potential product savings may also be illusory. For example, someone selling automatic bars may tell us that free pouring of liquor wastes 2 to 3 ounces per bottle. We will agree with that. But we do not agree when we are told that if we save these ounces, we can sell them at $2.50 each and, hence, save $5.00 to $7.50 per bottle, all because we have the automatic bar. Simply not wasting the ounces is no guarantee that customers will come in and buy them. You have only a certain number of customers. If you are wasteful, it costs you more product to serve them. Consequently, you save the cost of the liquor with the automatic bar. The fact that you have automation does not cause you to save an amount equivalent to the sales price of each drink. If that were the case, you should buy two or three automatic bars.

Energy efficiency is another noteworthy concern. One of the potential advantages of newer equipment is a more efficient energy usage pattern. Unfortunately, there are many bogus "energy-misers" on the market. You must be aware of the potential falsity of these exorbitant claims.

Sometimes operators purchase energy-saving equipment that they really do not need. For example, it may be futile to purchase an expensive oven that guarantees less energy use as well as less meat shrinkage. If you cook your roast beef at 250°F instead of at 375°F, you can accomplish almost the same savings. In addition, existing equipment sometimes can be modified to gain the same savings. And the modification might be a much cheaper alternative.

We have indicated that there are some potential problems with labor savings. To reiterate, we usually need a certain number of employees just to open the doors. We cannot very easily replace them with machines. Usually only the largest operations might save a bit of labor over the long run.

If you are purchasing a capital item primarily to effect a reduction in future operating expenses, you must do your homework very, very carefully. Speculation about future costs is a hazardous undertaking. The pitfalls are many, but the potential to save a considerable amount of money in the long run makes us eager to take our chances.

DIRECT PURCHASE

Should you go straight to the manufacturer and purchase your FFE items? Or should you go through the local dealer? The choice is not always clear. Most of the time, it is a matter of personal taste. If you buy direct, the AP price obviously is lower. But since you usually must put up the cash and provide your own transportation and installation, the costs can quickly increase. If you bypass the local dealer, there is a good chance that you will need to provide your own maintenance and other supplier services.

In our experience, operators have been sucked in too easily with this "let's bypass the local dealer" routine. When your equipment breaks down, who will help you? If you have your own maintenance crew, no problem. But if not, well, there is something to be said for having your friends waiting in the wings to help you.

DEMONSTRATION MODELS

Many manufacturers and dealers use FFE models—items in their showrooms, those at industry trade shows, or those used by a traveling salesperson—for demonstration purposes. In many cases, you might be able to purchase these items and save a considerable amount of money. If you buy this type of FFE, normally you must (1) put up the total amount of the AP price in cash, (2) take the item as is, and (3) usually provide your own transportation and/or installation. These items normally are inexpensive primarily because they are used products, thereby somewhat depreciated already in value.

There is generally a very good savings associated with this opportunity. If you can live with the absence of supplier services, have the cash in your pocket, and can handle all necessary installation chores, you should save quite a bit of money.

There is a downside, though, to consider. For instance, you may not be able to obtain state-of-the-art items. Most FFE available may not fit your needs exactly; you may have to compromise too much to take advantage of the savings. In addition, you may be unable to obtain adequate maintenance contracts or, if you do get them, they may be shorter than you would like to have.

EQUIPMENT PROGRAMS

In our discussion of nonalcoholic beverages in Chapter 24, we introduced the concept of an equipment program. Recall that under this program you are able to use a company's machinery as long as you are using its food, beverage, or cleaning product that is dispensed with this machinery. For instance, you might be able to receive "free" use of a laundry system if you agree to purchase all laundry chemicals from a specific firm. Of course, the machinery is not "free," since the chemicals normally are priced to take into account the value of the equipment.

In some instances, you cannot buy the juice, soap, cola, or what have you, that you want without taking the machine. As this might represent a tying agreement, some companies will sell the product without the machine, but they usually keep the surcharge on the product, so you might just as well take the "free" machine since you will be paying for it anyway.

Some operators resent an equipment program arrangement because they believe that the supplier will get rich by extracting a surcharge every time they purchase the products used in the machinery. In other words, you might pay over and over again the initial cost of the machinery.

However, in some instances, there may not be a surcharge. The equipment itself might represent only a form of discount to you. Or the supplier may be willing to toss in the equipment if you buy a large supply of products over a long period of time. Or the supplier might merely be motivated to ensure that the products are dispensed properly. Furthermore, most suppliers maintain the equipment, freeing you from a costly headache.

In our experience, equipment programs have generally been advantageous to the hospitality operator. We periodically compare the cost of coffee with and without machinery, and the coffee with machinery usually turns out to be only a few pennies more per pound than the cost without the machinery. And we do not need to purchase, install, and maintain coffee-brewing equipment.

CUSTOM FFE

Generally, you are motivated to purchase standardized FFE. That is, usually you do not want to purchase anything that violates height, width, veneer, and other standards.

Customized FFE are very expensive. It may not be worth the extra cost and inconvenience to procure such items. Aside from the normally high AP price, there are other major costs of purchasing custom FFE: (1) the company producing the item you want may go out of business, which can be troublesome if it is the only firm capable of maintaining and servicing that item; (2) if it is a very odd piece of custom work, it is unlikely that you can borrow against its value; (3) there may be several bugs in the item, which could increase operating costs and aggravation in the long run; (4) there probably is no future trade-in value; (5) the manufacturer may be forced to pass on to you cost overruns; and (6) it is possible that the item or items may not be ready on time—there could be a production and/or installation delay.

You might be able to save some of the expense of customized FFE if you can locate a supplier who has merchandise that is part standard, part customized. For instance, some kitchen equipment manufacturers produce standard stainless steel tables that allow some limited customization by the purchaser.

There are, however, several potential advantages of customized FFE. For instance: (1) operating savings may be available; (2) the items may be easier to operate, maintain, and clean; (3) they may be more attractive; (4) you can customize your image; (5) usually you can get exactly what you want; and (6) in the long run, the lifetime cost of these items can be more attractive than that associated with their standard counterparts. In fact, a custom installation may be economical in a hospitality operation because it will fit exactly the space and need for which it was designed. The idea of buying stock material is not a good one if it means getting something that is less than exactly what you want.

NEW VERSUS USED FFE

Occasionally, a buyer may come across merchandise that, while technically classified as used, could actually have suffered little or no use. For instance, kitchen equipment offered by trade show exhibitors at "show-special" prices may be just as good as new. Also, FFE manufacturers and dealers sometimes have "freight-damaged" items that they are willing to sell for a fraction of their original AP prices. Some of these damaged products may need a lot of work before they can be put into service. However, many of them may have only cosmetic damage; a couple of bumps and bruises may be inconsequential when you are purchasing, say, work tables.

Of course, most used items available for purchase have been in use for some time. In most cases, these items can be purchased for a small fraction of their original selling prices; experience shows that you can save as much as 70 percent of new AP prices. Again, as with most bargains of this type, you normally are required to put up the cash and take the items as is. Often there are secondhand dealers in your area who specialize in this type of merchandise. These persons, though, usually are not prepared to service what they sell.

You sometimes can purchase used merchandise from a new products dealer who makes a market in trade-in items. Quite often, a local new products dealer will have available like-new merchandise that recently was exchanged for more modern models. If you are on good terms with these dealers, they may even call you to let you know about something recently available that might be useful to you.

The trade papers often carry ads soliciting purchasers of used FFE. In our experience, most hospitality operators are leery of these arrangements. They have no qualms about dealing with someone local, or someone with whom they are familiar, but it is unusual for these businesspersons to answer ads placed by unknown, individual operators.

At times, an auctioneer is hired by a hospitality operator to liquidate the FFE. More than likely, a tax collector, or lender, forecloses on the hospitality operation and hires an auctioneer to liquidate the property to satisfy past debts. In our experience, if you know what you are doing, you can catch an extremely attractive bargain at these auctions. (See Figure 27.3.)

Some hospitality operators seek out auctioneers and other persons who are involved in liquidation procedures, such as attorneys, trustees,

FIGURE 27.3. FFE sometimes are purchased at an auction. Normally these items are sold as is, where is, but despite these disadvantages, a huge savings is possible. (Courtesy G. Robert Deiro and Norman Kaye.)

escrow companies, and title companies. These operators want to be on any mailing lists that are used to advertise liquidation sales. The obvious advantage of being on a mailing list is learning about potentially attractive opportunities. The drawback, though, is the possibility of making an impulse purchase that will not suit your needs.

The major potential advantage of used merchandise, of course, is the huge reduction in the purchase price. And, if you are lucky, you can obtain an item that has a long, useful life remaining. Unfortunately, several disadvantages might be incurred if you procure used FFE. You might acquire (1) obsolete merchandise, (2) an energy guzzler, (3) an item that is inefficient in its need for floor space, (4) merchandise that is expensive to maintain, or (5) an item that does not meet current fire, health and safety, and building codes. You must also consider (6) the time needed to seek out these bargains, (7) the time needed to examine the items before purchasing them, (8) the fact that the item lacks a guarantee, (9) the possibility that replacement parts are no longer available, (10) possible damage to your image, and (11) the inability to predict exactly the amount of money needed to recondition the item, if necessary.

Buying used FFE is a gamble; you must take a risk in order to reap the savings. You can minimize your risk, though, if you confine your purchases to nonmechanical pieces as well as small wares, such as pots and pans. The risk-averse buyer should shy away from mechanical items, especially those with complex computerized control systems.

VERSATILITY

Whenever possible, you should try to purchase versatile equipment, that is, equipment that can do more than one job. For instance, tilt kettles are popular in many kitchens because they can be used to satisfy so many different production requirements. The tilt kettle can be used as a grill, a steam kettle, and a braising pan.

Versatility is increasingly important today because the cost of space in the hospitality operation is very expensive. Our places of business are located in prime retail areas. Hence, the cost of the real estate is high, which means that we are motivated to reduce the size of our production facilities and increase the size of our income-producing facilities, such as the dining room and lounge. We cannot do this unless we are willing to pay a little more for versatility.

COMPACTNESS

Expensive real estate makes it necessary to purchase several FFE items that have the virtue of compactness. For instance, kitchen and laundry equipment that require less space can be very valuable to you in the long run. Likewise, fold-away types of furniture are valuable. These items certainly will cost more initially, but their convenience and space-saving capabilities cannot be ignored.

As a related issue, you must be concerned with the overall weight of the FFE items you are considering for purchase. You may have, for instance, a building structure that is incapable of supporting very heavy pieces of production equipment. Or there may not be a sufficiently large opening in your facility to permit delivery of the equipment to its final resting place.

COMPATIBILITY

You should attempt to ensure that new purchases will intermingle easily with your current stock of FFE. New FFE items should be compatible with the existing stock in many ways, such as aesthetically and functionally. Otherwise, you might experience some production problems and/or some damage to your overall image in the eyes of your customers. In some cases, such as with a systems sale, you have no choice; you must purchase compatible merchandise that will meet your specific needs.

APPEARANCE

Your image is a precious commodity in the hospitality business. You must do whatever is feasible to protect and enhance it. One way to do this is to select FFE items that have a high-quality appearance.

Manufacturers of similar FFE items often compete strictly on superficial appearance differences. For instance, counter fixtures may vary somewhat—veneers, width, height, and so forth may differ a bit from one manufacturer to another. These are not substantial differences, but they could be very important. If customers will see the FFE items, it may behoove you to spend a few extra dollars to ensure that what they see pleases them.

BRAND NAME

In our experience, most hospitality operators use this selection factor almost exclusively to purchase replacement FFE. Some are not necessarily concerned with brand names when they purchase an item for the first time. But once they have had a bit of experience with an item, either a good one or a bad one, the memory of it remains very strong. Consequently, it should be expected that brand-name recognition probably always will be a major selection factor.

There is something to be said for the effect that some brand names might have on your image. For instance, some of your customers may recognize high-quality brand names for refrigeration. If it is important for you to display one of these brand-name fixtures on your premises, your purchasing decision becomes an easy task.

Another dimension to the brand-name selection factor is the "halo effect" that a hospitality operator can develop as he or she gains experience with a certain brand of merchandise. The halo effect suggests that if you have had a good experience with a certain brand name, not only are you predisposed to purchase the same brand-name merchandise when it is time to replace some worn-out FFE, but you also will tend to feel more positive about that particular manufacturer's entire product line. Consequently, the brand-name selection factor gains in importance as your experience with the items increases.

If you invite input from users when you are developing your FFE purchasing strategy, you almost always can expect them to think in terms of brand names. Most users are familiar with certain brands that were

636 FURNITURE, FIXTURES, AND EQUIPMENT

used in some other place of employment. Or persons who attended, say, a culinary school, learned their crafts on particular brands of kitchen equipment and are apt to favor them.

PORTABILITY

This could be a very important selection factor for kitchen equipment. For instance, a hospitality operation that enjoys a good deal of banquet trade will enjoy the convenience of portability. Being able to rearrange the equipment to suit the specific needs of a party is a major advantage.

Mobile FFE also create another advantage, namely, the ability to move the items so that deep cleaning can be performed more easily and effectively. Also, a serviceperson will be able to perform his or her tasks more quickly if the items are not stationary.

Mobility also means that if a piece of machinery breaks down, there may be no need to have it repaired in place. The serviceperson can remove the item easily, replace it with a loaner item, and proceed to take the broken item to the shop where it can receive the proper attention. Employees then do not need to sidestep a serviceperson while trying to perform their duties.

Portable equipment also tends to retain its value over the long run. Since it is easy to move, it can be removed from service and sold easily.

Of course, portable items do not come cheap. They cost more because of their convenience and ability to accommodate several needs. In some hospitality operations, their initial cost will generate significant savings (as well as higher trade-in value) over the years.

EASE OF CLEANING

All FFE items must be cleaned periodically. The amount of time needed to clean these items will vary with the quality of items purchased. For instance, you expect to pay a bit more for an item that is very easy to clean. You gain an advantage, though, when employees are more motivated to clean it than another similar item. Furthermore, clean FFE, especially clean equipment, should last longer under normal operating conditions. Your lifetime cost for an easy-to-clean item, therefore, can shrink appreciably.

To save labor, you might consider purchasing self-cleaning devices. For instance, self-cleaning ovens, dispensing equipment, ventilation ducts, and exhaust fans are very convenient items to own. You are assured of clean equipment if you purchase these types of items, but you must be willing to pay a higher AP price as well as be willing to incur additional energy costs over their lifetimes, as self-cleaning items normally require a good deal of expensive energy in their operation. The convenience and labor savings, though, could easily exceed these costs.

EASE OF MAINTENANCE

Most equipment requires some sort of repair and maintenance. The amount required impacts directly on the total operating costs you will incur over the useful life of the items. The ease of providing a service also affects the total operating cost, primarily because the labor cost involved can increase dramatically if your equipment items require considerable effort to maintain.

It is a major mistake to overlook the maintenance requirements of any type of FFE. It is very tempting to ignore this potential problem because we may be blinded temporarily by an attractive AP price. This usually turns out to be false economy. Labor costs will continue to rise. We should strive to build a hedge against this inflationary expense by seeing to it, as much as possible, that we minimize future labor requirements whenever we can.

DEGREE OF AUTOMATION

Some saving can be earned if we purchase equipment that provides some labor-saving opportunity. For instance, we may be able to save a bit of labor cost if we use automated broilers. The related labor costs, such as payroll taxes, represent additional savings. Furthermore, if we can reduce the number of required work hours, we may be able to reduce the number of employees needed, which implies that we could economize on space needed.

In our experience, labor saving is very difficult to attain. Unless you operate a very large facility, it is very difficult to trim even a little bit of your payroll budget lest you risk alienating your guests with poor service. Consequently, it is difficult to justify automated equipments' higher AP price strictly with the potential amount of labor savings.

Instead, you should judge automated equipment on its ability to provide standardized products and on its ability to assist your control efforts in the hospitality operation. For instance, fully automated espresso machines will allow you to serve consistent coffee products quickly and easily. Furthermore, those with enhanced diagnostic capabilities, advanced computer controls, and several digital readouts can be operated by less skilled employees who will not require extensive training. This streamlines both your quality control and cost control efforts.

Some automated equipment also allows us to control the cost of sales and the cash collected from guests. For instance, fully automated bar dispensing systems can pour an accurate, preplanned portion of liquor, record the liquor usage, and ring up the sale on the cash register.

AVAILABILITY OF REPLACEMENT PARTS

You must ensure that there will be an available inventory of spare parts for the FFE you want to purchase. If there is any doubt about this, you may want to reconsider the purchase, or you might want to buy immediately a spare parts inventory to protect yourself. Maintaining your own inventory exposes you to normal storage costs, costs you would rather leave to your supplier. But an additional cost of this type can pale in comparison to dealing with a broken machine that might need to be scrapped because of the lack of one or two parts.

In addition to the availability of parts, you also should consider the time lag that might exist between the ordering of a part and its delivery. The lead time can be very short, or, as in the case of foreign-made FFE, quite lengthy. A short lead time implies that the supplier maintains an inventory of parts locally, thereby increasing his or her cost of doing business. This cost eventually will be passed to you, but it might be far less burdensome than having a broken item hampering your production needs.

You should assume that you will not be able to obtain replacement parts if you purchase a used piece of equipment. While this is not always the case, you should be prepared always for this possibility when buying used items. For instance, only electronic cash registers are manufactured today. The old gear-driven models may be attractive additions to your lounge, but you will pay the price for this luxury when you need service and parts.

Parts and service also may be tough to obtain if you purchase technologically unique equipment that is just being introduced to the marketplace. There may be bugs in these types of items that have yet to be remedied. Or, worse yet, the manufacturer of a new item may drop the line due to lack of interest from other hospitality operators, which could leave you begging for parts and service. Furthermore, servicepersons may be unfamiliar with a new item.

A similar situation can develop if you purchase customized FFE. The probability is great that you will be unable to procure parts and service without expending a great deal of effort.

SUPPLIER SERVICES

The main supplier service you are concerned with is the proverbial "service after the sale." You definitely need repair and maintenance service, as well as replacement parts, during the warranty period. Also, you must have the appropriate information on economic value (i.e., installation and operating instructions) where applicable.

It would appear that service is one of the most, if not the most, important of the selection factors. You must have a trustworthy supplier if you do not have the capability of handling this type of service yourself. Not only will inadequately installed or serviced FFE increase your operating costs, they also will affect the quality of service you can provide to your guests. The specter of customer dissatisfaction is a fearful thing, and we are generally not eager to suffer its consequences.

After the warranty period and the break-in period expire, you may wish to engage other service providers to maintain your FFE. But at the outset, you will find that several things can and will go wrong. This is when you need help the most. The ability to help you might ensure an FFE supplier's place on your approved supplier list. Many suppliers sell FFE, but not too many of them sell FFE and service. You cannot afford to discover you have chosen the wrong type of supplier after placing your purchase order.

If you purchase FFE direct, you must be willing to forgo any type of "service after the sale." While some manufacturers of highly specialized equipment give you an 800 or 900 number you can call for basic assistance, you should always assume that you will be on your own when you buy direct. This may be acceptable to you for some items, such as some types of furniture. But for mechanical devices, if you have any doubt about your ability to help yourself, it may be a good idea to seek the services of a reputable equipment dealer.

EMPLOYEE SKILL LEVEL

Before purchasing any equipment that is complicated to use in production or service, you must ensure that the staff is able to comprehend its operating procedures. At the very least, employees must possess the aptitude to learn the operating procedures within a reasonable period of time.

You must also be certain that the new equipment, which represents change to the employees, will be accepted by everyone in the hospitality operation. Resistance to change has caused many a good idea to fall by the wayside. For instance, employees may resent an automatic bar installation. This does not mean that you should not invest in one of these machines, but you should be prepared to smooth the way for its implementation within the operation.

SOURCE OF ENERGY

Machinery can be operated with various energy sources. For instance, it may be possible to utilize natural gas, electricity, steam, oil, or solar power to operate some of your equipment. In some instances, there is no choice; for example, you may be stuck with an all-electric kitchen with no possibility of converting to an alternate energy source. If you do, however, have a choice available, you will want to consider equipment that can be powered by a less expensive source of energy. Or you might be interested in using only energy that is least damaging to the environment.

In general, to acquire equipment that can utilize less energy, an inexpensive energy source, and/or an energy source that is most favorable to

Need new equipment?
Here are 5 reasons to choose gas:

1 **Long-term gas supply outlook is good.**
America still has enough underground gas deposits to last well into the 21st century. They lie in places where they're harder to get, but the work of getting them is already under way.
Add new sources like gas from coal – longer term technologies, too – and there could be enough gas to last indefinitely.

2 **Restaurants have high priority for gas.**
Right after our residential customers, you have the highest priority for continued gas service under federal guidelines.

3 **Gas will continue to be the best value.**
All forms of energy are facing increased costs these days, and projections by energy

experts show that natural gas will continue to keep its longtime position as your best energy value.

4 **Gas is America's most efficient energy.**
According to the U.S. Council on Environmental Quality, gas appliances use less of America's total energy supply.

5 **New gas equipment makes the most efficient energy even more efficient.**
More and more commercial equipment is being made with new energy-saving features, like fast convection cooking and infrared broiling.
If it's replacement time for any of your equipment, remember– it's smart to stay with gas. **AGA** American Gas Association

FIGURE 27.4. The type of energy a piece of equipment requires is an important selection factor. (Used through the courtesy of the American Gas Association.)

our environment, you must be willing to pay a significantly greater AP price for it. As with the potential saving of any type of operating cost in the future, usually we must be willing to invest something today to reap the benefit tomorrow. For instance, a natural gas-powered machine may cost more initially than a standard electric one. In addition, it may cost more to install it. You hope, though, that you will save enough money down the road to make such an investment economically attractive. (See Figure 27.4.)

EXCESS CAPACITY

In some cases, you may need to decide whether your current FFE purchase should include some consideration of the potential growth of your business. When buying equipment, especially kitchen equipment, you might consider the possibility that two or three years beyond, you will need equipment that can handle twice the number of customers you currently serve. The question, then, is "Should you buy kitchen equipment that handles the current customer load only, or should you purchase excess capacity equipment now?"

If the larger equipment is available today at an attractive AP price, you might consider purchasing it. If not, you probably should avoid the larger items for several reasons: (1) you often can buy equipment that has add-on capability, (2) you will waste money maintaining a larger-than-necessary piece of equipment, (3) you have capital tied up in the larger equipment that might be best used in some other income-generating activity, and (4) there is no guarantee that your business eventually will increase according to your expectations.

It is more difficult to add on to the physical plant when your customer count increases. Also, the costs of construction and so forth tend to increase considerably in just a short period of time. Consequently, it may be advisable to erect a physical structure that can service your needs down the road. But the FFE probably should be purchased as the need arises.

ADD-ON CAPABILITIES

If you anticipate an increase in business in the near future, you might want to consider purchasing FFE items that can be modified and adapted easily to service the added business. You should expect to pay a bit more today for this feature.

Possibly, you might discuss your needs with your supplier and agree to purchase the added capacity later on from that person if he or she will take this into consideration when setting the AP price of the items you currently wish to purchase.

WARRANTY

It is unusual for any FFE item to be sold without some manufacturer's warranty. The typical warranty generally covers parts and repair for 12 to 24 months.

The main issue with a warranty is not the warranty itself, since just about every item has one, but the convenience, or lack thereof, with which you can receive satisfaction if you must have an item serviced. For instance, you may need to ship the item to the factory for repairs. Or you may need to wait too long for the work to be performed, which can cause customer dissatisfaction if there is considerable downtime in your operation.

Warranties are only as good as the intention and ability of the manufacturer, and/or the dealer, to honor them. In our experience, the best warranty is the supplier's reputation for ensuring customer satisfaction.

If you purchase FFE items direct, the warranty provision might be very limited. Or there may not even be a warranty for items shipped direct. But when you purchase direct, you may have to surrender this benefit.

CODE COMPLIANCE

The local governments normally enforce several laws governing fire, health and safety, and building procedures that must be adhered to by all businesspersons. The FFE that we purchase must meet the existing legal codes. For instance, equipment that we purchase must meet health district codes, safety codes, electrical codes, noise pollution codes, and so forth. If you buy new equipment, you would expect it to satisfy the current legal requirements. Used equipment may not, so a bit of caution is needed to ensure that you do not purchase something only to find out later on that the government will disallow its use in your establishment.

There are several organizations that endorse certain types of FFE. Buyers normally look for their "seals of approval" when purchasing these items. The most common endorsements are made by NSF International—sanitation certification; Underwriters Laboratories (UL)—electrical safety certification; American Gas Association (AGA)—gas safety certification; National Fire Protection Association (NFPA)—fire safety certification; and American Society of Mechanical Engineers (ASME)—steam safety certification.

In some parts of the country, you may need to purchase items that carry these or other appropriate seals of approval. In Clark County, Nevada, for example, all food contact equipment used in food services must carry the NSF International seal.

FINANCING THE PURCHASE OF FFE

When purchasing capital items, almost invariably the subject of financing the purchase arises. In most cases, you must devote as much thought to the financing of the purchase as you do to the various selection factors discussed in this chapter.

Purchasing FFE is not an everyday occurrence. We do not expect to pay for many of these items by writing a check on our current bank account. Rather, we often must determine the various alternative financing arrangements available to us and decide which one, or ones, we can use to our best advantage.

Of course, for some FFE purchases, we may indeed be able to finance them with money that currently sits in our bank account. So, one financing alternative is the use of our own personal funds (i.e., we can fiance an FFE purchase through the normal cash flow of the hospitality operation). Quite often, though, we might use a bit of personal cash and supplement it with some sort of installment credit. For instance, we might be able to make a down payment to a dealer and convince the dealer to carry a personal promissory note for the remainder of the balance owed. We expect to pay the current market interest rate to the dealer, as he or she is acting as our lender in this transaction, as well as our FFE dealer.

Working a credit arrangement with the dealer may be to your advantage for several reasons. For instance, he or she may know you very well and dispense with the normal credit checks and other costly loan application fees, thereby saving you a bit of money. You also might be able to combine some sort of discount with your purchase, such as a cash discount, if you pay your final installment before the due date.

In our experience, FFE suppliers are a bit more inclined to grant favorable credit terms than are the food and beverage suppliers. While not all these suppliers may be willing to grant large amounts of credit, perhaps you might consider dealing only with those who are willing to finance your purchases regardless of the dollar amount.

If you arrange an installment-payment plan with a dealer, normally he or she will expect you to make a down payment equal to one-third of the purchase price, make monthly payments (to include interest and principal), and sign a "security agreement," which grants the dealer the right to foreclose and take back the FFE item if you fail to make your installment payments. Usually the loan term will not exceed 36 months.

Some dealers and manufacturers are willing to accept credit cards for payment. This is an expensive option, though, for buyers and suppliers. Credit card interest rates are usually much higher than rates the suppliers would charge if they extended credit themselves. Furthermore, suppliers accepting credit card payments must pay a fee to the credit card company; this added cost may be added to the AP prices buyers must pay for their FFE items.

You could use the FFE as collateral for a loan from a commercial lender. This is also an expensive alternative. For instance, the lenders normally require a relatively large down payment, as they are unwilling to finance more than 40 to 50 percent of the value of these items. They also assess a variety of credit expenses, such as loan origination fees. They require you to sign a security agreement. And, if you are dealing with a commercial bank, it might require you to maintain with it a noninterest-bearing checking account with a reasonably large balance; this increases the effective interest charges on your loan since you now have the use of less money than you originally borrowed.

Finally, you could opt for some sort of a lease arrangement for FFE items. While not all FFE are available for lease, you can lease a great number of items. For instance, leasing computers, ice machines, and refrigeration machinery is somewhat common in the food-service industry, whereas leasing television sets and laundry equipment is common in the lodging industry.

Leasing is a very expensive form of financing. For instance, with some leases, you pay and pay, but you never own the item. With others (such as "rent-to-own" plans), there is the opportunity, sometimes the requirement, to buy the item at the end of the lease period for some stated amount. The lessor normally requires you to purchase full insurance coverage for the leased items, which might be more than you would be willing to do if you owned them. Unless maintenance comes with the leased item, you may be required to spend more money for maintenance than you would consider spending if you owned the item. Furthermore, the lease payments are usually based on the FFE item's list price; hence, you do not have the opportunity to negotiate the underlying purchase price.

There are advantages to leasing. For one thing, you do not need to put up a major chunk of money as a down payment—this helps preserve your working capital. You also can experiment with new technology without making a long-term purchase commitment. And, generally, it is relatively easy to set up a lease arrangement—there is less paperwork and fewer other related problems with a lease than with a loan from a commercial lender. Unfortunately, these advantages aside, it is generally felt that leasing is almost always more expensive in the long run.

KEY WORDS AND CONCEPTS

Add-on capabilities	Contract supply house
AGA	Custom FFE
Appearance	Degree of automation
ASME	Delivery cost
Availability of replacement parts	Demonstration model
Brand name	Depreciable asset
Capital item	Design/build dealer
Capitalizing an expense	Detailed drawings
Code compliance	Direct purchase
Compactness	Downtime

Ease of cleaning

Ease of maintenance

Employee skill level

Equipment dealer

Equipment program

Exact name

Excess capacity

Financing the purchase of FFE

Freight-damaged

General and specific conditions

Impulse purchase

Installation and testing costs

Instructions to bidders

Intended use

Lifetime cost

Liquidation

Lowball bid

Management considerations when purchasing FFE

Net present value

New versus used FFE

NFPA

NSF International

Operating costs

Operating savings

Payback period

Portability

Purchasing FFE

Reconditioning versus replacement of FFE

Rent-to-own plan

Security agreement

Service after the sale

Show-special price

Source of energy

Supplier services

Systems sale

Trade-in value

Trade show

Types of FFE suppliers

UL

Versatility

Warranty

QUESTIONS AND PROBLEMS

1. What are some advantages of leasing FFE?

2. What are some disadvantages of leasing FFE?

3. A specification for a dining room table could include the following information:

   (a) _____

   (b) _____

   (c) _____

   (d) _____

   (e) _____

4. Briefly describe the concept of "capitalizing" an expense.

5. List some reasons that it might be advantageous to hire a consultant to assist in the development of FFE purchase specifications.

6. What are some possible disadvantages of purchasing reconditioned equipment?

7. When should your equipment purchase specification include detailed drawings?

8. The lifetime cost of an FFE item could include:

   (a) _____

   (b) _____

   (c) _____

   (d) _____

   (e) _____

9. Briefly describe the concept of "net present value."

10. What are some advantages and disadvantages of purchasing a personal computer direct from the manufacturer?

11. A specification for a microwave oven could include the following information:

    (a) _____

    (b) _____

    (d) _____

    (d) _____

    (e) _____

12. What are some advantages and disadvantages of purchasing customized kitchen equipment?

13. Why would an equipment dealer be willing to sell a demonstration model for much less than the normal purchase price?

14. When would "compactness of FFE" be an important selection factor?

15. When would "availability of replacement parts" be an important selection factor?

16. Briefly describe the concept of "payback period."

17. Why would a commercial lender require a borrower to sign a security agreement?

18. If you purchase a gas-powered clothes dryer, it will usually be more expensive than a similar electrically powered one. However, what would entice a buyer to consider spending more money for the gas-powered appliance?

19. What are some advantages of purchasing portable kitchen equipment?

20. What are some advantages and disadvantages of purchasing used FFE?

21. A specification for a walk-in refrigerator could include the following information:

    (a) _____

    (b) _____

(c) _____

(d) _____

(e) _____

22. What are some advantages and disadvantages of using a credit card to finance an equipment purchase?

23. What type of FFE items would you be willing to purchase from a local warehouse club? Why?

24. What are some advantages and disadvantages of equipment programs?

25. When would you select FFE strictly on the basis of brand name?

INDEX

Absentee owner, 321
Access rights, 622
Accounting service, 17
Accounts payable, 198, 201
Accounts receivable, 18
Accuracy in Menus, 53
Additives, *see* Chemical standards
Add-on capability, 641
Advanced Research Projects Agency, 334
Advertising service, 17, 598–603
  agency, 599, 600
  direct mail, 602–603
  magazine, 601
  newspaper, 599–600
  outdoor, 602
  printed matter, 601–602
  radio, 600
  telephone directory, 601
  TV, 600–601
Age at time of slaughter:
  meat, *see* Maturity class
  poultry, 445
Agency law, 44
Aging of cheese, 116, 415, 419
Aging of meat, *see* Meat, tenderization procedure
Agricultural Adjustment Act, 38
Agricultural Marketing Act, 126, 343, 499
Agricultural Marketing Agreement Act, 38
Agricultural price support and loan program, 126
Air freight, *see* Delivery
Air space, 427
Alarm system, 317
Alaska Seafood Marketing Institute, 474
Alcohol Beverage Commission (ABC), 15, 290
Alcohol content, 539–540
Allen, Robin Lee, 51
Alliant Foodservice, 331, 332
Alliant-LINK DIRECT, 331, 332
Allocation, *see* Product, allocation
American Angus Association, 506
American Can Company, 384
American Express, 200

American Gas Association (AGA), 640, 642
American Hotel & Motel Association (AH & MA), 24
American Society for Industrial Security, 323
American Society of Mechanical Engineers (ASME), 642
Amino acids, 509
Antitrust, 35, 38, 41
A-1 brand, 374, 380
Appearance, 635
Applied Foodservice Sanitation Certification Coursebook, 281, 285, 286, 302, 357, 359
Approved feeding program, 126
Approved payee list, 318
Approved supplier (list), 7, 93, 96, 206, 207, 208, 209, 217, 218, 219, 221, 237, 240, 319, 476, 570, 623, 639
Aquaculture, 464, 476
Architect, 16
Armour brand, 506
ARPANET, 334
Artificial foods, *see* Imitation (artificial) foods
Aseptic pack, *see* Packaging, aseptic
As-is (where-is), *see* Buying, as-is; Buying, as-is, where-is
Association meetings, 66
Attendance pattern, 333
Auction, *see* Buying, auction
Audit, *see* Independent (surprise) audit
Automatic bar, 542, 550, 629
Automation, 637

Backdoor selling, 68, 94, 222, 226, 239, 311, 317, 393
Background investigation (firm), 313, 315
Backhaul, 267
Back order, *see* Order, back
Bacteria, 409, 431, 434, 449, 468, 482, 523
  clostridium botulinum, 509
  disease-causing, 409, 452

  salmonella, 428, 433, 458, 521
  spoilage, 409, 410, 452
  staphyloccus, 458
Bank charges, 199
Banquet bar, 292
Barback, 561
Bar codes, *see* Universal Product Code (UPC)
Barnett, F. William, 51
Barter, *see* Exchange bartering
Barter group, 175
Bartlett, Michael, 322
Batty, Jennifer, 367
Beef chart, 517
Belman, David, 367
Bernstein, Charles, 25
Berton, Lee, 322
Best-if-used-by (consumed-by) date, 116, 558
Best's Insurance Reports, 609
Better Business Bureau (BBB), 570, 592, 612
Bid, 111, 117, 121, 168, 209, 225
  daily, 208–209
  fixed, 208
  low-ball, 122, 624, 625
  request (solicitation) for, 208, 390, 605, 609, 622, 624
  sealed, 208
Bill:
  itemized, 164
  of lading, 264. *See also* Title to goods
Billboard, 602
Bill-paying procedures, 242, 247, 257, 267, 314, 532, 594. *See also* Cash management; Payment (policy)
  cash on delivery (COD), 198, 199, 269–270
  credit card payment, 200, 596, 643
  invoices on account, 199–200
  paid-out, 199, 313
  service, 201
  stalling suppliers, 195
Bin card, 292, 293, 320, 457, 521, 543, 547
Bintliff, Russell, 323

BirdsEye brand, 336
Bleakley, Fred R., 157
Blind date, 411
Bloom, 516
Blowout sale, 184
Blue Goose brand, 346
Blumenthal, Karen, 232
Bohan, Gregory T., 71
Bonding (company), 316. *See also*
    Insurance, service
  fidelity, 315, 608
  performance, 605
  of supplier, 218–219
Bonus, 310
Botulism, 509
Bowen, John, 232
Brady, Mary Clare, 71
Brand name, 215, 539, 553. *See
    also* Packer's brand (grade)
  call, 534, 539
  controlled, 388
  furniture, fixtures, and equip-
    ment (FFE), 621, 635–636
  generic, 381
  house, 534, 546
  premium, 380, 534, 535, 540
  premium well, 535
  well, 534, 535, 540, 543, 544
Brannigan, Martha, 232
Break-in period, 639
Break point, 184, 389, 601
Brewer, 14
Brew pub, 534
Bribery, 308
Brix, 387
Brochure (flyer), 601
Broker, 13, 16, 17. *See also* Equip-
    ment, broker
Budgeting, 82, 91
Building code, 577, 619, 634,
    642
Building permit, 219
Bulkeley, William M., 231
Bulk pack, *see* Packaging, bulk
    pack
Bureau of Alcohol, Tobacco, and
    Firearms (BATF), 43
Burton, Thomas M., 366
Business ethics, *see* Ethics
Business license (bureau), 187,
    219, 591
Busted case, 115, 218, 332, 349,
    544
Butterball brand, 336
Butterfat (content), 414
Buyer:
  Advantage Program, 206
  beverage, 6
  colleagues, potential conflicts
    with, 102
  colleagues, relations with, 101–
    102
  equipment and nonfood sup-
    plies, 6
  food, 6
  hourly employees, potential
    conflicts with, 103

  hourly employees, relations
    with, 102–103
  pricing, 166–167
  problems of, 68–69
  profile (fact sheet), 162, 225,
    226, 332
  salesperson, relations with, 226–
    228
  self-improvement, 66
  supervisor, relations with, 87–
    101. *See also* Performance
    evaluation (of buyer)
  survey, 221
  user-buyer, 76, 77, 82, 91, 225,
    228, 229, 237, 239, 240,
    247, 277, 295, 309
Buyer's Guide, 206
Buying. *See also* Bid; Purchasing;
    Shopping procedures
  as-is, 171, 630, 632
  as-is, where-is, 188, 576
  auction, 570, 576, 620, 632
  bid, 122, 123, 124, 132, 207–
    209, 211, 216–217, 308,
    389, 408, 417, 567, 576,
    592, 593, 594, 604
  call sheet, 209
  cash and carry, 14, 211–212
  centralized, *see* Purchasing, cen-
    tralized
  certified, 521. *See also* United
    States Department of Agri-
    culture (USDA), Acceptance
    Service
  club, 14, 213, 354
  communal, 78
  co-op, *see* Purchasing, co-op
  cost-plus, 174–175, 210, 475,
    516
  daily quotation, 209
  direct, *see* Purchasing, direct
  forward, 211, 389, 393
  guide, 205
  market quote, 209
  open market, 209
  over, 100, 137
  panic, 167
  plan, 59–60, 75–76, 207–209,
    213, 221, 252
  reciprocal, 93, 205, 208, 216,
    225
  salvage, 187, 375
  service, 213
  shared, 78
Buyout:
  policy, 217–218
  sale, 184

Caesars Palace, 385
California Avocado Commission,
    336
California Cherry Advising Board,
    336
California Olive Committee, 114
California Walnut Board, 336
Campbell brand, 515, 558
Canceled check, 313

Canceled transaction (paperwork),
    314
Candling, 427
Canned Fruit Promotion Service,
    382
Can pressure, 437
Can sizes, 384
Capital item (investment), 565,
    577, 578, 581, 617
Capitalizing expenses, 577, 618,
    624
Captive audience, 98
Carlson, Eugene, 323
Cartilage, 501
Cash and carry, *see* Buying, cash
    and carry
Cash on delivery (COD), *see* Bill-
    paying procedures
Cash deposit, *see* Deposit
Cash flow, 643
Cash management, 171, 195–197,
    307
Cash rebate, *see* Rebate
Casper, Carol, 248
Catalog house, 16
Catch weight, 507
Caterer, 219
CD-ROM (catalog), 206, 331
Cello wrap, *see* Packaging, cello
    wrap
Cell pack, *see* Packaging, cell pack
Center for Advanced Purchasing
    Studies (CAPS), 71
Central distribution, 7, 41, 79–81,
    156, 220, 240, 393
  direct buying with, 20, 21
Certification, 521
Certified Angus Beef Program, 506
Certified Foodservice Professional
    (CFP), 66
Certified Foodservice Purchasing
    Manager (CFPM), 66
Certified grade, 410
Certified organic food, 506
Certified Purchasing Manager
    (CPM), 66
Chain of operating activities, 242,
    247, 327
  separation of, 311–312, 317,
    320
Chamber of commerce, 612
Chapman, Stephen, 322
Charlier, Marj, 25, 189
Chase, Marilyn, 51
C & H brand, 391
Checklist:
  for evaluating canned fruits,
    394–395
  for evaluating canned sliced
    peaches, 393
Check padding, 551
Chemical (standards), 116, 372,
    387, 397, 415, 416, 446,
    512, 521, 539
Cherry pick, 23, 169
Chicken of the Sea brand, 469, 477
Child Nutrition (CN) label, 387

Chill pack, *see* Product, preservation (processing)
Clayton Act, 38, 39
Cleaning service, 610–611
Cleaning supplies, 574–575
Cleaning tools, 575–576
Closed circuit television (CCTV), 317
Closeout sale, 184
Coca cola (Coke) brand, 222, 232, 552, 555, 556, 599
Code compliance, 622, 642
Coded date, *see* Dating code
Cohen, Laurie P., 25
Collateral, 622, 643
Collusion, 317
Color of product, *see* Product, color
Commercial grades, 448
Commercial hospitality operation, 4–5, 17
Commissary, 7, 13, 41, 79–81, 156, 220, 240, 257, 391, 393, 464, 572
Commission, 228, 599
Commission split, 607, 608
Commodity, 30, 164, 165, 172, 206, 409, 443, 449, 491
Commodity exchange, 172
Commodity futures market, 453
Common area maintenance (CAM) fee, 591, 594, 596
Common carrier, 260, 267, 269
Compactness, 634
Company goals, 117
Company's competitive position, 68
Compatibility, *see* Product, compatibility
Compensation (employee), 582. *See also* Purchasing, compensation for
Competitive pressure, 166
Computerization, 47–48, 206, 247, 272, 292, 293, 295, 320, 327–337, 374
  buyer applications, 329–336
  central, 330
  distributor applications, 327–328
  hardware, 213, 328, 331
  network, 330
  personal, 329, 331, 332, 333
  server, 330
  software, 213, 327, 328, 331, 332, 333, 335
ComSource Canned Goods Specifications Manual, 120, 380, 390
ComSource Frozen Food Specifications Manual, 120, 380, 390
Conceptual skill, *see* Employee skill, conceptual
Conformation, 447
Consignment sale, 45
Construction contractor, 16, 620
Consulting proposal, *see* Proposal

Consulting service, 17, 170, 219, 603
Consumer grades, 426, 447
Container, *see* Packaging
Continental Organization of Distributor Enterprises, Inc. (CODE), 129, 388, 572
Continuing education, 66
Continuous government inspection, 127
Contract, 111, 245
  cleaning service, 170
  futures, 171, 172, 513
  house (supply), 14, 213, 620
  law, 43–44
  lien-sale, 605
  long-term, 170, 174, 175, 207, 214, 218, 228, 375, 388, 391, 393, 416, 417, 453, 492, 514
  maintenance, 288, 576, 577, 582, 606, 607, 630
  national, 7, 79, 598, 608
  purchase, 3
  service, 576, 606
Control, 82, 239, 242, 244, 247, 271, 272, 277, 289, 300–302, 320, 637
  cost, 80, 110, 123, 183, 242, 247, 330, 333, 637
  cycle, 252
  direct system, 82, 245
  documents (records), 65
  indirect system, 82, 245, 246, 320
  internal, 65
  only the expensive items, 301
  personnel, 551
  product, 95–96, 551
  quality, 67, 80, 81, 110, 123, 225, 242, 257, 406, 417, 418, 472, 491, 551, 637
  state, 15, 417, 532–533, 542, 544
Controlled atmosphere (packaging) (CAP), *see* Storage, controlled atmosphere
Convenience foods, 12, 46, 47, 371, 372, 502, 513. *See also* Efficiency foods; Value-added foods
  advantages, 46–47
  first generation, 47
Convenience of nonfood expense items, 567–568
Conventional profit markup, *see* Profit markup (margin; percentage)
Conversion weight, 446, 453. *See also* Drained weight; Trim; Yield (edible; servable; usable)
Co-op cordinator, 213
Coors of Las Vegas, 544
Copyright, 45, 110, 552, 553
Cosmetics-Devices Act, 36
Cost:
  actual, 183, 289, 293, 294, 310

advertising, 598
as-served, 31
as-used, 31, 567, 569, 571, 572, 573, 574, 575
back door, 363
benefit analysis, 301, 591
beverage, 262
capital, 535
carrying (charge), 147, 476
delivery, 328, 622, 624
edible portion (EP), 31, 46, 61, 67, 161, 178–183, 318, 492–493
energy, 639–641
expected, 182
fixed, 589, 590
food (product), 182, 183, 213, 262, 270, 293, 295, 296, 309, 310, 311, 329, 332
  percentage, 183
front door, 363
of goods sold, 294, 333
in-house, 23
installation, 620, 622, 624, 629, 640
insurance, 186, 270
interest, 18, 198, 200, 201, 215, 644
labor, 332, 333, 362
landed, 174
license renewal, 534
lifetime, 571, 623–625, 631–632, 636
limits, 117, 121
loan application (origination), 643
of money (capital), 147
nonfood, 262
operating, 571, 576, 624, 625, 629, 631, 637, 638
opportunity, 147, 197, 535
ordering, 63, 140, 147, 149, 150, 153, 154, 155, 170, 184, 185, 188, 210
overrun, 622, 631
of paying too early, 197–198
of paying too late, 198
  penalty, 198
plus, *see* Buying, cost-plus
portion, 387, 552
pouring, 535
receiving, 173
recipe, 267, 332, 333
shipping, 335
standard, 182, 183
storage, 137, 140, 141, 147, 149, 150, 153, 154, 155, 170, 184, 185, 186, 188, 373, 416, 476, 584, 638
target percentage, 183
testing, 624
theoretical, 182
transaction, 172, 173
transportation (delivery; freight), 475, 478
Council on Hotel, Restaurant, and Institutional Management (CHRIE), 51

Count, *see* Product, size
Country Pride brand, 459
Coupon refund, 171
Credit:
  card (payment), *see* Bill-paying procedures
  check, 643
  control, 416
  memorandum, 259
  rating, 198, 220
  slip, 200, 260, 264
  terms (period), 18, 49, 117, 170, 198, 200, 212, 215, 521, 533, 544, 557, 571, 643
Cremer, Marion L., 83, 104, 302
Crimeproofing Your Business: 301 Low-Cost, No-Cost Ways to Protect Your Office, Store, or Business, 323
Crustacean, 466, 479
Cryovac brand, 432, 451, 455, 459, 507, 515, 516
Crystallization, 437, 479
Curing, *see* Product, preservation (processing)
Customized merchandise (FFE), 571, 572, 631, 638
  advantages, 631
  disadvantages, 631–632
Cutting (can cutting) test, 385, 391, 392, 393, 419. *See also* Holding court

Daily Fruit and Vegetable Report, 341
Daisy chain, 174
Damitio, James W., 190
Data base, *see* Product, data base
Dating code, 270, 411, 541, 550, 558
Dealer, *see* Equipment, dealer
Decay allowance, 350
Decorating and remodeling service, 605–606
Dehydration, 271
Deiro, G. Robert, 633
Delivery:
  acceptance, 260–264
  air-express (freight), 269
  arrival, 255–257
  cash on delivery (COD), 269–270
  early morning, 272
  late, 99
  mailed, 268, 269
  night, 173, 272
  odd-hours, 173–174
  options, 168
  rejection, 257–260
  schedule, 138, 139, 140, 141, 154, 155, 214, 241, 291, 353, 390, 417, 543, 556
  ticket, 267
DelMonte brand, 380
DeLuca Liquor & Wine Ltd., 544
Demonstration model, 188, 630
Department of Labor, 582

Deposit, 44, 219, 310, 318, 546, 559, 571, 612
Depreciation, 565, 578, 581, 617, 630
Derived demand, 163
Designated-driver program, 534
Designer, 16, 620
Detailed drawings, 622
Determine product and service requirements, 60
Deveny, Kathleen, 366
DiDomenico, Pat, 322
Direct bartering, 175
Directing, 82
Direct purchase, *see* Purchasing, direct
Direct writer, 609
Discount, 21, 94–95, 209, 222, 631, 643
  accepting, 201–202
  blanket-order, 95, 169
  cash, 95, 171, 184, 195, 197, 198, 201, 215, 246, 557, 643
  forklift, 168
  operation, 16
  problems with accepting, 201–202
  promotional, 38, 95, 175, 201, 215, 553, 555, 557, 574, 584, 599
  quantity, 94, 95, 184, 201, 215, 375, 389, 542, 555, 557, 569, 572, 600, 601
  user, 607
  volume, 95, 169, 184, 201, 210, 212, 215, 375, 389, 557, 569, 572
Disposable ware, 567, 575, 579–581, 582
Disposal of stock, 64–65
Distiller, 14
Distribution center, 213
Distribution co-op, 388. *See also* Seller co-op
Distribution system:
  beer, wine, and distilled spirits, 14
  food, nonalcoholic beverages, and nonfood supplies, 11
  furniture, fixtures, and equipment (FFE), 15, 569
  national, 214
  services, 17, 569
Distributor, 17, 240
  broad-line, 13
  full-line, 13
  furniture, fixtures, and equipment (FFE), 16
  liquor, 15
  sales representative (DSR), 226, 240
  specialty, 13
Dittmer, Paul R., 248
Dole Packaged Foods Company, 176, 391
Donnelly, Richard, 51, 120
Dore, Ian, 120

Dot system, 265
Dowling, Susan, 83
Download, 330, 333
Down payment, 644
Downsize, 67
Downtime, 328, 620, 642, 643
Drained weight, 377, 385–386, 388, 391. *See also* Conversion weight; Trim; Yield (edible; servable; usable)
Drink fee, 560
Drink list, *see* Wine, list
Drink ticket, 550
Drop shipment, 269
Drucker, Peter, 52
Drug test, 313, 315
Drummond, Karen Eich, 83
Due bill, 600. *See also* Exchange bartering
Dunnage rack, 288
Durability, 579
DWI laws, 533

Eacho, Bill, 52, 157, 232
Eagle Vineyards, Ltd., 544
Ease of cleaning, 636
Ease of maintenance, 637
EcoLab, 575
Economic analysis, 302
Economic Order Quantity (EOQ), 148, 150, 154, 155, 156
  in dollars, 148, 149
  in units, 149
Economic value, 18, 21–22, 132, 168, 214, 222, 579, 591
  form, 18–19, 63, 164, 567
  information, 19, 387, 638
  place, 19
  time, 18
Economies of scale, 337
Edible by-product, *see* Meat, variety
Educate suppliers, 64
Efficiency foods, 12. *See also* Convenience foods; Value-added foods
Egg Products Inspection Act, 426
Egg sizes, *see* Product, size
86 menu items, 330
Eiler, James O., 52
E & J brand, 545
Electrical code, 642
Electronic Data Interchange (EDI), 48
Electronic mail (E-mail), 334
Employee benefits, 608
Employee skill, 576, 639
  conceptual, 81, 90
  interpersonal (human), 81, 90
  technical, 81, 88–90
Emulsifiers, 414, 415
End-of-period statement, 200
Endorsement, 130
End user services, 13, 16, 214
Energy efficiency, 629
Energy source, 639–641
Equal brand, 319

Equal-to-facing layer, 270
Equipment:
  broker, 16
  dealer, 16, 632, 639
    design/build, 620
    full-service, 16
    heavy equipment, 16
    secondhand, 632
    storefront, 16
  financing, 622, 642–644
  installation, 624
  loaner, 625
  manufacturer, *see* Manufacturer
  program, 556, 570–571, 630–631
  rental firm, 644
  self-cleaning, 636
  testing, 624
Escoffier, Auguste, 308
Escrow account, 201, 612
Ethics, 33–34, 68
Ethics code, 33–34, 95
Ethics in Hospitality Management:
  A Book of Readings, 51
Ethylene gas, 352
Evaluating suppliers and salespersons, 228–229
Exact name of product or service:
  alcoholic beverages, 537–538
  dairy products, 407–408
  eggs, 426
  fish, 465–467
  fresh produce, 343
  furniture, fixtures, and equip-
    ment (FFE), 623
  meat, 493–496
  nonalcoholic beverages, 553
  nonfood expense items, 572, 573
  poultry, 445–446
  processed produce and other
    grocery items, 376–377, 386
  services, 593
Excess capacity, 641
Exchange bartering, 175–178, 216,
  291, 598, 600. *See also* Direct bartering; Due bill;
  Trade out
Exclusive dealing, 38
Exclusive distributor, 164, 209,
  532, 552
Exclusive selling, 38
Exclusive territory, 15
Expediting, 245, 489
Expense item, 565
Expiration date, 116, 270
Express PAK, 554

Fabricator, 12
Fabrics, 582–583
Facciola, Michael L., 189, 232
Farmer, *see* Grower (farmer)
Farmer's market, 355
Farm-raised fish, *see* Aquaculture
Farquharson, John, 232
Fat covering, *See also* Feathering;
  Finish
  of meat, 501, 502
  of poultry, 447

Favoring suppliers, 92, 124
F & B Business, 52, 231, 248
Feathering, 501, 502, 503. *See also*
  Fat covering; Finish
Federal Food, Drug, and Cosmetic
  Act (FFDCA), 36, 37
Federal Trade Commission (FTC), 37
Feinstein, Andy, vi, 327
Fermentation, 372
Ferrari Carano, 544
Fidelity bond, *see* Bonding (com-
  pany)
Field inspector, 272
Financial service, 595–596
Financing, 18. *See also* Equip-
  ment, financing
Fin fish, 466
Finish, 501, 502, 503. *See also* Fat
  covering; Feathering
Fire code, 619, 633, 642
Fisher, Joseph W., 51
Fish and Game office, 480
Fjellman, Stephen M., 232
Flaked and reformed fish, 472
Flaked and reformed meat, *see*
  Meat, tenderization proce-
  dure
Flat:
  eggs, 431
  fresh produce, 349
Fleshing, 447
Foil pack, *see* Packaging, foil pack
Food Arts, 189, 190, 232, 366
Food and Beverage Operation:
  Cost Control and Systems
  Management, 141
Food-borne illness, 279, 433, 458,
  480
Food cost, *see* Cost, food (product)
Food and Drug Administration
  (FDA), 36, 37, 377, 428,
  433, 467
  Interstate Certified Shellfish
    Shippers List, 480
  Office of Seafood Safety, 476
Food marketing board, 336
FoodNet, 206, 231
Food Purchasing Pointers for
  School Foodservice, 59
FoodService Director, 52, 83, 231,
  366
Foodservice Purchasing Managers
  (FPM) Study Group of the
  National Restaurant Asso-
  ciation (NRA), 34, 66, 81
Forces affecting distribution sys-
  tems:
  economic, 29–33, 164
  ethical, 33–34
  legal, 33–45
  other (intangible), 49–50
  political, 33
  technological, 46–49
Forecast, 62, 333
  availability, 62
  price, 62
  sales, 333

Foreclosure, 643
Form of product, *see* Product,
  form
Form value, *see* Economic value,
  form
Fortified milk, 410
Forward buy, *see* Buying, forward
Foster Farms brand, 449
Franchise hospitality operation, 6,
  38, 79
Franchise law, 41–43
Franklin, Terry, 323
Fraud, 308, 311, 319
Free on board (FOB), 44
Free-range chicken, 446
Freeze drying, *see* Product preser-
  vation (processing)
Freezer burn, 373, 396, 397, 452
Freight-damaged item, 187, 632
Freshness date, 116, 387, 558
Fresh Western Marketing Inc., 347
Frigo brand, 417
Frosty Acres brand, 129
Fuchsberg, Gilbert, 323
Furniture, fixtures, and equipment
  (FFE), customized, *see* Cus-
  tomized merchandise (FFE)
Futures contract (market), *see* Con-
  tract, futures

Galardi Group, 89
Gaston, Jolie, 52
General Mills band, 388
Genetically engineered food, 46
Gerlin, Andrea, 322
Getler, Warren, 189
Gibson, Richard, 52
Gifts from suppliers, 92, 308
Gilbert/Robinson, Inc., 89
Gilbey's brand, 545
Glaze, 479, 481
Going-out-of-business sale, 375, 576
Golbon brand, 129
Goods Received Without Invoice
  slip, 268
Goodwill, 153, 279
Goodwin, John, 52
Goussak, Gregory, 322
Grading factors, *see* United States
  government grades, grading
  factors
Grass-fed beef, 501
Green Giant brand, 388
Green meat, *see* Meat, green
Green Sheet, 513
Griffin, Gerald G., 248
Gross weight, 270
Groundskeeping service, 596–597
Grower (farmer), 12, 13
  independent, 355, 418, 435, 437,
    443, 454, 516
Guarantee, 45, 188, 622, 624, 634,
  638, 639, 641–642
  expressed, 45
  extended, 606
  implied, 45
  period, 606, 638, 639

Guest history, 602
Guiffrida, Michael, 231
Gupta, Udayan, 71
Gutfeld, Rose, 51

Hall, Stephen S. J., 51
Halo effect, 635
Happy hour, 533
Hart Act, 39
Hayes, Jack, 25
Hazard Analysis and Critical Control Points (HACCP) System, 36, 37, 468
Health district (code), 187, 279, 291, 375, 409, 413, 476, 478, 480, 570, 575, 619, 633, 642
Heavy pack, 385, 386
Hedden, Jenny, 323
Hedging, 171–173, 453, 492
Heinz brand, 225, 374, 380, 531
Help competitors, 66
Hochstein, Mort, 25
Holding court, 391. *See also* Cutting (can cutting) test
Homogenization, 409
Hormones, 415, 446
Hospitality, 231
Hospitality Research Journal, 190
Hospitality in Review, 248
Hospitality and Tourism Educator, 51, 52, 323
Hosteur, 52, 157, 232
Hotel and Casino Law Letter, 52
Hotel and Motel Management, 231, 603
Hotel Access CD, 206,
House account, 227, 228, 230, 318, 319, 332, 353, 354, 389, 390, 407, 435, 453, 475, 596, 620
HRI Meat Price Report, 513
Humidity requirements, 279, 280–288
Hummrich, Richard C., 51
Hydroponic fresh produce, 353
Hyperlink, 335

Ice cream:
    competitive, 411
    French, 411
    premium, 411
    regular, 411
Ice pack, *see* Product, preservation (processing)
Ice spots, 479
Idaho potatoes, 349, 351
Image, 566, 567, 568, 578, 579, 581, 582, 583, 585, 634, 635
Imitation (artificial) foods, 472, 489, 512–513
Implementing the Supervisory Process: Theory and Practice, 83
Importer-wholesaler, 14, 15
IMPS/NAMP numbers, 495
IMPS numbers, 495, 496, 504, 508, 514

Incomplete shipment, 270
Independent (surprise) audit, 314–315, 317, 320, 333
Independent farmers, *see* Grower (farmer), independent
Independent hospitality operation, 6
Indian Harvest brand, 336
Individually quick frozen (IQF), *see* Product, preservation (processing)
Industry and government publications, 118
Information Superhighway, 333
Information value, *see* Economic value, information
Ingersoll, Bruce, 52
Ingredient room, 300
In-house laundry, 610
Injunctive power, 36
In-room minibar, 539
Inspection procedures, *see* Test procedures
Institutional can size, 384
Institutional hospitality operation, 4–5
Institutional Meat Purchase Specification (IMPS), 495, 507
Instructions to bidders,
    general, 117, 622
    specific, 117, 622
Insurance, *see* Bonding (company)
    broker, 609
    exclusive agent, 609
    group, 609
    liability coverage, 534, 622
    premiums, *see* Cost, insurance
    service, 269, 608–609
Insurance Institute of America, 307
Integrity (honesty) test, 313, 315
Intended use, 112, 116, 167
    alcoholic beverages, 537
    dairy products, 407
    disposable ware, 580
    eggs, 425
    fabrics, 583
    fish, 464
    fresh produce, 342–343
    furniture, fixtures, and equipment (FFE), 623
    meat, 490, 493, 516
    nonalcoholic beverages, 552–553
    permanent ware, 578
    poultry, 444–445, 449, 453
    processed produce and other grocery items, 376
    services, 592
Interest cost (charge), *see* Cost, interest
Interest group, 334
Interest income, 197, 200
Intermediary, 11, 17, 240
    beer, wine and distilled spirits, 14

food, nonalcoholic beverages, and nonfood supplies, 12
furniture, fixtures, and equipment (FFE),15
Internal Revenue Service (IRS), 43, 175
International Foodservice Manufacturers Association (IFMA), 49
International Society of Food Service Consultants (ISFSC), 130
Internet, 333–336
Interpersonal skill, *see* Employee skill, interpersonal (human)
Interstate Shellfish Sanitation Commission, 37
Introductory offer, 178, 184, 209, 375, 376, 493
Inventory:
    adjustments, 333
    available for the month (for sale), 183, 310
    average, 98
    beginning, 98, 183, 310, 333
    book, 320
    classification, 290–291
    control, 290–291, 293, 296, 320, 329, 330, 333
    costing, 329
    counting, 329
    critical item inventory analysis (control procedure), 301, 320
    ending, 98, 183, 310, 333
    file, 265
    full-case equivalent, 295
    in-process, 239, 291, 292, 294, 295, 296, 301, 315, 319, 330, 333. *See also* Purchasing, direct
    alcoholic beverages, 551
    cleaning tools, 576
    dairy products, 420
    disposable ware, 581
    eggs, 438
    fabrics, 583
    fish, 481–482
    fresh produce, 362–365
    meat, 524
    nonalcoholic beverages, 560
    nonfood expense items, 567
    other paper products, 584
    permanent ware, 579
    poultry, 458
    preparation and service utensils, 581
    processed produce and other grocery items, 398
    investment, 67
    just-in-time, 152
    management, 48, 60, 137–138, 140, 213, 265, 295, 337, 457
    minimize investment, 67
    obsolescence, 155, 218
    optimal amount (level), 137, 293
    padding, 310–311, 551

percentage of annual purchases, 100

percentage of annual sales volume, 99, 100

percentage of previous month's food cost, 99

percentage of total assets, 100

perpetual, 291–294, 457, 523, 547, 549

physical, 293, 294, 296, 310, 314, 318, 320, 330, 333, 550

purposes, 293

return on investment, 138, 247

returns, 69, 100, 117, 201, 216, 246, 251, 252, 260, 309, 314, 521

sales (control procedure), 301

shrinkage, 278, 310, 318, 492

skimming, 278

substitution, see Substitution

theft, 310

theoretical, 293, 320, 330

tracking, 330, 332

turnover, 98–99, 100, 101, 279, 288

unrecorded, 319

valuation, 47, 49

Invoice, 199, 200, 242, 247, 255, 257, 262, 264, 265, 267, 268, 291, 309, 310, 313, 315, 332, 333, 612. See also Packing slip

discrepancy (handling), 255–260

fictitious, 309

fraudulent, 309, 314

padded, 309, 314

reconcile with end-of-period statement, 200

scam, 309–310, 318

stamp, 262

Irradiation, 46, 452

Issuing (system), 64, 238, 277, 289, 290, 293, 297, 300

alcoholic beverages, 549–551

dairy products, 420

disposable ware, 581

eggs, 438

fish, 481

fresh produce, 362

meat, 523

nonalcoholic beverages, 559–560

poultry, 457

processed produce and other grocery items, 398

ITEX, 177

Jacob M. Braude's Complete Speaker's and Toastmaster's Library, 161

Job description, 91

Johnson, Kim, 51

Journal of Purchasing and Materials Management, v

Justice Department, 22

Kaye, Norman, 633

Key card, 317

KFC, 220

KFC National Purchasing Cooperative, Inc., 89

Khan, Mahmood, 273

Kickback, 34, 45, 100, 308, 309, 310, 318, 319, 543

Kilman, Scott, 189

Kimiecik, Rudolph, 323

Koenig, Richard, 52

Kosher chicken, 446

Kossen, Stan, 83

Kotschevar, Lendal H., 51, 120

Kraft Foodservice, 331

Label, see Packaging, label regulations (information)

Labor pool (availability), 90, 577

Labor savings, 329, 624, 629, 637

Lactation, 406

Lactose, 416

Lady Luck Casino Hotel, 385

Lamb chart, 518

Land O'Lakes brand, 336

Lane, Robert B., 273

Las Vegas Hilton, 298

Las Vegas Review Journal, 322

Laundry and linen supply service, 582, 610

Lead time, 152, 153, 154, 156, 213, 215–216, 247, 638

Leasing, 582

advantages, 644

company, 16, 620

disadvantages, 644

Lefever, Michael M., 248

LeGout brand, 515

Levinson, Charles, 141

Levy, Paul, 322

Lewis, Sinclair, 35

Libbey brand, 572

Licensed supplier, 187, 219, 605. See also Bonding (company), of supplier

License state, 15, 532–533, 544

Lien release, 606

Limiting rule, 127, 500, 504

partial, 128

Linen room, 583

Liparulo, Robert, 190

Lipin, Steven, 157, 202

Liquidation, 632

Liquor:

call, see Brand name, call

codes, 543

distributor, 15

house brand, see Brand name, house

license, 533, 534

light, 540

premium well, see Brand name, premium well

well, see Brand name, well

LISTSERV, 335

Live fish, 473, 479

Live-in-shell fish, 473, 479

Loan origination fees, see Cost, loan application (origination)

Lodging, 71, 364

Lorenzini, Beth, 322

Loss leader, 478

Loss Prevention Guide for Retail Businesses, 323

Lot (number), 387, 470, 480

Lotus, 123, 333

Low ball, see Bid, low-ball

Lug, 348, 349

Lundberg, Craig, 51

Lundberg, Don, 322

Mailing list, 334, 602, 633

Mail-order catalog, 620

Maintenance contract, see Contract, maintenance

Maintenance service, 606–607, 638, 644

Maintenance supplies, 576–578

Make-goods, 598

Make-or-buy analysis, 62–63, 168

Management considerations:

alcoholic beverages, 533–537

furniture, fixtures, and equipment (FFE), 618–621

meat, 487–493

nonalcoholic beverages, 552

nonfood expense items, 566–571

processed produce and other grocery items, 371–376

services, 589–592

Manitowac Equipment Works, 627

Manual list, 334

Manufacturer, 12, 13, 15

Manufacturer's agent, 13

Manufacturer's representative, 13, 17

Manufacturing grade, 410, 448, 467, 501, 502

Marbling, 500, 506

Marinade pack, see Product preservation (processing)

Marine Mammal Protection Act, 37

Marketing terms for fish, 466

Market research, see Research activities, market

Market terminology, 376, 381, 411, 446, 466, 496

Markup (percentage), see Profit markup

Marlock brand, 317

Marriott, 309

Martin, Richard, 25

MasterCard, 200

Materials budget, 98, 164

Material used to make items, 579, 581. See also Product, form

Maturity class, 500, 501–506

MBG (Meat Buyers Guide) numbers, 495

McAnnally brand, 436

McCormick brand, 336

McDonald's, 71
McGinley, 52
McMurray, Scott, 366
Meal credits, 178
Meat:
  basic cuts, 496
  carcass, 496, 497, 503
  green, 510
  imitation/artificial, 512–513
  Inspection Act, 35, 497
  portion cut, 491
  primal cut, *see* Meat, wholesale
    cut
  quarter, 504
  retail cut, 331, 495, 496, 497,
    504, 506, 507
  safety legislation, 35
  sausage, 496
  side, 490, 491, 496, 504
  standardized cut, *see* Meat,
    wholesale cut
  tag, 265–266, 268, 521
  tenderization procedure, 489,
    492, 509–511
    aging, 509–510; Cryovac, 510;
      dry, 509, 510
    beef electrification, 510
    chemical, 510–511
    cubing, 511
    flaked and reformed, 492, 511
    grinding, 511
    mechanical, 510, 511
    needling, 511
  types, 488
  variety, 451, 456, 495, 496
  wholesale cut, 491, 495, 496,
    497, 504, 506, 507, 510,
    511
Media buyer (service), 598, 599,
  600
Meltzer, Peter D., 190, 232
Menu planning, 333, 543
Menu price (pricing), *see* Price,
  menu
Merchandising, 219
Merchant wholesaler, *see* Distribu-
  tor
Merits, 599
MGM Grand Hotel, Casino &
  Theme Park, 299
Microorganism, 361
Microprocessor, 329
Microsoft Excel, 333
Middleman, *see* Intermediary
Military hospitality operation, 4–5
Military meat inspection, 498
Milk solids content, 414
Miller, Jack E., 83
Minimum weight per case for
  fresh produce, 350
Minor's brand, 455
Miscellaneous items, 584–585
Mixers, 559
Modeco brand, 317
Model building (research),
  62
Model number, 623

Modified-atmosphere packaging
  (MAP), *see* Product, preser-
  vation (processing)
Moffa, Jim W., 323
Moisture content, 378
Mollusk, 466, 479, 480
Mom and Pop operation, 76
Monarch brand, 129
Monopolistic competition, 32, 165
Monopoly, 32, 39, 166
Monopoly state, *see* Control, state
Moomaw, Paul, 189
Mooney, Richard L., v
Moonlighter, 592, 605, 612
Mothers Against Drunk Driving
  (MADD), 533
Move list, *see* Muzz-go list
Multimedia E-mail, 334
Multiunit hospitality operation, 6,
  146, 156, 240, 572
Muzz-go list, 184, 478, 493

Nabisco brand, 336
Nader, Ralph, 35
Nader's Raiders, 35
National Association of Meat Pur-
  veyors (NAMP), 120, 331,
  494, 495
National Association of Purchas-
  ing Managers (NAPM), 34,
  66, 81
National distribution, 123
National Fire Protection Associa-
  tion (NFPA), 642
National Live Stock and Meat
  Board, 130, 495, 496, 517,
  518, 519, 520
National Restaurant Association
  (NRA), 24, 62, 71, 81, 206,
  231, 464, 468
  Educational Foundation, v, 281,
    284, 285, 286, 302, 357, 359
Nation's Restaurant News, v, 24,
  25, 51, 52, 71, 104, 157,
  189, 190, 206, 231, 232,
  273, 322, 323, 366
Natural food, *see* Organic (natural;
  whole) food
Needling, *see* Meat, tenderization
  procedure
Negative selling, 604
Negotiations, 61, 170, 213, 557,
  593, 596, 597, 598, 604,
  607, 609, 644
Net present value (of money), 628
Net weight (contents), 270. *See
  also* Drained weight
Nevada Beverage Analyst, 544
Nevada Hospitality, 232
Nevada Liquor & Wine Ltd., 544
*Nevada State Purchasing Newslet-
  ter*, 323
New merchandise, 570, 632–634
New pack time, 389, 475
Newsgroup, 334–335
New York Coffee and Sugar Ex-
  change, 553

New York Mercantile Exchange,
  172
Nifda brand, 128, 129
Night drop, 272
Nitrites, 509
Nitrogen flush, 548
Nitrosamine, 509
Node, 330
Noise pollution (codes), 642
Noncommercial hospitality opera-
  tion, 4–5, 17, 448
Nondairy product, 416
North American Association of
  Food Equipment Manufac-
  turers (NAFEM), 66, 81
NSF International, 116, 130, 642
Nugget brand, 129, 477
Number of pieces per bird, 451
Nutrition, 219, 333, 362, 381, 405,
  410, 416, 432, 443, 452,
  465, 499, 533
Nutrition Labeling and Education
  Act, 40

O'Block, Robert L., 323
O'Brien, Timothy L., 83, 232, 323
Off-premises caterer, 45, 212
Oil dripping, 433
Oil spraying, 433
One-stop shopping, *see* Shopping
  procedures, one-stop
On-line services, 206
Ontario Pork Producers Marketing
  Board, 336
Operating activities, *see* Chain of
  operating activities
Operating savings, 624, 625–629,
  631
Operating supplies, 565
  schemes, 569–570
Opportunity buy, 193–188, 195,
  197, 199, 209, 219, 375,
  388, 555, 557
  qualitative aspects, 186–188
Order:
  back, 69, 100, 217, 259
  blanket, 169–170, 246
  change, 245
  emergency, 291
  limits, *see* Quantity limits
  minimum required, 212, 215,
    478, 543, 544, 556, 557, 584
  modifiers, 330
  purchase, *see* Purchase order
  short, 309
  size, 137, 138, 139, 140, 141,
    142, 147, 148, 154, 155,
    156, 239, 240, 246, 293
  standing, 212, 246, 316, 416,
    419, 557
  time, 137, 138, 141, 142, 151,
    154, 155
  tracking, 331
Ordering:
  combination approach, 146
  cost, *see* Cost, ordering

EOQ approach, *see* Economic Order Quantity (EOQ)
Levinson approach, 141–144, 146, 155, 239
methods of streamlining, 245–247
on-line, 328, 331–332, 333, 601
par stock approach, 138–141, 146, 155, 156, 239, 557
procedure, 48, 137, 138, 141, 212, 213, 214, 227, 239–247, 291, 295, 532, 556
  computerized, 48, 212–213, 329
  fax, 48, 240, 329
  schedule, 139, 154, 185
variations of the Levinson approach, 144–146
wireless system, 330
Organic (natural; whole) food, 116, 353, 372, 376, 387, 418, 506, 555
Ortega, Bob, 190, 232
Oscar Mayer brand, 332
Ossification, 501
Other paper products, 583–584
Outsourcing, 591
Overhill brand, 477
Overpour, 551
Overrun, 414–415
Overwrapping, 433
Oxidation, 397

Packaging, 19, 48–49, 122, 241, 254, 270, 373, 380, 580
aseptic, 48, 373, 383, 412, 414, 432, 540. *See also* Storage, controlled atmosphere
bag-in-the-box, 540, 548. *See also* Packaging, aseptic
bulk pack, 375, 508
cello wrap (pack), 361, 450, 471, 473
cell pack, 350, 455, 471
chill pack, *see* Product, preservation (processing)
coded (numbered), *see* Dating code
Cryovac, *see* Cryovac brand
economical, 173
environmentally safe, 383
foil pack, 507
gas-flushed pack, 451
ice pack, *see* Product, preservation (processing)
individually quick frozen (IQF), *see* Product, preservation (processing)
label regulations (information), 39–41, 387
layered, 349, 383, 450, 471
layout, 508
marinade pack, *see* Product, preservation (processing)
modified atmosphere packaging (MAP), *see* Product, preservation (processing)

personalized, 383, 385, 413, 539, 540, 541, 546, 554, 569, 579, 580
portion pack, 412
procedure, 115, 349–350, 383–385, 388, 413, 432, 450, 471, 508
repacking, 356, 456
reusable, 113
shatter pack, 451, 471
shingle pack, 508
shrink wrap, 432, 507
single-service, 319, 413, 553, 560
size, 113, 349, 373, 383, 384, 412, 431, 450, 470–471, 507, 540, 553, 575
slab packed, 115, 349, 350, 374, 383, 450, 471, 508
snap pack, 451, 471
steam-table pack, 507
type, 113, 349, 383, 412–413, 431–432, 450, 471, 507–508, 540–541, 554
Packed Under Federal Inspection (PUFI), 37, 467–468
Packer's brand (grade), 3, 128–130, 215, 255, 271, 332. *See also* Brand name
dairy products, 411–412
eggs, 428–429
fish, 469–470
fresh produce, 346–348
meat, 503, 504–507, 508, 509, 516
nonfood expense items, 569
poultry, 449
processed produce and other grocery items, 380–381, 386, 388, 391, 395
Packing medium, 377, 387, 473
Packing slip, 269
Paid-out, *see* Bill-paying procedures, paid-out
Pallets, 288
Paper-less office, 48
Parasites, 468
Par stock, 138, 139, 140, 169, 239, 246, 291, 292, 293, 296, 300, 301, 374, 544, 550, 557, 568, 572, 584
Pasteurization, 409, 410, 414, 415, 549
Patent, *see* Copyright
Patterson, Patt, v, 24, 25, 51, 71, 104, 157, 189, 190, 231, 232, 273, 366
Payback period, 625–628
Payment (policy). *See also* Bill-paying procedures; Cash management; Credit
history, 225
installment plan, 215, 619
objective of, 195
optimal, 195–199
terms, *see* Bill-paying procedures; Credit

Pepsi Cola (PepsiCo) brand, 220, 552, 556, 558
Perceived value equation, 31–33, 61
Perdue brand, 449
Performance bond, *see* Bonding (company)
Performance evaluation (of buyer), 69–70, 97
operational, 97
part-time buyer, 101
procurement, 97
Performance requirement, *see* Intended use
Perishable Agricultural Commodities Act, 38
Permanent (reusable) ware, 567, 578–579
Permissible puffery, 45
Perry, Phillip M., 323
Personalization of nonfood expense items, 211, 566, 567, 578, 584
Personnel recruiting and selection procedures, 253, 313
Pest control operator (company) (PCO), 570, 597
Pest control service, 597–598
Pesticides, 512
Physical barriers, 317, 320
Pick-up memo, 260, 261
Pilferage, 278, 296, 307, 308, 310, 312, 313, 314, 315, 316, 317, 319, 320, 420, 491, 492, 524, 579. *See also* Shoplifting
Pillsbury brand, 388, 391
Pizza Hut, 220
Place value, *see* Economic value, place
Plant visit, 63, 66, 206
Point of origin, 115
alcoholic beverages, 541–542
fish, 467, 473–475, 476
fresh produce, 350–351
meat, 511–512
Point-of-sale (POS) system, 329–330, 331
Polygraph, 313
Popularity index, 141–142
Pork chart, 519
Portability, 636
Porter, Mary, 83
Portion divider (PD), 142, 145, 178–182, 267
Portion factor (PF), 142, 145, 178–182, 267
Post messages, 334, 335
Postmix, 554, 555
Post-off, 542, 544
Potentially hazardous food, 352, 428
Pottorff, Susan, 51
Poultry Products Inspection Act, 35, 36, 446
Powers, Tom, v
Precosting (recipe costing), 182

Pre-cut fresh produce, 351, 352
Predatory pricing, 39
Preemployment testing, 315
Prefabricated meat, *see* Meat, portion cut
Premium well, *see* Brand name, premium well
Premix, 554, 555
Preparation and service utensils, 581
Present value (of money), 628
Preservation method, *see* Product preservation (processing)
Preservatives, *see* Chemical standards
Price:
  as purchased (AP), 21, 31, 46, 161, 317–318, 388–389, 416, 431, 453, 492–493, 513–514, 542–543, 555–556, 578, 623, 624
  bid compared to invoice price, 257
  case, 218, 544
  club, 14
  competition, 32, 166
  controlled, 416, 533, 542, 556. *See also* Control, state
  current compared to other suppliers' prices, 317–318
  daily cash, 492
  discrimination (legal and illegal), 38–39
  extended, 241, 257
  function of competitive pressure, 166
  function of supplier's cost, 164–165
  how determined by suppliers, 164–167
  index, 206
  influence on buyers, 162–164
  limits, 93
  list, 644
  maintenance (minimum), *see* Price, controlled
  menu, 182–183, 213, 536–537
  open-market, 172
  optimal, 161
  quotation, *see* Bid
  rule, 165
  show-special, 632
  update, 266–267
  war, 556
  ways to reduce, 167–183
Primary sources of products and services, 11, 13, 14, 17, 240
  beer, wine, and distilled spirits, 14, 15
  food, nonalcoholic beverages, and nonfood supplies, 12
  furniture, fixtures, and equipment (FFE), 15
Prime vendor account, 332
Principles of Food, Beverage, and Labor Cost Controls, 248

Processing method, *see* Product, preservation (processing)
Processor, 12, 13, 46. *See also* Fabricator
Procter & Gamble brand, 574
Procurement, 3
  prime-vendor, 210, 337
  single-source, 210
  sole-source, 210
Procurement grades, 448
Produce knife, 253
Produce Marketing Association, 110, 345
Produce Planner: The Price & Availability Report for the Foodservice Industry, 341
Product:
  adaptability, 574
  allocation, 388, 543
  availability, 328, 332
  color, 116, 351, 386, 432
  compatibility, 634–635
  data base, 328, 332
  ease (of use), 575
  effectiveness, 574
  form, 116
    dairy products, 413
    eggs, 432
    fish, 472–473, 476
    fresh produce, 351
    meat, 496, 508
    nonalcoholic beverages, 554–555
    permanent ware, 579
    poultry, 451–452
    preparation and service utensils, 581
    processed produce and other grocery items, 386
  identification, 109, 331
  length of service, 582
  odor, 575
  preservation (processing), 46, 115, 372, 476. *See also* Packaging
    alcoholic beverages, 542
    canned (bottled), 373, 386
    cello wrap (pack), *see* Packaging, cello wrap (pack)
    chill pack, 449, 452, 471, 473, 479
    controlled atmosphere, *see* Storage, controlled atmosphere
    curing, 508, 509
    dairy products, 413–414, 415
    dried, 372, 373, 386
    eggs, 433–434
    fish, 473
    freeze drying, 434
    fresh produce, 352–353
    frozen, 373, 386
    ice pack, 450, 452, 457, 471, 473, 479, 508
    individually quick frozen (IQF), 451, 471
    marinade pack, 451, 453, 471

  meat, 490–491, 508–509
  modified-atmosphere packaging (MAP), 471
  nonalcoholic beverages, 555
  poultry, 452
  processed produce and other grocery items, 386
  smoked, 508, 509
  spray drying, 434
  sun dried, 378
  waxing, 352, 361
  research, *see* Research activities, product
  safety, 570, 574–575, 577, 581, 642
  savings, 629
  shortage, 390
  size, 113
    dairy products, 412
    eggs, 429–431
    fish, 470, 476
    fresh produce, 348–349, 356
    maintenance supplies, 577
    meat, 506–507, 521
    permanent ware, 579
    poultry, 449–450
    processed produce and other grocery items, 381–383
  tagging, 332
  testing (factors), *see* Test procedures
  variety (type), 215, 567
  yield, *see* Yield (edible; servable; usable)
Production system, 117
Productivity, 330, 624, 628
Profit markup (margin; percentage), 18, 164, 165, 174, 175, 210, 437, 475, 537
Promissory note, 643
Proof, 534–535, 537
Proposal, 219, 604
Pull date, 116, 411, 414, 419
Pullet eggs, 430
Pulley, Brett, 232
Pull strategy, *see* Sales strategy, pull
Pulp temperature, 352
Purchase order, 43, 44, 111, 200, 239, 240–244, 246, 247, 254, 255, 257, 268, 293, 295, 314, 315, 330, 543, 573
  acknowledgment (acceptance), 43, 242
  draft system, 246
Purchasing, 3, 64. *See also* Bid; Buying; Shopping procedures
  activities, 58–67
  administering, 65, 75–82
  alcoholic beverages, 544–546
  bottom-line, firm-price, 169
  budgeting for, 82, 91
  centralized, 6, 81, 214
  cleaning supplies, 575
  cleaning tools, 576
  compensation for, 96–97

co-op, 6, 14, 78, 174, 213
cost-plus, *see* Buying, cost-plus
dairy products, 417–418
decentralized, 80
direct, 20, 44, 214, 277, 296,
    390, 579, 624, 629, 639, 642
director, 78, 79
discretionary, 590
disposable ware, 581
eggs, 435–437
evaluation, *see* Performance
    evaluation (of buyer)
fabrics, 583
fish, 476–478
fresh produce, 353–356
furniture, fixtures, and equip-
    ment (FFE), 621–623
impulse, 374, 568, 576, 621, 633
line-item, 168
maintenance supplies, 577
managerial approach, vi
meat, 514–516
nonalcoholic beverages, 556–
    557
nonfood expense items, 572–
    574
objectives, 67–68, 75, 91
organizing for, 65, 76–81
    co-ops, 78
    independent operations, 76–
        78
    multiunit chain operations,
        78–81
other paper products, 584
permanent ware, 579
personal, 93, 103
planning for, 75–76
policies, 7, 92–96, 97, 207
poultry, 454
preparation and service utensils,
    581
processed produce and other
    grocery items, 390–396
services, 592–594
staffing for, 81
stockless, 211, 389, 393, 476,
    544, 572, 578, 579, 584
supervising, 83
training, 97
unapproved source, *see* Sup-
    plier, unapproved (un-
    licensed)
vice president of, 6, 7, 78–80,
    96, 214, 240
will call, 211, 215
*Purchasing for Food Service Man-
    agers*, 83, 104, 302
*Purchasing Practices of Large
    Foodservice Firms*, 71
Pure Food Act, 35
Push strategy, *see* Sales strategy,
    push

Quality:
    assurance, 257
    availability, 131

buyer's role in determining,
    131–132
control, *see* Control, quality
equal to facing, 270
of finished work, 593
limits, 121
lower the standard of, 169
maintain standards of, 67
of materials used, 593
measures, 126–131
standards, 96
statement, 476
who determines, 125–126
Quantity Food Purchasing, 51, 112
Quantity limits, 93, 117, 121
Quantity limits provision, 39

Ragu brand, 336
Raw milk, 409
Rax Restaurants, 308
Ready-to-serve, 383
Rebate, 34, 45, 100, 171, 175, 215
Receiving, 64, 251–272, 289, 290,
    329
    additional duties, 264–267
    alcoholic beverages, 546–547
    blind, 268
    cash on delivery (COD), 269–
        270
    cleaning supplies, 575
    cleaning tools, 576
    clerk, 78
    computerized, 272
    dairy products, 418–419
    dating products, 264
    disposable ware, 581
    drop shipment, 269
    eggs, 437–438
    equipment, 253
    errors, 310
    essentials for, 253–255
    fabrics, 583
    facilities, 254
    fish, 478–480
    fresh produce, 356–358
    good practices, 270–271
    hours, 254
    inspection procedures, *see* Test
        procedures
    invoice, 255–267, 268, 269
    mailed, 269
    maintenance supplies, 577
    meat, 516–523
    nonalcoholic beverages, 557–
        559
    objectives, 252–253
    odd-hours, 268–269
    other methods, 267–270
    other paper products, 584
    permanent ware, 579
    personnel, 253
    poultry, 456–457
    pricing products, 264–265
    processed produce and other
        grocery items, 396
    reducing costs, 271–272

sheet (log), 262, 263, 266, 268,
    315, 521
standing order, 267
Recipe file, 267
Reciprocity, *see* Buying, reciprocal
Reconciling end-of-period state-
    ment, 200
Reconditioned (rebuilt; remodeled)
    merchandise, 620, 621, 634
Reconstitution (of product), 373,
    381, 386, 392, 434, 554
Recycling, 65, 113, 267, 383, 567,
    580, 595
Reed, Lewis, 120
References:
    employee, 313
    supplier, 220–221, 335, 594,
        604, 605, 611
Referral group (service), 6, 220
Refund, 44
Reid, R. Dan, 71
Relationship marketing, 226
Religious meat inspection, 498
Renaming fish, 465
Rent-to-own plan, 16, 644
Reorder point (ROP), 151, 154,
    155, 156, 291
Repacking (of product), *see* Pack-
    aging, repacking
Replacement (spare) parts, 637–
    638
Repossessed merchandise, 643
Request for Credit memorandum,
    258, 259, 260, 269, 310,
    314, 479
Required work schedule, 593
Requisition:
    purchase, 238–239, 241
    stock, 238, 265, 293, 296–300,
        312, 315, 320, 398, 523, 550
Research activities, 61, 79
    market, 125, 225, 226
    product, 225
Response option, 603
Restaurant Association Network,
    62, 206
Restaurant Business, 25
Restaurants & Institutions, 206,
    361
Restaurants USA, 71, 189, 190,
    322, 323, 367
Restricted access, *see* Storeroom,
    limited access
Resume-checking service, 315
Retail cut, *see* Meat, retail cut
Retailer, 11, 15, 16, 17
Return on investment, *See also* In-
    ventory, return on invest-
    ment
Returns and allowances, *see* In-
    ventory, returns
R & H brand, 436
Rickman, Ted, 232
Riegel, Carl D., 71
Ripeness, 116, 351
Ripening process, 351–352
Ripening room, 352

Risk-purchasing group, 609
Ritz, Cesar, 308
Roberts, Phil, 232
Robichaux, Mark, 190
Robinson-Patman Act, 38–39
Route salesperson, 212, 246, 251, 557
Routing software, 328
Royalties, 622
Ruggless, Ron, 25, 322
Run-of-the press, 599
Run-of-the-station, 600

Sacred hours, 174
Safe-driver program, 534
Safety (considerations), *see* Product, safety
Safety stock, 139, 140, 142, 151, 154, 156
Sales history, 333
Salesperson-buyer relations, *see* Buyer, salesperson, relations with
Sales strategy, 222–225
  pull, 222–225, 374, 380, 532
  push, 222, 376
Salmonella, *see* Bacteria
Salvage buy, *see* Buying, salvage
Salvage sale, 576
Salvage value, 571
Samples:
  free from suppliers, 93–94, 216, 226, 557
  measure of quality, 130
Sanitation, 278, 289
  certification exam, 278
Schilling, 388
Schmidgall, Raymond S., 190
Schneider, Elizabeth, 366
Schulman Meats & Provisions, 196, 243, 256, 259, 261
Schultz, Howard, 322
Scism, Leslie, 189
Scott Paper Company, 94
Scrambleez brand, 436
Seafood Price-Current, 476
Seafood safety legislation, 37
Seasonal change, 353
Sebastian, Pamela, 104
Security, 212, 296, 307–321, 611–612
  preventing problems, 312–321
  problems, 308–312
Security agreement, 643
Security and Crime Prevention, 323
Security Management, 323
Selection, 3
Selection and procurement plan, *see* Buying, plan
Selection and procurement policies, *see* Purchasing, policies
Selection factors:
  alcoholic beverages, 537–544
  cleaning supplies, 574–575
  cleaning tools, 575–576

dairy products, 407–416
disposable ware, 580
eggs, 425–435
fabrics, 582–583
fish, 464–476
fresh produce, 342–353
furniture, fixtures, and equipment (FFE), 623–642
maintenance supplies, 576–577
meat, 493–514
miscellaneous items, 584–585
nonalcoholic beverages, 552–556
nonfood expense items, 572–573
other paper products, 583–584
permanent ware, 578–579
poultry, 444–454
preparation and service utensils, 581
processed produce and other grocery items, 376–390
services, 592–594
Self-improvement, 66
Sell-by date, 116
Seller co-op, 38. *See also* Distributor co-op
Selz, Michael, 24, 190
Seminars, 66
Servable weight, *see* Drained weight; Yield (edible; servable; usable)
Service agreement, 606
Service contract, *see* Contract, service
Service style, 118
Serving size, 40
S.E. Rykoff (SER) brand, 129, 388
Sex of bird, 445, 446
Shatter pack, *see* Packaging, shatter pack
Shelf life, 46, 48, 115, 139, 155, 186, 208, 342, 343, 346, 353, 356, 361, 371, 373, 387, 389, 397, 444, 449, 450, 451, 457, 471, 479, 480, 481, 542, 548, 555
Shelf stable, 373
Shellfish, 466
Shelving, 288
Sherman Act, 35, 37
Shoplifting, 278, 308, 310, 579. *See also* Pilferage
Shopping (buying) procedures, 96
  one-stop, 64, 208, 210–211, 215, 217, 227, 240, 254, 272, 301, 337, 383, 405, 407, 413, 416, 514, 567, 573, 595, 596, 620
  advantages, 210
  disadvantages, 210–211
Shopping service, 315, 551
Shortage, *see* Product, shortage
Shrinkage, *see* Inventory, shrinkage
Shrink allowance, 271, 350
Shrink wrap, *see* Packaging, shrink wrap

Shucked fish, 466
Signature item, 449, 452, 489, 513, 514
Sipco brand, 515
Size of container, *see* Packaging, size
Skimming, 278
Slab pack, *see* Packaging, slab packed
Slacked out, 271
Small Business Administration (SBA), 605
Small Business Protection Act, *see* Robinson-Patman Act
Smirnoff brand, 545
Smoked, *see* Product, preservation (processing)
Snap pack, *see* Packaging, snap pack
Sodium nitrite, 509
Soft-scald procedure, 449
Solid pack, 385, 386
Sound control system, 317
Sourcing, 60
Space-available basis, 600
Specification, 109–110, 201, 207, 208, 209, 251, 254, 269
  advantages of, 110–111
  alcoholic beverages, 545
  dairy products, 417–418
  eggs, 435–436
  fish, 476–477
  formal, 111
  fresh produce, 354
  furniture, fixtures, and equipment (FFE), 621–623
  informal, 111
  information included, 112–117
  institutional meat purchase, *see* Institutional Meat Purchase Specification (IMPS)
  job, 81, 88–90, 91
  meat, 514–516
  nonalcoholic beverages, 557, 558
  nonfood expense items, 572–573
  potential problems with, 121–124
  poultry, 454–455
  processed produce and other grocery items, 390–391
  product, 8, 41, 109, 165, 219, 271, 331, 622
  purchase, 7, 79, 109, 166, 622
  services, 592–593
  what influences type of information included, 117
  who decides what information to include, 111
  who writes, 118
Specific gravity, 386
Spillage, 551
Splete, Heidi, 52, 248
Spoilage, 270, 278, 296, 300, 342, 349, 362, 387, 419, 420, 481, 516, 531, 540, 567

Spotter, *see* Shopping service
Spray drying, *see* Product, preservation (processing)
Spreadsheet, 329, 333
S.S. Pierce brand, 129
Staffing, 81
Stalling a supplier, *see* Bill-paying procedures, stalling suppliers
Standard:
 of fill, 40, 386
 of identity, 39–40, 376, 377, 407, 408, 414, 415, 445, 446, 451, 452, 467, 472, 493, 496, 537, 553
 of quality, 40, 113, 392
Standing order, *see* Order, standing
Stanford University, 334
Staphylococcus bacteria, *see* Bacteria
Star Kist brand, 469
State grades, 411, 448
Steam-table pack, *see* Packaging, steam-table pack
Stefanelli, John, vi, 323
Stephenson, Annie, 231
Steward (executive; kitchen), 6, 77, 91, 610
Steward sales, 93
Stockout (cost), 67, 99, 100, 117, 137, 140, 153, 154, 247, 264, 291, 516, 568, 577
Stockpot Soups brand, 223
Stock rotation, 278, 279, 289, 290, 353, 362, 397, 419, 438, 457, 481, 523, 549
Storage, 64, 117, 277–302, 332–333
 alcoholic beverages, 547–549
 beer, 549
 cleaning supplies, 575
 cleaning tools, 576
 controlled atmosphere, 48, 342, 352–353, 426, 433–434, 451, 471. *See also* Packaging, aseptic
 cost, *see* Cost, storage
 dairy products, 419–420
 disposable ware, 581
 distilled spirits, 547
 eggs, 426, 438
 fabrics, 583
 facilities, 290–300. *See also* Ingredient room; Storeroom
 fish, 480–481
 fresh produce, 358–362
 life, *see* Shelf life
 maintenance supplies, 577
 meat, 523
 needed to achieve objectives, 279–290
 nonalcoholic beverages, 559
 objectives, 278–279
 other paper products, 584
 permanent ware, 579
 poultry, 457

processed produce and other grocery items, 397–398
temperature and humidity requirements, 279, 280–288
wine, 547–549
Storeroom:
 equipment, 288
 layout, 290–291
 limited (restricted) access, 316, 319
 maintenance requirements, 288
 manager (duties), 238, 290–300
 open, 237, 296, 311
 personnel requirements, 289
 proximity to receiving and production areas, 288
 regulations, 290
 security requirements, 288
 space requirements, 280
 time requirements, 289–290
 working, 296
Stretching the accounts payable, 198
Subscription service, 220
Substitution:
 dairy products, 406, 407
 fish for meat, 489, 492, 512
 ingredients in recipes, 489
 poultry for meat, 451, 489, 512
 of product by employee, 311, 312
 of product by hospitality operator, 170, 332, 337, 374, 405, 412, 418, 437, 444, 445, 472, 489, 492, 509, 513, 514
 of product by supplier, 69, 116, 155, 217, 225, 258, 310, 396, 419
 soybean for meat, 489, 492, 512
 surimi for fish, 472
Sun-dried, *see* Product preservation (processing)
Sunkist brand, 346, 353, 558
Supervision, 82
Supervision, 83
Supervision in the Hospitality Industry, 83
Supervisor-buyer relations, *see* Buyer, supervisor, relations with
Supervisory style, *see* Supervision
Supplier, 205–230
 coffee, 552
 comfort stage, 229–230
 diplomacy, 63–64
 errors, 310
 facilities, 218
 firing, 229
 forms, 246, 543
 initial survey, 205–206
 insured, *see* Licensed supplier
 length of time in business, 217
 licensed, *see* Licensed supplier
 local, 214, 390, 579
 major activities, 222–226
 national, 214, 390
 potential, 205–206

relations with buyer, 222–226
selection (criteria), 60, 207–222
service, 19–20, 22–23, 31, 32, 68, 110, 132, 161, 168, 222, 389–390, 543–544, 556, 567, 575, 591, 638–639
size of firm, 217, 221
socially responsible, 220
track record, 217
trust, 353, 434–435, 438, 453, 475–476, 516, 638
unapproved (unlicensed), 187, 396, 480, 592
who owns hospitality operations, 220
willingness to sell storage, 219–220
Supply and demand, 29–31, 32, 165
Support function, 20
Supporting local suppliers, *see* Trade relations
Surcharge, 630, 631
Surimi, 472
Suspicious behavior, 312
Sutter Home Fre brand, 545
Syrup density, *see* Brix
Sysco brand, 129, 506
Sysco Supreme Angus Beef brand, 506
Systems sale, 569, 635

Tabasco brand, 225
Taco Bell, 220
Tagged fish, 480
Tannenbaum, Jeffrey A., 52
Tare weight, 270
Target cost percentage, *see* Cost, target percentage
Tariff, 543
Taste test, *see* Cutting (can cutting) test
Tax:
 import, 543
 personal property, 186
 sales, 187, 257
 use, 187, 257
Technical skill, *see* Employee skill, technical
Telephone salesperson, *see* WATS-line hustler
Telephone sales scams, 311
Temperature probe, 253, 437
Temperature requirements, 279, 280–288
Tenderization procedure, *see* Meat, tenderization procedure
Test procedures, 116–117, 395
The Bottomline, 322
The Chronicle of Higher Education, 323
Theft, 278, 307, 308, 312, 313, 314, 315, 316, 317, 319, 320, 547
The Jungle, 35

The Meat Buyers Guide, 120, 331, 494, 495, 506, 508, 514
The New Fresh Seafood Buyer's Guide, 120, 476
The Packer: The National Weekly Newspaper of the Fruit and Vegetable Industry, 341
The Perrier Group, 224
The Produce Marketing Association Fresh Produce Reference Manual for Food Service, 120, 344, 345, 353
The Restaurant: From Concept to Operation, 322
The Sale and Purchase of Restaurants, 323
The Seafood Leader, 476
The Spirit of Southern Nevada, 544
The Wall Street Journal, 24, 25, 51, 52, 71, 83, 104, 157, 189, 190, 202, 231, 232, 322, 323, 366, 440
The Washington Post, 322
Thienpont, Charles, 366
Third party liability, 608
Thomas Food Industry Register, 205–206
Tied-house laws, 15
Time- and temperature-sensitive food label, 49
Time efficiency software, 328
Time lock, 31
Time savings, 329
Time value, *see* Economic value, time
Time value of money, 628
Title to goods, 44. *See also* Bill, of lading
Toner-phoner, 311, 569–570
Topor, George, 25
Touch-screen technology, 330
Toxins, 468
Trace, Thomas L., 51
Trade association (standards), 116, 130, 354, 553
Trade center, 206
Trade dollars, 178
Trade-in allowance (value), 218, 571, 624, 631, 632, 636
Trade-out, 600. *See also* Exchange bartering
Trade relations, 64, 96, 227, 514
Trade show:
 exhibit, 188, 630, 632
 visit, 66, 206, 621, 622
Trading, *see* Exchange bartering
Training, 81, 97, 226, 239, 253
 on-the-job, 97, 342
Transfer Slip, 291
Transportation, 47
Transportation cost, *see* Cost, transportation (delivery; freight)
Trash compactor, 316
Trash fish, 465
Trim, 113, 350, 450, 470, 495, 504.

See also Conversion weight; Drained weight; Yield (edible; servable; usable)
Trust the supplier, *see* Supplier, trust
Truth-in-menu legislation (regulations), 115, 351, 405, 475, 512
Tying agreement, 38, 625, 630
Type of container, *see* Packaging, type
Types of hospitality operations, 4–5
Tyson brand, 449, 455

Ultra-pasteurized, *see* Pasteurization
Unapproved (unlicensed) supply source, *see* Supplier, unapproved (unlicensed)
Undercover agent, 315
Underpour, 551
Underwriters laboratories (UL), 642
Uniform allowance, 610
Uniform Commercial Code (UCC), 43
Uniform Resource Locator (URL), 335
Uniform System of Accounts for Hotels and Restaurants, 201
United Parcel Service (UPS), 269
United States Department of Agriculture (USDA), 35, 36, 110, 341, 376, 377, 380, 467, 468
 Acceptance Service, 118, 120, 456, 512, 521
 Agricultural Marketing Service (AMS), 126, 343, 377, 408
 Dairy Market News Branch, 119
 Fruit and Vegetables Division, 343, 377
 Livestock Division, 495
 Livestock & Feed Division, 499
 Poultry and Dairy Division, 408
 Daily Fruit and Vegetable Report, 341
 Food Safety Inspection Service (FSIS), 36
 Food Safety and Quality Service (FSQS), 377, 426, 447, 497, 499
 Fruit and Vegetable Market News Branch, 119
 Livestock Market News Branch, 119
 Poultry Market News Branch, 119
 Product Examination Service, 521
United States Department of Commerce (USDC), 37, 307, 468
 National Marine Fisheries Service, 467, 469

United States government grades, 112–113, 126–128, 215
 dairy products, 408–411
 eggs, 426–428
 fish, 467
 fresh produce, 344
 grading factors:
  dairy products, 409–411
  eggs, 427–428
  fish, 467
  fresh produce, 344
  meat, 500–503
  poultry, 447, 448
  processed produce and other grocery items, 377–378
 meat, 497–503
 nonalcoholic beverages, 553
 poultry, 446–449
 problems with use, 127–128
 processed produce and other grocery items, 377–380
 yield grades, 499. *See also* Yield range; Yield standard
Universal Product Code (UPC), 49, 254, 265, 267, 295, 330, 331
University of California at Los Angeles (UCLA), 334
University of California at Santa Barbara (UCSB), 334
University of Florida, 335
University of Nevada, Las Vegas, vi
University of Utah, 334
Usage pattern (rate), 151, 154, 156, 186, 241, 242, 289, 291, 329, 550, 568
 actual, 320, 331
 standard, 320
USA Today, 71
Used merchandise, 188, 570, 576, 577, 579, 620, 630, 638, 642
 advantages, 570, 576
 disadvantages, 570, 576
USENET, 335
User-buyer, *see* Buyer, user-buyer
U.S. Department of Defense, 334
U.S. Public Health Service's Milk Ordinance and Code, 409

Value, 31, 161, 555
Value-added foods, 12, 46, 63
Value analysis, 61, 118, 167–168, 195, 209
 of storage management procedures, 300–302
Van Warner, Rick, 322
Variance, 183
Variety meat, *see* Meat, variety
Variety of product, *see* Product, variety (type)
Veal chart, 520
Vending machine service, 607–608
Versatility, 634
Vintage, 155, 535, 539
Virtual discussion group, 335
Visa, 200
Visual pollution (codes), 602

Vitality brand, 554
Vitamin A, 410
Vitamin, D, 410
VNR's Encyclopedia of Hospitality and Tourism, 273

Walker, John R., 322
Walkup, Carolyn, 25, 52, 322
Wall racks, 288
Walt Disney World, 221, 232
Warehouse club, 620
Warfel, M.C., 83, 104, 302
Warranty, *see* Guarantee
Waste removal service, 17, 318, 594–595
Waters list, 534
WATS-line hustler, 311, 319, 569
Waxing, *see* Product, preservation (processing)
Weight:
    range, 449, 456, 470, 507
    residual, 330
Welland, Diane, 366
Whataburger, 308
What-if analysis, 62
Wheeler-Lea Act, 37
White Swan brand, 129
Whole food, *see* Organic (natural; whole) food

Wholesale club, 14, 168, 212, 381
Wholesale cut, *see* Meat, wholesale cut
Wholesome Meat Act, 35, 36, 497
Wholesome Poultry Products Act, 36, 446
Will call, *see* Purchasing, will call
William F. Harrah College of Hotel Administration, vi
Winchester, Sarah Hart, 71, 190
Wine:
    bag-in-box, *see* Packaging, bag-in-the-box
    bar, 548
    buying complications, 535–536
    cellar, 547
    dispensing unit, 548
    fortified, 548
    house, 535, 537
    jug, 548
    life cycle, 548
    list, 543, 546, 550
    maker, 14
    speculation, 536
    steward, 312, 546, 547, 550
Winning Foodservice Ideas, 322
Winston Industries, 626
Wood, Tom, 71
Workers' compensation, 608

Work-hour accumulation, 333
Working capital, 644
Working storeroom, *see* Storeroom, working
Work schedule, 333
Workstation, 330
World Wide Web (WWW), 335–336
Wynter, Leon E., 232

Yellow Pages directory, 601
Yield (edible; servable; usable), 113, 142, 161, 178, 181, 377, 446, 470. *See also* Conversion weight; Drained weight; Trim
    dairy products, 413
    fish, 470
    fresh produce, 350
    meat, 499, 502, 503–504
    poultry, 446, 448, 449, 450
Yield range, 504
Yield standard, 503
York, Michael, 322
Yorkshire brand, 558

Zachary, G. Pascal, 232